T0220771

Lecture Notes in Computer Science   11344

Commenced Publication in 1973
Founding and Former Series Editors:
Gerhard Goos, Juris Hartmanis, and Jan van Leeuwen

Meikang Qiu (Ed.)

Smart Computing and Communication

Third International Conference, SmartCom 2018
Tokyo, Japan, December 10–12, 2018
Proceedings

 Springer

Editor
Meikang Qiu ⓘ
Columbia University
New York, NY, USA

ISSN 0302-9743   ISSN 1611-3349 (electronic)
Lecture Notes in Computer Science
ISBN 978-3-030-05754-1   ISBN 978-3-030-05755-8 (eBook)
https://doi.org/10.1007/978-3-030-05755-8

Library of Congress Control Number: 2018963968

LNCS Sublibrary: SL3 – Information Systems and Applications, incl. Internet/Web, and HCI

This Springer imprint is published by the registered company Springer Nature Switzerland AG
The registered company address is: Gewerbestrasse 11, 6330 Cham, Switzerland

Preface

This volume contains the papers presented at SmartCom 2018: the Third International Conference on Smart Computing and Communication held during December 10–12, 2018, in Tokyo.

There were 302 submissions. Each submission was reviewed by at least three reviewers, and on average 3.5, Program Committee members. The committee decided to accept 44 papers.

Recent booming developments in Web-based technologies and mobile applications have facilitated a dramatic growth in the implementation of new techniques, such as cloud computing, big data, pervasive computing, Internet of Things, and social cyber-physical systems. Enabling a smart life has become a popular research topic with an urgent demand. Therefore, the Third International Conference on Smart Computing and Communication (SmartCom 2018) focused on both smart computing and communications fields and aimed to collect recent academic work to improve the research and practical applications in the field.

The scope of SmartCom 2018 was broad, from smart data to smart communications, from smart cloud computing to smart security. The conference gathered all high-quality research/industrial papers related to smart computing and communications and aimed at proposing a reference guideline for further research. SmartCom 2018 was held at Waseda University in Japan and its conference proceedings publisher is Springer.

SmartCom 2018 continued in the series of successful academic get-togethers, following SmartCom 2017 (Shenzhen, China) and SmartCom 2016 (Shenzhen, China).

We would like to thank our sponsors Springer LNCS, Waseda University, Columbia University, Beijing Institute of Technology, UINP Global Community, Birmingham City University, LD Research Inc., North America Chinese Talents Association, and Longxiang High Tech Group Inc.

November 2018

Meikang Qiu

Organization

General Chairs

Qing Yang — The University of Rhode Island, USA
Meikang Qiu — Columbia University, USA

Program Chairs

Zhong Ming — Shenzhen University, China
Rui Mao — Shenzhen University, China
Keke Gai — Beijing Institute of Technology, China

Local Chairs

Cheng Zhang — Waseda University, Japan
Celimuge Wu — University of Electro-Communications, Japan

Publicity Chairs

Peng Li — Aizu University, Japan
Suhua Tang — University of Electro-Communications, Japan

Host Chair

Zhi Liu — Shizuoka University, Japan

Finance Secretary

Hui Zhao — Henan University, China

Technical Program Committee

Vitor Jesus — Birmingham City University, UK
Jeremy Foss — Birmingham City University, UK
Mohammad Patwary — Birmingham City University, UK
Peter Bull — QA Ltd., UK
Yunxia Liu — Zhengzhou Normal University, China
Hui Wang — Changzhou University, China
Qingsong Shi — Zhejiang University, China
Jianbin Wu — Zhejiang Normal University, China
Yamin Li — Hubei University, China
Meng Shen — Beijing Institute of Technology, China

Adel Aneiba	Birmingham City University, UK
Hengjin Cai	Wuhan University, China
Matthew Roach	Swansea University, UK
Yan Zhang	Central South University, China
Jinguang Gu	Wuhan University of Science and Technology, China
Chunhua Deng	Wuhan University of Science and Technology, China
Guangyou Zhou	Central China Normal University, China
Bo Li	Wuhan University of Science and Technology, China
Jun Li	Wuhan University of Science and Technology, China
Yu Shi	Zhejiang Normal University, China
Degang Xu	Hubei University of Arts and Science, China
Hui Zhao	Henan University, China
Bharat Rawal	Pennsylvania State University, USA
Lixin Tao	Pace University, USA
Xiaofu He	Columbia University, USA
Wenjia Li	New York Institute of Technology, USA
Thomas Austin	San Jose State University, USA
Peng Zhang	Stony Brook University, USA
Jian Xiong	Shanghai Jiao Tong University, China
Haibo Zhang	University of Otago, New Zealand
Suman Kumar	Troy University, USA
Zhongming Fei	University of Kentucky, USA
Weigang Li	University of Brasilia, Brazil
Yue Hu	Louisiana State University, USA
Ukka Riekki	University of Oulu, Finland
Hao Hu	Nanjing University, China
Art Sedighi	Global Head of Cloud Architecture and Strategy, TD Bank, USA
Bo Luo	The University of Kansas, USA
Jinjun Xiong	IBM Research, USA
Emmanuel Bernardez	IBM Research, USA

Contents

A Two-Way Identity Authentication Scheme Based on Dynamic Password

Baohua Zhao[1,2,3], Ningyu An[2,3], Xiao Liang[2,3], Chunhui Ren[2,3(✉)], and Zhihao Wang[2,3]

[1] Faculty of Information Technology, Beijing University of Technology, Beijing 100124, China
zbh1984_1@126.com
[2] Global Energy Interconnection Research Institute Co., Ltd., Beijing 102209, China
anningyu@foxmail.com, 33180900@qq.com, ren1198997229@163.com, lanyiner2016@163.com
[3] Artificial Intelligence on Electric Power System State Grid Corporation Joint Laboratory (GEIRI), Beijing 100124, China

Abstract. In order to solve the security issues existed in RFID authentication in recent years. A mutual identity authentication scheme based on dynamic is proposed after describing and analyzing the problems that RFID authentication technology encounters, which can solve replay attack, man-in-the-middle attack and other security issues. In addition, this paper also describes the techno of Authentication technology. The method proposed refers to tags privacy level between Tag and Reader to achieve mutual authentication, it not only can enhance the privacy protection of the label carrier and protect the identity privacy of the Reader holder, but also has a certain effectiveness advantage.

Keywords: Mutual authentication · Internet of Things · Mobile RFID

1 Introduction

The Internet of Things (IoT) embeds or equips sensors into objects such as smart grids, railways, oil and gas pipelines to realize the integration of objects with the existing Internet, the integration of human society, information space, and physical systems [1]. The basic security facilities of the IoT are the key reasons that limit the continued development of the IoT. The authentication technology for "things" entering the network is the basis of IoT security. If this problem cannot be solved, it's meaningless to talk about the development of the IoT. The following is an authentication method for IoT.

For example, object A moves from area 1 to area 2. If object A wants to collect and transmit its information using the resources of area 2, it must get the permission of management organization of area 2. Therefore, object A needs to ask for identity authentication to management organization of area 2, which is used to prove that it is a legal and normal node in area 2.

This work is supported by the science and technology projects of SGCC (5455HJ170001).

M. Qiu (Ed.): SmartCom 2018, LNCS 11344, pp. 1–7, 2018.
https://doi.org/10.1007/978-3-030-05755-8_1

The characteristics of this identity authentication are as follows. First, the access to resources is random. In the future trends of IoT applications, such mobile roaming will be long-term and exist in large numbers. Second, the energy of nodes in the IoT, regardless they are dynamic or static, is limited, which indicates that their survivability is limited by their own power. Third, when the node joins the new access area and obtains the legal identity through identity authentication, it can obtain all the network resources provided by the access area. Finally, except to ensure the security of itself, the identity authentication protocol should not reduce the security of the access area and transport backbone network connected to it.

There are many authentication models for the network, such as PKI technology. After the emergence of the IoT, professionals applied them to the IoT. These technologies played a role in the initial, but with the development of the IoT technology, there are some problems as follows.

(1) In this type of model, the legitimacy of the central node is guaranteed by the certificate issued by the CA. Since the entity information in the certificate is not very clear, it is difficult to distinguish the entity with the same name in real world.
(2) They are too dependent on PKI, which result in poor scalability.
(3) The authentication process requires the intervention of third-party intermediaries, which complicates the authentication process.
(4) They are usually large computation, low efficiency, and high cost, etc.
(5) Existing methods do not involve random roaming, combined security, etc.

In order to solve these problems, professionals engaged in certification research have proposed many methods.

2 Research Status of IoT Authentication Technology

There are many authentication technologies in the IoT, such as hash-based, state-based, key-based encryption, key-based sharing, TinyPk, etc.

RFID authentication protocol based on hash function: The literature [2] proposed a hash function-based authentication protocol. The privacy and security of the protocol can be guaranteed because of the one-way feature of hash function. In addition, as we know, with a one-way hash function h(), let $z = h(ID)$, it is easy to calculate z from the ID, but it is impossible to derive the ID from z. This irreversibility can fight against eavesdropping attacks. Furthermore, the Reader has a random number r generated in each communication. The literature [3] uses the CRC (Cyclic Redundancy Code) algorithm to design the hash function h(). Combined with the updated tag ID, the algorithm can effectively resist playback attack and location detection. However, once the attacker illegally terminates a session, it is easy to cause ID update which will suffer the asynchronous attack or the Tag location detection attack, and cannot effectively resist the fake attack.

In a certain communication using state-based RFID authentication protocol [4], if an attacker maliciously blocked the last session, it is likely to make flag = 0, and the Tag ID is not updated. While in the background database, the Tag ID was updated by the server, which will cause a non-synchronization problem.

The RFID authentication protocol based on key encryption [5] has the disadvantage that in an RFID system with a large number of tags, the calculation of authentication is very difficult. In every authentication, the authentication system needs to check the key of each Tag while for those low-cost RFID Tags, they usually have very limited storage space and computing power.

TinyPK Sensor Entity Authentication [6] requires a Trust Center (CA). Usually, base station can act as CA. Any external organization (EP) in the authentication protocol must have a public/private key pair to establish contact with the sensor node, and its legal identity can be proved by processing public key signed by CA. The TinyPK authentication protocol uses a request-response mechanism. First, the EP sends a request message which contains two parts: (1) its own public key signed by CA; (2) an information validity value and time stamp which are signed by the EP's private key. The integrity of the information is guaranteed by the information validity value, and the time stamp is used to resist the replay attack. After the request packet arrives at the node, the first part of the packet is verified using the CA's public key, which can confirm the identity of EP and obtain the public key of the EP at the same time. Then the EP's public key is used to verify the second part of the packet. After that, we can obtain the information validity value and time stamp, which can be used to verify the legal identity of the third party.

In addition, literature [7] uses a one-way hash chain to implement a broadcast authentication μTESLA. Literature [8] uses Merkle Tree to construct a certification path based on the public key mecha-nism to reduce the communication overhead of authentication. Literature [9] proposes a layered-based authentication management scheme. All of these authentication protocols are designed for the traditional static nodes of the sensor network, lightweight is an advantage. However, none of them consider about the roaming scenario and the combined security requirements for the IoT.

3 Mobile IoT Identity Authentication Based on Dynamic Password

Compared with the traditional static passwords, dynamic password is generally produced by a terminal device using dynamic password algorithm. The dynamic password produced is varied with dynamic parameters. The dynamic password generation algorithm generally adopts a double operation factors. One is the identification code of the user identity which is fixed, such as the user's private key; the other is a variation factor, such as time, random number, counter value, etc. Different dynamic factors adopt different dynamic password authentication techniques.

It is undeniable that the dynamic password-based identity authentication system brings the gospel to the mobile IoT, which can solve problems we mentioned in the second chapter of this article. Its advantages, such as dynamics, one-off, randomness, multiple security, etc. fundamentally repair some security risks of traditional identity authentication systems. For example, it can effectively prevent replay attacks, eaves-dropping, guessing attacks, etc. However, as far as the current research results and usages are concerned, it also has deficiency and technical difficulties.

The existing dynamic password-based identity authentication system can only achieve one-way authentication, that is, the server authenticates the client, so attacks from the server side cannot be avoided. With the diversity of network applications, more and more network applications require two-way authentication to ensure the benefits of both parties. For example, in the registration phase of e-commerce, the client and server need to exchange their id and public key. In order to solve above problems, and further improve the security, reliability, flexibility and efficiency of mobile IoT, a dynamic mobile IoT identity authentication method is proposed in this paper. This method is based on the mechanism of public key infrastructure PKI and Privilege Management Infrastructure (PMI), and absorbs the essence of traditional trust model.

3.1 Scheme Design

Under the wireless network structure of mobile IoT, node authentication is usually divided into three stages:

The first stage is registration. Mobile node will register in the initial area A. The main purpose of this stage is to pre-deploy secret materials such as initial identification code, password and authentication information, etc.

Symbols and parameters involved in the scheme are as follows:

Qu: Indicates that the Reader has submitted an authentication request to the tag.

PWx: Indicates the access cipher group generated by the server. It is a 32-bit binary number that can represent the password stored in the Tag (when x is t) and the password stored in the back-end server (when x is i).

UIx: Indicates the identification code assigned by the server to the tag. It is a 32-bit binary number, which can respectively represent the identification code stored in the label (when x is t) and the identification code stored in the back-end server (when x is (i).

Rt: Indicates the random number generated by the tag, which is a 16-bit binary number.

Rr: Indicates the random number generated by the reader, which is a 16-bit binary number.

H(): indicates a one-way hash function, !!: Cascade operator, ==: compares whether the two are equal, →: send (Fig. 1).

Fig. 1. Node registration

During the registration stage, the server assigns a unique identification code (USER ID) and password to the electronic tag, and stores them both in the Tag and back-end database e. In the process of system authentication, the password stored in the Tag is compared with the password stored in the database. If they are equal, it means the node belongs to the system. Since PWi, UIi, PWt and UIt are generated by the server (or manufacturer) when the system is established, and they are encrypted and then distributed by the secure channel and stored in the corresponding tag and back-end database, they are considered to be safe and confidential.

The second stage is the authentication of the mobile node in the registration area.

The specific steps of the RFID system password authentication scheme are as follows:

(1) Reader → Tag: The Reader generates a random number Rr and then sends an authentication request Qu and Rr to the tag.

(2) Tag → Reader → Server: After receiving the authentication request Qu and the random number Rr, the Tag generates a random number Rt, and calculates PUIt = H(UIt!!PWt!!Rt!!Rr), and then sends (PUIt, Rt)to the reader. After the Reader receives it, it forwards (PUIt, Rt, Rr) to the server.

(3) Server: After receiving the (PUIt, Rt, Rr) sent by the reader, the local authentication server searches for UIi and PWi (1 < i < n) that satisfies PUIi == PUIt in the backend database, where PUIi = H(UIi!!PWi!!Rt!!Rr). If there exists such UIi and PWi, the authentication is passed and the process proceeds to step (4); otherwise, the authentication fails and the operation will be terminated. So the Tag can be identified by Reader through above process.

(4) Server → Reader → Tag: The server calculates PUIi = H(UIi!!PWi!!Rt) with UIi, PWi, Rt, and sends the calculated PUIi to the Reader. After the Reader receives it, it will forward it to the Tag.

(5) Tag: After the Tag receives the PUIi forwarded by the reader, it first calculates PUIt = H(UIt!!PWt!!Rt), and then verifies whether the PUIt is equal to PUIi. If they are equal, the authentication to the Reader is successful; otherwise, the authentication is failed. So the Reader can be identified by the Tag through above process (Fig. 2).

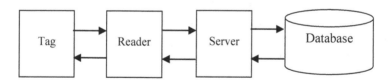

Fig. 2. Identification scheme

The third stage is to roam to the new area B (the visited area). How does the mobile node complete the authentication in the visited area with the assistance of the transmission backbone network? In this paper we assume that the static sensing network has been deployed, and there exists secure links among the sensor arears which are built on transmission backbone.

The mobile node A in the area A enters the area B through a period of time movement. Only node A accepts and passes the authentication from the manager of area B, it can enjoy the network service from the area B. The execution process of the roaming authentication protocol is shown in Fig. 3. The difference between it and the previous stage is that when the authentication server cannot find the node in the local database, it will issue a collaborative authentication request to the remote server cluster, and the remote server cluster will authenticate the node. If it still cannot be found in remote server cluster's database, the node will be considered to be an illegal node and be added to the blacklist, then refused to pass the authentication (Fig. 3).

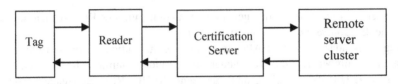

Fig. 3. Roaming authentication

4 Security Analysis

In order to verify the authentication scheme designed in this paper, a security analysis is carried out.

(1) Anti-replay attack: Whether password is sent from server or to server, it is one-time and irrelevant, namely, you can't deduce next password from the previous password. Therefore, it can resist the replay attack.

(2) Anti-man-in-the-middle attack: The protocol is two-way authentication, that is, user and server can authenticate each other. Generally, man-in-the-middle attack can break any protocol without encryption. Therefore, the public key encryption method is adopted in the transmission process. Even if the middleman can intercept the data transmitted between the server and the client, he still can't get the correct password because of lacking private key.

(3) High authentication strength: In this scheme, decryption, signed information verification, one-time password authentication are all used. So it has high security.

(4) Simple protocol structure: The whole authentication process can be completed by two communication parties and no third party is required. So the solution is easy to implement.

(5) Small interaction: Due to the use of one-time password generation mode in event synchronization, the number of communication times in the authentication process is small. And the amount of information exchange between two parties is small. Only two communications are required to achieve mutual authentication.

(6) Fractional attack vulnerability: The protocol adopts an event-based one-time password generation algorithm, which is different from the asynchronous one-time password generation mechanism used in challenge-response mode, so there is no fractional attack vulnerability.

5 Conclusion

With the increasingly growing applications of Internet of Things and RFID technologies, more security vulnerabilities are appearing in the RFID authentications, the requirements for its security are getting higher and higher. In order to solve the issue related to identity authentication existed in RFID applications in recent years. A mutual identity authentication scheme based on dynamic is proposed in this paper, which can better resist replay attack, man-in-the-middle attack, and has Simple protocol structure and small interaction. Therefore, the protocol can better satisfy the security requirements for mobile RFID applications. It has an effectiveness advantage and can make a positive contribution to the future RFID authentication applications.

References

1. Atzori, L., Iera, A., Morabito, G.: The Internet of Things: a survey. Comput. Netw. **54**(15), 2787–2805 (2010)
2. Cbien, H., Chen, C.: Mutual authentication protocol for RFID conforming to EPC class 1 generation 2 standards. Comput. Stan. Interfaces **29**(2), 254–259 (2016)
3. Dimitriou, T.: A lightweight RFID protocol to protect against traceability and cloning attacks. In: International Conference on Security and Privacy for Emerging Areas in Communications Networks, pp. 59–66. IEEE Press (2005)
4. Kang, S.Y., Lee, D.G., Lee, I.Y.: A study on secure RFID mutual authentication scheme in pervasive computing environment. Comput. Commun. **31**(18), 4248–4254 (2008)
5. Kaya, S.V., Sava, E.: Public key cryptography based privacy preserving multi-context RFID infrastructure. Ad Hoc Netw. **7**(1), 136–152 (2009)
6. Watro, R., Kong, D., Cuti, S.F., et al: TinyPK: securing sensor networks with public key technology. In: Proceedings of the 2nd ACM Workshop on Security of Ad Hoc and Sensor Networks, pp. 59–64. ACM (2004)
7. Perrig, A., Szewczyk, R., Tygar, J.D., et al.: SPINS: security protocols for sensor networks. Wirel. Netw. **8**(5), 521–534 (2002)
8. Du, W., Wang, R., Ning, P.: An efficient scheme for authenticating public keys in sensor networks. In: Proceedings of the 6th ACM International Symposium on Mobile Ad Hoc Networking and Computing, Urbana, pp. 58–67 (2005)
9. Ibriq, J., Mahgoub, I.: A hierarchical key establishment scheme for wireless sensor networks. In: Proceedings of 21st International Conference on Advanced Networking and Applications (AINA 2007), Niagara Falls, pp. 210–219 (2007)

Adaptive Quality Control Scheme to Improve QoE of Video Streaming in Wireless Networks

Minsu Kim and Kwangsue Chung[✉]

Department of Electronics and Communication Engineering,
Kwangwoon University, Seoul, South Korea
mskim@cclab.kw.ac.kr, kchung@kw.ac.kr

Abstract. Recently, with the spread of smart devices and the development of networks, the demand for video streaming has increased, and HTTP adaptive streaming has been gaining attention. HTTP adaptive streaming can guarantee QoE (Quality of Experience) because it selects the video quality according to the network state. However, in wireless networks, delay and packet loss rates are high and the available bandwidth fluctuates sharply. Therefore, QoE is degraded when the quality is selected on the basis of the measured bandwidth. In this paper, we propose an adaptive quality control scheme to improve QoE of video streaming in wireless networks. The proposed scheme calculates two factors, the buffer underflow probability and the instability, by considering the buffer state and the changes of quality level. Using these factors, the proposed scheme defines a quality control region that consists of four sub-regions. The video quality is determined by applying different control strategy to each sub-region. The results of experiments have shown that the proposed scheme improves QoE compared to the existing quality control schemes by minimizing the buffer underflow and the unnecessary quality changes and maximizing the average video quality.

Keywords: HTTP adaptive streaming · Quality of Experience
Wireless networks · Instability · Buffer underflow probability

1 Introduction

According to the Cisco Visual Networking Index, the proportion of video traffic currently on the Internet is estimated to be more than 70% and will increase to more than 82% in 2021 [1]. Therefore, HTTP adaptive streaming has been gaining attention to provide seamless streaming service for users. In HTTP adaptive streaming, the server stores an MPD (Media Presentation Description) describing video segments encoded at various bit rates and information about the media content. When the video streaming starts, the HTTP adaptive streaming client requests the MPD from the server. After receiving the MPD, the client selects the bit rate of the segment to be requested using the measured available bandwidth and the information described in the MPD. The available bandwidth is measured by the size of the last downloaded segment divided by the time taken to download it. HTTP adaptive streaming can guarantee QoE

© Springer Nature Switzerland AG 2018
M. Qiu (Ed.): SmartCom 2018, LNCS 11344, pp. 8–17, 2018.
https://doi.org/10.1007/978-3-030-05755-8_2

(Quality of Experience) of the video streaming by matching the available bandwidth and video quality to adaptively select the quality according to the network state [2].

However, HTTP adaptive streaming experiences QoE degradation due to unnecessary quality changes and buffer underflow in wireless networks [3]. The available bandwidth fluctuates abruptly even if there is no cross traffic because of interference between clients and fading of the channel in wireless networks. Also, the HTTP adaptive streaming client measures the available bandwidth after downloading the segment. Therefore, the fluctuations of bandwidth during segment download are not reflected appropriately in the bandwidth measurement [4].

In this paper, we propose an adaptive quality control scheme to improve QoE of video streaming in wireless networks. For each quality level, the proposed scheme calculates two factors, the buffer underflow probability and the instability, by considering the buffer state and the changes of quality level. Using these factors, the proposed scheme defines a quality control region that consists of four sub-regions, and the quality level is determined with different control strategy according to each sub-region.

The rest of this paper is organized as follows. In Sect. 2, we first describe the problems of HTTP adaptive streaming in wireless networks and the existing schemes to solve these problems. In Sect. 3, we describe the adaptive quality control scheme to improve QoE of video streaming in wireless networks. In Sect. 4, we evaluate the performance of the proposed scheme compared to the existing schemes. Finally, Sect. 5 concludes this paper.

2 Related Work

Figure 1 shows the QoE degradation problem in wireless networks. The available bandwidth is overestimated or underestimated in wireless networks because the instant throughput used in the bandwidth measurement is not able to reflect appropriately the fluctuations of bandwidth. When the available bandwidth is inaccurately estimated, the unnecessary quality changes and the buffer underflow occur, and the client utilizes the available bandwidth inefficiently.

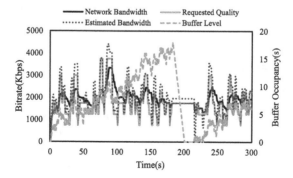

Fig. 1. QoE degradation problem in wireless networks.

To solve these QoE degradation problems in wireless networks, various schemes have been proposed. These schemes propose various bandwidth estimation methods for wireless networks and the quality control that takes additional consideration of the buffer state.

A throughput-based quality control scheme uses EWMA (Exponential Weighted Moving Average) of the previously downloaded segments to estimate the available bandwidth. We will denote this scheme as the conventional scheme [5]. Using EWMA improves an accuracy of the bandwidth measurement because it reflects instant fluctuations of the bandwidth and the previously measured bandwidth simultaneously. However, there is a problem that the weight parameter used in EWMA needs to be fixed depending on the type or the state of networks.

BBA (Buffer-Based Approach to Rate Adaptation) defines adaptation region that maps the buffer level to video quality level [6]. In the adaptation region, BBA selects the quality level according to buffer thresholds. These thresholds determine the optimal quality level that minimizes the buffer underflow. However, the unnecessary quality changes occur when the buffer level fluctuates near the buffer thresholds because these thresholds are fixed according to the number of quality levels.

JSQS (Joint Scheduling and Quality Selection) uses EWMA to measure the available bandwidth and selects the quality level based on the measured bandwidth [7]. To determine the optimal quality level in dense wireless networks, JSQS uses PID (Proportional-Integral-Derivative) controller to manage the quality control and the scheduling of segment request. However, the PID controller is too sensitive to the changes of each gain parameter that affect the performance.

OASVLS (Online Adaptive Scalable Video Layer Switching for Video Streaming) calculates the buffer underflow probability using the buffer state and the average reduction of buffer level [8]. OASVLS decreases the quality level when the buffer underflow probability is high and increases the quality level when the underflow probability is low. However, when the available bandwidth fluctuates abruptly, the average reduction of the buffer level is inaccurately estimated. Therefore, the client experiences the unnecessary quality changes.

SVAA (Smooth Video Adaptation Algorithm) selects the quality level by considering the buffer level, measured bandwidth, and requested quality observed within the predefined interval. The client decides target quality level to adapt the quality level smoothly [9]. However, SVAA is not able to respond quickly to the fluctuations of the bandwidth because it uses the average throughput in the bandwidth measurement.

3   Proposed Quality Control Scheme

Figure 2 shows the structure of the proposed quality control scheme. In the *bandwidth estimator*, the proposed scheme measures the available bandwidth and the *history manager* collects information about the measured bandwidth, the buffer level, and requested quality observed within a predefined interval. For each quality level, the *factor estimator* calculates the buffer underflow probability and the instability using the collected information. The *region manager* defines the quality control region that consists of four sub-regions using the calculated factors and switches the sub-region to another sub-region for minimizing the unnecessary quality changes caused by the wrong determined sub-region. The *quality controller* selects the quality level according to the control strategy in each sub-region, and the *segment requester* demands the segment corresponding to the selected quality level from the server.

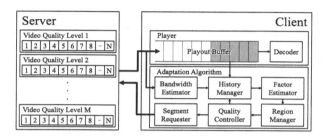

Fig. 2. Structure of the proposed quality control scheme.

As given in (1), the proposed scheme measures the available bandwidth using the segment length, τ, the download time of n th segment, D_n, and the bit rates of the n th segment, $R(l_n)$, corresponding to the quality level, l_n. l_n has the value from 1 to M; M denotes the value of maximum quality level. The measured bandwidth is smoothed using EWMA as given in (2). T_n is the instant bandwidth of the nth segment, T_n^s is the smoothed bandwidth, and α is a smoothing factor. We set the value of α equal to 0.8

$$T_n = \frac{R(l_n) \cdot \tau}{D_n} \tag{1}$$

$$T_n^s = \alpha \cdot T_{n-1}^s + (1 - \alpha) \cdot T_n \tag{2}$$

After the bandwidth measurement, the expected download time, D_{n+1}^{exp}, is calculated as given in (3) to estimate the changes of the buffer level. It denotes the predicted time when the next segment is downloaded in a given bandwidth.

$$D_{n+1}^{exp} = \frac{R(l_{n+1}) \cdot \tau}{T_n^s} \tag{3}$$

Using difference between the expected download time and previous download time, and changes of the quality level, the buffer underflow probability, $p_u(l_{n+1})$, is calculated as given in (4). $\hat{l}_n$ is the quality level that is previously selected by the proposed scheme. An increase in the expected download time and the quality level denotes that the stored data in the buffer have to be more consumed for seamless playback. Therefore, the higher underflow probability represents that the bit rates of the segment corresponding to the quality level exceeds the available bandwidth so that we need to decrease the quality level to minimize the risk of the buffer underflow.

$$p_u(l_{n+1}) = \left(\frac{1 + \tanh\left(\frac{D_{n+1}^{exp} - D_n}{D_n}\right)}{2} \right) \cdot \left(\frac{l_{n+1}}{l_{n+1} + \hat{l_n}} \right) \tag{4}$$

The proposed scheme calculates the instability, $p_i(l_{n+1})$, using (5), by considering the changes of quality level and the difference between the bit rates of two neighboring segments. To calculate the instability, we need to reflect the changes of the quality level observed from the past to the present. Therefore, the proposed scheme calculates the instability with the predefined interval. Length of the interval, m, indicates the number of segments to be considered for calculating the instability.

$$p_i(l_{n+1}) = \frac{\sum_{k=0}^{m-1}\left(|R(l_{n+1-k}) - R(l_{n-k})| \cdot (m - k - 1)\right)}{\sum_{k=0}^{m-1}\left(R(l_{n+1-k}) \cdot (m - k + 1)\right)} \tag{5}$$

Figure 3 shows the quality control region of the proposed scheme. The control region is divided into four sub-regions, and the appropriate sub-region for each quality level is determined by its value of the underflow probability and the instability. First of all, aggressiveness and conservativeness in the quality control are decided by the instability, and the quality level increases or decreases on the basis of the buffer underflow probability. Using the pair of the calculated factors corresponding to each quality level, the proposed scheme identifies where each quality level falls into the sub-regions. The sub-region that includes the most of quality levels is selected.

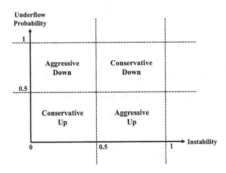

Fig. 3. Quality control region of the proposed scheme.

At the start of the streaming session, the proposed scheme is not able to calculate the instability because we need the information of the changes of quality level from the past to the present. Therefore, the proposed scheme adapts the quality level only after the client has downloaded more than m segments. When initial buffering starts, the proposed scheme selects the lowest quality level to fill the buffer and increases the quality level by one level at a time to utilize the bandwidth efficiently. When increasing the quality level, the proposed scheme maintains the current quality level until the number of requests of the corresponding quality level exceeds the value of the maintenance parameter, θ_n. Initial buffering ends when the buffer charging rate of the n th segment, γ_n is less than 0 or the buffer level exceeds the maximum buffer level. The buffer charging rate denotes how much buffer is consumed during the download of a segment and is calculated as given in (6). The maintenance parameter is determined as given in (7) using the difference between the maximum quality level, l_{max}, and the current quality level.

$$\gamma_n = \frac{\tau}{D_n} - 1 \tag{6}$$

$$\theta_n = l_{max} - l_n \tag{7}$$

After the initial buffering, the proposed scheme selects the quality level according to the determined sub-region. In the *aggressive down* region, the proposed scheme decreases the quality level due to the high underflow probability. As given in (8), the client selects the highest quality level that will not drop the buffer level during the download of the segment.

$$\hat{l}_{n+1} = \max\left\{ l_{n+1} \Big| \frac{T_n^s}{R(l_{n+1})} - 1 \geq 0 \right\} \tag{8}$$

We expect the abrupt changes of the quality level and the degradation of the average video quality when the instability is high. Therefore, in the *conservative down* region, the proposed scheme decreases the quality level according to the comparison between the bandwidth utilization of the nth segment, u_n, and expected bandwidth utilization, u_{n+1}^{exp}. The bandwidth utilization denotes how much of the bandwidth is occupied during the download of the corresponding segment. The expected bandwidth utilization is calculated as given in (9) using the buffer underflow probability and the instability, and the weight parameter, ε, is calculated as given in (10). As given in (11), the proposed scheme decreases the quality level when the expected bandwidth utilization is greater than the bandwidth utilization of the previous segment and maintains the previous quality level in the other cases.

$$u_{n+1}^{exp} = \varepsilon \cdot \frac{1}{p_i(\hat{l}_n - 1)} + (1 - \varepsilon) \cdot p_u(\hat{l}_n - 1) \tag{9}$$

$$\varepsilon = \frac{|R(\hat{l}_n - 1) - R(\hat{l}_n)|}{R(\hat{l}_n - 1) + R(\hat{l}_n)} \tag{10}$$

$$\hat{l}_{n+1} = \begin{cases} \hat{l}_n - 1, & if u_{n+1}^{exp} \geq u_n \\ \hat{l}_n, & else \end{cases} \tag{11}$$

When the buffer underflow probability and the instability are low, we expect that there is no risk of the buffer underflow. However, we need to consider the increase in the instability caused by the abrupt increase of the quality level. In the *conservative up* region, the proposed scheme calculates the target buffer occupancy, β_{tar}, as given in (12). The buffer occupancy, β_n, is the ratio of the current buffer level and the maximum buffer level, B_{max}. Using (13), the proposed scheme calculates the target quality level, l_{tar}, whose buffer occupancy after downloading the segment of the corresponding quality level is higher than the target buffer occupancy. The proposed scheme increases the quality level by one level only when the previous quality level is lower than the target quality level, as given in (14).

$$\beta_{tar} = \beta_n \cdot \left(1 - e^{-0.5} \cdot p_i(\hat{l}_n + 1) \cdot p_u(\hat{l}_n + 1)\right) \tag{12}$$

$$l_{tar} = \min\left\{l_{n+1} \Big| \frac{1}{B_{max}} \cdot \left(B_n + \tau - \tau \cdot \frac{l_{n+1}}{T_n^s}\right) \geq \beta_{tar}\right\} \tag{13}$$

$$\hat{l}_{n+1} = \begin{cases} \hat{l}_n + 1, & if\, \hat{l}_n \leq l_{tar} - 1 \\ \hat{l}_n, & else \end{cases} \tag{14}$$

In the *aggressive up* region, the proposed scheme aims to quickly utilize the available bandwidth. Therefore, as given in (15), the proposed scheme selects the quality level that is higher by one level than the previous quality level.

$$\hat{l}_{n+1} = \hat{l}_n + 1 \tag{15}$$

The proposed scheme selects the quality level according to the control strategy of the determined sub-region each time the segment is downloaded. However, the buffer underflow probability and the instability are appeared differently depending on whether the quality level is high or not. For example, if the client selected the highest quality level before, the underflow probability of other quality levels is calculated to low. Therefore, the proposed scheme selects the lower sub-regions and will not decrease the quality level until the buffer underflow occurs. In another case, the underflow probability of other quality levels is calculated to high so that the proposed scheme selects the upper sub-regions and will not increase the quality level for a long time. Therefore, the client utilizes the bandwidth inefficiently.

To solve these problems due to the wrong determined sub-region, the proposed scheme calculates the quality indicator, Q_{amp}, using (16). The quality indicator is calculated using the difference between the current quality level and the minimum quality level, l_{min}, or the maximum quality level.

$$Q_{amp} = \begin{cases} 0, & if\, |l_{min} - \hat{l}_n| \leq |l_{max} - \hat{l}_n| \\ 1, & else \end{cases} \tag{16}$$

As shown in Fig. 4, after the downloading the segment, if the value of Q_{amp} is 0, the upper sub-regions switch to the lower sub-regions, whereas, if the value is 1, the lower sub-regions switch to the upper sub-regions. However, when the sub-regions switch to other sub-regions frequently, the unnecessary quality changes occur because of the abrupt changes in the control strategy. Therefore, the proposed scheme switches the sub-regions to other sub-regions only when the bandwidth utilization of the current segment exceeds the length of the segment.

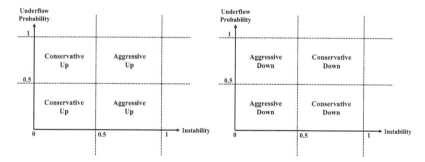

Fig. 4. Switching of the sub-regions (left: Q_{amp} is 0, right: Q_{amp} is 1)

4 Performance Evaluation

In order to evaluate the performance of the proposed scheme, we constructed a network topology as shown in Fig. 5 and implemented the HTTP adaptive streaming player with an NS-3 (Network Simulator) [10]. In the wireless environment as shown in Fig. 6, we evaluate the performance between the proposed scheme and the existing quality control schemes.

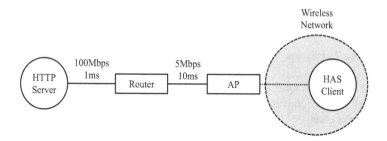

Fig. 5. Network topology.

The server offers seven video qualities including 750, 1250, 1750, 2250, 3000, 3750, 4500 kbps, and the length of the segment is set to 2 s. The experiments are performed for 200 s, and we compare the performance of the proposed scheme to two existing schemes, the conventional scheme [5] and BBA [6].

Figure 7 shows the changes in the video quality level and the buffer level of each scheme. All schemes do not experience the buffer underflow, but the conventional scheme changes the quality level unnecessarily because it selects the quality level based on the inaccurately measured bandwidth. BBA experiences a high number of the quality level changes because the buffer level fluctuates near the buffer thresholds.

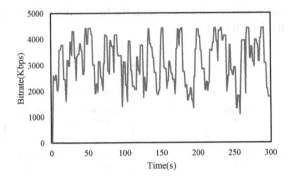

Fig. 6. Available bandwidth in wireless networks.

The proposed scheme selects the quality level by using the buffer underflow probability and the instability, instead of using the measured bandwidth. Therefore, the proposed scheme minimizes the unnecessary quality changes.

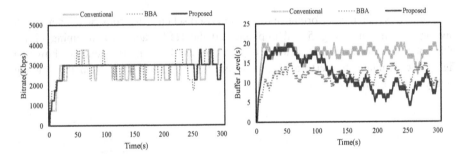

Fig. 7. Changes in the quality level (left) and the buffer level (right).

Figure 8 shows the QoE comparison of the quality control schemes. The average video quality of the conventional scheme and BBA are lower than the proposed scheme, and the changes in the quality level of the proposed scheme are almost one-third of the compared schemes.

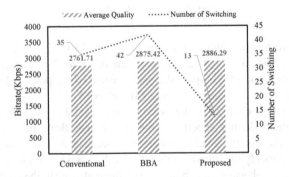

Fig. 8. QoE comparison of the quality control schemes.

5 Conclusion

In this paper, we have proposed the adaptive quality control scheme to improve QoE of video streaming in wireless networks. For quality control, the proposed scheme calculates two factors, the buffer underflow probability and the instability. Based on these factors, the proposed scheme defines the quality control region that consists of four sub-regions and applying different control strategy according to each sub-region. The proposed scheme selects the quality level using the control strategy of the determined sub-region. Experimental results have shown that the proposed scheme improves QoE by minimizing the unnecessary quality changes and the risk of the buffer underflow and maximizing the average video quality.

In future work, we plan to implement the proposed scheme in a real video player and evaluate the performance using complicated network scenarios with other quality control schemes.

Acknowledgement. This work was supported by Institute for Information & communications Technology Promotion (IITP) grant funded by the Korea government (MSIT) (No. 2017-0-00224, Development of generation, distribution and consumption technologies of dynamic media based on UHD broadcasting contents).

References

1. Cisco Visual Networking Index: Forecast and Methodology, 2016–2021. Cisco System Inc., San Jose, June 2017
2. Kua, J., Armitage, G., Branch, P.: A survey of rate adaptation techniques for dynamic adaptive streaming over HTTP. IEEE Commun. Surv. Tutorials **19**(3), 1842–1866 (2017)
3. Aguayo, M., Bellido, L., Lentisco, C.M., Pastor, E.: DASH adaptation algorithm based on adaptive forgetting factor estimation. IEEE Trans. Multimed. **20**(5), 1224–1232 (2017)
4. Bedogni, L., et al.: Dynamic adaptive video streaming on heterogeneous TVWS and Wi-Fi networks. IEEE/ACM Trans. Netw. **25**(6), 3253–3266 (2017)
5. Li, Z., et al.: Probe and adapt: rate adaptation for HTTP video streaming at scale. IEEE J. Sel. Areas Commun. **32**(4), 719–733 (2014)
6. Huang, T., Johari, R., McKeown, N., Trunnell, M., Waston, M.: A buffer-based approach to rate adaptation: evidence from a large video streaming service. In: Proceedings of the ACM Conference on SIGCOMM, pp. 187–198, August 2014
7. Miller, K., Bethanabholta, D., Caire, G., Wolisz, A.: A control-theoretic approach to adaptive video streaming in dense wireless networks. IEEE Trans. Multimed. **17**(8), 1309–1322 (2015)
8. Chen, S., Yang, J., Ran, Y., Yang, E.: Adaptive layer switching algorithm based on buffer underflow probability for scalable video streaming over wireless networks. IEEE Trans. Circ. Syst. Video Technol. **26**(6), 1146–1160 (2016)
9. Tian, G., Liu, Y.: On adaptive HTTP streaming to mobile devices. In: Proceedings of the International Packet Video Workshop, pp. 1–8, December 2013
10. The Network Simulator NS-3. <http://www.nsnam.org>

Travel Review Analysis System with Big Data (TRAS)

Chakkrit Snae Namahoot[1,2(✉)], Sopon Pinijkitcharoenkul[3],
and Michael Brückner[4]

[1] Department of Computer Science and Information Technology,
Faculty of Science, Naresuan University, Phitsanulok, Thailand
chakkrits@nu.ac.th
[2] Center of Excellence in Nonlinear Analysis and Optimization,
Faculty of Science, Naresuan University, Phitsanulok, Thailand
[3] Information Technology Center, Pibulsongkram Rajabhat University,
Phitsanulok, Thailand
sopon_b@psru.ac.th
[4] Department of Educational Technology and Communication,
Faculty of Education, Naresuan University, Phitsanulok, Thailand
michaelb@nu.ac.th

Abstract. This paper introduces a process for online travel review analysis in Thai language employed in a recommender system supporting travelers (TRAS). The process covers three main categories: attractions, accommodation, and gastronomy. The filtering and queuing results gained with MapReduce build the input for three main steps: (1) the analysis process for element scores, (2) the analysis process for the total scores of the reviews, and (3) the travel guidance system based on users' selections. The extensive tests revealed that the system operates properly regarding functional and non-functional requirements. We employed 60,000 travel reviews containing all categories to test the analysis process for steps (1) and (2). We found that the number of adjectives and modifiers in each review affects the time used for analysis. In contrast to previous recommender systems, TRAS applies a more diverse and transparent rating and ranking approach. Travelers can select the features they are interested in and get personalized results, so that a given location might achieve different rankings for different travelers.

Keywords: Big data · Data analysis · MapReduce · Decision support system

1 Introduction

At present, the tourism industry in Thailand is receiving increasing attention. General travel information and specific reviews are important in planning and deciding where to visit. Potential travelers find tourist information on many Websites. Visitors can find information about tourism to make decisions and plan for tourism. However, with so much information available on the Internet, they need to spend a lot of time searching to make sure they get all information they need to make informed decisions. The information retrieved from the Internet covers such items as attractions,

M. Qiu (Ed.): SmartCom 2018, LNCS 11344, pp. 18–28, 2018.
https://doi.org/10.1007/978-3-030-05755-8_3

accommodation, hotel and restaurants but cannot be acknowledged whether the tourist information is good or not. Travelers mostly read reviews or comments from other travelers who have been to that place before. The reviews contain the pros and cons and can be used as identifying alternatives or for planning decisions. Travel information online reviews, particularly high-score reviews from tourists who have been there, can be used to support decision making on travel planning, for example, for choosing tourist places, accommodations, or restaurants. Due to the large number of reviews that users often encounter, it takes a lot of time reading those reviews and making informed decisions based on the results.

Regarding the tool, the large amount of data impedes analysis and processing of useful information within a reasonable time [1, 2]. To analyze these large data sets in data warehouse-like fashion such specialized pieces of software as Hadoop and Hive have been employed. The software library Hadoop enables the processing of large amounts of data, whereas Hive builds an SQL-like interface for extracting, manipulating and managing the data.

Attacking the problem mentioned above, we have developed a system for extracting and analyzing data from online travel reviews in Thai language with Hadoop and Hive. TRAS uses a novel approach with both qualitative and quantitative ranking analysis of user selected components found in traveler reviews on accommodation, attractions and gastronomy.

Another point that needs attention is the recognition of out-of-date reviews, which contents may be of no use at the time of decision making. The Traveler Review Analysis System (TRAS) analyses the posting dates of reviews and uses only those reviews that have been posted during the past 18 months of system run, whereby both Christian Era (AD) and Buddhist Era (BE) can be handled. Reviews without date are dismissed.

Previously published recommender systems do not take into account such features as date or reviews, key contents of facilities and food offered, among others. Instead they focus on overall ratings as the number of stars (hotels) and the number of positive and negative words used in the reviews divided by the total number of those words.

2 Related Work

The extraction of knowledge from only online hotel reviews using fuzzy logic [3] is a research that extract online reviews from travelers who stay at the hotel by building a knowledge base ontology of tourism. The ontology contains a glossary of terms that define level of scores from 1 (very poor) to 5 (very good) and the context-free grammars construction. Also the knowledge extraction task is to calculate the level of scores of the review sentences which is divided into two levels: (1) specific context/subject scores such as hotel features, and (2) overall scores using specific scores from (1) and a fuzzy calculation system. This research uses only online reviews in English and does not support Thai language. The emphasis is on data extraction, and the overview analysis uses a simple fuzzy rule based on hotel facilities.

A similar research covered the development of an ontology knowledge base for automated online news analysis [4] by considering the importance of words. Using the term frequency-inverse document frequency (TF-IDF) in the news content to gather appropriate words for the development of the ontological knowledge base and weighting of key words in the news content. Only the number of important words influences the analysis but not the position of the words in the texts, although this may be important for understanding the meaning of message.

Data mining and customer feedback summary [5] is a research that analyze customer reviews of online merchants and summarize a positive and negative opinion. There are three parts in the process: (1) use of data mining techniques and natural language processing techniques to mine the characteristics of the product from customer feedback, (2) analysis of each comment to indicate whether the comment is positive or negative, and (3) the conclusion of the above steps. This provides very helpful information for other customers and also the producer/owner of the product who can continue to adjust the products, yet again there is only a summary of positive and negative opinions without further details of the characteristics.

Jian et al. [6] conducted a research to analyze big data relating hotel customer responses based on cloud data. Hadoop was deployed on a cloud server for data collection and analysis together with WebCrawler to collect the feedback. Techniques of Neural networking and unsupervised learning were used in the analysis of the comments to understand their meaning. Hadoop and the K-means algorithm were used to arrange and update the data in the database.

3   System Architecture Design

3.1   Big Data

Big data is often labeled as the 3Vs: (1) Volume, i.e. the size of the data, (2) the Variety of data: structured, semi-structured and unstructured, and (3) the Velocity of data processing [7]. The problem of large data is data processing, and the software we use for processing large data comprises:

- Hadoop: an open source software developed by Java which is designed to accommodate a wide variety of structured and unstructured data and can process large data. The first version of Hadoop has two main components, the Hadoop Distributed File System (HDFS) and MapReduce. HDFS serves as a storage area. This stores large data classified into large subdirectories at a large number of Data Nodes. There is a Master Node that specifies the location of the data stored in the Data nodes. MapReduce works as the data processor to analyze data in the form of Map and Reduce function so that the system can distribute them in parallel to many Hadoop machines.
- Hive: a data warehouse system for Hadoop that easily facilitates data summary. It is a query tool that stores information in HDFS with SQL language instead of MapReduce programming. Hive is responsible for translating SQL statements into MapReduce. Large-scale data analysis using Hadoop Pig and Hive [8] is a research that presents large-scale data analysis using Hive, which runs in SQL format. There is also a research on Hive software that works on Hadoop [9] such as Facebook's

Data Infrastructure team presented loading and adding data with Hive, which looks at the data in tabular form.

3.2   System Process

In the process of analyzing online travel reviews, three main subjects (categories) of tourist information are covered: tourist attractions, accommodation and restaurants. An overview of the system process is presented in Fig. 1.

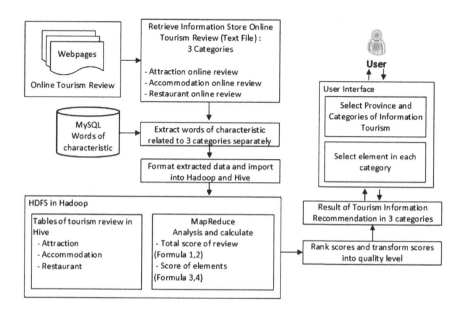

Fig. 1. System process

User: selects province (e.g., Phitsanulok Province) and categories of tourism information (attraction, accommodation and restaurant) they are interested in.

Select element in each category, for example a user selects accommodation category and refines by elements of service, cleanliness of a place and price.

The process used by the system is as follows (see formulas in the next section):

- Store online travel reviews related to attractions, accommodations and restaurants to a text file, then extract feature data, such as words of characteristics (adjectives) describing attractions, hotels and restaurants.
- Format and import the data into tables in Hive.
- Analyze and calculate the score of three types of tourist information review: the total score of reviews (Formula 1 and 2), score of all elements and score of the selected elements (Formula 3 and 4), rank the scores and transform them into quality levels.
- Display the results with ranking scores and quality levels.

3.3   Extraction of Review Characteristics from Big Data

A database is created to collect the words of the characteristics that describe important features of tourism information as used in the extraction process. The following types of words have been categorized:

- A word that indicates the quality, appearance, and characteristic of tourist attractions, accommodation and restaurants, such as stunning, beautiful, cheap, far, poor, bad, like, favor etc. 3 values of the words of characteristic: 1 represents positive, 0 represent fair and −1 represent negative words of review.
- Words that extend the words of characteristic as prefix (freaking, bloody (โกรต), very, a lot, (มาก)), suffix (a lot, so much (มาก)) etc.
- Words that indicating opposite, such as not (ไม่), for example not good, not ok, not so good, not bad, or not far.

All categorized words have a value level that is used in the analysis: the value of −2, −1, 0, 1, and 2 to show the levels of bad, fair and good (can be calculated from Table 1). The symbols +, − and 0 are "status symbols". The concepts of the item characteristics are extracted from our tourism ontology [10, 11].

Table 1. An example of words (characteristic) value calculation from review

Review: not clean, very nice location, cheap compared to quality, I like the room a lot even it smells bad, service is ok

Prefix modifier	Words of characteristic	Suffix modifier	Opposite modifier	Word value calculation	Sum of word value
-	Clean (+1)	-	Not (-)	−1	−1
Very(+1)	Nice (+1)	-	-	1 + 1	2
-	Cheap (+1)	-	-	1	1
-	Like (+1)	a lot (+1)	-	1 + 1	2
-	Smell (−1)	Bad (−1)	-	−1 + −1	−2
-	Ok (0)	-	-	0	0

Information obtained by the extraction process is then formatted and stored on Hive.

3.4   Review Analysis Process

In this process, the score of the adjectives extracted from Sect. 3.3 is calculated in three steps: (1) the total score of review, (2) the score of all elements, and (3) the score of selected elements by users, see the following algorithm.

Pre-process:

1. Input a review text and check the date of the review and exclude those without dates or with a date older than 18 months.

2. Classify elements and words identify them in each category as follows: Elements of attraction (convenience, service, atmosphere, facility, good place, and others), accommodation (convenience, service, clean place, food, atmosphere, price, and others) and restaurant (service, atmosphere, taste, price, music, fast delivery).
3. In each category (attraction, accommodation or restaurant), list all names (e.g. name of attraction, hotel, restaurant) to be analyzed.

Process:

Initialization: Review (ri) = 1, Words of characteristic = 0
Count all elements of each category and return number of all element (a)
Count words of characteristic in each review and return number of words (n)
      Return position of each word
If position of words of characteristic is next to each other (no extended words) then
      Return the words with value (compared to the words and value in database)
If not (there is extended word) check types of extended words and calculate values of words of characteristic (Table 1)
      Return number of words (n) of characteristic in each review
Compute score of each review using formula 1
      Return score of each review (pr)
Do until review (i) = m (all review)
Compute score of all review using formula 2.
      Return total score of all review (pr_{sum})
Compute score of all elements (pe_{all}) in each category using formula 3
      Return score of all elements (pe_{all})
Transform score into a quality level (very good, good, fair, bad, very bad, Table 2)
      Return a quality level for user Interface (Tourism Recommendation System with an Online Tourist In-formation Reviews Analysis):
User selects province, category with elements
      Return number of selected elements (s) according to the interface
Compute score of selected elements (pe_{select}) in each category using formula 4
Display elements found, recommend names in each selected category with total score of review (pr_{sum}), the quality level
Terminate after the last review to be processed

The score of each review pr is computed as

$$pr = \frac{\sum_{i=1}^{n} Wc_i}{n} \tag{1}$$

where Wc_i is the value of each word of characteristic i to n, n is a number of words characteristic found in each review.
      The score of all reviews pr_{sum} is computed as

$$pr_{sum} = \frac{\sum_{i=1}^{m} Pr_i}{m} \tag{2}$$

where pr_i the score of each review i to m, and m is the number of review found.

The score of all elements pe_{all} is computed as

$$pe_{all} = \frac{\sum_{i=1}^{a} Ca_i}{a} \tag{3}$$

where Ca_i is the score of each element i to a, and a is the number of all elements found in each category.

The score of user selected elements is

$$pe_{select} = \frac{\sum_{i=1}^{s} C_i}{s} \tag{4}$$

where C_i the score of each element i, and s is the number of selected elements in each category.

All scores (1)–(4) are then transformed into quality levels which are as follows:

From Table 1, word values can be divided into 5 levels (2 (very good), 1(good), 0 (fair), −1 (bad), −2 (very bad)) which is a level of measurement of class interval data. Thus, the class width can be calculated as (maximum score − minimum score)/number of class which is (2−(−2))/5 = 0.8 and score interval of quality level is as follows: Score ranges from 1.21 to 2.00 indicates a very good quality level, 0.41 to 1.20 indicates a good quality level, −0.40 to 0.40, indicates a fair quality level, −1.20 to −0.41 indicates a poor quality level and −2.00 to −1.21 indicates a very poor quality level.

Table 2. Quality level and score of all reviews (pr_{sum}), score of each element and score of all elements (pe_{all}) relating accommodation category

Element of accommodation	Number of reviews (m)	$(\sum Pr_i)$	$\sum C_i$	Quality level of elements
Service	4	(−1) + (1) + (2) + (2) = 4	1	Good
Atmosphere	1	0	0	Fair
Convenience	2	(1) + (−1) = 0	0	Fair
Food	6	(1) + (−1) + (1) + (−2) + (−1) + (1) = −1	−0.17	Fair
Price	4	(−1) + (−1) + (−1) + (1) = −2	−0.5	Bad
Clean place	3	(−1) + (−1) + (−1) = −3	−1	Bad
Others	1	(−1) = −1	−1	Bad
Sum	21	−3	$\sum Ca_i = -1.67$	Fair (−0.24)
pr_{sum} = −3/21 = −0.14 (quality level = fair)				
pe_{all} = −1.67/7 = −0.24 (quality level = fair)				

In Table 2 examples of calculations and scores of all reviews (pr_{sum}), scores of each element and scores of all elements (pe_{all}) of the accommodation category are presented.

4 Result and Discussion

To test the development of the tourism recommendation system, three main categories of approximately 60,000 online tourist information reviews have been used: attractions, accommodations, and gastronomy. The results are as follows: Fig. 2 shows the total score of all ten reviews regarding Phitsanulok United Guest House, which is 0.97 (the

Phitsanulok United Guest House				
Review no.	Number of words characteristic (n)	Wc_i	Pr	Quality of Review
1	3	3	1.00	Good
2	15	12	0.80	Good
3	4	1	0.25	Fair
4	7	8	1.14	Good
5	5	5	1.00	Good
6	2	2	1.00	Good
7	2	3	1.50	Very Good
8	3	3	1.00	Good
9	4	4	1.00	Good
10	5	5	1.00	Good
		Total Score of Reviews	0.97	
		Quality level	Good	

Fig. 2. Total score based on all reviews regarding Phitsanulok United Guest House

Phitsanulok United Guest House				
element (a)	No of word (m)	Ca_i	Pe_{all}	Quality of level of element
Convenience	1	1	1.00	Good
Service	5	5	1.00	Good
Clean place	24	22	0.92	Good
Food	1	0	0.00	Fair
Atmosphere	2	0	0.00	Fair
Price	2	2	1.00	Good
Other	15	16	1.07	Good
		Total Score of Elements	0.71	
		Quality level	Good	

Fig. 3. Sample score calculation results from all elements.

sum of score of each review is divided by the number of all reviews (9.69/10 = 0.97). Then the score of 0.97 is transformed into a quality level, which means that the Phitsanulok United Guest House has a good quality level based on the ten reviews.

Figure 3 shows the results of the total score analysis of all selected elements for Phitsanulok United Guest House which is 0.71 (total score of all elements is divided by the total number of all elements (4.99/7 = 0.71). The result of the analysis shows that Phitsanulok United Guest House has good quality based on selected elements.

Figure 4 displays the screen when the user selects Phitsanulok Province, all categories, and two, four and four elements from attraction, accommodation and restaurant, respectively. The system calculates the scores as described and the results are sorted from highest to lowest total score (Fig. 5).

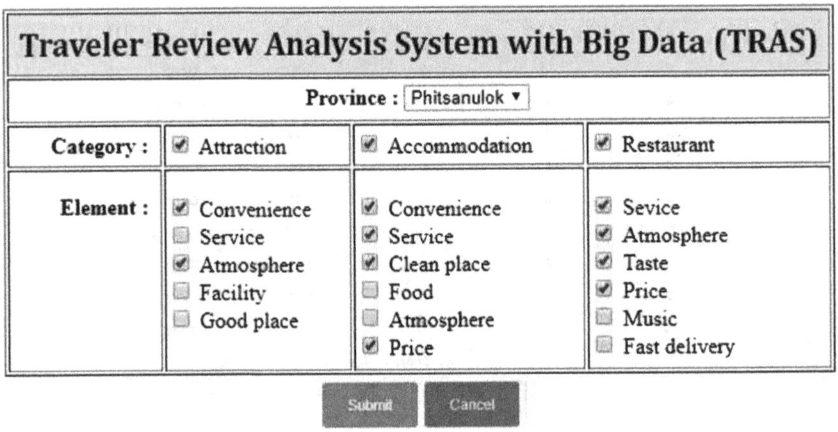

Traveler Review Analysis System with Big Data (TRAS)

Province : Phitsanulok ▼

Category :	☑ Attraction	☑ Accommodation	☑ Restaurant
Element :	☑ Convenience	☑ Convenience	☑ Sevice
	☐ Service	☑ Service	☑ Atmosphere
	☑ Atmosphere	☑ Clean place	☑ Taste
	☐ Facility	☐ Food	☑ Price
	☐ Good place	☐ Atmosphere	☐ Music
		☑ Price	☐ Fast delivery

Submit   Cancel

Fig. 4. User interface of TRAS

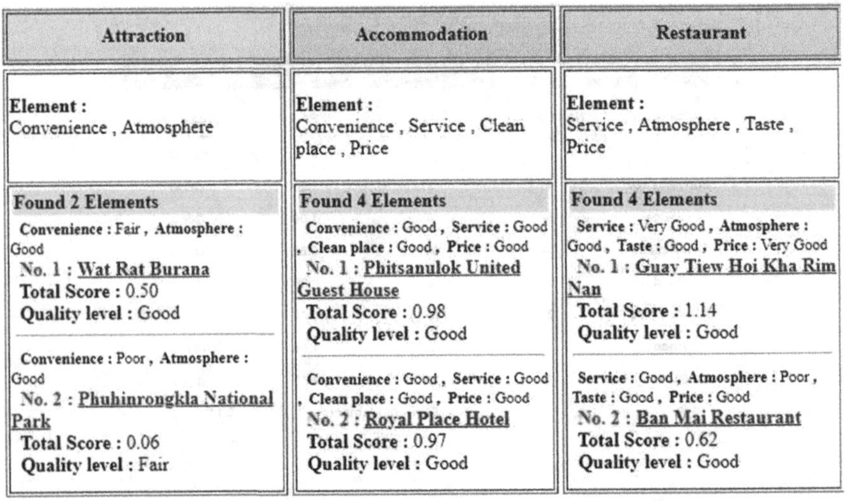

Attraction	Accommodation	Restaurant
Element : Convenience , Atmosphere	Element : Convenience , Service , Clean place , Price	Element : Service , Atmosphere , Taste , Price
Found 2 Elements	**Found 4 Elements**	**Found 4 Elements**
Convenience : Fair , Atmosphere : Good No. 1 : Wat Rat Burana Total Score : 0.50 Quality level : Good	Convenience : Good , Service : Good , Clean place : Good , Price : Good No. 1 : Phitsanulok United Guest House Total Score : 0.98 Quality level : Good	Service : Very Good , Atmosphere : Good , Taste : Good , Price : Very Good No. 1 : Guay Tiew Hoi Kha Rim Nan Total Score : 1.14 Quality level : Good
Convenience : Poor , Atmosphere : Good No. 2 : Phuhinrongkla National Park Total Score : 0.06 Quality level : Fair	Convenience : Good , Service : Good , Clean place : Good , Price : Good No. 2 : Royal Place Hotel Total Score : 0.97 Quality level : Good	Service : Good , Atmosphere : Poor , Taste : Good , Price : Good No. 2 : Ban Mai Restaurant Total Score : 0.62 Quality level : Good

Fig. 5. Personalized TRAS recommendations for Phitsanulok Province

Table 3 shows a comparison of features of similar systems developed previously and TRAS.

Table 3. Comparative results with the [3] and [6]

System features	[3]	[6]	TRAS
Hotel review	✓	✓	✓
Tourism recommendation	✗	✗	✓
Ranking overview	✓	✓	✓
Ranking tourism features	✗	✗	✓
Mobile application	✗	✗	✓
Analysis with total score quality level	✓	✗	✓
Selected scores of tourism information	✗	✗	✓
Analysis with big data analytic tools	✗	✓	✓

5 Conclusion and Further Work

In this research, the Traveler Review Analysis System (TRAS) based on an online tourist information reviews analysis process using big data has been developed. TRAS analyzes travel information in Thai language and covers three main categories: attractions, accommodations, and gastronomy. Review data are extracted, transformed and stored using Hadoop and Hive applications. Individual and overall scores are calculated considering adjectives and modifiers. The results are displayed as recommendations via the user interface. Users can select province, travel elements and travel categories, and then the system ranks the items individually selected by the users.

In contrast to previously developed recommender systems, TRAS takes into account requirements selected by users and ranks the locations individually. This may lead to different ranking results for different travelers. Additionally, TRAS is available as a smartphone application and can therefore be accessed on the spot.

The results of approximately 60,000 test cases show that the system operates properly. In terms of timing, we employed approximately 7,000 reviews of travel information from the three categories to test the analysis process. The number of adjectives and modifiers affects the time used for analysis. This is because the system checks all adjectives, pre-modifiers, including post-modifiers of the adjectives before performing the analysis.

A limitation of TRAS is inherent to the concept of traveler reviews: fake reviews posted by parties close to the item of review cannot be spotted easily and subsequently excluded. For the next version of TRAS, we plan to employ only reviews posted on high quality Websites that check the plausibility of reviews and ask reviewers to unveil their hotel reservations, tickets and so forth. It remains to be seen, though, how much information will be left after using this strategy.

References

1. Snae, C., Pawarawat, N.: A study of internet user behaviour using techniques of data mining and temporal ontology. In: The Third Naresuan Research Conference, Phitsanulok, Thailand, 28–29 July 2007 (2007). (in Thailand)
2. Snae, C., Brückner, M.: Data cleaning and clustering of internet log files based on a temporal ontology. In: The Third Mahasarakham International Workshop on AI (MIWAI 2009) (2009)
3. Kitwattanathaworn, P., Angsakul, T., Angsakul, C.: Knowledge extraction system from online hotel review using fuzzy logic. J. KMUTNB **23**(2), 363–377 (2013)
4. Chotirat, W., Boonrawd, P., Wichian, S.N.: Developing an ontology knowledge based for automatic online news analysis. Inf. Technol. J. **7**(14), 13–18 (2011)
5. Hu, M., Liu, B.: Mining and summarizing customer reviews. In: Proceedings of the 2004 ACM SIGKDD International Conference on Knowledge Discovery and Data Mining, pp. 168–177 (2004)
6. Jian, M.S., Fang, Y.C., Wang, Y.K., Cheng, C.: Big data analysis in hotel customer response and evaluation based on cloud. In: 19th International Conference on Advanced Communication Technology (ICACT) (2017). https://ieeexplore.ieee.org/document/7890201/. Accessed 21 Aug 2018
7. Bhosale, H.S., Gadekar, D.P.: A review paper on big data and hadoop. Int. J. Sci. Res. Publ. **4**(10), 1–7 (2014)
8. Dhawan, S., Rathee, S.: Big data analytics using hadoop components like pig and hive. Am. Int. J. Res. Sci., Technol., Eng. Math. (AIJRSTEM) **2**, 88–93 (2013)
9. Thusoo, A., et al.: Hive - a warehousing solution over a map-reduce framework (2009). https://research.facebook.com/publications/hive-a-warehousing-solution-over-a-map-reduce-framework/. Accessed 18 July 2018
10. Namahoot, C.S., Panawong, N., Brückner, M.: A tourism recommendation system for thailand using semantic web rule language and K-NN algorithm. INFORMATION **19**(7), 3017–3024 (2016)
11. Namahoot, C.S., Brückner, M., Panawong, N.: Context-aware tourism recommender system using temporal ontology and Naïve Bayes. In: Unger, H., Meesad, P., Boonkrong, S. (eds.) Recent Advances in Information and Communication Technology 2015. AISC, vol. 361, pp. 183–194. Springer, Cham (2015). https://doi.org/10.1007/978-3-319-19024-2_19

Vulnerability Assessment for PMU Communication Networks

Xiangyu Niu[1(✉)], Yue Tong[2], and Jinyuan Sun[1]

[1] Department of Electrical Enginnering and Computer Science,
University of Tennessee, Knoxville, TN 37996, USA
`xniu@vols.utk.edu, jysun@utk.edu`
[2] OSIsoft, 1700 Market St, STE 2200, Philadelphia, PA 19103, USA
`atong@osisoft.com`

Abstract. The smart grid is introducing many salient features such as wide-area situational awareness, precise demand response, substation automation. These features are enabled by data communication networks that facilitate the collection, transfer, and processing of a wide variety of data regarding different components of the smart grid. As a result, the smart grid's heavy dependence on data inevitably poses a great challenge to ensure data integrity and authenticity. Even though with defending mechanisms like firewalls deployed, the internal network can no longer be deemed physically isolated. Additionally, the experience with information security in common computer network reveals that flawed designs, implementations, and configurations of the communication network introduce vulnerabilities. These vulnerabilities open opportunities for attackers to launch cyber attackers. In this paper, we attempt to gain more insights with respect to the cyber security of the current PMU network technologies by exploring, validating, and demonstrating vulnerabilities.

Keywords: Vulnerability assessment · Cyber security · Smart grid

1 Introduction

A smart grid revitalizes the legacy electricity grid with modern communications to deliver real-time information and enable the near-instantaneous balance of supply and demand management. Naively, smart grid devices can directly be connected to the Internet. However, as data size, latency and reliability requirements for different smart grid applications vary widely, a number of communication systems and network structures have been proposed specifically for the smart grid.

In the past, legacy power grid was designed for local operations with limited remote control. The security of the legacy power grid largely relies on its physical isolation from the outside world, i.e. the airgappedness. For smart grid, most communication technologies are designed to support some monitoring/controlling applications as Supervisory Control and Data Acquisition

© Springer Nature Switzerland AG 2018
M. Qiu (Ed.): SmartCom 2018, LNCS 11344, pp. 29–38, 2018.
https://doi.org/10.1007/978-3-030-05755-8_4

(SCADA), Energy Management Systems (EMS), Distribution Management Systems (DMS), etc. For SCADA system, It is utilized for Distribution Automation (DA) and computerized remote control of Medium Voltage (MV) substations and power grids, and it helps electric utilities to achieve higher reliability of supply and reduce operating and maintenance costs. Connections between and DA/DMS control centers and EMS is typically provided via a high-performance IP Gateway or a similar node [3]. As a result, the air gap between the power grid internal network and the Internet has been increasingly blurring [10]. As such, even with defending mechanisms like Intrusion Detection System (IDS) and firewall deployed, the smart grid communication network can no longer be deemed as physically isolated. This lead to significant issues related to cyber attacks on the power grid. For instance, false data may mislead operation and control functions of control and monitor system such as EMSs. In a worst-case situation, carefully fabricated data could have potentially catastrophic consequences as suggested in [6]. In the past decade, there are a significant number of issues related to cyber attacks on the power grid. Likewise in the smart grid, before trusting and assigning critical responsibilities to a newly introduced network-related technology, we need to assess its potential vulnerabilities of all aspects, including the standards, software implementations, network configurations, etc. In this paper, we chose the PMU communication network because of its indispensable and critical role in the future smart grid as well as that the PMU network has not been under comprehensive vulnerability assessment in existing literature.

In the rest of the paper, we first revisit the concept, existing standard of PMU network in Sect. 2. Additionally, we present the evaluation setup for testing our protecting scheme in Sect. 3. Then, Sect. 4 covers the details of the penetration testing, including the procedures of the penetration testing, testing techniques, and a list of potential vulnerabilities to be explored. Finally, mitigation analysis is provided in Sect. 5.

2 Preliminary

2.1 Phasor Measurement Units and PMU Network

Synchrophasors are time-synchronized numbers that represent both the magnitude and phase angle of the sine waves found in electricity. The synchronization is attained by a real-time sampling utilizing calibrating signals from the Global Positioning System (GPS) technology. Synchrophasors are measured by high-speed monitors called Phasor Measurement Units (PMUs) that are 100 times faster than SCADA. PMU measurements record grid conditions with great accuracy and offer insight into grid stability or stress.

For the typical architecture of a PMU network, a utility company usually deploys PMUs at intersecting locations of its power system. PMUs send the measured data to the local PDCs within the same utility. Local PDCs send the concentrated data to a central data repository called SuperPDC, usually hosted by the regional Independent System Operator (ISO). A "publisher-subscriber" model can describe the data communication in a PMU network, where PMUs or downstream PDCs publish data while upstream PDCs subscribe to receive measurement data from the subscribed PMUs.

2.2   IEEE C37.118 Protocol

The purpose for IEEE 37.118 Protocol is to facilitate data exchange among measurement, data collection, and application equipment. It provides a defined, open access method for all vendors to use to facilitate the development and use of synchrophasors. It is a simple and direct method of data transmission and accretion within a phasor measurement system, which may be used directly or with other communication protocols. A number of standards have been proposed for the communication between PMUs and PDCs. Although IEC 61850-90-5 has several unique features over C37.118 [4]. However, its adoption is still limited and proper investigation of its features, requirements, and limitations is required. In this paper, we still use C37.118 and IP over Ethernet as the main communication protocol for PMU network.

To simplify widespread adoption of synchrophasor measurement technology and facilitate the use of other communication protocols for phasor data transmission, IEEE C37.118 is split into two standards, one with measurement requirements and the other with the data transfer requirements. This allows other communication protocols and systems to be used with phasor measurement systems supporting the original purpose of the standard.

In [1], IEEE C37.118 standard defines four types of messages: data, configuration, header, and command, which are briefly introduced as follows. A typical communication scenario when the data source operates in commanded mode is depicted in Fig. 2. For simplicity, header message is not shown which may be requested by the control center using command message.

- **Data Frame** transfer real-time measurements data from PMU or PDC to the receiving device (PDC or SuperPDC, correspondingly). An IEEE C37.118 data frame is captured in Fig. 1. A data frame consists of a header that species the message length, the source ID (i.e. sender's ID), a time-stamp, and other status information (e.g. source and quality of the data). Data blocks follow the header. Each data block contains a PMU's real-time measurements with the timestamp specified in the header.
- **Configuration Frame** is sent by PMU/PDC to notify the receiving device the configuration information of the data message, including the number of channels, types, and scaling factor, etc. Configuration frames are intended to be read by machines.
- **Command Frame** is sent from a data concentrator (a PDC or a SuperPDC) to its source devices (PMUs or PDCs, correspondingly) to coordinate the communication (start/stop data transfer, request for configuration frames, etc.).
- **Header** information is human readable descriptive information sent from the PMU/PDC but provided by the user.

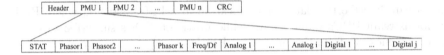

Fig. 1. The structure of a PMU data block.

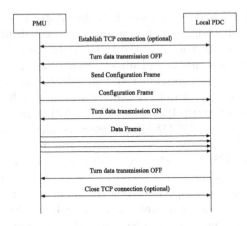

Fig. 2. A typical data transmission process by C37.118 protocol.

3   Experimental Setup

3.1   A Small Scale Prototype of Synchrophasor Network

For the purpose of conducting protection of the PMU network, we set up a small-scale prototype of the PMU network, which is depicted in depicted in Fig. 3. In the prototype, PDC and PMU are connected to their respective gateways. The gateways have access to the wireless local area network which simulates physical distance between PMU and PDC. Additionally, since our primary concern is on the communication side, the PDC does not store synchrophasor data to a database server.

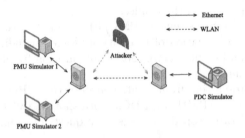

Fig. 3. A small scaled PMU communication network prototype.

We adopt the openPDC [2] as the PDC server in the prototype. In addition to a real PMU device, we emulate the PMUs with computers running PMU simulators provided by iPDC Khandeparkar and Pandit [5], which is an open-sourced Linux software package written in C++ and adheres to the IEEE C37.118. Note that using PMU simulators does not affect the validity of our research findings, since we concentrate on the testing the performance of proposed communication protocol and the software implementations, which are independent of the data acquisition process.

3.2   CURENT Hardware Testbed

To validate our proposed system in real world scenario, we also test on Hardware Testbed located in Center for Ultra-Wide-Area Resilient Electric Energy Transmission Networks (CURENT) as shown in Fig. 4. It provides broad time scales in one system - microseconds for power electronics to milliseconds and seconds for power system event. It also integrates real-time communication, protection, and control.

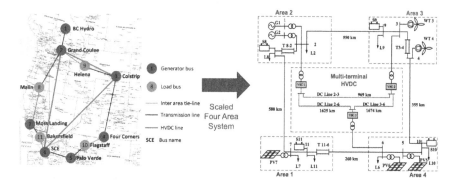

Fig. 4. Power electronic converter based Hardware Universal Grid Emulator setup in CURENT center.

This system is based on the reduced model of the NPCC testbed. A remote load center including L12 and L13 is fed by a local generator, two inter-connected systems, and offshore wind through multi-terminal HVDC (MTDC). This system will allow testing and verification of power system control algorithms considering renewable energy sources and the investigation of the impact from the MTDC system to the power grid.

4   Vulnerability Assessment for PMU Communication Networks

4.1   Reconnaissance

In the reconnaissance stage, we eavesdrop the traffic at both penetration points by packet sniffing with Wireshark. The presence of PMU and PDC were successfully confirmed by the capture of C37.118 frames. In particular, the captured C37.118 CONFIG frames also leaked the PMUs' configuration information.

4.2 Vulnerability Exploration

The goal of exploration phase is to validate the possible weaknesses of the PMU network, which are deduced from the information leaked from the reconnaissance phase. Evaluating the information gathered in the reconnaissance phase and also taking into the public information about the C37.118 standards, we list vulnerabilities that we will manually explore and validate during the exploration phase in Table 1.

Table 1. Vulnerabilities to be validated in the exploration phase

Cause of vulnerabilities	Possible attacks	Testing technique
Lack of encryption	Eavesdropping, Replay	Packet sniffing
Lack of user authentication	Impersonation man-in-the-middle attack	Packet sniffing Packet injection
Lack of message authentication	Frame modification	Packet sniffing Packet injection
Unexpected frames	Denial-of-Service Packet injection	Fuzzing
Lack of input validation	SQL injection code injection	Packet injection

We briefly explain the listed vulnerabilities as follows. (1) as we have already discovered in the reconnaissance phase, all C37.118 frames are transferred in clear. Hence, not only can attackers intercept and eavesdrop configuration frames but it is also possible for attackers to eavesdrop for command and data frames. (2) as the C37.118 standard does not specify any user authentication mechanism, it is possible for the attackers to impersonate a legitimate publishing or subscribing devices and confuse, mislead, or sabotage other parties in the PMU network. (3) as the case of lacking user authentication, neither C37.118 includes any message authentication mechanism. As a consequence, all frames are subject to frame modifications; a receiving device is unable to distinguish legitimated frames and modified frames. We use packet sniffing and packet injection to validate this vulnerability. (4) as a stateful protocol, a device that runs C37.118 protocol manages its transition of states based on its current state and the frames it receives. If the coming frames are expected under the current state, the device should make the state transitions accordingly. If not, the device should also handle for the case properly. (5) PMUs or PDCs may not properly validate input, which leads to code injection attacks.

4.3   Exploit Development

A Practical Data Stream Hijacking over C37.118. In this section, we demonstrate a practical false data injection attack. Specifically, we show that how the attack impacts the wide-area monitoring system (WAMS). Consider a scenario where a PMU network is employed in a wide area to obtain current, voltage and frequency measurements and to maintain the situational awareness of the potential inter-area oscillations.

In this demonstration, we show that a false injection attack targeting a PMU network can change the result of situational awareness and misleads the operator. A false injection attack is illustrated in Fig. 5 and consists of the following procedures:

1. An attacker penetrate the PMU network. This is usually done by compromising employee's email accounts, web servers, social engineering, etc.
2. The attacker eavesdrops the data communication between PDC and PMU. The data frame includes the source and destination IP addresses, port numbers, the ID of destination PDC, the message format, etc.
3. Initiate TCP flooding attack to local PDC or specific PMU. The main purpose of this step is trying to affect data availability, after which PDC will reset the system by re-initiating one or multiple PMUs. Note that if the system uses UDP as transport layer protocol, the attacker can choose other DoS attack scheme.
4. Attacker intercepts the configuration frame and uses the configuration frame to construct a false data stream. Based on the goals of the attacker, the data stream can be generated randomly or carefully manipulated using domain knowledge.
5. Wait for a good time such that the attacker can do the most damage to the power system and inject a false command frame to the PMU to turn off the data frame. Then, the attacker sends pre-generated measurement data to local PDC by fabricating forged data frames containing the falsified data.

We demonstrate this attack on CURENT hardware testbed. The first scenario we tested is random injection attacks where the attacker only tries to interrupt the normal operations of the WAMS. After starting the attacks, the attacker hijacks the data stream transmission and keeps sending zero value bus voltage, current, and frequency. Figure 6a showed the screenshot captured during a random false injection attack.

Figure 6b illustrates the target false data injection attack which a generator trip event is generated to mislead the operator. Based on this manipulated situational awareness, the operator or automatic control is deceived and harmful consequences may happen.

Test with WECC 179-Bus Power System. In this section, we show that how the attack impacts the wide-area monitoring of the WECC 179-bus system model [9]. The applied faults include six three-phase faults at 0s, 40s, 80s, 120s,

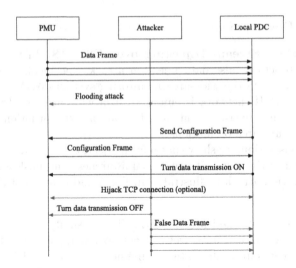

Fig. 5. A practical data stream hijacking attack on PMU network.

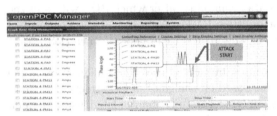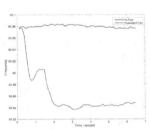

(a) The demonstration of our data hijacking attack in CURENT hardware testbed.

(b) A false generator trip event is injected to the small scale PMU network.

Fig. 6. A practical data stream hijacking over C37.118.

160s and 200s near bus 83 (Malin substation) on lines 83# -172, 83# -170, 114# -124, 115# -130, 83# -94 and 83# -98 ("#" indicates the fault bus) to simulate a cascading failure. In other words, by replaying the rotor angles obtained from the dynamic simulation on the respective PMU simulators, we can completely reproduce the behavior of the PMU network during the cascading failure. Figure 7a captures the angles differences on potential out of step (POOS) interfaces of 1-234, 14-23. As seen in the figure, the data received by the PDC provides the correct situational awareness: the angle difference between POOS's keeps climbing as the cascading failure takes place.

In this demonstration, we show that a data stream hijacking attack targeting a PMU network can change the result of situational awareness such that the contingencies vanish from the situational awareness and, thus, blinds the operator. The data stream hijacking attack was launched at the 35th second, which is just

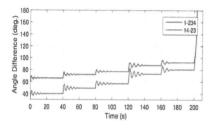

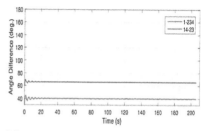

(a) Normal angle difference over simulation time.

(b) Manipulated angle difference by data stream hijacking over simulation time

Fig. 7. The demonstration of our data hijacking attack for WECC 179-bus system.

prior to the application of the first fault. The attacker hijacks the data stream transmission and keeps replaying to the PDC the rotor angle measurements of all the 12 PMUs between 30th to 35th second it obtained through eavesdropping.

As shown in Fig. 7a, during the attack, the resulting visualization of the angles difference between interface 1-234 and 14-23 were manipulated such that the inter-area angle differences keep unchanged. Based on this manipulated situational awareness, the operator or automatic control is blinded and fails to apply preventative controls to mitigate the inter-area oscillation.

5   Countermeasures and Mitigations

In this section, we talk about solutions or best practices to deal with the above vulnerabilities to prevent security breaches in reality.

Packet sniffing and packet injection can be greatly mitigated by employing SSL/TLS (Secure Socket Layer/Transport Layer Security) or IPSec (Internet Protocol Security) to encrypt the packets between electronic security perimeters (ESP) of PDC and PMU [8]. To counteract packet injections, we must authenticate packets' origin and ensure the integrity of packets on the fly. Both can be accomplished by SSL/TLS or IPSec, which utilize the public key infrastructure (X.509) certificates to authenticate a legitimate host on the PMU network, and use message authentication code (in SSL/TLS) or integrity check value (in IPSec) to make sure that the data are intact during their transmission. Thorough fuzzing test against the services and applications of PMU networks are very helpful to find the design and implementation flaws and errors. It is of great importance to eliminate the found flaws and errors before a PMU and PDC can be put into real use. To prevent SQL injection attack, best practice and programming guidelines regarding the database related development such as The Open Web Application Security Project [7] should be enforced in the developments of services and applications of PMU networks. Additionally, bugs or errors in the implementation of these security mechanisms can also undermine the security. Therefore, it would be more secure to employ multiple defenses in tandem to minimize the risk of data spoofing attacks when SSL/TLS falls short.

References

1. IEEE Standard for Synchrophasor Data Transfer for Power Systems. IEEE Std C37.118.2-2011 (Revision of IEEE Std C37.118-2005), pp. 1–53, December 2011. https://doi.org/10.1109/IEEESTD.2011.6111222
2. Grid Protection Alliance: OpenPDC Project (2014). http://openpdc.codeplex.com/
3. Hong, S., Lee, M.: Challenges and direction toward secure communication in the SCADA system. In: 2010 Eighth Annual Communication Networks and Services Research Conference (CNSR), pp. 381–386. IEEE (2010)
4. Khan, R., McLaughlin, K., Laverty, D., Sezer, S.: Analysis of IEEE C37. 118 and IEC 61850-90-5 synchrophasor communication frameworks. In: Power and Energy Society General Meeting (PESGM), pp. 1–5. IEEE (2016)
5. Khandeparkar, K., Pandit, N.: iPDC - free phasor data concentrator (2014). https://ipdc.codeplex.com/
6. Liang, G., Zhao, J., Luo, F., Weller, S.R., Dong, Z.Y.: A review of false data injection attacks against modern power systems. IEEE Trans. Smart Grid 8(4), 1630–1638 (2017)
7. OWAS Testing Project: SQL injection prevention cheat sheet (2014)
8. Stewart, J., Maufer, T., Smith, R., Anderson, C., Ersonmez, E.: Synchrophasor security practices. In: 14th Annual Georgia Tech Fault and Disturbance Analysis Conference (2011)
9. Sun, K., Luo, X., Wong, J.: Early warning of wide-area angular stability problems using synchrophasors. In: Proceedings of IEEE PES General Meeting, pp. 23–26 (2012)
10. Young, E.: CyberSecurity: how safe is your smart grid? (2014)

Proposal of Parallel Processing Area Extraction and Data Transfer Number Reduction for Automatic GPU Offloading of IoT Applications

Yoji Yamato[✉][iD], Hirofumi Noguchi, Misao Kataoka, Takuma Isoda, and Tatsuya Demizu

NTT Network Service Systems Laboratories, NTT Corporation,
Tokyo 180-8585, Japan
yamato.yoji@lab.ntt.co.jp

Abstract. Recently, IoT (Internet of Things) technologies have been progressed. To overcome of the high cost of developing IoT services by vertically integrating devices and services, Open IoT enables various IoT services to be developed by integrating horizontally separated devices and services. For Open IoT, we have proposed Tacit Computing technology to discover the devices that have data users need on demand and use them dynamically and an automatic GPU (graphics processing unit) offloading technology as an elementary technology of Tacit Computing. However, it can improve limited applications because it only optimizes parallelizable loop statements extraction. Therefore, in this paper, to improve performances of more applications automatically, we propose an improved method with reduction of data transfer between CPU and GPU. This can improve performance of many IoT applications. We evaluate our proposed GPU offloading method by applying it to Darknet which is general large application for CPU and find that it can process it 3 times as quickly as only using CPUs within 10 h tuning time.

Keywords: Open IoT · GPGPU · Automatic offloading

1 Introduction

As IoT (Internet of Things) technology has progressed (e.g., Industrie 4.0 [1–3]), various IoT applications have appeared. Typical IoT applications collect data via IoT devices, analyze and visualize the data by cloud technology on OpenStack [4] (e.g., [5–8]) using Spark [9], Storm [10] or MapReduce [11]. However, current IoT applications tend to be one-off solutions in which devices, network, and services are vertically integrated for specified targets, and this incurs much cost. To reduce costs and develop various services, researchers have investigated Open IoT (e.g., Tron project's Open IoT Platform [12]), which shares devices for multiple applications (e.g, [13–17]).

© Springer Nature Switzerland AG 2018
M. Qiu (Ed.): SmartCom 2018, LNCS 11344, pp. 39–54, 2018.
https://doi.org/10.1007/978-3-030-05755-8_5

One example Open IoT application is sharing network cameras of multiple organizations in a town for multiple purposes such as searching for lost pets and discovering terrorists using OpenCV [18]. However, in this example, image processing of camera videos for multiple purposes requires much calculation resources.

Additionally, systems have been upgraded to make the best use of recent advances in hardware to adapt to various usages such as IoT. Some providers use special servers with powerful GPUs (Graphics Processing Units) to process graphic applications or special servers with FPGAs (Field Programmable Gate Arrays) to accelerate specific signal processing. For example, AWS (Amazon Web Services) [19] provides GPUs and FPGAs for users to use on demand. Microsoft's search engine Bing tries to use FPGAs to optimize search processing [20].

We can now develop various IoT applications rapidly using service coordination technologies such as [21–25] in Open IoT environments. Users also expect to run their applications with high performance to utilize the recent advances in hardware. However, to achieve high performance, we need to program and configure appropriate applications considering heterogeneous hardware and be able to use technology such as CUDA (Compute Unified Device Architecture) [26] and OpenCL (Open Computing Language) [27].

To enable users' IoT applications to utilize GPUs and FPGAs easily, a new Open IoT platform is expected to analyze application logic and offload processing to GPUs and FPGAs automatically when general purpose applications are deployed.

We previously proposed Tacit Computing as an Open IoT platform that provides users with personalized services by discovering and coordinating appropriate resources for users dynamically. And we also proposed an automatic GPU offloading method of deployed applications logics using GA (Genetic Algorithm) as an elemental technology of Tacit Computing [28]. However, the work of [28] targets automatic extraction of appropriate parallelizable area and cannot improve performances of some applications. Therefore, in this paper, to improve performances of more applications automatically, we propose an improved method with reduction of data transfer between CPU and GPU and evaluate it.

2   Existing Heterogeneous Hardware Technologies

For GPGPU that uses GPU computational power not only for graphics processing, CUDA is a major development environment. To control heterogeneous hardware such as GPUs, FPGAs, and many core CPUs uniformly, OpenCL is a widely used standard specification. CUDA and OpenCL need not only C language extension but also additional descriptions such as memory copy between GPU or FPGA devices and CPUs. Because of these programming difficulties, there are few CUDA and OpenCL programmers.

For easy GPGPU programming, there are technologies that specify parallel processing areas by specified directives and compilers transform these directives into device oriented codes on the basis of specified directives. OpenACC [29] is one of the directive-based specifications, and the PGI compiler [30] is one of the directive-based compilers. For example, users specify OpenACC directives on C/C++/Fortran codes to process them in parallel, and the PGI compiler checks the possibility of parallel processing and outputs and deploys execution binary files to run on GPUs and CPUs. And also IBM JDK offloads Java program with lambda expression [31].

In this way, CUDA, OpenACC, and others support GPU offload processing. However, although parallel processing on a GPU itself can be performed, sufficient performance is hard to obtain. For example, when users use an automatic parallelization technology like the Intel compiler [32] for multicore CPU, possible areas of parallel processing such as "for" loop statements are extracted. However, naive parallel execution performances with GPUs are not high because of overheads of CPU and GPU memory data transfer. To achieve high performances with GPU such as fluid calculation [33], CUDA needs to be tuned by highly skilled programmers or appropriate offloading area need to be searched for by the PGI compiler or others [34,35]. The work of [28] extracts appropriate parallel processing area automatically using GA, there are some applications which cannot improve performances because of CPU-GPU memory data transfer.

Therefore, it is difficult for users without GPU skills to achieve high performances. Moreover, if users use automatic parallelization technologies, to obtain high performance, it takes a long time of try and error for each loop statement is parallelized or not, and there are applications which are not be improved.

We aim to appropriately offload logics of general applications such as analysis and image processing for IoT services to GPU in sufficiently short time. This enables users to reduce total cost because although GPU resources are increased, CPU resources such as virtual machines are greatly decreased.

Note that our offload processing is run in the background of actual IoT application uses. Our Tacit Computing [28] uses appropriate devices on the basis of users' requests and builds ad hoc services. For example, Tacit Computing uses image processing functions and network cameras to build continuous monitoring services for a specified person by switching network cameras in a town. In this example, we provide users with trial use services on the first day, perform offloading of image analysis in the background, and offer reasonably priced production services from the second day.

3   Proposal of Automatic GPU Offloading Method

3.1   GPU Offloading Using GA for Tacit Computing

Tacit Computing realizes Open IoT concept by discovering appropriate devices and coordinates them dynamically [28] using service coordination technologies such as [36–40]. There is an example of using a camera and an image identification program to identify images with cameras in town, discover cameras monitoring elderly people wandering around, and deliver the elderly people images to their families. In the case where the application is dynamically built in this way, since the device to be used is determined by the timing of that time, the processing is often inefficient. Therefore, Tacit Computing improves performances of applications such as image analysis during operation by offloading specific process to heterogeneous hardware such as GPU equipped with devices or home gateways. To control FPGA, we consider to use OpenCL SDK [41] based on the idea of [42].

To offload the function processing, Tacit Computing extracts the offload area from source codes of applications for users, outputs the intermediate language, deploys the binary file derived from the intermediate language on the verification machine, executes it, and verifies the offload effect. After repeating the verification and determining the appropriate offload area, Tacit Computing deploys the binary file to the production environment and provides it as a production service.

Here, we explain offloading steps using Fig. 1.

In 1-1, Tacit Computing identifies applications for users such as image analysis and specifies them to the automatic offloading function. In 1-2, the automatic offloading function analyzes application source codes and determines the application processing structure such as a loop statement, a specific library call such as FFT (Fast Fourier Transformation), or so on. In 1-3, the automatic offloading function detects offloadable logics to GPU or FPGA such as loop statement and FFT and extracts intermediate language for offload logics. In 1-4, it outputs intermediate files. As we explain in detail in the next subsection, intermediate language extraction occurs not only once. To search for appropriate offloading area, extraction and execution are repeated recursively.

In 2-1, the automatic offloading function deploys the binary file derived from the intermediate language to the machine equipped with GPU and FPGA in a verification environment. In 2-2, it executes deployed files and measures offloading performances. To set the area to be offloaded more appropriately by using performance measurement results, the automatic offloading function returns to step 1-3 and extracts another pattern. In 2-3, it determines the final pattern to specify offloading area and deploys binary files to the production environment of baremetel or container servers [43] for the user using [44] or [45]. In 2-4, after the binary files deployment, to show the performances to users, performance test cases are extracted from the test case DB (database) and extracted cases are automatically executed by Jenkins or other tools. In 2-5, information such as price, performance, and so on based on the performance test results are presented to users, and users decide whether to start the IoT service. Here, we can use existing technologies such as [46] for batch deployment to production environments and [47] for automatic tests.

An automatic GPU offloading is a process for repeating steps 1-3 to 2-2 in the preceding subsection and obtaining offload code to be deployed in step 2-3.

There are various IoT applications, but typical examples are image processing for camera videos and machine learning processing for large amounts of sensor data analysis, which have many loop processes. Therefore, the work of [28] aims

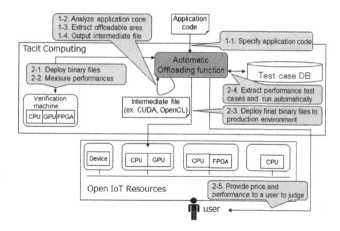

Fig. 1. Steps of automatic offloading

to enhance application throughput by offloading loop operations of applications to GPU automatically.

However, as described in Sect. 2, high performance needs parallel processing of an appropriate area. In particular, because of memory data transfer between CPU and GPU, performances sometimes do not improve unless the data size or the number of loops is large. Moreover, the combinations of individual loop statements that can be accelerated by parallel processing are sometime not the maximum performance configurations depending on memory process status and timing of memory data transfers. For example, when #1, #5, and #10 loop statements can be made faster by parallel processing than CPU processing in 10 loop statements, a three-parallelization combination of #1, #5, and #10 is not always the fastest configuration.

Therefore, to automatically extract appropriate offloading areas from general programs that do not assume parallelization, the work of [28] proposal is first to check all loop statements to determine whether they can be parallelized or not and second to repeat performance verification trials in the verification environment using GA for parallelizable loop statements to search for the highest performance pattern. By holding and recombining better performance processing patterns as gene parts after narrowing them down to parallelizable loop statements, we can search for high performance parallel processing patterns efficiently.

GA is a combinatorial optimization technique that simulates biological evolution [48]. Flows of GA are Initialization, Evaluation, Selection, Crossover, Mutation, and Complete Judgment.

However, the work of [28], although it is possible to search for an appropriate loop statement for offloading, there are inefficient cases such as CPU and GPU data transfer occurs for each loop. And even if it offloads loop statements there are cases high performances cannot be achieved because loop number is small. Therefore, improvable applications are limited.

3.2 Reduction of Data Transfer Number

Specifications of OpenACC and others define not only directives of GPU parallel processing instructions but also directives of data transfer instructions of CPU to GPU or GPU to CPU.

Therefore, in this paper, we propose to designate data transfer using explicit instruction directives together with extraction of parallel processing in GA to reduce inefficient data transfer. For each individual generated by GA, the proposed method analyzes the reference relations of the variables data used in loop statements, and does not transfer data every time for each loop but transfers data outside the loop when each loop does not need variables data every time using data transfer instruction directives.

We describe details specifically. The type of data transfer includes data transfer from CPU to GPU and data transfer from GPU to CPU.

– Data transfer from CPU to GPU

If the variable defined or set on the CPU program side and the variable referenced on the GPU program side overlap, it is necessary to transfer data from CPU to GPU, and data transfer is specified. The position to designate the data transfer is the loop statement GPU processed or the loop statement higher than the loop statement, which is the highest level loop which does not include the setting and definition of the corresponding variable. The insertion position of the data transfer directive is immediately before the loop such as "for", "do" and "while".

– Data transfer from GPU to CPU

If the variable set on the GPU program side and the variable referenced, set, defined or global variable on the CPU program side overlap, it is necessary to transfer data from GPU to CPU, and data transfer is specified. The position to designate the data transfer is the loop statement to be processed by GPU or the loop statement higher than it, which is the highest level loop which does not include reference, setting and definition of the corresponding variable. The insertion position of the data transfer directive is immediately before the loop such as "for", "do" and "while". Here, setting is included so as to take into consideration the case where the setting is executed by an "if" statement.

In this way, by explicitly instructing data transfer so as to collectively perform data transfer in the upper loop as much as possible, it is possible to avoid inefficient data transfer in which data is transferred every time for each loop.

3.3 Proposed GPU Offloading Method

Subsection 3.1 method can extract appropriate offloading loop statements and Subsect. 3.2 method can prevent inefficient data transfer.

However, even if those methods are adopted, there are applications which are not suitable for GPU. Efficient GPU offloading needs much loop number of offloading process. Thus, for pre step of full scale offloading area search, we propose to investigate loop number using a profiling tool. Because a profiling tool can investigate each line execution time, we can exclude applications which do not have 10 million loops beforehand, for example.

Here, we explain a proposed method with these ideas.

Firstly, the proposed method analyzes applications to search offloading area and understands loop statements such as "for", "do", "while". Next, it executes sample processing to investigate each loop number using a profiling tool and judges to proceed full-scale offloading area search whether applications have a certain number of loops.

When it starts a full-scale offloading search, it moves GA processing.

In Initialization, all parallelizable loop statements of application codes are mapped to genes after all loop statements are checked to determine whether they can be parallelized or not. We set the gene value as 1 for GPU parallel processing and 0 for non-GPU processing. Genes are generated specified individual numbers which gene values are assigned 0 and 1 randomly. At this timing, the code corresponding to the gene is added data transfer instruction based on the variables data reference relations in loop statements which are run on GPU.

In Evaluation, source codes corresponding to genes are compiled and deployed on a verification machine, and then benchmark performances are measured. The goodness of fit of a gene corresponds to each code performance. In Selection, genes that have high goodness of fit are selected on the basis of each value, and genes with specified individual numbers are selected. In our method, Selection is based on roulette selection proportional to goodness of fit and elite selection of one individual that has a gene that has maximum goodness of fit. In Crossover, with a specified crossover rate Pc, some genes are exchanged between selected individuals at one point, and children individuals are generated. In Mutation, at a specified mutation rate Pm, each value of an individual's gene is changed from 0 to 1 or 1 to 0.

Next generation genes are generated with specified number after Mutation. Then, as same as Initialization, the proposed method adds data transfer instruction, and moves to Evaluation, Selection, Crossover and Mutation steps recursively.

In Complete Judgment, after a specified number of generations is repeated for GA operations, GA is completed and the gene that has the best goodness of fit is an answer.

We deploy a maximum performance code corresponding to the gene with the maximum goodness of fit in production environments and provide it to users.

Figure 2 shows a processing image of GA with data transfer reduction.

4   Implementation

In this section, we explain the implementation to evaluate the effectiveness of the proposed method. Because the objective of this paper is to evaluate the

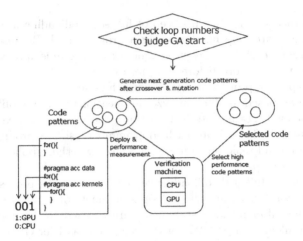

Fig. 2. Image of GPU offloading area search

effectiveness of automatic GPU offloading, we use the existing PGI compiler to control GPU for C/C++ applications.

C/C++ languages are widely used in OSSs and proprietary software development and are used to develop many applications. Our target is not scientific computing but IoT applications for general users, so we evaluate general applications like image processing for CPU to evaluate effectiveness.

GPU processing is controlled by a PGI compiler. PGI compiler is used for C/C++/Fortran languages to understand OpenACC. Bytecode for a GPU can be extracted by specifying parallel processable parts such as "for" loop statements by OpenACC directive #pragma acc kernels and executed on a GPU. Furthermore, for processes that have dependencies among loop statements and cannot be processed in parallel, an error is issued when a parallel processing directive is specified. The PGI compiler also can specify data transfer by specifying #pragma acc data copyin/copyout/copy directives.

Here, we explain the outline of the implementation. We implement the implementation by Perl 5 and Python 3.7, and it proceeds as shown in Fig. 3. Perl program controls GA processing and Python program parses source codes. Before all processing in Fig. 3, we prepare C/C++ codes to improve performances and benchmark tools to measure performances.

When a C/C++ application is specified, this implementation analyzes C/C++ code, detects "for" loop statements and understand the program structure such as variables data used in the "for" statements. For parsing, we python program uses parsing libraries of LLVM/Clang [49] libClang python binding.

The implementation executes the benchmark and counts the loop number of each "for" statement which is parsed firstly to obtain the prospect that the application has GPU offloading effect or not. To count the number of loops, we use gcov [50]. As profiling tools, gprof (GNU Profiler) [51] and gcov (GNU Coverage) are major and since both can investigate the number of execution of each line, either one can be used. In this test, only applications with loop counts of 10 million times or more are targeted, but this value can be changed.

General applications for CPUs are not implemented to consider parallel processing. Thus, we first need to exclude loop statements in which parallel processing itself is impossible. For each "for" statement, the implementation tries to insert the parallel processing #pragma acc kernels directive and judges whether an error occurs during compiling. There are several types of compile errors. Examples include external routines called in "for" statements, plural parallel processing directives specified for different tier loops in nest loops, "break" statements in "for" loop stops processes halfway, and data dependence in "for" statements. The types of compile errors vary depending on applications. These compile errors are excluded from GPU processing, and the implementation does not insert #pragma acc kernels directives.

Compile errors are difficult to automatically correct, and correcting errors may not improve performance much. #pragma acc routine directives may avoid external routine calls errors, but GPU processing including external routine calls may not be high performance because external calls may become a bottleneck. Nest loop errors do not occur in this case because the implementation tries each "for" loop one by one. In the case of "break" statements, the number of loops in parallel processing must be fixed, and this needs programming. When there is data dependence, parallel processing itself cannot be executed.

Here, the implementation re-counts "for" statements that do not cause errors when parallel processing is performed. If the counted "for" parallelizable loop statements are A, A is the gene length. Gene value 1 corresponds to #pragma acc kernels directive, and 0 corresponds to no directive. Application codes are mapped to A length genes. A specified number of individual genes is prepared as the initial setting. Initial genes are created so as to assign 0 and 1 randomly. The implementation adds parallel directives #pragma acc kernels to C/C++ "for" statements when corresponding gene values are 1.

At this timing, the part to be processed by the GPU is determined. Based on the reference relation of the variable data in the "for" statement analyzed by Clang, data transfer from CPU to GPU and GPU to CPU are specified based on the proposed rule of Sect. 3. Specifically, variables that require data transfer from CPU to GPU are specified by #pragma acc data copyin directives, and variables that require data transfer from GPU to CPU are specified by #pragma acc data copyout directives. If copyin and copyout overlap with each other on the same variable, they are summarized by #pragma acc data copy directive to simplify the description.

C/C++ codes added #pragma acc kernels and #pragma acc data directives are compiled by the PGI compiler on a verification machine using a GPU. The implementation deploys compiled binary files and measures performances using benchmark tools.

After performances of all individuals are measured, the implementation sets goodness of fit to each gene on the basis of each performance result, selects individuals on the basis of the set goodness of the fit value, and processes evolution operation of crossover, mutation, or copy so as to create the next generation of individuals.

Evolution calculations are executed by GA for each generation of individuals. If an individual that has the same pattern exists in a previous generation, compiling and performance measurement are skipped and the previous performance measurement value is adopted to reduce GA tuning time.

After a specified number of generations of GA operations, C/C++ code with maximum performance is the result of the offloading area search.

Individual number, generation number, crossover rate, mutation rate, goodness of fit setting, selection algorithm are GA parameters and conditions, and we set them in Sect. 5. By automatically conducting the above processing, our proposed method enables GPU offloading, which needs much time and skill conventionally.

- Analyze a code of C/C++
- Specify for loop statements from a code
- Run benchmark tool, Count loop numbers of each loop statement using gcov and judge to proceed
- Check each for loop statement parallelizability
  - Add OpenACC parallel processing of #pragma acc kernels directive to each for statement and Compile
    - When there are compile errors, Remove #pragma acc kernels from corresponding for statements and Exclude these for statements from GA cycles
  - Count for statements with no compile error and set gene length

- Map C/C++ code to gene and Prepare individuals of specified number
  - Configure #pragma acc data copyin/copyout/copy based on variables relations in for loop statements
  - Compile C/C++ code with "kernels and data" directives corresponding to each gene pattern
    - When there are compile errors of plural parallel processing directives for nest loop statements, Set performance processing time of this individual as same as time-out
  - Deploy binary files on a verification machine with CPU/GPU
  - Run binary files and Measure benchmark tool performances
- Measure performances of all individuals, Set goodness of fit value for each individual and Select high performance individuals based on goodness of fit
- Execute Crossover and Mutation for selected individuals and Generate next generation individuals

- Repeat GA processing for each generation individuals
  - If there occurs a same pattern individual which exists in previous generation, Skip compile and measurement and adopt previous measurement value

- After specified generations of GA processing, Select the maximum performance code pattern

Fig. 3. Outline of the implementation

Using this implementation, we verified a sample application of laplace equation solve with Jacobi method [52] which cannot be improved by our previous work with GA loop optimization [28]. In the result, it showed more than 30 times performance and we confirmed our implementation validity.

5   Evaluation

5.1   Evaluation Method

Evaluated Applications. We use Darknet which does image processing using deep learning because many users use them in Open IoT environments.

Darknet [53] is a neural network framework written by C language and it can process not only image analysis but also classification, detection and so on. In this evaluation, we confirm improvements of elemental image processing of object detection and image editing. We verify C language Darknet as one example of image processing for CPU in this paper although there are of course many types of image processing and libraries for GPU. In an Open IoT environment, image processing is often necessary for automatic monitoring from camera videos. Moreover, there are cameras with GPUs such as Axis cameras. For benchmark for tuning, we use a sample application of detection and nightmare which is equipped. Sample image data is 768 * 576 pixels with 24 bit color for detection and 352 * 448 pixels with 24 bit color for nightmare. And nightmare layer parameter is set to 5.

Experiment Conditions. In evaluation experiments, we measure performances of Darknet for each individual of each generation by using benchmark tools. We analyze performance change during GA generation transitions. After specified generation calculations, the code pattern of maximum performance at that time is the result of the offloading area search.

Parameters and conditions of GA are as follows.

Gene length: Number of parallelizable "for" loop statements. 75 for Darknet. Darknet has more than 171 "for" statements.

The number of individuals M: No more than gene length. 30 for Darknet.

The number of generations T: No more than gene length. 20 for Darknet.

Goodness of fit: (Processing time)$^{-1/2}$. When processing time becomes shorter, goodness of fit becomes larger. By setting $(-1/2)$ power, we prevent narrowing of search range due to too high goodness of fit of specific individuals with short processing times. If the performance measurement does not complete in 3 min, a timeout is issued, and processing time is set as 1000 s to calculate goodness of fit. The length of timeout is set on the basis of performance measurement characteristics. If processing is done by only CPUs for test data in the environment in Fig. 4, Darknet takes 108.28 s.

Selection algorithm: Roulette selection and Elite selection. Elite selection means one gene with maximum goodness of fit must be reserved for the next generation without crossover or mutation.

Crossover rate Pc: 0.9

Mutation rate Pm: 0.05.

Experiment Environment. We use physical machines with NVIDIA Quadro K5200 for verifications. The CUDA core number of NVIDIA Quadro K5200 is 2304. We use PGI compiler community edition v17.10 and CUDA toolkit v9.1. Figure 4 shows an experiment environment and environment specifications. Here, a client note PC specifies C/C++ application codes, codes are tuned on a verification machine, and fixed codes are deployed in an IoT environment for users after GA tuning.

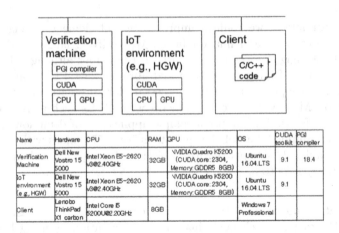

Fig. 4. Experiment environment

5.2   Performance Results

Two applications were confirmed to improve. Due to the characteristics of GA, it does not converge at the same number every time. For that reason, we tried five GA calculations for each application and the graph chose a typical trial that converges not so quick or not so slow among 5 times calculations.

Figure 5 shows maximum performance change of Darknet in each generation with GA generation transitions. The vertical axis shows how many times faster GPU offloading was than using only CPUs, with 1 being equivalent to the CPU processing time. From Fig. 5, performances can be improved and converged after 10 generations, and GPU offloading using GA generation transitions is about 3 times faster than CPU processing code (processing time is shortened from 108.28 to 36.28 s). Average trial time of each gene evaluation was within 3 min including timeout cases. Therefore, maximum GA time was estimated to be about one day, but GA actually extracted an appropriate offloading area within 10 h. After some generations, there were multiple individuals with the same pattern that had high goodness of fit, so compiling/measurements could often be skipped for same gene patterns.

We set small number of individuals and generations because we assume a production service will start within one or half a day. Therefore, performance improvement will sometimes not converge before the service starts. However, we think tuning about 20 generations will achieve higher performance than only CPU processing based on these results.

5.3   Discussion

Our previous work [28] confirmed more than 10 times performances using GA offloading method for simple applications such as matrix manipulation and multiresolution analysis [54]. In this time, Darknet performance improvement is

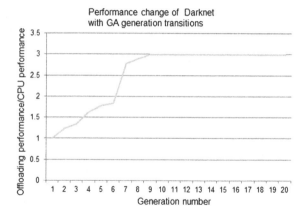

Fig. 5. Performance change of Darknet with GA generation transitions

about 3 times. This is because this application is large which have more than 100 loop statements and improvable parts are limited in the whole applications.

Therefore, we discuss cost performance. GPU boards like NVIDIA Tesla cost about 1,000 USD. Therefore, hardware with a GPU costs about twice as much as hardware with a CPU only. Generally in data centers, hardware and system development and verification cost is about 1/3 the total cost, electricity and operation/maintenance cost is more than 1/3, and other expenses such as service orders is the other 1/3. In the AWS case, a GPU instance with one GPU costs about 650 USD/month, which is the same as hosting a general dedicated server. Therefore, we think improving performances by 3 times in IoT applications that take much time such as image processing will have a sufficiently positive cost effect even though the hardware price twice.

In addition, by using gcov or gprof, it is possible to search improvable applications efficiently by preliminarily specifying applications that take a lot of execution time of loop processing.

Second, we discuss time to start production services. Based on these experiments, when we assume about 3 min for one individual trial, offloading area search takes 20 h for 20 individuals and 20 generations in the maximum case. However, compiling and performance measurement of an individual that has the same pattern as a previous one can be skipped, so we estimate that we can complete GA processing within 7 h. Because many cloud, hosting, and network services take about half a day before production service starts from the initial order, automatic offloading within half a day after trial use can be acceptable for many users.

To search for an offloading area within a shorter time, we can process each individual performance measurement on multiple machines in parallel. Changing the length of timeout also can reduce GA tuning time on the basis of each application characteristic (e.g., the length of timeout is set to a processing time twice as long as that for only a CPU). Because these experiments use few individuals and generations, we set a high crossover rate Pc to search for a wide area and search for certain degree answers relatively fast.

We will study parameters of GA and data transfer patterns to search for more high performance results within short time.

6   Conclusion

In this paper, we proposed an automatic GPU (graphics processing unit) offloading technology as a new elemental technology of an Open IoT (Internet of Things) platform to utilize GPU resources for user applications in Open IoT environments. Our proposed method has two characteristics. The first is to enable users without the special skills needed to use CUDA (Compute Unified Device Architecture) to run their applications with high performances by using GPUs. The second is to improve general large applications for CPUs.

Our proposed method detects "for" loop statements from application source codes and searches for appropriate offloading areas by the trial and error of GA (Genetic Algorithm) on the basis of actual benchmark performance results with reduction of memory data transfer between CPU and GPU based on variables reference relations in loop statements. For C/C++ applications, we implemented the proposed technology using the PGI compiler to verify its effectiveness. We evaluated performance improvements for Darknet which does image analysis using deep learning. Even though this application has more than 100 "for" loop statements, we found that this application showed about 3 times performances of only CPU use. Our technology is run in the background of actual IoT application uses. For example, we extract an appropriate offloading area during trial use of first half day and then offer reasonably priced production services from the latter half day.

In the future, we will study ways to search for higher performance results with short time by modifying GA parameters and data transfer patterns. Moreover, we will use OpenCL as an intermediate language of offloading to control FPGAs (field programmable gate arrays) and GPUs uniformly and study how to provide optimum resource sizes of GPU for offloading.

References

1. Hermann, M., et al.: Design principles for industrie 4.0 scenarios. In: Working Draft. Rechnische Universitat Dortmund (2015)
2. Evans, P.C., et al.: Industrial internet: pushing the boundaries of minds and machines. Technical report of GE (2012)
3. AWS IoT Platform. https://aws.amazon.com/iot/how-it-works/?nc1=h_ls
4. Sefraoui, O., et al.: OpenStack: toward an open-source solution for cloud computing. Int. J. Comput. Appl. **55**(3), 38–42 (2012)
5. Yamato, Y., et al.: Fast and reliable restoration method of virtual resources on OpenStack. IEEE Trans. Cloud Comput. **6**, 572–583 (2015)

6. Yamato, Y., et al.: Development of low user impact and low cost server migration technology for shared hosting services. IEICE Trans. Commun. **J95-B**(4), 547–555 (2012)
7. Yamato, Y.: Key points of telecommunication carriers' shared hosting servers replacement project. J. Soc. Project Manag. **15**(3), 3–8 (2013)
8. Yamato, Y., et al.: Software maintenance evaluation of agile software development method based on OpenStack. IEICE Trans. Inf. Syst. **E98-D**(7), 1377–1380 (2015)
9. Zaharia, M., et al.: Spark: cluster computing with working sets. In: 2nd USENIX Conference on Hot Topics in Cloud Computing (2010)
10. Marz, N.: STORM: distributed and fault-tolerant realtime computation (2013)
11. Dean, J., et al.: MapReduce: simplified data processing on large clusters. In: OSDI 2004, pp. 137–150, December 2004
12. TRON project. http://www.tron.org/
13. Yamato, Y.: Ubiquitous service composition technology for ubiquitous network environments. IPSJ J. **48**(2), 562–577 (2007)
14. Yamato, Y., et al.: Context-aware ubiquitous service composition technology. In: The IFIP International Conference on Research and Practical Issues of Enterprise Information Systems (CONFENIS 2006), pp. 51–61, April 2006
15. Yamato, Y., et al.: Study of user customize sevice composition technology based on BPEL extension. IPSJ J. **51** (2010)
16. Yamato, Y., et al.: Study and development of user customize service composition and change-over using BPEL engine. IEICE Trans. Commun. **J91-B**, 1428–1439 (2008)
17. Yamato, Y., et al.: Context-aware service composition and component change-over using semantic web techniques. IEEE ICWS **2007**, 687–694 (2007)
18. OpenCV. http://opencv.org/
19. AWS EC2 instance type. https://aws.amazon.com/ec2/instance-types/
20. Putnam, A., et al.: A reconfigurable fabric for accelerating large-scale datacenter services. In: ISCA 2014, pp. 13–24, June 2014
21. Yamato, Y., et al.: Study of service control function for SOAP-REST mash-up service. IPSJ J. **51**(2) (2010)
22. Yamato, Y., et al.: Abstract service scenario generation method for ubiquitous service composition. IIEICE Trans. Commun. **J91-B**, 1220–1230 (2008)
23. Yokohata, Y., et al.: Context-aware content-provision service for shopping malls based on ubiquitous service-oriented network framework and authentication and access control agent framework. In: IEEE CCNC 2006, pp. 1330–1331 (2006)
24. Moriya, T., et al.: Development of building alarm system on service delivery platform. IEICE Trans. Commun. **J93-B**(4) (2010)
25. Yamato, Y., et al.: Development of service processing agent for context aware service. IEICE Trans. Commun. **J91-B**(12) (2008)
26. Sanders, J., et al.: CUDA by Example : An Introduction to General-Purpose GPU Programming. Addison-Wesley, Boston (2011). ISBN 0131387685
27. Stone, J.E., et al.: OpenCL: a parallel programming standard for heterogeneous computing systems. Comput. Sci. Eng. **12**, 66–73 (2010)
28. Yamato, Y., et al.: Automatic GPU offloading technology for open IoT environment. IEEE Internet Things J. (2018)
29. Wienke, S., Springer, P., Terboven, C., an Mey, D.: OpenACC—first experiences with real-world applications. In: Kaklamanis, C., Papatheodorou, T., Spirakis, P.G. (eds.) Euro-Par 2012. LNCS, vol. 7484, pp. 859–870. Springer, Heidelberg (2012). https://doi.org/10.1007/978-3-642-32820-6_85

30. Wolfe, M.: Implementing the PGI accelerator model. In: ACM the 3rd Workshop on General-Purpose Computation on Graphics Processing Units, pp. 43–50 (2010)
31. Ishizaki, K.: Transparent GPU exploitation for Java. In: The Fourth International Symposium on Computing and Networking (CANDAR 2016), November 2016
32. Su, E., et al.: Compiler support of the workqueuing execution model for Intel SMP architectures. In: Fourth European Workshop on OpenMP, September 2002
33. Himeno. http://accc.riken.jp/en/supercom/himenobmt/
34. Tanaka, Y., et al.: Evaluation of optimization method for Fortran codes with GPU automatic parallelization compiler. IPSJ SIG Technical Report, no. 9 (2011)
35. Tomatsu, Y., et al.: gPot: intelligent compiler for GPGPU using combinatorial optimization techniques. In: The 7th Joint Symposium Between Doshisha University and Chonnam National University, August 2010
36. Yamato, Y., et al.: Study and evaluation of context aware service composition using BPEL engine. Inf. Technol. Lett. **6**, 447–449 (2007)
37. Yamato, Y., et al.: Study of service control function for web-telecom coordination service. IEICE trans. commun. **J91-B**, 1417–1427 (2008)
38. Nakano, Y., et al.: Implementation and evaluation of wrapper system that creates web services from web applications. IPSJ J. **49**(2), 727–738 (2008)
39. Yamato, Y., et al.: Evaluation of service composition technology through field trial of shopping support service. IPSJ J. **48**(2), 755–769 (2007)
40. Yamato, Y., et al.: Study of service composition engine implemented on cellular phone. Inf. Technol. Lett. **4**, 269–271 (2005)
41. Altera SDK for OpenCL. https://www.altera.com/products/design-software/embedded-software-developers/opencl/documentation.html
42. Yamato, Y.: Optimum application deployment technology for heterogeneous IaaS cloud. J. Inf. Process. **25**(1), 56–58 (2017)
43. Yamato, Y.: OpenStack hypervisor, container and baremetal servers performance comparison. IEICE Commun. Express **4**, 228–232 (2015)
44. Yamato, Y.: Performance-aware server architecture recommendation and automatic performance verification technology on IaaS Cloud. Serv. Orient. Comput. Appl. **11**, 121–135 (2016)
45. Yamato, Y.: Server selection, configuration and reconfiguration technology for IaaS cloud with multiple server types. J. Netw. Syst. Manag. (2017). https://doi.org/10.1007/s10922-017-9418-z
46. Yamato, Y., et al.: Development of template management technology for easy deployment of virtual resources on OpenStack. J. Cloud Comput. **3**, 7 (2014). https://doi.org/10.1186/s13677-014-0007-3
47. Yamato, Y.: Automatic verification technology of software patches for user virtual environments on IaaS cloud. J. Cloud Comput. **4**, 4 (2015). https://doi.org/10.1186/s13677-015-0028-6
48. Holland, J.H.: Genetic algorithms. Sci. Am. **267**, 66–73 (1992)
49. Clang. http://llvm.org/
50. GCOV. http://gcc.gnu.org/onlinedocs/gcc/Gcov.html
51. GPROF. http://sourceware.org/binutils/docs-2.20/gprof/
52. Laplace equation source. https://github.com/parallel-forall/cudacasts/tree/master/ep3-first-openacc-program
53. Redmon, J., et al.: Real-time grasp detection using convolutional neural networks. In: IEEE International Conference on Robotics and Automation (ICRA), May 2015
54. Beylkin, G., et al.: Multiresolution representation of operators with boundary conditions on simple domains. Elsevier ACHA **33**(1), 109–139 (2012)

Performance Evaluation of Industrial OPC UA Gateway with Energy Cost-Saving

Hanjun Cho and Jongpil Jeong[✉]

Department of Smart Factory Convergence, Sungkyunkwan University,
Suwon, Gyeonggi-do 16419, Republic of Korea
{jhj0955,jpjeong}@skku.edu

Abstract. OPC UA is an international standard that defines communication technology and data processing method in smart factory. Many industry standards and protocols accept the OPC UA specification. Therefore, OPC UA plays an important role in Smart Factory by supporting high interoperability among various protocols. ARM processors are typical CPUs and are used in many embedded systems due to their structural simplicity and low power consumption. However, existing plants still use x86 processors with high power consumption and price. Today, changing from smart factories to new processors has high entry barriers due to the huge cost and lack of experiments taking into account realistic indicators. Therefore, in this paper, we propose OPC UA Gateway that accommodates OPC UA specification on industrial device platform based on ARM processor. We evaluate performance based on indicators such as Publish Interval, Sampling Interval, Subscription Restriction, Encryption and Security Guidelines. Our experimental results show about 66% reduction in operating costs compared to x86 processors.

Keywords: OPC UA · IIoT · Industrial Internet of Things
Industrial Gateway · ARM CPU

1 Introduction

Recently, advances in information and communication technology are increasing the number of Various types of data in sensors and communication devices, thus increasing a variety of protocols. In the manufacturing sector, productivity

This research was supported by Basic Science Research Program through the National Research Foundation of Korea (NRF) funded by the Ministry of Education (NRF-2016R1D1A1B03933828) and the MSIT (Ministry of Science and ICT), Korea, under the ITRC (Information Technology Research Center) support program (IITP-2018-08-01417) supervised by the IITP (Institute for Information & communications Technology Promotion) and the Gyeonggi Techno Park grant funded by the Gyeonggi-Do government (No. Y181802).

© Springer Nature Switzerland AG 2018
M. Qiu (Ed.): SmartCom 2018, LNCS 11344, pp. 55–66, 2018.
https://doi.org/10.1007/978-3-030-05755-8_6

is enhanced through process-based automation based on programmable Logic Controller (PLC) and embedded device. This process-specific automation uses industrial Ethernet/IP, Profile, CC-Link, and other industrial Ethernet protocols specific to each PLC vendor. In addition, each process is vertically integrated and consists of an optimal system. In the industrial 4.0, smart factory plans implement an intelligent manufacturing system that increases productivity and efficiency, reduces energy consumption, and enables immediate response to consumer needs. For this purpose, it is essential to communicate data between each process and the upper system in the smart factory. The OPC Foundation standardized industrial protocol OPC UA for data integration and is expanding standards for real-time data communication and security [1]. This paper proposes a platform to apply the Industry Protocol OPC UA to industrial field equipment with limited resources. The proposed OPC UA Gateway on RISC-based Arm CPU cores for reducing power consumption in the OPC UA framework. The expected benefits are high efficiency in server operations and low power savings. We will evaluate the performance of OPC UA server based on x86 CPU and OPC UA server based on ARM processor [2].

The OPC Unified Architecture (OPC UA) is a provider-independent communication protocol for industrial automation applications. It is based on a client-server architecture and allows seamless communication from individual sensors and actuators to the ERP system or cloud. The OPC UA is platform-independent and features built-in safety mechanisms. Because the OPC UA is flexible and completely independent, it is considered the ideal communication protocol for the implementation of Industry 4.0 [3]. In addition, OPC UA provides the closest implementation to industry 4.0 through scalability, modeling, security, and a variety of services. For more information about OPC UA, see Sect. 2.

The ARM processor architecture, designed for mobile and embedded systems, has been successful in entering the server market. Microsoft first announced ARM-based PCs at Las Vegas (Las Vegas)'s Computer Electronics Show (CES). ZT Systems also announced a server powered by six ARM Cortex-A9 processor cores consuming up to 80 watts of system power, less than the power consumption of the Intel Xeon series processors. Therefore, there is a trend toward adopting a multi-core ARM processor to build an efficient energy server for executing Intel processor-based computing tasks. To reduce recent server costs, there is an emerging investment in ARM processors that benefit from air-cooled and low-power consumption [4]. Another reason to adopt an ARM processor is to help reduce the complexity of the motherboard due to the accumulation of devices such as rack-mounted blade servers, the low heat characteristics of the ARM processor, and the scattering layout, resulting in reduced power consumption and cost savings. Therefore, we propose the OPC UA Server part of the proposed system using the advantages of the ARM processor. A detailed description of the ARM processor is given in Sect. 2.

In this paper, we propose a node control and data collection system using OPC UA technologies through OPC UA gateway. We propose the possibility of power saving using Arm CPU and acquire the system which can be reliable, real time monitoring and control through OPC UA [5,6]. This paper is the first step to optimize the field device platform using OPC UA technology.

This paper is configured as follows: Sect. 2 deals with related research. Section 3 describes the architecture and service architecture of OPC UA Gateway proposed in this paper. In Sect. 4, the power consumption of the existing x86 based system and the Arm CPU system is described in detail, and experimental setup and results are shown to observe actual savings. Finally, Sect. 5 concludes with a conclusion and future work.

2 Related Work

2.1 OPC UA Overview

The OPC UA provides a more complete information structure than the traditional OPC (Classic OPC), more secure information openness, more secure information, a more secure, open and reliable information exchange mechanism between servers and customers. OPC UA is a mechanism that makes moving data more flexible and adaptable between enterprise-type systems, allowing control, monitoring devices and sensors to exchange global data in real time.

OPC UA is designed to connect databases, analytical tools, Enterprise Resource Planning (ERP) systems, or other enterprise systems with real data. Real data is generated by interacting with processes that generate and control real data such as sub-administrators, sensors, actuators, and monitoring devices. OPC UA uses an extended platform, multi-security model, multiple transport units, and sophisticated information model to allow even a minimum-unit specific controller to interact freely with server applications. OPC UA can communicate very complex plant information with huge amounts of data. OPC UA is a sophisticated, extensible, and flexible mechanism for securely connecting customers and servers [7,8].

2.2 OPC UA Services

OPC UA is reliable and secure. It makes it easier than ever to model objects, make them useful, and make them widely available across enterprise applications. Objects have a single level of data, complex processes, systems, or plant-wide levels. Object is a mixture of data values, metadata, and relationships. Take the Dual Loop controller as an example. The Dual Loop controller Object links the setpoint variable and the actual value of each loop variable. These variables refer to variables that include metadata, such as other variables, such as temperature unit or setpoint high/low, text description, and so on. Object makes it possible to subscribe to notify when a data value changes or a metadata value changes. Customers can connect to one object to get a small amount of data (a single data value), or a vast amount of information about the controller and operational details. The OPC UA consists of a client and a server. The client device elaborates the information and the server device provides the information. However, as seen on the loop controller, the UA server performs much more sophisticated tasks than the Modbus TCP, EtherNet/IP, and ProfiNet IO servers [9].

2.3   ARM Processors

Many producers choose the ARM architecture because of its low power consumption and simplicity. ARM's RISC keeps all instructions simple and uniform in length, and unlike complex instructions, special designs allow RISC processors to require less registers and less circuitry. In addition, uniform length instructions provide better performance in instruction pipeline techniques where ARM processors take full advantage of the processing circuitry. Therefore, ARM's simple architecture is cooler than Intel X86 architecture [10], but still has excellent performance. Thanks to the unique design of the ARM processor, ARM relies on high energy efficiency [11] to take control of the embedded system market. For example, Apple products, the Iphone, and the Ipad product line, both ARM processors, as well as many mainstream operating systems, are available for ARM deployment, and Microsoft has also announced plans to support ARM-based systems in January 2011 [12]. Over the years, ARM processors have gained computing power to participate in server end-computing competition. According to industry reports, for example, several manufacturers have already built their ARM-based servers. The total power consumed by the ARM Cortex-A8 processor (with solid state disks) is less than 80 W at 16 * 2 GHz computing speed.

Most servers or data centers these days employ X86 architecture processors. The Intel Xeon series processors account for about two-thirds of the server market. The high-end server processor, the IBM Power series, penetrated with 20% share, while Intel's strongest competitor, AMD, occupied only 8.5%. ARM-based servers are still new players in the server market compared to X86 architecture processors and only 2.3% have chosen users. Thus, replacing current high-power-consuming processors with ARM processors can potentially save power in the data center, and ARM processor-based servers are good candidates for new evolution to high-efficiency computing [13].

3   OPC UA Gateway for Industrial IoT Platforms

3.1   System Architecture

It is a system that converts to OPC UA protocol, which is industry 4.0 standard protocol for industrial protocol, without changing the installation of various industrial legacy protocol control systems used in existing industrial field, and it is possible to minimize the time, cost and change in construction of smart factory. In addition, by providing OPC UA protocol conversion function, it is possible to secure the security of existing industrial control system not considering security, and to perform data interlocking and monitoring function in integrated environment [14]. The proposed part of this paper is the OPC UA Gateway part of Device Level's OPC UA Server. The overall system shown in Fig. 1 is a plot for monitoring and data collection at industrial sites, as detailed in the following.

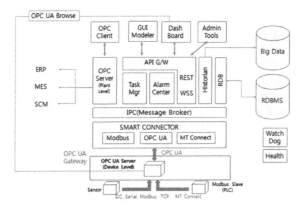

Fig. 1. System architecture.

OPC UA Gateway is the lowest part of the proposed system. OPC UA Gateway part is OPC communication and it is interlocked with the upper Smart Connector part and the lower field device by default. Since OPC UA communication is based on Server Client communication, this part acts as OPC UA Server. The OPC UA Gateway has an address space for data acquisition and modeling from the field device. In this system, the OPC UA Browse receives data from the OPC UA Gateway. The OPC Client includes both the field device at the bottom and the Smart Connector at the top. In this paper, we evaluate the data collection speed according to the structural characteristics of the OPC UA Gateway CPU and the power consumption according to the CPU usage. When evaluating, consider factors that may affect data collection speed and CPU usage. For example, we considered factors such as Security Policy, Publish Interval, and Sampling Interval that could affect communication in the experiment. OPC UA Gateway enables OPC communication with upper Smart Connector part as well as various kinds of data in conjunction with sensors such as Modbus and OPC DA field communication protocols. MTConnect is one of the most widely used protocols in factory machines and robots. In the United States, there is a strong trend to implement smart factories based on MTConnect standards. Since most robots in Korea accept MTConnect, they can cover a lot of numbers by converting them in the gateway. It is a module for easy selection and automation by the user without any program for each protocol. It supports standardized protocol and can accept other private protocols.

Smart Connect receives the address information of all OPC UA (device level) servers on the DB through the message broker, and then publishes the data back to the connected OPC UA server as a message broker.

IPC - Message broker is a service type that runs on external server and uses MQTT protocol. The message broker receiving the inquiry request from the smart connector sends a subscription request to inquire the address of all OPC Servers (device level) stored in the DB to the RDB Handler, and the RDB

Handler transmits the address information to the smart connector through the message broker again.

The API Gateway is a module that transfers the information collected from the server to the external service level system so that each service system can acquire the data through the API Gateway without directly accessing the device. This eliminates the need to transfer data from one device to multiple systems. This can save time for establishing a communication program according to system interworking.

Task Manager is a module that manages commands such as control, setting, and inquiry from client or external service system. Task Manager manages tasks that allow multiple client commands to be shared at the same time, determine priorities, and process commands in parallel with the device.

Alarm/Condition and Event is a module that generates and manages alarms or events through logical operation according to defined condition delivered from a node. It delivers values to clients in real time according to the situation.

The Historian service is used to store a large number of types and amounts of data coming from sensors at the field or PLC. The data includes elements for analyzing data such as key, value, time, destination, and so on. The data is delivered to the topic that is formatted through the message broker. The database uses MongoDB to store large amounts of data.

3.2   Implementation of Power and Cost-Reduced OPC UA Gateway

OPC UA Gateway, which acts as OPC UA protocol conversion and data collection server in the proposed system, can reduce power consumption and cost than existing industrial devices. There are a lot of CPUs used in embedded systems, but the specificity, the structural advantage, and the energy conservation technique are different for each CPU. The architecture of the ARM Core Series proposed in this paper can be minimized not only by the CPU architecture itself, but also by peripheral support elements such as interrupt controllers, memory interfaces, and memory accelerators [15].

3.3   Features and Benefits

The main features of the system including OPC gateway proposed in this paper are as follows. First, vertical integration of the protocol is possible. The provision of a single data source facilitates the addition of new devices and facilitates the understanding of data relationships by managing the entire data in a single logical tree of tags. Second, you can have a variety of device connectivity. Provides OPC-UA Server service function and can cope flexibly with various interface driver such as OPC-UA Client, Modbus, and MT Connect. Third, higher system interworking is possible. It supports various high-level system interfaces such as MES and ERP in the industrial field. Fourth, customization is possible. IoT device interface support and special type of nonstandard device dedicated interface are possible. In addition, OPC UA modeling function allows user to build desired system.

4   Experimental Results and Analysis

4.1   OPC UA Gateway Specification

The OPC UA Gateway proposed in this paper requires CPU usage equivalent to that of a PC to drive OPC UA servers at the device level and ensure seamless data flow to the field devices and the connection of Smart Connect. Currently, PLC and RTU for data acquisition in the factory market use x86 CPU with CISC structure or Arm CPU with RISC structure, but no performance evaluation has been done. In this paper, We compare X86 OPC UA Server with CISC architecture and Arm CPU OPC Server with RISC structure. One of the things related to profitability in the factory is low power, which cannot be subtracted from ARM processors. The ARM processor is a RISC architecture with 32 bits of instructions and internal registers. RISC (Reduced Instruction Set Computer) has a simpler instruction structure and fewer instructions than CISC (Complex Instruction Set Computer), so it can process faster and more efficiently. Most processors used in the Host PC (laptop, desktop) are CISC. This processor requires a cooling fan to cool down because it generates a lot of heat, but RISC does not need a cooling fan. A device without a cooling fan reduces its volume and consumes less power. Therefore, most embedded systems prefer the RISC architecture. In this paper, we propose a multi - protocol gateway system based on low power OPC UA communication. The proposed multi - protocol gateway system is designed to be independent of the CPU board and the base board so that it can be attached and detached through the connection connector. Therefore, it is possible to increase the ease of hardware replacement and the maintenance efficiency. It is possible to selectively use a wired or wireless communication such as an existing code division multiple access and Ethernet, a satellite navigation device, and a low power wireless communication depending on the installation place and environment [16].

For comparative evaluation, Intel x86 CPU and Arm CPU are selected and the performance of these CPU is evaluated according to the scenario. Table 1 shows the selected Intel x86 CPU and Arm CPU for performance evaluation.

Table 1. The comparison of SPEC according to CPU.

Parameter	Intel ATOM	Cubieboard6
Processor	X5-E8000 UP TO 2.00 GHz	Cortex A9 quad core
Memory	2 GB	2 GB
Operating System	Ubuntu 14.04	Debian GNU/Linux 8
Kernel	Linux 3.10.0-141	Linux 3.10.37

4.2   Problem Formulation

The basic relationship between device performance, power consumption and energy efficiency are shown as follows. The power consumed by the processor is directly proportional to the clock frequency (f). Instruction Count is the number of commands generated by a program through a compiler. Number of cycles per command (CPI) is the reciprocal of the construction per cycle (IPC), which represents the average number of clock cycles required to perform a command. Clock cycle time (T cycle) is time taken for one clock cycle. This trade-off between lower power and better performance leads to the existence of an optimum point for minimal energy usage with a tight performance improvement at a certain specific CPU frequency. To implement a better performance computer system, three elements must be reduced simultaneously, but these three factors conflict with each other. For example, an effort to reduce the number of commands in a program can result in more cycles (i.e., CPI) being designed to do more with a single command. Conversely, efforts to reduce the CPI are likely to increase the number of commands. Thus, the design that best matches the three factors mentioned above will improve the performance of the CPU. There are three ways to reduce the size of the components to improve CPU performance. Methods to reduce the number of commands include reducing the size of a program, using good algorithms, or optimizing command codes using optimization compilers. Methods for reducing the CPI include using the RISC command structure. The purpose of the experiments presented in this paper is to compare x86 CPU and Arm CPU with different CPU frequencies and structures. We also examine how the sampling rate and the number of monitored items affect each CPU usage and power consumption [17].

4.3   Experimental Environment

We used the open source OPEN62541 SDK for performance evaluation and configured the embedded OPC UA server environment using Arm CPU and x86 CPU. In this paper, UA Binary encoding and UA TCP communication protocol, which are known to exhibit optimal communication performance, have been selected in the previous research. Table 1 shows the specifications of the Arm CPU system and the x86 system to run the OPC UA server. OPC UA client used UA Expert commercial client to measure periodic read performance. In the first experiment, the performance of Arm CPU and x86 CPU was analyzed by measuring the response time according to the number of nodes monitored by the server. In this experiment, the minimum, average, and maximum values of the return time were measured when each read and write service was requested 1000 times.

In the second experiment, CPU utilization according to the number of items to be monitored was compared and compared in Arm CPU and x86 CPU, respectively. The number of monitored items in the server was measured in 10 units from 10 to 100. In addition, parameters such as Publishing Interval, Subscription, Sampling Interval, and security guidelines were considered. The Publishing

Interval is set to 1000 ms and the Sampling Interval to 1000 ms. Adjusting the Publishing Interval and Sampling Interval adjusted the data change detection time. All tested scenarios increased almost linearly with the number of items monitored. The results are shown in Fig. 3. In the third experiment, we compared the CPU utilization values of the Arm CPU and the x86 CPU according to the server sampling rate. The results are shown in Fig. 4. In the last four experiments, the actual power consumption of the Arm CPU and x86 CPU servers was measured. In the fourth experiment, the security policy of the server was set as a secure channel, and the use of CPU was maximized by including both the Sign process and Encrypt process of Message Security. The publishing interval was set to 100 ms and the sampling interval to 100 ms. The result is shown in Fig. 5.

4.4 Results

Cyclic read performance varied with the amount of nodes being monitored. The measurement results are shown in Fig. 2. Left Fig shows the response time of Arm CPU Server. Also, by setting the security policy to none and omitting the message process and the encryption process, the CPU load is reduced and the fastest response is obtained. The security policy between server-clients is set to Basic256Sha256 secure channel and the response time of arm CPU is measured. In addition, Message Security Mode uses both Sign and Encrypt. As a result, the read and write service times have increased as the number of items monitored increases. It also took more time than when the server did not set up secure. As a result, the read service and write service time increased as the number of items monitored increased. The write service could get a faster response than the read service. Right Fig shows the response time of an x86 CPU. It was configured the same as the ARM CPU and the measured results showed a faster response time than the ARM CPU. The monitored node means the value coming from the sensor or the PLC, and the response speed to this means the real time performance of the smart factory. In addition, security is very important in Smart Factory through connection of many IoT devices. OPC UA Gateway has strong security and real-time data transfer.

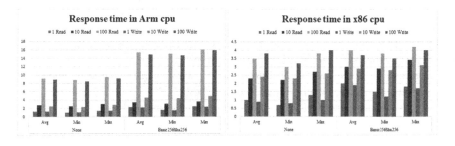

Fig. 2. OPC Server response time.

Figure 3 shows the CPU usage based on the number of Monitored Items. Parameters such as Publishing Interval, Subscription, Sampling Interval, and Security Policy are considered. The Publishing Interval is set to 1000 ms and the Sampling Interval to 1000 ms, which is the result of measuring the CPU usage according to the number of nodes monitored by the Server. The amount of change increased linearly. On the Coretex A9 ARM Core CPU with 100 monitoring nodes, the CPU usage of the OPC UA Server was 2.1 times higher than that of the x86 CPU. Also, the subscription response time according to the security policy showed that the Arm CPU server used about 3.5 times as much as the x86 CPU server. However, when the security policy of both CPUs is None, the average response time of Monitored Node is less than 10 ms, and when the security policy is Basic256Sha256, it is less than 15 ms.

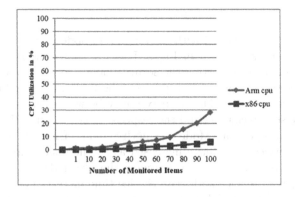

Fig. 3. The comparison of CPU utilization according to number of monitoring nodes.

The results of the third experiment are shown in Fig. 4. This experiment investigated the relationship between the change of node data monitored by the server and the amount of CPU usage. The Sampling Interval is the setting for how fast the Server will detect data changes. The faster the sampling interval, the more accurate the information about the data change, but the higher the CPU usage. The result of the arm CPU is 3.5% when the sampling interval is 500 ms, 56% when the sampling interval is 100 ms, and 89% when the sampling interval is 10 ms. The result of the x86 CPU is 2.6% when the sampling interval is 500 ms, 32% when the sampling interval is 100 ms, and 64% when the sampling interval is 10 ms. x86 had less CPU usage than arm.

The results of the last experiment are shown in Fig. 5. Figure 5 shows the power consumption of each Arm CPU and x86 CPU OPC UA Server. On a Coretex A9 ARM Core CPU for 480 s, the power consumption of the OPC UA Server was measured about 0.3 times less than the x86 CPU. Theoretically, CPU usage and power consumption are proportional, but basically, Arm CPU is designed for low-power environments such as mobile/embedded. As a result,

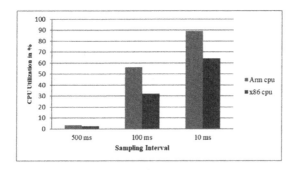

Fig. 4. The comparison of CPU utilization by sampling interval.

the Arm CPU Server consumed less electricity than the x86 CPU Server. Experimental results show that when the number of monitored items is 100, the CPU usage of the Arm CPU OPC UA Server is higher than that of the x86 CPU server. However, the power consumption of the Arm CPU server is about 0.3 times smaller.

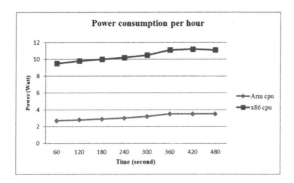

Fig. 5. The comparison of power consumption.

5 Conclusion

In this paper, we proposed an OPC UA gateway system applied on industrial IoT device platform with limited resources. The proposed OPC UA gateway system can be converted to the OPC UA protocol, which is an industry 4.0 industrial protocol standard platform, without changing the installation of various industrial legacy protocol control systems used in existing industrial sites. Therefore, it is possible to minimize time, cost, and changes when constructing Smart Factory. It also provided OPC UA protocol translation capabilities to ensure security for existing industrial systems that are not considered for security. Data interlock and monitoring functions can be performed in an integrated environment. In this paper, our experimental results show about 66% reduction in operating costs compared to x86 processors. Future studies plan to study Delay Reduction algorithms of certificate-based communications used by OPC UA Server and Client to connect secure channels.

References

1. OPC Foundation: OPC UA Part 1 - Overview and Concepts 1.03 Specification. http://www.opcfoundation.org. Accessed Oct 2015
2. Gul, S., Aftab, N., Rani, A.: A comparison between RISC and CISC microprocessor architectures. Int. J. Sci. Eng. Adv. Technol. (IJSEAT) 4(5), 254–259 (2016)
3. Cavalieri, S., Chiacchio, F.: Analysis of OPC UA performances. Comput. Stand. Interfaces 36(1), 165–177 (2013)
4. Cupek, R., Ziebinski, A., Franek, M.: FPGA based OPC UA embedded industrial data server implementation. J. Circ. Syst. Comput. 22(08), 1350070 (2013)
5. Huang, J.-D., Hsieh, H.-C.: Design of gateway for monitoring system in IoT networks. In: Proceedings of IEEE International Conference and IEEE Cyber, Physical and Social Computing (2013)
6. Qian, Z., Ruicong, W., Qi, Ch.: IOT gateway: bridging wireless sensor networks into Internet of Things. In: Proceedings of IEEE/IFIP 8th International Conference on Embedded and Ubiquitous Computing (EUC), December 2010
7. OPC Foundation: OPC UA Part 2 - Security Model 1.03 Specification. http://www.opcfoundation.org. Accessed Nov 2015
8. OPC Foundation: OPC UA Part 3 - Address Space Model 1.03 Specification. http://www.opcfoundation.org. Accessed July 2015
9. Cavalieri, S., Salaa, M.G., Scroppo, M.S.: Integrating OPC UA with web technologies to enhance interoperability. Comput. Stand. Interfaces 61, 45–64 (2018)
10. Jaggar, D.: ARM Architecture and Systems. In: IEEE Micro, vol. 17, no., pp. 9–11, August 1997
11. Fitzpatrick, J.: An interview with Steve Furber. Commun. ACM 54(5), 34–39 (2011)
12. Microsoft Announces Support of System on a Chip Architectures From Intel, AMD, and ARM for Next Version of Windows, January 2011
13. Pang, B.: Energy consumption analysis of arm-based Syste. Aalto University School of Science Degree Programme of Mobile Computing, p. 68, August 2011
14. Veichtlbauer, A., Ortmayer, M., Heistracher, T.: OPC UA integration for field devices. In: 2017 IEEE 15th International Conference on Industrial Informatics (INDIN), November 2017
15. Mittal, S.: A survey of techniques for improving energy efficiency in embedded computing systems. Int. J. Comput. Aided Eng. Technol. VI(4), 450–459 (2014)
16. Intel: System Programming Guide, Part 1 64 and IA-32 Architectures. vol. III, no. A, pp. 14–36 (2011)
17. Abou-Of, M.A., Sedky, A.A., Taha, A.H.: Power-energy simulation for multi-core processors in benchmarking. Adv. Sci. Technol. Eng. Syst. J. 2(1), 255–262 (2017)

Travel-Time Prediction Methods: A Review

Mengting Bai[1], Yangxin Lin[1], Meng Ma[2(✉)], and Ping Wang[1,2,3(✉)]

[1] School of Software and Microelectronics, Peking University, Beijing, China
{baimt,martinlin,pwang}@pku.edu.cn
[2] National Engineering Research Center for Software Engineering,
Peking University, Beijing, China
mameng@pku.edu.cn
[3] Key Laboratory of High Confidence Software Technologies (PKU),
Ministry of Education, Beijing, China

Abstract. Near-future Travel-time information is helpful to implement Intelligent Transportation Systems (ITS). Travel-time prediction refers to predicting future travel-time. Researchers have developed various methods to predict travel-time in the past decades. This paper conducts a review focusing on literatures, including techniques proposed recently. These methods are categorized as model-based and data-driven methods. We elaborate two common model-based methods, namely queuing theory and cell transmission model. Data-driven methods are categorized as parametric models (linear regression, autoregressive integrated moving average model and Kalman filter) and non-parametric models (neural network, support vector regression, nearest neighbors and ensemble learning). These methods are compared from data, prediction range and accuracy. In addition, we discuss several solutions to overcome shortcomings of existing methods, and highlight significant future research challenges.

Keywords: Travel-time prediction · Model-based · Data-driven
Parametric · Non-parametric

1 Introduction

Travel-time prediction is a critical component of Intelligent Transportation Systems (ITS) [1]. It plays an important role in the implementation of Advanced Traveler Information System (ATIS) and Advanced Traffic Management Systems (ATMS) [2]. Travel-time information can be applied as input or auxiliary data of dynamic navigation, congestion control, accident detection and so on. Therefore, it is significant to study travel-time prediction methods. Predicting future travel-time is a complex task because travel-time changes in different periods due to the weather, road conditions, drivers' habits, etc. It is crucial to understand these fluctuations and develop accurate travel-time prediction algorithms. Therefore, predicting travel-time requires complex traffic models or data-driven models that can learn traffic patterns from data.

In recent years, a variety of travel-time prediction methods have been proposed. These methods use different technologies and have their own advantages and disadvantages. Contributions of our work are as follows: **(a)** we classify travel- time

M. Qiu (Ed.): SmartCom 2018, LNCS 11344, pp. 67–77, 2018.
https://doi.org/10.1007/978-3-030-05755-8_7

prediction methods as model-based and data-driven methods, and provide some brief descriptions of these methods; **(b)** we compare model-based and data-driven methods in terms of datasets, prediction range, and accuracy; **(c)** we discuss several solutions to overcome shortcomings of existing methods, and highlight future research challenges.

2 Problem Statement

Travel-time can be generally defined as the time to reach a destination or cross a link. Travel-time prediction refers to the prediction of current or future travel-time. There are two ways to predict travel-time, namely direct prediction methods and indirect prediction methods. We usually utilize parametric or non-parametric methods to fit the functional relationship of travel-time data, and predict travel-time in the near future directly [3]. We predict time-space speed by using historical data such as flow, density, occupancy, or average speed, and then calculate travel-time indirectly [3].

The problem generally consists of three components, namely data collection, data processing and travel-time prediction. Traffic data is collected by loop detectors, radar monitors, the global positioning systems, etc. Data can be stored in historical database after pre-processing, such as missing data completing, data aggregation and so on. Some algorithms can be employed to predict travel-time in the near future with historical data and real-time data.

3 Classification of Travel-Time Prediction Methods

Various travel-time prediction methods have been proposed in the past decades. We categorize these methods as model-based and data-driven methods (See Fig. 1).

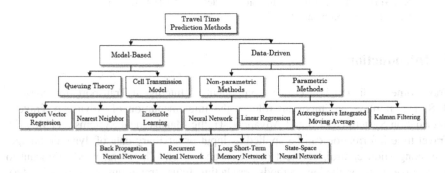

Fig. 1. Classification of travel-time prediction methods

The model-based methods predict future travel-time by building traffic models using traffic parameters (such as density, flow, and speed). They estimate traffic condition over time. This paper describes two common traffic models of travel-time prediction, namely queuing theory [4–6] and Cell Transmission Model [7–10].

The data-driven methods predict travel-time by mining potential patterns. We classify data-driven methods into two categories: parametric and non-parametric models. Common parametric models include Linear Regression [11–13], Autoregressive Integrated Moving Average [14–17] and Kalman Filtering [17–21]. Non-parametric models of travel-time prediction include Neural Networks (Back Propagation Neural Network [22, 23], State-Space Neural Network [24, 25], Recurrent Neural Network [26, 27], and Long Short-Term Memory Network [28, 29]), Support Vector Regression [30–32], Nearest Neighbors [33–35], and Ensemble Learning methods [36–39].

4 Review of Travel-Time Prediction Methods

4.1 Model-Based Methods

This kind of methods builds models using traffic data, such as flow, speed and density. It can describe the collective behavior of numerous vehicles, or the individual behavior of a vehicle. Table 1 lists the description and performance of these methods.

4.1.1 Queuing Theory

The queuing theory model generally utilizes historical data to analyze the length of the waiting queue, number of vehicles waiting in the queue and waiting time to obtain statistical patterns, and then predicts travel-time.

Takaba et al. [4] employed a sandglass model and a time-delay model to predict travel-time using data from Mejiro Street, Tokyo. The error rate (ER) was about 11–24%. They found that the performance of the sandglass model was more stable than the time-delay model. Akiva et al. [5] proposed a framework called DynaMIT to predict travel-time. However, it is not suitable for long-term forecasting. Skabardonis et al. [6] used a time-space model to predict travel-time on the main roads. They conducted experiments on Washington and Lincoln Avenue. The ER was less than 5%.

4.1.2 Cell Transmission Model

The Cell Transmission Model (CTM) can describe the formation, propagation and elimination of waiting queues and back-propagation of crowded waves. In CTM models, roads are divided into fixed-length units. Vehicles travel from one cell to another adjacent one.

Juri et al. [7] combined statistical forecasting techniques with CTM simulation to forecast short-term travel-time online. The advantage of the framework is that it is flexible and can take advantage of online data. Wan et al. [8] utilized Link-Node CTM to provide a probability distribution of travel-time. Xiong et al. [9] proposed a three-stage highway travel-time prediction framework. Seybold [10] proposed an improved CTM (CTM-v) model, and carried out experiments using data from E4 highway. The mean percentage error (MPE) of the proposed model was reduced by 16%. We find that the least squares (LS) and total least squares (TLS) methods can optimize parameters of CTM, thus improving the accuracy of CTM.

Table 1. Description and performance of model-based methods

Literature	Prediction model	Data		Prediction range	Accuracy
		Source	Location		
[4]	Queuing theory	Length of queue, flow, travel-time	Mejiro street (4.4 km)	5 min	**ER: 5–18%**
[5]	Queuing theory	Length of queue, travel-time	Boston highway	–	–
[6]	Queuing theory	Flow, occupancy, signal cycle	M street, Lincoln Avenue	7 min	**ER: <5% (in a cycle)**
[7]	CTM	Flow, speed	Highway simulation	–	**ER: <15%**
[9]	CTM	Flow, speed	M4	5 min	–
[10]	CTM-v	Flow, speed	E4 N (7.4 km)	–	**MPE: 19%**

4.2 Data-Driven Methods

The idea of data-driven methods is to fit a mapping function between variables to approximate the real situation with a large quantity of historical data.

4.2.1 Parametric Methods

Parametric methods generally assume that all data satisfies a certain distribution and train models according to pre-defined rules. Table 2 shows the description and performance of these parametric methods.

Linear Regression. LR model assumes that the function of travel-time prediction is a linear function of traffic variables.

Kwon et al. [11] employed a LR model to predict highway travel-time with data from I-880S in California. The mean absolute percentage error (MAPE) was lower than 23%. Zhang et al. [12] used a LR model with time-varying coefficients to predict travel-time. The ER on I-880 data increased from 5% to 24%. The ER on I-405 data was about 8–14%. Sun et al. [13] exploited the multi-variable local LR model to predict the speed using data from US-290 highway. The mean relative error (MRE) was 11.38%. The results showed that the performance of the local LR model was better than k-nearest neighbors and kernel smoothing methods.

Autoregressive Integrated Moving Average. ARIMA models convert a non-stationary time series into a stationary one, and fit a regression function of current values and lag values of variables and random error.

Oda et al. [14] experimented with ARIMA using vehicle sensor data collected on a 7 km highway. The ER was less than 13.9%. Zhicharevich et al. [15] applied the KARIMA model which combined a Kohonen network with ARIMA to predict short-term travel-time. Xia et al. [16] combined a Seasonal ARIMA with an adaptive Kalman Filter. They utilized detector data on I-80 highway and reported MAPE was 5.34%. The model can continuously adjust forecasting results as real-time data is available. Sun et al. [17] forecasted travel-time of origin-destination pairs by combining

SARIMA with KF. The results showed that the mean absolute error (MAE) and MAPE of the model were both less than 7%, which was better than SARIMA and KF.

Kalman Filtering. KF theory uses a state-space model of a linear stochastic system which consists of a state equation and an observation equation. The theory optimally estimates the state of system by input and output observation data.

Chen et al. [18] conducted experiments using simulation data from I-80 in New Jersey with a relative root square error (RRSE) less than 2.8%. Ji et al. [19] established KF equations for dynamic travel-time prediction. The MRE of the model was 1.6%. Ojeda et al. [20] proposed an adaptive KF for travel-time prediction online. The simulation experiment performed with ER less than 9%. Liu et al. [21] combined simple exponential smoothing (SES) with KF. The experiment showed that the mean absolute relative error (MARE) of ESES was 3.1% which was better than KF and SES. We think that KF methods can optimize smoothing factors over time, thus improving the performance of SES when traffic conditions change suddenly.

Table 2. Description and performance of parametric methods

Literature	Prediction model	Data		Prediction range	Accuracy
		Source	Location		
[11]	LR	Flow, travel-time, occupancy	I-880N&S (10 km)	5–60 min	**MAPE: 7.7–23%**
[12]	Time-varying LR	Flow, travel-time, occupancy, speed	I-880N (6 km) I-405 (32 km)	I-880: <60 min I-405: <90 min	**MAPE: I-880:7–24% I-405:8–14%**
[13]	local LR	Speed	US-290N (2.5 km)	25 min	**MRE: 11.38%**
[14]	ARIMA	Flow, occupancy	National route 16, Japan (7 km)	5 min	**ME: <13.9%**
[16]	SARIMA, KF	Flow, occupancy	I-80 (14.5 km)	5 min	**MAPE: 5.34%**
[17]	SARIMA, KF	GPS data	Commercial centers in Luohu and Futian, Shenzhen	5 min	**MAE: 4.88% MAPE: 6.38% RMSE: 20.34%**
[18]	KF	Travel-time	I-80	5 min	**MARE: <2.1% RRSE: <2.8%**
[19]	KF	Travel-time	Haining road, Zhoujiazui road, Yalujiang road	–	**MRE: 1.6‰ MARE: 2.13‰**
[20]	KF, CTM	Flow, speed	Highway simulation (10.5 km)	45 min	**ER: <9%**
[21]	KF, SES	Travel-time	Highway (17.7 km)	5 min	**MARE: 3.1%**

4.2.2   Non-parametric Methods

Non-parametric methods make none assumptions about distribution of the data. They learn from data and train models directly or indirectly. Table 3 shows the description and performance of non-parametric models in some researches.

Table 3. Description and performance of non-parametric methods

Literature	Prediction model	Data		Prediction range	Accuracy
		Source	Location		
[22]	BPNN	Travel-time	US-290 (27.6 km)	5–25 min	**MAPE: 7.4–17.9%**
[23]	BPNN	Travel-time, GPS data	Hwy35 (22 km)	3 h	**MSE: <3%**
[24]	SSNN	Travel-time, speed	A13 simulation (8.5 km)	1 min	**MRE: 1.6%**
[25]	SSNN	Travel-time	Binhe road (8 km)	2 min	**MAPE: 7.34%**
[26]	BPNN RNN	Travel-time	Interstate, intercity and urban areas	–	**BPNN: MAPE: <17.3% MARE: <12.3% RNN: MAPE: <5.4% MARE: <5.2%**
[27]	TDRN	Flow, density	I-5 simulation (8 km)	15 min	**MPE: <15%**
[28]	LSTM	Travel-time	British highway	15–60 min	**MRE:0.17–0.77**
[29]	LSTM-DNN	Travel-time	I-80	5–60 min	**MAPE: 1–7.3%**
[30]	SVR	Speed	National highway, Taiwan	3 min	**MRE: <4.5% RMSE: <7.4%**
[31]	OL-SVR	PeMS data	California highway	5 min	**Off-peak MAPE: <9% Peak MAPE: <23.4%**
[32]	SVR, IGA	Travel-time	Peace road, Langfang city	5 min	**MRE: 9.7% MAPE: 12.4%**
[33]	k-NN	Travel-time	Gyeongbu highway (3.4 km)	5–30 min	**MAPE: 4.3–14.8%**
[34]	1-NN	Flow, speed, travel-time	No.1 highway, Taiwan (88 km)	5 min	**MAPE: <8.6%**
[35]	Mk-NN	Speed	Korea highway (1800 km)	0–6 h	**MAPE: <3.3% RMSE: <3.5%**
[39]	RF	Flow, speed	GPS simulation	6–30 min	**RMSE: <7.5%**
[36]	GB	Travel-time	I-95S	5–30 min	**Off-peak MAPE: 2.3–14.8% Peak MAPE: 8.7–18.4%**
[37]	RF, k-NN	Travel-time	Bus 232, 249	–	**MAPE: 6.9–14.29%**
[38]	RF, GB	GPS data, speed	Porto city	–	**RF MRE: 17–29% GB MRE: 24–29%**

Neural Networks. As for travel-time prediction, we generally utilize travel-time or speed data as input to train NNs.

Back Propagation Neural Network. Park et al. [22] established a BPNN model and found the MAPE was 7.4–18%. Wisitpongphan et al. [23] designed a BPNN model with three hidden layers to predict travel-time. The mean squared error (MSE) of the proposed model was less than 3%.

State-Space Neural Network. Lint et al. [24] proposed a framework to process missing data. The MRE of the model was 1.6%. Li et al. [25] exploited a Bayesian SSNN with terminal conditions. Compared with the SSNN model, the training time of BSSNN reduced by 90 min, and MAPE also decreased by 0.17%. We conclude that using control factors to limit confidence intervals can shorten training time of neural network, accelerate convergence, and enhance stability.

Recurrent Neural Network. Yun et al. [26] conducted an experiment and found the MAPE of RNN was 12% less than BPNN. We think the reason is that RNN has a short-term memory and performs better at processing time series data than BPNN. Ickes et al. [27] used a Genetic Algorithm (GA) to improve the performance of Time-Delayed Recurrent Network (TDRN). The experiment showed the MPE of the model was less than 15%.

Long Short-Term Memory Network. Duan et al. [28] utilized travel-time data to verify the performance of LSTM. The MRE of LSTM was 0.17–0.77. Liu et al. [29] proposed a LSTM-DNN model using travel-time data on I-80 highway and found MAPE less than 7.3%. We believe that the model can mine the short-term and long-term correlation patterns of travel time data. However, it takes a long time to train models.

Support Vector Regression. The basic idea of SVR is to map the training data from the low-dimensional space to the high-dimensional feature space by fitting a function. SVR models can construct a separated hyperplane with the largest margin in the high-dimensional feature space.

Wu et al. [30] used speed data to predict travel-time using SVR. The MRE of SVR was less than 4.5% and the RMSE was less than 7.4%. Castro-Neto et al. [31] proposed an online SVR (OL-SVR) model using PeMS data. The result showed that the MAPE was less than 9% in off-peak hours, while the MAPE was less than 23.4% in peak hours. Gao et al. [32] exploited Immune Genetic Algorithms (IGA) to optimize SVR parameters. The experiment reported the MAPE of the model was 12.4%.

Nearest Neighbors. The Nearest Neighbors algorithm is also known as k-nearest neighbors (k-NN). In k-NN models, if most similar samples of a sample in the feature space belong to a certain class, the sample also belongs to the class. The k-NN regression method utilizes historical data of neighbors to predict travel-time.

Lim et al. [33] combined a point-detection system with an interval-detection system to predict travel-time. The MAPE of the proposed model was 4.3%–14.8%. Wang et al. [34] proposed an improved 1-NN model and showed that the MAPE was less than 8.6%, and the MPE was less than 16.2%. Tak et al. [35] proposed a multi-layer k-NN (Mk-NN) travel-time prediction framework for cloud systems. The framework conducted data classification, global matching, and local matching. The result showed that Mk-NN was 8 times faster than k-NN, and the MAPE and RMSE were less than 3.5%. We believe that the multi-layer matching process reduces searching space and computational complexity, making it a promising method.

Ensemble Learning. The main idea of EL is to predict travel-time based on the voting results of multiple classifiers.

Zhang et al. [36] built a Gradient Boosting (GB) regression method using travel-time data from I-95 highway. The MAPE was 8.7%–18.4% during peak periods, and 2.3%–14.8% during off-peak periods. Yu et al. [37] combined RF with k-NN (RFNN). The MAPE of RFNN was less than 14.3%. Gupta et al. [38] employed RF and GB models to predict travel-time of taxis in Porto. The MRE of RF was 17%–29% and the MRE of GB was 24–29%. Hamner et al. [39] applied a context-dependent Random Forest (RF) method to predict travel-time. The RMSE of the model was less than 7.5%. We conclude that GB regression methods perform better than RF regression methods. It is because GB models pay more attention to samples with larger prediction errors, while samples in RF are randomly selected. However, RF requires less time than GB to train models because RFs can be trained in parallel.

5 Open Issues

We classify travel-time prediction methods as model-based and data-driven methods. They have different applicable scenarios, advantages and disadvantages.

Most of model-based methods are suitable for short-distance short-term prediction on highways and urban roads. These methods have well-defined traffic models and a mature theoretical system. However, these methods have poor transferability.

Data-driven methods can be used for short-term and long-term prediction on highways. There are a few studies applied to urban roads. Most data-driven methods are suitable for non-linear, high-dimensional data. However, most methods have numerous parameters and lack interpretability. Only a few methods are partly inter-pretable, such as k-NN, SSNN and EL methods.

We discuss some solutions to overcome shortcomings of existing methods, and highlight significant research challenges in the future as follows.

(1) Data processing: Existing data-processing algorithms always assume that noise is a known distribution, while realistic noise is difficult to describe. Therefore, it is worthwhile to study new algorithms. Excessive data can increase calculation of models, such as k-NN. Cluster methods can be used to select high-quality data.

(2) Combining spatial information: Travel-time in target roads can be affected by vehicles from upstream and downstream. Correlation metrics of roads may help to improve accuracy of methods. In addition, data mining algorithms can be exploited to analyze traffic data to monitor whether the traffic condition changes or not.

(3) Hybrid methods: Hybrid algorithms can have a better performance. SSNN can capture spatial information but has a short memory. It is a potential method to combine SSNN with LSTM. Furthermore, Mk-NN can be applied to select training samples of GB. The high-quality samples may improve the accuracy of GB.

(4) Deep learning algorithm: Deep learning methods have been exploited to many fields in recent years. Deep Belief Network (DBN), which consists of several RBMs, can learn the potential patterns and trends from data. Therefore, it is worthy to study travel-time prediction with DBN models.

6   Conclusion

This paper reviews travel-time prediction methods in the past decades. These methods are classified as model-based and data-driven methods. Besides, these models are compared from datasets, prediction range, and accuracy. Last but not least, some solutions are proposed to overcome shortcomings of existing methods. Although there are so many methods to predict travel-time, many problems still need to be solved in the future.

Acknowledgement. This work is supported in part by National Key R&D Program of China No. 2017YFB1200700 and National Natural Science Foundation of China No. 61701007.

References

1. Figueiredo, L., Jesus, I., Machado, J.A.T., Ferreira, J.R.: Towards the development of intelligent transportation systems. In: 2001 Proceedings of Intelligent Transportation Systems, pp. 1206–1211 (2001)
2. Zhang, J., Wang, F.Y., Wang, K., Lin, W.H., Xu, X., Chen, C.: Data-driven intelligent transportation systems: a survey. IEEE Trans. Intell. Transp. Syst. **12**, 1624–1639 (2011)
3. Chen, H., Rakha, H.A.: Multi-step prediction of experienced travel times using agent-based modeling ★. Transp. Res. Part C **71**, 108–121 (2016)
4. Takaba, S., Morita, T., Hada, T., Usami, T.: Estimation and measurement of travel time by vehicle detectors and license plate readers. In: Vehicle Navigation and Information Systems Conference, pp. 257–267 (1991)
5. Ben-Akiva, M., Bierlaire, M., Burton, D., Koutsopoulos, H.N., Mishalani, R.: Network state estimation and prediction for real-time traffic management. Netw. Spat. Econ. **1**, 293–318 (2001)
6. Skabardonis, A., Geroliminis, N.: Real-time estimation of travel times along signalized arterials. Transportation & Traffic Theory (2005)
7. Juri, N.R., Unnikrishnan, A., Waller, S.T.: Integrated traffic simulation-statistical analysis framework for online prediction of freeway travel time. Transp. Res. Rec. J. Transp. Res. Board **2039**, 24–31 (2007)
8. Wan, N., Gomes, G., Vahidi, A., Horowitz, R.: Prediction on travel-time distribution for freeways using online expectation maximization algorithm. In: Transportation Research Board 93rd Annual Meeting (2014)
9. Xiong, Z., Rey, D., Mao, T., Liu, H.: A three-stage framework for motorway travel time prediction. In: IEEE International Conference on Intelligent Transportation Systems, pp. 816–821 (2014)
10. Seybold, C.: Calibration of fundamental diagrams for travel time predictions based on the cell transmission model. VS Verlag für Sozialwissenschaften (2015)
11. Kwon, J., Coifman, B., Bickel, P.: Day-to-day travel time trends and travel time prediction from loop detector data. Transp. Res. Rec. J. Transp. Res. Board **1717**, 1819–1825 (2000)
12. Zhang, X., Rice, J.A.: Short-term travel time prediction ★. Transp. Res. Part C **11**, 187–210 (2003)
13. Sun, H., Liu, H.X.: Short-term traffic forecasting using the local linear regression model. Center for Traffic Simulation Studies (2002)

14. Oda, T.: An algorithm for prediction of travel time using vehicle sensor data. In: International Conference on Road Traffic Control, pp. 40–44 (1990)
15. Zhicharevich, A., Margalit, Y.: Travel Time Prediction Problem RTA Freeway
16. Xia, J., Chen, M., Huang, W.: A multistep corridor travel-time prediction method using presence-type vehicle detector data. J. Intell. Transp. Syst. **15**, 104–113 (2011)
17. Sun, J., Zhang, C., Chen, S.K., Xue, R., Peng, Z.R.: Route travel time estimation based on seasonal model and Kalman filtering algorithm. J. Chang. Univ. **34**, 145–151 (2014)
18. Chen, M., Chien, S.: Dynamic freeway travel-time prediction with probe vehicle data: link based versus path based. Transp. Res. Rec. J. Transp. Res. Board **1768**, 157–161 (2001)
19. Ji, H., Xu, A., Sui, X., Li, L.: The applied research of Kalman in the dynamic travel time prediction. In: International Conference on Geoinformatics, pp. 1–5 (2010)
20. Ojeda, L.L., Kibangou, A.Y., De Wit, C.C.: Online dynamic travel time prediction using speed and flow measurements. In: Control Conference, pp. 4045–4050 (2013)
21. Liu, X., Chien, S.I., Chen, M.: An adaptive model for highway travel time prediction. J. Adv. Transp. **48**, 642–654 (2015)
22. Park, D., Rilett, L.R.: Forecasting freeway link travel times with a multilayer feedforward neural network. Comput.-Aided Civ. Infrastruct. Eng. **14**, 357–367 (2010)
23. Wisitpongphan, N., Jitsakul, W., Jieamumporn, D.: Travel time prediction using multi-layer feed forward artificial neural network (2012)
24. Lint, J.W.C.V., Hoogendoorn, S.P., Zuylen, H.J.V.: Accurate freeway travel time prediction with state-space neural networks under missing data. Transp. Res. Part C **13**, 347–369 (2005)
25. Li, X., Wang, C., Shi, H.: A travel time prediction method: Bayesian reasoning state-space neural network. In: 2010 2nd International Conference on Information Science and Engineering (ICISE), pp. 936–940 (2010)
26. Yun, S.Y., Namkoong, S., Rho, J.-H., Shin, S.-W., Choi, J.-U.: A performance evaluation of neural network models in traffic volume forecasting. Math. Comput. Model. **27**, 293–310 (1998)
27. Ickes, W., et al.: Short Term Freeway Traffic Flow Prediction Using Genetically-Optimized Time-Delay-Based Neural Networks **7**, 219–234 (1999)
28. Duan, Y., Lv, Y., Wang, F.Y.: Travel time prediction with LSTM neural network. In: IEEE International Conference on Intelligent Transportation Systems, pp. 1053–1058 (2016)
29. Liu, Y., Wang, Y., Yang, X., Zhang, L.: Short-term travel time prediction by deep learning: a comparison of different LSTM-DNN models. In: IEEE International Conference on Intelligent Transportation Systems, pp. 1–8 (2017)
30. Wu, C.H., Ho, J.M., Lee, D.T.: Travel-time prediction with support vector regression. IEEE Trans. Intell. Transp. Syst. **5**, 276–281 (2004)
31. Castro-Neto, M., Jeong, Y.S., Jeong, M.K., Han, L.D.: Online-SVR for short-term traffic flow prediction under typical and atypical traffic conditions. Expert Syst. Appl. **36**, 6164–6173 (2009)
32. Gao, P., Hu, J., Zhou, H., Zhang, Y.: Travel time prediction with immune genetic algorithm and support vector regression. In: World Congress on Intelligent Control and Automation, pp. 987–992 (2016)
33. Lim, S., Lee, C.: Data fusion algorithm improves travel time predictions. IET Intell. Transp. Syst. **5**, 302–309 (2011)
34. Wang, J.Y., Wong, K.I., Chen, Y.Y.: Short-term travel time estimation and prediction for long freeway corridor using NN and regression. In: International IEEE Conference on Intelligent Transportation Systems, pp. 582–587 (2012)
35. Tak, S., Kim, S., Oh, S., Yeo, H.: Development of a data-driven framework for real-time travel time prediction. Comput.-Aided Civ. Infrastruct. Eng. **31**, 777–793 (2016)

36. Zhang, Y., Haghani, A.: A gradient boosting method to improve travel time prediction. Transp. Res. Part C **58**, 308–324 (2015)
37. Yu, B., Wang, H., Shan, W., Yao, B.: Prediction of bus travel time using random forests based on near neighbors. Comput.-Aided Civ. Infrastruct. Eng. **33**, 333–350 (2017)
38. Gupta, B., Awasthi, S., Gupta, R., Ram, L., Kumar, P., Rohit Prasad, B., Agarwal, S.: Taxi travel time prediction using ensemble-based random forest and gradient boosting model. In: Rajsingh, E.B., Veerasamy, J., Alavi, Amir H., Peter, J.Dinesh (eds.) Advances in Big Data and Cloud Computing. AISC, vol. 645, pp. 63–78. Springer, Singapore (2018). https://doi.org/10.1007/978-981-10-7200-0_6
39. Hamner, B.: Predicting travel times with context-dependent random forests by modeling local and aggregate traffic flow. In: IEEE International Conference on Data Mining Workshops, pp. 1357–1359 (2011)

The Influence of Sleep on Opportunistic Relay in Linear Wireless Sensor Networks

Haibo Luo[1,2,3]([✉]), Zhiqiang Ruan[1,2,3], and Fanyong Chen[1,2,4]

[1] College of Computer and Control Engineering, Minjiang University,
350108 Fuzhou, China
robhappy@qq.com
[2] Digital Fujian IoT Laboratory of Intelligent Production, 350108 Fuzhou, China
[3] Industrial Robot Application of Fujian University Engineering Research
Center, Minjiang University, 350108 Fuzhou, China
[4] School of Electrical Engineering, Anhui Polytechnic University, 241000
Wuhu, China

Abstract. In linear wireless sensor networks, if the nodes can listen and receive packet at any time, a better balance between energy consumption and delay can be achieved by using opportunistic relay (such as TE-OR). In order to further reduce the network power consumption, the nodes need to be properly in a dormant state, which will affect the performance of opportunistic relay. Taking TE-OR algorithm as an example, this paper studies the effect of sleep on opportunistic relay. The simulation results show that in order to achieve the delay performance of the TE-OR algorithm without sleep, the duty cycle should reach more than 60%. In addition, it is difficult to optimize the energy consumption and delay performance simultaneously for the opportunistic relay with sleep.

Keywords: Linear wireless sensor networks · Sleep · Opportunistic routing
Energy efficiency · Latency

1 Introduction

When nodes are deployed along the linear geographic area, a linear wireless sensor networks (LWSNs) can be constructed. LWSNs can be widely applied to monitoring rivers, tunnels, bridges, roads and so on [1, 2]. In the application of the linear topology network, the deployment path length of nodes ranges from tens of meters to hundreds of kilometers, so the network may have tens or even thousands of sensors/executors. In addition to the common characteristics of wireless sensor networks, compared with other topologies, linear topology networks have longer link and more hops, resulting in greater delay and more uneven network energy consumption. Therefore, these two problems of improving energy-efficiency and reducing packet latency can't be addressed well at the same time in LWSNs [3].

In our previous work, we proposed a joint optimization strategy of delay and energy consumption based on the residual energy of nodes for linear topological networks, and analyzed an opportunistic relay selection algorithm (TE-OR [4]). However,

M. Qiu (Ed.): SmartCom 2018, LNCS 11344, pp. 78–86, 2018.
https://doi.org/10.1007/978-3-030-05755-8_8

this algorithm assumes that nodes in the network can listen and receive packets at any time. In order to further save energy, nodes need to enter the sleep state at the right time according to the protocol. In linear networks, if each node works according to a certain duty cycle, and if there is no coordination and scheduling between nodes, there are two disadvantages to the opportunistic relay selection scheme we designed: (1) when relaying packets, some of the backward listening nodes may be dormant, so the 'deviation of sending energy updating' will occur in these nodes, and eventually result in performance degradation or even failure of the algorithm. (2) when duty-cycled TE-OR is implemented, some nodes in forward set will be dormant during relaying period, so it will inevitably affect the performance of the algorithm. Theoretically, the lower the duty cycle of nodes, the worse the performance of TE-OR algorithms. Taking TE-OR as an example, this paper analyzes the effect of duty cycle of nodes on the performance of opportunistic relay selection in LWSNs by simulation.

2 Related Works

There are many routing algorithms and protocols in WSNs [5–9], but most of them are not suitable for LWSNs, or need to be optimized to be applied in LWSNs. For example, flooding is often used to discover route in WSNs, but not in LWSNs, because nodes in WSNs are often deployed randomly, and the topology of LWSNs may be known beforehand. Based on this, a variety of routing algorithms have been designed for linear networks according to the application characteristics and requirements. These algorithms construct single-layer [10–14] or multi-layer network topology [15–19]. At the same time, nodes in the network can be deployed statically [10, 12–14, 16–19] or dynamically [11, 15]. Lv et al. [19] designed an opportunistic routing strategy in linear networks based on the optimal transmission power control of nodes, thereby optimizing energy efficiency. Luo et al. [13] also proposed an opportunistic relay selection method (ENS_OR) for one-dimensional linear wireless sensor networks. In ENS_OR algorithm, the optimal transmission distance of energy consumption is analyzed and the transmission power is assumed to be dynamically adjusted by nodes. However, ENS_OR algorithm does not consider packet latency.

Inspired by the opportunistic routing strategy, we have designed opportunistic relay method to dynamically select the best forwarder, so as to balance the energy consumption between nodes and guarantee the end-to-end delay. To do this, we firstly assume that nodes can receive messages at any time, and studies the strategy of collecting residual energy of nodes in linear topology network, then takes the residual energy of nodes as a key parameter for opportunistic forwarding priority. Furthermore, taking network energy consumption and data end-to-end delay as joint optimization objectives, the adaptive opportunistic relay selection strategies with fixed transmitting power are studied, and TE-OR algorithms are proposed [4]. Compared with existing methods, the proposed algorithm can significantly balance the energy consumption between nodes while minimizing the delay of time-critical packets and network energy consumption.

3 System Settings

3.1 Network Model

Linear topology network model is shown in Fig. 1. In this topology model, there are M wireless sensor nodes and a sink node. The hardware architecture of all sensor nodes is the same, that is, their sensor/actuator types, communication units and energy supply mode are the same. On the one hand, the sensor node is responsible for collecting and sending data, or receiving remote commands and messages and driving controller/executor operations, on the other hand, it can also act as a router to forward data. Sink node is responsible for data aggregation processing, and acts as a gateway between the network and the external network (such as the Internet) for data upstream and downstream protocol conversion and interactive processing. For deployment purposes, sensor nodes are often battery-powered and therefore require low-power operations, whereas sink can be powered by adapters or is energy-intensive.

In this linear network model, the nodes are about equidistant from each other, and the distance between any two adjacent nodes is D_N. Considering the linearity and simplicity of the network link, each node has a unique network address form 1 to M (ID number), and the ID number corresponds to its geographical location, that is, the node numbered M is nearest to sink, while the node numbered 1 is farthest from sink in geographical location. The communication range of a node is $R = nD_N$, when the node N_i sends data, there are $2n$ nodes in the communication range ($\{N_j | i - n \leq j \leq i + n\}$) to hear the packet.

In TE-OR algorithm, the next hop forwarder N_c must satisfy:

$$\underset{i+1 \leq c \leq i+n}{argmax} \left[\frac{2E_{Tx}(k, R) \times RE_c}{n} + \lambda c \right] \tag{1}$$

Where $E_{Tx}(k, R)$ is the transmission power, RE_c is the residual energy of node N_c, and λ is the coordination factor between energy consumption and latency. The data types are divided into emergency messages and ordinary messages. TE-OR utilize different λ value to relay different type of messages. When the node N_i forwards a packet, it is assumed that forwarder candidates will not sleep, that is, all of them can receive packets at any time. According to the optimized formula, the forwarding priority of the forwarders is calculated, and then the data is broadcast. these nodes with higher priority will relay the packet, thus achieving a balance between energy consumption and delay.

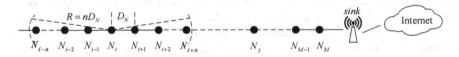

Fig. 1. Network model of LWSNs

3.2 Simulation Parameters

We use MATLAB to analyze the influence of duty cycle on TE-OR algorithm. The parameter settings are consistent with TE-OR. In addition, in order to study the effect of length of sleep time on energy consumption, the listening and sleep power is set to be 0.5 mW and 1μW respectively. The duty cycle is set to 20%–70%, and the total number of nodes varies between 100–500. The active time of the nodes is fixed to 10 ms, but the start time of active period is random, and the source node does not generate packets in a fixed period of 1S, but randomly delays sending data in 1S. In order to compare the performance of different situations, the time points of packet generation under different parameters are consistent. In addition, the performance of TE-OR algorithm at different duty cycle is compared with a non-scheduled deterministic routing algorithm. All nodes in the algorithm are not sleeping, and the packet is always transmitted at the optimal transmission distance of energy consumption, that is, node N_i always transmits message to N_{i+1}. However, since there is only one source node, we should avoid all packets being transmitted along a fixed route. To do so, the first hop relay will be selected in turn from N_4 to N_1. That is, the route of the first packet is $\{N_4 \rightarrow N_8 \rightarrow N_{4x}\}$, the second packet is $\{N_3 \rightarrow N_7 \rightarrow N_{4x-1}\}$, and the fourth packet is $\{N_1 \rightarrow N_5 \rightarrow N_{4(x-1)+1}\}$. The route of the fifth packet is exactly the same as that of the first packet, and so on. Obviously, this is a deterministic relay method (EOR, Energy Optimal Relay) that always chooses the optimal transmission distance for energy efficiency.

4 Performance Evaluation Results

Figure 2 shows the packet loss rate varying with the network size when the node has different duty cycles. We can see that regardless of the duty cycle, the packet loss rate increases as the number of nodes increases. When the total number of nodes is fixed, the smaller the duty cycle, the higher the packet loss rate. When the duty cycle is higher than 50%, the packet loss rate of TE-OR can be maintained below 10%, and the increase rate with the increase of network size is not large. However, when the duty cycle is 40%, the packet loss rate of TE-OR is significantly increased, and will be higher than that of EOR algorithm When duty cycle is less than 40%. With the further reduction of duty cycle, the packet loss rate will also rise rapidly. When the duty cycle is 20%, the packet loss rate reaches 83.36% and 100% respectively when the total number of nodes is 100 and 300.

Figure 3 shows the average energy consumption of one packet successfully transmitted. This metric is defined as the average energy consumption of a single node that has been successfully relayed to sink node under a certain duty cycle and network size, that is, the average total energy consumption of a single node divided by the total number of packets successfully transmitted to sink. Considering the additional energy consumption due to packet loss, this metric reflects the actual energy cost of successfully relaying a packet. Figure 3 shows the maximum, minimum and average energy consumption under different duty cycles. When the duty cycle is 20% and the number of nodes is 200–500, the average energy consumption reaches 0.0041 J,

0.0183 J, 0.1192 J and 0.1530 J respectively, which is much larger than that of other duty cycles, so it is not shown in the graph. It can be seen that when the duty cycle is 50%, the average energy consumption and the difference between different network sizes are minimal. If we gradually reduce the duty cycle, the mean and difference will increase, and gradually expand the duty cycle, the mean value will increase, but the difference will not be significantly increased. Furthermore, we can see that when the duty cycle of TE-OR is less than 30%, the average energy consumption performance drops to the level of EOR algorithm.

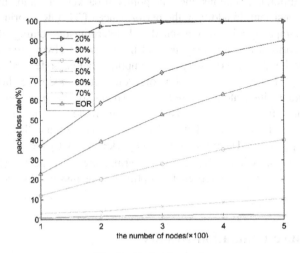

Fig. 2. Packet loss rate

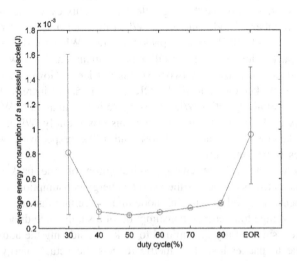

Fig. 3. Average energy consumption of a successful packet

Figure 4 illustrates the average residual energy of all nodes when the linear network link disconnection happens. We can see that the performance change of average residual energy is similar to the packet loss rate, that is, the smaller the duty cycle, or the larger the network size, the higher the average residual energy. This is because the data link is single for large data transmission with only one data source in linear topology networks, when the packet loss rate is high, packets cannot be transmitted to the back end of the link easily. Therefore, the nodes at the back end of the link still have high residual energy until the network is disconnected, so the final average residual energy value is higher. Moreover, because of the high packet loss rate and the consistent generation time of packet under all duty cycle, the network survival time of lower duty cycle is longer, as can be seen in Fig. 5. Furthermore, because nodes in EOR are active all the time, its network lifetime is the shortest.

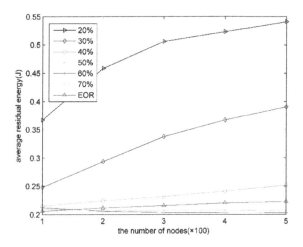

Fig. 4. Average residual energy

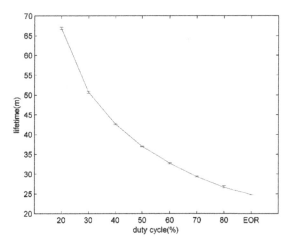

Fig. 5. Network lifetime

Figures 6 and 7 show the normal and time-critical packet delays of duty-cycled TE-OR algorithm at different duty cycles. In addition, to facilitate the observation, the latency of EOR is plotted in these two figures. It needs to be explained that the messages in the EOR algorithm are neither normal nor time-critical. As can be seen from both figures, the average latency decreases with the increase of duty cycle for both normal and time-critical packets, and increases linearly with the increase of the total number of nodes in the linear network, which is coincident with the previous discussion. It must be pointed out that even if the duty cycle of TE-OR reaches 20%, its latency is still lower than that of EOR, which is only 4 nodes per hop. Furthermore, compared with non-sleep TE-OR when the network size is 500, the duty cycle of all nodes in the network must be higher than 60% and 50% respectively to achieve the latency performance of time-critical and normal packets.

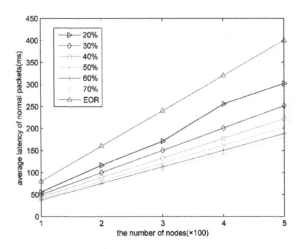

Fig. 6. Average latency of normal packets

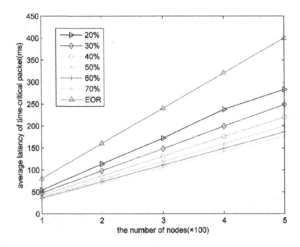

Fig. 7. Average latency of time-critical packet

5   Conclusions

Taking TE-OR algorithm as an example, this paper analyzes the effect of sleep on the opportunistic relay selection algorithm. We conclude that if a node starts its working window completely randomly and works according to the same duty cycle, and if we want to meet certain delay requirements, it must increase the duty cycle of all nodes. in order to achieve the latency performance of the non-sleep TE-OR algorithm, the duty cycle must be greater than 60%. The increase of duty cycle can reduce the packet loss rate and the average energy consumption of a single successful packet, but it will greatly shorten the network life cycle, even close to the deterministic routing algorithm without sleep (such as EOR algorithm). It can be seen that it is difficult to optimize the performance of energy consumption and latency at the same time for the duty-cycled opportunistic relay method, and deterministic relay without scheduling and sleep is even more unfavorable to the network life. In the future, we will study a sleep scheduling scheme for linear topological networks to optimize the energy consumption while guaranteeing the performance of latency.

Acknowledgement. This work was supported by the National Nature Science Foundation of China (Grant number: 61871204); Fujian provincial leading project (Grant number: 2017H0029); the Scientific Research Program of Outstanding Young Talents in Universities of Fujian Province; the Key Project of Natural Foundation for Young in Colleges of Fujian Province (Grant number: JZ160466); the Scientific Research Project from Minjiang University (Grant number: MYK16001); Scientific Research Starting Foundation of Anhui Polytechnic University (s031702004), and Funded by Industrial Robot Application of Fujian University Engineering Research Center,Minjiang University (MJUKF-IRA201805).

References

1. Santi, P., Blough, D.M.: The critical transmitting range for connectivity in sparse wireless ad hoc networks. IEEE Trans. Mob. Comput. **2**(1), 25–39 (2003)
2. Behnad, A., Nader-Esfahani, S.: Probability of node to base station connectivity in one-dimensional ad hoc networks. IEEE Commun. Lett. **14**(7), 650–652 (2010)
3. Varshney, S., Kumar, C., Swaroop, A.: Linear sensor networks: applications, issues and major research trends. In: Proceedings of International Conference on Computing, Communication & Automation (ICCCA), pp. 446–451. IEEE, New York (2015)
4. Luo, H., He, M., Ruan, Z.: Time-aware and energy-efficient opportunistic routing with residual energy collection in wireless sensor networks. Int. J. Commun Syst **30**(10), 1–12 (2017)
5. Liu, Y.X., Liu, A., Guo, S., et al.: Context-aware collect data with energy efficient in cyber-physical cloud systems. Futur. Gener. Comput. Syst. https://doi.org/10.1016/j.future.2017.05.029
6. Liu, Z., Tsuda, T., Watanabe, H., et al.: Data driven cyber-physical system for landslide detection. Mob. Netw. Appl., 1–12 (2018)
7. Phi, L.N., Ji, Y., Liu, Z., et al.: Distributed hole-bypassing protocol in WSNs with constant stretch and load balancing. Comput. Netw. **129**, 232–250 (2017)
8. Gai, K., Choo, K.K.R., Qiu, M., et al.: Privacy-preserving content-oriented wireless communication in internet-of-things. IEEE Internet Things J. **5**(4), 3059–3067 (2018)

9. Zhou, H., Wang, X., Liu, Z., et al.: Resource allocation for SVC streaming over cooperative vehicular networks. IEEE Trans. Veh. Technol. **67**(9), 7924–7936 (2018)

10. Yoon, S., Ye, W., Heidemann, J., et al.: SWATS: wireless sensor networks for steamflood and waterflood pipeline monitoring. IEEE Netw. **25**(1), 50–56 (2011)

11. Lai, T.T., Chen, W.J., Li, K.H., et al.: TriopusNet: automating wireless sensor network deployment and replacement in pipeline monitoring. In: Proceedings of the 11th International Conference on Information Processing in Sensor Networks, pp. 61–72. ACM, New York (2012)

12. Sikora, M., Laneman, J.N., Haenggi, M., et al.: Bandwidth- and power-efficient routing in linear wireless networks. IEEE Trans. Inf. Theory **52**(6), 2624–2633 (2006)

13. Luo, J., Hu, J.Y., Wu, D., et al.: Opportunistic routing algorithm for relay node selection in wireless sensor networks. IEEE Trans. Ind. Inform. **11**(1), 112–121 (2015)

14. Behnad, A., Nader-Esfahani, S.: On the statistics of MFR routing in one-dimensional ad hoc networks. IEEE Trans. Veh. Technol. **60**(7), 3276–3289 (2011)

15. Jawhar, I., Mohamed, N., Al-Jaroodi, J., et al.: An efficient framework for autonomous underwater vehicle extended sensor networks for pipeline monitoring. In: Proceedings of IEEE International Symposium on Robotic and Sensors Environments (ROSE), pp. 124–129. IEEE, New York (2013)

16. He, B., Li, G.: PUAR: performance and usage aware touting algorithm for long and linear wireless sensor networks. Int. J. Distrib. Sens. Netw. **10**(8), 505–521 (2014)

17. Heinzelman, W.B., Chandrakasan, A.P., Balakrishnan, H.: An application-specific protocol architecture for wireless microsensor networks. IEEE Trans. Wirel. Commun. **1**(4), 660–670 (2002)

18. Varshney, S., Kumar, C., Swaroop, A.: Leach based hierarchical routing protocol for monitoring of over-ground pipelines using linear wireless sensor networks. Procedia Comput. Sci. **125**, 208–214 (2018)

19. Lv, X., Hao, J., Jia, X., et al.: Optimal power control based opportunistic routing in linear wireless sensor networks. In: IEEE Control Conference, pp. 8402–8407. IEEE, New York (2016)

Reconfigurable Hardware Generation for Tensor Flow Models of CNN Algorithms on a Heterogeneous Acceleration Platform

Jiajun Gao[1], Yongxin Zhu[1,2(✉)], Meikang Qiu[3], Kuen Hung Tsoi[4],
Xinyu Niu[4], Wayne Luk[5], Ruizhe Zhao[5], Zhiqiang Que[5], Wei Mao[6],
Can Feng[6], Xiaowen Zha[6], Guobao Deng[6], Jiayi Chen[6], and Tao Liu[6]

[1] School of Microelectronics, Shanghai Jiao Tong University, Shanghai, China
zhuyongxin@sari.ac.cn
[2] Shanghai Advanced Research Institute, Chinese Academy of Sciences,
Shanghai, China
[3] Harrisburg University of Science and Technology,
Harrisburg 17101, PA, USA
[4] Shenzhen Corerain Technologies Co. Ltd., Shenzhen, China
[5] Imperial College London, London, UK
[6] The Commercial Aircraft Corporation of China, Shanghai, China

Abstract. Convolutional Neural Networks (CNNs) have been used to improve the state-of-art in many fields such as object detection, image classification and segmentation. With their high computation and storage complexity, CNNs are good candidates for hardware acceleration with FPGA (Field Programmable Gate Array) technology. However, much FPGA design experience is needed to develop such hardware acceleration. This paper proposes a novel tool for design automation of FPGA-based CNN accelerator to reduce the development effort. Based on the Rainman hardware architecture and parameterized FPGA modules from Corerain Technology, we introduce a design tool to allow application developers to implement their specified CNN models into FPGA. Our tool supports model files generated by TensorFlow and produces the required control flow and data layout to simplify the procedure of mapping diverse CNN models into FPGA technology. A real-time face-detection design based on the SSD algorithm is adopted to evaluate the proposed approach. This design, using 16-bit quantization, can support up to 15 frames per second for 256*256*3 images, with power consumption of only 4.6 W.

Keywords: FPGA · Framework · CNNs · Hardware acceleration

1 Introduction

In the era of big data, massive data is collected in people's everyday life. How to extract high semantic information and conduct efficient data analysis from these raw data is always a hot topic recently. Convolutional Neural Networks (CNNs) [1] based algorithms have achieved great performance and high accuracy in many applications related to computer vision, such as object detection [2] image segmentation [3] and

© Springer Nature Switzerland AG 2018
M. Qiu (Ed.): SmartCom 2018, LNCS 11344, pp. 87–96, 2018.
https://doi.org/10.1007/978-3-030-05755-8_9

speech recognition [4]. State-of-the-art CNN-based object detection algorithms like SSD [5], YOLO [6], etc. have been applied to realistic applications and can reach near-human accuracy.

However, the CNN algorithms are very computationally intensive which becomes a major issue in their application to real time tasks on embedded devices. Due to their highly-parallel and bit-oriented architecture, FPGAs have been widely adopted to accelerate these algorithms. According to survey [7], FPGA-based accelerators achieve higher performance in terms of execution time compared with CPUs, consume much less power than GPUs, and tend to be more flexible and configurable than ASICs.

FPGAs can provide high performance for specified network topology at a time through off-line reconfiguration. To implement one CNN model with FPGA, designers should understand the network topology and the flow control with FPGA modules. It is not friendly to the developers who focus on high level machine learning models or neural network architectures. Moreover, off-line reconfiguration also takes considerable efforts and add to complexity of application development [8]. To make FPGAs accessible to a broad community of CNN application developers who are versed in CNN algorithms but lack hardware design experience, we provide a design tool, CNNBUILDER, to help deal with the challenge. Our main contribution in this paper is a reconfigurable hardware generation tool for CNN algorithms targeting a heterogeneous acceleration platform and we make our contributions as follows:

(1) We propose a design tool, CNNBUILDER, which adopts a unified structure to cover different CNN models and save them locally as model description files. This enables our approach to support a high-level programming interface adopted by TensorFlow.

(2) To enable automation of flow control and FPGA re-configuration, we adopt a directed graph structure to describe a design in a model description file.

(3) A memory management facility has been developed to automate memory address allocation to adaptively generate data layout to make the most effective use of limited on-chip resources.

This paper aims to make energy-efficient FPGA accelerator easy to use, and to extend the versatility and improve designer productivity in project development. The rest of the paper is organized as follows: Sect. 2 introduces related work on mapping high-level neural network models to FPGAs. Section 3 introduces relevant CNNs and FPGA accelerator architectures. Section 4 presents our proposed framework design, including unified data structure design, memory allocator design and flow control design. Section 5 provides evaluation result with SSD model to show the improvement in performance and productivity.

2 Related Work

There exists some similar work in this area on mapping high-level neural network models to FPGAs. Sharma et al. [9] devised a design tool DNNWEAVER that automatically generates a synthesizable accelerator for given (DNN, FPGA) pair from a high-level specification in Caffe. Wang et al. proposed a framework DeepBurning [10] to simplify the procedure of mapping diverse neural networks into FPGAs.

Compared with the above two frameworks, our approach exposes a high-level programming interface based on TensorFlow model files instead of Caffe in [9] and [10]. Secondly, similar to DNNWEAVER [9] and DeepBurning [10], our design tool covers multiple neural network models and maps them into FPGA. However, our approach follows a streaming architecture and does not involve instructions, while DNNWEAVER adopts an instruction set architecture. Lastly, DNNWEAVER [9] and DeepBurning [10] only support FPGA implementations, while our approach supports both CPU and FPGA technologies. The device type can be configured through script files, which allows easy realization of heterogeneous acceleration.

3 Background

3.1 CNN

A typical CNN model always contains an input and an output layer, as well as multiple hidden layers. The most frequently used layers in CNN are: convolutional layer, pooling layer and activation layer. The CNN algorithm we implement with CNNBUILDER in this paper is SSD [5], and its structure is shown in Fig. 1. SSD's architecture builds on the VGG-16 architecture but discards the fully connected layers. VGG-16 is used to extract feature maps and after that SSD applies 3*3 convolution filters for each cell to make predictions.

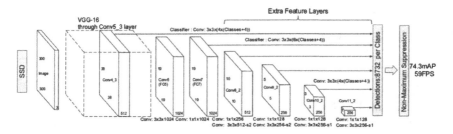

Fig. 1. SSD architecture

3.2 FPGA Accelerator Architecture

The architecture of our proposed FPGA accelerator, shown in Fig. 2, takes several components into consideration, including computation units design (mainly convolution computation unit), on-chip memory, external memory and interaction between the on-chip data and the off-chip data. Convolution is the most important unit for CNN-based algorithm which convolves the input feature maps with the convolutional kernel and produces the output feature map. Because of the on-chip memory resource constraint, it is hard to fit the entire CNN into FPGA board. So, all data for processing are stored in external memory first, and then cached in on-chip buffers layer by layer before they are processed by computation units. In addition, there is also an AXILite Bus which is responsible for the control logic between FPGA Program logic (PL) and the processor (PS). The convolution computation unit is mainly based on design in [2].

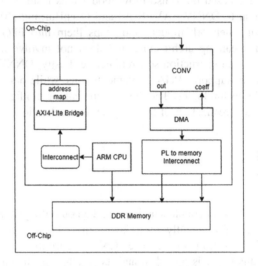

Fig. 2. FPGA accelerator architecture

4   Design Tool Description

4.1   Overview

Figure 3 depicts the overall architecture of our approach. We define three kind of files:

(1) **Model description file.** A unified structure, which will be described in the next section, is adopted to support different CNN models. This file contains the essential information of the computation dataflow graph of a specific CNN model.
(2) **Coefficient data file.** The weight parameters of each layer will be captured as binary files with layer name. These files will be loaded into an FPGA afterwards.
(3) **Data layout configuration file.** This file is used to describe the size of input feature map and output feature map. With this file, our tool can pre-allocate memory space automatically.

As depicted in Fig. 3, CNNBUILDER automatically transforms the programmer-provided CNN model files generated by a TensorFlow platform to model description file, coefficient files and data layout configuration files. Then, with these files, our design tool maps CNN models into an FPGA. In this way, developers can start with TensorFlow and training models. Our tool can then be used to produce an FPGA implementation from TensorFlow descriptions.

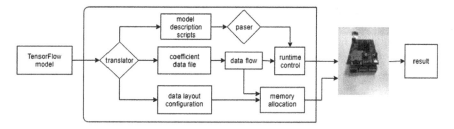

Fig. 3. Framework of CNNBUILDER

4.2 Unified Data Structure Design

Our approach provides a unified data structure to abstract away the details of FPGA accelerator design. We use Google's protocol buffer to design the structure and abstract different kinds of CNN models into this structure. We define **DFGNode** to capture different layers in CNN models and it contains the following information:

- **Name** is the name of the node, which is always the same as the corresponding layer in the model. It is the unique ID to identify the node.
- **Input** represents the input node or input nodes of current node.
- **Operation** represents the operation to be executed in this node. The operations CNNBUILDER supports now are: convolution, max-pooling, fully-connected.
- **Device Type** can be set to be either FPGA or CPU, which decides whether to use FPGA accelerator for current node.
- **Data Type** can be set as FLOAT or FIXED32 or FIXED16, which corresponds to the device type. If the device type is set as CPU, data type will be FLOAT. If the device type is set as FPGA, data type should be FIXED32 or FIXED16.
- **Operation parameter** contains necessary information of operation parameters and every node contains one operation parameter.

We have defined different operations to support different CNN models. Details of these operations are shown as follows:

Input for input node: There is only one node with input operation in specified CNN model. It contains dimension information of the input feature map.

Conv2D for convolution: device type can be FPGA or CPU to operate on different platforms. As mentioned in FPGA accelerator architecture, we have designed adding bias, activation, pooling (max-pooling2*2 in this paper), and batch normalization in convolution module and set some signals to activate corresponding functions. Activation in table can be ReLU, Tanh, Sigmoid, and the default value for activation param means no activation function is used.

MaxPool2D for max-pooling: This node is designed for CPU platform. We subsample each 2*2 window of input feature map to a single maximum pooled output. The height and width of the window are fixed to 2.

FullyConnected for fully connected: Fully connected layer is implemented as matrix multiplication between weight matrix with dimensions (rows * columns) and input matrix with dimensions.

There are some operations with no parameters, such as **Drop-out**. We use the structure to store the information of the model. Figure 4 shows a convolution node and a max-pooling node in model description script.

```
node {                                    node {
  name: "convolution"                       name: "maxpool"
  input: "input_layer_name"                 input: "input_layer_name"
  op: "Conv2D"                              op: "MaxPool2D"
  device: FPGA                              device: CPU
  type: T_FIXED32                           type: T_FLOAT
  conv2d_op_param {                         max_pool2d_op_param {
    depth: 32                                 kernel_size: 2
    kernel_size: 3                            stride: 2
    pad: 1                                  }
    stride: 1                             }
    activation_fn: "Relu"
    use_maxpool_2x2: false
    use_batch_norm: false
    use_bias: true
  }
}
```

Fig. 4. Conv2D and MaxPool2D in model description file

4.3   Memory Allocator Design

This part will elaborate the design of memory management interface to allocate memory automatically. Besides model description file, we also extract coefficient data files and data layout configuration files. Coefficient data files contain the parameters of each layer. And the data layout configuration files include the size of input feature map and output feature map, as well as the shape of the coefficient tensors.

The memory allocator is based on a Best-fit with Coalescing algorithm with basic functions including memory allocation, release, and fragment management. The idea behind this algorithm is to divide the memory into a series of memory blocks, each of which is managed by a block data structure. From the block structure, information such as the base address of the memory block, the usage state of the memory block, the block size, the pointer to the previous and the next block can be obtained. The entire memory can be represented by a block structure with a double-linked list as shown in Fig. 5.

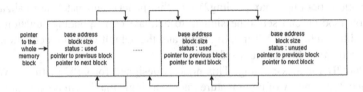

Fig. 5. Framework of memory allocator

The information of the shapes of the input feature map, the weight data and the intermediate feature map is included in the data layout configuration files. Based on layout configuration files, a memory allocator will fetch and store data sets to pre-allocated addresses. It will allocate memory of the same size depicted in the configuration files for each layer. After that, input feature map and weight data will be loaded to specified address in the tool at first and then be loaded into on-chip buffers when related operation are performed. Our approach makes use of pairs of layer name and base address to save information for flow control, which will be covered in the next section.

4.4   Automatic Parser and Runtime Control Design

For each model description file generated with unified data structure, we design a parser to map the specified CNN model into FPGA. For these **DFGNode**s except input node, we can use directed edges with input node as source and current node as target to construct a **Data Flow Graph (DFG)**. DFG is a class that contains essential information of the computation dataflow graph of a specific CNN model. With **DFG**, we realize runtime control as shown in Fig. 6.

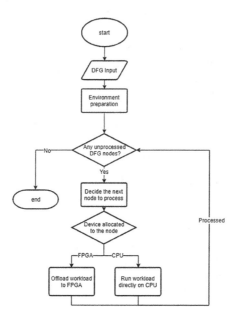

Fig. 6. Runtime control flowchart

Firstly, memory allocator will conduct environment preparation. Then, our design tool searches for the input node in **DFG** and find the starting address of the corresponding data by the name of current node. After that, it loads these data into an on-chip buffer through DMA. It will detect the status register of DMA until the end of the

DMA transfer. It fetches the information of the node and sets related signals by writing registers including starting signal of computation. The intermediate output feature map will be dumped to specified address through DMA and saved as input of next node. For any unprocessed **DFGNode**, our tool repeats the process until all nodes in DFG are traversed. After that, it returns pairs of the name of output node and the starting address of the corresponding data.

5   Evaluation

5.1   Implementation Details

The FPGA based accelerator is provided by Shenzhen Corerain Technology. It is built on a Xilinx Zynq ZC706 board which consists of a Xilinx XC7Z045 FPGA, a dual ARM Cortex-A9 Processor and 1 GB DDR3 memory. The FPGA XC7Z045 is programmed with the convolutional neural network accelerator mentioned in this paper. The ARM processor is used to initialize the accelerator and run our design tool. All designs run on a single 150 MHz clock frequency and the DDR3 memory has a data-path width of 64 bits. The ARM core reorganizes the input feature map and coefficient data, and then stores them to specified address generated by memory allocator described in the previous section. The FPGA accelerator accesses the DRAM memory through AXI switches.

Our design tool aims to map trained CNN model into FPGA and focuses on the inference instead of training models. Since it differs in FPGA platforms and the design of FPGA accelerator compared with prior work, it is hard to compare the proposed design tool with them directly. Here is the evaluation method in this paper: an experienced engineer knows deep learning and FPGA accelerator design well from Corerain Technology write the code to drive FPGA manually and the time used will be compared with the corresponding design in our approach. Meanwhile, the accuracy and power consumption will also be evaluated.

Application. In this paper, our design tool maps trained SSD5 model into FPGA. In order to be better implemented on the FPGA, the SSD5 model is adjusted with input size of 256*256*3.

In experiments, we map the well-trained SSD model onto FPGA with our design tool and records the time it takes to complete a round of network forward-propagation with the input set. We are going to compare the performance of using and not using CNNBUILDER. Function correctness is based on FDDB (Face Detection Data Set and Benchmark) [11] to evaluate the accuracy.

5.2   Experimental Results

Performance and Power, we use FDDB [11] as input and record the run time it takes to process the feature maps with and without our tool targeting FPGA design. Our tool can support CPU as well and we also record the time taken on CPU platform. The results are shown in Table 1. *MC* represents manually-coded driver for the application and it is a reference for our design tool in our experiments, which is denoted as *AG* (Automatic Generation).

Compared with manually coded implementation, automatic generated drivers from our approach contains more software operations which leads to extra time consumption. As shown in Table 1, the average convolution time using our tool is 150 ms, which is very close to 142 ms with manually coded implementation. In manually coded implementation, the lines of code to be handwritten is nearly a thousand and for each CNN model, these implementations need to be modified manually.

Table 1. Our design tool with FPGA and CPU implementations

Device	FPGA	CPU
Platform	ZC706	Intel Core i5
Compiler	Vivado	GCC (4 cores)
Clock	150 MHz	2.30 GHz
Precision	32-bit fixed-point	32-bit floating-point
MC Conv. time	142 ms	366 ms
AG Conv. time by CNNBUILDER	150 ms	366 ms
MC power	4.3 W	-
AG power by CNNBUILDER	4.6 W	-

FPGA's power consumption is obtained from the board using a power meter. With no program running, the power consumption of the FPGA board is 3.6 w. When implementing the SSD algorithm, the power consumption of designs developed with our tool is 4.6 w, only 1.07 times of that with manually-coded driver.

Accuracy. In this experiment, FDDB [11] is used to evaluate the functional correctness and the accuracy of position coordinates and size of face detection frame with our design tool. The result of manually coded implementation and our design tool is the same and the true positive rate reaches up to 82.76% in the case of a false positive number of 50. The result of golden-reference application implemented with SSD model is 82.92% with the same false positive number. Considering accuracy loss due to the fixed-point operation, the precision loss is bearable. Besides, we compare the results of intermedia layers to find that the results generated by manually coded implementation and our design tool are identical.

6   Conclusion

This paper presents a design tool, CNNBUILDER, to simplify the design flow of CNN-based accelerators for machine learning and extend the versatility of the CNN-based accelerators. Our approach makes it easy for software developers to compose CNN models and implement their applications. Our approach adopts a unified data structure to store the information of different CNN models and then map them into FPGA. With our design tool, application developers without FPGA design experience can easily implement their design on the energy-efficient FPGA platform containing both FPGA and CPU. Meanwhile, we show that the accuracy of designs from our approach is guaranteed with only minor overhead in run time and power consumption. Our design tool improves the productivity of CNN based accelerator implementation by significantly reducing the time required to modify designs manually for new models.

Acknowledgment. This work is partially supported by National Key Research & Development Program of China (2017YFA0206104), Shanghai Municipal Science and Technology Commission and Commercial Aircraft Corporation of China, Ltd. (COMAC) (175111105000), Shanghai Municipal Science and Technology Commission (18511111302, 18511103502), Key Foreign Cooperation Projects of Bureau of International Co-operation Chinese Academy of Sciences (184131KYSB20160018) and Shenzhen Corerain Technologies Co. Ltd.

References

1. LeCun, Y., Bengio, Y., Hinton, G.: Deep learning. Nature **521**(7553), 436–444 (2015)
2. Zhao, R., Niu, X., Wu, Y., Luk, W., Liu, Q.: Optimizing CNN-based object detection algorithms on embedded FPGA platforms. In: Wong, S., Beck, A.C., Bertels, K., Carro, L. (eds.) ARC 2017. LNCS, vol. 10216, pp. 255–267. Springer, Cham (2017). https://doi.org/10.1007/978-3-319-56258-2_22
3. Ronneberger, O., Fischer, P., Brox, T.: U-Net: convolutional networks for biomedical image segmentation. In: Navab, N., Hornegger, J., Wells, W.M., Frangi, Alejandro F. (eds.) MICCAI 2015. LNCS, vol. 9351, pp. 234–241. Springer, Cham (2015). https://doi.org/10.1007/978-3-319-24574-4_28
4. Long, J., Shelhamer, E., Darrell, T.: Fully convolutional networks for semantic segmentation. In: Proceedings of the IEEE Conference on Computer Vision and Pattern Recognition - CVPR 2014, pp. 3431–3440 (2015)
5. Liu, W., et al.: SSD: single shot multibox detector. In: Leibe, B., Matas, J., Sebe, N., Welling, M. (eds.) ECCV 2016. LNCS, vol. 9905, pp. 21–37. Springer, Cham (2016). https://doi.org/10.1007/978-3-319-46448-0_2
6. Simonyan, K., Zisserman, A.: Very deep convolutional networks for large-scale image recognition. arXiv preprint arXiv:1409.1556v6 (2014)
7. Abdelouahab, K., et al.: Accelerating CNN inference on FPGAs: a survey (2018)
8. Lacey, G., Taylor, G.W., Areibi, S.: Deep learning on FPGAs: past, present, and future. arXiv e-print 2 (2016)
9. Sharma, H., et al.: From high-level deep neural models to FPGAs. In: 2016 49th Annual IEEE/ACM International Symposium on Microarchitecture (MICRO), Taipei, Taiwan, pp. 1–12 (2016)
10. Wang, Y., et al.: DeepBurning: automatic generation of FPGA-based learning accelerators for the neural network family. In: Design Automation Conference, pp. 1–16. IEEE (2016)
11. FDDB: A Benchmark for Face Detection in Unconstrained Settings. Technical Report UM-CS-2010-009, Deptartment of Computer Science, University of Massachusetts, Amherst (2010)

Image Segmentation Algorithm Based on Spatial Pyramid and Visual Salience

Jingxiu Ni[1,2(✉)], Xu Qian[2], Guoying Zhang[2], Aihua Liang[1], and Huimin Ju[1]

[1] Engineering Integrated Experimental Teaching Demonstration Center, Beijing Union University, Beijing 100101, China
njxl211@163.com
[2] School of Mechanical, Electronic and Information Engineering, China University of Mining and Technology, Beijing 100083, China

Abstract. An image segmentation algorithm based on Spatial Pyramid and visual salience is proposed in the paper. The segmentation algorithm is divided into five steps. The first step is extracting the global features of images to be processed. The second step is dividing the image into some sub-blocks according to different scales. And the third step is extracting the sub-block features of different scales and connecting the features sequentially. The fourth step is calculating the salience of different sub-blocks. The last step is segmenting the salient objects from the source image. The segmentation algorithm detects salient parts of image by means of both color histogram and spatial pyramid. The significance of pixels can be calculated by means of color and pattern. The algorithm assigns different weights to different pixels and sub-blocks. According to experiment results, the segmentation algorithm proposed in the paper outperforms other segmentation in precision, recall and time complexity.

Keywords: Image segmentation · Spatial pyramid · Visual salience Similarity · Feature fusion

1 Introduction

Instead of being attracted by the whole images, people always take interest in certain salient parts of the images. The salient parts are different from the background in such features as texture, color and intensity. It is an important research topic to find and segment the salient objects from images. Image segmentation plays a key role in image processing and image understanding. Therefore, image segmentation attracts many researcher at home and abroad and develops dramatically.

2 Related Work

Bag of words (briefly, BoW) [1] are widely applied in image classification and segmentation. Bag of words are characterized by the formation of multiple clustering centers according to the features, and the construction of a visual dictionary according

© Springer Nature Switzerland AG 2018
M. Qiu (Ed.): SmartCom 2018, LNCS 11344, pp. 97–103, 2018.
https://doi.org/10.1007/978-3-030-05755-8_10

to the clustering centers. Then, the features of the image are mapped to a visual dictionary to obtain the histogram of the image in image classification or segmentation. Bag of words needs to be improved in many aspects. Firstly, the color histogram stresses the frequency of color feature, but it neglects the spatial information of the image. Secondly, the semantics of the image is represented by the semantic words of the clustering center, which is likely to lose the important details. Finally, K-means clustering is generally adopted, resulting in poor classification performance.

Some researchers are trying to take full advantage of spatial information of images. In [2], Suryanto gets the spatial information of the interesting blocks in images according to color histogram and voting. The method takes the pixel position into full consideration [3] proposed the spatially ordered patch, the area of interest is divided into many blocks, and each sub-block is assigned a weight, which means the importance of every sub-block. In [4], Li distinguished the area of interest in the image by means of the saliency of each sub-block. In [5], Kavitha provided the spatial information of the sub-blocks by dividing images into fixed size. Besides, Kavitha adopted complicated feature which combines color and texture. In [6], Ali took full advantage of the color histogram taken from the sub-blocks which are segmented in the shape of a triangle, and provides the position of sub-blocks through the triangle area.

3   Image Features Under Spatial Pyramid

In order to find the salient parts of images, it is critical to find the difference of the salient pixels from the surrounding pixels.

3.1   Spatial Pyramid

As is known to all, color histogram performs excellently in describing the global feature of images. Meanwhile, the fatal shortcoming of color histogram is its disability in providing the position information of pixels or sub-blocks. Some researches have tried to divide one image into many sub-blocks. Many studies have proved the fact that simple sub-block method is prone to lose color information. At the same time, current segmentation methods often ignore the significance of each sub-block or each pixel.

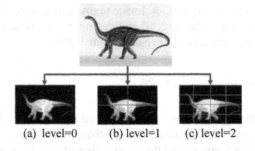

(a) level=0   (b) level=1   (c) level=2

Fig. 1. Multi-scale division of image

The paper takes full advantage of Spatial Pyramid in [7] to provide the position of pixels and sub-blocks. Since the segmentation model proposed in the paper provides both the histogram and the spatial information, the algorithm can promote the segmentation precision. Besides, the paper tries its endeavor to calculate the visual salience of pixels and sub-blocks. In this way, full consideration is given to both the global feature and the local feature of images.

An image can be divided at different scales, which corresponds to different levels (see Fig. 1). Level 0 means the original image without any division. Level 1 means that the image is divided into four sub-blocks of the same size. Level 2 means that each sub-block will be divided into four smaller sub-blocks of the same size. And the operation will be repeated until the size of the smallest sub-block reaches a threshold.

After division procedure, the color histogram of each sub-block at different levels will be extracted and then joined orderly into a complicated eigenvector. The feature vector includes the position information and the color histogram. Hence, the feature vector provides the global feature and local feature by means of multi-scale division.

3.2 The Complicated Feature Vector

In the spatial pyramid model, image is divided at different scale or different level. Let the division level be denoted as l. The sub-blocks at different levels should be appointed corresponding weights, since different levels means different importance. Let the weight of level l be α_l, the calculation of α_l can be stated as follows,

$$\alpha_l = \frac{1}{4^l} \tag{1}$$

At the scale l, the original image is divided into several sub-blocks denoted as B_l^i, $i \in \{1, 2, ..., N\}$, $l \in \{0, 1, 2\}$, N is the number of sub-blocks at level l. The color histogram of each sub-block, denoted as T_l^i, can be calculated as follows,

$$T_l^i = H_l(i) \tag{2}$$

Where $H_l(i)$ is the normalized color histogram of the sub-blocks under the scale l. By joining each features of all the sub-blocks under different levels, the eigenvector of the image can be obtained. Let the eigenvector be V, and V can be calculated as follows,

$$V = \left(\alpha_0 T_0^1, \ \alpha_1 T_1^1, \ \alpha_1 T_0^2, \ ..., \ \alpha_1 T_1^{2^{2l}} \right) \tag{3}$$

3.3 Color Difference and Pattern Difference

Let color difference be denoted as $C(r_x)$, in which r_x is the area where the color difference is formulated. The color difference can be calculated in two steps. The first step is to divide the image into sub-blocks. The i-th sub-block is denoted as $r_i(i = 1,2,\ldots M)$. The second step is to calculate the color difference $C(r_x)$ as follows,

$$C(r_x) = \sum_{i=1}^{M} \|r_x - r_i\|_2 \tag{4}$$

In order to detect the salient parts in image, the difference among sub-blocks should be measured properly. While calculating the salience of different sub-blocks, it is necessary to select a reference sub-block. The reference pattern P_R is obtained as follows:

$$P_R = \frac{1}{N} \sum_{x=1}^{N} P_x \tag{5}$$

Where P_x is the candidate sub-block. If the difference between P_x and the reference block is large, P_x will be more salient. The number of sub-blocks is denoted as N.

4   Image Segmentation Algorithm Based on Spatial Pyramid and Visual Salience

4.1   Calculating Difference and Salience

The salient parts in image is prone to differ from its surrounding parts in both pattern and color. The algorithm proposed in the paper detects the salient parts by means of combining the pattern difference with color difference. The difference of sub-block p_x is denoted as $D(p_x)$, which can be calculated as follows:

$$D(p_x) = P(p_x).C(p_x) \tag{6}$$

Where $D(p_x)$ is the saliency of sub-block p_x. $P(p_x)$ is the pattern difference of sub-block p_x. $C(p_x)$ is the color difference of sub-block p_x. The greater $D(p_x)$ means that the sub-block as p_x is more significant in pattern.

Statistics suggest that the salient part is prone to appear in the middle half part of the image [8]. The distribution probability of salient pixels or salient sub-block p_x accords with Gaussian distribution. If denote the distribution probability as $G(p_x)$, the salience of sub-block p_x can be calculated as follows:

$$S(p_x) = G(p_x).D(p_x) \tag{7}$$

Where $S(p_x)$ is the salience of sub-block p_x.

4.2   Image Segmentation Algorithm Based on Spatial Pyramid and Visual Salience

The segmentation algorithm proposed in the paper detects salient parts of a image by means of both color histogram and spatial pyramid. Based on the previous calculation of salient sub-blocks, the optimized saliency assign a weight W_l^i for all the pixels $B_l^i(i = 1, 2, \ldots, 2^{2l})$. The weight W_l^i is calculated according to the saliency of the pixel (m, n), namely $s(m,n)$. The calculation formula is as follows:

$$W_l^i = \sum\nolimits_{(i,j) \in B_l^i} S(m, n) \tag{8}$$

The detailed procedure of the segmentation algorithm is listed as follows:

Step 1 Divide the image into many sub-blocks, and each sub-block is denoted as B_l^i;

Step 2 Assign a corresponding weight $\alpha_l = \frac{1}{4^l}$ for each sub-block as B_l^i;

Step 3 Extract the color histogram as T_l^i from each sub-block as B_l^i and calculate the color salience as $C(B_l^i) = \sum_{j=1}^{M_l} \left\| T_l^i - T_l^j \right\|$ for each sub-block as B_l^i, where $T_l^j = \frac{1}{M_l} \sum_{i=1}^{M_l} T_l^i$;

Step 4 Extract the pattern as P_l^i from each sub-block and calculate the pattern salience as $P(B_l^i) = \sum_{j=1}^{M_l} \left\| P_l^i - P_l^i \right\|$ for each sub-block as B_l^i, where $P_l^j = \frac{1}{M_l} \sum_{i=1}^{M_l} P_l^i$;

Step 5 Calculate the difference as $D(B_l^i) = P(B_l^i) \cdot C(B_l^i)$ for each sub-block as B_l^i;

Step 6 Calculate the probability distribution function as $G(B_l^i)$ for each sub-block as B_l^i according to Gaussian Distribution;

Step 7 Calculate the salience as $S(B_l^i) = D(B_l^i) \cdot G(B_l^i)$ for each sub-block as B_l^i;

Step 8 Cluster the sub-blocks according to their spatial information and segment the image according to the clustering result.

5   Experiments

The image segmentation experiments are carried out on PASCAL VOC2012 dataset (see Fig. 2). Compared with the traditional multiscale segmentation results in [9], the segmentation algorithm in this paper and the segmentation algorithm based on wavelet transform in [10] are more complete and accurate.

Fig. 2. Segmentation images of PASCAL VOC2012

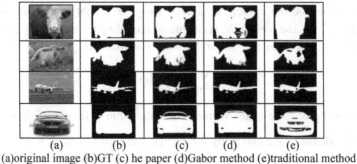

| | (a) | (b) | (c) | (d) | (e) |

(a)original image (b)GT (c) he paper (d)Gabor method (e)traditional method

Fig. 3. Comparison of different segmentation results

As shown in Fig. 3(a-1)–(a-4). Take Fig. 3(a-4) as an example, the segmentation results show that the traditional multi-scale segmentation method has the wrong segmentation, since the ground at the bottom of the car and some background behind the car are mistakenly segmented as targets. The segmentation results produced by the paper are closer to the benchmark. Figure 3(a-3) demonstrates that the wavelet-based segmentation method can hardly separate the fuselage part of the plane from the background, while the slender wing part of the plane is classified as the background.

6 Conclusion

An image segmentation algorithm based on spatial pyramid and visual salience is proposed in the paper. The segmentation algorithm detects salient parts of image by means of both color histogram and spatial pyramid. What's more, the algorithm assigns different weights to different pixels and sub-blocks. According to experiments, the segmentation algorithm proposed in the paper outperforms other segmentation in Precision, Recall and time complexity.

References

1. Ali, N.M., Jun, S.W., Karis, M.S., Ghazaly, M.M., Mohd, M.S.A.: Object classification and recognition using Bag-of-Words (BoW) model. In: 2016 IEEE 12th International Colloquium on Signal Processing and its Applications, CSPA 2016, pp. 216–220 (2016)
2. Suryanto, Kim, D.H., Kim, H.K.: Spatial color histogram based center voting method for subsequent object tracking and segmentation. Image Vis. Comput. **29**(12), 850–860 (2011)
3. Kim, H.U., Lee, D.Y., Sim, J.Y., Kim, C.S.: SOWP: spatially ordered and weighted patch descriptor for visual tracking. In: 2015 IEEE International Conference on Computer Vision (ICCV), Santiago, pp. 3011–3019 (2015)
4. Li, G., Xie, Y., Lin, L., Yu, Y.: Instance-level salient object segmentation. In: 2017 IEEE Conference on Computer Vision and Pattern Recognition (CVPR), Honolulu, HI, 2017, pp. 247–256 (2017)

5. Kavitha, C., Rao, B.P., Govardhan, A.: Image retrieval based on color and texture features of the image sub-blocks. Int. J. Comput. Appl. **15**(7), 33–37 (2011)
6. Ali, N., Bajwa, K.B., Sablatnig, R.: Image retrieval by addition of spatial information based on histograms of triangular regions. Comput. Electr. Eng. **54**, 539–550 (2016)
7. Xie, L., et al.: Improved spatial pyramid matching for scene recognition. Pattern Recogn. **82**, 118–129 (2018)
8. Jiang, X., Feng, K., Lin, H., Tang, J., Zhou, Z., Li, J.: Active contours driven by local gaussian distribution fitting and local robust statistics. J. Inf. Hiding Multimed. Signal Process. **9**(1), 89–98 (2018)
9. Dakua, S.P., Abinahed, J., Al-Ansari, A.: A PCA-based approach for brain aneurysm segmentation. Multidimens. Syst. Signal Process. **29**(1), 257–277 (2018)
10. Chetih, N., Messali, Z., Serir, A., Ramou, N.: Robust fuzzy c-means clustering algorithm using non-parametric Bayesian estimation in wavelet transform domain for noisy MR brain image segmentation. IET Image Proc. **12**(5), 652–660 (2018)

Fast Implementation for SM4 Cipher Algorithm Based on Bit-Slice Technology

Jingbin Zhang[1], Meng Ma[2(✉)], and Ping Wang[2,3,4(✉)]

[1] School of Electronics Engineering and Computer Science, Peking University,
Beijing, China
zhangjingbin@pku.edu.cn
[2] National Engineering Research Center for Software Engineering,
Peking University, Beijing, China
{mameng, pwang}@pku.edu.cn
[3] School of Software and Microelectronics, Peking University, Beijing, China
[4] Key Laboratory of High Confidence Software Technologies,
Peking University, Ministry of Education, Beijing, China

Abstract. The SM4 block cipher algorithm used in IEEE 802.11i standard is released by the China National Cryptographic Authority and is one of the most important symmetric cryptographic algorithms in China. However, whether in the round encryption or key expansion phase of the SM4 algorithm, a large number of bit operations on the registers (e.g., circular shifting) are required. These operations are not effective to encryption in scenarios with large-scale data. In traditional implementations of SM4, different operands are assigned to different words and are processed serially, which can bring redundant operations in the process of encryption and decryption. Bit-slice technology places the same bit of multiple operands into one word, which facilitates bit-level operations in parallel. Bit-slice is actually a single instruction parallel processing technology for data, hence it can be accelerated by the CPU's multimedia instructions. In this paper, we propose a fast implementation of the SM4 algorithm using bit-slice techniques. The experiment proves that the Bit-slice based SM4 is more efficient than the original version. It increases the encryption and decryption speed of the message by an average of 80%–120%, compared with the original approach.

Keywords: SM4 · Bit-slice technology · Block cipher algorithm
Substitution-Box (S-box) · Efficiency

1 Introduction

With the rapid development of Internet applications such as virtual digital currency and blockchain, how to obtain sensitive information (e.g. trade data) in a safe and private manner has become an open issue [1–3]. Traditional block encryption algorithms (e.g., DES, AES, and SM4 etc.) widely used in various fields are indispensable choices to solve this problem. However, these block cipher algorithms often require a large number of logical shift operations which serially operates on every words, so that the

© Springer Nature Switzerland AG 2018
M. Qiu (Ed.): SmartCom 2018, LNCS 11344, pp. 104–113, 2018.
https://doi.org/10.1007/978-3-030-05755-8_11

efficiency of implementation is not high, that cannot meet the high real-time require-ment for trade data transmission in virtual currency and blockchain.

SM4 is a symmetric key algorithm released by the China National Cryptographic Authority, which is simple in design and can be applied to various smart devices, suitable for virtual digital currency and blockchain applications. In this paper, we describe an efficient implementation for SM4 algorithm based on bit-slice technologies in hardware and software to improve the performance. Bit-slice technology has already been applied in multiple cypher algorithms, such as DES [4], AES [5], Serpent [6] and Whirlpool [7] etc., to speed up the software speed. It breaks down of encryption process into a series of logical bit operations using XOR, AND, OR, and NOT logical gates, so that N parallel encryptions are possible on a single N-bit micro-processor [8], i.e., simultaneous execution of N logical gates. When implemented on a micropro-cessor with a N-bit register width, different with using traditional approach which puts cryptographic blocks into different words to process serially, in the bit-slice imple-mentation, each bit in the register acts as a 1-bit processor conducting a different encryption, so that N encryptions are done in a parallel way [5]. In other words, bit-slice implementation places the same bit of N encryption blocks into one word. For example, a register records all the first bit values of N encryption blocks. It is equiv-alent to remove the bit-level operations inside all registers and operates all blocks at the same time on the register level. Then, we can utilize the SIMD instruction set to optimize the parallel processing efficiency. In addition, compared to traditional table-based implementations, the bit-slice implementation are safer against attacks such as caching and timing attacks [9].

The rest of this paper is organized as follows: Sect. 2 reviews the SM4 cipher algorithm. In Sect. 3, we propose the fast implementation for SM4 algorithm based on bit-slice technologies. In Sect. 4, we experimentally analyze the encryption efficiency and throughput of bit-slice SM4. Finally, Sect. 5 concludes the paper.

2 SM4 Cipher Algorithm

The SM4 block cipher algorithm, formerly known as SMS4 algorithm, has been widely performed in the Chinese National Standard for Wireless LAN WAPI (Wired Authentication and Privacy Infrastructure) [3]. In the SM4 algorithm, it has a block length of 128 bits and a key length of 128 bits. Both the encryption process and the key expansion process use a 32-rounds nonlinear iterative structure. The decryption algo-rithm has the same structure as the encryption algorithm, except that the using order of the round keys is reversed, i.e., the decryption round keys are the reverse sequence of the encryption round keys. Therefore, we only introduce the SM4 encryption process in the following, shown in Algorithm 1.

2.1 Round Keys Generation

The encryption key is 128-bit long and is denoted as $EK : (ek_0, ek_1, ek_2, ek_3)$, where ek_i is 32 bits long, i.e., $ek_i \in Z_2^{32}, \forall i \in \{0, 1, 2, 3\}$. The round keys can be represented as $RK : \{rk_0, rk_1, \ldots, rk_{N-1}\}$, where $rk_i \in Z_2^{32}, \forall i \in \{0, 1, \ldots, N-1\}$ and N is the number of encryption rounds, i.e., $N = 32$. Round keys are generated by the encryption key through the key extension process. Given an encryption key $EK : (ek_0, ek_1, ek_2, ek_3)$, the round key is generated by following two steps:

- **Step 1.** Generating initial intermediate keys: $K = (k_0, k_1, k_3, k_4) = (ek_0 \oplus fk_0, ek_1 \oplus fk_1, ek_2 \oplus fk_2, ek_3 \oplus fk_3)$, where $\{fk_0, fk_1, fk_2, fk_3\}$ are the system parameters, in which each $fk_i \in Z_2^{32}, \forall i \in \{1, 2, 3, 4\}$.
- **Step 2.** Generating round keys: for $\forall i \in \{0, 1, \ldots, N\}$, $rk_i = k_{i+4} = k_i \oplus T'(k_{i+1} \oplus k_{i+2} \oplus k_{i+3} \oplus ck_i)$, where $\{ck_0, ck_1, \ldots, ck_{N-1}\}$ are another fixed hyperparameters and T' function is same as T function in round encryption process, except the linear transform L is modified to L', represented as $L'(w) = w \oplus (w <<< 13) \oplus (w <<< 23)$, where w is an input word with 32 bits and the symbol operation $<<< i$ indicates that circular shifting the bits in the word i times to the left. Other operations of T' are same as T summarized in the Sect. 2.2.

Algorithm 1 SM4 encryption algorithm

Input: 4×4 bytes Plaintext $X(x_0, x_1, x_2, x_3)$, 4×4 bytes key EK
Output: 4×4 bytes Cyphertext $Y(y_0, y_1, y_2, y_3)$
1: Round keys $RK \leftarrow KeyExtension\ (EK)$
2: **for** *round* $i \leftarrow 0$ *to* $N - 1$ **do**
3:     **procedure** $F(x_i, x_{i+1}, x_{i+2}, x_{i+3}, rk_i)$:
4:         $x \leftarrow x_{i+1} \oplus x_{i+2} \oplus x_{i+3} \oplus rk_i$
5:         **procedure** $T(x)$:
6:             Nonlinear transformation $\tau(x) \rightarrow x'$
7:             Linear transformation $L(x') \rightarrow x''$
8:         **endprocedure**
9:         $x_{i+3} \leftarrow x'' \oplus x_i$
10:     **endprocedure**
11:     $Y \leftarrow (x_{N+3}, x_{N+2}, x_{N+1}, x_N)$
12: **End**

2.2 Basic Round Encryption

Suppose that the 128-bit plaintext input is $X : (x_0, x_1, x_2, x_3)$, and for the round key $rk_i \in RK$, the encryption transform is:

$$x_{i+4} = F(x_i, x_{i+1}, x_{i+2}, x_{i+3}, rk_i) = x_i \oplus T(x_{i+1} \oplus x_{i+2} \oplus x_{i+3} \oplus rk_i)$$

where, F is the basic round encryption function and its encryption process is shown in Fig. 1. T is the synthetic replacement function, which is a reversible transformation composed by a nonlinear transformation τ and a linear transformation L, represented as $T(x) = L(\tau(x))$. Finally, the 128-bit cyber text is represented as $Y : (y_0, y_1, y_2, y_3) = (x_{35}, x_{34}, x_{33}, x_{32})$.

The **nonlinear transformation** τ consists of four parallel s-boxes. For an input $x : (b_0^x, b_1^x, b_2^x, b_3^x)$, $i \in \{0, 1, 2, 3\}$, its output is denoted as $y \in Z_2^{32}$:

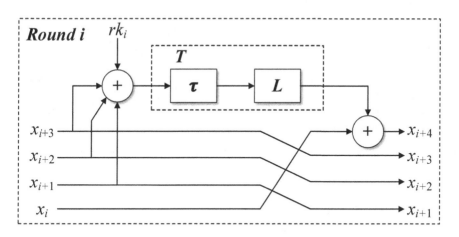

Fig. 1. The pipeline of basic round function in SM4 algorithm.

$$\left(b_0^y, b_1^y, b_2^y, b_3^y\right) = \left(Sbox\left(b_0^x\right), Sbox\left(b_1^x\right), Sbox\left(b_2^x\right), Sbox\left(b_3^x\right)\right)$$

where, $\forall b_i^x$ or b_i^y is a byte, and $Sbox(\cdot)$ is a nonlinear transformation function, fixed for one byte input and one byte output.

The input of **linear transformation** L is the output of the nonlinear transformation τ. Assume that the input is $y \in Z_2^{32}$, the output $z \in Z_2^{32}$ can be denoted as,

$$L(y) = y \oplus (y <<< 2) \oplus (y <<< 10) \oplus (y <<< 18) \oplus (y <<< 24)$$

The decryption transformation of the algorithm is the same as the encryption transformation, except the order of the round keys are used: the order of the encryption round keys is: $(rk_0, rk_1, \ldots, rk_{31})$; the order of the decryption round keys is: $(rk_{31}, rk_{30}, \ldots, rk_0)$.

3   Bit-Slice SM4 Implementation

This section introduces the optimization of bit-slice implementation for SM4 algorithm in storage form, nonlinear transformation τ, and linear transformation L.

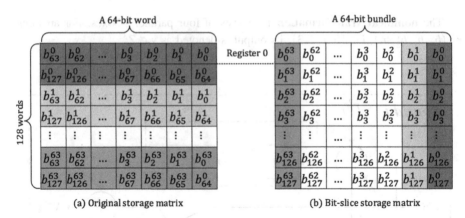

Fig. 2. Transformation from the original storage form to the bit-slice storage form on the 64-bit machine.

Algorithm 2 Bit-slice bundle generation

    Input: $128 \times M$ original storage matrix S
    Output: $128 \times M$ Bit-slice storage matrix S'
1: **for** all *words* **do**
2:     **for** all *bits* in the *word* **do**
3:         $bundle'.loc \leftarrow M \times \left\lfloor word.loc \% \frac{128}{M} \right\rfloor + bit.loc$
4:         $bit'.loc \leftarrow \left\lfloor \frac{word.loc}{\frac{128}{M}} \right\rfloor$
5:         Put the value at the bit' of $bundle'$ in S'
6:     **end**
7: **end**

3.1 Microprocessor Store Optimization

We now need to encrypt the 128-bit plaintext block. If encryption on the M-bit microprocessor, it requires $128/M$ words of memory for storage. For traditional implementation, it simply group 128 bits into $128/M$ words and record them in different registers in big endian form. Then, substitution and replacement operations frequently perform bit-level shifting operations, which is not conducive to efficient encryption. For bit-slice implementation, we operate with M inputs at a time, in which the same bits of the M inputs are then placed into respective locations of the corresponding word. For example, on a 64-bit machine, the traditional storage is that 128-bit inputs are divided into two parts stored in different words respectively, shown in Fig. 2(a), where b_j^i is the jth bit of the ith input block, $\forall i \in [0, 63], j \in [0, 127]$. Figure 2(b) is the storage form for bit-slice implementation, records same bits of M input blocks into one word for parallel processing, e.g., Register 0 stores the first bit of all input blocks. The word storing nth bits of M input blocks is called as bundle n, $\forall n \in [0, 127]$.

On the M-bit microprocessor, a word is M bits long. Obviously, the jth bit of the ith input block, i.e., b_j^i, is stored at the $j\%M$ bit of the $i\left(\frac{128}{M}\right) + \left\lfloor\frac{j}{M}\right\rfloor$ word, in the original storage matrix. The Algorithm 2 describes the process transforming the traditional storage matrix into bit-slice storage matrix, which rearranges that each bit of the word be placed at the bit $\left\lfloor\frac{128 \times word.loc}{M}\right\rfloor$ of the bundle $M\left\lfloor word.loc\%\frac{128}{M}\right\rfloor + bit.loc$, where $word.loc$ is the raw number and $bit.loc$ is the column number in the original storage matrix.

The algorithm need be called twice, respectively to the plaintext encryption, and to convert the decrypted text into the original storage form. Obviously the latter is the reverse of the above processes. In addition, various fixed parameters and system parameters are also pre-converted into the bit-slice storage form before encryption and decryption.

3.2   Round Function Optimization

The core of the entire SM4 algorithm, whether encryption or key expansion, is the round function F, which mainly consists of a nonlinear transformation τ and a linear transformation L. In this subsection, we present the optimization for nonlinear transformation and the optimization for linear transformation optimization based on SIMD instructions.

Nonlinear Transformation Optimization. The nonlinear transformation is actually four parallel S-boxes, so the problem roots in how to implement the S-box substitution in bit-slice style storage form, which is the difficulty of the SM4 bit-slice implementation. In the original implementation, the SM4 S-box is defined as a table, and the input substitutions are implemented by looking up the table when encrypting and decrypting. However, in actual implementation, the look-up method not only requires a large amount of memory space to store tables, but also cannot process data in the bit-slice storage form. Therefore, in order to make the S-box operation bit-sliceable, we must proceed from the definition of the S-box to understand the mathematical logic of the S-box function clearly and completely. If the input data x is a row vector $(b_7, b_6, \cdots, b_0)$, the S-box function is mathematically defined as follows:

$$Sbox(x) = I(xA + c)A + c$$

where, c is a constant 0xd2, and A is defined as a 8×8 matrix:

$$A = \begin{bmatrix} 1 & 1 & 1 & 0 & 0 & 1 & 0 & 1 \\ 1 & 1 & 1 & 1 & 0 & 0 & 1 & 0 \\ 0 & 1 & 1 & 1 & 1 & 0 & 0 & 1 \\ 1 & 0 & 1 & 1 & 1 & 1 & 0 & 0 \\ 0 & 1 & 0 & 1 & 1 & 1 & 1 & 0 \\ 0 & 0 & 1 & 0 & 1 & 1 & 1 & 1 \\ 1 & 0 & 0 & 1 & 0 & 1 & 1 & 1 \\ 1 & 1 & 0 & 0 & 1 & 0 & 1 & 1 \end{bmatrix}$$

The function $I(x)$ is the inverse of x under $GF(2^8)$, using the modular polynomial:

$$m(x) = x^8 + x^7 + x^6 + x^5 + x^4 + x^2 + 1$$

Matrix multiplication and addition are relatively simple and cost low computation time. If we can quickly and efficiently calculate the inverse element of x, we can quickly calculate the solution of S-box function. One possible way is to calculate the inverse elements on the finite field GF. In general, solving the inverse elements on the finite field GF, we use the extended Euclidean algorithm. However, the extended Euclidean algorithm is not efficient because it involves a large number of division operations and cannot be parallelized. Therefore, we need find another way to calculate the inverse elements on the finite field GF efficiently.

In order to inverse element efficiently, we can use the method proposed by Canright et al. [10, 11]. First, using the isomorphism between $GF(2^8)$ and $GF(2^8)/GF(2^4)$ to represent $GF(2^8)$ as a polynomial (in y) over $GF(2^4)$. Then, using $GF(2^4)/GF(2^2)$ we can similarly represent $GF(2^4)$ as linear polynomials (in z) over $GF(2^2)$. Finally, we use $GF(2^2)/GF(2)$ to represent $GF(2^2)$ as linear polynomials (in w) over $GF(2)$. In other word, we convert the original polynomial form where the coefficient of each term is in $GF(2^8)$, into a polynomial form where the coefficient of each item is in $GF(2^4)$. The operation is repeated for each coefficient until the coefficients are fully transformed into $GF(2)$. Finally, we can transform the operation into a set of polynomials:

$$r(y) = y^2 + \tau y + v = \left(y + Y^{16}\right)(y + Y)$$

$$s(z) = z^2 + Tz + N = \left(z + Z^4\right)(z + Z)$$

$$t(w) = w^2 + w + 1 = \left(w + W^2\right)(w + W)$$

The reason for this transformation is that on such these normal basis, we can use the divide and conquer method to find the inverse of the low level coefficient, and then combine the results of the operation by the linear operation of multiplication and addition to get the inverse of the high level coefficient. Due to space limitations, the specific calculation steps can refer to [10, 11], which has a discussion of the details of the operation. In this way, the inverse operation on the natural basis can be completely converted into a linear operation. By comparing the correspondence between the original polynomial basis and the coefficients of the normal basis, we can obtain the coefficient conversion matrix when changing the basis. Therefore, the transformation between the polynomial basis and the normal basis is also a linear operation. Thus all inverse operations can be represented as linear operations. The algorithm discussed above is to deal with non-bit-slice inputs. However, since it is already linear algorithms, we can automatically generate S-box functions receiving bit-slice inputs by tracking the changes in each bit during the execution of the algorithm. So far, the part of the nonlinear transformation τ has also been solved.

Linear Transformation Optimization. The linear transformation L is much simpler than the nonlinear transformation, including a series of shifting and XOR operations.

Based on the bit-slice storage form, the circular shifting operations can be converted into the operations of word-level sequence transformation. For example, in Fig. 3, if the input block has 3 bits, there are three words for storing the different bits of each blocks. Therefore, the function of $B \oplus (B < < < 2)$ can be completed directly by the word-level XOR, without performing bit-level operations.

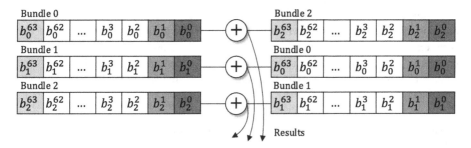

Fig. 3. The word-level operations for function of $B \oplus (B < < < 2)$.

4 Experiments

Based on above designs, we developed a public bit-slice SM4 component for virtual digital currency applications. In order to evaluate the performance of the bit-slice implementation in ubiquitous environment, we chose two heterogeneous network devices to execute the encryption and decryption process, including a high-performance PC server and an edge-side sensor node. Table 1 summarizes the experiment environment.

Table 1. The configurations of experiment environment.

Personal computer	CPU	Intel(R) Xeon(R) 64-bit CPU E5−2620 v3 @ 2.40 GHz
	Memory	64G
	OS	Ubuntu 16.0.4
Edge node	CPU	Broadcom BCM2836 32-bit Cortex-A7 CPU @900 MHz
	Memory	1G
	OS	Raspbian Jessie

We run virtual currency applications on the above two different devices respectively, and evaluate the performance of original SM4 implementation and bit-slice SM4 implementation in encryption efficiency under different size of inputs. The experiment results are shown in Fig. 4, where (a) shows the performances on the PC server, and (b) shows the performances on the edge node. The abscissa is the size of plaintext inputs, and the ordinate is the encryption time. When performing SM4 encryption on the PC, the bit-slice implementation is up to 122% faster than the original implementation in average. For example, encrypting 100 Mb plaintext inputs on the PC, the bit-slice implementation takes 1805 ms, compared the original implementation takes 3992 ms. Similarly, when performing SM4 encryption on the edge node, the bit-slice implementation is up to 81% faster than the original implementation in average. For example, encrypting 100 Mb plaintext inputs, the bit-slice implementation takes 4644 ms, compared the original implementation takes 8258 ms.

It can be seen that the bit-slice method can significantly accelerate the SM4 encryption process averaging over 100%, regardless of network devices. Based on the above experiments, we can see that bit-slice implementation effectively encrypts and decrypts large-scale inputs. In addition, bit-slice approach can leverage the multi-core characteristic of devices to increase the encryption parallelism on the bit level, thereby further increasing the speed.

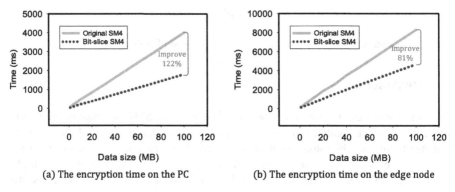

(a) The encryption time on the PC   (b) The encryption time on the edge node

Fig. 4. The comparisons between original SM4 implementation and bit-slice SM4 implementation on encryption time.

5   Conclusion

In this paper, we propose a bit-slice implementation approach for SM4 cipher algorithm and develop a public cipher component for the virtual digital currency applications. We introduced the encryption process of the SM4 algorithm, and detail how to implement efficient storage and parallel encryption of multiple input blocks using bit-slice technology on microprocessor utilizing the SIMD instructions. Experimental results prove that the bit-slice based SM4 is more efficient than the original version especially when processor has more bits. It increases the encryption and decryption speed of the message by an average of 80%–120%, compared with original approach. In the future, we will devote to establish a public bit-slice optimization framework for more cipher algorithms. By doing this, Internet applications can choose and apply a suitable cipher algorithm to guarantee transformation information security.

Acknowledgement. This work is supported in part by National Key R&D Program of China No. 2016YFB0800603, No. 2017YFB1200700, and National Natural Science Foundation of China No. 61701007.

References

1. Lin, I.C., Liao, T.C.: A survey of blockchain security issues and challenges. Int. J. Netw. Secur. **19**, 653–659 (2017)
2. Atzei, N., Bartoletti, M., Cimoli, T.: A survey of attacks on ethereum smart contracts (SoK). In: Maffei, M., Ryan, M. (eds.) POST 2017. LNCS, vol. 10204, pp. 164–186. Springer, Heidelberg (2017). https://doi.org/10.1007/978-3-662-54455-6_8
3. Pu, S., et al.: Boolean matrix masking for SM4 block cipher algorithm. In: International Conference on Computational Intelligence and Security, pp. 238–242(2018)
4. Biham, E.: A fast new DES implementation in software. In: Biham, E. (ed.) FSE 1997. LNCS, vol. 1267, pp. 260–272. Springer, Heidelberg (1997). https://doi.org/10.1007/BFb0052352
5. Rebeiro, C., Selvakumar, D., Devi, A.S.L.: Bitslice implementation of AES. In: Pointcheval, D., Mu, Y., Chen, K. (eds.) CANS 2006. LNCS, vol. 4301, pp. 203–212. Springer, Heidelberg (2006). https://doi.org/10.1007/11935070_14
6. Anderson, R.: Serpent: a proposal for the advanced encryption standard (1998)
7. Scheibelhofer, K.: A bit-slice implementation of the whirlpool hash function. In: Abe, M. (ed.) CT-RSA 2007. LNCS, vol. 4377, pp. 385–401. Springer, Heidelberg (2006). https://doi.org/10.1007/11967668_25
8. Zhang, W.T., Bao, Z.Z., Lin, D.D., Rijmen, V., Han, Y.B., Verbauwhede, I.: RECTANGLE: a bit-slice lightweight block cipher suitable for multiple platforms. Sci. China Inf. Sci. **58**, 1–15 (2015)
9. Matsui, M., Nakajima, J.: On the power of bitslice implementation on intel Core2 processor. In: Paillier, P., Verbauwhede, I. (eds.) CHES 2007. LNCS, vol. 4727, pp. 121–134. Springer, Heidelberg (2007). https://doi.org/10.1007/978-3-540-74735-2_9
10. Canright, D.: A very compact S-Box for AES. In: Rao, J.R., Sunar, B. (eds.) CHES 2005. LNCS, vol. 3659, pp. 441–455. Springer, Heidelberg (2005). https://doi.org/10.1007/11545262_32
11. Canright, D.: A very compact rijndael S-box. Technical Reports Collection 4–5 (2005)

Static Analysis of Android Apps Interaction with Automotive CAN

Federica Panarotto[1], Agostino Cortesi[2], Pietro Ferrara[3(✉)],
Amit Kr Mandal[2,4], and Fausto Spoto[1]

[1] Università di Verona, Verona, Italy
federica.panarotto@gmail.com,fausto.spoto@univr.it
[2] Università Ca' Foscari, Venezia, Italy
{cortesi,amitkr.mandal}@unive.it
[3] JuliaSoft Srl, Verona, Italy
pietro.ferrara@juliasoft.com
[4] BML Munjal Univesity, Gurgaon, Haryana, India
amitmandal.nitdgp@gmail.com

Abstract. Modern car infotainment systems allow users to connect an Android device to the vehicle. The device then interacts with the hardware of the car, hence providing new interaction mechanisms to the driver. However, this can be misused and become a major security breach into the car, with subsequent security concerns: the Android device can both read sensitive data (speed, model, airbag status) and send dangerous commands (brake, lock, airbag explosion). Moreover, this scenario is unsettling since Android devices connect to the cloud, opening the door to remote attacks by malicious users or the cyberspace. The OpenXC platform is an open-source API that allows Android apps to interact with the car's hardware. This article studies this library and shows how it can be used to create injection attacks. Moreover, it introduces a novel static analysis that identifies such attacks before they actually occur. It has been implemented in the Julia static analyzer and finds injection vulnerabilities in actual apps from the Google Play marketplace.

1 Introduction

Car industry is quickly introducing Android devices in cars, to provide new infotainment options to the driver. Various existing Android apps already connect to the car and provide info about the status of its hardware, the history of its movements or the driving style. Moreover, they connect to the Internet, hence gather information about the nearby area or the presence of parking slots. Such possibilities enhance the driving experience, but are also security concerns since apps can leak arbitrary data, including sensitive information on car, movements and drivers [7]. Moreover, they can send dangerous commands: lock or unlock the car, activate its brakes, turn the engine on or off, accelerate, turn on the windshield wipers, and so on. Hence, such apps need very high security standards, or the might otherwise expose driver and passengers to serious physical threats.

© Springer Nature Switzerland AG 2018
M. Qiu (Ed.): SmartCom 2018, LNCS 11344, pp. 114–123, 2018.
https://doi.org/10.1007/978-3-030-05755-8_12

In particular, injection of data and commands by a malicious user or by the outside world should be forbidden, as well as the unconstrainted communication of sensitive data about the car and its sensors.

This article targets OpenXC[1], an open-source library for the programmatic connection of Android apps embedded in cars to the hardware of the car. The Google Play Store already contains various apps that use this library. The Automotive Grade Linux Foundation Workgroup uses OpenXC for low level access to internal car information[2]. The *traffic tamer app challenge*[3] (dealing with the traffic in London) uses OpenXC. Apps connect to OpenXC services to read sensitive data or send commands, by using its API methods. In terms of information flow and taint analysis [10], such methods are sources and sinks of tainted data, respectively. Injection attacks occur when the user or the external world injects data or commands that reach a sink; privacy issues occur when sources are used to read sensitive data that flows towards the outside world. Static taint analysis of Java has already been widely applied to identify injection attacks, for instance in the Julia analyzer [5]. This article leverages and instantiates this approach to automatically verify apps that use OpenXC; it reports several examples of Android apps where our technique finds vulnerabilities, automatically, and compares the results with those of other static analyzers. The theory and implementation of the injection analysis of Julia is already fully described in [5] and is only briefly introduced in Sect. 3, since it is not the topic of this article.

Modern vehicles connect their embedded hardware, such as sensors and actuators, through an electronic bus. External devices can be plugged in the bus through an OBD II port and send AT commands. The most adopted connection device is the ELM327, whose AT commands are publicly available online[4]. The CAN bus protocol is the most widely adopted standard bus in both USA and Europe. It was meant to be fast and robust, hence uses unauthenticated and unencrypted communication. However, the CAN is nowadays connected to the driver and external world, even to the Internet, by using smartphones and tablets plugged in via Bluetooth or USB. This paves the way to security attacks to the car and to privacy leaks of the transferred data [1,3,6]. An attacker might even be granted complete control over the vehicle's systems [3]. More recently, authentication has been added [12]; this increases latency time but does not completely solve injection issues, nor applies to legacy systems.

There are a few software layers for connecting to the CAN, trying to become the industry standard. This article focuses on one such layer, namely, on OpenXC, since it is free, open-source and already distributed on Google Play. OpenXC is an automotive middleware and hardware platform supported by Ford Motors as an evolution of its AppLink technology. Alternatives layers

---

[1] http://openxcplatform.com

[2] http://docs.automotivelinux.org/docs/apis_services/en/dev/reference/signaling/architecture.html#reusing-existinglegacy-code

[3] https://traffic.devpost.com/

[4] https://www.sparkfun.com/datasheets/Widgets/ELM327_AT_Commands.pdf

Fig. 1. A schematic description of the connection between car and OpenXC.

```
public interface VehicleManager {
  public @UntrustedDevice Measurement get(@DeviceTrusted Class<? extends Measurement> msrmttp);
  public @UntrustedDevice VehicleMessage get(@DeviceTrusted MessageKey key);
  public @UntrustedDevice VehicleMessage request(@DeviceTrusted KeyedMessage msg);
  public boolean send(@DeviceTrusted Measurement msg);
  public boolean send(@DeviceTrusted VehicleMessage msg);
  public String requestCommandMessage(@DeviceTrusted CommandType type);
  public void request(@DeviceTrusted KeyedMessage msg, Listener lstnr);
  public void addListener(@DeviceTrusted Class<? extends Measurement> msrmttp, Listener lstnr);
  public @UntrustedDevice String getVehicleInterfaceDeviceId();
  public @UntrustedDevice String getVehicleInterfaceVersion();
  public @UntrustedDevice String getVehicleInterfacePlatform();
}
public interface Measurement {
  public interface Listener {
    public void receive(@UntrustedDevice Measurement msrmt);
  }
}
public interface VehicleMessage {
  public interface Listener {
    public void receive(@UntrustedDevice VehicleMessage msg);
  }
}
public interface UserSink {
  public void receive(@UntrustedDevice VehicleMessage msrmt);
}
public interface ApplicationSource {
  void handleMessage(@UntrustedDevice VehicleMessage msg);
}
public interface UsbVehicleInterface {
  boolean write(@DeviceTrusted byte[] bytes);
}
public interface NetworkVehicleInterface {
  boolean write(@DeviceTrusted byte[] bytes);
}
public interface BluetoothVehicleInterface {
  boolean write(@DeviceTrusted byte[] bytes);
}
```

Fig. 2. Java classes from OpenXC and their source/sink specifications for Julia.

are MirrorLink[5], largely used but shown insecure [8], and the new Automotive Grade Linux[6]. The results of this article can be extended to such alternatives once injection sources and sinks are identified, by using the same approach as in Sect. 4.

Figure 1 shows data flows between car, smartphone and the Internet, through OpenXC. The hardware side is an OBD II device with an installed firmware,

---

[5] https://mirrorlink.com
[6] https://www.automotivelinux.org

called Vehicle Interface (VI). It is configured by default in read-only mode, to access the vehicle's data by translating CAN messages into the OpenXC message format. Messages can then be pushed to a host device. To send commands and data to the VI (and hence to the car), the bus configuration must be set to `raw_writable`. The software side is OpenXC, a library whose Java API allows Android apps, coded in Java, to read and write commands to the CAN. To pass these commands as messages, OpenXC exports them as `Parcelables` consumed by `Services`, as typical in Android: there, *services* are abstractions of a remote data processor, where communication takes place, transparently, through remote procedure calls between the components of a distributed system. OpenXC services are *bound*, meaning that the app receives a stub object whose methods handle, transparently, the interprocess method calls. By invoking such methods, this allows direct and fast communication between software components. The OpenXC Android manifest exports a `com.openxc.remote.VehicleService` towards the hardware of the car and another `com.openxc.VehicleManager` service towards the Java client app. An app can bind the latter service and use Java code for creating objects of a class `VehicleMessage` to interact with the CAN. The OpenXC API consists of Java classes, including interfaces and stubs for the above services. The main class for interacting to the CAN is the above mentioned `VehicleManager`. It exports methods that allow an app to read and write measurements, send commands to the CAN, register listeners for receiving data updates and access sensitive information about the hardware VI. The full description of this API is available online[7]. Figure 2 reports just methods and listeners of `VehicleManager` that are relevant to this article. In terms of taint analysis, we anticipate that such methods are either sources of sensitive data or sinks of dangerous commands, or even both at a time.

2   Examples of Injections in Android Apps Using OpenXC

We analyzed open-source, third-party apps using OpenXC, mostly from https://github.com/openxc; two come from the Google's Play Store, in Dalvik bytecode, and have been translated into Java bytecode through `dex2jar` and `apktool`. We classify these apps on the basis of our findings.

A Privacy Breaking App. Rain Monitor[8] uses OpenXC to access sensitive data: car location, windshield status and speed. It sends it to a remote web service, that uses it to inform drivers about showers in their area. The status of the HTTP request and of the windshield are also logged. These are injections: flow of sensitive data into dangerous operations. In this case, the operations divulge sensitive data, violating privacy. Rain Monitor also reads the car position from the CAN and logs it. Hence, anybody with access to the logs can reconstruct the movements of the vehicle, a clear privacy issue. This code builds a URL by

---

[7] http://android.openxcplatform.com/reference/com/openxc/VehicleManager.html
[8] https://github.com/openxc/rain

using latitude and longitude. This is a URL injection (sensitive data flowing into an Internet address), possibly inherent to the task performed by this app.

An App that Injects Data into the CAN. OpenXC Enabler[9] is a tutorial app meant to test and document most functionalities of OpenXC. It shows the possibility of typing and sending arbitrary messages to the CAN (see Fig. 3). The user formats the messages as requested by the protocol, *i.e.*, CAN bus number, ID of a target sensor or actuator and a value containing multiple CAN signals, in JSON format, such as {"bus": 1, "id": 43,

Fig. 3. OpenXC enabler apps.

"value": "0x0102003040506ABCD"}. That message gets sent to the sensor or actuator. This app features a flow of information from user input into the CAN, that is, an injection of data into the CAN.

Apps that Keep CAN Data Inside their Logic. Shift Knob[10] tracks vehicle information from the CAN and provides to the driver haptic and visual suggestions about good driving style, by vibrating the shift knob. Clearly, it accesses CAN data, but keeps it inside the app. Data is reported in the app's UI, but never divulged externally, for instance through the Internet. Hence, this app does not feature any injection. Night Vision[11] "adds night vision to a car with off-the-shelf parts. The webcam faces forward [...] and uses edge detection to detect objects on the road". It uses OpenXC only for listening to the headlamps status. When the headlamps are turned on, a listener starts the main activity of the app. Sensitive data (the state of the headlamps) is only used inside the logic of the app and does not escape from it. Hence, this app does not feature any injection. Dynamic Skip Fire[12] is "used [...] to showcase Tula Technology's for cars"[13]. It shows the fuel efficiency rate of 7–15% through optimized combustion and reduced engine pumping losses. We downloaded this app from the Play Store but could not find its source code. Hence, we analyzed its behavior in the Android emulator and looked at its bytecode. Also this app uses sensitive data inside its internal logic only.

An App Where CAN Data Flows into a Database, Sanitized. MPG[14] stores trips information, fuel consumption and efficiency into a local SQLite database. Hence this app builds an information flow from sensitive data from the CAN into a database. This could allow a dangerous SQL-injection, but data undergoes sanitization before the database update and no SQL-injection occurs.

---

[9] https://play.google.com/store/apps/details?id=com.openxcplatform.enabler

[10] http://openxcplatform.com/projects/shift-knob.html

[11] http://openxcplatform.com/projects/nightvision.html

[12] https://apkpure.com/dsf/com.ntt.customgaugeview

[13] https://www.tulatech.com/dsf-overview/

[14] https://github.com/openxc/mpg

3   Taint Analysis for Java and Android

Our work builds on the Julia static analyzer [11] for Java and Android bytecode, based on abstract interpretation [4]. Julia starts the analysis from a set of entry points and builds a semantic model of the execution of a program. Namely, all methods reachable, recursively, from the entry points get analyzed. The selection of the entry points can be done in three ways: (i) they are **main** methods; (ii) they are public methods (this is the default); (iii) they are public and protected methods. A larger set of entry points induces a larger set of reachable methods, weaker method call patterns and, in general, more warnings. The selection of the entry points is different in Android, whose execution model heavily relies on event handlers. Hence, Julia scans the Android manifest, looking for XML elements declaring services, activities, receivers and content providers. Then Julia creates a synthetic method that simulates the lifecycle of such components (*e.g.*, an activity starts with a call to `onCreate()`, followed by calls to `onStart()`, `onStop()` and `onResume()`). This method is then an entry point [9].

Among its checkers, Julia includes the Injection checker for a sound information flow analysis [5]. It propagates tainted data along all possible information flows. Boolean variables stand for program variables. Boolean formulas model explicit information flows. Namely, their models are a sound overapproximation of all taintedness behaviors for the variables in scope at a given program point. For instance, the abstraction of the **load k** bytecode instruction, that pushes on the operand stack the value of local variable k, is the Boolean formula $(\check{l}_k \leftrightarrow \hat{s}_{top}) \wedge U$, stating that the taintedness of the topmost stack element after this instruction is equal to that of local variable k before the instruction; all other local variables and stack elements do not change (expressed by a formula U); taintedness before and after an instruction is distinguished by using distinct hats for variables. There are such formulas for each bytecode instruction. Instructions that might have side-effects (field updates, array writes and method calls) need some approximation of the heap, to model the possible effects of the updates. The analysis of sequential instructions is merged through a sequential composition of formulas. Loops and recursion are saturated by fixpoint. The resulting analysis is a denotational, bottom-up taint analysis, that Julia implements through efficient binary decision diagrams [2].

The taint analysis of Julia uses a dictionary of sources and sinks for Android. Sources include methods accessing sensitive information about the user or device, or reading data from UI widgets; sinks include methods for logging or for database or network manipulation. The analysis of a source forces the corresponding Boolean variable to true. At each sink, the analyzer checks if the corresponding Boolean local variable is definitely false. In that case, no flow of tainted data into that sink is possible; otherwise, Julia issues a warning, reporting a potential flow of tainted data into the sink. This approach uses a single Boolean mark for all sources. Hence, it is inherently impossible to distinguish different origins of tainted data. However, this limitation justifies its scalability.

4   Instantiation to OpenXC

Figure 2 reports the methods of OpenXC that either produce (*sources*) sensitive, tainted data, that should not flow into sensitive locations, or receive (*sinks*) data that must be untainted, since it might flow into the CAN. This information was in the mind of the library developers, and is not explicit in code. To use the taint analysis of Julia, it must be first made explicit, in a format that Julia understands. Currently, Julia allows one to instantiate its taint analysis with the addition of sources and sinks, given either as an XML file or as annotated interfaces. This article exploits the latter possibility. Namely, the annotated interfaces in Fig. 2 are given to Julia before the analysis, with annotations for sources (`@UntrustedDevice`) or sinks (`@DeviceTrusted`). For instance, methods `get` receive a parameter that specifies the kind of information that must be read from the CAN. Hence, that parameter must not be freely in control of the user of the application, or otherwise she might be able to build an injection into the CAN device. That is, it is a sink. Moreover, the value returned by such `get` methods discloses sensitive information about the car. Consequently, it must be used in a proper way or otherwise privacy might be jeopardized. Hence, it is a source. Also the parameter of the `receive` method of the listeners is a source, since it carries data reporting updates about the car status. Hence, it is annotated as `@UntrustedDevice`. Note that these annotations must be manually provided for OpenXC, once and for all. They cannot be automatically inferred, either statically or dynamically, since they follow from the intended semantics of OpenXC, which is only described in its plain English documentation. Any other taint analyzer would need that same information.

Once Julia receives such annotated interfaces, it can perform a taint analysis, aware of those extra sources and sinks. Sources are marked as tainted during the analysis and propagated. Sinks are checked for taintedness at the end of the analysis: if they are tainted, Julia issues a warning about a potential injection.

5   Experiments

We have analyzed the apps from Sect. 2 with the taint analysis of Julia, instantiated with the annotation in Fig. 2. The analyses require up to 3 min per app on a standard desktop Intel Core i7 with 16GB of RAM. We have monitored and captured the network traffic of the apps, in the Android emulator of Android Studio and with the VI simulator[15] by WireShark[16].

The analysis of Rain Monitor issues the following injection warnings:

```
CheckWipersTask.java:111:XSS-injection into method "execute"
CheckWipersTask.java:114:Log forging into method "w"
CheckWipersTask.java:117:Log forging into method "d"
FetchAlertsTak.java:68:Log forging into method "d"
FetchAlertsTak.java:76:URL injection into method "<init>"
```

---

[15] https://github.com/openxc/openxc-vehicle-simulator
[16] https://www.wireshark.org/

These correspond to the injections informally discussed in Sect. 2. By analyzing the network traffic with Wireshark, we have found a package sent to the IP address 2.17.206.167, that corresponds to a company that supplies Internet services such as a cloud database. This is definitely a dangerous injection, but not exactly a cross-site scripting (XSS) injection, as Julia suggests, since it cannot distinguish the source of tainted data. Moreover, the status of the HTTP request and the status of the windshield get logged into a file (second and third warning). The former is an example of data coming from the external world (the HTTP server might be compromised and send any possible status); the latter is an example of sensitive car data. Sensitive data (latitude and longitude) is read from the CAN, logged (fourth warning) and later used to build a URL (fifth warning). The latter points to a remote web service that tracks the position of the car and the weather. This is a potential privacy breach. Hence, the analysis only issues true alarms here, although inherent to the task of the app.

The analysis of OpenXC Enabler issues seven injection warnings, including:

```
SendCanMessageFragment.java:110:Device injection into method "send"
NetworkPreferenceManager.java:53:Log forging into method "w"
```

The first corresponds to the injection discussed in Sect. 2. Namely, data coming from user-controlled widgets flows into the send method and hence to the CAN. The second corresponds to the other discussed in the same section, about the flow of user-controlled preferences into the logs. Another warning is similar to the first (line 127 of DiagnosticRequestFragment.java). Four more warnings are similar to the second, that is, they warn about data from the preferences of the app (hence under user control) that can flow into logs (line 480 of SettingsActivity.java, line 69 of PreferenceManagerService.java and line 72 of TraceSourcePreferenceManager.java) or into the specification of a file name (path-traversal: line 72 of viewTraces.java). These warnings are true alarms. The analysis of the network traffic shows many ack packages sent to the VI simulator and some non-empty packages, unfortunately coded in hexadecimal, corresponding to commands sent from the user to the CAN bus simulator.

For Shift Knob, Night Vision and Dynamic Skip Fire, Julia issues no warning. This is in line with the fact that sensitive data from the CAN flows in a controlled way inside those apps and never reaches critical operations nor leaves the device. The analysis of the network traffic reports packages from the VI simulator, that is, the CAN information, and from no other interesting IP address. We have no analysis for the other two apps since, during emulation, they crashed repeatedly.

For MPG, Julia issues only one warning, at line 343 of MpgActivity.java. There, an option from Android preferences (hence controlled by the user) is used in a call to Thread.sleep. This allows a denial-of-service injection by setting a large integer value in the preferences. More interestingly, Julia does not issue any warning where a method insertOrThrow is used to update an SQL database. Julia does consider the query to that method as potentially tainted, but that method is not in the list of sinks provided to Julia, since it is known to sanitize data used to perform the query. Hence, no warning is issued there. We have no network traffic analysis since the app crashed repeatedly during emulation.

The last results are relevant, since they show the power of the tool: not only did it identify several real issues, but it did not issue false alarms here. In these experiments, we have used the Injection checker of Julia, that performs a taint analysis. Julia includes other checkers, that issue other warnings on these apps. They are not injections, nor security issues, but mainly related to potential bugs and inefficiencies. As such, they are not considered here.

We have analyzed the same apps with other static analyzers: FindBugs[17], SpotBugs[18], SonarQube[19], Qark[20] and FlowDroid[21]. They do not identify any of the above injections. Some of them do issue warnings tagged as *security issues*, by using some syntactical check of the code. Namely, SonarQube complains about the fact that some public fields should have been declared as `final`, since they are never modified; or that some visibility modifier is too weak; it also complains about calls to `File.delete()` with no check on the returned value, which in Java is meant to inform about the outcome of the operation. Julia would issue the same warnings, had the corresponding checkers been turned on; however, it does not tag them as security issues but rather as bugs or inefficiencies. Dynamic Skip Fire has not been analyzed with these tools, since they do not work on bytecode. Qark issues warnings about a too small `minSdkVersion` in the `AndroidManifest.xml`, which is known to allow some security problems; it also warns about the run-time registration of Android broadcast receivers, that might allow some form of data hijacking. FlowDroid issues Android security warnings about writing information in a log file, since it warns at *all* logging calls. The same happens for method `putString`, that FlowDroid assumes to *always* inject tainted data into an intent. These are simple syntactical checks of the code, since the analyzers do not make any effort in proving that the risk is real or only potential, which results in false alarms. These analyses are only pattern-matching. Julia avoids such false alarms through a taintedness analysis of data. Moreover, FlowDroid issues no warning about information flow from/to the CAN. FindBugs and SpotBugs issue no security warnings on these apps.

6   Conclusion

This article instantiated the taint analysis of Julia [5] with a specification of sources and sinks for OpenXC. The resulting taint analysis finds security vulnerabilities in actual third-party apps interacting with the car CAN bus. They are injections, that is, either a safeness issue (the user of the app or the external world can control safety critical aspects of the car) or a privacy issue (sensitive data about the car escape into the external world). Comparison with five other tools for static analysis shows that only Julia is able to spot such issues.

---

[17] http://findbugs.sourceforge.net
[18] https://spotbugs.github.io
[19] https://www.sonarqube.org
[20] https://github.com/linkedin/qark
[21] https://github.com/secure-software-engineering/FlowDroid

The actual relevance of the injection issues depends from the level of privacy and security required by a car manufacturer. In any case, the importance of these results can also be read the other way around: since the Injection checker of Julia is sound (that is, it considers all execution paths), then there is no injection into the CAN if Julia does *not* issue any warning. This allows one to understand where are the only injection risks.

References

1. Avatefipour, O., Hafeez, A., Tayyab, M., Malik, H.: Linking received packet to the transmitter through physical-fingerprinting of controller area network. In: IEEE Workshop on Information Forensics and Security (WIFS 2017), Rennes, France, pp. 1–6, December 2017
2. Bryant, R.: Symbolic Boolean manipulation with ordered binary-decision diagrams. ACM Comput. Surv. **24**(3), 293–318 (1992)
3. Checkoway, S., et al.: Comprehensive experimental analyses of automotive attack surfaces. In: 20th USENIX Security Symposium, SanFrancisco, CA, USA. USENIX Association, August 2011
4. Cousot, P., Cousot, R.: Abstract interpretation: a unified lattice model for static analysis of programs by construction or approximation of fixpoints. In: POPL, pp. 238–252 (1977)
5. Ernst, M.D., Lovato, A., Macedonio, D., Spiridon, C., Spoto, F.: Boolean formulas for the static identification of injection attacks in Java. In: Davis, M., Fehnker, A., McIver, A., Voronkov, A. (eds.) LPAR 2015. LNCS, vol. 9450, pp. 130–145. Springer, Heidelberg (2015). https://doi.org/10.1007/978-3-662-48899-7_10
6. Koscher, K., et al.: Experimental security analysis of a modern automobile. In: 31st IEEE Symposium on Security and Privacy (S&P 2010), Berleley/Oakland, California, USA, pp. 447–462. IEEE Computer Society, May 2010
7. Mandal, A.K., Cortesi, A., Ferrara, P., Panarotto, F., Spoto, F.: Vulnerability analysis of android auto infotainment apps. In: Proceedings of the 15th ACM International Conference on Computing Frontiers, pp. 183–190. ACM (2018)
8. Mazloom, S., Rezaeirad, M., Hunter, A., McCoy, D.: A security analysis of an in-vehicle infotainment and app platform. In: 10th USENIX Workshop on Offensive Technologies (WOOT 2016). USENIX Association, Austin, August 2016
9. Payet, É., Spoto, F.: Static analysis of android programs. Inf. Softw. Technol. **54**(11), 1192–1201 (2012)
10. Sabelfeld, A., Myers, A.C.: Language-based information-flow security. IEEE J. Sel. Areas Commun. **21**(1), 5–19 (2003)
11. Spoto, F.: The Julia static analyzer for Java. In: Rival, X. (ed.) SAS 2016. LNCS, vol. 9837, pp. 39–57. Springer, Heidelberg (2016). https://doi.org/10.1007/978-3-662-53413-7_3
12. Wang, Q., Sawhney, S.: VeCure: a practical security framework to protect the CAN bus of vehicles. In: 4th International Conference on the Internet of Things (IOT 2014), Cambridge, MA, USA, pp. 13–18. IEEE, October 2014

Opportunistic Content Offloading for Mobile Edge Computing

Hao Jiang, Bingqing Liu, Yuanyuan Zeng$^{(\boxtimes)}$, Qian Li, and Qimei Chen

School of Electronic Information, Wuhan University, Wuhan, China
{jh,liubbq,zengyy,whusandra,chenqimei}@whu.edu.cn

Abstract. It has been envisioned that future Mobile Edge Computing (MEC) paradigm is enabled with cache ability. Considering some
of the content requests are highly concentrated, the popular contents
will be repeatedly requested. To prevent frequent extra content request
that will burden network backhaul, Base station (BS) with cache ability and even mobile user with the exact content can provide flexible
content offloading on-consume. In this paper, we propose an opportunistic content offloading scheme by predicting the opportunistic content
providers among mobile users and edges for MEC paradigm. At first,
we propose to predict the opportunistic mobile content providers with
popular contents according to historical data record. We then propose
the opportunistic content offloading algorithm modeled by Stackelberg
game. During the process, we consider mobile content consumer and content providers including mobile users and MEC server (e.g., BS) as the
relationship of "leader-followers" in Stackelberg game. Based on the prediction of opportunistic connection with neighboring content provides,
we design an iterative algorithm to reach the optimal equilibrium pricing with fast convergence. Our simulations are based on the real dataset
provided by China Mobile Communications Corporation. The simulation
results show our scheme can efficiently alleviate the network backhaul.
During the peak hours, the number of content unloaded by our method
accounts for 34.5% of the original total content load, thus effectively
reducing the content overload pressure of the BS.

Keywords: Mobile edge computing · Content offloading
Opportunistic offloading · Prediction · Stackelberg game

1 Introduction

According to Cisco's mobile network outlook report, global mobile data traffic
will grow to 292EB in 2019, of which 97% data traffic is generated by smart

This work was supported in part by the National Natural Science Foundation of China
under Grant 61702387, in part by the National Key Research and Development Program under Grant 2017YFB0504103 and Grant 2017YFC0503801, in part by the Development Program of China (863 Program) under Grant 2014AA01A707, and in part by
the Natural Science Foundation of Hubei Province of China under Grant 2017CFB302.

© Springer Nature Switzerland AG 2018
M. Qiu (Ed.): SmartCom 2018, LNCS 11344, pp. 124–133, 2018.
https://doi.org/10.1007/978-3-030-05755-8_13

mobile devices. One interesting phenomena is that content requests are highly concentrated, so some popular contents are repeatedly requested. The redundant content request will burden the network backhaul a lot. Traditional centralized mobile cloud computing services cannot effectively match the explosive growth of the massive network edge data. A new paradigm called Mobile Edge Computing is proposed in mobile computing. ETSI firstly proposed the concept of MEC in 2014. MEC refers to a technology that deeply integrates base stations and Internet services based on the 5G evolution architecture. Base station (BS) with cache ability and even mobile user with the exact content can provide flexible content offloading on-consume. Content offloading exploits complementary networks to deliver content data interested, thereby reducing network backhaul overload. Current mobile offloading techniques mainly involve MEC server by using WiFi, Femtocell, etc. Due to the limited coverage of the MEC server, the content offloading efficiency is also limited.

In this paper, we firstly propose to predict the opportunistic content providers among the neighborhood of mobile users, in order to find the local popular content that will be repeatedly requested. For content offloading, we consider the mobile content consumer and content providers including mobile users and MEC server (e.g., BS) as the relationship of "leader-followers" in Stackelberg game. The initial pricing in Stackelberg game is set according to the predicted content consume, so as to speed up the game process to equilibrium.

The main contributions of the paper includes:

(1) Considering the characteristics that content requests are with highly concentrated and some of the popular contents are repeatedly requested, We propose an opportunistic content offloading scheme by predicting the opportunistic content providers with popular and repeatedly cached contents among mobile users and edges for MEC paradigm.
(2) The opportunistic content offloading scheme is modeled by Stackelberg game, in which the content consumer and content providers including mobile users and MEC server (e.g., BS)are formulated as "leader-followers" game relationship. During the process, the prediction based on historical data predicts the opportunistic content providers that can be used to provide an initial pricing to speed the equilibrium convergence.
(3) Our simulation is implemented with real dataset provided by China Mobile Communications Corporation. The game process in our scheme is with fast convergence to equilibrium that is suitable for realistic situations. Beyond this, Our scheme also provides efficient alleviation of network backhaul.

The rest of this paper is organized as follows: system model and overview of our method are presented in Sect. 2. Section 3 propose a prediction algorithm for opportunistic content providers. Section 4 discussed the optimal solution using Stackelberg game. Experimental results are analyzed in Sect. 5. Section 6 is conclusion.

2   Related Work

With the emergency of cloud computing, many researches that focus on saving energy and expanding the capabilities of mobile devices have done in mobile cloud computing. Research [1] proposes a novel approach of using dynamic cloudlet-based MCC model, DECM, to gain the benefits of green computing. Their approach was an effective mechanism that could enable mobile users to address green IT within a dynamic complicated wireless environment. Research [2] proposed a novel approach solving the problem of data allocations in cloud-based heterogeneous memories, which could be applied in big data for smart cities. Moreover, Gai et al. [3] proposed a model called EA-HCM, which was designed to solve the energy minimization problem on heterogeneous computing that is an NP-hard problem. However, with the development and application of Internet of Things technology, traditional cloud computing cannot meet the requirements of low latency, high reliability, and data security for application services. A new computing paradigm called Mobile Edge Computing (MEC) has emerged.

Content offloading for mobile edge computing systems has attracted significant attention in recent years. Joseleal [4] presents a lightweight and efficient framework called User-Level Online Offloading Framework (ULOOF), for mobile computation offloading. ULOOF is equipped with a decision engine that minimizes remote execution overhead, while not requiring neither superuser privileges on the mobile device nor modifications to the underlying operating system. Tang and He [5] study the multi-user computation offloading problem in MEC from a behavioral perspective. Based on the framework of prospect theory (PT), they cast the users' decision making of whether to offload or not as a PT-based non-cooperative game and propose a distributed computation offloading algorithm to achieve the Nash equilibrium. X chen [6] propose a game theoretic approach for the computation offloading decision making problem among multiple mobile device users for mobile-edge cloud computing. The proposed approach can achieve efficient computation offloading performance.

Furthermore, for the aspect of current mobile data content offloading methods, it mainly based on WiFi network, Femtocell. In terms of WiFi-based method, Lee [7] analyzed the performance of the WiFi-based 3G mobile data offloading scheme by analyzing the mobile devices of 100 volunteers accessing the WiFi data in two weeks and a half. The results show that WiFi can effectively offload about 65% of mobile data while saving 55% of power consumption. Balasubramanian [8] studied the data of mobile vehicles accessing 3G and WiFi networks in three cities. The availability of 3G and WiFi networks was 87% and 11% respectively.

For Femtocell-based content offloading, which mainly focuses on the licensed frequency band. The content generated by the user's mobile device is not transmitted via the macrocell network base station. Therefore, the Femtocell can effectively reduce the load pressure on the cellular network and improve the service quality of users. Ramaswamy [9] considered the interference between cells as a Gaussian random variable and explored the Femtocell's backlinking capability.

However, most of the proposed content offloading frameworks in MEC do not consider user mobility, cannot predict when users are in proximity, can provide content for each other. Then, based on this, we design a content offload strategy for users according to the predicted specific content needs of content consumer.

3 System Model

We consider the opportunistic content offloading for MEC paradigm as shown in Fig. 1. Each base station is equipped with an MEC server and the mobile data provided by the BS is stored in the MEC server. For content consumer, content can be obtained either from the MEC server (e.g., BS) or from other mobile users caching the same content. For example, the UE1 cache the popular content that may be also needed by UE2. UE2 can obtain the content either from the MEC server or from user1 that depends on the cost. Our scheme provides the prediction ability to find the possible content provides and the opportunistic content offloading by fully utilize the cache ability of mobile users.

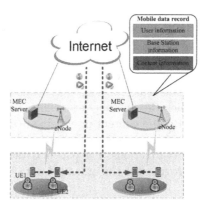

Fig. 1. System model

4 Prediction for User Opportunistic Content Provid

We consider a one-hour time scale, and the day is divided into 24 h. In each time period, we will firstly seek for the opportunistic content provider for each content consumer. We construct complex network in which nodes represent users and edges represent the content provide relationship between users. By constructing a complex network, the user opportunistic content provide prediction problem is transformed into the problem of link prediction in the graph.

We analyzed multi-dimensional features from the three aspects of network topology, user mobility and Internet behavior characteristics. Three topology features including Common Neighbor index, Salton index and Adamic-Adar index were selected. In terms of user mobility features, the distance between the hotspot is exploited to characterize the similarity of users. We use Haversine formula to calculate the distance in geographic space. Based on the frequency sequences of user accessing the base station, pearson similarity and Kullback-Leibler divergence are calculated. Based on the classic indicator Common Neighbor index, we takes the number of content provide as weights to obtain the similarity indicators based on the content provide behavior [10]. In the following formula, $n(u, v)$ is the number of times users provide content to each other.

$$Protimes\_WCN(u, v) = \sum_{z \in \Gamma(n) \cap \Gamma(v)} n(u, z) + n(z, v) \tag{1}$$

Similarly, in terms of user Internet behavior features, we introduce the features based on the duration of surfing the Internet and data content. Moreover, we exploit the Jaccard similarity of Internet content. Finally, using these extracted features as input information, random forest model is exploited to predict user content provide behavior.

5 Content Offloading Algorithm Based on Stackelberg Game

In the Stackelberg game, there are two kinds of rational players, leaders and followers. The content consumers are considered as leaders. Leaders influence the amount of data content which the followers are willing to provide by determing the pricing strategies. The BS and content providers are considered as followers. Followers adjust the content strategies according to the leader's pricing strategy to maximize the system utility functions. The part of data content that the leader obtains from the content providers is the offloaded data based on opportunistic content provide.

5.1 Utility Function and Nash Equilibrium

We designed utility functions for BS, content providers and content consumer respectively to reflect the reward that participants receive. For the leader, the utility function of content consumer is composed of data content income and payment expenses. $\sum_{j \in Followers} f_j$ is the amount of data content that followers provide for the leader. We took the form of a logarithm function to represent the leaders' gain for data content. The leader's utility function is calculate by

$$U_0 = \alpha \log \left(1 + \sum_{j \in Followers} f_j\right) - p \tag{2}$$

where α is a parameter related to user experience, p denotes the total price published by the leader.

Under a given pricing scheme, the provider decides on the providing content to maximize its expected revenue. For the follower i, the utility function is composed of the benefits and costs of providing content to the content consumer.

$$U_i = \frac{f_i}{\sum\limits_{j \in Followers} f_j} \cdot p - f_i c_i \tag{3}$$

where f_i denotes the total providing content, c_i denotes the cost of unit content.

The goal of game theory is to find solutions to game problems so that participants eventually reach a stable equilibrium. Nash equilibrium is a solution to the non-cooperative game. We firstly prove that Nash equilibrium exists in the Stackelberg game model proposed in this paper.

Lemma 1. *There is a Nash equilibrium in the Stackelberg game model proposed in this paper.*

Proof. In the Stackelberg model, the follower i determines the data content strategies according to the total price p published by the leader. The follwer's content strategy is a bounded closed set in Euclidean space, and the utility function is continuous in its strategy space, and the first order partial derivative is:

$$\frac{\partial U_i}{\partial f_i} = -\frac{f_i p}{\left(\sum\limits_j f_j\right)^2} + \frac{p}{\sum\limits_j f_j} - c_i \tag{4}$$

The second order partial derivative is:

$$\frac{\partial^2 U_i}{\partial f_i^2} = -\frac{2p\left[\sum\limits_j f_j - f_i\right]}{\left(\sum\limits_j f_j\right)^3} < 0 \tag{5}$$

Therefore, the follower's utility function is a strictly concave functioin, which ensures that a Nash equilibrium point exists in the Stackerberg game model proposed in this paper.

5.2   Distributed Iterative Algorithm

We exploited distributed iterative algorithm to solve the optimal pricing and mobile data offloading problem. We predict users' total content consume based on the average content during the previous days. For a single user, the predicted total content is denoted as Q and the unit cost is denoted as c_i, then the initial total price announced by the leader is $p_0 = Q \cdot \min(c_i)$. By predicting the data content consume of users, we can effectively reduce the number of iterations in the game model, thus improving the efficiency of the algorithm.

In the two stage Stackelberg game, at each moment τ, the leader announces the pricing strategy p to followers. According to the total price p, followers seek to find the optimal content strategy by solving the multiple quadratic equation.

$$
\begin{cases}
-\dfrac{f_1 p}{\left(\sum\limits_j f_j\right)^2} + \dfrac{p}{\sum\limits_j f_j} - c_1 = 0 \\[4mm]
-\dfrac{f_2 p}{\left(\sum\limits_j f_j\right)^2} + \dfrac{p}{\sum\limits_j f_j} - c_2 = 0 \\[4mm]
\qquad\qquad \vdots \\[2mm]
-\dfrac{f_n p}{\left(\sum\limits_j f_j\right)^2} + \dfrac{p}{\sum\limits_j f_j} - c_n = 0
\end{cases}
\tag{6}
$$

According to the multiple quadratic equation, the optimal content strategy is:

$$
f_i = \frac{(n-1)\,p}{\sum\limits_j c_j} \left(1 - \frac{(n-1)\,c_i}{\sum\limits_j c_j} \right)
\tag{7}
$$

If the utility of the leader also reaches the maximum at this time, all participants in the game have reached the Nash equilibrium. Otherwise, at the next moment, the leader continues to iterate on the pricing strategy according to Eq. (8), where λ is the adjustment step size, and announces the new price p to followers. The iterating stops until the utility of leader reaches its maximum.

$$
p(\tau + 1) = p(\tau) + \lambda
\tag{8}
$$

Algorithm 1. Iterative algorithm for solving Nash equilibrium

---

Input *records*: recorded information
Output p: pricing strategy, f: content strategy
Step-1: Predict user opportunistic content provide based on Random Forest;
Step-2: For each user u_i in user set U, calculate mobile user collection that may access the same base station at the same time period as user u_i: $E(u_i) = \{v_1, v_2, ...v_{m(u_i)}\}$;
Step-3: For each user v_j in $E(u_i)$, filter on the content dimension by determine whether the interest set of user u_i and user v_j is an empty set, obtain the content providers collection $\phi(u_i)$ of user u_i.
Step-4: Calculate the predicted total content Q of user u_i after content consume analysis.
Step-5: Calculate the initial total pricing $p_0 = Q * min(c_i)$ of user u_i;
Step-6: Calculate the utility function $U_0(\tau)$ of user u_i, while $U_0(\tau) <= max\{U_0\}$, jump to Step-7 and Step-8, otherwise end while.
Step-7: Iterate over the total pricing p according to equation(8), for each follower in $\phi(u_i)$ calculate the content strategy f_i according to equation(7);
Step-8: $\tau = \tau + 1$, jump to Step-6.

---

6   Experiment and Evaluation

6.1   Data Description

Our simulation is based on real dataset provided by China Mobile Communication Coporation. The dataset consists of a 24 day mobile Internet detail records of users(UDRs), covering all the Internet records by 1,614,291 users in a 24 day, from 2014/11/21 to 2014/12/13. To verify the method, we select active users with more than 20 records from the original dataset.

6.2   User Opportunistic Content Provide Prediction

In this part, we select the data stream from 2014/12/01 to 2014/12/08 as the training set, the data stream on 2014/12/09 as the test set. We use accuracy and recall as evaluation indicators for the forecasting algorithm. Figure 2 plots the accuracy and recall rate for different time periods. Compared with the algorithm that only considering the traditional network structure features and unsupervised algorithm, Our algorithm significantly improved the accuracy of the prediction, which remained at around 0.8 at all times.

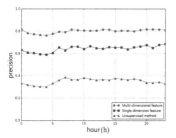 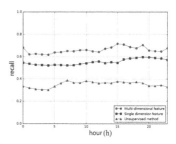

Fig. 2. Precision and recall of user content provide prediction algorithm

6.3   Content Offloading

The data records from 2014/12/01 to 2014/12/09 are used to verify the effectiveness of data offloading algorithm based on Stackelberg game. Take a content consumer with 5 followers including the edge device and 4 content providers as an example. The predicted data content of him is 1 Mb. As shown in Figs. 3 and 4, when price p is increasing from the initial price, the utility of the leader gradually increases. When $p^* = 0.34$, all participants reach the Nash equilibrium in the Stackelberg model. Figure 4 shows the data content strategies changing with different price. With the increasing price, followers are encouraged to provide more data content for the content consumer.

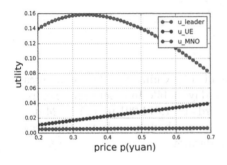

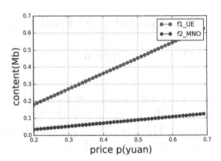

Fig. 3. Utility function

Fig. 4. Data content strategies

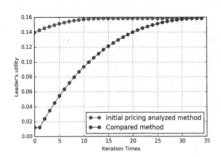

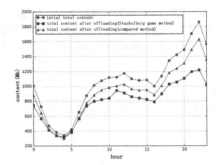

Fig. 5. Iterations numbers

Fig. 6. Content load of BS

Iteration Times. We further compared the number of iterations of the algorithm proposed in this paper with the compared method in which the initial price is 0. As shown in Fig. 5, compared to the method with an initial pricing of 0, our method, which analyze the initial pricing by predicting the data content consume of users, can quickly receive the optimal pricing and reduce the number of iterations. The efficiency of the algorithm has been improved.

Amount of Offloaded Content. Figure 6 shows the data content load of the BS after applying the mobile data offloading strategies in 24 h. During the peak period of content 22 h, the amount of offloaded data content accounts for 34.5% of the original content load. Also, we use the content offloading method in reference [11] for comparative experiments. It can be seen from the figure that the offloading ratio of the comparison method is lower than the content offloading ratio based on the Stackelberg game. The experiment shows that the mobile data offloading algorithm based on Stackelberg game can effectively reduce the data content pressure of the BS.

7   Conclusion

For the future MEC paradigm, the large-volume data content of repeated content request in the networks will burden the backhaul. Considering the content visit shows great pattern with popularity and repetition, we propose the opportunistic content offloading scheme by efficiently predicting the possible content provides among the varied neighborhood based on historical data. The offloading process is formulated by Stackelberg game to make tradeoff between different content providers of MEC server and mobile users cache the contents. Our scheme is simulated with real dataset provided by China Mobile Communication Corporation. The results show our scheme provides fast convergence to game equilibrium that is suitable for realistic situations. By fully utilizing the mobile users that may share the popular contents, our scheme provides efficient alleviation of network backhaul. For future work, we will consider using GPS positioning data to improve the accuracy of the user's location information.

References

1. Gai, K., Qiu, M., Zhao, H., Tao, L., Zong, Z.: Dynamic energy-aware cloudlet-based mobile cloud computing model for green computing. J. Netw. Comput. Appl. **59**(C), 46–54 (2016)
2. Gai, K., Qiu, M., Zhao, H.: Cost-aware multimedia data allocation for heterogeneous memory using genetic algorithm in cloud computing. IEEE Trans. Cloud Comput. **PP**(99), 1 (2016)
3. Gai, K., Qiu, M., Zhao, H.: Energy-aware task assignment for mobile cyber-enabled applications in heterogeneous cloud computing. J. Parallel Distrib. Comput. **111**, 126–135 (2017)
4. Neto, J.L.D., Yu, S., Macedo, D.F., Nogueira, J.M.S., Langar, R., Secci, S.: ULOOF: a user level online offloading framework for mobile edge computing. IEEE Trans. Mob. Comput. **PP**(99), 1 (2018)
5. Tang, L., He, S.: Multi-user computation offloading in mobile edge computing: a behavioral perspective. IEEE Netw. **32**(1), 48–53 (2018)
6. Chen, X., Jiao, L., Li, W., Fu, X.: Efficient multi-user computation offloading for mobile-edge cloud computing. IEEE/ACM Trans. Netw. **24**(5), 2795–2808 (2016)
7. Lee, K., Lee, J., Yi, Y., Rhee, I., Chong, S.: Mobile data offloading: how much can WiFi deliver? In: International Conference, pp. 1–12 (2010)
8. Balasubramanian, A., Mahajan, R., Venkataramani, A.: Augmenting mobile 3G using WiFi. In: International Conference on Mobile Systems, Applications, and Services, pp. 209–222 (2010)
9. Ramaswamy, V., Das, D.: Multi-carrier macrocell femtocell deployment-a reverse link capacity analysis. In: Vehicular Technology Conference Fall, pp. 1–6 (2009)
10. Lü, L., Zhou, T.: Link prediction in weighted networks: the role of weak ties. EPL **89**(1), 18001 (2010)
11. Han, B., Hui, P., Kumar, V.S., Marathe, M.V., Pei, G., Srinivasan, A.: Cellular traffic offloading through opportunistic communications: a case study. ACM (2010)

Image Annotation Algorithm Based on Semantic Similarity and Multi-features

Jingxiu Ni[1,2(✉)], Dongxing Wang[2], Guoying Zhang[2], Yanchao Sun[2], and Xinkai Xu[1,2]

[1] Beijing Union University, Beijing 100101, China
njxl211@163.com
[2] School of Mechanical, Electronic and Information Engineering,
China University of Mining and Technology, Beijing 100083, China

Abstract. The paper proposed an image annotation algorithm based on semantic similarity and multi-feature fusion. The annotation algorithm draws lessons from the method of semantic extraction in natural language processing, and establishes the corresponding semantic trees for some common scenes. The scene semantic tree is constructed based on the visual features of the specific scene in the image set. Firstly, the visual features of scene images are extracted, and then the visual features are clustered by fuzzy clustering. According to the clustering results, the images are grouped, clustered at different nodes according to visual features, and the images are further grouped. After the scene semantic tree is constructed, the algorithm will extract the visual features of the image to be annotated. Furthermore, the image moves from the item node to a leaf node in the scene semantic tree according to its visual features, and the semantic keywords which appear in the route constitute the tags of the image.

Keywords: Semantic tree · Image annotation · Multi-feature fusion
Semantic similarity · Fuzzy clustering

1 Introduction

With the rapid development of image acquisition equipment and network technology, it is necessary for people to manage all kinds of images captured by monitors efficiently. Since traditional understanding of images is mainly based on the visual features of images, there lies an insurmountable semantic gap between the results of image retrieval and people's needs. It is far from satisfactory to extract the primary visual features of an image. On the contrary, more and more applications need to extract the senior semantic information of the image. Based on this, the high-level semantics include emotional semantics and scene semantics. There is a growing demand for advanced emotional semantics, such as joy, anger, sadness, weather analysis. Mining high-level semantics is a hot topic and semantic annotation of images is also a meaningful research direction.

© Springer Nature Switzerland AG 2018
M. Qiu (Ed.): SmartCom 2018, LNCS 11344, pp. 134–142, 2018.
https://doi.org/10.1007/978-3-030-05755-8_14

2 Related Work

Image annotation involves learning features, annotation correlation, loss function design and incomplete labeling for processing training data [1]. Learning features aims mainly at finding proper features for image annotation. A popular method of learning feature is Convolutional Neural Networks (briefly CNN) [2, 3]. CNN can learn the key features in image classification and object detection. CNN is now gradually shifting from learning global features [4] to learning local features [5], because local features are more effective in recognizing the foreground objects in the image. In addition, tag-level smoothness [6, 7], image-level smoothness [4, 6, 7], low rank assumption [8] and semantic hierarchy [6] are also hot directions in image annotation. However, these correlation researches mainly focus on the positive correlation of the annotations, and there are few studies on the negative correlation such as the mutual exclusion of the different annotations [9]. The processing of incomplete annotations is another important research direction of semantic annotation [6, 10, 11]. The contributions of the paper are not limited to just one of the above four research directions, but are related to the above four directions simultaneously. Since most image annotation algorithms are not comprehensive, it is very meaningful to deal with incomplete annotated words. While providing more tagging words for the image, we find the correlation of tagging words, and try to ensure that the tagging words provided for the image can reflect the different unique contents of the image more comprehensively, so as to eliminate the semantic gap between automatic image tagging and manual image tagging.

3 Semantic Model of Scene Images

The paper adopts the semantic extraction mechanism of Natural Language Processing (NLP) to construct a semantic tree for each scenario. The parent node of one node contains the common semantics of both the current node and its sibling node. In order to distinguish one node from its sibling node, the annotation of the node should discard the semantics of its parent node. All the images in the scene are gathered at the root node, which also represents the most abstract semantics in the scene. At the training stage, training set is utilized to build one semantic tree related to a scene. The semantic tree contains both the visual features and the semantics.

3.1 Scene Related Semantic Tree

In the semantic tree, each node corresponds to a subset of the scene images. The tags related to this subset are fuzzily clustered to get the core tags that represent the semantics of the subset, and at the same time the semantics of the node. These core tags can represent this subset of images. The parent node of one node contains the common semantics of both the current node and its sibling node. In order to distinguish one node from its sibling node, the annotation of the node should discard the semantics of its parent node. All the images in the scene are gathered at the root node, which also represents the highest level of abstraction in the tree. And the tree root represents the most common semantic annotations. The semantic information is more and more specific from the root node to the leaf node, and accordingly images of node are less and less. At the training stage, training set is utilized to build one scene semantic tree related to a specific scene. The scene semantic tree contains not only the visual features of the images, but also the semantics represented by the image tags. At the image annotation stage, the image is first categorized into a certain scene according to the global visual feature of the image. Then the image will go through from the root node to one leaf node by matching the image feature with the node feature, and consequently the set of annotation words of all matched nodes from the root node to the leaf node will be found, which constitute the semantic annotation of an image.

Representation of Semantic Tree. The formal representation of scene semantic tree is listed in formula 1.

$$T = \{t_1, t_2, \ldots, t_k\} \tag{1}$$

Where t_k is the semantic tree related to the k-th scene, and t_k is a tuple consisting of two parts (see formula 2). The first part is the division of scene image set as $t_{v_{node}}^k$ according to visual features. The second part is the tags distribution as t_{word}^k.

$$tk = \{t_{v_{node}}^k, t_{word}^k\} \tag{2}$$

Let image set of the k-th scene be P^k, P^k can be denoted as:

$$P^k = \{P_{img}^i\} \tag{3}$$

Where $i = 1, 2, \ldots, k$, $img = \{1, 2, \ldots, n_k\}$, and k is the amount of scenes, and n_k is the amount of images in the k-th scene. Each node, denoted as N_{node}^k corresponds to an image subset, denoted as P_{node}^k, and P_{node}^k can be expressed as:

$$P_{node}^k = \{P_{inode}^k\} \tag{4}$$

Where $inode = 1, 2, \ldots, I_{node}$ and I_{node} is the amount of node. Therefore, P^k can be denoted as:

$$P_k = \bigcup_{i=1}^{node} P_{inode}^k \tag{5}$$

Division of Image Set. The image set is divided by means of N-cut [12] according to its visual eigenvalues, and then the corresponding binary tree structure is produced. N-cut is a kind of graph segmentation methods. Let graph be $G = (V, E)$, where V is the vertex set, and E is the edge set. The graph G can be divided into two parts as A and B. Let the weight of edge E be $w(E)$, and the division be $DIV(A, B)$ (see formula 6).

$$DIV(A,B) = \sum_{a \in A, b \in B} w(a, b) \tag{6}$$

In graph segmentation, the weight sum of cut edges should be minimal, and the size of two vertex sets A and B should be similar. If an image is regarded as the node of the graph, and the similarity between the two images is regarded as the weights of edges in graph G, the segmentation of image sets can be regarded as an N-cut segmentation problem. Consequently, the image sets can be organized in the form of binary trees.

3.2 Algorithm of Constructing Semantic Tree

The following is the detailed algorithm of constructing the semantic tree.

Input: distribution of semantic words of scene image set denoted as $W=(w1, w2, ...,wk)$, image set denoted as $P^k=\{p^k_{img}\}$ and the depth limit as depth.

Output: semantic tree $tk= \{t^k_{vnode}, t^k_{word}\}$。

The procedure of algorithm is listed as follows:

(1) calculate the scene image set $P^k=\{p^k_{img}\}$;
(2) calculate the visual feature set $vnode_0$ of P^k;
(3) cluster the semantic tags of P^k and adopt the cluster result $word_0$ as the tags of root node;
(4) $j=0$;
(5) for $i=j$ to depth:

according to the node as N^i_{node} and its   corresponding image set as $P^i=\{p^k_{img}\}$,img$=\{1,2,...,n_k\}$:

(6)   calculate the visual features as $vnode_i$ of P^k ;
(7)   cluster the tags of P^k and adopt the cluster result as the node $word_i$ as the tags of the node N^i_{node};
(8)   If count(vnode)>1 then
(9)   cut the cluster result into two parts as vnode1 and vnode2;
(10)   divide the image set into two parts as L and R according to the cut of visual features;
(11) $j=i+1$;
(12)   Repeat from step 2 on image sub-set L;
(13)   Repeat from step 2 on image sub-set R;
(14)   end if
(15) end for

4 Image Annotation Algorithm Based on Semantic Similarity and Multi-feature Fusion

In the process of constructing scene semantic model, Probabilistic Latent Semantic Analysis (PLSA) in [13] can be adopted to assist scene semantic clustering. PLSA realizes the co-occurrence of visual features and semantic annotations through the combination of polynomial distribution and conditional distribution. In this way, a specific correspondence between visual features and semantic annotations is established. Hofmann proposed PLSA model based on latent Semantic Analysis (LSA) and probability statistics, and used EM algorithm to solve the parameters in the model. The probabilistic model of the PLSA model for image annotation is shown in Fig. 1.

Fig. 1. Illustration of PLSA model for image annotation

In Fig. 1, S is source image set, T is the hidden topic set, and L is the label set. Probability of tags appearing in source image s_i is denoted as $p(s_i)$, probability of tags in topic t_k appearing in s_i is denoted as $p(t_k|s_i)$, and probability of label lj appearing in topic is denoted as $p(l_j|t_k)$. In PLSA model, the distributions as $p(t_k|s_i)$ and $p(l_j|t_k)$ obey polynomial distribution, and the parameters in the polynomial distribution can be estimated by means of Expectation and Maximization (EM) algorithm. In this way, the matrix of co-occurrence between semantic annotation words and visual features can be established, and the image annotation model can be established.

The parameters of two polynomial distributions of the PLSA algorithm are estimated according to the EM algorithm, and the corresponding relationship between the documents to be annotated and the words to be annotated is obtained.

In this paper, an image annotation method based on scene semantic tree is proposed. The image annotation method uses scene semantics as a bridge to construct a semantic binary tree, which can refine the scene semantics layer by layer. The scene semantics tree represents the corresponding relationship between the annotation words and visual features. Scene semantic model needs to use semantic annotation words to represent the image semantics, so it is necessary to establish a certain relationship between the image and the annotation words, which can be expressed in the form of co-occurrence matrix between the image and the annotation words.

The image set of the k-th scene can be denoted as $S^k = \{S_i^k\}$, where S_i^k is the i-th image in the k-th scene. Each image S_i^k contains both the visual features and the semantic information of the image, therefore S_i^k can be denoted as $S_i^k = \{V_i^k, W_i^k\}$, where V_i^k is the visual feature vector and W_i^k is the tag vector. V_i^k can be denoted as $V_i^k = \{V_i^k1, V_i^k2, \ldots, V_i^km\}$, and W_i^k can be denoted as $W_i^k = \{W_i^k1, W_i^k2, \ldots, W_i^kn\}$.

The main task of scene semantic model is to find out the corresponding relationship among image set, visual feature and tag set. Due to the advantages of co-occurrence matrix in dealing with the relationship between different sets, the co-occurrence matrix between image visual features and annotation words can be used to represent the image and visual features, and the corresponding relationship between image and semantic annotation words. The matrix $SV = \{SV_{s \times m}\}$ means the correlation between image set S and visual feature set V. The matrix $SW = \{SW_{s \times n}\}$ is the correlation between image set S and semantic tag set W. With the help of the two matrices as SV and SW, the correlation matrix VW between visual feature set V and semantic tag set W can be calculated as $VW = \{VW_{m \times n}\}$.

The probability of occurrence of each image S_i^k is represented by the joint conditional probability of each visual feature $V_i^k v$. Let the distribution probability of semantic tags and visual features be denoted as $P(W_i^k w, V_i^k v)$, then the calculating method is listed as follows:

$$P\left(W_i^k w, V_i^k v\right) = P(V_i^k v) \sum_{i=1}^{N_k} P\left(W_i^k w | S_i^k\right) P(S_i^k | V_i^k v) \qquad (7)$$

Where $P\left(W_i^k w | S_i^k\right)$ is the distribution of tag set over image set, and $P(S_i^k | V_i^k v)$ is the distribution of image set over visual feature set. According to the maximum likelihood criterion, the parameters of the model can be estimated by maximizing the logarithmic likelihood function L, and L can be obtained as follows:

$$L = \sum_v \sum_a VW_{va} \log P\left(V_i^k v, W_i^k w\right) \qquad (8)$$

The maximum likelihood function can be solved by a standard expectation maximization (EM) algorithm to estimate the parameters.

In this way, the probability distribution matrix of co-occurrence between semantic annotation words and visual features can be established, and the image annotation model can be established.

The core idea of building a scene semantic tree is to represent the semantic structure of the scene by tree structure. Therefore, the root node contains all the training images of the scene, and the semantic annotations of the root node represent the semantic concept with the highest frequency of the scene. The unique semantic concepts in the scene appear in the leaf nodes. Accordingly, the images containing these unique semantics also gather in the leaf nodes. The semantic tree represents the progressive semantic relationship from the root node to the leaf node. The construction of scene semantic tree is based on the visual features of images. Therefore, scene semantic tree includes the relationship between semantic concepts and visual features. In image annotation, the image is first classified into specific scenes according to the visual features of the image to be annotated, and then a leaf node is accessed through iterative matching from the root of the scene semantic tree corresponding to the scene, and the annotation words corresponding to the path are obtained.

5 Experiments

Corel5k is the standard data set of image annotation experiments. It has 50 kinds of semantic scenes, and each scene has 100 images. It is widely used to measure the performance of annotation algorithms. Therefore, in order to test this data set, 90 images of each scene in Corel5k are used as training images, and the other 10 images are used as test images.

In this experiment, the performance difference among the annotation algorithm in this paper and three image annotation algorithms were analyzed. The above Table 1 gives the annotation results. The image annotation algorithm proposed in the paper is close to the PLSA-GMM [13] algorithm in terms of the total annotation rate, and the annotation accuracy is improved.

Table 1. Annotation results of different algorithms

Groun d Truth	Close-up, leaf, Plants	Clouds, sky, sun, tree	Birds, nest, tree	Frost, ice, sky, Tree
The paper	Leaf, plants, ste ms, Lily, flowers	Clouds, sky, sun, mountain,tree	Birds, nest, tree, fl owers, Grass	Frost, ice, tree, wood, winter
PLSA-GMM	Leaf, plants, textu re, Pepper, lily	Clouds, sun, land, clock, storm	Birds, nest, tree, Branch, wood	Frost, ice, fruit, Cr ops, rapids

5.1 Precision and Recall of Annotation Algorithm

Recall can reflect the integrity of image retrieval results, while Precision represents the accuracy of correct image retrieval. The results of TM [14], CRM [15] and PLSA-GMM [13] are compared under the same image set and its labeled word set. The performance comparison results of the different models are shown in Table 2.

Table 2. Performance comparison for different annotation models

	TM	CRM	PLSA-GMM	The paper
Recall	0.34	0.70	0.73	0.75
Precision	0.20	0.59	0.59	0.69

It is not difficult to see from the experimental results that the model annotation performance of this algorithm is improved compared with TM, CMRM, CRM and PLSA-GMM models (see Fig. 2).

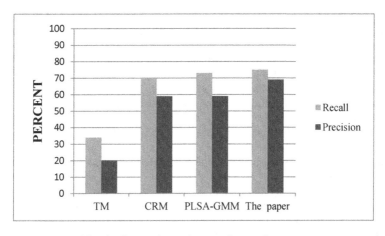

Fig. 2. Comparison of annotation performance

6 Conclusion

In the paper, a hierarchical semantic annotation algorithm is proposed. The algorithm takes full advantage of the global and local features of images, and plays different roles in image classification. Another contribution of this algorithm is to construct a semantic tree according to the specific scene. The annotation algorithm proposed in the paper organized the scene-related semantic tags according to the visual characteristics of the image, and consequently obtains a more reasonable model background for the subsequent semantic annotation work.

References

1. Wu, B., Fan, J., Liu, W., Ghanem, B.: Diverse image annotation. In: 30th IEEE Conference on Computer Vision and Pattern Recognition, CVPR 2017, pp. 6194–6202 (2017)
2. LeCun, Y., Boser, B., Denker, J.S., Henderson, D., et al.: Backpropagation applied to handwritten zip code recognition. Neural Comput. **1**(4), 541–551 (1989)
3. Ren, S., He, K., Girshick, R., Sun, J.: Faster R-CNN: towards real-time object detection with region proposal networks. In: NIPS 2015, pp. 91–99 (2015)
4. Johnson, J., Ballan, L., Li, F.: Love thy neighbors: image annotation by exploiting image metadata. In: ICCV 2015, pp. 4624–4632 (2015)
5. Gong, Y., Jia, Y., Leung, T., Toshev, A., Ioffe, S.: Deep convolutional ranking for multilabel image annotation. arXiv preprint arXiv:1312.4894 (2013)
6. Wu, B., Lyu, S., Ghanem, B.: ML-MG: multi-label learning with missing labels using a mixed graph. In: ICCV 2015, pp. 4157–4165 (2015)
7. Wu, B., Lyu, S., Hu, B.G., Ji, Q.: Multi-label learning with missing labels for image annotation and facial action unit recognition. Pattern Recogn. **48**(7), 2279–2289 (2015)
8. Cabral, R.S., Torre, F.D., Costeira, J.P., Bernardino, A.: Matrix completion for multi-label image classification. In: NIPS 2011, pp. 190–198 (2011)

9. Cao, X., Zhang, H., Guo, X., Liu, S., Meng, D.: SLED: semantic label embedding dictionary representation for multi-label image annotation. IEEE Trans. Image Process. **24**(9), 2746–2759 (2015)

10. Wu, B., Lyu, S., Ghanem, B.: Constrained submodular minimization for missing labels and class imbalance in multi-label learning. In: AAAI 2016, pp. 2229–2236 (2016)

11. Li, Y., Wu, B., Ghanem, B., Zhao, Y., Yao, H., Ji, Q.: Facial action unit recognition under incomplete data based on multi-label learning with missing labels. Pattern Recogn. **60**, 890–900 (2016)

12. Shi, J., Malik, J.: Normalized cuts and image segmentation. IEEE Trans. Pattern Anal. Mach. Intell. **22**(8), 888–905 (2000)

13. Hofmann, T.: Unsupervised learning by probabilistic latent semantic analysis. Mach. Learn. **42**(1), 177–196 (2001)

14. Salami, S., Shamsfard, M.: Integrating shallow syntactic labels in the phrase-boundary translation model. ACM Trans. Asian Low-Resour. Lang. Inf. Process. **17**(3) (2018)

15. Moran, S., Lavrenko, V.: Sparse kernel learning for image annotation. In: Proceedings of the ACM International Conference on Multimedia Retrieval, pp. 113–120 (2014)

One Secure IoT Scheme for Protection of True Nodes

Yongkai Fan[1,2(✉)], Guanqun Zhao[1,2], Xiaodong Lin[1,2],
Xiaofeng Sun[1,2], Dandan Zhu[1,2], and Jing Lei[1,2]

[1] Beijing Key Lab of Petroleum Data Mining, China University of Petroleum,
Beijing, China
fanyongkai@gmail.com
[2] Department of Computer Science and Technology,
China University of Petroleum, Beijing, China

Abstract. As a new generation of information technologies, IoT has been applied into many industrial fields and made great contributions to our everyday life. However, vulnerability of IoT constrains the application of IoT, especially, when the node used in IoT systems is malicious one which may break the system and leakage vital data (for example, nodes used by patient to transfer condition data). To tackle the security concerning, we propose one secure IoT framework used to protect true nodes and ensure the secure operation. Firstly, we introduce two types of IoT classic architectures and summarize the security challenges, then we give an introduction and comparison of several IoT security frameworks. At last, we propose our scheme for protecting the safety of IoT nodes in the perception layer.

Keywords: IoT · Security · Security framework · IoT node

1 Introduction

IoT (internet of things) is a novel notion of modern information technologies with no definition in common use yet. The gist of IoT paradigm is the ubiquity of all sorts of objects around us are able to have an interaction with each other and achieve their common goals collectively [1]. In short, IoT represents a linkage between heterogeneous entities which render services in traditional Internet by means of plunking for communications between objects and people. In the current trend of global communication, IoT has gradually evolved into a global "smart object" network [2]. It has also been mentioned that the term IoT represents a technology for interconnecting smart objects into a global network via the Internet [3]. Another definition is that it semantically refers to "the only addressable network of global interconnected objects based on standard communication protocols" [4]. IoT is also known internationally as a "sensor system", that is, a concept of the expansion of sensor networks into objects, and it is also a new revolution of the Internet [5]. In a manner of speaking, IoT delegates a new exposure of informatics.

© Springer Nature Switzerland AG 2018
M. Qiu (Ed.): SmartCom 2018, LNCS 11344, pp. 143–152, 2018.
https://doi.org/10.1007/978-3-030-05755-8_15

IoT has influenced several aspects and has many application scenarios. Here we select representative application areas as examples to show how the IoT exchanges the human living and manufacturing field.

(1) Smart industry. It can provide a more automatic management for better security and effectiveness in a company. For example, hovering the phones on NFC-tagged posters, users can automatically get information from relevant network services and purchase the needed tickets [6]; in addition, ubiquitous computing and sensor technology can make food supply more efficiency [7]. (2) Smart medical treatment. In modern society, high-calories food and decreasing amount of exercise cause a hidden danger on people's health. With the monitoring of wearable devices, the abnormal physical data will be stored in hospitals, which offers a timely information to doctors for potential patients to provide an early protection for users and reduce pressure of medical institution. (3) Smart home. There are many kinds of sensors used on intelligent devices in house, and collected information by sensors is used by individuals who own the network. For instance, a home monitoring system is created by the expansion of computer networks to help doctors monitor their patients. (4) Smart grid. Smart grid has been capable of supplanting the traditional gridline with a view to better service quality. Through the combination of IoT, smart grid can be seen as an intelligent grid delivering electric energy to users, in return consumers can adjust their choices autonomously [8]. (5) Smart transportation. Through the wireless networks, the smart vehicles are able to contact with each other, apperceive and share different traffic information efficiently. Besides, a driver's travel can be scheduled by the intelligent transportation system for better safety, efficiency and reliability. (6) Smart city. It is likely to be a multivariate comprehensive framework, which is used to manage the public affairs of a city through information and communication technology [9]. And as a comprehensive framework, smart city is an integration of different services and applications in one conurbation. (7) Utilities. Applying IoT technologies in gym, the fitness data can be collected and uploaded in time; application in museums can give an automatic explanation in view of conditions of the stream of people, reducing the pressure of management. Public gardens can set up self-regulation systems for plants and public devices by setting proper sensors at all places, offering a better environment for citizens. The water monitoring system use sensors to ensure the quality of people's drinking water, while the electric monitoring system can alter light intensity over time with the use of photo sensors.

From the examples in earlier sentences, we can come to a decision that IoT flourishes our life to a large extent. However, with the popularity of smart devices handling sensitive data, the security considerations related to IoT should not be ignored for the safety and secure utilization of IoT [10]. The remainder of this paper is organized as follows: We first introduce two classic IoT architectures in Sect. 2. In Sect. 3, the security goals and challenges in IoT will be presented in detail. Then we introduce several IoT security frameworks and give a comparison in Sect. 4. Finally, we propose our secure scheme for nodes used in perception layer in Sect. 5.

2 IoT Architecture

According to the recent researches [4, 6, 7, 11, 12], there are two main kinds of architectures of IoT architectures as shown in Fig. 1. The obvious distinction between them is the repartition of layers, as shown in the Fig. 1(a) and (b).

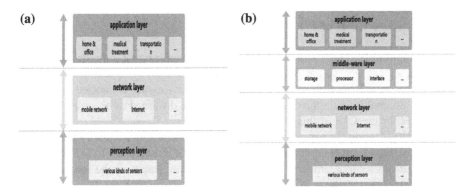

Fig. 1. (a) The three-layer-architecture of IoT. (b) The four-layer-architecture of IoT.

From the Fig. 1(a) [11], we can see that there are three layers in the general architecture of IoT: (1) Perception Layer is also called the sensor layer, which is the bottom of the general architecture. It contains many kinds of sensors, for example, photoelectric sensors, acoustic sensors, infrared sensors or any other kinds of sensor networks. The main propose of perception layer is to identify objects and acquire their status information, store these data and deal with them later. (2) Network Layer is seated in the middle of the general architecture. It is responsible for transmitting, transferring the data collected by sensors in perception layer to different kinds of information processing systems, which through the communication networks. (3) Application layer is the top layer, responsible for realizing different kinds of practical applications belonging to IoT in the light of the users' needs. No matter what kinds of derivative architectures will be constructed in the future, it is necessary to use the three-layer-scheme as a benchmark for improving and achieving.

To build a versatile and flexible IoT multi-level architecture for more functions, a four-layer-architecture which is called as SoA-based architecture is proposed [12]. As shown in Fig. 1(b), middle-ware layer is introduced to connect diverse services or functional units through protocols and interfaces, including information processing systems, which take actions according to the data-processing results. Additionally, it can link the database in which the data storage with the system. What's more, the middle-ware layer is service-oriented that can ensure the same service type among the connected equipment.

3 IoT Security

Although the IoT has brought convenience to human beings, there are also potential security threats and possible attacks. If we want to apply applications or service in IoT safely and effectively, the first thing is to figure out what should we take into consider for the IoT security.

3.1 The Secure Goals of IoT

(1) **Confidentiality.** This characteristic is designed to ensure that only the authorized consumer can access the information. The confidentiality is a crucial security property in IoT because a lot of measurement devices are connected with each other. So, making sure the collected data won't be disturbed or be stolen by other devices for the sake of this aim.

(2) **Integrity.** During the period of data communication, it is important to prevent the sensitive data from being leaked by variety kinds of interference. In IoT, while the applications receive tampered data, wrong operation status can be measured and the system may make a wrong feedback.

(3) **Availability.** Availability is a property which can make sure that the authorized consumer can access the needed data whenever and wherever. Because of the real-time requirements of IoT, the useful information is needed to be transferred timely, unless some services cannot run correctly. Thus, availability is a vital security feature for IoT [6].

3.2 The Security Challenges in IoT

In the consideration of security goals, mail security challenges faced in IoT has to be thought over. We summarize the challenge may be faced and has a simple description of it in Table 1:

Table 1. The main security challenges in IoT.

Challenge	Description
Detection	Either malicious behaviors or malicious nodes will cause a damage in IoT. So, in such a sophisticated circumstance, we need a detection mechanism consisting of two modules. One is intrusion detection while the other is malicious node detection. The proposal of the former detection is finding out abnormal behaviors in all the processing flow and give a feedback for appropriate countermeasures. The latter one aims at chasing down malicious nodes and executing an isolation or clearance
Transmission protection	Because of the inherent limited nature, information leakage is more easily to happen in IoT with tons of data transmitted. An attacker may intercept data in transit and tampering with it, which has an impact on the data integrity and confidentiality. Consequently, people need to take effective methods to avoid attacks during data transmission

(continued)

Table 1. (*continued*)

Challenge	Description
Access control	Access control is a kind of authentication for IoT nodes and users, which makes it possible that only the users with effective identity can access specific systems, carry out sensitive operations or gain needed data. When non-permission users call on a visit, the system will reject the request and send a feedback to managers. Some representative mechanisms have been put forward in recent years such as [13–15]. Besides, multifarious access control systems are proposed in view of different principles [16–18]
Recognition	Services and applications in IoT take advantage of received data and meet users' demands. As a consequence, the application layer may cause a battery of security issues without accurate recognition mechanisms, defending untrusted services for trusted users. In most cases, consumers do not have the abilities to distinguish the quality of an application, as anyone is seemed to provide a secured service with delicate camouflage
Data privacy	With the usage of wearable devices and home appliances, more and more private data are stored in intelligent devices or even in cloud. Once there is a physical attack or software flaw, the private information stored can be destroyed or leaked. Therefore, efficacious light-weight security policies need to be put forward for IoT devices with resource and performance constraints

4 Comparison of Several Security Frameworks for IoT

There are some researchers propose appropriate solutions for resisting security threats mentioned in Sect. 3. We select four popular and typical security frameworks or techniques for different fields of IoT to show the security consideration of them. First, we'll give a brief description of each framework and then compare frameworks to show the differences and features of them.

A. Brief Introductions to the Four Frameworks.

(1) Access control system [20]. In this control system, sensors are open to users with mobile devices, and these mobile devices have less ability to track down who is using the resources or data. Here researchers propose an architecture, which is directed against this issue. The proposed framework [20] consists of four parts as Fig. 2(a): the cloud, the mobile clients, the IoT nodes, and the gateway. *The Cloud* plays a role of server, which receives the request from the mobile clients. It can provide variety kinds of services to clients and transmit web requests to IoT nodes. *The Mobile Clients* execute the following function. Once launching to applications, they'll register with the sensors; besides, clients can collect sensor data and initiate authorization requests regularly; what' more, the mobile clients receive the web response and then present it to users. Different *IoT Nodes* have different functions. They can only connect with the gateways, because the nodes only trust the gateway server. *The Gateway* can send usable sensor lists as well as connection requests. If there is any request passed to the sensor, the cloud can know which gateway to choose. Then the specific gateway will

send the information to IoT nodes. (2) Smart cyber infrastructure [19]. Figure 2(b) shows one security framework for IoT, which is used to carry out security developments of intelligent infrastructures [19]. There are four layers in this framework: IoT End Node layer, Network layer, Service layer and Application layer. *End Node Layer* consists of many IoT devices, and the information collected from the real world can be passed to the next layer through this layer. The most significant components in this layer are sensors and actuators. *Network Layer* is designed to conduct data between the end nodes and the fog or cloud. In this layer there is a secure gateway, which is responsible for controlling access to defend against cyber-attacks that might appear. Then the secure data which passed through the gateway can be sent for further processing through networks. *Service Layer* acts as an interface between the next two layers. Because of the lack of memory and computing capacity of IoT devices, all the needed energy and resources are provided as cloud or fog services. *Application Layer* can provide services to devices and users through applications. The most important aspect of the layer is data sharing, so it's of vital importance to avoid information leaks and maintain data privacy. (3) SecIoT [20]. The SecIoT framework (shown in Fig. 2 (c)) is responsible for improving the security in IoT through three modules: authentication, access control and risk indicator. *Authentication* is in the center of the architecture. It connected with data providers and data consumers, so the authentication is divided into user authentication and device authentication. Because the IoT exists in the network ecosystem, providing support for security protocols is crucial, as the security of IoT depends on the realizing degree in some extent. *Access Control* is responsible for identifying whether the users have abilities to access specific data, while the role-based solution is a prevalent mechanism for protecting safety. Different roles are assigned to different users, and thus users with variety kinds of roles can carry out dissimilar jobs. *Risk indicator* can help customers to apperceive security risks better. The security indicator is generated according to asset identification, threat identification and risk evaluation. The asset identification can make sure the asset which should be protected, the threat identification is able to identify the probable threat, and the risk evaluation can evaluate the results and influence caused by threat. (4) Cloud ecosystem [21]. Cloud Ecosystem has three layers called gathering layer, transmitting layer and applying layer shown in Fig. 2(d) [21]. *Gathering Layer* is the bottom of this architecture consisting of sensors and base stations. The sensor nodes have secure localization capability, and can sample, process, communicate complicated data, and send it to the Base station, which acts as a secure gateway. *Transmitting Layer* consists of transceivers and towers, and both of them are responsible for transmitting data between base station and cloud and prevent eavesdropping as well. *Applying Layer*'s main part is the cloud. It can make sure that only the authorized users have the ability to access and avoid privilege escalation.

B. Comparison

After reviewing four typical security frameworks of IoT, we compare them in different evaluation directions in Table 2. Giving a description and comparison of different security frameworks can help people to take appropriate security measures with the necessary technology in different IoT fields.

There are other schemes proposed [16–18] in IoT, they mainly focus on the application layer and network layer, which are responsible for consumer identity and

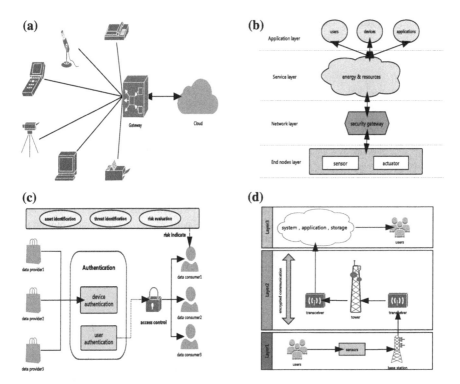

Fig. 2. (a) Access control system. (b) Smart cyber infrastructure. (c) SecIoT. (d) Cloud ecosystem.

data interchange. As a common knowledge, reliable data source is much more important for consideration the security goals we mentioned before, however, there is a short board on the conception layer's security universally. So for the sake of protecting the security of the source data, we put forward a novel scheme.

5 Our Proposal

As we all know, there are many kinds of sensors used in IoT, no matter above mentioned schemes or other frameworks, sensors are used for collecting data from the real world, and then data is transferred and stored for further use. In order to protect the security of the data gathered by sensors, we propose a scheme to give an identification of normal nodes and malicious modes based on several security solutions. The purpose of the scheme is to protect data reliability and security from the beginning of the whole communication process.

The proposed scheme is used in the perception layer between IoT nodes and the key node. There are five main parts in our scheme which is shown as Fig. 3.

(1) **Dacty_Module.** The first step is to extract the unique device information of the IoT node, and then generate a dactylogram of each device. After this process, every

Table 2. Comparison of several security frameworks for IoT.

Framework	IoT component	Security control	Security protocol and technology	Application
A: Access control system	Cloud, gateways, sensors	Null	Web socket, CoAP protocol	Access control of users
B: Smart cyber infrastructure	Cloud, gateways, sensors, actuators	Light-weight encryption, sensor authentication, intrusion detection, anti-jamming strategy, identity authentication, abnormal behavior analysis	Communication protocol for mobile communication network, wireless sensor network communication protocol	Ensure the security of intelligent infrastructure such as the smart home and smart buildings
C: SecIoT	Cloud, sensors	Device and user authentication, role-based access control, risk indication	PKI, out-of-band communication technology, single sign-on mechanism, multi-channel security protocol	Ensure the security of communication between IoT devices
D: Cloud ecosystem	cloud, sensors, base station, storage, communication towers	Access control, identity authentication	Wireless communication protocol, SSDLC, data analysis	Ensure the security of sensors based on the cloud

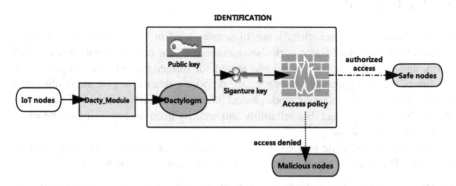

Fig. 3. The proposed scheme in perception layer.

equipment in IoT has a unique identity that will be used as an attribute of the device.

(2) **PKGen_Module.** It will generate a public key for further use. In this step, the system or the trusted third party will produce a public key with some parameters. The public key is used for generating a signature key in the next step.

(3) **SKGen_Module.** The main goal of this module is generating signature key. Here we use the public key along with the dactylogram produced in the first step to carry out the process. As a result, the dactylogram will be a part of the signature key as an attribute.

(4) **Sig_Module.** Here, the system will sign collected data with the public key and the signature key. Here we need to define an access policy, in which there are security nodes' dactylograms included. Of course, the malicious nodes' dactylograms are not in the policy. After that, we use the signature key with the unique dactylograms to sign the collected data.

(5) **Verify_Module.** In the last step of our scheme, the module will carry out a verification on the basis of previous steps. Using the public key, signature key and defined access policy to verify the device's identify. The principle is if the attribute in signature is a part of the policy, the device is safe. Otherwise, the device is considered as a malicious node and access denied.

We are still on our way to do some extensive experiments; the proposed scheme seems useful and effective according to our initial experimental results. Moreover, security analysis is under its way and there are lots of work need to be done in order to make sure our proposed scheme can meet the security requirement.

6 Conclusion

IoT has the advantages of high efficiency, low cost, and high scalability. With the development of IoT, security issues have become more serious. Because people put great emphasis on services provided by the IoT environment, safety issues have not led to adequacy attention. This article introduces IoT security-related knowledge and introduces four different security frameworks in IoT. In addition, we give a brief comparison of them, and then introduces our new scheme simply. Our future work will focus on the theoretical analysis and extensive experiments to prove our scheme can be a useful and improvement of security goals in IoT.

References

1. Atzori, L., Iera, A., Morabito, G.: The internet of things: a survey. Comput. Netw. **54**(15), 2787–2805 (2010)
2. Giusto, D., Iera, A., Morabito, G., Atzori, L.: The Internet of Things. Springer, New York (2010). https://doi.org/10.1007/978-1-4419-1674-7. ISBN 978-1-4419-1673-0
3. The Internet of Things, ITU Internet Reports (2005). http://www.itu.int/internetofthings/

4. INFSO D.4 Networked Enterprise & RFID INFSO G.2 Micro & Nano systems. In: Co-operation with the Working Group RFID of the ETP EPOSS, Internet of Things in 2020, Roadmap for the Future, Version 1.1, 27 May 2008
5. Vermesan, O., et al.: Internet of things strategic research and innovation agenda. River Publishers Series in Communications, p. 7 (2013)
6. Maheswari, S.U., et al.: A novel robust routing protocol RAEED to avoid DoS attacks in WSN. In: 2016 International Conference on Information Communication and Embedded Systems (ICICES). IEEE (2016)
7. Ilic, A., Staake, T., Fleisch, E.: Using sensor information to reduce the carbon footprint of perishable goods. IEEE Pervasive Comput. 8(1), 22–29 (2009)
8. Siano, P.: Demand response and smart grids—A survey. Renew. Sustain. Energy Rev. 30, 461–478 (2014)
9. Hao, L., et al.: The application and implementation research of smart city in China. In: 2012 International Conference on System Science and Engineering (ICSSE). IEEE (2012)
10. Fan, Y., Liu, S., Tan, G., et al.: Fine-grained access control based on trusted execution environment. Futur. Gener. Comput. Syst. (2018)
11. Mahmoud, R., et al.: Internet of things (IoT) security: current status, challenges and prospective measures. In: 2015 10th International Conference for Internet Technology and Secured Transactions (ICITST). IEEE (2015)
12. Xu, L.D., He, W., Li, S.: Internet of things in industries: a survey. IEEE Trans. Ind. Inform. 10(4), 2233–2243 (2014)
13. Anggorojati, B., et al.: Capability-based access control delegation model on the federated IoT network. In: 2012 15th International Symposium on Wireless Personal Multimedia Communications (WPMC). IEEE (2012)
14. Chen, H.C.: Collaboration IoT-based RBAC with trust evaluation algorithm model for massive IoT integrated application. Mobile Netw. Appl., 1–14 (2018)
15. Sanchez, P.M., Lopez, R.M., Skarmeta, A.F.G.: PANATIKI: a network access control implementation based on PANA for IoT devices. Sensors 13(11), 14888–14917 (2013)
16. Pereira, P.P., Eliasson, J., Delsing, J.: An authentication and access control framework for CoAP-based internet of things. In: IECON 2014-40th Annual Conference of the IEEE Industrial Electronics Society, pp. 5293–5299. IEEE (2014)
17. Bernabe, J.B., Ramos, J.L.H., Gomez, A.F.S.: TACIoT: multidimensional trust-aware access control system for the internet of things. Soft. Comput. 20(5), 1763–1779 (2016)
18. Guoping, Z., Wentao, G.: The research of access control based on UCON in the internet of things. J. Softw. 6(4), 724–731 (2011)
19. Monir, S.: A Lightweight Attribute-Based Access Control System for IoT (2016)
20. Huang, X., Craig, P., Lin, H., et al.: SecIoT: a security framework for the internet of things. Secur. Commun. Netw. 9(16), 3083–3094 (2016)
21. Rahman, A.F.A., Daud, M., Mohamad, M.Z.: Securing sensor to cloud ecosystem using internet of things (IoT) security framework. In: Proceedings of the International Conference on Internet of things and Cloud Computing, p. 79. ACM (2016)

Predicted Mobile Data Offloading for Mobile Edge Computing Systems

Hao Jiang, Duo Peng, Kexin Yang, Yuanyuan Zeng, and Qimei Chen[✉]

School of Electronic Information, Wuhan University, Wuhan, China
{jh,pandapeng,yiren,zengyy,chenqimei}@whu.edu.cn

Abstract. Mobile Edge Computing (MEC) has emerged as a promising technology to meet with the high data rate, real-time transmission, and huge computation requirements for the ever growing future wireless terminals, such as virtual reality devices, augmented reality, and the Internet of Vehicles. Due to the limitation of licensed bandwidth resources, mobile data offloading should be considered. On the other hand, WiFi AP that works on the abundant unlicensed spectrum can provide good wireless services under light-loaded areas. Therefore, in this paper we leverage WiFi AP to offload some devices from SBS. To effectively perform the offloading process, we build a multi-LSTM based deep-learning algorithm to predict the traffic of SBS. According to the prediction results, an offline mobile data offloading strategy has been proposed, which has been obtained through cross entropy method. Simulation results demonstrate the efficiency of our prediction model and offloading strategy.

Keywords: Mobile data offloading · Deep learning
Mobile Edge Computing

1 Introduction

With the development of wireless communication, the number of mobile users increased sharply and thus the computation amount have become extremely huge, which brings some stiff challenges such as latency, data rate and computation capability [1].

As a key technology of 5G, Mobile Edge Computing (MEC) provides possibility for wireless devices by bringing computing and cashing resources to the network edge [2]. MEC servers are deployed in close proximity of the Small Base Stations (SBSs) to execute delay-sensitive and context-aware applications to the users [3]. Therefore, the use of the storage and computation capabilities of MEC can effectively increase the system efficiency as investgated in [4].

This work was supported in part by the Fundamental Research Funds for the Central Universities under Grants 2042018kf1009 and 204208kf10002, and in part by the National Natural Science Foundation Program of China under Grants 61371126.

© Springer Nature Switzerland AG 2018
M. Qiu (Ed.): SmartCom 2018, LNCS 11344, pp. 153–162, 2018.
https://doi.org/10.1007/978-3-030-05755-8_16

Owing to the explosive growth of mobile data and the limitation of licensed resources, mobile data offloading, which can lease the burden of high-loaded SBSs, should be considered [5]. As shown in [6] and [7], offloading users from SBS to WiFi is a promising solution. Inspired by this, we build a system model which combines MEC system with mobile data offloading. In the proposed model, all of the user data would be stored in the MEC previously. By some detection, parts of the users can be offloaded to the WiFi network. Existing works do not take into account both the particularity of mobile data contents (different types of contents require different data transmission rates) and the real-time traffic load of SBS.

Motivated by this, we propose a predicted content-based offloading mechanism for MEC system to further improve the system performance in the paper. The contents are divided into different categories according to their data transmission rate. And users with lower data transmission rate contents are considered to have lower priority, which will be offloaded first. Thus, the most important problem for us is to decide which users to be offloaded.

The main contributions of this paper are summarized as follows:

- Considering that the offloading process occurs on overloaded SBS, accurate traffic prediction results are needed. We build a prediction model based on multi-LSTM, and the prediction value can be a guide for offloading.
- By utilizing the prediction value and considering the user priority, we propose an offloading algorithm based on cross entropy method (CE method) to decide which users to be offloaded to WiFi, and maximize the system throughput.
- Based on actual data from a Usage Detail Records (UDR) data set collected in Jinhua, some simulations have been conducted to validate the applicability of our proposed mechanism. It's obvious that the mechanism can effectively improve the system performance.

The remaining part of this paper is organized as follows. The system model and problem formulation are presented in Sect. 2. Section 3 shows the traffic prediction model and the offloading strategy. In Sect. 4, we evaluate the performance of the proposed mechanism. The whole paper is concluded in Sect. 5.

2   System Model and Problem Formulation

2.1   System Model

We consider a scenario with one SBS, one WiFi AP, and N users, as shown in Fig. 1. There is an MEC server in close proximity of each SBS so that the transmission delay can be greatly reduced, and we assume that users with low data rate requirements will be offloaded to WiFi first if the SBS traffic exceeds the threshold. We further assume that there is a central controller, which can send the content to the MEC and switch the users to WiFi.

The progress of the proposed model can be described as follows. First, the traffic prediction value is used to determine which user groups may be offloaded.

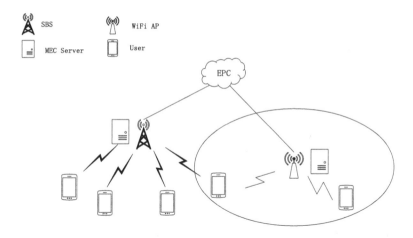

Fig. 1. System model.

Then, we decide to offload some of these users to WiFi according to their priorities and the system throughput after offloading, until the traffic of the SBS is below the threshold. Moreover, the data transmission rate of users must be ensured.

The throughput of the system contains two parts:

- WiFi Throughput:
  The saturation throughput of a WiFi network with n users can be analyzed with a discrete-time Markov chain (DTMC) model, which can be expressed as Eq. 1.

$$R_w (n) = \frac{P_{tr} P_s E [P]}{(1 - P_{tr}) T_\sigma + P_{tr} P_s T_s + P_{tr} (1 - P_s) T_c}, \tag{1}$$

  where P_{tr} and P_s are the probabilities at least one transmission in a slot time and transmission being successful, respectively. T_σ, T_s and T_c are the WiFi parameters. The average packet size is denoted as $E [P]$ [8].
- SBS Throughput:
  Considering the diverse access needs of different users, the throughput of each user can be expressed according to the Shannon-Hartley theorem as follows.

$$R_c (u) = B_u \log_2 (1 + SNR_u), \tag{2}$$

  where B_u denotes the bandwidth obtained by user u. SNR_u is the signal-to-noise ratio (SNR) between the SBS and user u. Therefore, the total throughput of the target SBS can be expressed as

$$R_s = \sum_u R_c (u), \tag{3}$$

For the different access requirements of users, our system model will consider the actual needs of each user to formulate an offloading strategy.

2.2   Problem Formulation

Mobile data offloading can be regarded as a problem to maximize the whole system throughput while guaranteeing the users' data rate requirements and release the traffic burden of SBS.

According to Eqs. 1 and 2, the total throughput of the system can be expressed as

$$R = \sum_{k=1}^{K} \sum_{i=1}^{N_s^k} \left(1-a_i^k\right) R_c\left(u_i^k\right) + R_w \left(N_w + \sum_{k=1}^{K} \sum_{i=1}^{N_s^k} a_i^k\right), \tag{4}$$

where K is the number of divided categories, N_s^k denotes the total number of users that access content k on the SBS. u_i^k denotes the i-th user accessing content k. a_i^k is the offloading indicator where $a_i^k = 1$ means that u_i^k needs to be offloaded and $a_i^k = 0$ otherwise. It can be expressed as

$$a_i^k = \delta \lambda_i^k, \tag{5}$$

where

$$\delta = \begin{cases} 0, if\, T_p \leq T_{th}, \\ 1, otherwise, \end{cases} \tag{6}$$

where T_p and T_{th} denote the traffic load and the traffic threshold of the SBS, respectively.

The optimization problem to maximize the system throughput among all users can be formulated as

$$\max_{\{a_i^k\}} R, \tag{7}$$

subject to

$$\left(1 - a_i^k\right) R_c\left(u_i^k\right) \geq \left(1 - a_i^k\right) R_{th}^k, \forall k, \tag{8}$$

$$\frac{R_w}{N_w + \sum_{k=1}^{K} \sum_{i=1}^{N_s^k} a_i^k} \geq \max_k \left\{R_{th}^k\right\}, \tag{9}$$

$$\sum_{k=1}^{K} \sum_{i=1}^{N_s^k} \left(1 - a_i^k\right) T_i^k \leq T_{th}, \tag{10}$$

Constraint Eq. 8 ensures the throughput of each SBS user, while constraint Eq. 9 guarantees the average throughput of each WiFi user. Constraint Eq. 10 denotes the traffic load of SBS should be below the traffic threshold after offloading.

Note that users with lower data transmission rate requirements are considered to have lower priority, and would be first defined as potential offloaded objects if the traffic of SBS is over the threshold. To make an offloading strategy, we also need to consider the benefit of reducing the SBS traffic load and the change in system throughput, i.e., our goal is to find the optimal solution for Eq. 7 with low-priority users offloaded first.

3   Traffic Prediction and Offloading Strategy

3.1   Traffic Prediction

From Eq. 6, δ is determined by the prediction result, which means the accuracy of prediction will directly affect the performance of the system. In order to predict SBS traffic accurately, multi-LSTM is applied to build a deep learning model.

For the purpose of solving the Vanishing Gradient Problem of Recurrent Neural Networks (RNN) [9], the Long Short Term Memory (LSTM) model [10] was put forward. The structure of LSTM has the ability to decide the memory unit to forget some of the previous information, so that it can easily store and access information over long periods of time. Then, the model can be used to process longer time series without vanishing gradient. Moreover, the LSTM layer can control the flow of information well. Furthermore, multi-LSTM can make the model deeper, and it adds levels of abstraction of input at higher layers.

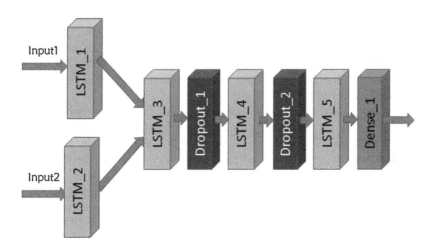

Fig. 2. Traffic prediction model.

Therefore, in this paper we build a multi-LSTM model which can predict the value determined by previous traffic sequence. Besides, the number of users on the SBS can also directly affect the traffic load, i.e., the more users represent the higher traffic. Our deep learning model is depicted in Fig. 2, in which $Input1$ and $Input2$ represent the traffic sequence of the SBS and the number of users, respectively.

3.2   Offloading Strategy

Due to the non-convexity and nonlinearity of the combinatorial optimization problem in Eq. 7, we have great difficulties obtaining the optimal solution [8].

Therefore, an algorithm based on cross entropy method (CE method) [11] is adopted to get the approximate solution while reducing the computational cost.

CE method translates the original problem into a stochastic estimation problem, and works through adjusting the probability distribution according to the sampling result generated by a specialized mechanism until minimizing the cross-entropy or Kullback CLeibler divergence. In the objective function Eq. 7, the goal is to maximize the system throughput determined by a_i^k while meeting the constraints Eqs. 8–10. To solve the problem with CE method, we treat a_i^k as Bernoulli variable ϕ and sample it with the method of rejection sampling in the iterative process.

As mentioned above, users on overloaded SBS (i.e., $\delta = 1$) will be defined as potential offloaded objects. If there are multiple overloaded SBSs, we will perform the offloading operations one by one for each SBS. So we only discuss the situation of one SBS.

First, since low-priority users are preferred to be offloaded first, the candidate user set $\mathcal{U}$ can be reduced to $\sum_{k=1}^{k_1} \delta N_s^k$ users, of which k_1 indicates the highest priority of users need to be offloaded when the SBS traffic is exactly below the threshold. Note that we assume that the smaller k, the lower the priority. Then, we can generate candidate solutions for the offloading strategy. We use Φ to generalize the decision policy, and the Bernoulli variable $\phi \in \Phi$ is determined by the probability $p(\phi)$ of each user.

Second, we can obtain ϕ by comparing the $p(\phi)$ of each user with a random value between 0 and 1, which indicates whether to offload it. If $p(\phi)$ is greater than the random value, ϕ is set to 1, otherwise 0. We can get the value of all ϕ as a candidate strategy Φ of offloading. In this way, we generate M candidate strategies, note that they must meet the constraints Eqs. 8–10.

After obtaining those M candidate strategies, the total throughput in Eq. 4 can be calculated, which can clearly indicate the system performance. Then we sort those M candidate strategies by their performance, and select the strategies which represent the top N ($N < M$) results to increase the probability of better performance in next iteration. The probability $p(\phi)$ of each user can be updated after each iteration:

$$p(\phi)^{(j+1)} = \frac{\sum_{m=1}^{M} \phi^{(j,m)} \eta^{(j,m)}}{N}, \tag{11}$$

where $\eta^{(j,m)}$ is an indicator of whether the performance of the strategy is ranked in the top N:

$$\eta^{(j,m)} = \begin{cases} 1, R\left(\Phi^{(j,m)}\right) \geq R\left(\Phi^{(j,N)}\right), \\ 0, otherwise, \end{cases} \tag{12}$$

where $R\left(\Phi^{(j,N)}\right)$ indicates the result of the N-th strategy in the j-th iteration. To avoid the solutions converging to local extremum, different from [8], we use factors μ and ξ to further update the probability. Where μ ($0 < \mu \leq 1$) is used to control the information amount learned from the current strategy, and

---

Algorithm 1. Algorithm of offloading strategy.

Input: M, N, convergence threshold ε, μ and ξ;
Output: $\Phi^{(j,1)}$
1: Calculate k_1 and determine the candidate user set $\mathcal{U}$;
2: **repeat**
3:    Generate M candidate strategies by sampling, each should satisfy constraints Eqs. 8–10;
4:    Rank these M strategies based on Eq. 4, and select the N-th strategy;
5:    **if** $\dfrac{\left|R\left(\Phi^{(j,1)}\right) - R\left(\Phi^{(j,2)}\right)\right|}{R\left(\Phi^{(j,1)}\right)} \leq \varepsilon$ **then**
6:       Convergent
7:    **else**
8:       Update $p(\phi)$ based on Eqs. 11–13, in which μ and ξ are utilized to avoid converging to local extremum;
9:    **end if**
10: **until** complete the iteration or convergent
11: **return** $\Phi^{(j,1)}$ as the approximate solution of Eq. 7;

ξ represents the update step size of the probability, that is, current probability is related to the probability distribution of the previous ξ steps:

$$p(\phi)^{(j+1)} = \mu \cdot p(\phi)^{(j+1)} + \frac{(1-\mu)}{\xi}\sum_{i=0}^{\xi} p(\phi)^{(j-i)}, \tag{13}$$

From Eq. 13, we can see that with the increase of μ, more information will be learned each time when the probability is updated. And with the increase of ξ, the update of the current probability is related to the probability of longer time steps. The two factors jointly control the update of the probability to prevent converging to local extremum. Through multiple iterations, an approximate optimal strategy is finally obtained. The algorithm is illustrated in Algorithm 1.

4   Simulation Results

In this paper, we use a Usage Detail Records (UDR) data set collected in Jinhua to simulate the scenario and execute offloading strategy.

4.1   Traffic Prediction Results

We set the coverage distance threshold $500m$ of each SBS and then count the changes in the SBS traffic and the number of users in a randomly selected region in Jinhua as input to the traffic prediction model. The design of the model structure and the selection of hyperparameters in Fig. 2 are shown below. Then, we divide the data set into two parts of training and experiment, and use the data of lasting 4 days to evaluate the prediction result and make an offloading strategy.

Parameters	Setting
Input dim of LSTM_1/LSTM_2	50
Output dim of LSTM_1/LSTM_2	200
Output dim of LSTM_3	256
Output dim of LSTM_4	256
Output dim of LSTM_5	512
Output dim of Dense_1	1
Drop out	0.2

The normalized mean-squared error (NMSE) is utilized as an evaluation indicator for traffic prediction performance. As shown in Fig. 3, the traffic prediction results for four areas of different sizes have pretty small errors, which prove the accuracy of our prediction model. And it is obvious that with the increase of the size, our prediction value is getting closer to the real traffic, that is, the error of traffic prediction gradually decreases, which means that our model performs better in larger area.

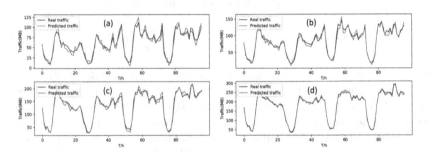

Fig. 3. Traffic prediction results for areas of different sizes. (a) $5\,km^2$, NMSE $= 0.0134$; (b) $10\,km^2$, NMSE $= 0.0061$; (c) $20\,km^2$, NMSE $= 0.0037$; (d) $30\,km^2$, NMSE $= 0.00081$.

4.2   Offloading Strategy Performance

During the offloading phase, we classify users into 3 categories with different priorities according to the content information contained in UDR.

First, we select one SBS with large historical traffic, set the traffic threshold to 3000KB and place 6 WiFis evenly around it. Once the traffic on the SBS exceeds the set threshold, offloading will be executed. The result is shown in Fig. 4, where (a) indicates the number of the offloaded users over time and (b) indicates the total throughput of the system. The horizontal axis is a time axis with a time span of 4 days. After dividing one day into the daytime, evening and night, it's easy to see that offloading mainly occurs during the daytime and evening, which is in line with the daily life habits of users. Besides, (b) shows that the system throughput has increased significantly after offloading because of the increase of the SBS and WiFi utilization.

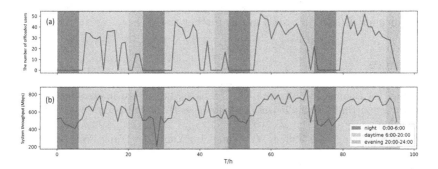

Fig. 4. Offloading in different time in single-SBS scenario.

On the other hand, a $5\,km^2$ area including 89 SBSs is selected to discuss the scenario of multiple SBSs. The number of offloaded users and throughput changes with time in this scene are shown in Fig. 5. Different from Fig. 4, the phenomenon in the multi-SBS scenario is more regular. From the curves we can see that the offloading still concentrates in the daytime and the evening while no offloading appears at night. After offloading, the throughput of the system has still increased significantly as before, which means that our offloading strategy performs well not only in single-SBS but also in multi-SBS scenario.

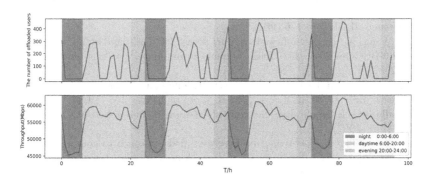

Fig. 5. Offloading in different time in multi-SBSs scenario.

5   Conclusion

In this paper, we have implemented the prediction model and offloading strategy to improve the system performance. First, the multi-LSTM model is used to predict the traffic of SBS, aiming to provide a guideline for mobile data offloading.

After that, the offloading strategy based on CE method is applied to maximize the system throughput while guaranteeing the data transmission. The simulation results demonstrate the applicability of our proposed method. Furthermore, the influence of the number of WiFi APs and the traffic threshold on the offloading performance should be discussed in our further research.

References

1. Bastug, E., Bennis, M., Medard, M., Debbah, M.: Toward interconnected virtual reality: opportunities, challenges, and enablers. IEEE Commun. Mag. **55**(6), 110–117 (2017)
2. Wang, S., Zhang, X., Zhang, Y., Wang, L., Yang, J., Wang, W.: A survey on mobile edge networks: convergence of computing, caching and communications. IEEE Access **5**, 6757–6779 (2017)
3. Tran, T.X., Hajisami, A., Pandey, P., Pompili, D.: Collaborative mobile edge computing in 5G networks: new paradigms, scenarios, and challenges. IEEE Commun. Mag. **55**(4), 54–61 (2017)
4. Zhang, H., Guo, J., Yang, L., Li, X., Ji, H.: Computation offloading considering fronthaul and backhaul in small-cell networks integrated with MEC. In: 2017 IEEE Conference on Computer Communications Workshops (INFOCOM WKSHPS). IEEE, pp. 115–120 (2017)
5. Aijaz, A., Aghvami, H., Amani, M.: A survey on mobile data offloading: technical and business perspectives. IEEE Wirel. Commun. **20**(2), 104–112 (2013)
6. Feng, G., Xia, F., Zhang, Y., Su, D., Lv, H., Wang, H., Lv, H.: Optimal cooperative wireless communication for mobile user data offloading. IEEE Access **6**, 16224–16234 (2018)
7. Zhang, Y., Hou, F., Cai, L.X., Huang, J.: QoS-based incentive mechanism for mobile data offloading. In: GLOBECOM 2017–2017 IEEE Global Communications Conference. IEEE, pp. 1–6 (2017)
8. Li, P., Feng, K.: Energy-efficient channel access for dual-band small cell networks. In: GLOBECOM 2017–2017 IEEE Global Communications Conference. IEEE, pp. 1–6 (2017)
9. Bengio, Y., Simard, P., Frasconi, P.: Learning long-term dependencies with gradient descent is difficult. IEEE Trans. Neural Netw. **5**(2), 157–166 (1994)
10. Schmidhuber, J., Hochreiter, S.: Long short-term memory. Neural Comput. **9**(8), 1735–1780 (1997)
11. Deng, L.Y.: The cross-entropy method: a unified approach to combinatorial optimization, monte-carlo simulation, and machine learning. Technometrics **48**(1), 147–148 (2006)

A Monte Carlo Based Computation Offloading Algorithm for Feeding Robot IoT System

Cheng Zhang[1]([✉]), Takumi Ohashi[2], Miki Saijo[2], Jorge Solis[3], Yukio Takeda[2], Ann-Louise Lindborg[4], Ryuta Takeda[5], and Yoshiaki Tanaka[6,7]

[1] Department of Computer Science and Communications Engineering, Waseda University, Tokyo 169-0072, Japan
cheng.zhang@akane.waseda.jp
[2] Tokyo Institute of Technology, Tokyo 152-8550, Japan
[3] Department of Engineering and Physics, Karlstad University, Karlstad, Sweden
[4] Camanio Care AB, Norgegatan 2, 4tr, 164 32 Nacka, Sweden
[5] Leave a Nest Co. Ltd., Tokyo 162-0822, Japan
[6] Global Information and Telecommunication Institute, Waseda University, Tokyo 169-8555, Japan
[7] Department of Communications and Computer Engineering, Waseda University, Tokyo 169-8555, Japan

Abstract. Ageing is becoming an increasingly major problem in European and Japanese societies. We have so far mainly focused on how to improve the eating experience for both frail elderly and caregivers by introducing and developing the eating aid robot, Bestic, made to get the food from plate to the mouth for frail elderly or person with disabilities. We expand the functionalities of Bestic to create food intake reports automatically so as to decrease the undernutrition among frail elderly and workload of caregivers through collecting data via a vision system connected to the Internet of Things (IoT) system. Since the computation capability of Bestic is very limited, computation offloading, in which resource intensive computational tasks are transferred from Bestic to an external cloud server, is proposed to solve Bestic's resource limitation. In this paper, we proposed a Monte Carlo algorithm based heuristic computation offloading algorithm, to minimize the total overhead of all the Bestic users after we show that the target optimization problem is NP-hard in a theorem. Numeric results showed that the proposed algorithm is effective in terms of system-wide overhead.

Keywords: Eating robot · IoT · Computation offloading

1 Introduction

"100-Year Life Society" is a cutting-edge concept proposed by the Japanese government, which indicates that society should support people's well-being even

© Springer Nature Switzerland AG 2018
M. Qiu (Ed.): SmartCom 2018, LNCS 11344, pp. 163–171, 2018.
https://doi.org/10.1007/978-3-030-05755-8_17

in super-aging society. To put it into practice, the essential is to track data of actual field, interpret, and compare with the scientific literature to make a decision in elderly-care context. However, the most aging society, Japan, is facing a fatal problem that the supply/demand ratio of caregiver is expected to worsen as 87% in 2025 to 77% in 2035 [13]. It means that there is no room for caregivers to not only engage in daily care work but also track every single event precisely for elderly.

In our Japan-Sweden academia-industry international collaboration project, a robotic assistive device and a camera system that keeps track of their food intake has been proposed [12,14]. We have so far mainly focused on how to improve the eating experience for both frail elderly and caregivers by introducing and developing the eating aid, Bestic, made to get the food from plate to the mouth, controlled by the users. One of our strategies is to expand the functionalities of Bestic to create food intake reports automatically so as to decrease the undernutrition among frail elderly and workload of caregivers through collecting data via a vision system connected to the Internet of Things (IoT) system (see Fig. 1). A camera attached to Bestic will take pictures of the food. Then the food pictures are upload to the cloud server through cellular network or Wi-Fi access point, to be analyzed by the cloud server. The transfer of resource intensive computational tasks to an external cloud server is called *computation offloading* [6].

Since the storage and computation capability of Bestic is very limited, computation offloading is proposed to do the heavy nutrition data analysis from the picture taken by Bestic camera.

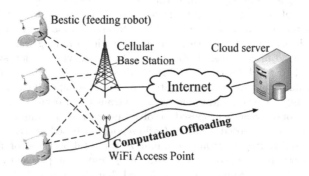

Fig. 1. IoT robot system architecture.

The main contributions of this paper are as follows:

- We consider minimizing the total overhead of all the Bestics in use, in which the overhead is defined as the weighted sum of consumed time, energy and monetary cost (if the task is offloaded to the cloud server), and prove that the target optimization problem is NP-hard [10]. This differentiates our work from existing works that minimize the individual overhead of each user by non-cooperative game.

- We propose a Monte Carlo algorithm based heuristic, which has the advantage of enumeration algorithm and Monte Carlo algorithm.
- We validate our proposed enumeration Monte Carlo heuristic (EMCH) algorithm through numeric analysis. The numeric results show the effectiveness of the proposed EMCH algorithm.

2   Related Work

Computation offloading has been extensively researched in the past, and has been identified as a solution to solve the local resource scarcity problem. The survey paper by Deshmukh et al. [6] identified that the network problem, latency, energy efficiency as well user experience and ease of development are important factors for computation offloading.

Many works has concentrated on single-user computation offloading problem. Barbera et al. [4] revealed the feasibility of both mobile computation offloading and mobile software/data backups in real-life scenarios in terms of network bandwidth cost and energy cost. Huang et al. [11] proposed a dynamic computation offloading algorithm to save energy while satisfying given application execution time requirement. These works only considered single-user case and monetary cost in computation offloading is ignored.

Multiple users computation offloading problem has also been studied, mainly through non-cooperative game theoretic approach. Chen et al. [5] formulated the computation offloading decision making problem among multiple mobile users as a multi-user computation offloading game. Zhang et al. [16] proposed a similar game under multiple mobile user scenario to minimize each mobile user's overhead, which is defined as combination of time and energy consumption as well as monetary cost. Barbarossa et al. [3] investigated the multiple users computation offloading problem to jointly minimize the computation and communication resources. These works do not consider the case when the multiple user cooperates with each other to transmit data and execute tasks, either locally or in remote cloud server.

Gai et al. [8] focused on the energy-saving problem and consider the energy wastes when tasks are assigned to remote cloud servers or heterogeneous core processors. Gai et al. [9] proposed a dynamic energy-aware cloudlet-based mobile cloud computing model focusing on solving the additional energy consumptions during the wireless communications by leveraging dynamic cloudlets based model. These works only focus on the energy aspect of computation offloading for cloud computing. They ignored monetary cost and time delay of the system.

Different from aforementioned related works, we consider multiple Bestic users cooperatively offload their computation tasks to the cloud server in this paper. The objective is to minimize the overall overhead (defined as a combination of monetary cost, energy cost, and time consumed) of the system, which is different from the non-cooperative game approach with the objective to minimize each individual user's (player's) overhead.

3   System Model

System model is introduced in this section. It is assumed that there is a set of $\mathcal{N} = \{1, 2, .., N\}$ Bestic users in the IoT system. For each Bestic device, the pictures are taken by the camera on the Bestic for nutrition data analysis. There are two ways for Bestic users to do nutrition data analysis: (i) to do the nutrition data analysis locally in Bestic device; (ii) to offload the pictures to the remote cloud and let the cloud to do the nutrition data analysis. This is called computation offloading in our IoT architecture.

For the first way, it may take a long time for nutrition data analysis since the Bestic device only has very limited computation capability and limited memory. For the second way, the nutrition data analysis is expected to be quicker soon since the cloud has high computation capability and large memory, but communication cost and time is incurred when transmit the data from local Bestic device to the cloud.

For Bestic user $n \in \mathcal{N}$, there is a computation task $\mathcal{H}_n := (\beta_n, \gamma_n)$. This task can be either executed locally in Bestic devices, or on cloud through computation offloading. β_n is the size of input computation data including the food pictures and the code for nutrition data analysis, and γ_n is the overall number of CPU cycles needed for completing the computation task $\mathcal{H}_n$.

(1) *Bestic local computing*: when execute the task locally in Bestic devices, the computation time is defined as $t_n^l = \frac{\gamma_n}{s_n^l}$, where s_n^l is Bestic n's computation power in CPU cycles per second.

The energy for computation is as $e_n^l = \varepsilon_n \gamma_n$, where ε_n is the energy consumption per CPU cycle. The overhead for Bestic local computing can be calculated as in Eq. (1).

$$\Phi_n^l = \sigma_n^t t_n^l + \sigma_n^e e_n^l \tag{1}$$

where $\sigma_n^t, \sigma_n^e \in [0, 1]$ denote user's preference for time consumption and energy consumption, respectively. In the extreme case, when $\sigma_n^t = 0, \sigma_n^e = 1$, user cares about energy consumption and do not care about time consumption. When $\sigma_n^t = 1, \sigma_n^e = 0$, user cares about time consumption and do not care about energy consumption.

(2) *Cloud computing*: The task $\mathcal{H}_n$ of Bestic user n can be offloaded to the cloud, and the cloud will do the nutrition data analysis for Bestic user.

When execute the task remotely in cloud, extra network transmission time and communication cost is needed. The transmission time, which depends on the data size β_n and transmission rate r_n, is calculated as $t_{n,o}^c = \frac{\beta_n}{r_n}$. The energy for offloading task from Bestic device to cloud is calculated as $e_n^c = \frac{q_n \beta_n}{r_n}$ where q_n is users transmission power. The execution time on cloud for task $\mathcal{H}_n$ is denoted as $t_{n,e}^c = \frac{\gamma_n}{s_n^c}$. There is also monetary cost incurred for network data transmission, which is defined as $m_{n,o}^c = g(\beta_n)$, where $g(\cdot)$ is the monetary cost function. $g(\cdot)$ is a function of transmit data β_n, and also is determined by the specific pricing strategy of network operators [15]. For example, there is *usage based pricing* scheme, in which the charge $m_{n,o}^c$ is proportional to the transmit data β_n.

For the cloud computing, we consider *public cloud*, which is provided by cloud service provider such as Amazon AWS [1]. Users can use pay-as-you-go pricing plan. The public cloud service providers provide different kinds of pricing plans. For example, Amazon AWS's two kinds of pricing plans are *on-demand pricing* and *spot pricing* [2]. We denote the cloud computing price as p^c in yen per second. The cost for cloud computation can be calculated as $m_{n,e}^c = p^c t_{n,e}^c$.

The overhead for Bestic local computing can be calculated as in Eq. (1).

$$\Phi_n^c = \sigma_n^t(t_{n,o}^l + t_{n,e}^l) + \sigma_n^e e_n^c + \sigma_n^m(m_{n,o}^c + m_{n,e}^c) \tag{2}$$

where $\sigma_n^m \in [0,1]$ denotes user's preference for monetary cost.

4   Problem Formulation

There is a planner tries to minimize the overall overhead of the whole system, i.e.,

$$\min_{\mathbf{o}} \sum_{n \in \mathcal{N}} \Omega_n \tag{3}$$

subject to

$$t_{n,o}^l + t_{n,e}^l \leq T_n, \text{or } t_n^l \leq T_n, \forall n \in \mathcal{N} \tag{4}$$

$$e_n^c \leq E_n, \text{or } e_n^l \leq E_n, \forall n \in \mathcal{N} \tag{5}$$

$$m_{n,o}^c + m_{n,e}^c \leq M_n, \forall n \in \mathcal{N} \tag{6}$$

$$o_n \in \{0,1\} \forall n \in \mathcal{N} \tag{7}$$

where Ω_n is defined as in Eq. (8)

$$\Omega_n = o_n \Phi_n^c + (1 - o_n)\Phi_n^l \tag{8}$$

where $o_n \in \{0,1\}$ indicates the computation offloading decision; if $o_n = 1$, user n offloads computation task to the cloud; if $o_n = 0$, user n computes the task locally. And $\mathbf{o}$ is defined as $\mathbf{o} = (o_1, ..., o_N)$. T_n is the time tolerance, or time budget of user n. The time to process task $\mathcal{H}_n$ should not be over than this time budget T_n. E_n is the energy budget of user n. The energy consumption for task $\mathcal{H}_n$ should not exceed the energy budget E_n. M_n is the monetary budge of user n. The monetary cost of task $\mathcal{H}_n$ should not be bigger than monetary budget M_n.

Please note that existing works [5,16] that proposed game theoretic approach tried to minimize each individual user's overhead Ω_n instead of the system-wide overhead $\sum_{n \in \mathcal{N}} \Omega_n$.

The problem formulation in this paper is reasonable since the Bestic feeding robot can be installed in nursing home and then performance of the overall system is important to the nursing home managers. The nursing home managers, performing as the planner, try to optimize the problem defined in Eq. (3).

Algorithm 1. Proposed EMCH Algorithm

1:	Initialize all the parameters in (3)
2:	Initialize the optimal result $p0 = 0$
3:	**if** $N < \hat{N}$:
4:	Enumerate all the possible **o** to find the solution.
5:	Set the optimal result to $p0$.
6:	**else:**
7:	**for** i in $[1, 2^{\hat{N}}]$:
8:	randomly generate solution $\mathbf{o}_i$
9:	**if** constraints (11-13) are satisfied:
10:	**if** the objective function result $< p0$:
11:	Set the result to $p0$.
12:	**else:**
13:	Continue
14:	**end if**
15:	**else:**
16:	Continue
17:	**end if**
18:	**end for**
19:	**end if**
20:	*Ouput*: $p0$ and the corresponding solution.

5   Proposed Monte Carlo Based Algorithm

In this section, we firstly show that the problem defined in Sect. 4 is a NP-hard non-convex problem, then a Monte Carlo heuristic algorithm is proposed to solve the problem.

For the problem defined in Eq. (3), we have the following Theorem 1.

Theorem 1. *The problem defined in (3) is NP-hard.*

For this theorem, we do not give detailed proof. Instead, we give the explanation on how to proof it. It is noticed that the problem defined in (3) can be reduced as a classic mixed integer programming problem. A mixed integer programming problem has already been identified as NP-hard. Therefore, the problem in (3) is NP-hard.

Furthermore, it is obvious that objective function in (3) is non-linear and non-convex. When the number of Bestic users N is small, the enumeration method can be applied to solve this problem. The optimal result can be obtained by the enumeration method. However, the time complexity of enumeration method is rather high when there are a large number of Bestic users.

We propose a enumeration Monte Carlo heuristic (EMCH) algorithm to get results. The main idea of the EMCH algorithm is as follows. When the number of Bestic users is less than a threshold, $\hat{N}$, the enumeration method is utilized, in which all the possible solutions are evaluated to get the one that optimize the objective function. When the number of Bestic users is more than $\hat{N}$. Instead of enumeration method that enumerate to get the result, only a part of possible solutions are sampled randomly, to get the solution that minimizes the value of objective function.

The proposed algorithm is shown in Algorithm 1.

6   Numerical Results

In this section, the performances of our *proposed EMCH* algorithm are evaluated by comparing it with the case of Bestic local computing by all users (*BLCA*) and the case of cloud computing by all users (*CCA*).

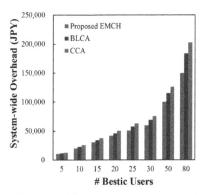
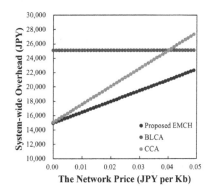

(a) System-wide overhead comparison among proposed EMCH, BLCA and CCA.

(b) System-wide overhead changes with the network price.

Fig. 2. Simulation results.

The computation task is the nutrition data analysis from pictures. The input data size β_n is assumed as 25000 Kb, and the number of CPU cycle γ_n is 5000 Megacycle. While the Bestic computation power s_n^l is 500 MHz, the cloud computation power s_n^c is 10000 MHz. The energy consumption per CPU cycle ε_n is 0.5 J. Users preference for time, energy and monetary cost σ_n^t, σ_n^e, σ_n^m are all set to 1, which means that users pay equal attention to all of these factors. If there is no other illustration, the network price r_n is assumed as 5000 Kb/s, and the cloud computing price p^c is 0.0582 yen per second. Please note that this cloud computing price is made from Amazon EC2 cloud computing price plans [2].

Figure 2(a) shows the system-wide overhead changes with the number of Bestic users. The more the Bestic users, the higher the system-wide overhead. Compared with the overhead of *BLCA* and *CCA*, the overhead of *proposed EMCH* is lowest for all different number of users.

Figure 2(b) shows the system-wide overhead changes with the network price. While both the system-wide overhead of *proposed EMCH* and *CCA* are increased with network price, that of *BLCA* keeps unchanged. And the system-wide overhead of *proposed EMCH* is lower than that of *CCA*.

7 Conclusions

In this paper, we proposed a Monte Carlo algorithm based heuristic computation algorithm, which has the advantage of enumeration algorithm and Monte Carlo algorithm, to minimize the total overhead of all the Bestic after we showed that the target optimization problem is NP-hard in a theorem. Numeric results showed that the proposed EMCH algorithm is effective in terms of system-wide overhead. In the future, we will consider the privacy and security problem of the nutrition data (such that in [7]) since these data is individual user's private data and protection is required.

Acknowledgements. This work was carried out as a part of the SICORP under the responsibility of the Japan Science and Technology Agency (JST) and was supported in part by JSPS KAKENHI JP17H03162.

References

1. Amazon Web Services Inc: Amazon AWS Cloud computing. https://aws.amazon.com. Accessed June 2018
2. Amazon Web Services Inc: Amazon EC2 Pricing. https://aws.amazon.com/ec2/pricing/. Accessed June 2018
3. Barbarossa, S., Sardellitti, S., Lorenzo, P.D.: Joint allocation of computation and communication resources in multiuser mobile cloud computing. In: 2013 IEEE 14th Workshop on Signal Processing Advances in Wireless Communications (SPAWC 2013), pp. 26–30, June 2013
4. Barbera, M.V., Kosta, S., Mei, A., Stefa, J.: To offload or not to offload? The bandwidth and energy costs of mobile cloud computing. In: 2013 Proceedings IEEE International Conference on Computer Communications (INFOCOM 2013), pp. 1285–1293, April 2013
5. Chen, X., Jiao, L., Li, W., Fu, X.: Efficient multi-user computation offloading for mobile-edge cloud computing. IEEE/ACM Trans. Netw. **24**(5), 2795–2808 (2016)
6. Deshmukh, S., Shah, R.: Computation offloading frameworks in mobile cloud computing: a survey. In: 2016 IEEE International Conference on Current Trends in Advanced Computing (ICCTAC), pp. 1–5, March 2016
7. Gai, K., Choo, K.R., Qiu, M., Zhu, L.: Privacy-preserving content-oriented wireless communication in Internet-of-Things. IEEE Internet Things J. **5**(4), 3059–3067 (2018)
8. Gai, K., Qiu, M., Zhao, H.: Energy-aware task assignment for mobile cyber-enabled applications in heterogeneous cloud computing. J. Parallel Distrib. Comput. **111**, 126–135 (2018)
9. Gai, K., Qiu, M., Zhao, H., Tao, L., Zong, Z.: Dynamic energy-aware cloudlet-based mobile cloud computing model for green computing. J. Netw. Comput. Appl. **59**, 46–54 (2016)
10. Garey, M.R., Johnson, D.S.: Computers and Intractability; A Guide to the Theory of NP-Completeness. W. H. Freeman & Co., New York (1990)
11. Huang, D., Wang, P., Niyato, D.: A dynamic offloading algorithm for mobile computing. IEEE Trans. Wirel. Commun. **11**(6), 1991–1995 (2012)

12. Lindborg, A.L., Solis, J., Saijo, M., Takeda, Y., Zhang, C.: Design approach of a robotic assistive eating device with a multi-grip and camera for frail elderly's independent life. In: ICRA 2017 Workshop on Advances and Challenges on the Development, Testing and Assessment of Assistive and Rehabilitation Robots: Experiences from Engineering and Human Science Research, vol. 1, p. 21 (2017)
13. METI of Japan: Study meeting report on providing long-term care service according to future care demand (2016). (in Japanese). https://goo.gl/ohNAE9. Accessed June 2018
14. Solis, J., Lindborg, A.L., Saijo, M., Takeda, Y., Zhang, C., Takeda, R.: Japan-Sweden academia-industry international collaboration: challenges in developing a robotic assistive eating device for frail elderly's independent life. In: 2017 Joint Workshop on Social Interaction and Multimodal Expression for Socially Intelligent Robots and the Workshop on the Barriers of Social Robotics Take-up by Society, WS-SIME+ Barriers of Social Robotics 2017, Lisbon, Portugal, August 2017, vol. 2959, pp. 61–65 (2017)
15. Zhang, C., Gu, B., Yamori, K., Xu, S., Tanaka, Y.: Oligopoly competition in time-dependent pricing for improving revenue of network service providers with complete and incomplete information. IEICE Trans. Commun. **E98–B**(1), 30–32 (2015)
16. Zhang, J., Xia, W., Yan, F., Shen, L.: Joint computation offloading and resource allocation optimization in heterogeneous networks with mobile edge computing. IEEE Access **6**, 19324–19337 (2018)

Collective Behavior Aware Collaborative Caching for Mobile Edge Computing

Hao Jiang[1], Hehe Huang[1], Ying Jiang[2], Yuan Wang[1], Yuanyuan Zeng[1(✉)], and Chen Zhou[3]

[1] School of Electronic Information, Wuhan University, Wuhan, China
{jh,hhhuang,wangyuan_ashiny,zengyy}@whu.edu.cn
[2] School of Data and Computer Science, Sun Yat-Sen University, Guangzhou, China
jiangy32@mail.sysu.edu.cn
[3] China Ship Development and Design Center, Wuhan, China
zhouchen@whu.edu.cn

Abstract. In Mobile Edge Computing (MEC) paradigm, popular and repetitive content can be cached and offloaded from nearby MEC server in order to reduce the backhaul overload. Due to hardware limitation of MEC devices, collaboration among MEC servers can greatly improve the cache performance. In this paper, we propose a Collective Behavior aware Collaborative Caching (CBCC) method. At first, we propose to discover the collective behavior of users by using content-location similarity network fusion algorithm. our analysis is based on real dataset of usage detail records and explore the heterogeneity and predictability of collective behavior during content access. Based on it, we propose a collaborative relationship model that relies on the collective behavior. Then, the collaborative caching placement is formulated by solving a multi-objective optimization problem. Our simulations are based on the real dataset from cellular systems. The numerical results show that the proposed method achieves performance gains in terms of both hit rate and transmission cost.

Keywords: Collaborative caching · Collective behavior · 5G · MEC

1 Introduction

Currently, cellular networks are under great pressure due to the exponential growth of wireless data traffic. A recent report by Cisco projects that mobile data traffic will reach 49.0 exabytes per month by 2021 [4]. This traffic growth is leading to greater pressure on the transmission link especially. Meanwhile, MEC

This work was supported in part by the National Natural Science Foundation of China under Grant 61702387, in part by the National Key Research and Development Program under Grant 2017YFB0504103 and Grant 2017YFC0503801, in part by the Development Program of China (863 Program) under Grant 2014AA01A707, and in part by the Natural Science Foundation of Hubei Province of China under Grant 2017CFB302.

© Springer Nature Switzerland AG 2018
M. Qiu (Ed.): SmartCom 2018, LNCS 11344, pp. 172–181, 2018.
https://doi.org/10.1007/978-3-030-05755-8_18

has become a promising technology to solve this problem by providing caching and computational capabilities on the edge of networks.

In this paper, we firstly analyze a usage detail records (UDR) data set, which is a real data set and contains the content and location information of users' access records. We then explore the heterogeneity and predictability of users' individual behavior and collective behaviour. We focus on the predictability of users' access behavior and find that collective behaviour is more helpful than individual behavior. Additionally, the combination of content and location features can also improve the predictability to a certain degree. Despite the heterogeneity among users, we find that a user group is more valuable for prediction than an individual. Motivated by these results, we propose a CBCC method for fifth-generation (5G) cellular networks. The main idea of the CBCC is the utilization of collective behavior in the design of the collaborative relationship and the caching placement. In particular, the motivation is to maximize the hit rate and minimize the transmission cost.

2   Related Work

Mobile edge computing (MEC) makes it possible to deploy and provide service locally, which is close to the users, by enabling the computation and caching capability at radio access networks (RAN) [8]. Thus, MEC can improve the quality of experience (QoE) by reducing the latency and decrease the transmission cost.

Caching contents on the edge of the network is regarded as a solution to alleviate the pressure of network transmission [12]. The state-of-the-art RRH caching methods can be classified into collaborative caching methods and non-collaborative caching methods. In non-collaborative caching, RRHs with a certain amount of cache contents respond to the requests of users individually. When an RRH is requested for content not in its local cache, the RRH asks the Internet for a copy.

In general, there are two subcategories of collaborative caching: one is based on the location feature and the other is based on the content feature. The basis of the first subcategory is that the request of a user is received by all base stations in a neighborhood, and then one or a certain number of base stations is responsible for the service. For example, in [3], the authors use a hexagonal grid with inter-cluster center distance so that nearby small base stations (SBSs) are grouped into disjoint clusters and can provide service together.

The basis of the second subcategory is that the request for specific content (regardless of which user it is received from) can be responded to by all the RRHs that have already cached this content. For example, [1,11] both adopt the idea. By contrast, in [1], several base stations may cache a certain part of the same content, and the user has to collect the complete content from a series of base stations. In [11], users can choose from all the base stations that cache the content they need according to the channel condition.

3   Analysis of User Behavior

We now analyze a UDR data set to explore some characteristics. Human behavior has been long analyzed, and the long-tail distribution and power-law distribution of user behavior have been verified from different perspectives, namely, visited locations and visit times. In this section, we attempt to further explore access behavior.

We conduct the analysis with a data set generated in Jinhua, China. The data span 23 days and mainly include detailed user network access information.

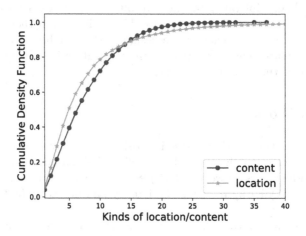

Fig. 1. The diversity of users' access behavior in terms of location and content features.

First, we obtain an overview of the diversity of users with respect to the content and location features. The diversity of users is defined as the number of unique contents or locations they have visited. As shown in Fig. 1, users' access behavior has a limited range of location and content features.

After confirming users' behavior are limited, we come to the exact benefit of using user groups instead of individuals. We use the normalized entropy to measure the gap between these two strategies. Figure 2 shows the CDF of the normalized entropy of individual users and user groups, Fig. 2(a) shows the normalized entropy of the content feature, and Fig. 2(b) shows the normalized entropy of the location feature.

According to the above analysis, several factors can contribute to the description and prediction of user behavior. First, as many studies have demonstrated, the locations and contents visited by a user are limited. Thus, good performance can be achieved with limited resources. Second, users show great diversity of group behavior according to their preferences. Based on these phenomena, we propose a CBCC method in which both the location and content features are considered to form a user similarity matrix, and user groups are divided according to the similarity matrix. Finally, the user groups are used to determine the

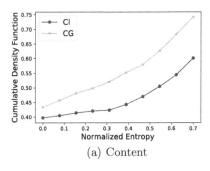 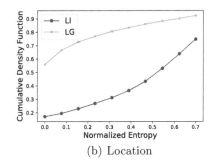

(a) Content   (b) Location

Fig. 2. The normalized entropy of the content and location features for user groups and individual users. (a) The normalized entropy of the content feature in user groups (CG) and individual users (CI). (b) The normalized entropy of the location feature in user groups (LG) and individual users (LI).

collaborative relationships among RRHs, and the caching is arranged according to the relationship.

4   System Model and Problem Formulation

4.1   System Model

As shown in Fig. 3, we discuss the system based on the infrastructure in [10]. In this paper, we assume that there are M contents in the Internet, denoted as $C = \{C_1, C_2, ..., C_M\}$ with sizes $S = \{S_1, S_2, ..., S_M\}$. We consider a set of RRHs $B = \{B_1, B_2, ..., B_N\}$, where B_i refers to the i-th RRH. Each RRH is equipped with limited local caching capacity, and the size of the local caches are $V = \{V_1, V_2, ..., V_N\}$. The cache matrix is formed in (1).

$$\begin{bmatrix} Q_{11} & \cdots & Q_{1M} \\ \vdots & \ddots & \vdots \\ Q_{N1} & \cdots & Q_{NM} \end{bmatrix}, \tag{1}$$

where $Q_{ij} = 1$ indicates the existence of C_j in the local cache of B_i, and $Q_{ij} = 0$ indicates that C_j is not cached on B_i.

In this paper, we consider a collaborative method, in which T disjoint RRH groups are formed after several procedures, namely, $\phi = \{\phi_1, \phi_2, ..., \phi_T\}$, and each group consists of a certain number of RRHs. The request matrix is formed in (2).

$$\begin{bmatrix} P_{11} & \cdots & P_{1M} \\ \vdots & \ddots & \vdots \\ P_{N1} & \cdots & P_{NM} \end{bmatrix}, \tag{2}$$

where P_{ij} refers to the probability that users request B_i for C_j.

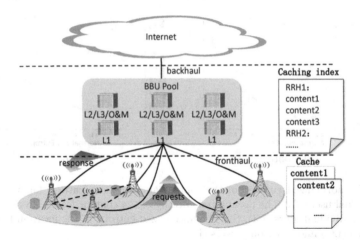

Fig. 3. The system infrastructure. The whole system consists of three layers. The bottom layer of the system is RRH layer, which is nearest to users, all of these RRH have caching capability. Requests are sent to different RRHs based on the users' locations. The second layer is the BBU pool layer. The BBU pool layer has computational capability for resource scheduling. The top layer is Internet, which is responsible for the core business, e.g., obtaining all the content.

When a request is received by an RRH (local RRH), the RRH first checks its local cache for the content. If the content exists in its local cache, it is sent directly to the user. Otherwise, the BBU pool receives a request and searches the caching index for a copy. Then, a copy is obtained from the collaborative RRH or the Internet.

4.2 Problem Formulation

Generally, we are interested in a service with both better quality and lower cost. Therefore, we define the problem as a multi-objective optimization problem. One of the objectives is the hit rate of the requests, and the other is the transmission cost. We define the hit rate as the percentage of requests that can be responded to by the RRHs, whether a local RRH or a collaborative RRH. The hit rate can be formulated as in (3).

$$Hit\left(Q\right) = \sum_{i=1}^{N}\sum_{j=1}^{M}(P_{ij}\cdot Q_{ij} + P_{ij}\cdot(1 - Q_{ij})\cdot$$

$$\left(1 - \prod_{k\in\phi^i, k\neq i}(1 - Q_{kj})\right)) \tag{3}$$

$$\text{s.t.} \sum_{j=1}^{M}Q_{ij}S_j \leq V_i, i \in [1, N],$$

where $\left(1 - \prod_{k\in\phi_i,k\neq i}(1 - Q_{kj})\right)$ is the indicator function, which means C_j is in the local cache of one of the RRHs in ϕ^i, and ϕ^i is the RRHs that are in the same group as B_i. $P_{ij} \cdot Q_{ij}$ indicates that the request for C_j on B_i can be responded to by B_i, and $P_{ij}\cdot(1 - Q_{ij})\cdot\left(1 - \prod_{k\in\phi^i,k\neq i}(1 - Q_{kj})\right)$ indicates that the request for C_j on B_i is responded to by an RRH in ϕ^i rather than B_i. This constraint represents the cache capacity constraint of RRHs.

We define the transmission cost of the requests in two separate parts, one is the transmission cost among collaborative RRHs, namely, $Cost_{RRH}$, and the other is the transmission cost of obtaining contents from the Internet, namely, $Cost_{Inter}$. We assume that $Cost_{Inter} = 1$ and $Cost_{RRH} = \gamma$, where $0 < \gamma \leq 1$. Thus, the total transmission cost can be calculated as in (4).

$$
\begin{aligned}
Cost\,(Q) = \sum_{i=1}^{N}\sum_{j=1}^{M} P_{ij} \cdot \prod_{k\in\phi^i}(1 - Q_{kj}) + \\
P_{ij} \cdot (1 - Q_{ij}) \cdot \left(1 - \prod_{k\in\phi^i,k\neq i}(1 - Q_{kj})\right) \cdot \gamma
\end{aligned}
\tag{4}
$$

where first item represents the total cost of obtaining content from the Internet and second item represents the total cost of obtaining content from collaborative RRHs.

5 Collective Behavior Aware Collaborative Caching

5.1 Cooperative Caching Placement

In this paper, we will design the collaborative relationship among the RRHs based on user groups rather than individuals. The user groups are determined according to the fused similarity network. We denote user groups as $\varphi = \{\varphi_1, \varphi_2, ..., \varphi_T\}$. Generally, RRHs that serve the same group should be considered to be collaborative RRHs.

As mentioned before, the caching placement is obtained by solving the optimization problem in (5).

$$
\begin{aligned}
&\underset{Q}{\operatorname{argmax}} \quad Hit\,(Q) \\
&\underset{Q}{\operatorname{argmin}} \quad Cost\,(Q) \\
&\text{s.t.} \quad \sum_{j=1}^{M} Q_{ij}S_j \leq V_i, \quad i \in [1, N], \\
&\qquad\quad Q_{ij} \in [0, 1].
\end{aligned}
\tag{5}
$$

In this paper, we analyze (5) according to game theory, we try to prove the existence of Nash equilibria (NE). First, we define a normal-form game as a tuple (N, A, u) according to [6], where

- N is a finite set of n players, indexed by i;
- $A = (A_1, ..., A_n)$, where A_i is a finite set of actions available to player i. Each vector $a = (a_1, ..., a_n) \in A$ is called an action profile;
- $u = (u_1, ..., u_n)$, where u_i is a payoff function for player i.

N refers to the set of players that includes the hit rate and transmission cost, A refers to the caching actions, and u refers to the hit rate or transmission cost defined in (5). Let $(N, (A_1, ..., A_n), u)$ be a normal form game; then, the set of mixed strategies for player i is $S_i = \prod(A_i)$. Based on Brouwer's fixed point theorem, we design the function $f : S \to S$ by $f(s) = s'$ in (6) according to [6].

$$s_i'(a_i) = \frac{s_i(a_i) + \varphi_{i,a_i}(s)}{\sum_{b_i \in A_i} s_i(b_i) + \varphi_{i,b_i}(s)} \qquad (6)$$

where φ is defined in (7).

$$\varphi_{i,a_i}(s) = \max\{0, u_i(a_i, s_{-i}) - u_i(s)\}. \qquad (7)$$

Intuitively, this function maps a strategy profile s to a new strategy profile s' in which each player's actions that are better responses to s receive increased probability mass. The function f is continuous since each φ_{i,a_i} is continuous because S is convex and compact and f must have at least one fixed point. Now, we prove that the fixed point must be a NE.

Consider an arbitrary fixed point s. We define a_i' as a point in the support of s, for which $u_{i,a_i'}(s) \leq u_i(s)$, namely, we have $\varphi_{i,a_i'}(s) = 0$. Since s is a fixed point of f, there must be $s_i'(a_i') = s_i(a_i')$. According to (6), the denominator must be 1, namely, for any $i \in N$ and $b_i \in A_i$, $\varphi_{i,b_i}(s)$ must equal 0. From the definition of φ, this can only occur when no improvement can be obtained regardless of the changes made on the pure strategy. Therefore, s is a NE and we can conclude that the problem in (5) must have at least one NE. We use NSGA-II [5] to obtain the Pareto optimal set and then make a selection from the set based on the NE according to [9]. Finally, a simple rounding strategy is used to generate the final solution of the caching placement.

6   Numerical Result

6.1   Description of Dataset

We use the UDR data set introduced in Sect. 3 to evaluate the proposed algorithm. We select the 4000, 6000, and 8000 users that generate the most records as the data sets for the experiments.

We compare CBCC with five reference algorithms, starting with the CMP. Previous studies have proved that CMP outperforms most of the non-collaborative caching methods [7,13]. To demonstrate the advantages of CBCC from different perspectives, we adopt 3 algorithms, namely, cooperative caching based on location (CCBL), cooperative caching based on content (CCBC), and cooperative caching based on RRH (CCBR). CCBR uses the location and content features of the RRHs instead of those of users. The last reference algorithm is ratio collaborative caching (RCC), which combines the non-collaborative caching method in [2] with the collaborative relationship designed by CBCC. In RCC, the contents to be cached are selected randomly, but contents with higher preference have higher probability of being cached.

6.2   Performance Evaluation of CBCC

For simplicity, we assume that each content is the same size and that each RRH has the same cache size. To evaluate our method, we compare the transmission cost and hit rate of CBCC against those of the previously mentioned methods. Figure 4 plots the total hit rate and local hit rate under all six methods for different numbers of users (4000, 6000, and 8000) in the system.

As shown in the figure, the CBCC has the highest total hit rate and local hit rate, regardless of the number of users. The total hit rate of RCC is almost as high as that of CBCC; however, the local hit rate performance of RCC decreases substantially and becomes the worst caching method.

CMP, in which no collaborative relationships are adopted, shows the worst performance. All the hit rates decrease slightly as the number of users increases from 4000 to 8000. One possible reason is that the content diversity increases along with the number of users. Thus, the popularity skew decreases, and the prediction becomes increasingly difficult.

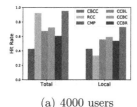   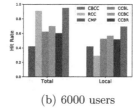   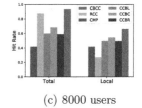

      (a) 4000 users   (b) 6000 users   (c) 8000 users

Fig. 4. The total hit rates and local hit rates for 4000, 6000 and 8000 users. (a) The total hit rates and local hit rates for 4000 users. (b) The total hit rates and local hit rates for 6000 users. (c) The total hit rates and local hit rates for 8000 users.

The transmission cost is shown in Fig. 5. When considering the transmission cost, CBCC still outperforms the other methods. With no collaborative relationship, CMP obtains a stable cost that is not influenced by γ. While the

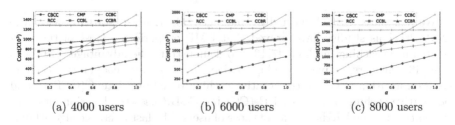

(a) 4000 users   (b) 6000 users   (c) 8000 users

Fig. 5. The transmission cost for 4000, 6000 and 8000 users. (a) The transmission cost for 4000 users. (b) The transmission cost for 6000 users. (c) The transmission cost for 8000 users.

performances of CCBL, CCBC and CCBR are nearly stable at a high cost with different γ, the curve of the RCC shows a steep gradient.

The cache size can affect the result. In Fig. 6, we analyze the hit rate and cost for different cache sizes, with the number of users fixed at 4000 and γ fixed at 0.4. The cache size is selected uniformly from the discrete set $\{3, 4, ..., 15\}$.

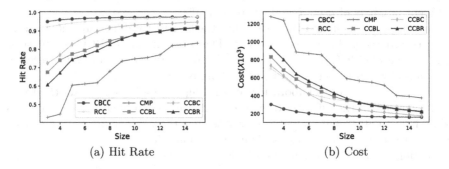

(a) Hit Rate   (b) Cost

Fig. 6. The hit rate and transmission cost versus cache size. The cache size is varied within the range [3,15]. (a) The hit rate versus cache size. (b) The transmission cost versus cache size.

According to the above results, CBCC achieve performance gains in both hit rate and transmission cost due to the proper design and utilization of the collaborative relationships.

7   Conclusion

The popular and repetitive content requests for cellular network lead to increasingly regorous transmission pressure, and numerous caching methods based on MEC have been proposed to alleviate the pressure. In this paper, we propose a collaborative caching method based on user collective behavior, which is motivated by the concept of the sharing economy where resources are reused by users with similar preferences. On the basis of a thorough analysis of real data set from cellular systems, we find that most user's access contents and locations are within a limited range. Based on these results, we design a collaborative caching method. We propose the caching method by solving a multi-objective optimization problem, in which both the hit rate and the transmission cost are considered. The multi-objective optimization problem is analyzed and solved according to game theory. The performance gain of the proposed caching method is validated with a large data set generated from real networks and is compared with several representative caching methods. The results show that our method is outperforms the other methods in terms of both hit rate and transmission cost. We also show that the performance of our method is stable over time and regardless of the cache size.

References

1. Altman, E., Avrachenkov, K., Goseling, J.: Coding for caches in the plane. arXiv preprint arXiv:1309.0604 (2013)
2. Blaszczyszyn, B., Giovanidis, A.: Optimal geographic caching in cellular networks. In: 2015 IEEE International Conference on Communications (ICC), pp. 3358–3363. IEEE (2015)
3. Chen, Z., Lee, J., Quek, T.Q., Kountouris, M.: Cooperative caching and transmission design in cluster-centric small cell networks. IEEE Trans. Wirel. Commun. **16**(5), 3401–3415 (2017)
4. Cisco: Cisco visual networking index: Global mobile data traffic forecast update, 2016–2021 white paper (2016). http://www.cisco.com/c/en/us/solutions/collateral/service-provider/visual-networking-index-vni/mobile-white-paper-c11-520862.html
5. Deb, K.: A fast elitist multi-objective genetic algorithm: NSGA-ii. IEEE Trans. Evolut. Comput. **6**(2), 182–197 (2000)
6. Jiang, A.X., Leyton-Brown, K.: A tutorial on the proof of the existence of nash equilibria. University of British Columbia Technical report TR-2007-25 (2009)
7. Liu, D., Yang, C.: Energy efficiency of downlink networks with caching at base stations. IEEE J. Sel. Areas Commun. **34**(4), 907–922 (2016)
8. Liu, J., Ahmed, E., Shiraz, M., Gani, A., Buyya, R., Qureshi, A.: Application partitioning algorithms in mobile cloud computing: taxonomy, review and future directions. J. Netw. Comput. Appl. **48**(C), 99–117 (2015)
9. Miyamoto, T., Noguchi, S., Yamashita, H.: Selection of an optimal solution for multiobjective electromagnetic apparatus design based on game theory. IEEE Trans. Magn. **44**(6), 1026–1029 (2008)
10. Peng, M., Yan, S., Zhang, K., Wang, C.: Fog-computing-based radio access networks: issues and challenges. IEEE Netw. **30**(4), 46–53 (2016)
11. Peng, X., Shen, J.C., Zhang, J., Letaief, K.B.: Backhaul-aware caching placement for wireless networks. In: 2015 IEEE Global Communications Conference (GLOBECOM), pp. 1–6. IEEE (2015)
12. Xu, X., Liu, J., Tao, X.: Mobile edge computing enhanced adaptive bitrate video delivery with joint cache and radio resource allocation. IEEE Access **5**(99), 16406–16415 (2017)
13. Yang, C., Yao, Y., Chen, Z., Xia, B.: Analysis on cache-enabled wireless heterogeneous networks. IEEE Trans. Wireless Commun. **15**(1), 131–145 (2016)

Implementation of Distributed Multi-Agent Scheduling Algorithm Based on Pi-calculus

Bairun Li, Hui Kang, and Fang Mei[✉]

JiLin University, ChangChun 130012, China
meifang@jlu.edu.cn

Abstract. Currently, efficient use of distributed resources is a research hotspot. Considering that the structure of a distributed communication system is prone to change and many distributed algorithms are still based on the serial underlying model, this paper proposes a distributed multi-agent model based on Pi-calculus. This model takes advantage of Pi-calculus parallel computing, including using channels to transfer information. Besides this, the model combines multi-agent technology to further improve parallelism, enabling distributed resources to be used more efficiently. This paper uses the classic algorithm of heterogeneous scheduling in distributed environments, the heterogeneous earliest finish time (HEFT) algorithm as an example to apply the model by creating different topologies of the task scheduling graph. And then implement the model with Nomadic Pict using channels to transmit information and assigning tasks to multiple agents. We can prove that the distributed multi-agent model based on Pi-calculus can make use of distributed resources more efficiently compared with traditional C++ language combined with multithreading and Socket communication mechanisms assigning tasks to multiple clients.

Keywords: Distributed · Task scheduling · Pi-calculus · Multi-Agent HEFT

1 Introduction

The efficient use of distributed resources is a research hotspot that attracts much attention today. The task scheduling problem is a classical problem in the field of distributed computing. The task scheduling has many applications, including analyzing calculated mass data and remote control of the machine. Distributed computing systems can be divided into two types: isomorphic distributed computing systems and heterogeneous distributed computing systems, depending on the types of computers and the computer networks they use. In a heterogeneous distributed computing system, the hardware and software of each computer, and

---

Supported by CERNET Innovation Protect(NGII20170506).

M. Qiu (Ed.): SmartCom 2018, LNCS 11344, pp. 182–195, 2018.
https://doi.org/10.1007/978-3-030-05755-8_19

the communication protocols between the computer network hardware or networks that make up the system are different. With the development of computer systems and networks, Isomorphism is relative, and heterogeneity is absolute [1]. Efficient task scheduling is the key to achieving high performance computing in heterogeneous systems. The task scheduling problem was demonstrated to be NP-complete [2], and it has been extensively studied by domestic and foreign research institutions due to its criticality.

Pi-calculus [3] was developed by Robin Milner, a famous British scientist and Turing Award winner in 1991. It is a calculation model that describes and analyzes concurrent systems for formal analysis and description of system models in various domains. Pi-calculus extends the communication system calculus and allows the name of the channel to be transferred in the communication, enabling Pi-calculus to describe the dynamic changes in communication topology. So Pi-calculus has powerful expressive capabilities, and at the same time it inherits the concise and elegant semantic theory of communication system calculus, that is bisimulation. It is best suited to describe parallel processing algorithms.

The task scheduling environment is distributed. At present, a large number of model assumptions and algorithms have been proposed for DAG task scheduling of heterogeneous distributed computing systems. The DAG task scheduling model and HEFT algorithm of heterogeneous distributed computing systems proposed by H. Topcuoglu in 2002 are one of the best-known models and algorithms [4], and many scholars have improved and optimized them later. However, most of the existing studies are based on the serial underlying model. Pi-calculus is a parallel programming model, so it is logical to do parallel computational research with it. Intelligence, agency, learning, cooperation, continuity of agent-oriented technology make agent quite suitable for the implementation of distributed task scheduling. Therefore, the combination of the two will further enhance its parallelism. The advanced concurrent programming language, Nomadic Pict [5], not only implements the core of Pi-calculus but adds agent-related functions, which are most rational for implementing the model. Experiments on task scheduling graphs with different topological structures show that the HEFT algorithm implemented by distributed multi-agent model based on Pi-calculus is more efficient than the traditional C++ language combined with multithreading and Socket communication mechanisms assigning tasks to multiple clients.

2   Related Information

2.1   Agent

Agent refers to a computing entity [6] that resides in a certain environment, can continue to function autonomously, and has characteristics such as residency, reactivity, sociality and initiative. It is also a software entity that performs a specific task for users, has a degree of intelligence to allow autonomous execution of part of the task and interacts with the environment in a suitable way. Because the ability of a single agent to solve the problem is limited, many problems often require the cooperation of multiple agents to solve the problem. Then the MAS (Multi-Agent System) is created. MAS is a loosely coupled system composed of multiple agents. They achieve cooperation and coordination between agents along some form of communication or indirect communication mechanism, and thus accomplishing goals together [7].

2.2 HEFT Algorithms

The task scheduling model is generally expressed by using a DAG (directed acyclic graph) [8]. The general DAG is represented by G(T, E) as shown in Fig. 1. T is a set of tasks, which is represented by $T = \{t_i | i \in [1, n]\}$, where n is the number of tasks; E is a set of directed edges with weights, which is represented by $E = \{e_{ij} | e_{ij} < t_i, t_j >, e_{ij} \in T \times T\}$. $e_{ij} \in E$ is the dependency relationship between task t_i and t_j, and t_j must be executed after t_i is completed. At this time, t_i is a predecessor task of t_j and t_j is a successor task of t_i. The ingress task does not have a predecessor task and the egress task does not have a successor task. If there are multiple ingress tasks, then build a virtual ingress task, the communication overhead between it and each ingress task is zero; if there are multiple egress tasks, the communication overhead between it and each egress task is zero. The HEFT algorithm is one of the most famous heterogeneous scheduling models and algorithms. The algorithm is divided into two main steps:

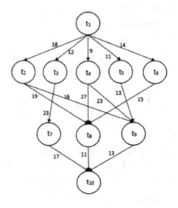

Fig. 1. Channel graph between the processes of the first stage

1. Calculate the value of the upward rank of each task [2], and then determine the task priority level based on the value of the arrival rank. The calculation method of the uprank value is shown in formula (1).

$$uprank\,(n_i) = \overline{w_l} + \max_{n_j \in succ(n_i)} (\overline{c_{l,j}} + uprank\,(n_j)) \qquad (1)$$

Where $succ(n_i)$ is the direct successor to task node n_i, $\overline{c_{l,j}}$ is the average communication time of edge $E_{i,j}$, and $\overline{w_l}$ is the average calculation time of task node n_i.

2. The choice of processor: let each task choose the processor that allows the task to be completed the earliest. Based on the principle of insertion, that is to say, consider the free time between tasks in all processors. If there are constraints in the free segments that satisfy the constraints between the tasks and are sufficient for the current task to execute, then you can choose the processor that can finish the current task as early as possible and insert into the free segment. The satisfaction constraint here means that the current task start in the processor free segment is greater than or equal to the ready_time of the task on the processor. The calculation of ready_time is shown in formula (2).

$$\text{ready}_{time(n_i,p_j)} = \max_{n_j \in pred(n_i)} \{fin(n_j) + c(p(n_j),pj)\} \tag{2}$$

Where $pred(n_i)$ denotes the immediate precursor set of node n_i, $fin(n_j)$ denotes the completion time of node n_j, $p(n_j)$ denotes the processor where node n_j is located, and $c(p_x,p_y)$ represents the communication time between processor p_x and processor p_y.

3   Multi-Agent Distributed HEFT Algorithm Modeling and Implementation

3.1   Modeling Related Data Structures

The spreadsheet programming of Pi-calculus is used in the modeling process [9].

Definition 1. *The table constant Nil, the constructor Cons(V,L), and n elements of the table are defined as follows:*

$$Nil \overset{def}{=} (k).k(nc).\overline{n}$$

$$Cons(V,L) \overset{def}{=} (k).new\ vl(Node < kvl > |V < v > |L < l >)$$

Where:

$$Node(kvl) \overset{def}{=} k(nc).\overline{c} < vl >$$

$$[V_1, \cdots, V_n] \overset{def}{=} Cons(V_1, Cons(\cdots Cons(V_n, Nil) \cdots))$$

Definition 2. *Operation used to read the element at position k in table L:*

$$L < k > \overset{def}{=} \overline{k} < nc > .c(vl).P | Cons(V,L) < k >$$

Where:
v: Interface of element interaction information
l: Interface of the tail table interaction information

3.2   Task Node Layering

In order to improve the use of agents efficiently, this paper will layer the task nodes [10]. Specify the ingress node's task level as 0, that means level = 0. Traverse the DAG task graph from top to bottom, and use the maximum number of communication edges from the task node to the ingress node as the level value of the task node, and thus the level value of the task node vi equals to the maximum level value of all its predecessors plus 1. The formula is shown in formula (3).

$$level(vi) = Max(level(vj)) + 1, vj \in pred(vi) \tag{3}$$

3.3   Modeling

This paper combines multi-agent technology based on Pi-calculus to model the HEFT algorithm. The core idea of the model is to separate the control part and the calculation part of the algorithm into controlling agent and computation agent [11], and thus deploy them on different physical machines [12]; each process can send and receive messages in parallel through channels.

The first stage needs to calculate the rank value of each task node.

$$O = readBasicData(nname, pname).(initAllList)(\overline{os}$$
$$< nodeList, rankList, levelList > |S)$$

Process O is responsible for reading the basic data from the node file and the processor file, and constitutes a corresponding task schedule chart linked list and processor linked list.

$$S = createAgents(cagent, agent1, agent2, ..., agentn).(migrate($$
$$agent1, agent2, ..., agentn)|os < nodel, rankl, levelList > .$$
$$calculateLevelList(nodel, levelList).(\overline{SA_i} < nodel, rankl, levelList >$$
$$|\overline{sp} < nodel, rankl, levelList > |P))$$

The S process is a startup process. The first step is to create all agents including the controlling agent and each computing agent. The controlling agent starts each computing agent and allows each computing agent to migrate to specified processor location. At the same time, each node is stratified according to the node linked list received from os channel and the linked list information is sent to the computing agent. The task schedule diagram linked list named nodel, rank value list named rankl, and level node list named levelList are sent to process P along the channel sp.

$$P = (sp(nodel, rankl, levelList) + qp(nodel, tempRankl,$$
$$levelList).updateRankl(rankl, tempRankl)).(if(levelList == nil)$$
$$then (sort(rankl).\overline{step2} < rankl >) else \overline{levelList} < nc > .c(vl).$$
$$pq < rankl, levelList, l, v > |Q|Cons(V, L) < levelList >)$$

Process P receives the linked list information from the channel sp, and can also receive the linked list of rank values of the calculated one layer of nodes returned by the Q process described later along the qp channel and update the total rank value list. Then they all need to pass the following judgment: If each layer of linked list is processed and the rank value of each node is calculated, all rank values are sorted from the largest to the smallest, then the priority of the task node is obtained. The ordered rank list is sent to the second stage of the algorithm along the channel step2 as an input parameter; otherwise, each time a layer of node list is taken out and sent to process Q.

$$Q = (pq(rankl, levelList', level).match(level).allocateTaskToAgents(Ai)$$
$$\overline{QAi} < rankl, level, sIndex, eIndex > +returnResult(rankl', eIndex).$$
$$updateRankl(rankl, rankl').levelFinish(level, eIndex).(if(true)$$
$$then \ \overline{qp} < nodel, tempRankl, levelList' >))$$

Process Q receives the layer node linked list from the channel pq, assigns the layer node to different computing agents to calculate. The layer label, the layer start node label and the layer end node label are sent to process Ai along QAi channel, or receives the calculated rank linked list and the label of the last node that has been calculated from the channel AiQ, and update the total rank value list, and if the layer node is calculated, information such as the calculated temporary rank value list is sent to process P along the channel qp.

$$Ai = SAi(nodel, rankl, layerList).allocateToAgents(rankl,$$
$$layer, sIndex, eIndex).calulateRank(rankl, layer, sIndex, eIndex).$$
$$\overline{returnResult} < rankl, eIndex >$$

Process Ai receives the task scheduler linked list, layer node list information from channel SAi, and receive relevant information from a certain node list from channel QAi, calculate the rank value of each task node and send the updated temporary rank value list to process Q along the channel AiQ.

Channel graph between the processes of the first stage is shown in Fig. 2:

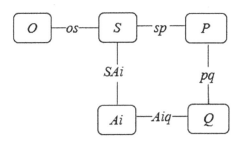

Fig. 2. Channel graph between the processes of the first stage

The second-stage processor needs to select the processor that can complete the current task node at the earliest time based on an insertion-based policy.

$$P = \bar{a} < rankl, prol >$$

Process P will send the ordered rank table rankl and the processor linked list prol along channel a to process Q.

$$Q = a(rankl, prol).(Case\ rankl\ of\ Nil? \Rightarrow END.Else \Rightarrow \overline{rankl} < nc > .c(vl).$$
$$if(searchparent(v, id)\ not\ null) \Rightarrow \bar{b} < v.parent, v.id, prol, timel > else \Rightarrow$$
$$insert(newtimel, v.id).\overline{sendq} < l, prol > |Cons(V, L) < rankl) >$$

Process Q will judge whether the table is empty after receiving the rank table along channel a. If it is empty, it indicates that all task nodes have selected the most suitable processor, and the entire algorithm is completed. Otherwise, a pending node in the rank table is taken out. If there is a parent node, the parent node table structure of the task node needs to be sent to process O for further processing. If there is no father node in current processing node, there is no need to calculate, and each node corresponding to the processor in the processor time linked list timel should be 0. Then the function insert can be called to complete the processor selection, and the current processor has already processed and looped to process the next lower priority task node.

$$O = [b(parentl, id, prol, timel) + c(parentl, id, prol, timel)].\overline{tl} < nc > .c(vl).\bar{h}$$
$$< v, parentl, id, prol, l > |Cons(V, L) < timel >$$

The timel of process O received from channel b takes out one of the nodes and sends out the node along channel h.

$$R = h(tnode, parentl, id, prol, timel).\overline{pl} < nc > .c(vl).\bar{g}$$
$$< v, tnode, id, prol, l, timel > |Cons(V, L) < parentl >$$

Process R receives the linked list information from channel h, takes out an unprocessed node in parent node structure parentl of the current node, then sends it out along the channel g, where rtime is the ready_time of a certain node on a certain processor.

$$S = [g(pnode, rtime, id, prol, parentl, timel) + e(pnode, rtime, id, prol, parentl,$$
$$timel)].\overline{cl} < n1c1 > .c1(v1l1).\overline{v1} < n2c2 > .c2(v2l2).\bar{e} < pnode, rtime, id, l1, v2,$$
$$parentl, timel, Cons(V, L) < prol > |Cons(V, L) < vl >$$

Process S is also a process of taking out a node. The node taken out is the id and one of the timeslices in a certain processor of the processor table structure. The first valuing $\overline{cl} < n1c1 > .c1(v1l1)$ is to fetch the table structure of a certain processor. The second valuing $\overline{v1} < n2c2 > .c2(v2l2)$ of the entry of the table structure is the value that was taken out for the first time, that is to say, in order to retrieve the id of the processor and send the id along channel e.

$$U = [e(pnode, rtime, id, prol, pid, parentl, time, l) + d(pnode, rtime, id, prol,$$
$$parentl, timel, l)].(Case\ l\ of\ Nil? \Rightarrow \bar{e} < pnode, rtime, id, prol, parentl,$$
$$timel > .Else \Rightarrow \bar{l} < nc > .c(vl').\bar{d} < pnode, rtime, id, l', prol, pid, parentl,$$
$$timel, l' > |Cons(V, L) < l >$$

In order to find the scheduling situation of the parent node of the current processing node, process U is created to loop through timeslices of the processor table structure. This step is to take a timeslice and send it to process T along channel d.

$$T = d(pnode, rtime, id, prol, period, pid, parentl, timel, l).id(period.id =$$
$$pnode.id) \Rightarrow (if(period.id = pid) \Rightarrow if((period.id = pid) \Rightarrow (if(rtime.value$$
$$< period.etime) \Rightarrow rtime.value = period.etime)else \Rightarrow if(rtime.value <$$
$$period.etime + pnode.communication) \Rightarrow rtime.value = period.etime+$$
$$pnode.communication).(Case\ timel\ of\ Nil? \Rightarrow insert(timel, id).Else \Rightarrow$$
$$\bar{c} < parentl, id, prol, timel, id >)$$

The previous processes are designed to take nodes primarily for loop processing nodes. Process T receives channel information, where period is a processor timeslice. The first step is to determine whether the timeslice used by the processor is a parent node of the current node. If it is not, then it needs to continue to fetch the next timeslice processing; if it is, then it is determined whether the processor where the father node is located is the same as the processor that currently calculates ready_time. If there is no communication overhead, there is no need to add communication time when calculating ready_time, otherwise it is added. Then determine if timel is empty, that is to say, determine whether the ready_time of all processors has been calculated. If so, call the insert function, otherwise continue to calculate the ready_time of the next processor of the current node.

Channel graph between the processes of the second stage is shown in Fig. 3:

3.4   Algorithm Implementation

After modeling based on Pi-calculus, this paper will use Nomadic Pict [13] to implement the model. Nomadic Pict [14] is very close to Pi-calculus based on Pict [11]. In addition, it adds the related functions of the agent. The following is the flow of the HEFT algorithm based on multi-agent:

(1) Create all agents, controlling agents to start each computing agent.
(2) Read the basic data, generate corresponding task schedule diagram linked list and processor linked list, and layer the task schedule diagram linked list, send these basic linked list information to each computing agent.

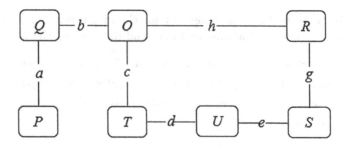

Fig. 3. Channel graph between the processes of the second stage

(3) Take out a layer of nodes to form a layer node list, if each layer node is processed, go to step 7
(4) Rationally assign the nodes in the layer node list to each computing agent.
(5) The computing agent calculates the rank value of the task node. If its child node is empty, the node's rank value is the average calculation time of the node. Otherwise, the child node is looped. If the child node's rank value plus the communication overhead with the node is greater than the node rank value, the node rank value is updated and sent to the controlling agent.
(6) If the controlling agent receives the calculation of the rank values of all the nodes in the layer, update the total rank value list and go to step 3.
(7) Sort all nodes according to the rank value and get the sorted list of nodes.
(8) Take out a node from the sorted list of nodes. If the node's parent is empty, the earliest start time of the node is 0. Select the processor whose finish time is earliest and insert it; otherwise, the earliest start time is calculated for each processor, and the processor with the earliest finish time is selected for insertion until all the task nodes are scheduled to complete.

4   Comparison of Experimental Results

This paper uses Nomadic Pict assigning tasks to multiple agents by channel and C++ language assigning tasks to multiple clients to implement the HEFT algorithm. The experimental environment of the algorithm: 6 PCs in the LAN, the centos system under the Linux platform, the version number is 6.3, the memory of the virtual machine is 1024M, and the hard disk is 20G.

In the experiment, taking into account the complexity of the topology structure in the task scheduling map under distributed environment, for integrity, the experimental data was divided into two cases of breadth-first DAG and depth-first DAG. For each situation, we set the number of nodes to 20, 40, 60, 80, and 100 as an example. The algorithm runs an average of 20 results in seconds.

4.1   Breadth-First Horizontal Comparison

The breadth-first gradient use cases for calculating the number of agents 2, 4, and 6 respectively are compared with the experimental results shown in Figs. 4,

5 and 6. It can be seen that under the same number of nodes with the same breadth, the Nomadic Pict with multi-agent technology runs at 1/3 or even less than the C++ language, and the advantage is maintained as the number of nodes increases. It is not difficult to infer that in the case of breadth priority, the number of nodes continues to increase, and Nomadic Pict will further exert its parallelism and maintain its advantages.

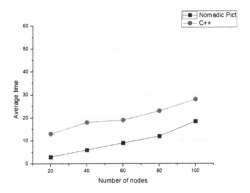

Fig. 4. Comparison of real time when the agent is 2 in the case of breadth first

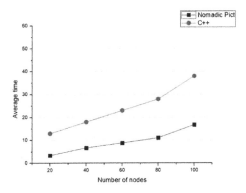

Fig. 5. Comparison of real time when the agent is 4 in the case of breadth first

4.2 Depth-First Vertical Comparison

Depth-priority gradient use case experiment results are shown in Figs. 7, 8 and 9. It is not difficult to see that in the depth-first case, the Nomadic Pict still runs faster than C++, even if this advantage is slightly less than the breadth-first

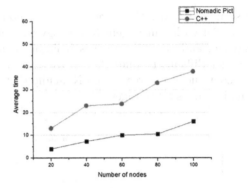

Fig. 6. Comparison of real time when the agent is 6 in the case of breadth first

advantage. However, its growth trend is more stable. With the increase in the number of nodes, this advantage will continue to be maintained. Therefore, it is not difficult to infer that the number of nodes continues to increase in the depth-first case. The HEFT algorithm based on the combination of multi-agent technology and Nomadic Pi-calculus model will still maintain its advantages.

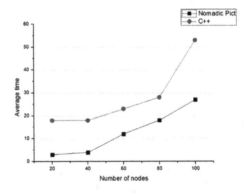

Fig. 7. Comparison of real time when the agent is 2 in the case of depth first

4.3 Comparison of Execution Time When the Number of Computing Agents is Different

In this paper, when the breadth first is selected, the comparison of the execution time of the number of agents 1, 2, 4, and 6 under the same node structure is shown in Fig. 10.

Analysis of Fig. 10 can lead to the conclusion that when the number of nodes is small, the execution time becomes longer as the number of computing agents

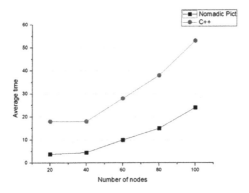

Fig. 8. Comparison of real time when the agent is 4 in the case of depth first

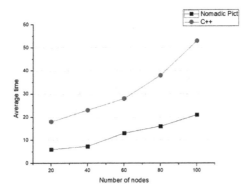

Fig. 9. Comparison of real time when the agent is 6 in the case of depth first

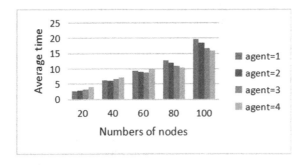

Fig. 10. Comparison of execution time when the number of computing agents is different in the case of breadth first

increases. The reason is that as the number of computing agents increases, communication overhead increases. With the increase of the number of nodes, the relationship between nodes is more complicated, and the increase in the number of agents will increase the degree of parallelism, not only gradually offset the communication overhead, but shorten the time further. Therefore, this feature is very suitable for distributed environments where the number of nodes is large and the relationships between nodes are very complicated. Combined with Fig. 2, the experiment uses only three computers with 6 agents running in parallel to calculate the time, shortening the time to about 1/3 of the traditional model. If a larger computer cluster, this algorithm model can greatly improve the speed of calculation.

5   Conclusion

This paper studies the distributed heterogeneous scheduling algorithms firstly, and uses the Pi-calculus and fusion multi-agent technology to model the HEFT algorithm. And then use Nomadic Pict to implement the model. The experimental results show that distributed multi-agent model based on Pi-calculus has great advantages in distributed task scheduling. It is also not difficult to assert that not only in distributed task scheduling, but the model can be applied in more distributed scenes. In addition, the structure of the distributed communication system is easy to change, and Pi-calculus supports the transmission of the channel name, which can easily realize the change of the complex communication system structure. Therefore, the model has certain advantages and prospects across the distributed domain. In the future, the multi-agent HEFT algorithm can be implemented on other distributed platforms such as JADE [15] for further comparison.

References

1. Tanenbaum, A.S.: The Distributed Operating System, 1st edn. Electronic Industry Press, Beijing (2008). (USA) LU LI-NA, Translation
2. Hu, T.C.: Parallel sequencing and assembly line problems. Oper. Res. **9**(6), 841–848 (1961)
3. Milner, R.: Functions as processes. Math. Struct. Comput. Sci. **2**(2), 119–141 (1992)
4. Topcuoglu, H., Hariri, S., Wu, M.Y.: Performance-effective and low-complexity task scheduling for heterogeneous computing. IEEE Trans. Parallel Distrib. Syst. **13**(3), 260–274 (2002)
5. Wojciechowski, P.T.: Nomadic Pict: language and infrastructure design for mobile computation. ACM Trans. Program. Lang. Syst. **32**(4), 0164–0925 (2010)
6. Mukun, C., Kiang, M.Y.B.D.I.: BDI agent architecture for multi-strategy selection in automated negotiation. J. Univ. Comput. Sci. **18**(10), 1379–1404 (2012)
7. Yu, B., Zhang, C., Li, W.J.: Pi-calculus modeling for the multi-agent collaborative system. J. Xidian Univ. **41**(6), 76–82 (2014)

8. Stavrinides, G.L., Karatza, H.D.: Scheduling multiple task graphs with end-to-end deadlines in distributed real-time systems utilizing imprecise computations. J. Syst. Softw. **83**(6), 1004–1014 (2010)
9. Milner, R.: Communicating and Mobile Systems: The Pi-Calculus. Cambridge University Press, Cambridge (1999)
10. Jing-mei, L.I., Dong-wei, S.U.N., Qi-long, H.A.N.: Research on static task scheduling based on heterogeneous chip multi-processor. J. Chin. Comput. Syst. **12**(34), 2770–2774 (2014)
11. Ilie, S., Bădică, C.: Multi-agent approach to distributed ant colony optimization. Sci. Comput. Program. **78**(6), 762–774 (2013)
12. Jin, C., Zhang, Y., Wang, C.: Distributed multiagent-based ant colony algorithm. Appl. Res. Comput. **35**(3), 666–670 (2018)
13. Sewell, P., Wojciechowski, P.T., Unyapoth, A.: Nomadic Pict: programming languages, communication infrastructure overlays, and semantics for mobile computation. ACM Trans. Program. Lang. Syst. (TOPLAS) **32**(4), 12 (2010)
14. The Nomadic Pict System.http://www.cs.put.poznan.pl/pawelw/npict
15. Zafar, K., Baig, R., Bukhari, N., et al.: Route planning and optimization of route using simulated ant agent system. Int. J. Comput. Appl. **4**(8), 457–478 (2010)

SmartDetect: A Smart Detection Scheme for Malicious Web Shell Codes via Ensemble Learning

Zijian Zhang, Meng Li, Liehuang Zhu[(⊠)], and Xinyi Li

School of Computer Science and Technology, Beijing Institute of Technology,
Beijing, China
{zhangzijian,menglibit,liehuangz,2120171114}@bit.edu.cn

Abstract. The rapid global spread of the web technology has led to an increase in unauthorized intrusions into computers and networks. Malicious web shell codes used by hackers can often cause extremely harmful consequences. However, the existing detection methods cannot precisely distinguish between the bad codes and the good codes. To solve this problem, we first detected the malicious web shell codes by applying the traditional data mining algorithms: Support Vector Machine, K-Nearest Neighbor, Naive Bayes, Decision Tree, and Convolutional Neural Network. Then, we designed an ensemble learning classifier to further improve the accuracy. Our experimental analysis proved that the accuracy of SmartDetect—our proposed smart detection scheme for malicious web shell codes—was higher than the accuracy of Shell Detector and NeoPI on the dataset collected from Github. Also, the equal-error rate of the detection result of SmartDetect was lower than those of Shell Detector and NeoPI.

Keywords: Smart detection · Malicious web shell code · Data mining

1 Introduction

High-speed Internet access provided by web technologies has enhanced web experience for users. However, user data remains susceptible to security attacks because these technologies do not provide security to users. Therefore, web server attacks have become one of the most dangerous Internet problems. Canali and Balzarotti found that almost half of the hackers use web shells for their attacks [1].

To create backdoors in servers, hackers often upload web shells that enable remote control and administration of these servers. Attackers explore and discover web-specific vulnerabilities and configuration loopholes, such as Cross-Site Scripting and SQL injection, to expose the administrator's interfaces [2]. After hackers gain control of the server, they can arbitrarily upload and download files, view databases, execute commands, elevate their privileges, and subsequently control the entire network of the enterprise. This can have devastating

© Springer Nature Switzerland AG 2018
M. Qiu (Ed.): SmartCom 2018, LNCS 11344, pp. 196–205, 2018.
https://doi.org/10.1007/978-3-030-05755-8_20

consequences. Therefore, it is very important to develop a precise method for detecting web shells.

The commonly used methods for the detection of web shell codes can be categorized into three main groups: static detection, dynamic detection, and statistical detection. The static detection method uses the regularization feature to match the malicious commands. Dynamic detection determines the threat by using system commands and abnormal network traffic [3]. Statistical detection uses entropy, longest word, index of coincidence, signature, and the compression rate to detect the web shell codes.

Moreover, several automatic detection tools have been developed that have better efficiency than the manual detection of web shell codes. For instance, Shell Detector [4] is a static detection tool. It can find both the original and encoded web shells. NeoPI is a statistical detection tool to detect obfuscated and hidden web shell codes. Unfortunately, both tools have low precision and high equal-error rates.

This research proposes a model that overcomes these concerns to a large extent. Our main contributions are as follows:

- We compared SmartDetect with five existing data mining algorithms: Support Vector Machine (SVM), K-Nearest Neighbor (KNN), Naive Bayes (NB), Decision Tree (DT), and Convolutional Neural Network (CNN), for web shell detection. To improve the detection accuracy, we propose SmartDetect, a smart scheme for detecting malicious web shell codes.
- We applied ensemble learning to improve the accuracy of the proposed scheme. To the best of our knowledge, this is the first study that constructs an ensemble classifier for detecting malicious web shell codes.
- Our experimental analysis showed that the precision of the ensemble classifier was higher than that of the existing classifiers such as Shell Detector and NeoPI. In addition, the equal-error rate of the ensemble classifier was lower than that of the Shell Detector and NeoPI.

2   Related Work

In this section, we have investigated several studies from the last decade on malicious web shell detection. These studies can be divided into four categories.

Starov et al. [2] performed a comprehensive study on web shells. They used several static and dynamic detection methods, and they checked the visible and invisible features generated by popular malicious shells. The result demonstrated that 25% shells were missed in the sample set even for the best detection system at that time.

Tu et al. [5] proposed a detection method to identify malicious codes by using the optimal threshold values. They calculated the score for malicious signatures and malicious functions of the source code. An optimal threshold value was determined to select the suspicious files whose signature total score exceeded the threshold value. The system received a true positive rate of 79.9% and a false positive rate of 2.0%.

Yi Nan et al. [6] proposed a detection scheme for semantics-based web shells by using an abstract syntax subtree extraction algorithm. This algorithm could locate the malicious behavior of web shell files by using the risk assessment table of nodes. However, it could not detect certain specific shells.

Wrench et al. [7] proposed a shell classification approach based on the similarities of the files to known malwares. They proposed four ways of classifying shells based on their similarities: their aim was to produce representative similarity matrices. Then, the matrices were visualized and interpreted graphically. However, the existing web shells that detected malicious shells were not flexible enough. Our proposed method, SmartDetect, can be used to manage the deduplication and deobfuscation of web shell data sets.

3   Preliminaries

3.1   Web Shell

Based on their complexity and available functions, web shells can be basically divided into three categories: complex web shells, simple web shells, and web shells that contain one command line [8]. The complex web shells contain all the features of Trojans. They usually need to call the system's key commands such as exec and system. They are concealed using code encryption. Simple web shells include only the function of uploading files. Their file sizes are small. The web shells that contain one command line can be used flexibly because they can be used as separate files or as parts of a normal file. Therefore, it is difficult to detect these web shells by using ordinary methods.

For identification, web shells can be basically divided into two categories. One category is non-encoded web shells, and the other is encoded web shells. Non-encoded web shells store their source code without being encoded. Thus, we can detect the commands directly. Encoded web shells contain commands that are obfuscated. For example, hackers always use base64_encode to encode the commands [9].

3.2   Ensemble Classifier

Dietterich [10] theoretically proved that ensemble classifiers have better classification accuracy than single-component classifiers. Miranda Dos Santos [11] proved this fact empirically. The error rate of ensemble classifiers could be reduced by implementing multiple base classifiers if the accuracy of each base classifier was over 50%. For the detection of web shells, we used ensemble classifiers to improve the detection accuracy because web shells are of different types, and we can detect these web shells using different basic detectors. Our study uses bagging to realize the ensemble classifier. Bagging, namely Breiman's bootstrap aggregating method, is a straightforward way to obtain high efficiency [12]. A number of sampling sets are produced by using bootstrap sampling. We used each sampling set to train a distinct classifier; then, we combined these classifiers by using the simple voting method.

4   SmartDetect

We propose SmartDetect: a smart code detection scheme for malicious web shells. The concrete scheme consists of three steps. The first step was to preprocess the collected data. Second, we used the bootstrap sampling measure to generate five sample sets and train five classifiers separately. Finally, we used bagging to design an ensemble learning algorithm by which the malicious web shell codes could be precisely detected.

4.1   Data Preprocessing

We obtained web shell samples from some publicly available data sets on the web [13–16]. Given the complexity and diversity of web shells, there were a number of data sets having entirely different structures; all of these could not be used directly for our scheme. However, we preprocessed the collected data by identifying a number of similar web shell codes. In this paper, we mainly deal with the malicious web shell codes with the PHP script language. We performed the following steps:

- First, we filtered the web shell codes by checking the PHP tags. Then, the web shell codes with non-PHP script languages were deleted. Subsequently, we obtained 1404 PHP files [13–15] with web shell codes.
- Second, we removed the web shells with syntactic meaning, whitespaces, and comments. After this procedure, we had 826 shells.
- Code obfuscation was used to prevent reverse engineering [17]. Although the obfuscation technique could protect the proprietary code, it could also be used by web shell authors to hide the malicious code. We used the UnPHP deobfuscation service [18,19] for automatically deobfuscating the shells.

The normal PHP files were collected from an open source software developed by multiple PHP projects [20–25]. In fact, we eventually collected a total of 8045 PHP files.

4.2   Feature Extraction

We used the Opcode bi-gram model to extract the features. Here, Opcode [26] is part of the instructions that specify the operation to be performed. The content of the instructions were determined by the instruction specifications of the previous step. In addition, certain operands are usually required by the instruction. The possible instructions do not require explicit operands. These operands may be the values in the registers, the values in a stack, the values in a memory block, or the values in an input or an output port. We used PHP's VLD [27] extension to view the Opcode of the PHP file. The N-Gram model is based on the assumption that the occurrence of the nth word is only related to the preceding $N - 1$ words. The probability of the entire sentence is the product of the probabilities of the occurrences of the words that make up the sentence.

The flowchart for the feature extraction model is as follows:

Algorithm 1. Feature Extraction Algorithm

Input:
    PHP Files F.
Output:
    Features $\mathcal{F}$.
1: *Put F into VLD extension module.*
2: *Obtain Opcode O.*
3: *Put O into Bi-Gram model.*
4: **return** $\mathcal{F}$.

4.3   Model Training

We first used SVM, KNN, NB, DT, and CNN to train fives classifiers by using the above-mentioned training sets to obtain a well-performing classifier. The architecture for web shells classification is shown in Fig. 1.

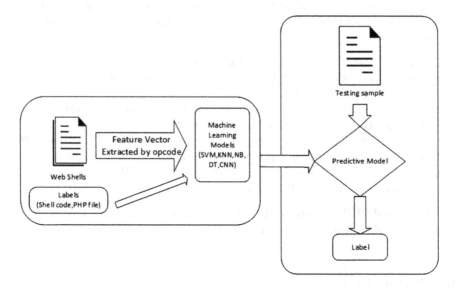

Fig. 1. Architecture for web shell codes' classification

We illustrate the technical details by using the SVM-based malicious web shell codes as an example. The model uses the following formula.

$$min\frac{1}{2}\|\omega\|$$

$$s.t.\ y_i(\omega^T x_i + b) \geq 1, i = 1, 2, ..., m$$

Then, the RBF kernel is defined as follows:

$$\kappa(x_i, x_j) = exp(-\frac{\|x_i - x_j\|^2}{2\sigma^2}).$$

4.4   Ensemble Learning

We continue to apply bagging to design the ensemble learning algorithm to further improve accuracy. Bagging can be applied to a parallel model where there is no strong dependency between the individual learners and can be generated simultaneously.

The algorithm for building a bagging model is shown in Fig. 2.

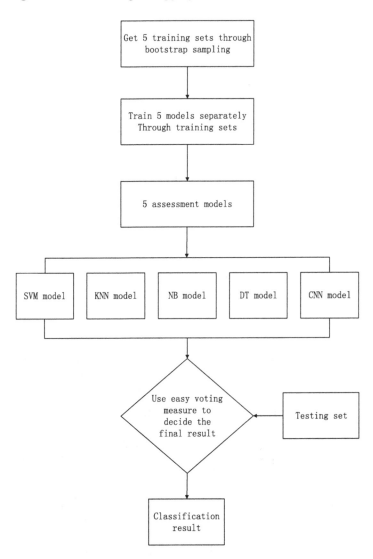

Fig. 2. Experimental flowchart for bagging

Algorithm 2. Ensemble-Learning-Based Detection Algorithm

Input:
    1. Basic classifier: C,
    2. The iteration of training: t. The total iteration T is 5,
    3. Training set: S.
Output:
    Ensemble of classifiers: C_t.
1: $t = 1$
2: while $t < T$
3:   $S_t \leftarrow$ *the subset of training set generated through bootstrap sampling*
4:   *Using S_t to create basic classifier C_t*
5:   $t{+}{+}$
6: **return** *C(Ensemble of classifiers C_t by simple voting measure)*

---

5   Performance Analysis

We compared the accuracy of our proposed scheme with the existing detection tools. The experimental flowchart is shown in Fig. 2.

We first compared the accuracy of the proposed scheme. For this, we considered five data mining algorithms: SVM, KNN, NB, DT, and CNN. The results are shown in Fig. 4.

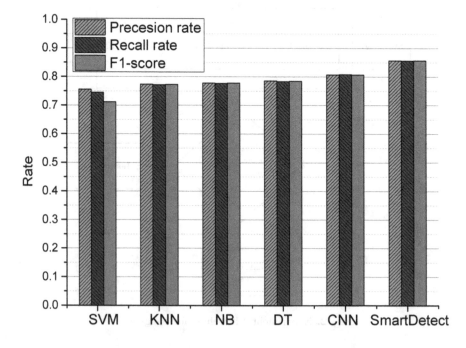

Fig. 3. Architecture for web shells' classification

From the table, we can see that the best basic classifier is from the CNN-based detection scheme. Its precision reaches 80.7%, which is higher than that of other algorithms. Our ensemble classifier achieved the highest precision of 85.7% (Fig. 3).

Then, we compared the error rate. The ROC curve is shown in Fig. 4.

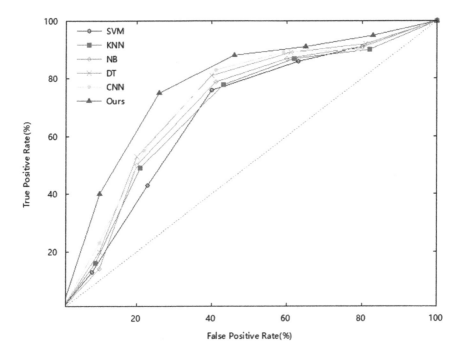

Fig. 4. Architecture for web shells classification

From the figure, we can see that the error rate of the proposed detection scheme is far superior to that of existing detection schemes.

6   Conclusion

The damage caused by web shells can be extremely serious. Unfortunately, the existing detection methods are not very effective. In this study, we developed SmartDetect, an ensemble learning model to detect web shells. Five learning algorithms were applied. Our experimental results proved that the precision of our ensemble learning algorithm increased by at least 5% as compared with the basic learning algorithm. It is difficult to detect web shells using a single classifier because there are various kinds of web shells; therefore, we used the ensemble classifier.

Our experimental analysis also showed that the precision of the ensemble classifier was higher than that of the existing classifiers such as Shell Detector and NeoPI, whereas the equal-error rate of the ensemble classifier was lower than that of NeoPI.

With the advent of the intelligent age [28,29], the use of machine learning methods to detect malicious code is becoming increasingly significant. Moreover, the methods used in our research can be applied to other malicious-code detection fields. In our future studies, we could investigate web shells that are hidden in test images.

Acknowledgment. This work is partially supported by China National Key Research and Development Program No. 2016YFB0800301 and National Natural Science Foundation of China No. 61872041.

References

1. Canali, D., Balzarotti, D.: Behind the scenes of online attacks: an analysis of exploitation behaviors on the web. In: NDSS 2013, 20th Annual Network and Distributed System Security Symposium, San Diego, CA, United States, 24–27 February 2013 (2011)
2. Starov, O., Dahse, J., Ahmad, S.S., Holz, T., Nikiforakis, N.: No honor among thieves: a large-scale analysis of malicious web shells. In: Proceedings of the 25th International Conference on World Wide Web, International World Wide Web Conferences Steering Committee, pp. 1021–1032 (2016)
3. Xue, L., Ma, X., Luo, X., Chan, E.W.W., Miu, T.T.N., Gu, G.: LinkScope: toward detecting target link flooding attacks. IEEE Trans. Inf. Forensics Secur. **13**(10), 2423–2438 (2018)
4. http://www.shelldetector.com
5. Tu, T.D., Guang, C., Xiaojun, G., Wubin, P.: Webshell detection techniques in web applications. In: Proceedings of the International Conference on Computing, Communication and Networking Technologies (ICCCNT), pp. 1-7 (2014)
6. Yi Nan, H.C.L.L., Yong, F.: Semantics-based webshell detection method research. Res. Inf. Secur. **3**(2), 145–150 (2017)
7. Wrench, P.M., Irwin, B.V.: Towards a PHP webshell taxonomy using deobfuscation-assisted similarity analysis. In: Proceedings of the Information Security for South Africa (ISSA), pp. 1-8 (2015)
8. Kolbitsch, C., Livshits, B., Zorn, B., Seifert, C.: Rozzle: de-cloaking internet malware. In: Proceedings of the IEEE Symposium on Security and Privacy 2012, pp. 443-457 (2012)
9. Exploitable PHP functions. https://stackoverflow.com/questions/3115559/exploitable-php-functions
10. Dietterich, T.G.: Ensemble methods in machine learning. In: Kittler, J., Roli, F. (eds.) MCS 2000. LNCS, vol. 1857, pp. 1–15. Springer, Heidelberg (2000). https://doi.org/10.1007/3-540-45014-9_1
11. Miranda Dos Santos, E.: Static and dynamic overproduction and selection of classifier ensembles with genetic algorithms. Ph.D. thesis, École de technologie supérieure (2008)
12. Breiman, L.: Bagging predictors. Mach. Learn. **24**(2), 123–140 (1996)
13. Webshell open source project. https://github.com/tennc/webshell
14. Common PHP webshells. https://github.com/JohnTroony/php-webshells

15. Nikicat's webshells collection project. https://github.com/nikicat/web-malware-collection
16. Gai, K., Qiu, M.: Blend arithmetic operations on tensor-based fully homomorphic encryption over real numbers. IEEE Trans. Ind. Inform. $4(8)$, 3590–3598 (2018)
17. Wrench, P.M., Irwin, B.V.: Towards a sandbox for the deobfuscation and dissection of PHP malware. In: Proceedings of the Information Security for South Africa (ISSA), pp. 1–8 (2014)
18. UnPHP - the online PHP decoder. https://stackoverflow.com/questions/3115559/exploitable-php-functions
19. Gai, K., Choo, K.-K.R., Qiu, M., Zhu, L.: Privacy-preserving content-oriented wireless communication in internet-of-things. IEEE Internet Things J. $5(4)$, 3059–3067 (2018)
20. Wordpress project. https://github.com/WordPress/WordPress
21. A PHP blogging platform. https://github.com/typecho/typecho
22. A web interface for MySQL and MariaDB. https://github.com/phpmyadmin/phpmyadmin
23. A PHP framework for web artisans. https://github.com/laravel/laravel
24. The symfony PHP framework. https://github.com/symfony/symfony
25. Yii 2: the fast, secure and professional PHP framework. https://github.com/yiisoft/yii2
26. Opcode. http://www.php-internals.com/book/?p=chapt02/02-03-02-opcode
27. Visual leak detector. https://github.com/KindDragon/vld
28. Gai, K., Qiu, M., Xiong, Z., Liu, M.: Privacy-preserving multi-channel communication in edge-of-things. Futur. Gener. Comput. Syst. **85**, 190–200 (2018)
29. Zhu, L., Li, M., Zhang, Z., Zhan, Q.: ASAP: an anonymous smart-parking and payment scheme in vehicular networks. IEEE Trans. Dependable Secur. Comput. (TDSC) **PP**(99) (2018)

An Optimized MBE Algorithm on Sparse Bipartite Graphs

Yu He$^{(\boxtimes)}$, Ronghua Li, and Rui Mao

ShenZhen University, Nanhai Ave 3688, Shenzhen,
Guangdong, People's Republic of China
329686183@qq.com

Abstract. The maximal biclique enumeration (MBE) is a problem of identifying all maximal bicliques in a bipartite graph. Once enumerated in a bipartite graph, maximal bicliques can be used to solve problems in areas such as purchase prediction, statistic analysis of social networks, discovery of interesting structures in protein-protein interaction networks, identification of common gene-set associations, and integration of diverse functional genomes data. In this paper, we develop an optimized sequential MBE algorithm called sMBEA for sparse bipartite graphs which appear frequently in real life. The results of extensive experiments on several real-life data sets demonstrate that sMBEA outperforms the state-of-the-art sequential algorithm iMBEA.

Keywords: Biclique enumeration · Sparse bipartite graphs

1 Introduction

As a natural abstraction of complex relationships in data, the graph model has been widely used in various applications, such as social networks, recommendation systems and bioinformatics. Such graph data typically contains dense substructures. Finding the dense substructures from a graph, such as cliques, bicliques, and k-cores is an important operator in graph data mining and network analysis.

In this paper, we focus on a particular type of substructure, i.e., the biclique, and study the problem of enumerating all maximal bicliques in a bipartite graph. The *biclique* is a fundamental dense substructure in graph theory and it has a long history of applications [17]. For example, in recommendation systems, the relation between users and items, such as liking, purchasing and rating, can be modeled as a user-item bipartite graph. A biclique in this bipartite graph consists of a set of users U and a set of item V such that every user in U has liked every item in V. Finding such a maximal biclique yields a set of users who share the common interest, and is useful for predicting the users' purchase intention.

Many graph mining tasks rely on enumerating maximal bicliques. Notable examples include learning context-free grammars [26], finding correlations in databases [9], data compression [1], role mining in role-based access control [7],

© Springer Nature Switzerland AG 2018
M. Qiu (Ed.): SmartCom 2018, LNCS 11344, pp. 206–216, 2018.
https://doi.org/10.1007/978-3-030-05755-8_21

and process operation scheduling [19]. In bioinformatics, a variety of biological mining problems can be modeled as a problem of identifying maximal bicliques in bipartite graphs, such as the phylogenetic tree construction [2,3,14,15], protein-protein interaction networks analysis [10,25], genephenotype analysis [6], miRNA regulatory module prediction [12] and genotypes/diseases relation modeling [18].

Although there are many of applications, the problem of enumerating all maximal bicliques (MBE) in a bipartite graph is shown to be **NP**-hard, thus it is impossible to solve it in polynomial time unless $P = NP$. In the literature, many backtrack enumeration algorithms were proposed. Among them, the state-of-the-art algorithm is a DFS (depth-first search) backtrack enumeration algorithm proposed in [29]. However, such a sequential algorithm has some unnecessary processes that is time-consuming.

Specifically, we proposed an improved sequential algorithm which leverages the sparsity of most real-life bipartite graphs to optimize the time-consuming maximality checking and the candidate generation procedures in iMBEA. By a careful analysis, we show that with our optimization, the time complexity of our improved sequential algorithm can be reduced from $\mathcal{O}(2^n(nH))$ to $\mathcal{O}(2^n(n + H^3))$, where H is the upper bound of degrees in the graph. Clearly, when H is not very large, our algorithm can be very efficient. The main contributions of this work are summarized as below.

- We propose an improved sequential algorithm for the MBE problem by considering the sparsity of most real-life bipartite graphs.
- We propose theoretical proof for the complexity of sMBEA.

The rest of the paper is organized as follows. Section 1.1 reviews the related work. We state the problem definition in Sect. 2.1. We overview iMBEA in Sect. 2.2, we propose optimized serial algorithm sMBEA in Sect. 3.1. We report the experimental results in Sect. 4. Finally, we conclude this work in Sect. 4.3.

1.1   Related Work

As an important branch of modeling the graph properties, a huge amount of studies are proposed to solve the MBE problem. These studies can be roughly classified into three categories: (1) *exhaustively searching*, (2) *graph inflation* and (3) *frequent itemset mining*.

The most intuitive approach entails exhaustively building all possible subgraphs and checking each for maximality. Some studies reduce the search space by placing one or more restrictions on the original problem, including maximum input degree [24], arboricity [8], minimum biclique size [15,23] and figure-of-merit values [21]. [29] takes advantages of bipartite structure and performs a DFS-like search scheme with pruning optimization.

Another kind of approaches relies on graph inflation. [16] proposes to transform the bipartite graph to two complete graphs with bipartite edges, and solve the maximal clique enumeration on this general graph [2,15,20,25]. However, the inflation operation greatly increases the data scale and is unable to take advantage of bipartite graph structures. These approaches are neither practical nor scalable.

Some studies build the connection between MBE and database field and try to solve MBE with the help of database algorithms. [27] models a transaction database as a bipartite graph, with a one-to-one correspondence between frequent closed item sets and maximal bicliques. A correspondence between maximal bicliques of a general graph and frequent closed item sets has been shown in [13], leading to the suggestion that FPclose and similar frequent item set mining methods [8,16,22,23,28] may be helpful in enumerating maximal bicliques. An algorithm LCM-MBC is presented in [11]. LCM-MBC is improved upon LCM [5].

The most related work to ours is [29]. In [29], Zhang et al. combine backtracking with branch-and-bound techniques to efficiency prune the search space. The key difference between [29] and our work is that [29] does not consider the graph sparsity and is a sequential algorithm, while our work utilizes the graph sparsity to greatly accelerating the maximality checking process.

2 Preliminary

2.1 Problem Definition

Let $G = (U \cup V; E)$ be a bipartite graph, U and V are two disjoint vertex set without intra-edges. Let $n_U = |U|$, $n_V = |V|$ and $m = |E|$. Without loss of generality, denote $n_U \geq n_V$. A graph $G'(V'; E')$ is called induced subgraph of G if and only if $V' \subseteq U \cup V$, $E' \subseteq E$. Based on G and G', the *maximal biclique* can be defined as:

Definition 1 *(Maximal Biclique).* *A biclique $B = (L, R)$ is a induced subgraph of G with $L \subseteq U$, $R \subseteq V$. $B = (L, R)$ is said to be maximal if and only if there is no other biclique $B'(L', R')$ in G such that $L \subset L'$, $R \subset R'$.*

Example 1. *Figure 1 shows a bipartite graph. As can be seen, the set $\{\{u_1, u_2, u_3\}, \{v_1\}\}$ is a biclique, and $\{\{u_1, u_2, u_3\}, \{v_1, v_2\}\}$ is a maximal biclique. Similarly, we can easily check that $\{\{u_1, u_2, u_3\}, \{v_2\}\}$ is a biclique, while $\{\{u_1, u_2, u_3, u_4\}, \{v_2\}\}$ is a maximal biclique.*

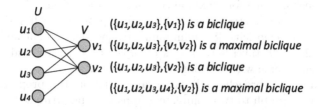

Fig. 1. Running example: biclique and maximal biclique

Thus, the **Maximal Biclique Enumeration** (MBE) problem is formulated as:

Definition 2 (*Maximal Biclique Enumeration*). *Given a bipartite graph G, the* MBE *problem aims to enumerate the maximal biclique set $\mathcal{B}_G$.*

Example 2. *Consider the bipartite graph in Fig. 1. Clearly, the output of our* MBE *problem is $\mathcal{B}_G = \{(\{u_1, u_2, u_3\}, \{v_1, v_2\}); (\{u_1, u_2, u_3, u_4\}, \{v_2\})\}$.*

2.2   Recap of iMBEA

Inspired for the classic maximal clique-finding method [3] which has shown to have optimal time complexity in [25,29] propose a sequential algorithm called iMBEA. Compared with exhaustive search, iMBEA combines backtracking with branch-and-bound techniques to efficiency prune the search space.

We initialize the candidate vertex set $P = V$, $L = U$ and the processed vertex set $R = \emptyset$, $Q = \emptyset$. Note that the vertices in P are sorted by the non-decreasing order of common neighbor size, so that try to balance the searching tree.

At each node of the search tree, iMBEA iteratively adds a vertex $v \in P$ to R to form new R', $R' = R \cup \{v\}$. L' is generated by removing all vertices not connected to v in L. Consequently, Q' is updated by eliminating vertices not connected L', while P' keeps the vertices which partially connect to vertices of L' in P. Next, we check the maximality of biclique $B(L', R')$, i.e., if no vertex in Q' is fully connected to vertices in L', $B(L', R')$ is a maximal biclique. Then iMBEA recursively searches the new node $\langle L', R', P', Q' \rangle$ until P is empty or any vertex in Q is fully connected to vertices in L.

3   The Proposed **MBE** Algorithms

3.1   The sMBEA Algorithm

We first definite some useful notations in Table 1 which will be frequently used in analyzing our algorithms.

Although there exist a large number of applications based on bipartite graph analysis, the sparsity of bipartite graphs that frequently appear in real-life applications has not been well explored for devising efficient algorithms. For example, most previous solutions for the MBE problem did not utilize the sparse nature of real-life bipartite graphs. In this work, we first make use of the sparsity of bipartite graph to solve the MBE problem and propose an optimized algorithm *sMBEA* based on the state-of-the-art sequential iMBEA.

sMBEA shrinking candidates set P and checking set Q to improve efficiency without affecting the final results, that is calculating SP, SQ and replace P, Q.

To proof our shrinking strategy is useful, we first analyze original algorithm. The essence of iMBEA is a process of DFS (Depth First Search) backtrack enumeration. The description of iMBEA shows in Sect. 2. Let T_{ie} be the time taken in each node of the iMBEA DFS-tree. We can easily derive that T_{ie} mainly includes

---

Algorithm 1. sMBEA(G, P, Q, L, R)

Input: G, P, Q, L, R

Output: All maximal bicliques

1 $i \leftarrow 0$;

2 **while** $P \neq \varnothing$ **do**

3 $\quad$ $x \leftarrow P[i++]; R' \leftarrow R \cup \{x\}; L' \leftarrow \{u \in L | (u, x) \in E(G)\}$;

4 $\quad$ $\overline{L} \leftarrow L \backslash L'; C \leftarrow \varnothing; P' \leftarrow \varnothing; Q' \leftarrow \varnothing; isM \leftarrow true$;

5 $\quad$ $N_{L'}$ $N_{L'} = \bigcup_{l \in L'} N_l$

6 $\quad$ $Q \leftarrow N_{L'} \cap Q$;

7 $\quad$ $P \leftarrow N_{L'} \cap P$;

8 $\quad$ **for** $q \in Q$ **do**

9 $\quad\quad$ $N_q \leftarrow \{u \in L' | (u, q) \in E(G)\}$;

10 $\quad\quad$ **if** $|N_q| = |L'|$ **then**

11 $\quad\quad\quad$ $isM \leftarrow false$;

12 $\quad\quad\quad$ break;

13 $\quad\quad$ **else if** $|N_q| > 0$ **then**

14 $\quad\quad\quad$ $Q' \leftarrow Q' \cup \{q\}$;

15 $\quad$ **if** isM **then**

16 $\quad\quad$ **for** $p \in P, p \neq x$ **do**

17 $\quad\quad\quad$ $N_p \leftarrow \{u \in L' | (u, p) \in E(G)\}$;

18 $\quad\quad\quad$ **if** $|N_p| = |L'|$ **then**

19 $\quad\quad\quad\quad$ $R' \leftarrow R' \cup \{p\}$;

20 $\quad\quad\quad\quad$ $S \leftarrow \{u \in \overline{L} | (u, p) \in E(G)\}$;

21 $\quad\quad\quad\quad$ **if** $|S| = 0$ **then**

22 $\quad\quad\quad\quad\quad$ $C \leftarrow C \cup \{p\}$;

23 $\quad\quad\quad$ **else if** $|N_p| > 0$ **then**

24 $\quad\quad\quad\quad$ $P' \leftarrow P' \cup \{p\}$;

25 $\quad\quad$ **OUTPUT**(L', R')

26 $\quad\quad$ **if** $P' \neq \varnothing$ **then**

27 $\quad\quad\quad$ sort(P');

28 $\quad\quad\quad$ sMBEA(G, L', R', P', Q');

29 $\quad$ $Q \leftarrow Q \cup \{x\} \cup C$;

30 $\quad$ $P \leftarrow P \backslash \{x\} \backslash C$;

---

two parts: (i) the time cost for checking maximality (denoted by $T(f_q)$); (ii) the time overhead for candidates generation (denoted by $T(f_p)$).

For $T(f_q)$, we can easily derive from Algorithm 1 line 8–14, the time complexity for checking maximality can be bounded by $\mathcal{O}(nH)$, where H the upper bound of the degrees in the bipartite graph G.

Table 1. Notations

Notation	Description
P	Candidates set
Q	Checking set, to detect biclique maximality
R	Nodes set that extend from P
L	Common neighbors of R
$N_{L'}$	$N_{L'} = \bigcup_{l \in L'} N_l$
SP	$SP = N_{L'} \cap P$
$\overline{SP}$	$\overline{SP} = P \backslash SP$
SQ	$SQ = N_{L'} \cap Q$
$\overline{SQ}$	$\overline{SQ} = Q \backslash SQ$
P'	$\{p \mid N_p \cap L' \neq \varnothing, p \in P\}$
n	$n = |V|$
H	Upper bound of the degrees in G
N	Total thread number

For $T(f_p)$, we need to traverse all candidates in P to generate a new candidate set P' for the next recursion. Note that P is initially set to V, so the largest size of P is n. As a result, the time complexity for candidate generation is $T(f_p) = \mathcal{O}(nH)$.

Putting it all together, we have

$$T_{ie} = T(f_q) + T(f_p) = \mathcal{O}(nH). \tag{1}$$

The iMBEA does not consider the sparsity of the bipartite graph. In this work, we make use of the sparsity of bipartite graph to improve the efficiency of iMBEA. Our improved sequential algorithm sMBEA is shown in Algorithm 1.

Since $Q = (SQ \cup \overline{SQ})$, $P = (SP \cup \overline{SP})$, we claim that each node $q \in \overline{SQ}$ has no opportunity for maximality checking in next recursion. This is because q has no neighbor in L' and will not insert into the set Q'. Similarly, every node $p \in \overline{SP}$ also does not insert into the new candidate set P'.

Based on the above observation, the efficiency of the algorithm can be improved by shrinking the variables Q, P to SQ, SP respectively, because the sets $\overline{SQ}, \overline{SP}$ can be safely removed without losing accuracy. However, computing the sets SQ, SP will take $\mathcal{O}(n)$ costs. It can be shown that in $sMBEA$, the time complexity taken in each node in the DFS enumeration tree is

$$T_{se} = \mathcal{O}(n + H^3). \tag{2}$$

Since the number of nodes in the DFS recursion tree is 2^n in the worst case, the total time complexity of $iMBEA$ is

$$T_i = \mathcal{O}(2^n(nH)). \tag{3}$$

Likewise, the total time complexity of *sMBEA* is

$$T_s = \mathcal{O}(2^n(n + H^3)). \tag{4}$$

Clearly, in spare bipartite graph with $n >> H^2$, our algorithm will be much faster than the state-of-the-art iMBEA as confirmed in our experiments.

By the above analysis, we are able to get the following results.

Proposition 1. *Except for searching in DFS-tree root node, the superiority of optimization will loss.*

Proof. During the process of DFS, when search in root node(that is $L = U$), $\Theta(|P|) = |V|$, and in sparse G, $|V| >> H^2$, so T_s is better than T_i, However, after get new candidates P', and $\Theta|P'| = H^2$, when search forward, the superiority of optimization will loss because $\Theta(|P|) = H^2$.

Proposition 2. *In dense bipartite graph(When $\mathcal{O}(n) = H$), T_i is better than T_s.*

Proof. When $\mathcal{O}(n) = H$, the sparsity of bipartite graph G is too low, and G is a dense graph. $T_i = \mathcal{O}(2^n H^2)$, $T_s = \mathcal{O}(2^n H^3)$ and the calculation of SP, SQ has relative high cost. However, in actual life, dense bipartite graph is rare, so our method is always effective to solve MBE problem in practice.

4   Experiment

In this section, we conduct extensive experiments on both synthetic and real-world graphs to evaluate the performance of the proposed algorithms.

4.1   Experimental Configuration

Comparison Methods. In this section, our proposed algorithms are denoted as sMBEA. We implement iMBEA [29] as baseline.

We conduct all experiments on a commodity machine equipped with a 2.40 GHz Intel(R) Xeon(R) x86_64 E5-2630 v3 processor with 32 cores and 256 KB L2 cache (per core), 20 MB L3 cache (share), and 32G memory.

Evaluation Metrics. For sequential algorithms, we use Speedup Ratio (SR) [4] to evaluate their efficiency as:

$$SR_i = \frac{T_{base}}{T_i}. \tag{5}$$

In (5), T_{base} is the running time of the baseline. T_i is the running time of algorithm i.

Table 2. Dataset statistics

Dataset	$|U|$	$|V|$	$|E|$	d_{avg}	Remark
Occupation	229,307	101,730	250,945	2.1887	User-occupation
Youtube	124,325	30087	293,360	4.7192	User-group
Location	225,498	53,407	293,697	2.6049	Entity-location
Country	592,414	2,302	637,134	2.1510	Entity-country
ActorMovies	511,463	383,640	1,470,404	5.7498	Actor-movie
Wiki_Cat	2,036,440	182,947	3,795,796	3.7279	Article-category

4.2 Experiments on Real-World Graphs

We evaluate and compare the performance of different methods on five real data sets. Table 2 demonstrates the statistics of the five data sets. d_{avg} is the overall average degree. As shown in Table 2, these data sets exhibits different characteristics. Note that the largest data set: Wiki_Cat contains millions of vertices and edges. To the best of out knowledge, this is the first work aims to solve the MBE problem on bipartite graphs with such scale. All data sets can be obtained from http://konect.uni-koblenz.de/.

Performance of Sequential Algorithms. Table 3 lists the experiment results for two sequential algorithms sMBEA and iMBEA. As demonstrated in Table 3, with the help of utilizing sparsity property, sMBEA outperforms iMBEA on all data sets. The average speedup ratio is 178.82%. Another notable observation is that sMBEA runs much faster on Country data set which has lowest overall average degree than other data sets. This observation implies the sparsity property can help to accelerate MBE tasks.

Table 3. The result of the running time (in seconds) and speedup ratio for the real data

	iMBEA	sMBEA	Speedup Ratio
Occupation	9,173	**5,206**	176.20%
Youtube	12,127	**7,620**	159.15%
Location	5,917	**2,958**	200.03%
Country	898	**519**	173.03%
ActorMovies	44,384	**23,594**	188.12%
Wiki_Cat	275,125	**155,971**	176.39%

4.3   Experiments on Synthetic Graphs

In order to validate the theoretical analysis and evaluate the performance of sMBEA, we conduct experiments on several synthetic bipartite graphs.

Performance on Graphs with Different H. To validate the complexity analysis of sMBEA in Sect. 3.1, we generate three sets of random bipartite graphs: $\mathcal{G}_{(40000,5000)}$, $\mathcal{G}_{(80000,5000)}$ and $\mathcal{G}_{(160000,5000)}$. The subscript of $\mathcal{G}$ indicates the vertex number of U and V respectively. Each graph set contains five random bipartite graphs with different degree bound $H \in \{50, 100, 150, 200, 250\}$. We run experiments on all three graph sets for iMBEA and sMBEA respectively.

Table 4 lists the experimental results for all graph sets. Furthermore, to illustrate the trend of speedup ratio for different H, we report the speedup ratio curve for three graph sets in Fig. 2. We can observe that the speedup ratio for three graphs sets follow the same trend: when the degree bound H increases, the speedup ratio decreases. The trend becomes significant when the vertex number of graph is small. This observation validate the complexity analysis of sMBEA. When the bipartite graph is sparse, i.e., $H \ll |V|$, sMBEA can achieve better performance than iMBEA does.

Table 4. The result of the running time (in seconds) with different degree bound H

H	Method	$\mathcal{G}_{(4e4,5e3)}$	$\mathcal{G}_{(8e4,5e3)}$	$\mathcal{G}_{(16e4,5e3)}$
50	iMBEA	12	20	38
	sMBEA	**7**	**11**	**22**
100	iMBEA	22	28	45
	sMBEA	**15**	**17**	**30**
150	iMBEA	69	44	56
	sMBEA	**60**	**31**	**40**
200	iMBEA	253	92	75
	sMBEA	**245**	**78**	**55**
250	iMBEA	877	229	115
	sMBEA	**866**	**215**	**92**

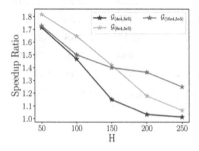

Fig. 2. The speedup ratio curve of three graph sets for different degree bound H.

5   Conclusion

In this paper, we study the Maximal Biclique Enumeration (MBE) problem on huge biparatate graphs. Based on the state-of-the-art sequential MBE algorithm: iMBEA, we exploit the graph sparsity to optimize the time complexity of maximality checking in iMBEA and propose the improved version of iMBEA: sMBEA. Extensive experiments on both synthetic data and real-world data demonstrate that: The optimization based on graph sparsity can greatly accelerate MBE.

References

1. Agarwal, P.K., Alon, N., Aronov, B., Suri, S.: Can visibility graphs be represented compactly? Discrete Comput. Geom. **12**(3), 347–365 (1994)
2. Alexe, G., Alexe, S., Crama, Y., Foldes, S., Hammer, P.L., Simeone, B.: Consensus algorithms for the generation of all maximal bicliques. Discrete Appl. Math. **145**(1), 11–21 (2004)
3. Bron, C., Kerbosch, J.: Algorithm 457: finding all cliques of an undirected graph. Commun. ACM **16**(9), 575–577 (1973)
4. Brown, R.G.: Maximizing beowulf performance. In: Annual Linux Showcase & Conference (2000)
5. Cheng, Y., Church, G.: Biclustering of expression data. In: 2000 Proceedings of Intelligent Systems for Molecular Biology (2000)
6. Chesler, E.J., Wang, J., Lu, L., Qu, Y., Manly, K.F., Williams, R.W.: Genetic correlates of gene expression in recombinant inbred strains. Neuroinformatics **1**(4), 343–357 (2003)
7. Colantonio, A., Di Pietro, R., Ocello, A., Verde, N.V.: Taming role mining complexity in RBAC. Comput. Secur. **29**(5), 548–564 (2010)
8. Eppstein, D.: Arboricity and bipartite subgraph listing algorithms. Inf. Process. Lett. **51**(4), 207–211 (1994)
9. Jermaine, C.: Finding the most interesting correlations in a database: how hard can it be? Inf. Syst. **30**(1), 21–46 (2005)
10. Johnson, D.S., Yannakakis, M., Papadimitriou, C.H.: On generating all maximal independent sets. Inf. Process. Lett. **27**(3), 119–123 (1988)
11. Kaytoue-Uberall, M., Duplessis, S., Napoli, A.: Using formal concept analysis for the extraction of groups of co-expressed genes. In: Le Thi, H.A., Bouvry, P., Pham Dinh, T. (eds.) MCO 2008. CCIS, vol. 14, pp. 439–449. Springer, Heidelberg (2008). https://doi.org/10.1007/978-3-540-87477-5_47
12. Kreek, M.J., Nielsen, D.A., LaForge, K.S.: Genes associated with addiction. NeuroMol. Med. **5**(1), 85–108 (2004)
13. Li, J., Li, H., Soh, D., Wong, L.: A correspondence between maximal complete bipartite subgraphs and closed patterns. In: Jorge, A.M., Torgo, L., Brazdil, P., Camacho, R., Gama, J. (eds.) PKDD 2005. LNCS (LNAI), vol. 3721, pp. 146–156. Springer, Heidelberg (2005). https://doi.org/10.1007/11564126_18
14. Li, J., Liu, G., Li, H., Wong, L.: Maximal biclique subgraphs and closed pattern pairs of the adjacency matrix: a one-to-one correspondence and mining algorithms. IEEE Trans. Knowl. Data Eng. **19**(12), 1625–1637 (2007)
15. Liu, G., Sim, K., Li, J.: Efficient mining of large maximal bicliques. In: Tjoa, A.M., Trujillo, J. (eds.) DaWaK 2006. LNCS, vol. 4081, pp. 437–448. Springer, Heidelberg (2006). https://doi.org/10.1007/11823728_42

16. Makino, K., Uno, T.: New algorithms for enumerating all maximal cliques. In: Hagerup, T., Katajainen, J. (eds.) SWAT 2004. LNCS, vol. 3111, pp. 260–272. Springer, Heidelberg (2004). https://doi.org/10.1007/978-3-540-27810-8_23

17. Malgrange, Y.: Recherche des sous-matrices premières d'unematrice à coefficients binaires. applications à certainsproblèmes de graphe. In: Proceedings of the DeuxièmeCongrès de l'AFCALTI, pp. 231–242 (1962)

18. Mash, D.C., Adi, N., Qin, Y., Buck, A., Pablo, J., et al.: Gene expression in human hippocampus from cocaine abusers identifies genes which regulate extracellular matrix remodeling. PLoS One $2(11)$, e1187 (2007)

19. Mouret, S., Grossmann, I.E., Pestiaux, P.: Time representations and mathematical models for process scheduling problems. Comput. Chem. Eng. $35(6)$, 1038–1063 (2011)

20. Mukherjee, A.P., Tirthapura, S.: Enumerating maximal bicliques from a large graph using mapreduce. IEEE Trans. Serv. Comput. $10(5)$, 771–784 (2017)

21. Mushlin, R.A., Kershenbaum, A., Gallagher, S.T., Rebbeck, T.R.: A graph-theoretical approach for pattern discovery in epidemiological research. IBM Syst. J. $46(1)$, 135–149 (2007)

22. Peeters, R.: The maximum edge biclique problem is NP-complete. Discrete Appl. Math. $131(3)$, 651–654 (2003)

23. Sanderson, M.J., Driskell, A.C., Ree, R.H., Eulenstein, O., Langley, S.: Obtaining maximal concatenated phylogenetic data sets from large sequence databases. Mol. Biol. Evol. $20(7)$, 1036–1042 (2003)

24. Tanay, A., Sharan, R., Shamir, R.: Discovering statistically significant biclusters in gene expression data. Bioinformatics 18(Supp. 1), S136–S144 (2002)

25. Tomita, E., Tanaka, A., Takahashi, H.: The worst-case time complexity for generating all maximal cliques and computational experiments. Theor. Comput. Sci. $363(1)$, 28–42 (2006)

26. Yoshinaka, R.: Towards dual approaches for learning context-free grammars based on syntactic concept lattices. In: Mauri, G., Leporati, A. (eds.) DLT 2011. LNCS, vol. 6795, pp. 429–440. Springer, Heidelberg (2011). https://doi.org/10.1007/978-3-642-22321-1_37

27. Zaki, M.J., Hsiao, C.J.: Charm: an efficient algorithm for closed itemset mining. In: Proceedings of the 2002 SIAM International Conference on Data Mining, pp. 457–473. SIAM (2002)

28. Zaki, M.J., Ogihara, M.: Theoretical foundations of association rules. In: 3rd ACM SIGMOD Workshop on Research Issues in Data Mining and Knowledge Discovery, pp. 71–78 (1998)

29. Zhang, Y., Chesler, E.J., Langston, M.A.: On finding bicliques in bipartite graphs: a novel algorithm with application to the integration of diverse biological data types, p. 473. IEEE (2008)

IoT Framework for Interworking and Autonomous Interaction Between Heterogeneous IoT Platforms

Seongju Kang and Kwangsue Chung[(✉)]

Department of Electronics and Communication Engineering,
Kwangwoon University, Seoul, South Korea
sjkang@cclab.kw.ac.kr, kchung@kw.ac.kr

Abstract. The IoT (Internet of Things) connects with various devices over the Internet and provides a high-level service by interacting between devices. However, heterogeneous characteristics such as communication protocols and message types limit the scope of interaction between IoT platforms. To solve the problem of the fragmented IoT market, the oneM2M global initiative defined a horizontal M2M service layer. Since conventional platforms work based on syntax data, servers and gateways do not understand the meaning of exchanged data. Semantic Web technologies which give meaning to information has been studied in many fields to realize platform understand the data. In this paper, we propose an IoT framework that is based on the oneM2M standard to ensures the interoperability of heterogeneous IoT platform. In addition, the proposed framework interacts autonomously with all objects by applying semantic Web technologies. All data generated by connected device and sensor are described as semantic data. The platform understands the data based on the ontology and performs the autonomous interaction. Users manage rules and devices via the Web client's management interface. Finally, interoperability evaluation is presented through an experiment of interworking and rule-based interaction between heterogeneous platform devices in real IoT environment.

Keywords: oneM2M global initiative · Semantic web technologies
Ontology · Interoperability · Autonomous interaction

1 Introduction

Devices have evolved for user convenience while providing remote control and monitoring. As devices have been connected to the Internet and various M2M communication technologies have emerged, a number of IoT platforms have emerged that provide services through interaction between devices. IoT devices provide to users a high level of service by interacting with other devices in the same service domain. The conventional platforms are designed vertical silo of IoT domain that uses specific protocols, message format, and so on. The vertical service layer is optimized for information processing and communication functions between devices and applications However, a proxy is required for interoperability between the vertical IoT domain [1].

M. Qiu (Ed.): SmartCom 2018, LNCS 11344, pp. 217–225, 2018.
https://doi.org/10.1007/978-3-030-05755-8_22

To address the problem of the fragmented IoT market, seven SDOs (Standards Developing Organizations) have established the oneM2M Global Initiative [2]. The oneM2M standard defined service functions commonly used in IoT environment as CSFs (Common Service Functions) which horizontalized the service layer. The oneM2M define a resource as URI (Uniform Resource Identifier) and provide a RESTful API method for all service. The oneM2M standard enables to be built scalable IoT systems and ensures communication level interoperability between heterogeneous IoT platforms.

Platforms based on IoT standard are ensured communication level interoperability. To process raw data generated by devices that does not have computing power such as sensor devices, the platform must to know the meaning of data. Through semantic Web technology, the platform can process data on its own by understanding the meaning of raw data. The semantic Web is an extension of the current Web, giving meaning to information through a well-defined vocabulary, allowing the computer to understand the information on its own. Raw data is expressed as semantic data via semantic Web technology. The platform provides intelligent services that process sensor values by themselves or perform new interactions based on peripheral data.

In this paper, we propose IoT framework based on the oneM2M standard for communication level interoperability. The proposed framework links a vendor devices' API to oneM2M RESTful API and supports the general input/output format to the user. In addition, raw data generated by devices and sensors are represented as semantic data. Our framework performs rule-based autonomous interactions.

The remainder of this paper is organized as follows. In Sect. 2, we first describe the oneM2M standard and the semantic Web technologies. In Sect. 3, we describe the proposed IoT framework. In Sect. 4, we evaluate the interoperability of the proposed framework with performing experiments between heterogeneous IoT platform in real IoT environment. Finally, Sect. 5 concludes this paper.

2   Related Works

For interoperability between isolated IoT platforms, seven SDOs, Korea (TTA), Europe (ETSI), China (CCSA), USA (ATIS/TIA) and Japan (TTC/ARIB) have established the oneM2M Global Initiative 2015. Figure 1 shows the oneM2M system architecture. oneM2M consists of four functional nodes: IN (Infrastructure Node), MN (Middle Node), ASN (Application Service Node), and ADN (Application Dedicated Node) [4]. IN is cloud server that integrates and manages data, and the MN is a middleware that manages devices in a local and connects IN and IoT devices. ASN and ADN represent devices, and ADN is a device that operates only on the oneM2M standard platform. CSE (Common Service Entity) is a logical entity that includes various CSFs. AE (Application Entity) is an entity that provides application logic to provide monitoring and remote-control service. Functional nodes consist of at least one of CSE and AE. The oneM2M standard defines a service as a URI and provides it as a RESTful API on the platform. It has a URI form <CSE>/<AE>/<ASN or ADN> according to hierarchical service structure. Each service is provided based on CSF using MCC (M2M Communication CSE) and MCA (M2M Communication AE). The oneM2M standard platform supports protocol bindings such as HTTP, CoAP, MQTT, and WebSocket, enabling communication between heterogeneous protocols.

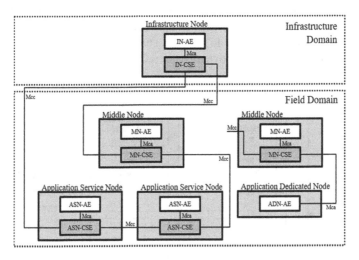

Fig. 1. oneM2M system architecture.

The oneM2M standard realizes communication level interoperability. However, even if the oneM2M based platform supports interworking between heterogeneous IoT platforms, cannot understand the meaning of the information exchanged. For providing intelligent and autonomous service at IoT platforms, they must have an ability of the understanding meaning of a resource. Semantic Web technologies enable a machine to understand the meaning of data and to infer new knowledge through relationships between data. LOD (Linked Open Data) is the most fundamental concept to realize semantic Web technology. The RDF (Resource Description Framework) for representing the LOD concept has been standardized by the W3C (World Wide Web Consortium) [3]. The RDF enables semantic modeling of XML data. The ontologies are composed OWL (Ontology Web Language) and RDFS (RDF Schema) which are the upper languages of RDF [7, 8]. The ontologies define the resource class and the attributes between the classes through semantic vocabularies. The ontology is an important technology for realizing semantic Web technology and has been used for interoperability in many previous studies [5, 6]. SPARQL (Semantic Protocol and RDF Query Language) is an RDF and RDFS query language. SWRL (Semantic Web Rule Language) provides strength reasoning function in OWL-based ontologies.

3   Proposed IoT Framework

In this paper, we propose IoT framework for interworking and autonomous interaction between heterogeneous platforms through oneM2M IoT standard and semantic Web technologies. Figure 2 shows the architecture of the proposed framework. Our framework is composed IoT server, middleware, Web client, and things. The IoT server consists of CI (Communication Interface), RR (Resource Registration), OI (Device Management), DM (Device Management), and SM (Service Management) modules. The CI module supports the various protocols binding such as HTTP, CoAP, and MQTT. The connected devices construct as the oneM2M resource at the RR module. OI module registers the resource to IoT server. The DM and SM modules monitor the status of devices and services and dynamically reconfigure them.

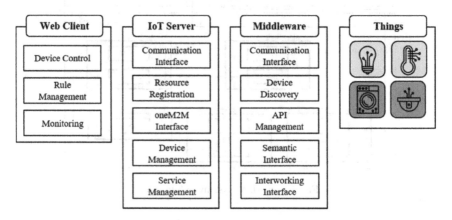

Fig. 2. Proposed IoT framework architecture.

When the device is connected to the network, the IoT server registers the device as a oneM2M resource. And for managing device dynamically, the IoT server performs a health-check mechanism of the device at the DM module. The data generated from the device registered is integrated into the oneM2M resource through monitoring from the SM module and is reported the event about the data generated by the middleware through the CI module.

Middleware connects between IoT server and device. There is the DD (Device Discovery) module to search connected device on a network. DD module gets the device information such as a manufacturer number, device model, and so on. Semantic Interface (SI) module represents raw data as semantic data. API of the discovered device in DD module is translated at AM (API Management) module to the oneM2M RESTful API. When a user sends a device control request to the platform, AM searches the API of the device and then transmits the API to the II (Interworking Interface) module. II module retrieves data from device or performs control request based on the API of the discovered device directly. The SI module uses the semantic Web technology for interaction between the IoT device and the sensor device which has limited computing power. Since the IoT platform only reports the syntax information of data, the current IoT system has limited range to perform the autonomous interaction. The SI analyzes oneM2M resource parameters managed by RR and converts them into semantic data. Raw data is represented as semantic data by IoT framework based on ontologies. The platform understands the resources that occur in all devices or sensors by representing as semantic data. Therefore, the middleware creates and executes interactions rule based on the relationship between data through semantic query. The middleware ensures semantic level interoperability through the ontology. Figure 3 shows an ontology to operate within the IoT framework by simplifying the *oneM2M base ontology* [9]. The SI module manages all semantic vocabularies. The ontology is used to execute the interaction rules for all oneM2M resource through semantic vocabularies. All devices and services are represented as the thing and the service class on ontology and the user-based rules are described as the function class.

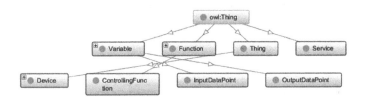

Fig. 3. Ontology design for representing raw data as semantic data

Figure 4 shows the oneM2M and semantic resource registration process. When thing connects to the local network, things announces its own information to the middleware. Announced information is described as semantic data in the SI module. And middleware forwards the information to the IoT server. The IoT server registers forwarded information as a oneM2M resource.

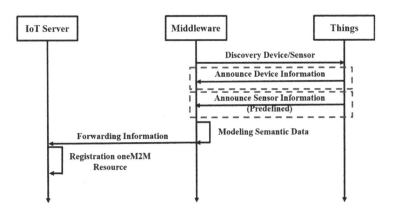

Fig. 4. oneM2M and semantic resource registration process.

The Web client consists of DC (Device Control), RM (Rule Management), and DMO (Device Monitoring) modules for easy management and control connected devices and sensors. The DMO module allows the user to confirm the status of the connected device. The DC module provides a function to directly control the device. And the RM module allows the user to create rules which interact between IoT platform devices. For example, a user can create the rule 'when the power of the A device is turned on, turn off the power of the B device'. Figure 5 shows the process of managing interaction rules via the Web client and performing the rules. The user sends the request about the creation and deletion of the interaction rule at the RM module. The IoT server reports request message about the rule to the SI module of the middleware. The SI module creates/deletes the rule using the semantic vocabularies defined in the ontology. When the device or sensor reports resource updating to middleware, the SI module searches the rule involved that event. If the rule exists, the SI module requests the API of the actuator to the AM module and forwards API to the II module. Finally, the event about the interaction that performed in the middleware are notified to the IoT server, and the IoT server updates the oneM2M resource.

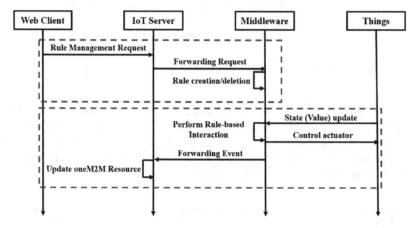

Fig. 5. Rule management and rule-based interaction process.

The proposed IoT framework ensure interoperability for devices and sensors in the vertical domain. All devices or sensors are registered as equivalent formatted resources. Since our framework based on oneM2M, it provides general input/output data point by oneM2M RESTful API. The middleware manages and executes interaction rules by representing raw data as semantic data. Therefore, the proposed platform provides intelligent and automated services. The user controls the device and creates the interaction via the Web without expert skill and knowledge of the API.

4   Implementation and Evaluation

As shown in Fig. 6, we set up the experimental testbed to evaluate the interoperability of our framework in real IoT environment. The IoT server is based on Mobius, an open source platform provided by OCEAN, which runs on a Linux OS desktop with Ubuntu installed [10]. The middleware works on Raspberry Pi 3B + and is implemented in the Eclipse development environment. The semantic module was developed using the Jena framework, a library based on Java language [11]. For the experiment, the devices belong to Alljoyn, Philips Hue, Nest platform. And sensor devices are implemented on Raspberry Pi 3B + using temperature/humidity, ultrasonic and illuminance sensor. We assume sensor devices have a constrained computing resource. Therefore, sensor devices return only the sensor value and the sensor identity tag.

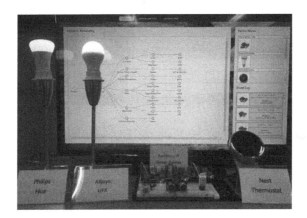

Fig. 6. Experimental testbed in real IoT environment

Figure 7 shows the results of the discovery in the DD module when the Philips platform and Alljoyn Platform devices connect to the local network. Since the oneM2M standard manages services in URI format middleware constructs URI using each device's metadata to avoid duplicate URIs. The sensor devices are registered in the same mechanism as the IoT device using a predefined identity tag as metadata.

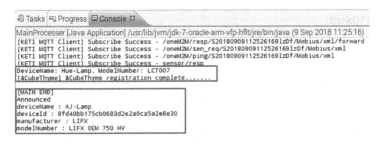

Fig. 7. Discovering device in the middleware

In the first experiment, we control the connected device on the Web client. Figure 8 shows the result of the controlling the brightness of the Hue lamp. We control the lamp of Philips platform without expert knowledge of the device's API. When the proposed framework receives request command, the AM module searches Philips platform's API and then forwards to the II module. The II module executes the requested service directly.

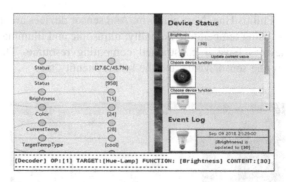

Fig. 8. Performing remote control of Hue lamp brightness.

In the second experiment, we evaluate the interoperability between different IoT platforms by executing rule-based interaction in the proposed framework. We have created the following rule: 'If the ultrasonic sensor detects the distance less than 5 cm, turn the power of the Hue lamp on'. Figure 9 shows the result of the performing remote control of Hue lamp. We confirmed that lamp turn on when the distance less than 5 cm.

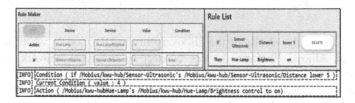

Fig. 9. Rule-based interaction between Philips platform and sensor device

5   Conclusion

In this paper, we point out the limitations and problems of the traditional vertical IoT platform and propose a solution of a horizontal interworking system based on the oneM2M standard. We also proposed a mechanism to create rules and perform interactions based on ontologies for autonomous interactions in the service platform. The IoT server manages resources based on the oneM2M standard and provides various protocol bindings to ensure interoperability of communication levels. Middleware provides semantic level interoperability that describes raw data as semantic data and performs rule-based interactions. We confirmed that the proposed framework allows the interoperability among Nest, Alljoyn, Philips platform devices and sensor devices in actual IoT environment. In addition, we have confirmed that the user-defined rules on the platform are autonomously executed through the ontology.

Acknowledgment. This work was supported by Institute for Information & communications Technology Promotion (IITP) grant funded by the Korea government (MSIT) (No. 2017-0-00167, Development of Human Implicit/Explicit Intention Recognition Technologies for Autonomous Human-Things Interaction).

References

1. Desia, P., Sheth, A., Anantharam, P.: Semantic gateway as a service architecture for IoT interoperability. In: Proceedings of the IEEE International Conference on Mobile Service, pp. 313–319, July 2015
2. Swetina, J., Lu, G., Jacobs, P., Ennesser, F., Song, J.: Toward a standardized common M2M service layer platform: introduction to oneM2M. IEEE Wirel. Commun. **21**(3), 20–26 (2014)
3. The RDF Document. https://www.w3.org/standards/techs/rdf#w3c_all
4. oneM2M-TS-0001. "oneM2M Functional Architecture Technical Specification," v3.12.0, July 2018
5. Mazayev, A., Martins, J.A., Correia, N.: Interoperability in IoT though the semantic profiling of objects. IEEE Access **6**, 19379–19385 (2017)
6. Maarala, A.I., Su, X., Riekki, J.: Semantic matching for context-aware Internet of Things applications. IEEE Internet of Things J. **4**(2), 461–473 (2017)
7. OWL 2 Web Ontology Language Primer. https://www.w3.org/TR/owl2-primer/
8. RDF Schema. https://www.w3.org/TR/rdf-schema/
9. oneM2M Base Ontology. http://www.onem2m.org/technical/onem2m-ontologies
10. Mobius. http://developers.IoTocean.org/archives/module/mobius
11. Jena Framework. https://jena.apache.org/index.html

Improvement of TextRank
Based on Co-occurrence Word Pairs
and Context Information

Yang Wang, Hua Yin[✉], and Minwei He

Information School, Guangdong University of Finance and Economics,
Guangzhou, China
yinhua@gdufe.edu.cn

Abstract. TextRank, a widely used keyword extraction algorithm, considers the relationship between words based on the graph model. However, Words with high frequency have more opportunities to co-occur with other words. Extracting keywords based on co-occurrence relationships ignores some unrecognized words, and TextRank only constructs a graph model from a single document. It leads to less efficiency in some related documents for missing the context information in the documents collection. In this paper, A smart improvement algorithm for TextRank is promoted. Firstly, for introducing external document features and considering the relationship between documents, all co-occurrence word pairs from the documents collection are extracted by associate rule mining. Then the co-occurrence frequency in TextRank score formula is replaced with the mutual information between the co-occurrence word pairs, which considers some less co-occurrence word pairs. Moreover, the context entropy of the words in the collection are calculated. At last, a new TextRank score formula is constructed, in which the context entropy pluses the replaced score formula with different weights. For testing the effectiveness, an experiment, considering five scoring weights combination, compares the improvement algorithm with the original TextRank and TF-IDF based on two different type of datasets (a public Chinese dataset and a financial dataset crawled from the internet). The experiment results show that with the same weight of the two parts, the improved TextRank algorithm is superior to the others.

Keywords: TextRank · Keyword extraction · Co-occurrence word pairs
Mutual information · Context entropy

1 Introduction

Natural Language Processing (NLP) is an important research direction in artificial intelligence. It is widely used in text sentiment analysis [1], information retrieval system [2], automatic question answering system [3], etc. Among them, keyword extraction is the core step. Zhao et al. [4] classify this field from linguistics, cognitive science, complexity science, psychology and social sciences. Chang et al. [5] also summarized the existing achievements used in various keyword extraction methods and

© Springer Nature Switzerland AG 2018
M. Qiu (Ed.): SmartCom 2018, LNCS 11344, pp. 226–235, 2018.
https://doi.org/10.1007/978-3-030-05755-8_23

the future development direction. They both believe that keyword extraction will inevitably generate new ideas, models and methods with the development of technology, and its application will become more and more extensive.

The keyword extraction algorithm includes supervised and unsupervised method. The unsupervised method can generate keywords directly without manual labels, which is more practical and convenient in practical work, and thus has received extensive attention. TextRank [6] is an unsupervised method based on graph model. After being proposed by Mihalcea R in 2004, it is continually improved by many scholars. In 2010, Liu [7] combined the topic model of the document with the graph model, used LDA to calculate the distribution of words under the theme, and then calculated the distribution of words under the document, finally calculated the PageRank score of all words. In 2014, Wang et al. [8] combined the word vector with the graph model, introduced the semantic relevance of the word, and added the relevance score formula of the word to improve the scoring formula. Xia et al. also used word vector techniques [9] to cluster the word vectors of TextRank word graph nodes to adjust the voting importance of nodes within the cluster, calculate the random jump probability between the nodes, generate the transfer matrix. Finally, the importance score of the node is obtained through iterative calculation. Zhou et al. [10] used FastText to characterize the document set. This method was based on the implicit topic distribution idea and the difference in semantics between vocabulary to construct the transition probability matrix of TextRank. In 2017, Florescu et al. [11] proposed the PositionRank method, which introduced the position of words in the document and improved the restart probability in the scoring formula. The above methods improved the TextRank scoring formula from different aspects, but they did not consider the external document related to the target document. Introducing external information would largely enrich the vocabulary and improve the efficiency. Moreover, TextRank still depended on the word frequency. The high frequency words have more opportunities to generate the co-occurrence relationship.

For reducing the computing consumption and introducing the external information, we firstly extract all co-occurrence word pairs by association rules mining from a document collection [12]. Then we replace the word frequency in TextRank scoring formula with the mutual information of co-occurrence word pairs. It can consider pairs of words with fewer co-occurrences. However, if a word in a document collection has no co-occurrence relationship with other words, it will be missed. So, we combine the mutual information of the co-occurring word pairs with the context entropy [13], and improve the TextRank scoring formula by weighting these two parts.

2   The Main Idea of TextRank

TextRank extracts a keyword list from a document. Suppose that there is a document d. it includes a set of words $\{w_1, w_2, w_3, \ldots, w_n\}$, where w_i represents the ith word in the document. The keyword extraction is to calculate the score of each word $R(w_i)$, and rank the score to select keywords.

For computing the word score, TextRank represents the document d by the graph $G = (V, E)$, where the vertex set V represents the word set $\{w_1, w_2, w_3, \ldots, w_n\}$ in the document and the edge set E represents the relationship between two words. $e(w_i, w_j)$ represents co-occurrence frequency between two words. So, the word scoring formula is as shown in (1).

$$R(w_i) = \lambda \sum_{j:w_j \to w_i} \frac{e(w_j, w_i)}{O(w_j)} \cdot R(w_j) + (1 - \lambda) \cdot r(w_i) \qquad (1)$$

Where λ is the damping coefficient and is usually taken as 0.85. it indicates that each node has a probability of $1 - \lambda$ to randomly jump to other nodes. $O(w_i)$ represents the degree of the outflow of the node w_j. $r(w_i)$ is the restart probability, which is usually 1/N and N is the total number of nodes in the graph.

The keyword score in TextRank largely depends on the co-occurrence frequency between two words. The higher the frequency, the greater the chance of co-occurrence with other words. And TextRank is more suitable for a single document. If it is used to extract keywords from a document collection, the current score formula will suffer some problems and miss the context information.

3 An Improvement Based on Co-occurrence Word Pairs and Context Information

We think that the higher co-occurrence frequency of words does not represent the importance of the word. Words with less co-occurrence frequency in a document might be important, if we consider it in a document collection. Considering the co-occurrence word pairs from a document collection will provide more information about the word. It will eliminate the influence of polysemous words, make the expression of the theme more accurate. And using the co-occurrence word pairs to extract keywords considers the co-occurrence word pairs in a document collection, which has less computing consumption than original way in TextRank. Because only consider the co-occurrence word pairs, only the co-occurrence words will be searched out. The way of scoring non-co-occurring words should be considered comprehensively. Considering above problems, we propose a smart improvement of TextRank based on co-occurrence word pairs and context information.

3.1 The Improvement Algorithm Description

The improvement algorithm is divided into three steps: (1) Text preprocessing; (2) Co-occurrence word pairs extraction; (3) Keywords weight score computing. The main pseudo code of the algorithm is as following:

Begin:
Input: document set $D = \{d_1, d_2, \ldots, d_n\}$, and document $d = \{w_1, w_2, w_3, \ldots, w_n\}$
(1) Extract a set of co-occurrence word pairs $A\{(w_i, w_j)\}$ in D
(2) Calculate the co-occurrence word pair mutual information $PMI(w_i; w_j)$ in A
(3) Calculate the context entropy $LCE(w_i), RCE(w_i), LCE(w_j), RCE(w_j)$ of the words w_i, w_j
(4) Calculate the keyword score $R(w_i)$, as in formula (2) and sort

$$R(w_i) = \alpha \left[\lambda \sum_{j:w_j \to w_i} \frac{PMI(w_i, w_j)}{O(w_j)} \cdot R(w_j) + (1 - \lambda) \cdot r(w_i) \right] + \beta \cdot$$
$$\frac{LCE(w_i) + RCE(w_i) + LCE(w_j) + RCE(w_j)}{2} \tag{2}$$

$PMI(w_i, w_j)$ represents the mutual information between the words w_i, w_j, $LCE(w_j)$ and $RCE(w_j)$ respectively represent the left context entropy and the right context entropy of w_j, respectively, and α and β respectively represent the weights of the two items. Where $\alpha + \beta = 1$.
Output: keyword list
End

3.2 Calculating Mutual Information of Co-occurrence Word Pairs

The co-occurrence word pairs extraction mainly adopts the method of association rule mining [14]. Each document is regarded as a transaction T, and the collection D of the document is a transaction database. Each word in the document after text preprocessing is treated as an item i. Since the co-occurring word pairs discussed in this paper are two-tuples, it is similar to extracting frequent binomial sets. The degree of support and confidence of co-occurring word pairs is calculated by calculating the co-occurrence rate of words.

Definition 1: Co-occurrence rate [15], $P(w_i, w_j)$ is the co-occurrence rate of word w_i and w_j, it refers to the probability that these two words co-occur in the same language unit, that is, their joint probability in text space, as shown in formula (3):

$$P(w_i, w_j) = \sum_{t \in T} P(t)P(w_i \mid t)P(w_j \mid t) \quad \forall w_i, w_j \in W \tag{3}$$

Suppose there is a topic set T and a word set W in the document collection D. The topic set of the document collection D is determined by the common theme of the field contained in the document. $d_i \in D$ represents the i-th document, and $t_k \in T$ represents the kth topic in the document space, $w_m \in W$ are the word that appears in the document collection.

If the subject t_k appears, the conditional probability that the word w_m appears can be expressed as $P(w_m \mid t_k)$. Then we compute the support and confidence of the word pairs by the associate rule mining algorithm.

$$\text{Support}(w_i, w_j) = P(w_i, w_j) \tag{4}$$

$$\text{Confidence}(w_i, w_j) = \frac{1}{2}\left(\frac{P(w_i, w_j)}{p(w_i)} + \frac{P(w_j, w_i)}{p(w_i)}\right) \tag{5}$$

We obtain the frequent binomial set R according to the threshold of support and confidence. R is a set of co-occurrence word pairs. And we calculate all the co-occurrence word pairs' point mutual information PMI (w_i, w_j), which is used to replace $e(w_i, w_j)$ in the original TextRank scoring formula.

$$\text{PMI}(X; Y) = \log\frac{p(x, y)}{p(x)p(y)} = \log\frac{p(x|y)}{p(x)} = \log\frac{p(y|x)}{p(y)} \tag{6}$$

3.3 Calculating the Context Entropy

When we use the point mutual information of the co-occurrence word pair to replace the co-occurrence frequency in the formula of TextRank, it really can increase the context information. But analyzing a large number of documents, we find that the keywords of the document may appear in only single document. It does not appear in the other document. For example, some specific place names or some specific terminology. That means the word pairs, not in the co-occurrence word pairs set, will not be considered, which will lead the first part of TextRank to be Zero. So, we should consider the words with less co-occurrence relationship. The idea of the new word detection [16] gives us some inspirations. We compute the context entropy of word and add it to the scoring formula. The technology can effectively extract the specific words that have not co-occurred in the document collection.

Therefore, this paper introduces the left context entropy and the right context entropy [13] for a word. Given a word w in the document d, $A = \{a_1, a_2, \ldots, a_s\}$ is the word set appearing on the left side of word w, $B = \{b_1, b_2, \ldots, b_s\}$ is the word set appearing on the right side of word w. we can calculate the left context entropy of word w: LCE(w) and the right context entropy: RCE(w) as the following formula.

$$\text{LCE}(w) = \frac{1}{n}\sum\nolimits_{i=1}^{s} C(a_i, w) \ln\left(\frac{C(a_i, w)}{n}\right) \tag{7}$$

$$\text{RCE}(w) = \frac{1}{n}\sum\nolimits_{i=1}^{t} C(w, b_i) \ln\left(\frac{C(w, b_i)}{n}\right) \tag{8}$$

Where $C(a_i, w)$ is the co-occur frequency of a_i and w, and $C(w, b_i)$ is the co-occur frequency of w and b_i.

4   Experiment

4.1   Experimental Datasets

Since the keyword extraction effect will vary from dataset to dataset, we need to use multiple different datasets to verify the performance of the algorithm. So we chose two datasets, one is a publicly available multi-domain dataset, another one is a dataset crawled from the internet in the specific financial fields.

The first dataset selected the Netease news dataset [17] collected by Professor Liu Zhiyuan of Tsinghua University in 2011. The dataset includes 13702 news stories captured from Netease News, a mainstream news media in China. We randomly selected 50 stories, which include a wide range of article topics, such as science, technology, politics, sports, art, society, and military. All articles have keywords that are manually labeled by the site editor, and each article also contains titles and summaries.

The second dataset is a specific financial dataset. Using web crawling technology to crawl 500 financial news reports from http://www.caijing.com.cn/, a finance website in China. Each article has at least two manually labeled keywords, along with the title and body. Table 1 shows the parameters of the two datasets.

Table 1. Comparison of two datasets

Dataset attributes	Dataset one	Dataset two
Number of documents	50	50
Number of word number	61257	28495
Unique words	3541	2784
Number of artificial keywords	158	126
Average keyword length	3.16	2.52
Field	Science, technology, politics, sports, art, society and military	Finance

4.2   Comparative Experiments

Considering the computational complexity of the experiment, we randomly select 50 documents for text preprocessing. Firstly, we remove the stop words from the document, which can greatly save search space and improve search efficiency. We use the stop word library provided by Sichuan University Machine Intelligence Laboratory. After that, we do the word segmentation processing by Jieba, from a Chinese open-source project. Because the keywords are always some nouns or verbs, further word-of-speech filtering is needed. We obtain the collection of nouns and verbs by word-of-speech filtering. Secondly, we extract the co-occurrence word pairs by the associate rule mining. At last we run the improved TextRank algorithm.

TFIDF and TextRank are chosen to be compared with the improved algorithm. TFIDF and TextRank are the current mainstream keyword extraction algorithm, which are still widely used. That is why we choose the two typical algorithms to compare with the new algorithm. We have considered five parameters setting of α and β shown as the following table (Table 2).

Table 2. parameters setting of α and β in the improved TextRank

Parameters setting 1	Parameters setting 2	Parameters setting 3	Parameters setting 4	Parameters setting 5
Mutual information improvement only $(\alpha = 1, \beta = 0)$	Context entropy improvement only $(\alpha = 0, \beta = 1)$	Both join at the same time $(\alpha = 0.5, \beta = 0.5)$	Both join at the same time $(\alpha = 0.25, \beta = 0.75)$	Both join at the same time $(\alpha = 0.75, \beta = 0.25)$

$$Precision = \frac{\text{The predicted correct number}}{\text{The predicted correct number} + \text{The prediction errors number}} \quad (9)$$

$$Recall = \frac{\text{The predicted correct number}}{\text{The predicted correct number} + \text{Original correct sample number}} \quad (10)$$

$$F\text{-}measure = \frac{2 * Precision * Recall}{Recision + Recall} \quad (11)$$

4.3   Experimental Results and Analysis

We compared TFIDF, TextRank and the improved TextRank algorithm with five different parameter settings on the two datasets. The results are showed in Tables 3 and 4.

Table 3. Results on the first dataset

Method	Precision	Recall	F-measure
TFIDF	0.197	0.247	0.215
TextRank	0.225	0.287	0.239
Setting1	0.188	0.241	0.240
Setting2	0.175	0.220	0.241
Setting3	0.293	0.331	0.305
Setting4	0.261	0.299	0.284
Setting5	0.241	0.280	0.245

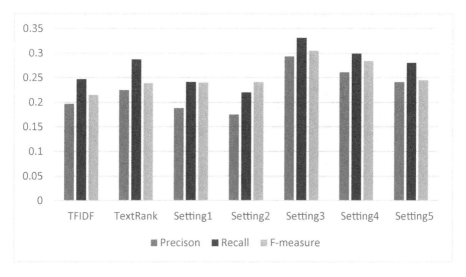

Fig. 1. Results on the first dataset

From Table 3 and Fig. 1, The improved algorithm in Setting1 and Setting2 are obviously inferior to TFIDF and TextRank. But the improved algorithm in the other three settings are all better than TFIDF and TextRank. It means that we should consider the two parts in the new scoring formula together. Furthermore, we find that the results of the improved algorithm in Setting3 is the best. Therefore, we can set the parameter α and β as 0.5 separately.

Table 4. Results on the second dataset

Method	Precision	Recall	F-measure
TFIDF	0.198	0.235	0.225
TextRank	0.230	0.285	0.235
Setting1	0.187	0.235	0.239
Setting2	0.178	0.222	0.245
Setting3	0.302	0.336	0.315
Setting4	0.271	0.303	0.288
Setting5	0.243	0.286	0.259

From Table 4 and Fig. 2, The results of these two datasets are a little different, but in general the results are similar. The results are better than TFIDF and TextRank on both datasets in Setting3, but the difference between the improved algorithm and TextRank in the second dataset is bigger than in the first dataset. It is concluded that the results in a specific field will be better than in the multiple fields.

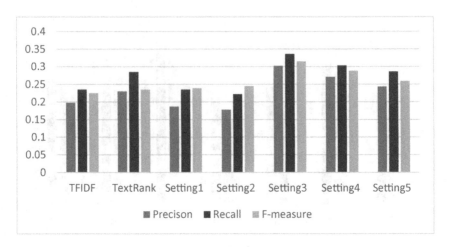

Fig. 2. Results on the second dataset

By performing multiple experiments and comparing the convergence speeds of these algorithms to the optimal solution, it is found that the convergence rate of the Setting 3 is better than other algorithms.

5 Conclusion and Future Work

This paper is an improvement of the traditional TextRank algorithm. Aiming at the problem that TextRank relies too much on word frequency and has less efficiency in the documents collection, we extract co-occurrence words to calculate their mutual information. For the problem that TextRank don't consider unco-occurring words, we introduce the context entropy, thus improve the efficiency of the algorithm. However, there are still some problems in the new algorithm. For example, it is not considered from the semantic level of the document. Therefore, the next research direction is to start from the word vector. We will try to use Word2Vec [18] to improve the accuracy of the results.

Acknowledgments. This work was supported by Science and Technology Program of Guangzhou, China (No. 201707010495), Project supported by Guangdong Province Universities, China (No. 2015KTSCX046), Foundation for Technology Innovation in Higher Education of Guangdong Province, China (No. 2013KJCX0085) and Foundation for Distinguished Young Talents in Higher Education of Guangzhou, China (No. 2013LYM0032).

References

1. Zhao, Y.Y., Qin, B., Liu, T.: Sentiment analysis. J. Softw. **21**(8), 1834 − 1848 (2010). (in Chinese). http://www.jos.org.cn/1000-9825/3832.html
2. Wang, Y., Jia, Y., Liu, D., Jin, X., Cheng, X.: Open web knowledge aided information search and data mining. J. Comput. Res. Dev. **52**(02), 456–474 (2015). (in Chinese)
3. Ou, S., Tang, Z.: A question answering method over library linked data. J. Libr. Sci. China **41**(06), 44–60 (2015). (in Chinese)
4. Zhao, J., Zhu, Q., Zhou, G., Zhang, L.: Review of research on automatic keyword extraction. J. Softw. **28**(09), 2431–2449 (2017). (in Chinese)
5. Chang, Y., Zhang, Y., Wang, H., Wan, H., Xiao, C.: Features oriented survey of state-of-the-art keyphrase extraction algorithms [J/OL]. J. Softw. 1–25 (2018). (in Chinese)
6. Mihalcea, R., Tarau, P.: TextRank: bringing order into texts. In: Proceedings of EMNLP, pp. 404–411 (2004)
7. Liu, Z.Y., Huang, W.Y., Zheng, Y.B., Sun, M.S.: Automatic keyphrase extraction via topic decomposition. In: Proceedings of EMNLP, pp. 366–376 (2010)
8. Wang, R., Liu, W., Mc Donald, C.: Corpus-independent generic keyphrase extraction using word embedding vectors. In: Proceedings of Software Engineering Research Conference, p. 39 (2014)
9. Xia, T.: Extracting keywords with modified TextRank model. Data Anal. Knowl. Discov. **1**(02), 28–34 (2017). (in Chinese)
10. Zhou, J., Cui, X.: Keyword extraction method based on word vector and TextRank [J/OL]. Comput. Appl. Res. **05**, 1–5 (2019). (in Chinese)
11. Florescu, C., Caragea, C.: A position-biased pagerank algorithm for keyphrase extraction. In: Proceedings of AAAI, pp. 4923–4924 (2017)
12. Chang, P., Feng, N.: A co-occurrence based vector space model for document indexing. Chin. J. Inf. Process. **26**(01), 51–57 (2012). (in Chinese)
13. Huo, S., Zhang, M., Liu, Y., Ma, S.: New words discovery in microblog content. Pattern Recogn. Artif. Intell. **27**(02), 141–145 (2014). (in Chinese)
14. Agrawal, R., Srikant, R.: Fast algorithms for mining association rules. In: Proceedings of International Conference on Very Large Databases, pp. 487–499 (1994)
15. Hofmann, T.: Unsupervised learning by probabilistic latent semantic analysis. Mach. Learn. **42**(1–2), 177–196 (2001)
16. Luo, Z., Song, R.: An integrated method for Chinese unknown word extraction. In: Proceedings of ACL SIGHAN Workshop (2003)
17. Liu, Z., Chen, X., Zheng, Y., et al.: Automatic keyphrase extraction by bridging vocabulary gap. In: Fifteenth Conference on Computational Natural Language Learning. Association for Computational Linguistics, pp. 135–144 (2011)
18. Mikolov, T., Chen, K., Corrado, G., et al.: Efficient estimation of word representations in vector space. Computer Science (2013)

Augmenting Embedding with Domain Knowledge for Oral Disease Diagnosis Prediction

Guangkai Li[1], Songmao Zhang[1(✉)], Jie Liang[2], Zhanqiang Cao[3],
and Chuanbin Guo[2]

[1] MADIS, Academy of Mathematics and Systems Science,
Chinese Academy of Sciences, University of Chinese Academy of Sciences,
Beijing 100190, China
liguangkai15@mails.ucas.ac.cn, smzhang@math.ac.cn
[2] Department of Oral and Maxillofacial Surgery,
Peking University School and Hospital of Stomatology, Beijing 100081, China
Liangjie.pkuss@gmail.com, guodazuo@sina.com.cn
[3] Information Center, Peking University School and Hospital of Stomatology,
Beijing, China
caozhanqiang@pkuss.bjmu.edu.cn

Abstract. In this paper, we propose to add domain knowledge from the most comprehensive biomedical ontology SNOMED CT to facilitate the embedding of EMR symptoms and diagnoses for oral disease prediction. We first learn embeddings of SNOMED CT concepts by applying the TransE algorithm prevalent for representation learning of knowledge base. Secondly, the mapping from symptoms/diagnoses to biomedical concepts and the corresponding semantic relations defined in SNOMED CT are modeled mathematically. We design a neural network to train embeddings of EMR symptoms and diagnoses and ontological concepts in a coherent way, for the latter the TransE-learned vectors being used as initial values. The evaluation on real-world EMR datasets from Peking University School and Hospital Stomatology demonstrates the prediction performance improvement over embeddings solely based on EMRs. This study contributes as a first attempt to learn distributed representations of EMR symptoms and diagnoses under the constraint of embeddings of biomedical concepts from comprehensive clinical ontology. Incorporating domain knowledge can augment embedding as it reveals intrinsic correlation among symptoms and diagnoses that cannot be discovered by EMR data alone.

Keywords: Biomedical ontology · Embedding · Diagnosis prediction
EMR data

1 Introduction

Applying advanced AI technologies to discovering knowledge implied in electronic medical records (EMRs) has always been important and compelling in the domain of biomedical informatics. Early efforts focus on constructing rules or using lexical/ linguistic methods to extract features from EMRs [1], whereas state-of-the-art works

© Springer Nature Switzerland AG 2018
M. Qiu (Ed.): SmartCom 2018, LNCS 11344, pp. 236–250, 2018.
https://doi.org/10.1007/978-3-030-05755-8_24

exploit machine learning approaches, especially classification and clustering algorithms to predict the probability of diagnosis, survival or morbidity [2–6]. In recent years, the word embedding technique has made distinctive achievements in natural language processing tasks [7–11]. Inspired by the rationale of embedding, we designed a model of diagnosis prediction in one of our previous studies [12], where symptoms and diagnoses in EMRs are represented as continuous vectors in high-dimensional, real-valued space and trained using artificial neural network. The evaluation on real-world EMR data shows that our model outperforms widely-used classification methods under various kinds of metrics.

Biomedical ontologies contribute to probably the most successful application of the Semantic Web technology, by modeling domain conceptualizations so that systems or search engines built upon them can interoperate with each other by sharing the same meaning. A lot of biomedical ontologies have been developed, often of large scale, for instance, the Foundational Model of Anatomy (FMA) [13] and Adult Mouse Anatomy (MA) [14] for anatomy, National Cancer Institute Thesaurus (NCI) [15] for disease, and Systematized Nomenclature of Medicine-Clinical Terms (SNOMED CT) [16] for clinical medicine. These ontologies have been utilized in many AI-based applications including semantic annotation, information retrieval, data integration, question-answering, reasoning, and decision making. In this paper, to further our previous study [12], we propose to add domain knowledge from biomedical ontologies to facilitate the embedding of symptoms and diagnoses for oral disease prediction.

The data we use comes from Peking University School and Hospital of Stomatology (PKUSS), one of the most prestigious hospitals in China for oral diseases. PKUSS has been enhancing the development of EMR information systems and over the years has accumulated a large amount of clinical data. The stomatologic data is of high dimensionality and complexity, and has been less studied in AI community. We collected more than 7,000 patients' records from eleven PKUSS departments, and developed a comprehensive set of ways to extract symptoms as well as diagnoses from raw EMR data [12], as shown in Table 1.

Table 1. The PKUSS datasets with symptoms and diagnoses extracted

Dataset	Record	Symptom	Diagnosis
Pediatric dentistry	669	609	6
Oral & maxillofacial surgery	728	211	8
Laser dentistry	569	190	7
Emergency	371	242	6
Oral medicine	425	253	4
Prosthodontics	1135	321	3
Geriatric dentistry	320	286	2
General dentistry	407	283	3
Orthodontics	671	886	4
Periodontology	1016	706	3
Implant dentistry	897	111	6

To incorporate biomedical domain knowledge, we utilize the most comprehensive clinical ontology SNOMED CT and learn embeddings of its biomedical concepts by applying TransE [24], a prevalent algorithm for representation learning of knowledge base. Visualization and computation of similarities of concepts illustrate that the learned vectors can reflect the semantic correlation among concepts. Afterwards, we map the symptoms and diagnoses in PKUSS datasets to SNOMED CT concepts whose semantic relations are used for augmenting the embedding of EMRs. Concretely, we mathematically model the closeness of symptoms/diagnoses with their mapped biomedical concepts and the linearity of a concept with those in its semantic relations in continuous vector space. These two constraints are specified as regularization terms of the loss function that our neural network-based embedding model pursues to minimize in training. The mathematical modeling is inspired by so-called semantically smooth embedding proposed in [17], which only uses types of concepts for representation learning of knowledge graph. In our model, not only type hierarchies but also attribute relationships defined in SNOMED CT are involved. Moreover, embeddings of EMR symptoms and diagnoses and ontological concepts are trained coherently, where for the latter the TransE-learned vectors are used as initial values. As a result, under the support of domain knowledge, the prediction performance in accuracy, weighted precision, recall and f1-score has all increased on seven out of eleven PKUSS datasets compared with the embedding solely based on EMR data.

The contribution of our study in this paper can be summarized as a first attempt to learn distributed representations of EMR symptoms and diagnoses under the constraint of embeddings of biomedical concepts from comprehensive clinical ontology. The evaluation on real-world oral disease EMRs demonstrates that incorporating domain knowledge can augment embedding as it reveals intrinsic correlation among symptoms and diagnoses that cannot be discovered by EMR data alone.

The rest of the paper is organized as follows. Applying TransE to learn the distributed representation of SNOMED CT is described in Sect. 2. Under the support of such domain knowledge, we present a neural network model for embedding EMR symptoms and diagnoses in Sect. 3. The evaluation in Sect. 4 presents the result of representation learning of SNOMED CT and the prediction performance of diagnosis for eleven PKUSS datasets. Lastly, we introduce related work and compare with our own study, discuss the future directions and conclude the paper in Sect. 5.

2   Representation Learning of Biomedical Ontology

We present the extraction of biomedical concepts and their semantic relations from SNOMED CT followed by their embedding in continuous vector space in this section.

2.1   The Biomedical Ontology SNOMED CT

SNOMED CT is so far the most comprehensive, multi-lingual clinical terminology system in the world, covering subdomains of anatomy, morphology, disease, diagnosis, chemical product, surgical operation, and more. There are more than 300 thousand concepts and 7 million semantic relations specified in SNOMED CT, providing core and general biomedical terms that can be used to annotate EMRs in a semantic way. We choose SNOMED CT as source of the domain knowledge to augment the representation learning of symptoms and diagnoses in oral disease EMRs.

Each SNOMED CT concept is described by one preferred term and several synonyms, and concepts can be linked through two kinds of relationships, subtype and attribute relationships. Subtype relations actually compose the *is-a* hierarchical structure, and there are 19 such hierarchies in SNOMEDT CT rooted respectively by 19 top-level concepts. Both SNOMED CT subtype and attribute relationships between concepts are used in our approach. More precisely, we extract the sourceId, typeId, and destinationId from file "sct2_Relationship_Full_INT_20180131.txt" in the January 2018 SNOMED CT International Edition Release[1]. Take concept *Dental plaque* for example, whose SNOMEDT CT relations are obtained as triples in the following, where *Associative morphology, Causative agent* and *Finding site* are attribute relationships.

(Dental plaque, is a, Accretion on teeth)
(Dental plaque, Associative morphology, Accretion)
(Dental plaque, Causative agent, Superkingdom Bacteria)
(Dental plaque, Finding site, Tooth structure)

Symptoms present in EMRs can be correlated, for instance, in the PKUSS Oral Medicine dataset, symptoms "Dental plaque slight", "Dental plaque moderate" and "Dental plaque abundant" all describe the extent of plaques; and "Dental calculus (+)", "Dental calculus (++)" and "Dental calculus (+++)" are symptoms about calculi. As a matter of fact, plaques and calculi refer to different stages of food residues building up on tooth, which is not shown in EMR data *per se*. Such knowledge, however, can be identified in SNOMED CT, as shown by the relation triples for concept *Dental calculus* in the following.

(Dental calculus, is a, Accretion on teeth)
(Dental calculus, Associative morphology, Calculus)
(Dental calculus, Associative morphology, Accretion)
(Dental calculus, Finding site, Tooth structure)

The two concepts *Dental plaque* and *Dental calculus* share an *is-a* relation and two attribute relations in SNOMED CT, indicating certain correlation, which can be used to facilitate the predication based on EMR symptoms and diagnoses.

---

[1] https://www.nlm.nih.gov/healthit/snomedct/international.html.

2.2 Applying TransE to Learn the Representation of SNOMED CT Concepts

With the rise of word embedding in natural language processing, incorporating the idea into knowledge bases has become an important research trend, especially as seen in the knowledge graph community [18]. The goal is to embed an entity or semantic relation in knowledge base into a dense, real-valued vector or matrix in high-dimensional space, where the value of each dimension in the vector represents the projection of the entity/relation on some semantic dimension. Such vectors are also called distributed representations of knowledge base. These numerical representations are obtained by training on the whole knowledge base, usually of large scale, thus have a potential to reflect the correlation among concepts and individuals. Many such numerical methods have been proposed, including structured embedding (SE) [19], semantic matching energy (SME) [20], single layer neural networks (SL) [21], latent factor models (LF) [22], tensor factorization models (RESACL) [23], and translational models. Among these, the TransE model [24] becomes appealing for requiring fewer parameters, holding lower computational complexity, and that it has successfully demonstrated its outperformance on real-world, large-scale knowledge bases like WordNet and Freebase. We use TransE to learn vector representations of SNOMED CT concepts. Particularly, for a semantic relationship from one concept (head) to another (tail), TransE models the relationship vector to be the transition from the head vector to the tail vector in numerical space. The more correlated concepts defined in ontology, the more similar their learned vectors are in space.

3 Embedding of EMR Symptoms and Diagnoses Under the Support of SNOMED CT

We map EMR symptoms and diagnoses to SNOMED CT concepts whose semantic relations are used for learning the distributed representations. Suppose there are m EMRs in the training set whose symptoms are $S = \{symp_i\}_{i=1}^n$ and diagnoses $D = \{diag_i\}_{i=1}^l$. Mapping symptoms in S to SNOMED CT yields concepts $SC = \{sc_i\}_{i=1}^p$, whose number is normally less than that of symptoms as quite often multiple symptoms are matched to one concept, as exemplified by that symptoms "**Dental plaque slight**", "**Dental plaque moderate**" and "**Dental plaque abundant**" all correspond to concept *Dental plaque*. For the i-th concept in SC, suppose that the semantic relations specified in SNOMED CT are $T1_i = \{(sc_i, scattr_{i,j}, sc_{i,j})\}_{j=1}^{p_i}$. Similarly, we suppose that mapping diagnoses in D to SNOMED CT yields concepts $DC = \{dc_i\}_{i=1}^q$, where the i-th concept has semantic relations $T2_i = \{(dc_i, dcattr_{i,j}, dc_{i,j})\}_{j=1}^{q_i}$. In order to incorporate the SNOMED CT relation triples in embedding, we present the following propositions and model them mathematically.

Proposition 1. For any two symptoms $symp_i$ and $symp_j$ that are mapped to one SNOMED CT concept *Concept*, both $symp_i$ and $symp_j$ shall have the same embedding representation as *Concept*. This also holds for embeddings of diagnoses.

Proposition 2. The Embedding of a SNOMEDT CT concept can be represented by the embeddings of the concepts in its semantic relations in a linear way.

We construct adjacency matrix $W^{(1)} \in \Re^{n \times p}$ to represent correspondence between symptoms and their mapped concepts, and $W^{(2)} \in \Re^{l \times q}$ for correspondence between diagnoses and their mapped concepts, defined as follows.

$$W_{ij}^{(1)} = \begin{cases} 1 & \text{if the } i\text{-th symptom in } S \text{ is mapped to the } j\text{-th concept in } SC \\ 0 & \text{otherwise} \end{cases} \quad (1)$$

$$W_{ij}^{(2)} = \begin{cases} 1 & \text{if the } i\text{-th diagnosis in } D \text{ is mapped to the } j\text{-th concept in } DC \\ 0 & \text{otherwise} \end{cases} \quad (2)$$

Suppose matrix $F \in \Re^{p \times k}$ where its i-th dimension is the embedding of the i-th concept in SC, and matrix $G \in \Re^{q \times k}$ where its i-th dimension is the embedding of the i-th concept in DC. Now we can model Proposition 1 by minimizing R_1 defined in the following equation so that the distance between embeddings of the symptoms mapped to the same SNOMED CT concept becomes as small as possible.

$$R_1 = \frac{1}{2} \sum_{i=1}^{n} \sum_{j=1}^{p} \| C(i) - F(j) \|_2^2 W_{ij}^{(1)} + \frac{1}{2} \sum_{i=1}^{n} \sum_{j=1}^{q} \| V(i) - G(j) \|_2^2 W_{ij}^{(2)} \quad (3)$$

For Proposition 2, if SNOMED CT concept $concept_a$ has two relations $(concept_a, attribute_1, concept_1)$ and $(concept_a, attribute_2, concept_2)$ and the embeddings of $concept_1$ and $concept_2$ are E_1 and E_2, then the embedding of $concept_a$ can be represented as:

$$E = \alpha_1 E_1 + \alpha_2 E_2 \quad (4)$$

In (4), α_1 and α_2 are weights dependent on the importance of $attribute_1$ and $attribute_2$ to $concept_a$ respectively. To model Proposition 2, we define:

$$R_2 = \frac{1}{2} \sum_{i=1}^{p} \left\| F(i) - \sum_{(sc_i, scattr_{i,j}, sc_{i,j}) \in T1_i} \alpha_{scattr_{i,j}} E(sc_{i,j}) \right\|_2^2$$
$$+ \frac{1}{2} \sum_{i=1}^{q} \left\| G(i) - \sum_{(dc_i, dcattr_{i,j}, dc_{i,j}) \in T2_i} \alpha_{dcattr_{i,j}} E(dc_{i,j}) \right\|_2^2 \quad (5)$$

In (5), $E(sc_{i,j})$ represents the embedding of concept $sc_{i,j}$ in the semantic relation, and $\alpha_{scattr_{i,j}}$ the weight of how the embedding of $sc_{i,j}$ contributes to the embedding of sc_i, which depends on the weight of attribute in the relation. As normally cannot decide such weights, we set $\alpha_{scattr_{i,j}} = \frac{1}{p_i}$ where p_i is the number of semantic relations of the i-th concept in SC.

Our embedding model is a neural network with three layers, as illustrated in Fig. 1. Firstly, the input layer consists of n nodes, where n is the number of symptoms extracted from EMR data. We define function $C(\cdot)$ to map symptom element i of S to real vector $C(i) \in \Re^k$, where k represents the dimension of embedding representation. Similarly, we define function $V(\cdot)$ to map diagnosis element j of D to real vector $V(j) \in \Re^k$. Functions $C(\cdot)$ and $V(\cdot)$ respectively represent embeddings associated with each symptom and diagnosis in an EMR dataset, and we further add $E(\cdot)$ for embeddings of SNOMED CT concepts whose initial values are learned by TransE algorithm. The three functions are represented as a $n \times k$, $l \times k$, and $p \times k$ matrix of free parameter k.

Secondly, the hidden layer of our neural network uses the hyperbolic tangent function as an activation function and then makes adjustments by weights and bias terms [12]. Lastly, the output layer consists of l nodes, the number of diagnoses in EMR data, and we use a softmax function to obtain diagnosis with highest probability. Training is performed by looking for θ that maximizes a log-likelihood loss function defined as follows:

$$\mathcal{L}(y, \mathcal{O}; \theta) = \frac{1}{m} \sum_i^m \sum_j^l y_{ij} log \mathcal{O}_{ij} - R_1 - R_2 \tag{6}$$

In (6), $\mathcal{O}_{ij}$ is a normalized exponential function that computes the probability of the m-th EMR case determined as the j-th diagnosis, and R_1 and R_2 for modeling the influence of domain knowledge are used as regularization terms.

4   The Evaluation

We present the evaluation of our approach by two parts in this section: firstly, the result of applying TransE to learn distributed representations of SNOMED CT concepts, and secondly, feeding these into our neural network model to learn embeddings of the EMR symptoms and diagnoses in PKUSS datasets for oral disease prediction.

4.1   The Representation of SNOMED CT Concepts by TransE

The extraction of SNOMED CT resulted in a total of 396,877 concepts, 101 attributes and 2,666,776 semantic relations. We used the TransE algorithm provided in OpenKE[2], an open source software package for knowledge base representation learning, and set embedding dimension to be 100, batch size 10,000, learning rate 0.001, maximum training iterations 1,000, and used the L_1 norm.

---

[2] https://github.com/thunlp/OpenKE.

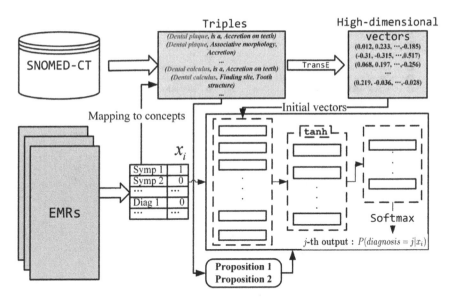

Fig. 1. Architecture of the symptom/diagnosis embedding model supported by domain ontology

Take the PKUSS Oral Medicine dataset for example, whose symptoms and diagnoses are mapped to 23 concepts in SNOMED CT. After training by TransE, each of these concepts is represented by a vector in a high-dimensional space. The distance between these vectors in space reveals the correlation of the concepts. For the purpose of validation, we visualize the high-dimensional vectors into 2D space by using a dimensionality reduction algorithm t-SNE [25], shown in Fig. 2. One can see that correlated concepts (in the same shape in Fig. 2) are positioned adjacently, as exemplified by the neighboring of *Dental plaque, Dental calculus* and *Soft deposit on teeth*, and the neighboring of *Dental crown, metal/polymer, Dental crown, metal*, and *Temporary crown*.

With vector representations available, we can compute their cosine similarity in high-dimensional space to reflect the semantic similarity of concepts, as follows.

$$csimilarity = \frac{E_i \cdot E_j^T}{\|Ei\| \cdot \|Ej\|} \tag{7}$$

In (7), E_i and E_j are the learned vectors of concepts, and the bigger the value of *csimilarity*, the more similar the two concepts. Table 2 lists the most similar concepts to *Dental plaque* computed, which are all of tooth and the first two specifically represent residues on tooth as same as *Dental plaque*, illustrating the validity of the distributed representations learned for concepts.

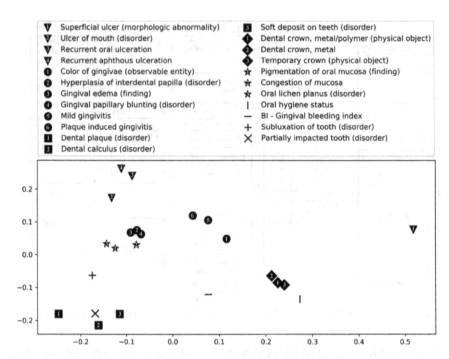

Fig. 2. Visualization of the distributed representations of SNOMED CT concepts by TransE.

Table 2. The SNOMED CT concepts that are mostly similar to concept *Dental plaque*.

Concept	Similarity
Dental calculus (disorder)	0.744
Soft deposit on teeth (disorder)	0.729
Subluxation of tooth (disorder)	0.635
Partially impacted tooth (disorder)	0.598

4.2   The Prediction of Diagnoses from the PKUSS EMRs

The vectors learned above are fed into our neural network model as initial values for SNOMED CT concepts. We set learning rate as 0.05 for stochastic gradient ascent and embedding dimension $k = 100$ for concept/symptom/diagnosis. The number of nodes in the hidden layer of our neural network is determined by empirical formula $nh = \sqrt{ni + no} + o$, where ni is the number of nodes of the input layer, no the output layer, and o a constant between 1 and 10. For the purpose of comparison, we selected five highly recognized classification methods: k-NN, logistic regression, C4.5, naïve Bayes, and SVM.

Tables 3, 4, 5 and 6 lists the prediction performance on eleven PKUSS datasets in terms of accuracy, weighted precision, weighted recall, and weighted f-score, respectively. The accuracy measures the percentage of those correctly classified over the whole records, whereas weighted metrics are used in multiclass classification tasks for computing weighted averages of the corresponding measure of each class. In these tables, the rightmost column in gray presents the performance of our augmented model under the support of domain knowledge, whereas other columns are the same as reported in our previous study [12]. While the embedding approach outperforms all five benchmark classifiers on every PKUSS dataset, incorporating SNOMED CT further increases the accuracy and weighted precision, recall and f-score on seven out of eleven datasets, i.e., the Pediatric Dentistry, Oral & Maxillofacial Surgery, Emergency, Oral Medicine, Prosthodontics, General Dentistry, and Implant Dentistry.

Table 3. The prediction accuracy (%) of classifiers on eleven PKUSS datasets.

Dataset	k-NN	Logistic regression	C4.5	Naïve Bayes	SVM	Embedding [12]	Embedding + ontology
Pediatric Dentistry	70.5	75.0	75.0	33.8	76.4	**77.2**	**78.7**
Oral & Maxillofacial surgery	70.9	81.7	68.9	58.7	79.7	**82.4**	**83.8**
Laser Dentistry	84.4	90.5	86.2	73.2	**91.3**	**91.3**	91.3
Emergency	72.3	71.0	71.0	64.4	72.3	**75.0**	**76.3**
Oral Medicine	89.5	83.7	90.6	80.2	86.0	**93.0**	**94.1**
Prosthodontics	**89.0**	87.7	85.1	70.3	86.4	**89.0**	**89.5**
Geriatric Dentistry	89.2	87.6	86.1	87.6	89.2	**92.3**	92.3
General Dentistry	75.9	**92.7**	75.9	61.4	90.3	**92.7**	**93.9**
Orthodontics	55.7	67.3	55.7	29.7	65.9	**70.2**	70.2
Periodontology	94.6	94.6	95.1	85.3	95.6	**96.0**	96.0
Implant Dentistry	80.1	80.1	80.6	19.8	80.6	**81.2**	**81.7**

Table 4. The weighted precision (%) of classifiers on eleven PKUSS datasets

Dataset	k-NN	Logistic regression	C4.5	Naïve Bayes	SVM	Embedding [12]	Embedding + ontology
Pediatric Dentistry	0.71	0.76	0.76	0.36	0.76	**0.77**	**0.79**
Oral & Maxillofacial surgery	0.75	**0.84**	0.77	0.65	0.80	**0.84**	**0.85**
Laser Dentistry	0.85	**0.91**	0.86	0.77	**0.91**	0.91	0.91
Emergency	**0.80**	0.75	0.72	0.64	0.72	0.75	**0.77**
Oral Medicine	0.89	0.82	0.90	0.84	0.84	**0.93**	**0.95**
Prosthodontics	**0.89**	0.87	0.85	0.78	0.86	**0.89**	**0.90**
Geriatric Dentistry	0.89	0.87	0.86	0.88	0.89	**0.92**	0.92
General Dentistry	0.76	**0.93**	0.80	0.66	0.90	**0.93**	**0.94**
Orthodontics	0.55	0.69	0.60	0.30	0.68	**0.73**	0.73
Periodontology	0.92	0.92	0.93	0.92	0.93	**0.95**	0.95
Implant Dentistry	0.72	0.77	**0.78**	0.76	0.76	0.76	**0.78**

As an example, consider EMRs containing two symptoms "Peripheral edema" and "Dental calculus (+++)" in the PKUSS Oral Medicine dataset. In the training set, EMRs with the symptoms present simultaneously are diagnosed as "Oral lichen planus", which is thus the classification result for those in the test set. Nevertheless, the test set contains cases whose diagnoses are not "Oral lichen planus" but rather "Light recurrent ulcer of mouth", thus classified wrongly. In SNOMED CT, the *finding site* of concepts *Mucous membrane edema* and *Recurrent ulcer of mouth* are both defined to be *Oral mucous membrane structure*, whereas *Oral lichen planus* has *finding site* at *Oral soft tissues structure*. With such knowledge augmented in the training process, EMRs with symptom "Peripheral edema" are more likely to be diagnosed as "Light recurrent ulcer of mouth", when the symptom and diagnosis are mapped to concepts *Mucous membrane edema* and *Recurrent ulcer of mouth*, respectively. Moreover, according to SNOMEDT CT, *Dental calculus* and *Dental plaque* are correlated and *Plaque induced gingivitis* is *due to Dental plaque*. With the availability of such knowledge, cases with symptom "Dental calculus (+++)" become less possible to be diagnosed as "Oral lichen planus".

Table 5. The weighted recall (%) of classifiers on eleven PKUSS datasets

Dataset	k-NN	Logistic regression	C4.5	Naïve Bayes	SVM	Embedding [12]	Embedding + ontology
Pediatric Dentistry	0.70	0.75	0.75	0.33	0.76	**0.77**	**0.79**
Oral & Maxillofacial surgery	0.70	0.81	0.71	0.58	0.79	**0.82**	**0.84**
Laser Dentistry	0.84	0.90	0.86	0.73	**0.91**	**0.91**	0.91
Emergency	0.72	0.71	0.71	0.64	0.72	**0.75**	**0.76**
Oral Medicine	0.89	0.83	0.90	0.80	0.86	**0.93**	**0.94**
Prosthodontics	**0.89**	0.87	0.85	0.70	0.86	**0.89**	**0.90**
Geriatric Dentistry	0.89	0.87	0.86	0.87	0.89	**0.92**	0.92
General Dentistry	0.75	**0.92**	0.79	0.61	0.90	**0.92**	**0.94**
Orthodontics	0.55	0.67	0.55	0.29	0.65	**0.70**	0.70
Periodontology	0.94	0.64	0.95	0.85	0.95	**0.96**	0.96
Implant Dentistry	0.80	0.80	0.80	0.19	0.80	**0.81**	**0.82**

On the other hand, prediction in the Laser Dentistry, Geriatric Dentistry, Orthodontics and Periodontology dataset has not been improved by the addition of domain knowledge. This can be caused by the granularity difference between EMR data and domain ontology. Take the Orthodontics dataset for example. Among its 886 symptoms, many describe concrete numerical values, as in "Crowding of teeth: upper dental arch I^O3 mm", "Crowding of teeth: upper dental arch II^O5 mm", and "Crowding of teeth: upper dental arch III^O9 mm". These values represent the position of upper and lower dental arch based on the first molar, which are crucial for diagnosing among "Angle's Class I", "Angle's Class II", "Angle's Class II Division 1", and "Angle's Class III". Such position values, however, are absent in

Table 6. The weighted f1-score (%) of classifiers on eleven PKUSS datasets

Dataset	k-NN	Logistic regression	C4.5	Naïve Bayes	SVM	Embedding [12]	Embedding + ontology
Pediatric Dentistry	0.69	0.74	0.74	0.31	0.76	**0.77**	**0.79**
Oral & Maxillofacial surgery	0.71	0.81	0.73	0.57	0.79	**0.82**	**0.84**
Laser Dentistry	0.84	0.90	0.85	0.71	**0.91**	**0.91**	0.91
Emergency	0.71	0.72	0.71	0.63	0.72	**0.75**	**0.76**
Oral Medicine	0.89	0.81	0.90	0.81	0.83	**0.92**	**0.94**
Prosthodontics	**0.89**	0.87	0.85	0.70	0.86	**0.89**	0.89
Geriatric Dentistry	0.89	0.87	0.86	0.87	0.89	**0.92**	0.92
General Dentistry	0.74	**0.92**	0.79	0.61	0.90	**0.92**	**0.94**
Orthodontics	0.53	0.68	0.57	0.26	0.66	**0.71**	0.71
Periodontology	0.93	0.93	0.94	0.88	0.94	**0.95**	0.95
Implant Dentistry	0.74	0.77	**0.78**	0.20	0.77	0.77	**0.79**

SNOMED CT, thus all the symptoms have to be mapped to one concept *Crowding of teeth*, under which our model fails to capture the concrete correlations.

5   Related Work, Discussion and Conclusions

The interest to exploit word embedding in biomedical informatics emerges as the technique has demonstrated its power in many research areas. This includes, for instance, training multiple word embeddings on different EMR notes so as to extract similar terms for chart reviews [27], applying the word2vec model to processing PubMed medical texts [26], using real-world EHR data for the purpose of medical concept representation learning [28, 29], comparing word embedding and machine learning methods in representing clinical notes for medical named entity recognition [30], modeling correlation of diseases in sparsity-based graph to facilitate diagnosis assignment [31], and many others. These works often learn vectors based on skip-gram models, compared with which our model targets diagnosis prediction by learning distributed representation of each symptom and diagnosis from EMR data. Moreover, we manage to incorporate domain knowledge from the most comprehensive clinical ontology SNOMED CT and the evaluation on oral disease datasets demonstrates the augmentation in performance.

Introducing additional semantic knowledge into embedding is becoming frequent when researchers realize the inadequacy of learning solely based on observed data [17]. The semantic information used are diverse, e.g., semantic categories of entities in semantically smooth embedding of knowledge graph [17], soft rules with confidence levels extracted automatically from knowledge graph in rule-guided embedding [32], WordNet synsets in context-sensitive embedding [33], RDFS assertions in ontology-aware embedding [36], and so on. On the other hand, adding semantic resources is comparatively less seen in embedding-based biomedical informatics research. Our work described in this paper is thus meaningful as a first attempt to learn distributed representations of EMR symptoms and diagnoses under the constraint of embeddings of biomedical concepts from comprehensive clinical ontology. As shown by our empirical results, incorporating such domain knowledge can facilitate embedding by revealing intrinsic correlation among symptoms and diagnoses that generally cannot be discovered by EMR data *per se*.

The performance improvement listed in Tables 3, 4, 5 and 6 is promising yet marginal, pointing the future directions of our work. The reason comes from limited mappings from symptoms and diagnoses in PKUSS data described in Chinese to SNOMED CT concepts, for which cross-lingual word embedding is definitely worth exploring [34]. Moreover, as analyzed above, the granularity difference between EMR data and domain ontology can impede effectiveness of the combined embedding, which has to be dealt with specific, novel modeling measures. Lastly, the very recent progress in aligning biomedical ontologies based on representation learning [35] shall be considered for strengthening the knowledge augmentation in embedding.

To summarize, we present to incorporate domain knowledge from biomedical ontologies to facilitate the embedding of EMR data for the task of diagnosis prediction. The evaluation on complex, real-world data for oral diseases validates the power of combining symbolic knowledge representation underpinned by logic and numerical representation of data trained by neural network.

Acknowledgements. This work has been supported by the National Key Research and Development Program of China under grant 2016YFB1000902, Projects of Beijing Municipal Science & Technology Commission, and the Natural Science Foundation of China grant 61621003.

References

1. Jonnalagadda, S.R., Adupa, A.K., Garg, R.P.: Text mining of the electronic health record: an information extraction approach for automated identification and subphenotyping of HFPEF patients for clinical trials. J. Cardiovasc. transl. Res. **10**(3), 313–321 (2017)
2. Sesen, M.B., Kadir, T., Alcantara, R.B., Fox, J., Brady, M.: Survival prediction and treatment recommendation with Bayesian techniques in lung cancer. In: AMIA Annual Symposium Proceedings, pp. 838 (2012)
3. Mani, S., Chen, Y., Elasy, T., Clayton, W., Denny, J.: Type 2 diabetes risk forecasting from EMR data using machine learning. In: AMIA Annual Symposium Proceedings, pp. 606–615 (2012)
4. Mani, S., Chen, Y., Arlinghaus, L.R., Li, X., Chakravarthy, B., Bhave, R.: Early prediction of the response of breast tumors to neoadjuvant chemotherapy using quantitative MRI and machine learning. In: AMIA Annual Symposium Proceedings, pp. 868–877 (2011)
5. Kawaler, E., Cobian, A., Peissig, P., Cross, D., Yale, S., Craven, M.: Learning to predict post-hospitalization VTE risk from EHR data. In: AMIA Annual Symposium Proceedings, pp. 436–445 (2012)
6. Kim, Y.J., Lee, Y.G., Kim, J.W., Park, J.J., Ryu, B., Ha, J.W.: Highrisk Prediction from electronic medical records via deep attention networks. arXiv preprint arXiv:1712.00010 (2017)

7. Bengio, Y., Ducharme, R., Vincent, P., Jauvin, C.: A neural probabilistic language model. J. Mach. Learn. Res. **3**(Feb), 1137–1155 (2003)
8. Mikolov, T., Chen, K., Corrado, G., Dean, J.: Efficient estimation of word representations in vector space. arXiv preprint arXiv:1301.3781 (2013)
9. Tang, D., Wei, F., Yang, N., Zhou, M., Liu, T., Qin, B.: Learning sentiment-specific word embedding for twitter sentiment classification. In: Proceedings of the 52nd Annual Meeting of the Association for Computational Linguistics, pp. 1555–1565 (2014)
10. Maas, A.L., Daly, R.E., Pham, P.T., Huang, D., Ng, A.Y., Potts, C.: Learning word vectors for sentiment analysis. In: Proceedings of the 49th Annual Meeting of the Association for Computational Linguistics, pp. 142–150 (2011)
11. Ganguly, D., Roy, D., Mitra, M., Jones, G. J.: Word embedding based generalized language model for information retrieval. In: 38th International ACM SIGIR Conference on Research and Development in Information Retrieval, pp. 795–798 (2015)
12. Li, G., Zhang, S., Liang, J., Cao, Z., Guo, C.: An embedding-based approach for oral disease diagnosis prediction from electronic medical records. In: 2nd International Conference on Medical and Health Informatics, pp. 125–133 (2018)
13. Rosse, C., Mejino Jr., J.L.: A reference ontology for biomedical informatics: the foundational model of anatomy. J. Biomed. Inform. **36**(6), 478–500 (2003)
14. Hayamizu, T.F., Mangan, M., Corradi, J.P., Kadin, J.A., Ringwald, M.: The adult mouse anatomical dictionary: a tool for annotating and integrating data. Genome Biol. **6**(3), R29 (2005)
15. Golbeck, J., Fragoso, G., Hartel, F., Hendler, J., Oberthaler, J., Parsia, B.: The national cancer institute's thesaurus and ontology. J. Web Semant. **1**(1) (2003)
16. Donnelly, K.: SNOMED-CT: the advanced terminology and coding system for eHealth. Stud. Health Technol. Inf. **121**, 279 (2006)
17. Guo, S., Wang, Q., Wang, B., Wang, L., Guo, L.: Semantically smooth knowledge graph embedding. In: Proceedings of the 53rd Annual Meeting of the Association for Computational Linguistics and the 7th International Joint Conference on Natural Language Processing, pp. 84–94 (2015)
18. Wang, Q., Mao, Z., Wang, B., Guo, L.: Knowledge graph embedding: a survey of approaches and applications. IEEE Trans. Knowl. Data Eng. **29**(12), 2724–2743 (2017)
19. Bordes, A., Weston, J., Collobert, R., Bengio, Y.: Learning structured embeddings of knowledge bases. In: AAAI, p. 6 (2011)
20. Bordes, A., Glorot, X., Weston, J., Bengio, Y.: A semantic matching energy function for learning with multi-relational data. Mach. Learn. **94**(2), 233–259 (2014)
21. Socher, R., Chen, D., Manning, C. D., Ng, A.: Reasoning with neural tensor networks for knowledge base completion. In: Advances in Neural Information Processing Systems, pp. 926–934 (2013)
22. Jenatton, R., Roux, L., Bordes, A., Obozinski, R.: A latent factor model for highly multi-relational data. In: Advances in Neural Information Processing Systems, pp. 3167–3175 (2012)
23. Nickel, M., Tresp, V., Kriegel, H. P.: A three-way model for collective learning on multi-relational data. In: ICML, pp. 809–816 (2011)
24. Bordes, A., Usunier, N., Garcia-Duran, A., Weston, J., Yakhnenko, O.: Translating embeddings for modeling multi-relational data. In: Advances in Neural Information Processing Systems, pp. 2787–2795 (2013)
25. Maaten, L.V.D., Hinton, G.: Visualizing data using t-SNE. J. Mach. Learn. Res. **9**(Nov), 2579–2605 (2008)
26. Minarro-Giménez, J.A., Marin-Alonso, O., Samwald, M.: Exploring the application of deep learning techniques on medical text corpora. Stud. Health technol. Inf. **205**, 584–588 (2014)

27. Ye, C., Fabbri, D.: Extracting similar terms from multiple EMR-based semantic embeddings to support chart reviews. J. Biomed. Inf. **83**, 63–72 (2018)
28. Choi, E., Schuetz, A., Stewart, W. F., Sun, J.: Medical concept representation learning from electronic health records and its application on heart failure prediction. arXiv preprint arXiv: 1602.03686 (2016)
29. Choi, Y., Chiu, C.Y.I., Sontag, D.: Learning low-dimensional representations of medical concepts. AMIA Summits on Transl. Sci. Proc. **2016**, 41 (2016)
30. Henriksson, A.: Representing clinical notes for adverse drug event detection. In: 6th International Workshop on Health Text Mining and Information Analysis, pp. 152–158 (2015)
31. Wang, S., Chang, X., Li, X., Long, G., Yao, L., Sheng, Q.: Diagnosis code assignment using sparsity-based disease correlation embedding. IEEE Trans. Knowl. Data Eng. **1**, 1 (2016)
32. Guo, S., Wang, Q., Wang, L., Wang, B., Guo, L.: Knowledge graph embedding with iterative guidance from soft rules. arXiv preprint arXiv:1711.11231 (2017)
33. Dasigi, P., Ammar, W., Dyer, C., Hovy, E. Ontology-aware token embeddings for prepositional phrase attachment. arXiv preprint arXiv:1705.02925 (2017)
34. Ruder, S., Vulić, I., Søgaard, A.: A survey of cross-lingual word embedding models. arXiv preprint arXiv:1706.04902 (2017)
35. Kolyvakis, P., Kalousis, A., Smith, B., Kiritsis, D.: Biomedical ontology alignment: an approach based on representation learning. J. Biomed. Semant. **9**(1), 21 (2018)
36. Diaz, G., Fokoue, A., Sadoghi, M.: EmbedS: scalable, ontology-aware graph embeddings. In: 21st International Conference on Extending Database Technology, pp. 433–436 (2018)

Regional Estimation Prior Network for Crowd Analyzing

Ping He[1], Meng Ma[2(✉)], and Ping Wang[1,2,3(✉)]

[1] School of Software and Microelectronics, Peking University, Beijing, China
{hepingheping, pwang}@pku.edu.cn
[2] National Engineering Research Center for Software Engineering,
Peking University, Beijing, China
mameng@pku.edu.cn
[3] Key Laboratory of High Confidence Software Technologies (PKU),
Ministry of Education, Beijing, China

Abstract. Crowd analysis from images or videos is an important technology for public safety. CNN-based multi-column methods are widely used in this area. Multi-column methods can enhance the ability of exacting various-scale features for the networks, but they may introduce the drawbacks of complicating and functional redundancy. To deal with this problem, we proposed a multi-task and multi-column network. With the support of a regional estimation prior task, components of network may pay more attention to their own target functions respectively. In this way, the functional redundancy can be reduced and the performance of network can be enhanced. Finally, we evaluated our method in public datasets and monitoring videos.

Keywords: Crowd analysis · Multi-column · Multi-task · Regional estimation
Various-scale features

1 Introduction

Crowd analysis from images or videos is a new technology for public safety monitoring, disaster management and design of public spaces. In many scenarios, such as traffic monitoring or sports events, estimating crowd count and distribution accurately can provide important information which is helpful to identify high-risk situations and make correct decisions [1]. Therefore, crowd analysis, especially crowd counting and distribution estimating, is very important for crowd flows monitoring and security services. In this paper, we concentrate on the field of estimating crowd count and generating distribution map from crowd images.

Many methods have been proposed for crowd counting with various approaches, such as detection-based methods, regression-based methods and density estimation-based methods [2]. Recently, density estimation-based methods are widely proposed and employed because they can estimate not only the number of people in crowd flows, but also the spatial distribution information of the crowd.

Like many other applications of computer vision, convolutional neural networks (CNN) are widely used for better performance. However, it is still a challenging task

M. Qiu (Ed.): SmartCom 2018, LNCS 11344, pp. 251–260, 2018.
https://doi.org/10.1007/978-3-030-05755-8_25

for researchers because crowd flows often come with non-uniform distribution and high clutter appearance. In such congested scenes, occlusions make it very difficult to detect every person accurately from images [3].

Compared with many other architectures, the networks with multiple columns and different filter sizes perform better in many cases [4–6]. One explanation is that separated columns with different filter sizes present various sizes of receptive fields. So, the networks with multiple columns have advantages for the task with various scale visual information. Intuitively, crowd analysis should be categorized to this kind of task. While the ability of extracting features has been enhanced with the increased columns, the complicated structure may introduce new problems, such as over fitting and functional redundancy [7].

Contributions of This Paper. In this paper, we aim to conduct crowd counting from an arbitrary image. To reduce the functional redundancy of components in networks, we discussed the relationships between multiple tasks and multiple columns. Then, we proposed a new useful subtask for target prior components. Furthermore, inspired by previous researches, we proposed a new multi-task and multi-column network to estimate the density maps and count for crowd flows. Finally, we evaluated the proposed method in public dataset and monitoring videos.

To summarize, in this paper we present: (1) A novel regional estimation task to boost the density map generation task; (2) A new network with 2 columns and 2 tasks for crowd counting and density map generation.

2 Related Works

The main methods for crowd analysis can be classified into the following categories: detection-based methods, regression-based methods and density estimation-based methods [2]. Both the CNN-based and traditional-based solutions can be used in the three categories. With the development of theoretical and experimental techniques for deep learning, most of the new methods are based on deep neural networks.

2.1 Detection-Based Methods

Many initial researches for crowd counting were based on detection approaches which use a moving window detector to find humans and count the number in crowd flows [8–10]. These methods need well-trained classifiers to classify humans and other objects. While detection-based methods are close to the way of human thinking intuitively, it is hard for them to deal with highly congested scenes because most of the persons in such images are obscured [11]. To tackle this problem, researchers attempted to count for crowd by regression.

2.2 Regression-Based Methods

Regression-based methods are deployed to learn the relations between the number of people and the scene features extracted from images [3, 12, 13]. These methods usually consist of two major components: a feature extraction algorithm to generate features from a picture of crowd and a regression model to estimate the number of people in the picture according to the extracted features.

2.3 Density Estimation-Based Methods

Regression-based methods follow the demand of counting the number of people, however, they ignore the crowd distribution, which may be critical spatial information for crowd analysis in many cases. To incorporate the spatial distribution information, Lempitsky et al. [14] proposed a method to learn a mapping between features of local patches and density map of the corresponding persons or objects.

More recently, various Convolutional Neural Network (CNN) based approaches are employed for density estimation and crowd counting [15, 16]. Although CNN based methods have better capability to extract features than traditional methods, scene scale variation in many crowd analysis tasks would make them difficult. To tackle the issue of scale variation, Zhang et al. [5] proposed a Multi-column CNN architecture (MCNN), so that it can extract features at different scales. In addition, they also introduced ShanghaiTech dataset, which is an annotated large-scale dataset for crowd analysis. Similar with MCNN, Sam et al. [6] proposed a Switching-CNN network (SCNN). It uses a classifier to choose the appropriate column for corresponding patches. In many other cases, multi-column and multi-scale methods are also proved to achieve lower count errors than single-scale ones [17, 18]. While multi-scale CNN methods demonstrate considerable success in many experiments, few researchers define the functions of each CNN column respectively, which would be critical for designing networks. One of the researches concerning this problem is the CNN-based Cascaded Multi-task architecture (Cascaded-MTL) proposed by Sindagi et al. [19]. Inspired by multiple tasks method [20], they designed an architecture with two columns: one has bigger convolutional filters in size and the other has smaller ones. However, the high-level prior provided by Sindagi et al. was depended on a classification task with the global count information of image, which may not enough for boosting the density estimation performance. In this paper, we designed a novel network structure to generate a new kind of high-level prior that contains not only the global count information but also the regional spatial information in an image.

3   Proposed Method

We designed a two-task and two-column network to generate density map and count the crowd. Different from many other multi-column methods, the column with bigger convolutional filters tends to learn high-level and large-scale features for the density estimation by a new task. So, to generate high-level and large-scale features becomes the major function of the bigger-filters column. In this way, different columns can focus on respective target features and avoid functional redundancy. Unlike Cascaded-MTL [19] with global count classification task, we proposed a new task: region average density estimation, which aims to learn spatial prior information and boost the major density map generation task. The new task is defined as to estimate the average density level for different regions of the target image. We choose this task for the following reasons:

- The new task is correlated to the major task, so it will not introduce confusion information for the major one.
- The supervisory information for the new task can be produced from the ground truth of the major task easily.
- The new task can be regarded as a large-scale and rough density map which mainly concerns the regional average density level in the image. This characteristic is helpful for the first column to pay more attention to extract large-scale features, therefore it can reduce the functional redundancy of two columns.
- Different from the image classification task proposed in the previous work, region density estimation task contains not only the global level count information but also the rough spatial information of crowd flows, which is helpful to boost the performance of the density estimation task.

Our proposed regional estimation prior CNN network (REP-CNN) has two columns for the two tasks. Separated columns contain the different network layers and different size of convolutional filters to present the large-scale and normal-scale receptive fields respectively. The major task for the network is to generate density map (the number of the crowd can be counted with the density map). Both columns are employed to the major task. To reduce the functional redundancy of the two columns, we proposed a new task for the column with large scale receptive fields.

The details of the proposed network are discussed in the following sub-sections.

3.1 Configuration of REP-CNN

The configuration of REP-CNN can be seen in Table 1. The network has 4 blocks: Large-scale Column, Normal-scale Column, Regional Estimation and Density Map Esti-mation. Convolutional and pooling layers are used in these blocks. Each convolutional layer is followed by a Parametric Rectified Linear Unit (PReLU) activation fun-ction.

Large-Scale Column. It consists of 8 convolutional layers and 2 max pooling layers. The aim of this block is to extract the large-scale features since the size of filters in this block is larger than Normal-scale Column. The output of this block are 8 large-scale feature maps.

Normal-Scale Column. It consists of 8 convolutional layers and 2 max pooling layers. It shares the first 2 layers with Large-scale column. This block is employed to extract the normal-scale features. The output of this block are 10 normal-scale feature maps.

Regional Estimation. This block consists of an adapt pooling layer and 3 convolutional layers. The adapt pooling layer resizes the feature maps from Large-scale Column into the size of 32×32. Function of the following convolutional layers is to estimate the number of people in each region. The size of filters in the first layer is 16×16 and the stride is 16 too. So, combined with the following layers, they are implementation of 4 fully connected layers which share the same parameters. The output of this block is a matrix with the size of 2×2 (the number of people in each region). In is paper, we define this matrix as the average density estimation for 4 regions of the image.

Density Map Estimation. This block consists of 3 convolutional layers and 2 transposed convolution layers. Transposed convolution layers are employed to resize the feature maps to the initial size of the input image. The output map is defined as the estimation of the density map.

Table 1. Configuration of REP-CNN

A: Large-scale Column	B: Normal-scale Column	C: Regional Estimation	D: Density map Estimation
conv9-16-1 conv7-32-1		adapt-pooling 32 × 32	conv3-24-1 conv3-32-1
conv9-16-1	conv7-20-1	conv16-128-16 conv1-64-1 conv1-1-1	conv-transpose conv-transpose
max-pooling			
conv7-32-1	conv5-40-1		
max-pooling			
conv7-16-1	conv5-20-1		conv1-1-1
conv7-8-1	conv5-10-1		

Note: Parameters of the convolutional layers are denoted as "conv-(kernel size)-(number of filters)-(stride)", max-pooling layers are con-ducted over a 2×2 pixel window with stride 2.

3.2   Prior Regional Estimation Task

This is the proposed task to estimate regional average density level. It aims to enhance the ability of exacting the large-scale features about crowd flow distribution for the first column. There are two blocks for prior information generation task. They are the Large-scale Column block and the Regional Estimation block. The input of the Large-scale Column block is the target image. And the output feature maps are fed into the Regional Estimation block to generate a regional density estimation. For simplicity, we use the number of people to represent the average density level in the region.

3.3   Density Map Generation Task

Generating density map is the major task of the proposed network. Three blocks are employed for the task: Large-scale Column, Normal-scale Column and Density map Estimation block. The input of Large-scale Column and Normal-scale Column is the target image. They generate and combine the feature maps. The combined feature maps are fed into Density Map Estimation block to generate the final density map. The overview of the Regional Estimation Prior CNN can be seen in Fig. 1.

3.4   Loss Functions

The loss function [5] for the density estimation task is defined as:

$$L_d = \frac{1}{2N} \sum_{i=1}^{N} \|F_d(X_i; \theta_A, \theta_B, \theta_D) - D_i\|_2^2 \tag{1}$$

where $F_d(X_i; \theta_A, \theta_B, \theta_D)$ is the estimated density map in the major task. X_i is the input image, and D_i is the ground truth density map of this image. θ_A, θ_B and θ_D are the parameters of the corresponding blocks shown in Table 1. The loss function for the prior regional estimation task is defined as:

$$L_r = \frac{1}{2N} \sum_{i=1}^{N} \|F_r(X_i; \theta_A, \theta_C) - R_i\|_2^2 \tag{2}$$

where $F_r(X_i; \theta_A, \theta_C)$ is the estimated regional score matrix (the estimated count of the crowd in each region) in the prior task. R_i is the ground truth region count matrix of this image. The final loss is defined as:

$$L = \lambda L_r + L_d \tag{3}$$

where λ is a weighting factor.

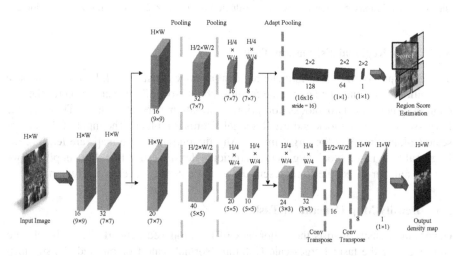

Fig. 1. Overview of the proposed Regional Estimation Prior CNN

3.5   Training Details

For every image in training set, 9 patches are cropped. The ground truth density map is generated according to the methods proposed by the previous researches [16]. The geometry-adaptive kernels are used to tackle the highly congested scenes. We produce the ground truth by blurring each head annotation using a Gaussian kernel. Each image is cropped into 9 patches at different locations. After cropping, we mirror the patches so that the number of images in training set is doubled. To generate the ground truth region scores for the prior task, we divided every density map in training set into 4 regions averagely and counted the density values in each region. The training and testing experiments were performed with Pytorch frame-work.

4   Experiments

4.1   Evaluation Metric

The absolute error (MAE) and the mean squared error (MSE) [1] are employed to evaluate the performance of proposed method. The MAE and MSE are defined as follows:

$$\text{MAE} = \frac{1}{N}\sum_{i=1}^{N}|C_i - C_i^{GT}| \tag{4}$$

$$\text{MSE} = \sqrt{\frac{1}{N}\sum_{i=1}^{N}(C_i - C_i^{GT})^2} \tag{5}$$

where N is the number of images. And C_i^{GT} is the ground truth of the crowd number in the image. C_i is the estimated count.

4.2   ShanghaiTech Dataset

The ShanghaiTech dataset was a large-scale dataset introduced by Zhang et al. [5] for crowd counting. The dataset contains 1198 images of crowd flows in many scenes with a total of 330,165 people. For every picture in the dataset, the positions of each person in it were annotated. The ShanghaiTech dataset consists of two parts: Part A and Part B with 482 images and 716 images respectively.

4.3   Experiment Results

We evaluated our proposed method in the Part A of ShanghaiTech dataset and compared the results with some previous works. The results are shown in Table 2. Our method is an improvement of Cascaded-MTL by introducing the regional estimation task. We only used 2 columns too. Compared with the previous multi-column methods, the REP-CNN reduced the MAE and MSE. The experiment results demonstrate that the novel network with the new prior task can enhance the accuracy for crowd counting and density estimation tasks. The density map samples generated by our method are shown in Fig. 2. The 3 columns are input images, ground truth of density maps and generated density maps.

Table 2. Results of different methods on the ShanghaiTech Part A dataset.

Method	MAE	MSE
MCNN [5]	110.2	173.2
SCNN [6]	90.4	135.0
Cascaded-MTL [19]	101.3	152.4
REP-CNN (ours)	**85.2**	**126.7**

Note: Comparing results of different methods on the ShanghaiTech Part A test set.

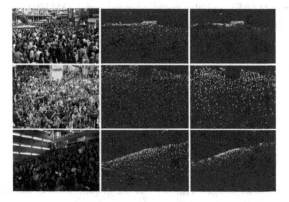

Fig. 2. Density estimation results using proposed method on ShanghaiTech dataset.

4.4   Monitoring Video Crowd Count and Situation Awareness

The monitoring videos are used to evaluated our method. The camera of this scene is installed over the elevator aisle exit in the subway station. The video is seriously blur and encounters severe occlusion. We counted the number of people in sampled frames and compared the results with the output count of REP-CNN. The observed counts are categorized into 7 approximate values: 0, 5, 10, 15, 20, 25 and 30. The comparison of observed approximate counts and method output is shown in Fig. 3. The generated density maps for the sampled frames are shown in Fig. 4. The results demonstrate that our method can count the number from video and get the periodic information of commuters in subway station. The crowd flow periodic information and the density maps are important to situation awareness and making correct decisions.

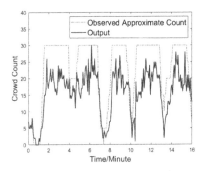

Fig. 3. Count results from video

Fig. 4. Density maps for sampled frames

This network consists of 2 columns and 2 tasks. The results show that it can get better performance than many 3-column networks. However, it does not demonstrate the architectures with 2 columns are better than the 3-column architectures because increased columns can extract various sizes of features. The disadvantage of increasing the number of columns is the increased risks of over-fitting and functional redundancy. But the increased tasks can provide different supervision information which may decrease the risks. Besides multiple tasks, transfer learning can introduce the knowledge of other dataset and other models, which may be a new approach to deal with overfitting and improve the performance of crowd analyzing.

5   Conclusion

In this paper, we proposed a two-column and two-task network to generate crowd density map and count the number of the crowd. The new regional estimation prior task is proposed to deal with functional redundancy problem. With the support of this task, components of network may pay more attention to their own target functions respectively. As a result, the functional redundancy can be reduced and the performance of network can be enhanced. In the end, we evaluated our method in public datasets and monitoring videos. The experiment results demonstrate that the new task can improve the performance for density map generation and crowd counting.

Acknowledgements. This work is supported in part by National Key R&D Program of China No. 2017YFB1200700 and National Natural Science Foundation of China No. 61701007.

References

1. Tota, K., Idrees, H.: Counting in dense crowds using deep features. CRCV (2015)
2. Sindagi, V.A., Patel, V.M.: A survey of recent advances in cnn-based single image crowd counting and density estimation. Pattern Recogn. Lett. **107**, 3–16 (2018)
3. Idrees, H., Saleemi, I., Seibert, C., Shah, M.: Multi-source multi-scale counting in extremely dense crowd images. In: Proceedings of the IEEE Conference on Computer Vision and Pattern Recognition, pp. 2547–2554 (2013)

4. Liu, J., Gao, C., Meng, D., Hauptmann, A.G.: Decidenet: counting varying density crowds through attention guided detection and density estimation. In: Proceedings of the IEEE Conference on Computer Vision and Pattern Recognition, pp. 5197–5206 (2018)

5. Zhang, Y., Zhou, D., Chen, S., Gao, S., Ma, Y.: Single-image crowd counting via multi-column convolutional neural network. In: Proceedings of the IEEE Conference on Computer Vision and Pattern Recognition, pp. 589–597 (2016)

6. Babu Sam, D., Surya, S., Venkatesh Babu, R.: Switching convolutional neural network for crowd counting. In: Proceedings of the IEEE Conference on Computer Vision and Pattern Recognition, pp. 5744–5752 (2017)

7. Li, Y., Zhang, X., Chen, D.: CSRNet: dilated convolutional neural networks for understanding the highly congested scenes. In: Proceedings of the IEEE Conference on Computer Vision and Pattern Recognition, pp. 1091–1100 (2018)

8. Felzenszwalb, P.F., Girshick, R.B., McAllester, D., Ramanan, D.: Object detection with discriminatively trained part-based models. IEEE Trans. Pattern Anal. Mach. Intell. **32**, 1627–1645 (2010)

9. Topkaya, I.S., Erdogan, H., Porikli, F.: Counting people by clustering person detector outputs. In: Proceedings of the IEEE International Conference on Advanced Video and Signal Based Surveillance, pp. 313–318 (2014)

10. Li, M., Zhang, Z., Huang, K., Tan, T.: Estimating the number of people in crowded scenes by mid based foreground segmentation and head-shoulder detection. In: Proceedings of the IEEE International Conference on Pattern Recognition, pp. 1–4 (2008)

11. Babu Sam, D., Sajjan, N.N., Venkatesh Babu, R., Srinivasan, M.: Divide and grow: capturing huge diversity in crowd images with incrementally growing CNN. In: Proceedings of the IEEE Conference on Computer Vision and Pattern Recognition, pp. 3618–3626 (2018)

12. Chan, A.B., Vasconcelos, N.: Bayesian poisson regression for crowd counting. In: Proceedings of the IEEE International Conference on Computer Vision, pp. 545–551 (2009)

13. Chen, K., Gong, S., Xiang, T., Change Loy, C.: Cumulative attribute space for age and crowd density estimation. In: Proceedings of the IEEE Conference on Computer Vision and Pattern Recognition, pp. 2467–2474 (2013)

14. Lempitsky, V., Zisserman, A.: Learning to count objects in images. In: Proceedings of the Advances in Neural Information Processing Systems, pp. 1324–1332 (2010)

15. Wang, C., Zhang, H., Yang, L., Liu, S., Cao, X.: Deep people counting in extremely dense crowds. In: Proceedings of the ACM International Conference on Multimedia, pp. 1299–1302 (2015)

16. Zhang, C., Li, H., Wang, X., Yang, X.: Cross-scene crowd counting via deep convolutional neural networks. In: Proceedings of the IEEE Conference on Computer Vision and Pattern Recognition, pp. 833–841 (2015)

17. Onoro-Rubio, D., López-Sastre, R.J.: Towards perspective-free object counting with deep learning. In: proceedings of the European Conference on Computer Vision, pp. 615–629 (2016)

18. Walach, E., Wolf, L.: Learning to count with CNN boosting. In: Proceedings of the European Conference on Computer Vision, pp. 660–676 (2016)

19. Sindagi, V.A., Patel, V.M.: CNN-based cascaded multi-task learning of high-level prior and density estimation for crowd counting. In: Proceedings of the IEEE International Conference on Advanced Video and Signal Based Surveillance, pp. 1–6 (2017)

20. Chen, J.C., Kumar, A., Ranjan, R., Patel, V.M., Alavi, A., Chellappa, R.: A cascaded convolutional neural network for age estimation of unconstrained faces. In: proceedings of the IEEE International Conference on Biometrics Theory, Applications and Systems, pp. 1–8 (2016)

RBD: A Reference Railway Big Data System Model

Weilan Lin[1], Fanhua Xu[1], Meng Ma[2(✉)], and Ping Wang[1,2,3(✉)]

[1] School of Software and Microelectronics, Peking University, Beijing, China
{linweilan, xufanhua, pwang}@pku.edu.cn
[2] National Engineering Research Center for Software Engineering,
Peking University, Beijing, China
mameng@pku.edu.cn
[3] Key Laboratory of High Confidence Software Technologies (PKU),
Ministry of Education, Beijing, China

Abstract. The subway line is complex and involves many departments, resulting in unstandardized storage of relevant data in the Metro department. Data systems between different departments cannot cooperate. In this paper, we propose Railway Large Data Platform (RBD) to standardize the large data of rail transit. A large data platform system is designed to store the complex data of rail transit, which can cope with complex scenes. Taking the construction of rail transit platform in Chongqing as an example, we have made a systematic example.

Keywords: Micro-service architecture · Root cause · Anomaly detection
Impact graph · Frequent subgraph mining

1 Introduction

With the rapid development of information technology, the mode of rail transit operation has gradually changed from single mode to multi-level, intelligent and comprehensive operation [1]. Globally, intelligent rail transit systems have been established in developed large cities or urban agglomerations, such as Tokyo [2]. Although there are some integration and interconnection within these systems, these rail transit information systems are still confined to a single traffic system. Large scale data exchange can not be implemented across systems. In the intelligent big data information interaction system, data is the information-based foundation of rail transit intellectualization [3]. With the continuous development of intelligent rail transit, rail transit data reflects the characteristics of unstructured, large-scale, low density, high hidden value. However, in the traditional one-way operation mode, the data types of rail transit at different levels are not uniform, the data types are complex. This makes rail traffic data difficult to manage and integrate.

At present, the main challenges are the lack of standardized large-scale data management platform, the lack of information sharing [4, 5]. Therefore, in order to realize the high-speed and effective operation of intelligent big data information exchange system, it is urgent to carry out standardized data collection, centralized

© Springer Nature Switzerland AG 2018
M. Qiu (Ed.): SmartCom 2018, LNCS 11344, pp. 261–270, 2018.
https://doi.org/10.1007/978-3-030-05755-8_26

storage, unified management and integrated services for the big data center of urban rail transit system. The contributions of this paper are as follows:

1. We establish a unified traffic data specification. Make every transportation department use urban mass transit data in an orderly way.
2. We design a related large-scale data platform architecture to coordinate and support the data needs of different transport departments.
3. Taking Chongqing rail transit system as an example, we have demonstrated an application scenario of the system. The practicability of the platform is proved.

The rest of this paper is organized as follows. Section 2 reviews related work. In Sect. 3 we designed a set of big data specification for rail transit big data area. In Sect. 4, based on this big data specification, we built a big data architecture and designed related storage models. In Sect. 5, taking Chongqing rail transit as an example, we introduce the data display and storage of the platform. Concluding are contained in Sect. 6.

2 Related Work

At present, the data sources of rail transit system are mainly log and sensor data, operation and maintenance data, ticket data and historical legacy data [6]. With the continuous development of intelligent rail transit, the data resources of rail transit system can not only rely on traditional file system or relational database for storage, but also need to introduce distributed database, including non-relational database [7].

There are many kinds of data in the rail transit system. It is a great challenge to the storage type, scalability, maintainability, security and other aspects of the data storage in the rail transit system [8, 9]. The data generated by rail transit operation can be divided into the following categories: text file, non-relational data, video stream file and relational data [10]. In terms of big data architecture, due to the large amount of unstructured traffic data, such as video data and monitoring data, and the need for strong real-time processing, most rail transit platforms use Mapreduce distributed computing framework and real-time data processing framework. Other structures were built on this basis [11, 12].

Through the statistical analysis of rail transit data over the years, using a large number of multi-source data for traffic decision-making can effectively alleviate the problem of congestion in the field of rail transit [13, 14]. However, most of the existing rail transit big data platforms can not take into account the real-time and high efficiency of rail transit data processing, and also can not take into account the large amount of rail transit data, heterogeneous and decentralized characteristics [15]. It is urgent solve the current hot issues of rail transit, such as short-term traffic flow prediction, traffic guidance, passenger travel analysis and other issues.

3   Big Data Specifications

Data classification is an important component of big data platform planning. The data specification of big data platform needs to consider the following factors: 1. Regional railway management mode, system structure and operation characteristics 2. Data generation, collection, storage, use process. 3. Data goals, aggregation, decomposability, relevance, adaptability and integrity. The purpose is to form a unified and standardized hierarchical data classification system to guide the use of regional railway operation data. Starting from the basic spatial static point data, spatial static network data, spatial static sequential network data and spatiotemporal dynamic network data can be formed by increasing the number of nodes involved. On the other hand, from the point of view of dynamic increase, static point time series data and spatiotemporal dynamic point data can be formed. The data classification is shown in Fig. 1.

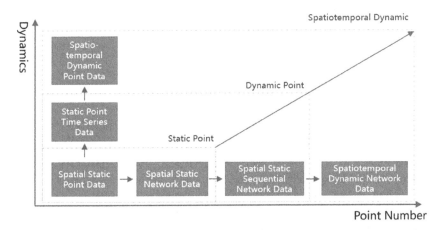

Fig. 1. Big data type of rail transit

The granularity of regional rail transit big data can be divided into point data and dynamic network, according to the dynamic can be divided into static point, dynamic point. Separate data from quadrants, as shown in the Fig. 2. Data types are divided into four quadrants.

The First Quadrant Data is Based on Static Points and Static Attributes. The layer mainly includes geographic nodes and networks, characterized by relatively static time and space, such as rail transit platform, including all the equipment in the platform, and natural fixed natural change points including slope points and curves. They take natural parameters as their main attributes.

The Second Quadrant Data are Static Points and Dynamic Attributes. The location of the data space in this quadrant is relatively fixed, but the attributes change with time. Specifically refers to the 1. Various stations facilities. 2. Operation service points contain physical vertices, such as passenger guidance points and ticket points. 3.

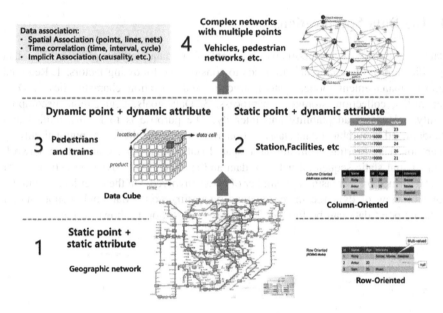

Fig. 2. Classification of mass transit data

Concept points such as resource maintenance points and event points. 4. Artificially added sites. 5. Rule-making points 6. Equipment on the road.

The Third Quadrant is Dynamic Point and Dynamic Attribute. Those points have characteristics that the spatial position and attribute of the quadrant point change with time, including pedestrians and trains. Take the train as an example. The location information of trains varies with time. At the same time, the speed and running state of each train also change with the change of position and time.

The Complex Network Consisting of the Points in the Above Quadrants is the Fourth Quadrant. The fourth quadrant includes vehicle and pedestrian networks, and relatively fixed rail transit routes, such as subway network topological path and tram network topological path. There are many nodes in the subway network. Nodes, tracks and vehicles are all affected by each other, forming a subway network together. The storage of the subway network has an important influence on the schedule and emergency response of the subway.

4 Architecture Design

4.1 Big Data Architecture

Big data is a collection of large and complex datasets, which is difficult to handle with manual data management tools. Challenges include receiving, storage, search, sharing, transmission, analysis, etc. Big data span four dimensions: volume, speed, diversity and accuracy, and transmit more frequently on the network.

We designed a big data system. The system consists of four parts: Data provision, data consumption, big data application, big data architecture. The raw data will enter the system from Data provision, and the system application layer will carry out a series of operations on the data. Through data application layer, data will be consumed by users (Fig. 3).

Big Data Architecture. The data analysis module is implemented by the big data architecture, which is divided into three layers. The most basic big data infrastructure layer is responsible for the distributed transmission and storage of the overall architecture, and manages the virtual resources and material resources. This layer is based on Hadoop and cooperates with the mongoDB database. Platform layer is responsible for the distributed organization of big data, based on geomesa, opentsdb, HBase to achieve six kinds of rail transit data forms and file storage, memory storage and other storage forms of storage, management. The processing layer of the big data architecture is responsible for computing and analyzing, including the functions of fragmentation, interaction, stream processing based on spark and hadoop. The whole big data architecture platform is coordinated and managed by zookeeper distributed cluster.

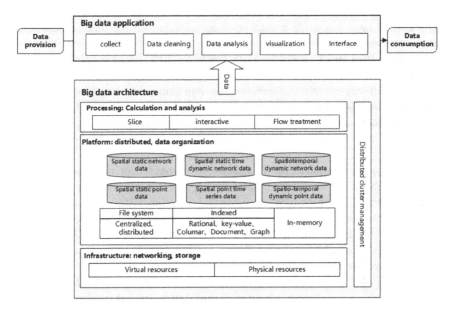

Fig. 3. Rail transit big data architecture

System Data Application Layer. The system data application layer includes five steps: collect, data cleaning, data analysis, visualization, interface. Big data application layer first collects the data in big data system, then cleans up the data and filters the valid data. Valid data will be analyzed in the next step, and the analysis structure will be collected by the data application layer and visualized. The data calculated by visualization are displayed in the user interaction layer.

4.2 Data Storage

The data types of traffic data platform designed in this paper include structured data and unstructured data at least, support multiple data types, and provide the same specification and easy to expand data definition and description language.

In the aspect of storage, we design a distributed, memory computing tool based on HBase to store different levels, which we call RBD (Reference Railway Big Data). RBD is divided into three levels, RBD basic layer RBD-1 is responsible for the storage of static data in urban rail transit, such as ramp, RBD time layer RBD-2 is responsible for the relative static space in urban rail transit, but some attributes change with time, such as card swiping machine, RBD space layer RBD-3 is responsible for urban rail transit. Spatiotemporal attributes are stored in changing data, such as trains and pedestrians.

RBD database is a geo-spatially oriented data management system that is built atop the Hbase database. The RBD is used to insert, enumerate, update and delete various time series data. The server supports sets of aggregation functions such as sum, min, max, avg, etc. to aggregate data over some period of time.

RBD-2 is facing a huge amount of time data. In view of the high consumption caused by the query of attributes and a large number of time nodes in the database, RBD's RBD-2 layer has made a number of optimization for the time storage of the database, including:

Each Data Item may Contain Multiple Attributes. RBD uses key value pairs. Each key value pair consists of attribute name and attribute value. For example, trains in urban rail transit may contain attributes such as train name, train length, train load, etc.

Attribute and Key Specification to Row ID. The use of attribute columns greatly increases the query time. We compress the attribute and the row data together, so that queries do not need to query multiple columns, only one query can accurately locate the data.

Using Mapping to Shorten the Length of Attributes. There are a lot of duplicate data in the database, just like a train number may appear in a large number of data rows. RBD assigns one UID to each metric, tag key and tag value, UID is three bytes of fixed length. We designed a spatio-temporal data index table. Users can design indexes according to the characteristics of the data. For the repeated data, the index is used to replace the data items which occupy a larger storage space. It saves storage space and improves query efficiency.

Store the Value of Each Time in an Hour Cycle and Merge it into a Column. Time information is not expressed in specific time, but is divided into hours according to time. Each time period is split in seconds, and each value represents data in one second. When merged into a row, the timestamp in the rowkey of the row is specified as the start time of the hour. This time is the base time of the time period. The column name of each column records the difference between the timestamp of the real data point and the start time (base) of the time period. If it's a second precision timestamp, you need four bytes, if it's a millisecond precision timestamp, you need eight bytes. But if the column name only has a difference value and the time period is one hour, then if it is second precision, the difference value range is 0–3600, only two bytes; if it is millisecond precision, the difference value range is 0–360000, only four bytes; so this design can save a lot of space compared to the real time stamp. In addition, all columns in the same row are merged into one column, and if the data is seconds accurate, 3600 columns in a row are merged into one column, and the Key-Value number is reduced from 3600 to only one.

The above process is illustrated in the Fig. 4. RBD-3 supports storage and efficient query of geographical space. RBD optimizes the storage of geographical space on the basis of hbase:

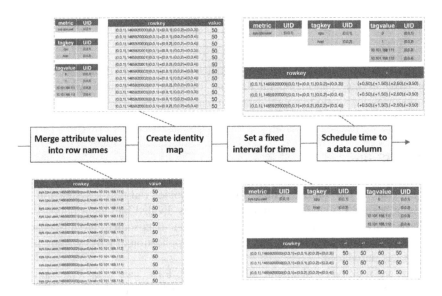

Fig. 4. Time series data representation

Geographic Information Representation Requires Space Filling Curve. We use Hilbert encoding to map two-dimensional information into one-dimensional space, as shown in the Fig. 5. Because the region of geographic location is a common scene in spatio-temporal database, it is a common operation to find its adjacent geographic location from a geographic location. Compared with row-major encoding and Z-order curve, the location of coded adjacent points in Hilbert curve is also adjacent in physical space. Hilbert coding can make the space-time three-dimensional data represented by one-dimensional data, which speeds up the traversal speed.

Design Different Queries Schema. In large-scale spatio-temporal databases, the query of data may face the problem of inefficiency. We design three kinds of schemas. According to the schema of spatio-temporal data search, according to the schema of attribute value search and according to the schema of data mark search, the data is copied into exactly the same three copies in each data storage.

Distributed Optimization for Query Logic. For the AND judgment in SQL statements move forward, OR and other binary operations move forward, so that the machine can be distributed to judge the logic, speeding up the efficiency of SQL statement execution.

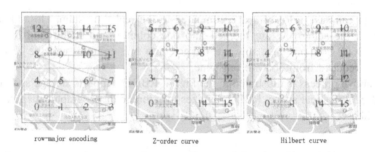

row-major encoding   Z-order curve   Hilbert curve

Fig. 5. Geocoding

The advantage of RBD system is to organize spatiotemporal data faster and better. Using RBD as the spatio-temporal database of urban rail transit system can well support storing the spatio-temporal data of trains and pedestrians, as well as stationary stations and equipment.

5 Case Study

Chongqing urban rail transit is one of the most complex rail transit systems in China because of terrain. Chongqing Shapingba Station is divided into eight floors. Passengers have many transfer modes in the station, and the data sources are miscellaneous. Taking the following four data as an example, the application of RBD system in urban rail transit is introduced.

There are four types of urban rail transit data. First, gate data. The traffic data platform records the gate data from the platform, which records the departure and arrival sites of each user passing through the gate. The OD matrix can be calculated by showing the passengers' departure from the gate to the destination station. Second, according to the crowd positioning. With the popularity of mobile internet, more and more passengers have mobile devices. Urban rail transit system can obtain a complete user movement curve through the crowd positioning provided by mobile app. Thirdly, through the user's historical travel data, analyze the periodic law. Fourthly, with the help of artificial intelligence technology, video data can be used to analyze the population density at a certain station location.

In the traditional model, these four data come from different data sources of rail transit system. Only by making a comprehensive analysis of the data from the four data sources can we get the appropriate conclusion.

On the RBD data platform, the data from the gate machine is the data of spatial static property changes, stored in the RBD-2 layer of the RBD data platform. Mobile terminal data contains location and time information, which is stored in the RBD-3 layer. The historical trajectory of population is spatio-temporal dynamic network data stored in the RBD-3 layer. Video data is space static, attributes transform data, in the form of video stored in the RBD-2 layer. On the platform of RBD, we have realized crowd analysis technology. Through video image analysis technology, we can automatically calculate the crowd density in the video line of sight of the train compartment and platform, and provide reference for the current travel comfort of the station or train number. Data stored in the database can be more accurately estimated by analyzing the spark streaming stream processing platform in the big data platform (Fig. 6).

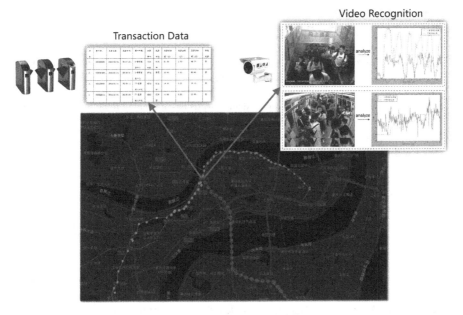

Fig. 6. Examples of RBD system display

The big data system extracts all kinds of data stored in the RBD system and puts them into the Hadoop platform. Secondly, we use spark computing model and a large number of historical user videos, in and out of the station data to train, modify the training results of the user's historical trajectory model. In the scenario of pedestrian travel planning, pedestrians submit their current location and destination to RBD system. The system sends the data to task queue and submits it to the spark streaming stream processing platform. Spark streaming uses previously trained models, real-time crowd location and context information to recommend the most comfortable route to users.

6 Conclusions

In this paper, we propose a big data normalization method for urban rail transit, which combs the data in urban rail transit according to the complexity and dynamics. So that it can well include the time and space complexity data in urban rail transit. Based on this specification, a big data structure of urban rail transit is constructed. The storage scheme of the structure is designed. With this framework, the standardized consistency of big data in urban rail transit is realized. We have demonstrated the feasibility of the system in a case study of Chengdu rail transit.

Acknowledgement. This work is supported in part by National Key R&D Program of China No. 2017YFB1200700 and National Natural Science Foundation of China No. 61701007.

References

1. Yu-Ping, X.U., Qin, G., Zhang, Z.: Study on utilization of big data of urban rail transit investigation. Railw. Transp. Econ. **4**, 024 (2015)
2. Zhang, X.: Historic data saving and application in urban rail transit building automation system. Urban Mass Transit **13**(11), 21–25 (2010). https://doi.org/10.3969/j.issn.1007-869X. 2010.11.006
3. Cong, H., University, N.N.: Study on big data analysis based running route tracking of urban rail train. Mod. Electron. Tech. **41**(5), 110–115 (2018)
4. Kim, W., Yong, H.K., Park, H.S., et al.: Analysis of traffic card big data by hadoop and sequential mining technique. J. Inf. Technol. Appl. Manag. **24**, 187–196 (2017)
5. Oneto, L.: Delay prediction system for large-scale railway networks based on big data analytics. In: Angelov, P., Manolopoulos, Y., Iliadis, L., Roy, A., Vellasco, M. (eds.) INNS 2016. AISC, vol. 529, pp. 139–150. Springer, Cham (2017). https://doi.org/10.1007/978-3-319-47898-2_15
6. Fumeo, E., Oneto, L., Anguita, D.: Condition based maintenance in railway transportation systems based on big data streaming analysis. Procedia Comput. Sci. **53**(1), 437–446 (2015)
7. Thaduri, A., Galar, D., Kumar, U.: Railway assets: a potential domain for big data analytics. Procedia Comput. Sci. **53**(1), 457–467 (2015)
8. Tianyun, S., Jun, L., Ping, L.I., et al.: Overall scheme and key technologies of big data platform for China Railway. Railw. Comput. Appl. **25**(9), 1–6 (2016)
9. Xiaoning, M.A., Ping, L.I., Tianyun, S.: System framework of railway big data application. Railw. Comput. Appl. **25**(9), 7–13 (2016)
10. Durazo-Cardenas, I., Starr, A., Tsourdos, A., et al.: Precise vehicle location as a fundamental parameter for intelligent self-aware rail-track maintenance systems. Procedia CIRP **22**(1), 219–224 (2014)
11. Jamshidi, A., Faghihroohi, S., Hajizadeh, S., et al.: A big data analysis approach for rail failure risk assessment. Risk Anal. Off. Publ. Soc **37**, 1495–1507 (2017)
12. Liu, J., Wang, X., Khattak, A.J., et al.: How big data serves for freight safety management at highway-rail grade crossings? A spatial approach fused with path analysis. Neurocomputing **181**(C), 38–52 (2016)
13. Zhu, L., Yu, F.R., Wang, Y., et al.: Big data analytics in intelligent transportation systems: a survey. IEEE Trans. Intell. Transp. Syst. **22**(99), 1–16 (2018)
14. Kim, K.W., Kim, D.W., Noh, K.S., et al.: An exploratory study on improvement method of the subway congestion based big data convergence. J. Korea Inst. Inf. Commun. Eng. **13**(2), 35–42 (2015)
15. Cheng, W., Tianyun, S.: Railway automatic ticketing and gate monitoring system based on big data analysis. Railw. Comput. Appl. **2015**(11), 42–45 (2015)

Artificial Intelligence Platform for Heterogeneous Computing

Haikuo Zhang[1,2,3](✉), Zhonghua Lu[1,2], Ke Xu[1,2], Yuchen Pang[4],
Fang Liu[1], Liandong Chen[5], and Jue Wang[1]

[1] Computer Network Information Center, Chinese Academy of Sciences,
Beijing 100190, China
`zhanghaikuo@cnnic.cn`
[2] University of Chinese Academy of Sciences, Beijing 100049, China
[3] China Internet Network Information Center, Beijing 100190, China
[4] University of Illinois at Urbana-Champaign, Champaign, IL 61820, USA
[5] State Grid Hebei Electric Power Company, Shijiazhuang 050022, Hebei, China

Abstract. Since the birth of artificial intelligence, the theory and the technology have become more mature, and the application field is expanding. In this paper, we build an artificial intelligence platform for heterogeneous computing, which supports deep learning frameworks such as TensorFlow and Caffe. We describe the overall architecture of the AI platform for a GPU cluster. In the GPU cluster, based on the scheduling layer, we propose Yarn by the Slurm scheduler to not only improve the distributed TensorFlow plug-in for the Slurm scheduling layer but also to extend YARN to manage and schedule GPUs. The front-end of the high-performance AI platform has the attributes of availability, scalability and efficiency. Finally, we verify the convenience, scalability, and effectiveness of the AI platform by comparing the performance of single-chip and distributed versions for the TensorFlow, Caffe and YARN systems.

Keywords: Artificial intelligence · Hadoop · Slurm · Schedule
TensorFlow · Caffe

1 Introduction

With the advent of the age of Internet of Things and mobile Internet, data are produced in various forms from all aspects of production and life. It is estimated that 80% of the data today is unstructured, and unstructured data are growing 15 times more rapidly than structured data [1]. The total number of data worldwide is expected to reach 40 zettabytes by 2020. Human beings have truly entered a data-centric era [2]. We see the great value of combining artificial intelligence (AI) with big data to handle increasing demand for computation. In recent years, deep learning has been widely used in speech recognition, machine translation, computer vision, and other fields. The high-performance computing cluster HPC is ideally suited for algorithms that emphasize big data computing represented by deep learning and provides a guarantee to build a reliable AI platform. With the rise of deep learning theory, the programming frameworks of many deep learning systems are continually emerging, and advancement in

© Springer Nature Switzerland AG 2018
M. Qiu (Ed.): SmartCom 2018, LNCS 11344, pp. 271–280, 2018.
https://doi.org/10.1007/978-3-030-05755-8_27

hardware GPUs is promoting the development of deep learning theory. Therefore, it is of great significance to apply Hadoop YARN, the most popular big data processing framework, to the unified resource management scheduling of deep learning frameworks [3].

This paper is organized as follows: The second section introduces related work required for heterogeneous computing AI platforms and a variety of deep learning frameworks. The third section details the overall architecture of an AI platform for GPU clusters, layering the components from the bottom up, and the underlying supporting hardware. In the fourth section, we propose a job scheduling management system for heterogeneous clusters, which explains the extension to the Slurm platform submission management system and the Yarn platform and improves the application layer. In the fifth section, we will carry out various experiments on the scheduling system to show that the system implemented in this paper is effective. The sixth section summarizes the article and looks forward at future research directions.

2 Related Work

With the upsurge of deep learning, there are a variety of deep learning frameworks, such as TensorFlow [4], Caffe [5], MXNet [6], Theano [7], and Lasagne [8]. Table 1 shows the three indicators of commonly used open source frameworks on GitHub: the number of stars, the number of forks and the number of contributors [9].

Table 1. Data statistics of open source frameworks

Frame	Mechanism	Support language	Stars	Forks	Contributors
TensorFlow	Google	Python/C++/Go/...	92195	59389	1357
Caffe	BVLC	C++/Python/MATLAB	23168	14151	264
Keras	fchollet	Python	26771	9767	638
CNTK	Microsoft	C++/Python/BrainScript	14001	3712	173
MXNet	DMLC	Python/C++/R/...	13322	4909	492
Torch	Facebook	Lua/LuaJIT/C	7739	2249	133
Theano	U. Montreal	Python/C++	8004	2419	328
Lasagne	Lasagne	Python	3390	918	64
PaddlePaddle	Baidu	C++/Python	1174	509	44

TensorFlow is a distributed deep learning framework developed by Google based on DistBelief and open source [10]. To some extent, TensorFlow shields users from low-level programming requirements such as CUDA [11] and encapsulates commonly used basic functions into interfaces. Caffe is one of the open-source deep learning frameworks on GitHub, and it was initially widely used in computer vision and has great advantages in image processing [12]. Commercial deep learning platforms include DistBelief, COTS [13], Adam, Baidu in-depth learning platform, Tencent's DI-X platform, and Kubernetes [14].

In traditional scheduling systems, LSF [15] and Kubernetes are currently open to support GPU management and scheduling. The operation mechanism of LSF is to submit deep learning program as a job and run it as well. The de novo scheduling system is currently limited to only a few commercial versions, with limited support functions.

3   Overall Architecture of AI Platform for GPU Clusters

The overall hardware system of the AI platform consists of 48 computing nodes, each of which is configured as a Dawn W780-G20 server. The shared storage system has a capacity of 400 TB, and each node is configured with a 1 TB high-speed solid-state disk as distributed storage.

The overall system architecture of the AI platform is shown in Fig. 1, which is called Yarn by the Slurm scheduler on the Linux system platform. The Yarn by the Slurm scheduler is an excellent in resource manager and scheduler and can manage scheduling system resources well. The YARN-based deep learning framework scheduling system is interfaced to Hadoop's distributed file system HDFS. HDFS is a distributed shared file system that can provide shared file systems on heterogeneous clusters and provides high reliability through redundant design [16]. The Slurm-based deep learning framework scheduling system is interfaced to a shared parallel file system. At present, the main distributed shared storage systems are GFS [17], HDFS [18], Lustre [19, 20] and parastor [21]. The HPC infrastructure provides a parallel file system to address the data-intensive application IO bottleneck and the problem of very large-scale data storage.

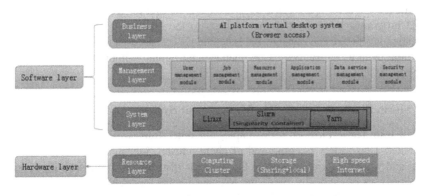

Fig. 1. System overall architecture diagram

At the same time, the Hadoop system is deployed on the cluster to allow Yarn to run for an extended time as a special application on all nodes of the system and accept Slurm management and scheduling. Yarn's own scheduling system manages and schedules Hadoop-based jobs on a virtual cluster consisting of available nodes allocated by Slurm as a secondary scheduling system. Users submit jobs to the job queue of

Yarn through Noah, manage and schedule jobs through a label-based scheduling method, and wait when the available node resources are insufficient [22]. By creating and maintaining dynamic sharing of available node lists for Slurm and Yarn, and dynamically adjusting the list in the form of atomic transactions based on the assignment and running state of the two, the Slurm scheduling of YARN can be implemented.

Taking Caffe2 as an example, in the management layer, there is a requirement for users to submit Caffe2 applications with their user accounts.

4 Job Scheduling Management System for Heterogeneous Clusters

The main task of the job scheduling management system on heterogeneous clusters is not the resource utilization of the system, but ensuring that the work submitted to the system is successfully started and completed. After ensuring that all jobs can be completed correctly, the job scheduling system will consider the problem of load balancing, that is, how to make the best use of the scheduling system resources. Job scheduling focuses on the completion of operations, rather than on resource utilization. Mainstream job scheduling systems include Condor, SGE, LSF and PBS [23]. For Yarn by the Slurm scheduler, we manage a distributed cluster as easily as running a standard process on a local machine. Users only need to write the script that involves of resource allocation and the execution command of programs at the beginning of the job submission.

In the following subsections, we will introduce Slurm and the YARN platform submission management systems. In the Slurm scheduling layer, plug-in improvements are made for the distributed TensorFlow to make distributed programs run as easily as normal programs. Because of improvements to the Hadoop YARN scheduling and application layers, we can manage and schedule GPUs based on the original supporting CPU and memory resources. This management greatly improves the computing capacity.

4.1 Slurm Platform Submission Management System

We will take TensorFlow as an example, but other frameworks are also supported. Distributed TensorFlow is composed of client, cluster, job, main service, basic task, server, and worker service. Based on the dynamic distribution of physical machines, it is necessary to dynamically parse the relevant parameters according to the physical machines provided by Slurm [24]. Each physical machine also needs to have its own functions and responsibilities, such as worker and PS, and each type has a different index number to distinguish different responsibilities. Finally, we use the list of clusters allocated and the name of each execution machine to find the corresponding index list. The plug-in can now dynamically parse the allocated resources and can automatically generate the overall communication network structure. Each machine can generate cable references to distinguish different tasks from different machines [25].

4.2   YARN Platform Submission Management System

The resource manager of YARN [26] can be regarded as a transaction processor. In YARN, the resource manager deals with six transaction types, each of which triggers the corresponding transaction processor. Each transaction involves the application, allocation, and recovery of management system resources. Scheduling algorithms mainly control the management and scheduling of system resources. In this paper, we extend the depth-first search algorithm to manage GPU clusters, which starts with the root node of the tree and traverses the tree as deeply as possible. That is, after the root node, the algorithm starts from the first child node of the root node, and the first child node traverses the first child node, thus reciprocating [27]. Depth-first search algorithm pseudo code such as Algorithm 1 shows:

Algorithm 1 Pseudo code for depth-first search algorithm
1.   Start
2.   Add a vertex to a queue
3.   Repeat
4.   When the queue is nonempty, the algorithm continues to execute and ends when it is empty.
5.   Gets the vertex v of the current queue and marks its status as already visited.
6.   If some of the subnodes of the vertex v have not been accessed
7.   Find the first W1 that is not accessed in the child node
8.   Update the state of W1 for access
9.   Send W1 into the queue
10. Otherwise, the vertex v is sent out of the queue

The DRF (Dominant Resource Fairness) algorithm is the main algorithm for resource management and scheduling of YARN, which can support multidimensional resource scheduling. The DRF algorithm, which has been proven to be very effective in managing and scheduling the CPU and memory resources, can manage and schedule non-single-dimensional resources effectively [28]. Therefore, in order to enable the Yarn by the Slurm scheduler to support GPU scheduling, this paper mainly expands on the basis of DRF. Through the DRF algorithm, the submission management system can be processed similar to a single resource management scheduling.

4.2.1   Extending YARN to Support Deep Learning Frameworks and Containers on GPU Clusters

We designed separate clients for each application and modified the code of Application Master. We do not change the original deep learning framework and container operation, but we increase the management and scheduling capabilities of the system resources. The application technology architecture is shown in Fig. 2.

The system architecture of TensorFlow application on YARN includes three components. The client is mainly responsible for the start-up of jobs and the acquisition of job execution status [29]. Application Master is used for the fragmentation of input data, starting and managing Container, executing log saving, etc. Container is a place where the job is performed. Container replaces native TensorFlow distributed programs

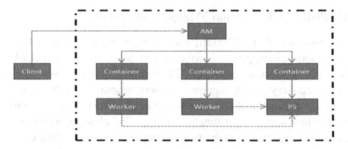

Fig. 2. TensorFlow on YARN architecture diagram

and automatically starts PS and Worker processes. Container reports the running status of the process to AM periodically and at the same time is responsible for the output of the application. PS is responsible for saving and updating parameters, and Worker is responsible for saving output.

The overall process of submitting the application through the client is shown in Fig. 3. The key to the client submission of the application is to obtain the unique Application ID and put all required information to start the ApplicationMaster into the data structure. In addition to monitoring the application, the management system also must parse and identify script information in the application submitted by the user and perform corresponding initialization.

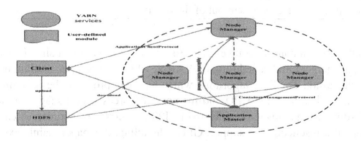

Fig. 3. Client submission application process

5   Experiments

In this paper, several experiments are designed to compare the performance of single version and distributed deep learning frameworks. We test the convenience and scalability of the overall platform environment for multiple deep learning frameworks using the proposed scheduling. We also test the efficiency of large-scale test cases in learning performance across multiple GPUs and multiple CPUs. The effectiveness of the scheduling system implemented in this paper is verified.

5.1   System Hardware Environment

There are 10 Dawn W780-G20 GPU servers, each configured with two Intel Xeon 2650v4 processors, with a double-precision floating-point peak of 4.455 billion times per second. Each single node is equipped with eight NVIDIA Tesla P100 GPU acceleration cards, with a double-precision peak of 1786 TFlops and a single-precision peak of 3534 TFlops. There are 80 NVIDIA Tesla P100 GPU acceleration cards. The computing storage network solution uses Infiniband high-speed network to configure a 108-port 56 Gb/s FDR large-port modular IB switch.

5.2   Experiment on Overall Scalability and Efficiency of Slurm Platform

To represent the AI platform usage practices, we tested the performance practice of a single node and a distributed TensorFlow using Caffe's deep learning framework experiment.

5.2.1   TensorFlow Deep Learning Framework Experiment

This test selects four sets of experiments carried out on 1, 2, 4, 8 multi-block GPUs. Experiment one is for TensorFlow running directly on a single node. Experiment two calls Slurm for dynamic node assignment tests. Experiment three is the TensorFlow environment test in a virtualization container. Experiment four is with a Slurm schedule Singularity-loaded TensorFlow container. The results of the experiments are shown in Fig. 4.

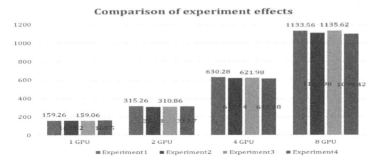

Fig. 4. Comparison of experiment 1234 effect

From the experimental results, four groups of experiments achieve linear speedup. The experimental method based on the Yarn by the Slurm scheduler is consistent with the data of the TensorFlow running on the bare machine. The gap is minimal. From this point of view, the overall availability of the AI platform is strong. Singularity has minimal impact on the performance of the platform as a whole, and the AI platform has good scalability. The platform provides a solid guarantee for future rapid iterative deep learning frameworks.

5.2.2   Performance Practice of Distributed TensorFlow

Eight GPUs have been able to meet the requirements of most deep learning training. To support the training and acceleration on the super-large-scale model, the plug-in of Slurm scheduling is added via programming so that the Slurm also seamlessly adjoins the distributed TensorFlow with the dynamic scheduling of Yarn. Figure 5 shows the performance test of distributed TensorFlow with 1, 2, 4, 8 nodes.

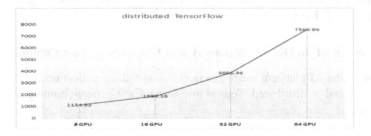

Fig. 5. Distributed TensorFlow effect diagram

From the performance results of the test, the extension of 8 GPU to 64 block GPU also achieves the effect of the linear speedup, reflecting the excellent scalability of the AI platform.

5.2.3   Caffe Deep Learning Framework Experiment

The Caffe framework effect diagram is shown in Fig. 6 to verify the availability and scalability of the high-performance platform.

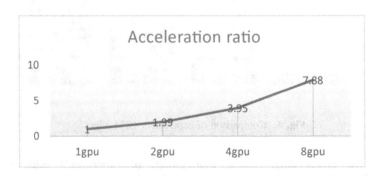

Fig. 6. Caffe framework effect diagram

6   Conclusion

To make the most advanced AI technology available in the network information center of CAS, we built an AI platform for mobile service computing to support multiple deep learning frameworks. In an era characterized by the rapid development of AI, an AI platform can serve scientists and engineers in various fields and meet the technical needs of large- and medium-sized enterprises. We have investigated the research status of AI platform-related technologies for mobile service computing at home and abroad, including TensorFlow, Caffe and commercial deep learning platforms. In the job scheduling management system for heterogeneous clusters, we improved the Yarn by the Slurm scheduler in the form of plug-ins, which not only enabled Slurm to support distributed TensorFlow more thoroughly but also made the program run as easily as ordinary programs. The YARN is improved to manage and schedule GPU resources on the basis of CPU and memory resources. This paper also extends the existing algorithm DRF of YARN. The management system has many important functions, such as job submission and user management. Finally, this paper achieves the goal of defining a linear acceleration ratio of GPU from single node to cross-node from multiple perspectives and meets the computational performance requirements of deep learning. Therefore, the AI platform on mobile service computing is very effective and reflects the effectiveness of the system in different deep learning frameworks.

Acknowledgments. This work was partly supported by the National Key R&D Program of China (No. 2017YFB0202202), the State Key Program of National Natural Science Foundation of China (No. 61702476).

References

1. Shanhai, W., Xinxing, J., Haiyan, Y.: Research on isolated word speech recognition based on deep learning neural network. Comput. Appl. Res. **32**(8), 2289–2291 (2015)
2. Gantz, J., Reinsel, D.: Digital Universe in 2020 [EB/OL]. https://www.emc.com/collateral/analyst-reports/idc-the-digital-universe-in-2020.pdf. Accessed 1 Dec 2012
3. Christiansen, B., Garey, M., Hartung, I.: SlurmOveview [EB/OL]. https://slurm.schedmd.com/SC17/SlurmOverviewSC17.pdf. Accessed 12 Dec 2017
4. Jeff, D., Rajat, M., et al.: (9 November 2015) TensorFlow: Large-scale machine learning on heterogeneous systems (PDF). TensorFlow.org. Google Research. Accessed 10 Nov 2015
5. Cybulska, M.: Assessing yarn structure with image analysis methods1. Text. Res. J. **69**(5), 369–373 (1999)
6. Pacelli, M., Caldani, L., Paradiso, R.: Performances evaluation of piezoresistive fabric sensors as function of yarn structure. In: 2013 35th Annual International Conference of the IEEE Engineering in Medicine and Biology Society (EMBC), pp. 6502–6505 (2013)
7. Ozturk, M., Nergis, B.U.: Determining the dependence of colour values on yarn structure. Color. Technol. **124**(3), 145–150 (2008)
8. Owens, J.D., Houston, M., Luebke, D., et al.: GPU computing. Proceed. IEEE **96**(5), 879–899 (2008)
9. Hou, S., Tan, M.T., Luo, X.G.: Application driven multi DSP processor array in high performance computing. Comput. Appl. Res. **28**(4), 1336–1338 (2011)
10. Nickolls, J., Dally, W.J.: The GPU computing era. IEEE Micro **30**(2), 56–69 (2010)
11. Hwu, W.M.W.: Introduction - GPU computing gems emerald edition. GPU Comput. Gems Emerald Ed. **27**, 599–600 (2011)
12. Pratx, G., Xing, L.: GPU computing in medical physics: a review. Med. Phys. **38**(5), 2685–2697 (2011)

13. Li, X.: A design of secret information system against internal network attack based on software container. Inf. Comput. **10**, 109–111 (2016)
14. Ubal, R., Schaa, D., Jang, B., et al.: Multi2Sim: a simulation framework for CPU-GPU computing, pp. 335–344 (2012)
15. IBM Platform LSF. http://www-03.ibm.com/systems/platformcomputing/products/lsf/
16. Wei, J.: Research on massive transaction record query system based on Hadoop. Nanjing University of Posts and Telecommunications, Nanjing (2013)
17. Ghemawat, S., Gobioff, H., Leung, S.-T.: The Google file system. In: 19th ACM Symposium on Operating Systems Principles, October 2013
18. Wikipedia contributors. Apache Hadoop [EB/OL]. https://en.wikipedia.org/wiki/Apache_Hadoop. Accessed 13 Dec 2017
19. Braam, P.J.: The Lustre storage architecture. Cluster File Systems, Inc. (2004). http://www.clusterfs.com
20. Wikipedia contributors. Lustre_(file_system) [EB/OL]. https://en.wikipedia.org/wiki/Lustre_(file_system). Accessed 31 Jan 2018
21. Wang, J., Gao F., Vazquez-Poletti, J.L., Li, J.: Preface of high performance computing or advanced modeling and simulation of materials. Comput. Phys. Commun. (211) (2017). (IF: 3.653)
22. Martin, A., Raponi, S., Combe, T., et al.: Docker ecosystem – vulnerability analysis. Comput. Commun. **122**, 30–43 (2018)
23. Slurm workload manager [EB/OL]. http://slurm.schedmd.com/slurm.html
24. Wang, J., Liu, C., Huang, Y.: Auto tuning for new energy dispatch problem: A case study. Future Gener. Comput. Syst. **54**, 501–506 (2016)
25. HuaiTe, Z., et al.: Hadoop Authoritative Guide, 2nd edn. Tsinghua University Press, Beijing (2011)
26. Zhao, H., Zhang, Y., Bradford, P.D., et al.: Carbon nanotube yarn strain sensors. Nanotechnology **21**(30), 305502 (2010)
27. Ramesh, M.C., Rajamanickam, R., Jayaraman, S.: The Prediction of yarn tensile properties by using artificial neural networks. J. Text. Inst. Proceed. Abstr. **86**(3), 459–469 (1995)
28. Debo, L.: Research of GPU cluster system based on YARN, Sun Yat-sen University, Guangzhou (2014)
29. Schwarz, E.R.: Certain aspects of yarn structure. Text. Res. J. **21**(3), 125–136 (1951)

Review on Application of Artificial Intelligence in Photovoltaic Output Prediction

Dianling Huang[1,2], Xiaoguang Wang[1(✉)], and Boyao Zhang[1,2]

[1] Computer Network Information Center, Chinese Academy of Sciences,
Beijing 100190, China
wangxg@cnic.cn
[2] University of Chinese Academy of Sciences, Beijing 100049, China

Abstract. With the development of photovoltaic, the distributed power grid has begun large-scale interconnection, which has an impact on the stability of the network. Distributed photovoltaic output is intermittent and stochastic. It is affected by climate and environment conditions such as sunlight, season, geography and time. It is difficult to accurately model and analyze the characteristics of distributed photovoltaic output. More and more artificial intelligence methods are applied to the photovoltaic output prediction and produce good results. This paper introduces the importance of photovoltaic prediction in photovoltaic power generation, then briefly gives what is artificial intelligence, and enumerates a large number of applications of artificial intelligence methods in photovoltaic power prediction. Finally, the direction of future research on photovoltaic power generation is proposed.

Keywords: Photovoltaic output · Prediction · Artificial intelligence
Machine learning · Deep learning

1 Introduction

Since twenty-first Century, the world's new energy has developed rapidly. With the advantages of renewable, easy access, green and clean, solar energy has become one of the main forces of new energy. According to REN21's Global Renewable Energy Status Report 2018, the total installed capacity of global photovoltaic power generation in 2017 was 98 GW, an increase of 29% over the same period last year. The installed capacity of new photovoltaic power generation was greater than the combined net installed capacity of coal, natural gas and nuclear power [1].

At the same time, with the rapid development of distributed generation, photovoltaic power generation will occupy a larger and larger market share, and will be combined with the existing power system into a more flexible, efficient and reliable power system, so that the whole society's energy efficiency is more efficient. Distributed generation, such as photovoltaic generation, has many advantages, but its interconnection will also bring many negative effects on the operation of the system. The ability of grid to accept photovoltaic power is closely related to space and time, and has certain randomness. It is a coordination decision-making problem between the power penetration capacity and operation mode. The factors that restrict PV power

© Springer Nature Switzerland AG 2018
M. Qiu (Ed.): SmartCom 2018, LNCS 11344, pp. 281–290, 2018.
https://doi.org/10.1007/978-3-030-05755-8_28

access to the grid include peak shaving at low valleys, sectional transmission capacity, system power flow, voltage, power quality and so on. Accurate power prediction of photovoltaic power station can make power dispatching department adjust dispatching plan in advance according to the predicted photovoltaic power, solve the problems arising from the coordination of photovoltaic power generation with load forecasting and power grid dispatching, further ensure the power quality of power grid, and save the installation of battery capacity, reduce the cost of photovoltaic power plants. Therefore, PV power forecasting is an effective way to increase the installed proportion of PV power generation and reduce its adverse impact on the grid.

The existing methods of PV output forecasting are varied, which are mainly divided into statistical methods and physical methods. Statistical methods are used to analyze the historical data, find out the inherent rules and use them for forecasting. Physical methods take meteorological forecasting data as input and use physical equations to predict. Artificial intelligence is a statistical method. With the development of artificial intelligence technology, more and more artificial intelligence methods such as Markov chain, neural network, regression analysis, support vector machine, least squares method are applied to photovoltaic output forecasting, and produce good results [2].

2   Introduction to Artificial Intelligence

Artificial intelligence is a branch of computer science. It understands and explores the essence of intelligence and reacts in a similar way to human intelligence. Artificial intelligence mainly studies robots, language recognition, image recognition, natural language processing, and expert systems and so on. It is a new technological science to study and develop theories, methods, technologies and application systems for simulating, extending and expanding human intelligence [3].

Artificial intelligence was born at a seminar in Dartmouth College in 1956. So far, it has three upsurge of development, namely, the early upsurge in 1950–1970, represented by symbolism, early reasoning system, early neural network (connectionism), expert system; the second upsurge in 1980–2000 represented by statistics, machine learning, neural network; and the third upsurge after 2006 which is characterized by the widespread use of large data, the emergence of deep learning, machine learning, and mass communication of AlphaGo [4] (Fig. 1).

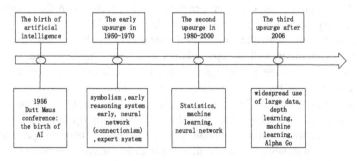

Fig. 1. Development of artificial intelligence

At present, in the third upsurge of development, artificial intelligence technology is flourishing and widely used in various fields. Machine learning, deep learning computer vision, natural language processing, robot and speech recognition are the core technologies of artificial intelligence.

Machine Learning. Machine Learning (ML) is a multi-disciplinary interdisciplinary, involving probability theory, statistics, approximation theory, convex analysis, algorithm complexity theory and other disciplines. Specialized in how to simulate or implement human learning behavior, in order to acquire new knowledge or skills, reorganize the existing knowledge structure so as to continuously improve their performance. It is the core of artificial intelligence and the fundamental way to make computers intelligent. It is widely used in various fields of artificial intelligence. It mainly uses induction, synthesis rather than deduction [5].

Deep Learning. Deep learning is a new field in machine learning research. Its motivation is to establish and simulate neural networks for analysis and learning. It simulates the mechanism of human brain to interpret data, such as images, sounds and text.

Computer Vision. Computer vision is a simulation of biological vision using computer and related equipment. Its main task is to process the captured pictures or videos to get the 3D information of the scene, just as humans and many other species do every day [6].

Natural Language. Processing Natural Language Processing is a science integrating linguistics, computer science and mathematics. It studies various theories and methods that can effectively communicate between humans and computers in natural language [7].

Robot. Integrating machine vision, automatic planning, and other cognitive technologies into minimal but high-performance sensors, brakes, and ingeniously designed hardware has spawned a new generation of robots.

Speech Recognition. Speech recognition is mainly concerned with automatic and accurate transcription of human speech technology [8].

In the prediction of PV output, machine learning and deep learning are mainly used. The relationship among them is shown in Fig. 2. Machine learning is a method of realizing artificial intelligence, and deep learning is a technology of realizing machine learning. Next, we will introduce machine learning and depth.

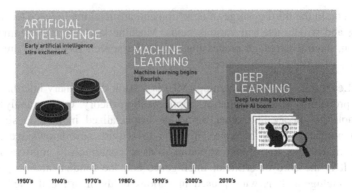

Fig. 2. The relationship between artificial intelligence, machine learning and deep learning [9]

2.1 Machine Learning

The concept of machine learning comes from early AI researchers. Machine learning is a general term for a class of algorithms that try to extract implicit rules from a large number of historical data and use them for prediction or classification. In short, machine learning is to use algorithms to analyze data, learn from it and make inferences or predictions. Unlike traditional handwritten software using specific instruction sets, we use a large amount of data and algorithms to "train" the machine, resulting in machine learning how to complete the task [10]. Subsequent paragraphs, however, are indented.

Machine learning mainly includes two kinds of learning methods, supervised learning and unsupervised learning. The so-called supervised learning means that the historical data used in training has labels, while unsupervised learning means that the historical data used in training hasn't labels. There is also a mixed learning method between them, called semi supervised learning [11].

In unsupervised learning, it is mainly to discover unknown structures or trends in data. Although the original data does not contain any tags, we want to integrate the data (grouping or clustering), or simplify the data (reducing dimensions, removing unnecessary variables, or detecting outliers). Therefore, the main classification of unsupervised algorithm includes:

- Clustering algorithm (Representation: K means clustering, system clustering).
- Dimension reduction algorithm (Representation: principal component analysis PCA, linear discriminant analysis LDA).

Supervised learning is to label historical data and use model prediction results. Supervised learning can be subdivided according to the type of prediction variable. If the prediction variable is continuous, then this is a regression problem. If the predictor is a discrete value of an independent class (qualitative or classified), then it is a classification problem. Therefore, the main categories of supervised learning include:

- Regression algorithm (linear regression, least squares regression, LOESS local regression, neural network, deep learning)
- Classification algorithms (Decision Tree, Support Vector Machine, Bayesian, K-Nearest Neighbor, Logical Regression, Random Forest).

2.2 Deep Learning

Since 2006, deep learning has emerged as a branch of machine learning. It is a method of data processing using multi-layer complex structure or multi-layer nonlinear transformation [12]. In recent years, deep learning has made breakthroughs in the fields of computer vision, speech recognition, natural language processing, audio recognition and bioinformatics [13]. Deep learning has been praised as one of the top ten technological breakthroughs since 2013 because of its considerable application prospects in data analysis. Deep learning method to simulate the human neural network, through the combination of multiple non-linear processing layer by layer abstraction of the original data, obtained at different levels of abstract features from the data and used for classification and prediction [14].

From the most primitive artificial neuron model, single-layer perceptron, back-propagation algorithm, convolution neural network, depth neural network, cyclic neural network, multi-channel neural network, depth learning in the development process has a bottleneck, but have been overcome one by one. Until now, deep learning has achieved excellent results in world-class competitions (Fig. 3).

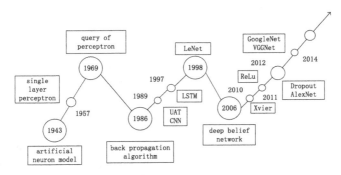

Fig. 3. Development history of deep learning [15]

3 Application of AI in PV Output Forecasting

3.1 Evaluation Criteria

Error evaluation index is used to evaluate the performance and prediction accuracy of power prediction model, and make the prediction effect of each prediction model in different photovoltaic power stations can be compared. At present, there are many kinds of error evaluation indicators, each of which is used to describe the specific error distribution law, and has certain pertinence, so there is no unified optimal error evaluation criteria. The evaluation criteria commonly used in short-term prediction of photovoltaic power generation are: average absolute error (MAE), average error percentage (MAPE) and root mean square error (RMSE). In this paper, the average error percentage (MAPE) and root mean square error (RMSE) are used as the error evaluation indexes. The mathematical expressions are as follows [16]:

$$\text{MAPE} = \frac{1}{N} \sum_{i=1}^{N} \left| \frac{t_i - T_i}{T_i} \right| \times 100\% \tag{1}$$

$$\text{RMSE} = \sqrt{\frac{1}{N} \sum_{i=1}^{N} (t_i - T_i)^2} \tag{2}$$

Among them, N is the number of samples in the test set, t_i is the power prediction value, T_i is the expected value. MAPE can reflect the proportional relationship between the error and the expected value, and RMSE describes the dispersion between the predicted value and the expected value.

3.2 Application of AI in PV Output Forecasting

In the early stage, the long-term and medium-term power forecasting was carried out by using the statistical analysis of historical meteorological data and historical output power data, mainly considering the latitude and longitude, perihelion, seasonal differences and other factors [17], which was basically used in the planning and design of photovoltaic power generation system and the medium-term and long-term power dispatch of grid-connected system. For example, Lorenz predicts the output power of regional photovoltaic power generation using the total solar radiation over the next three days provided by the European Centre for Mesoscale Weather Forecasting and combined with observations of photovoltaic power stations [18]. With the development of photovoltaic, the accuracy of photovoltaic output power prediction is becoming more and more important. Since then, most of the research has focused on the short-term prediction methods of photovoltaic power generation system.

With the development of artificial neural network, artificial intelligence is widely applied to short-term output forecasting of photovoltaic power generation.

Yu takes the weather conditions that affect the output of photovoltaic power generation system as the influencing factors, and establishes BP neural network to predict the output power, which can basically realize the short-term prediction of output power [19]. However, the influencing factors are too little to describe the changes of output power in a short time, resulting in poor prediction accuracy. Tao considers radiation effect analysis, temperature and weather patterns, and trains NARX networks to predict the output power of photovoltaic systems over the next few hours by obtaining clear sky conditions and weather data from the website over the next few hours [20]. In the reference [21], historical power generation, weather type index and atmospheric temperature prediction are used as input, and BP neural network is used to train and predict the daily hourly power generation. In the reference [22], similar day selection algorithm is proposed in the literature. The improved BP neural network (learning rate can be changed according to feedback error) is used to train and predict the power generation of the next 24 h. The MAPE of this method is 10.06% and 18.89% on sunny and rainy days, respectively. The improved network can improve the convergence speed of the network and reduce the computational burden. Similar day data as model input can enhance the adaptability of the model, but the integrity of historical data is more demanding. According to the intensity of illumination, the historical data can be divided into different subsets, which can effectively reduce the adverse effects of weather changes. In the reference [23], based on the mining of the characteristics of historical output data to improve the prediction accuracy, a photovoltaic ultra-short-term output prediction model with adaptive ability is proposed. Firstly, the SVM classifier is trained by the wavelet analysis and feature analysis of the historical output data, and then the output curve type is predicted by the established SVM classifier using the photovoltaic output data of the first 30 min. Finally, the auto-regressive and moving average model is combined with the curve type. And moving average model (ARMA) and artificial neural network model (ANN) select the appropriate method to predict photovoltaic output. ARMA, ANN and adaptive models are compared. The results show that the proposed model performs best in root mean square error (RMSE), mean absolute percentage error (MAPE) and Theil inequality coefficient (TIC). In the reference [24], by analyzing the correlation between photovoltaic power generation and meteorological factors, irradiance, temperature and humidity were selected as input variables of the prediction model. Then, a prediction model of photovoltaic ultrashort-term power output in the next 15 min is proposed, which uses the extraterrestrial radiation and Kalman filter to obtain the predicted irradiance, and then the temperature and humidity predicted by the continuous prediction method. Furthermore, the validity of the proposed model is verified by three consecutive days of actual data. The model has high prediction accuracy, especially at the inflection point of irradiance, the predicted value is in good agreement with the actual measured value.

Wang uses BP neural network to establish prediction models according to seasonal types respectively [25]; Yuan maps weather factors into daily type index as input of prediction model, establishes short-term output prediction model of photovoltaic power generation based on BP neural network, simplifies the prediction method of sub-model based on daily type [26]. Wang and Zhao considering that solar radiation and temperature are the two greatest factors affecting photovoltaic output, a prediction model of solar radiation based on uncertainty theory is established on the basis of the ambiguity of cloud amount and the double randomness of cloud cover coefficient. After the prediction of solar radiation and temperature of photovoltaic cells is realized, the photovoltaic output is calculated [27, 28]. The model calculates the PV output forecast value and realizes the prediction of PV output. In addition, Hou uses the grey forecasting theory to establish the forecasting model of photovoltaic power generation system to predict the future generation of photovoltaic power generation system based on historical data [29].

Support Vector Machine (SVM) and Neural Network (NN) were used to combine weather types and historical meteorological data to predict the photovoltaic output under different weather conditions. These methods improve the prediction accuracy to a certain extent, but the weather data often reflect the environmental conditions of larger areas, cannot accurately reflect the environmental conditions of photovoltaic panels, so the improvement of prediction accuracy is limited.

Using NWP data can improve the adaptability of forecasting models to weather changes and improve the prediction accuracy. In the reference [30], meteorological data combined with extraterrestrial irradiance and hourly temperature data provided by NWP predicted the light amplitude in the next 1 h to 3 h, and the MAPE predicted by RNN model with different time lengths were 18.53% to 20.33% respectively, which was superior to FNN. In the reference [31], NWP data from four locations around the photovoltaic power station under test are used to reduce the dimension of NWP data, and the sunshine index is taken as the output parameter. BP neural network is used to predict the illumination amplitude. The MSE of predicted results at different times in the next day is 20 to 50 respectively, which can obtain similar NWP data without local NWP data to improve the prediction performance of the model. Mellit divides the historical data into three weather types according to the daily average illumination amplitude, and then divides them into sunny, cloudy and cloudy weather types according to the set threshold [32]. The adaptive feedforward neural network (AFFNN) is used to train each weather type, and the hourly illumination amplitude prediction obtained by NWP is used to select the corresponding prediction model to predict power generation after one hours.

4 Summary

Artificial neural network and mechanical methods have more applications in photo-voltaic output prediction (see Fig. 4), while depth learning methods have less applications.

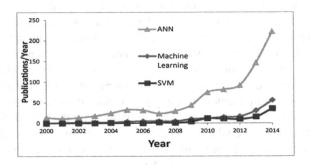

Fig. 4. Number of time the ANN, machine learning and SVM terms have been used in the original articles [33].

Artificial neural network and mechanics use relatively simple networks, such as BP neural network, SVM and so on, which can only extract the shallow structure of features. The generalization of these learning methods has been greatly limited. In deep learning algorithm, the importance of feature learning in the model is clearly high-lighted, and automation is achieved by layer-by-layer feature transformation. By learning the abstract features of the sample, the feature representation of the sample in the original space is transformed into a more abstract feature space, so as to obtain better prediction results and improve the generalization of the same model in dealing with different scenarios of photovoltaic prediction. On the other hand, the deep learning algorithm emphasizes that the depth of the model feature structure usually has five, ten or even hundreds of hidden layer nodes, so that the model contains more information, can be more widely taken into account the factors affecting photovoltaic output, providing a good way for fine analysis of photovoltaic output prediction.

References

1. REN21: Global Renewable Energy Status Report 2018. In: Organizing Committee of Guiyang International Forum on Ecological Civilization, Guiyang (2018)
2. Qian, Z., Cai, S.B., Gu, Y.Q.: Review of PV power generation prediction. Mech. Electr. Eng. Mag. **32**(5), 651–659 (2015)
3. Baidu Encyclopedia: Artificial Intelligence. https://baike.baidu.com/item/%E4%BA%BA% E5%B7%A5%E6%99%BA%E8%83%BD/9180. Accessed 11 June 2018
4. Gu, X.F.: Historical review and development history of artificial intelligence. Chin. J. Nat. **38**(3), 157–166 (2016)
5. Baidu Encyclopedia: Machine learning. https://baike.baidu.com/item/%E6%9C%BA%E5% 99%A8%E5%AD%A6%E4%B9%A0/217599?Fr=aladdin. Accessed 06 June 2018
6. Baidu Encyclopedia.: Computer vision. https://baike.baidu.com/item/%E8%AE%A1%E7% AE%97%E6%E6%BA%E8%E7%86%E8%A7%A7%89/2803351?Fr=aladdin. Accessed 04 July 2018
7. Baidu Encyclopedia: Natural Language Processing. https://baike.baidu.com/item/%E8%AE %A1%E7%AE%97%E6%9C%BA%E8%A7%E8%A7%A7%89/2803351?Fr=aladdin. Accessed 06 June 2018
8. Cao, J.Q.: Five core technologies of artificial intelligence. https://blog.csdn.net/sergeycao/ article/details/75254630. Accessed 17 July 2017
9. Michael, C.: What's the Difference Between Artificial Intelligence, Machine Learning, and Deep Learning?. https://blogs.nvidia.com/blog/2016/07/29/whats-difference-artificial-intelligence-machine-learning-deep-learning-ai/. Accessed 19 July 2016
10. Code_xzh: An article to understand the difference between AI, machine learning and in-depth learning. https://blog.csdn.net/xiangzhihong8/article/details/69935712. Accessed 08 Oct 2018
11. Wods_wang_219: Artificial Intelligence Learning Notes - Basic Concepts. https://blog.csdn. net/woods_wang_219/article/details/53519149. Accessed 08 Dec 2016
12. Lecun, Y., Bengio, Y., Hiton, G.: Deep learning. Nature **1**(7553), 436–444 (2015)
13. Deng, L., Yu, D.: Deep learning. Signal Process. **7**, 3–4 (2014)
14. Zhang, Q.L., Zhao, D., Chi, X.B.: Review for deep learning based on medical imaging diagnosis. Comput. Sci. **44**(b11), 1–7 (2017)
15. Gold FE: Deep learning: The history of in-depth learning. https://blog.csdn.net/u012177034/ article/details/52252851. Accessed 19 Aug 2016
16. Jing, B., Tan, L.N., Qian, Z., et al.: An overview of research progress of short-term photovoltaic forecasts. Electr. Meas. Instrum. **54**(12), 1–6 (2017)
17. Cheng, H., Cao, W.S.: Forecasting research of long-term solar irradiance and output power for photovoltaic generation system. In: 2012 Fourth International Conference on Computational and Information Sciences, pp. 1224–1227 (2012)

18. Lorenz, E., Hurka, J., Heinemann, D., et al.: Irradiance forecasting for the power prediction of grid-connected photovoltaic systems. IEEE J. Sel. Top. Appl. Earth Obs. Remote Sens. 2 (1), 2–10 (2009)
19. Yu, T.C., Chang, H.T.: The forecast of the electrical energy generated by photovoltaic systems using neural network method. In: 2011 International Conference on Electric Information and Control Engineering, ICEICE, pp. 2758–2761. IEEE (2011)
20. Tao, C., Duan, S., Chen, C.: Forecasting power output for grid-connected photovoltaic power system without using solar radiation measurement. In: IEEE International Symposium on Power Electronics for Distributed Generation Systems, pp. 773–777. IEEE (2010)
21. Yuan, X.L., Shi, J.H., Xu, J.Y.: Short-term power forecasting for photovoltaic generation considering weather type index. Proc. CSEE 33(34), 57–64 (2013)
22. Ding, M., Wang, L., Bi, R.: An ANN-based approach for forecasting the power output of photovoltaic system. Proc. Environ. Sci. 11(1), 1308–1315 (2011)
23. Gao, Y., Zhang, B.L., Mao, J.L., Liu, Y.: Machine learning-based adaptive very-short-term forecast model for photovoltaic power. Power Syst. Technol. 39(2), 307–312 (2015)
24. Wang, Y., Su, S., Yan, Y.T.: Very short-term PV power forecasting model based on Kalman filter algorithm and BP neutral network. Electr. Eng. 1, 42–46 (2014)
25. Wang, C.L.: Research on the short-term prediction of photovoltaic power output. Master, Nanchang University (2015)
26. Yuan, X.L., Shi, J.H., Xu, J.Y.: Short-term power forecast for photovoltaic generation based on BP neutral network. Renew. Energy Resour. 31(7), 11–16 (2013)
27. Wang, K.: Output prediction research of photovoltaic system considering multiple uncertainty factors. Master, School of Electrical and Electronic Engineering (2013)
28. Zhao, S.Q., Wang, M.Y., Hu, Y.Q., Liu, C.L.: Research on the prediction of PV output based on uncertainty theory. Trans. China Electrotech. Soc. 30(16), 213–220 (2015)
29. Hou, W., Xiao, J., Niu, L.Y.: Analysis of power generation capacity of photovoltaic power generation system in electric vehicle charging station. Electr. Eng. 4, 53–58 (2016)
30. Atsushi, Y., Tomonobu, S., Toshihisa, F., et al.: Decision technique of solar radiation prediction applying recurrent neural network for short-term ahead power output of photovoltaic system. Smart Grid Renew. Energy 04(6), 32–38 (2013)
31. Badia, A., Xavier, L.P.: Artificial neural network based daily local forecasting for global solar radiation. Appl. Energy 130(5), 333–341 (2014)
32. Mellit, A., Pavan, A.M., Lughi, V.: Short-term forecasting of power production in a large-scale photovoltaic plant. Sol. Energy 105, 401–413 (2014)
33. Cyril, V., Gilles, N., Soteris, K., Nivet, M.-L.: Machine learning methods for solar radiation forecasting - a review. Renew. Energy 105, 569–582 (2017)

Abnormal Flow Detection Technology in GPU Network Based on Statistical Classification Method

Huifeng Yang[1], Liandong Chen[1], Boyao Zhang[2], Haikuo Zhang[2,3,4],
Peng Zuo[4(✉)], and Ningming Nie[2]

[1] State Grid Hebei Electric Power Company, Shijiazhuang 050022, Hebei, China
[2] Computer Network Information Center, Chinese Academy of Sciences,
Beijing 100190, China
[3] University of Chinese Academy of Sciences, Beijing 100049, China
[4] China Internet Network Information Center, Beijing 100190, China
zuopeng2008@163.com

Abstract. Domain Name System (DNS), as the Internet "hub system" of basic resources services, mainly provides the basic services of domain name and IP address mapping. Abnormal flow detection technology plays an important role in the security service quality of Internet basic services, and it is also one of the important contents of Internet security research. The existing research mainly focuses on the analysis of network flow and other technologies at the data level, but in the context of network attacks, especially in the case of DDoS attacks, the accuracy and detection performance need to be improved. Based on the statistical method of high-performance abnormal flow detection technology, in this paper, the flow data are used for real-time statistical fitting, and the difference is made with the historical log data statistics. GPU parallel technology is used to improve the detection performance, which improves the accuracy and detection performance in the case of DDoS attacks on the network.

Keywords: Abnormal flow detection · Network flow · GPU

1 Introduction

With the increasing popularity of the Internet and the continuous penetration of production and life, people have become increasingly dependent on the Internet. At present, the Internet is not only a way to obtain and share information, but also a basic carrier for most traditional industries to conduct daily business negotiations. The diversity of Internet applications and the rapid growth of Internet scale have posed challenges to the safe operation of the Internet. Known as the "hub system" of the Internet, the field of Internet basic resources mainly includes domain name, IP and other core basic resources, and its security plays an important role in the overall security of the Internet.

Domain name system (DNS) is one of the most important basic services of the Internet. It identifies and locates the servers and service portals on the Internet by mapping and transforming the basic resources of the Internet, such as domain name and

© Springer Nature Switzerland AG 2018
M. Qiu (Ed.): SmartCom 2018, LNCS 11344, pp. 291–299, 2018.
https://doi.org/10.1007/978-3-030-05755-8_29

Internet Protocol Address (IP). DNS is a relatively mature global distributed database, providing highly readable, efficient and stable Internet identity resolution services for Internet. By the fourth quarter of 2017, a total of 332 million domain names were registered across the world through all top-level domain registrars [1]. As of December 2017, the total number of domain names in China reached 38.48 million, the number of top-level domain names of ".cn" reached 20.84 million, the annual growth rate of Chinese ".cn" domain names was 1.2%, the number of Chinese websites was 5.33 million, and the number of websites under ".cn" top-level domain names was 3.15 million, the annual growth rate exceeded 20% [2].

In recent years, there are more and more attacks on DNS, such as Domain Name Phishing, DNS DDoS, DNS Cache Poisoning, DNS Amplification Attack, and Client Flooding and so on. The security of domain name service is attracting more and more attention from the state. In the 13th Five-Year Plan for National Informationization, it is clearly stated that "the Internet domain name security system should be built to strengthen the detection and emergency disposal of the root and. CN and other important top-level domain name server anomalies". In this paper, we use big data analysis method to improve and optimize the traditional network abnormal flow detection technology, and use GPU method to improve processing speed, which gets better results.

2 Research Status

Currently, the vast majority of data exchanges between DNS services and terminals (mainly including requests and feedback) are conducted in plaintext and unencrypted ways. This will lead to user privacy being exposed to Internet communications, and the privacy vulnerabilities will be exploited by hackers. For example, hackers can collect user access traces (query time, access content, user IP address, etc.) and other information to analyze user habits. Aiming at this problem, many methods have been put forward to protect user privacy.

In 2003, Krishnamurthy et al. first applied sketch to abnormal detection and proposed a heuristic method to automatically set sketch parameters [3], and some researchers use different methods to detect abnormal traffic flow [4–6]. In 2007, Dewaele et al. used non-Gaussian fitting method to study the network abnormal flow between metropolitan area networks, mainly searching for abnormal flow data around the flow characteristics of network layer data in TCP/IP stack [7]. In 2011, Mikle et al. introduced this method into DNS flow analysis to look for abnormal flow at low flow levels and to find botnets from it [8]. In 2012, Lorna et al. proposed an abnormal detection method based on sketch summary data structure, using an exponential weighted smoothing model to find abnormal flow numbers for flow characteristics of network layer data (target IP address, etc.) [9]. In 2016, Xie and Xie et al. abstracted the network flow into three characteristic values: time stability, spatial correlation and flow periodicity, and established a three-dimensional Tensor data model. Based on this data model, they introduced the Tensor Completion method to solve the network flow recovery problem, and used the Sequential Tensor Completion Algorithm to optimize the calculation process [10].

3 GPU Abnormal Flow Detection Technology Based on Statistical Classification Method

In this paper, the statistical-based gamma distribution fitting technique is used to add the data features of application layer. We use network flow sketch and non-Gaussian multi-resolution statistical detection methods to calculate the difference with the historical log data. The abnormal flow detection based on data flow is completed, and the abnormal flow detection ability based on flow is improved by GPU parallel algorithm (Fig. 1).

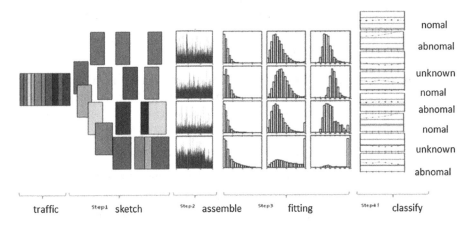

Fig. 1. Abnormal flow analysis based on gamma distribution

The algorithm maps the network flow to finite space by hash bucket method according to IP, domain name and other characteristics with time window as the basic unit. Then the data in the hash bucket are gathered by multiscale (Step 2). The gamma distribution is used to fit the convergent data at different scales (Step 3). And the alpha and beta parameters of the gamma distribution in each hash bucket are obtained. Mahalanobis distance is used to calculate the characteristic value, and the difference with the historical log flow is made to judge whether the abnormal is or not (Step 4).

The calculation method is shown in Table 1 as follows:

Table 1. Symbolic interpretation of algorithm models

Using symbols	Meaning
N	Hash function quantity
$n \in \{1, \ldots, N\}$	Hash function serial number, used to create hash bucket
M	Hash bucket size
$n \in \{1, \ldots, M\}$	Sketch output function of hash function h_n
J	Flow aggregation size
Δ_j	Flow aggregation scale
$X_{\Delta_j}^{n,m}(t)$	Flow aggregation hash time series
$\alpha_{\Delta_j}^{n,m} \ \beta_{\Delta_j}^{n,m}$	Gamma distribution fitting parameter (parameter α and parameter β)
$D_{\alpha^{n,m}} \ D_{\beta^{n,m}}$	Mahalanobis distance (parameter α and parameter β)
λ	Threshold

Step 1. Flow sketch

Using the unit time window T as the unit, the network flow is analyzed in the form of data packets. In each time window, six tuples like $\{t_i, \{x_{i,l}...l = 1, ...5\}\}$ are used to represent each packet, they are timestamp, original IP, target IP, source port, target port and query domain name respectively. I represents the packet of the time window, $i = 1, ..., I$. h_n $n \in \{1, ..., N\}$ is defined to represent N independent hash functions with different seeds. Definition M represents the size of a hash bucket. Definition F represents the eigenvalues of data packets, corresponding to the characteristic values of six tuples of packets. Each hash function h_n in the hash bucket can scatter the original flow P to the M dimensional sketch matrix. $X_{n,m} = \{(t_i, m_{n,j})\}_{n,m}$, among $m_{n,j} = h_n(F_i)$, $m_{n,j} \in \{1, ..., M\}$.

Step 2. Multiscale polymerization

The corresponding eigenvalues of the sketch matrix produced in the first step are superimposed according to a series of different scales to form a time-dependent sequence of $X_{\Delta_j}^{n,m}(t)$. Δ_j represents different scales. Through multi-scale aggregation, the graphs formed by $X_{\Delta_j}^{n,m}(t)$ time correlated sequences can be used as a probability density function (PDF) to provide data for the third step of gamma distribution fitting.

Step 3. Non Gaussian fitting (based on gamma distribution fitting)

In the sketch matrix, the gamma distribution is fitted to $\Gamma \alpha\Delta, \beta\Delta$ by using different scales of aggregate flow eigenvalues. Gamma parameters α (shape) and β (range) of different scales are produced during fitting $\Gamma \alpha, \beta$ distribution in this time window. Thus, the mapping from $X_{\Delta_j}^{n,m}(t)$ to gamma distribution parameter $\{\alpha_{\Delta_j}^{n,m}, \beta_{\Delta_j}^{n,m}\}$ is realized.

Step 4. Calculating reference values

For each h_n, the sample mean and sample variance are defined according to the α and β fitted by gamma distribution. For example, taking α as an example, defining $\alpha_{\Delta_j}^{m,R} = <\alpha_{\Delta_j}^{n,m}>_m$ and $\sigma_{m,\partial,\Delta_j}^2 = \ll\alpha_{\Delta_j}^{n,m}\gg_m$, $<\bullet>_m$ and $\ll\bullet\gg_m$ denote sample mean and sample variance respectively, $m \in \{1, ..., M\}$.

Step 5. Statistical distance

According to the reference value $\alpha_{\Delta_j}^{m,R}$ calculated by the fourth step, the distance between $\alpha_{\Delta_j}^{n,m}$ and the reference value is calculated by using the Markov distance. The formula is as follows:

$$(D_\alpha n, m)^2 = \frac{1}{J}\sum_{j=1}^{J}\frac{(\alpha_{\Delta_j}^{n,m} - \alpha_{\Delta_j}^{m,R})^2}{\sigma_{m,\alpha,\Delta_j}^2}$$

Similarly, the average reference value $\bar{\alpha}_{\Delta_j}^{n,m}$ of the same period in history can be obtained by analyzing the historical log, and the Markov distance from $\bar{\alpha}_{\Delta_j}^{n,m}$ to $\alpha_{\Delta_j}^{m,R}$ can be calculated. The specific formula is as follows:

$$(\bar{D}_\alpha n, m)^2 = \frac{1}{J} \sum_{j=1}^{J} \frac{(\bar{\alpha}_{\Delta_j}^{n,m} - \alpha_{\Delta_j}^{m,R})^2}{\bar{\sigma}_{m,\alpha,\Delta_j}^2}$$

When $\bar{D}_\alpha n, m \leq \lambda$ and $D_\alpha n, m \leq \lambda$, the eigenvalue is normal.

When $\bar{D}_\alpha n, m > \lambda$ and $D_\alpha n, m \leq \lambda$, the characteristic value is DDoS attack flow eigenvalue.

When $\bar{D}_\alpha n, m \leq \lambda$ and $D_\alpha n, m > \lambda$, the characteristic value is low flow abnormal access flow.

Other cases are suspected abnormal flow.

Step 6. Abnormal flow classification by abnormal sketch matrix

After calculating the abnormal eigenvalues of hash bucket according to the fifth step, abnormal flow data packets can be found according to these abnormal characteristics, so as to realize the function of abnormal flow detection.

This method combines historical log features to conduct real-time checking of flow data, and finds abnormal flow. Due to the high real-time requirement of abnormal flow analysis based on data volume and the need to analyze historical logs, performance is also one of the key indicators of the model.

4 Experiment and Analysis

In this paper, based on the statistical method of high-performance abnormal flow detection technology, the flow data is used for real-time statistical fitting, and the difference is compared with the historical log data statistics, which can detect abnormal flow more comprehensively (Fig. 2).

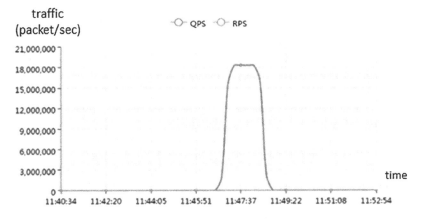

Fig. 2. DDOS attack flow characteristics

In the case of DDoS attacks on DNS, traditional abnormal flow detection based on five tuples of network packets (original IP, target IP, original port, target port and protocol number) is difficult to separate. After abnormal flow becomes the main flow, it confuses the statistical characteristics of traditional abnormal flow.

In this paper, sketch and non-Gaussian multiresolution statistical detection is studied by combining network flow and history log analysis. Without reducing the abnormal flow recognition rate of network flow, it can detect DDoS attack flow in time and reduce the misjudgment rate of useful flow under DDoS attack. At the same time, according to the content of application layer DNS message, the eigenvalue is abstracted by sketch, and the recognition rate of abnormal flow is improved.

At the same time, the abnormal flow detection performance is improved by combining GPU and CPU under large flow.

(1) Principle analysis

In the aspect of correctness, the characteristic value of historical log analysis is added to the original abnormal flow identification algorithm based on network flow. A single model is transformed into a hybrid model, and a specific DDoS attack flow can be identified on the basis of the original recognition rate.

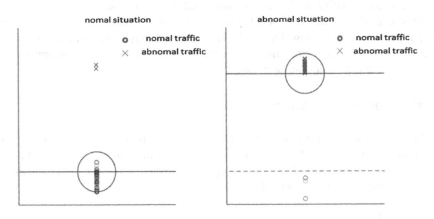

Fig. 3. Abnormal flow separation in DDoS attack

As shown in the Fig. 3 above, a flow-based network flow sketch abnormal detection method can effectively detect a small amount of abnormal flow in the case of non-DDoS attacks according to the main network flow characteristics. However, under DDoS attack, abnormal flow becomes the main flow, and abnormal flow detection based on this will judge normal flow as abnormal flow. In this paper, we will fit the fixed history log information and compare it with the current time window fitting mean. When the distance is greater than a specific threshold, DDoS attack scenarios can be effectively identified, as shown in the Fig. 3 on the right. In the case of DDoS attack, the fitted mean will bias attack flow characteristics. Therefore the flow that is close to the fitting mean of the flow is judged as abnormal flow. So we can find the characteristics of attack flow and support operators to clean up flow.

In terms of performance, GPU can be used to perform parallel computing for multiple sets of sample data that need to be fitted, as shown in Fig. 4. Grid represents GPU computing model. Each Grid contains multiple Block computing units. Each Block computing unit also contains multiple computing cores. $X_1 \sim X_n$ represents n sample data to be fitted. Because the data are independent of each other, the parallel computing capability of GPU can be used to optimize the multi-sample fitting process.

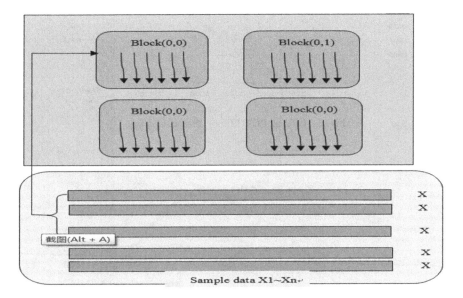

Fig. 4. GPU parallel fitting multiple sample data

Assuming that there are N sample data to be fitted, each Block of GPU has T computing cores. The Block number of GPU can be calculated according to the following formula: $block\_num = \frac{(N + (T-1))}{T}$. So the last Block calculates the fitting of $N\%T$ sample data. The other Block is the fitting of $\frac{N}{T}$ sample data.

(2) Experiment and analysis

This experiment realizes the combination of log analysis and flow based abnormal detection. By simulating the DDoS attack of DNS, DDoS flow can be detected and separated. Through NVIDIA Titan GK110B GPU parallelization, the maximum speed is 76.5 times faster.

Experiments show that gamma fitting takes a long time when the data volume is large and the hash bucket is large. When the gamma distribution is fitted, the data correlation between different eigenvalues is weak and the communication is less, which is suitable for large-scale parallel speed increase. In recent years, GPU technology has developed rapidly, and computing power has been greatly improved. At the same time, directRDMA and other technologies can be used to solve the problem of data copy performance between memorys. The practice shows that GPU parallel accelerated fitting can achieve better results (Fig. 5).

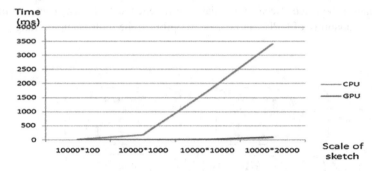

Fig. 5. CPU and GPU fitting time comparison

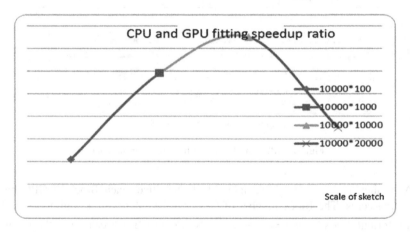

Fig. 6. CPU and GPU fitting speedup ratio

According to the test, this method has better GPU performance compared with serial fitting in the case of fine particle size fitting. But the speedup will decrease as the number increases (Fig. 6).

5 Conclusion

In this paper, based on the statistical method of high-performance abnormal flow detection technology, we adopt the flow data for real-time statistical fitting, and make a difference with the historical log data statistical data. We use GPU parallel technology to improve detection performance with the following innovations:

(1) It not only contains five tuples of Internet packets, but also uses DNS packet content as feature value, which improves the ability of abnormal detection.
(2) Adding historical log analysis to the flow-based analysis can enhance the ability to detect DDoS attacks on DNS.
(3) By using GPU parallel technology, the fitting performance of fine-grained network data flow is realized, and the abnormal flow can be detected more accurately.

As network security gets more and more attention, the accuracy and performance of network abnormal detection technology will become more and more prominent. This paper is hoped to provide some reference value for the future development of network abnormal flow detection technology.

Acknowledgments. This work was partly supported by the National Key R&D Program of China (No. 2017YFB0203102), the State Key Program of National Natural Science Foundation of China (No. 91530324).

References

1. Verisign. The domain name industry brief [EB/OL]. https://www.verisign.com/assets/domain-name-report-Q42017.pdf
2. CNNIC. The forty-first statistical report on China's Internet development [EB/OL]. http://www.cnnic.cn/hlwfzyj/hlwxzbg/hlwtjbg/201803/P020180305409870339136.pdf
3. Krishnamurthy, B., Sen, S., Zhang, Y.: Sketch-based change detection: methods, evaluation and applications. In: Proceedings of the 3th ACM SIGCOMM Conference on Internet Measurement (2003)
4. Estan, C., Varghese, G.: New directions in traffic measurement and accounting: focusing on the elephants, ignoring the mice. ACM Trans. Comput. Syst. (TOCS) **21**(3), 270–313 (2003)
5. Tang, J., Cheng, Y., Hao, Y., Song, W.: SIP flooding attack detection with a multi-dimensional sketch design. IEEE Trans. Dependable Secure Comput. **11**(6), 582–595 (2014)
6. Liang, G., Taft, N., Yu, B.: A fast lightweight approach to origin-destination IP traffic estimation using partial measurements. IEEE/ACM Trans. Netw. Special Issue Netw. Inf. Theory **14**(6), 2634–2648 (2006)
7. Dewaele, G., Fukuda, K., Borgnat, P., Abry, P., Cho, K.: Extracting hidden anomalies using sketch and non Gaussian multiresolution statistical detection procedures. In: Workshop on Large Scale Attack Defense (2007)
8. Mikle, O.: Detecting Hidden Anomalies in DNS Communication [EB/OL]. https://www.dns-oarc.net/files/workshop-201210/DNS-anomaly-OF.pdf
9. Luo, N.: Research and implementation of abnormal flow monitoring method based on synopsis data structure (2008)
10. Xie, K., Wang, L., Wang, X., Xie, G., Wen, J., Zhang, G.: Accurate recovery of internet flow data: a tensor completion approach. In: INFOCOM (2016)

Research on Data Forwarding Algorithm Based on Link Quality in Vehicular Ad Hoc Networks

Xiumei Fan[✉], Hanyu Cai, and Tian Tian

Faculty of Automation and Information Engineering,
Xi'an University of Technology, Xi'an 710048, China
xmfan@xaut.edu.cn

Abstract. Vehicular ad hoc networks (VANETs) realize remote data transmission via multi-hop communications. However, high relative vehicle mobility and frequent changes of the network topology inflict new problems on forwarding data in time. As a result, the robustness of the link is crucial to VANETs. In this paper, we present an efficient routing algorithm based on link quality named DFLQ. Firstly, we determine the range of forwarding according to the traffic density and the vehicle route. Then, we can compute the time of link maintaining on the basis of the position, speed and direction of the nodes. Also, we can estimate the quality of wireless channel based on the expected transmission count. Finally, the longest link maintenance time is chosen as the relay node to forward the data. Simulation results validate that the DFLQ improves packet delivery rate, reduces end-to-end delay and network overhead to a certain extent.

Keywords: VANETs · Link quality · Traffic density · Link maintenance time · Routing algorithm

1 Introduction

With the improving of people's living standard, there are more than 1 billion registered motor vehicles worldwide. As a result, lots of critical issues are becoming more serious, such as traffic congestion, traffic accidents and environmental pollution [1]. VANETs [2] is a temporary ad hoc network which enable vehicle-to-vehicle (V2V), vehicle-to-infrastructure (V2I) communications. The message will transfer within one-hop or multi-hop. A vehicle not only relay a packet, but also it can forward a packet. If the destination node is in the transmission range of the source node, the nodes will directly communicate. When the destination node is out of the range of communication, the message will depend on other nodes to relay the packet.

In VANETS, vehicles move with high and variable speed, causing frequent changes in the network topology, which leads the link between a source node and a destination node has become more and more fragile. VANETs has more requirements, such as the excellent adaptive of routing and better link quality.

© Springer Nature Switzerland AG 2018
M. Qiu (Ed.): SmartCom 2018, LNCS 11344, pp. 300–310, 2018.
https://doi.org/10.1007/978-3-030-05755-8_30

2   Related Work

Routing technology is also a promising and challenging subject in VANETs. Many protocols have been proposed. DSR [3] and AODV [4] have been proposed for years. An improved AODV algorithm based on link awareness is presented [5], which can predict the maintenance of the link by selecting vehicle information, including position, velocity, and acceleration. The MOPR algorithm [6] presents a prediction model to estimate the position of the vehicle at the next moment GPSR [7] is a classic routing algorithm based on location information. Due to high relative vehicle mobility and frequent changes of the network topology, it occurs some problems such as the unstable link, congestion, large delay.

In order to maintain the stability of V2V communication and avoid the sudden break, GPSR-L [8] aims at inter-vehicle communication links with frequent breaks, poor routing stability, and low data transmission efficiency in V2V. The algorithm solved the impact of speed on the GPSR routing through the lifetime concept, thereby enhancing the stability of the route. The RRMLI protocol [9] optimizes the routing mechanism of GPSR and uses the greedy algorithm to send RREQ message packet repair route to the destination node after the link is disconnected. LOUVRE [10] is improved on the basis of GPSR. LOUVRE transmits the estimation of traffic density through flooding mode, so many flooding messages can easily cause congestion and generate large transmission delay.

Based on the above analysis, the traditional routing algorithm is inefficient for VANETs. In this paper, we propose a novel link quality-based routing protocol, which can ensure the best connectivity of links between two vehicles in VANETs.

3   Date Forwarding Algorithm Based on Link Quality-DFLQ

Based on link quality, we proposed a date forwarding algorithm (DFLQ), which is on the basis of GPSR.

3.1   Related Definitions

- Definition 1-Link quality: It refers to the quality of link between the source node and the destination node in the process of vehicle sending data.
- Definition 2-Hello message: The contents of the Hello message include the node number I_n, the node location information D_n, the node speed V_n, the link label R_{ij}, the current link density K_{ij}, the node time stamp T_n, and the link maintenance time information T_l, as shown in Table 1.
- Definition 3-Neighbor node: It refers to nodes within communication range, and the nodes obtain the information of neighbor vehicles through Hello messages, including location, speed, direction of movement and density of vehicles.
- Definition 4-Jamming density K_j: It refers to the traffic flow density when the vehicle cannot move or move slowly owing to congestion.

- Definition 5-Optimum density K_m: It refers to the optimum density that is close to capacity of the road. Meanwhile, the value of traffic flow is maximum. The relationship between speed and density is shown in Fig. 1.

Table 1. Hello message content

I_n	D_n	V_n	R_{ij}	K_{ij}	T_n	T_l

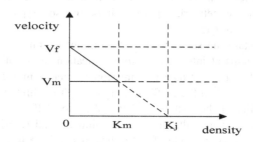

Fig. 1. The graph of vehicle speed-density

3.2 Vehicle Density Estimation

The value of the vehicle density can be calculated with the "velocity-density linear" model which is proposed by the Greenshields [11]. The speed-density linear model can be written as:

$$v = v_f \left(1 - \frac{k}{k_j}\right) \qquad (1)$$

v_f is the free speed of the vehicles when traffic density is very small; k_j is the maximum traffic density which road can load. The real-time traffic density k which unit is "vehicle/km" can be estimated by collecting the average speed of the traffic within a certain geographical area. We assume that the set $\{v_{i0}, v_{i1}, \ldots, v_{im}\}$ which is obtained by the vehicle at the slot t present the vehicular speed of the neighbor nodes and itself, where i is the periodic broadcast in $i - th$ slot and m is the number of neighbor nodes. Therefore, at time t the average speed of the vehicle and its neighbor nodes is:

$$\bar{v}_t = \frac{\sum_{j=1}^{m} v_{ij}}{m} \qquad (2)$$

After the n periodic broadcast, we can get set $\bar{v}\{\bar{v}_1, \bar{v}_2, \ldots, \bar{v}_n\}$, so the expectation of $\bar{v}_t$ is:

$$\bar{v} = \frac{\sum_{i=1}^{m} \bar{v}_l}{n} \tag{3}$$

The traffic density can be calculated with following formula:

$$k = k_j \left(1 - \frac{\bar{v}}{v_f} \right) \tag{4}$$

3.3 Link Maintenance Time (LMT)

In this paper, the calculation of LMT not only considers the distance between the vehicle nodes, the speed, and the coordinate position, but also takes the direction of the node into account. We can consider that the node i is in the effective communication range of node j when the link transmission distance d_{ij} is not great than the distance of vehicles R, the communication link can be established and obtained the data of GPS.

If the mobility node stays in the communication range of each other, so it represents the link is connecting, we can get the link expire time through the calculate TML which is called the link expire time. The value of LMT will increase to infinite. The link is connected always, or else it is will be broken. Therefore, it will select the node which have the maximum TML as the next forwarding node.

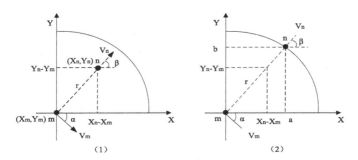

Fig. 2. Prediction model of link maintenance time

We can assuming that the nodes m and n can communicate with each other, the node m is obtained the position coordinates (X_m, Y_m), the motion velocity is v_m, the movement direction is α by the GPS device. The node n position coordinates are (X_n, Y_n), the velocity is v_m. α is the movement direction; the link maintenance time can be calculated by the mathematical model shown in Fig. 2.

Thus, from Fig. 2, it is clear that the segment a, b, c, d can be represented as $a = V_n cos\beta - V_m cos\beta$, $b = V_n sin\beta - V_m cos\alpha$, $c = X_n - X_m$, $d = Y_n - Y_m$. The transmission range between vehicles is γ, the time of experience is t, then in $Rt\Delta a$ mb need to meet the Pythagorean theorem:

$$(c+at)^2 + (d+bt)^2 = r^2 \tag{5}$$

Then the formula for solving the time t can be as follows (6):

$$t = \frac{-(ac+bd) + \sqrt{r^2(a^2+b^2) - (bc-ad)^2}}{a^2+b^2} \tag{6}$$

If the distance between the mobile nodes is always in the communication range of each other, it means that the link state between the nodes is always connected. Otherwise, the link state between the nodes is not always maintained, there exist a broken situation in the middle process. In the process of selecting the relay node, we choose the node with the largest time t as the optimal relay node by calculating the formula.

3.4   The Decision of Selecting the Relay Forwarding Node

The vehicles can get the higher speed when the vehicles density is smaller. In contrast, the speed of the vehicle will decrease if the traffic density is larger. If the traffic is congested, the speed will become zero. when the traffic reaches the crowded state, the speed is further reduced until the stagnation. Therefore, it is necessary to determine the forwarding range according to the different traffic density k. As shown in Fig. 3, The selection range of the relay node is limited to a certain region according to the distance coefficient $\frac{\mu}{k}$ which is in the range of $[0, 1]$, k is calculated by the formula (4), μ is used to adjust the forwarding range after several times and the initial value of μ is 0.064. This eliminates a number of neighbor nodes that do not meet the requirements, reducing complexity and the network overhead, end-to-end latency.

1. When the traffic is congested and the vehicle is in a stagnant state ($k \geq k_j$), the link quality between the nodes is in a steady state. Therefore, the greedy algorithm is used to forward the data, that is, the neighbor node closest in $\left[\frac{\mu}{k}R, R\right]$ to the destination node is selected as the relay node.
2. When the traffic density is relatively high ($k_m < k < k_j$), select the node with the longest link maintenance time (LMT) in $\left[\frac{\mu}{k}R, R\right]$ as the forward node. If there is no more than the node near it, then reduce μ.
3. When the traffic density is small ($k < k_m$), the number of nodes is small, the speed is high, so the link quality is poor. We select the node in the range of $\left[\frac{\mu}{k}R, R\right]$ with the longest link duration to forward. If there is no more than the node near it, then increase μ. If at this time still cannot find a neighbor node than own node close to the destination node, the peripheral forwarding mode is adopted.

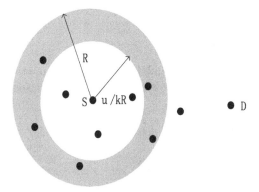

Fig. 3. Limits the forwarding range

3.5　DFLQ Forwarding Strategy

DFLQ forwarding strategy are as follows:

1. Each node in the network broadcasts the Hello message periodically and each node updates its own routing table in time when the neighbor nodes receive the data packets. If there exist the relevant information of node in the routing table, this information will be replaced by the new information. If this information does not exist in the routing table, it is added to the table and then go to step (2).
2. The node detects whether there is a destination node in the neighbor nodes. It forwards packets and the process of route is completed if the neighbor nodes exist. Otherwise, go to step (3).
3. To determine whether the current traffic density is greater than or equal to the blocking density of the road, that is $k \leq k_j$. If yes, the forwarding process will use the greedy method which choose the node which is nearest to the destination node to forward the data packet in the range $\left[\frac{\mu}{k}R, R\right]$. Otherwise, go to step (4).
4. To determine whether the current traffic density is greater than or equal to the optimal density of the road, that is $k_m \leq k \leq k_j$. If the forwarding range is limited to $\left[\frac{\mu}{k}R, R\right]$, the longest T_L is selected as the next hop forwarding node in this range, and the forwarding range is adjusted if the next hop node is not obtained. Otherwise, go to step (5).
5. The forwarding range is limited to $\left[\frac{\mu}{k}R, R\right]$, in which the T_L is selected as the next hop forwarding node, otherwise the forwarding range is adjusted.
6. Repeat the above steps until you find the destination node. If the optimization path can't be found, then to use this model continuously or transfer according to the peripheral forwarding mode.

4   Simulation Results

4.1   Simulation Modeling

We use VanetMobiSim [12] and NS2 [13] to establish a co-simulation platform. Simulation parameter settings are shown in Tables 2 and 3, respectively.

Table 2. VanetMobiSim parameter settings

Content	Parameter
Simulation area	1 km * 1 km–3 km * 3 km
Simulation time	200 s
Vehicle node type	Car
Number of vehicle nodes	20–160
Vehicle movement speed	0 m/s–17 m/s
Traffic light	10
Road speed limit	17 m/s
Vehicle movement model	IDM_LC

Table 3. NS2 simulation parameters

Content	Parameter
Simulation area	1 km * 1 km–3 km * 3 km
Vehicle movement mode	VanetMobSim
Traffic model	CBR
Number of vehicles	20–160
Vehicle communication range	250 m
MAC layer protocol	802.11

4.2   Simulation Results Analysis

The main performance parameters of this algorithm are packet delivery ratio, average end-to-end delay, and network overhead. Under the same condition of other parameters, the number of vehicle nodes on packet loss rate and average delay of different network protocols are analyzed. The number of vehicle nodes were set as 20, 40, 60, 80, 100, 120, 140, 160 respectively, and the eight groups of experiments were simulated for several times. The packet loss rate and average end to end delay in the network are calculated according to the number and time of packets received by all nodes.

Figure 4 shows the average end-to-end delay of the packet as the number of vehicles increases. The average end-to-end delay of DFLQ and GPSR is generally decreasing. Compare to the GPSR protocol, taken the forwarding range and direction into account when the DFLQ protocol selects the forwarding node, which can reduce the complexity of calculation and save time. However, the delay will raise with the increasing collision of packets in the network, while the density of vehicle increased.

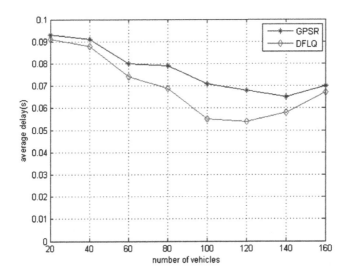

Fig. 4. The impact of the number of vehicles on the average delay

Figure 5 shows the change in the rate of delivery of packets with the increase in the number of vehicles. When the number of nodes changes from 20 to 160, the data arrival rate of the two routing protocols is greatly improved. When the number of nodes is between 20 and 60, there is low rate of data delivery. With the increase of node number, the data arrival rate of the DFLQ algorithm is also improved. The protocol effectively reduces the probability of finding the next hop node because it calculates the maintenance time of each link before execution, and then selects the longest link time as the message transmission path. When the traffic density is too large, a large number of packets will collide, which will inevitably lead to packet loss, resulting in a slight drop in delivery rate.

Set up another the size of the scene for 1 km * 1 km, 1.5 km * 1.5 km, 2 km * 2 km, 2.5 km * 2.5 km, 3 km * 3 km, and the number of nodes corresponds to 100, 150, 200, 250, 300 respectively.

As shown in Figs. 6 and 7, the end-to-end delay of the packets in the network tends to increase when the number of scenes and nodes becomes larger, and the packet delivery rate tends to decrease. The DFLQ protocol has a smaller increase than the GPSR. This is because the DFLQ protocol takes the factors of link maintenance time into account when selecting relaying nodes. When the scene is enlarged and the road topology is more complex, the link is still established between the nodes with better link quality, the end to end delay is reduced and the delivery rate of the packet is improved. The results show that the scalability of DFLQ algorithm is better than GPSR.

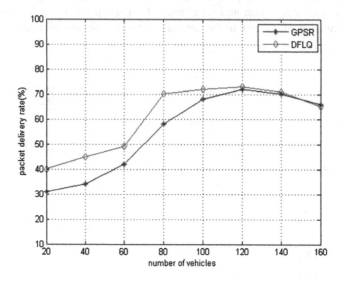

Fig. 5. The impact of the number of vehicles on the data delivery rate

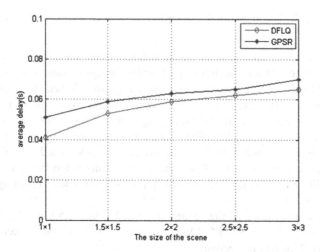

Fig. 6. The impact of size of scene on average delay

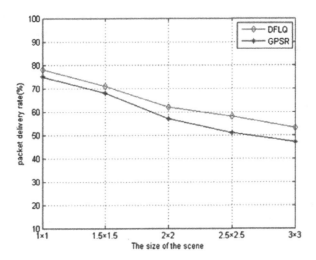

Fig. 7. The impact of the size of scene data delivery rate

5 Conclusion

In order to reduce the packet fragmentation problem caused by the rapidly changing topology in VANETs, we propose a routing and forwarding algorithm based on link quality (DFLQ). The algorithm makes full use of the vehicle's density, speed, location and road topology, which determines the forwarding range according to vehicle density to reduce end-to-end delay and ensures high packet delivery rate according to link maintenance time. The simulation results show that DFLQ is superior to the traditional algorithm in the urban environment, which can be applied to the environment with more nodes and more complicated traffic conditions.

Acknowledgments. This work was supported by Natural Science Foundation of China (No. 61272509), Beijing Natural Science Foundation (No. 4132049), Shanxi Province Hundred Talents Program, and the key research and development plan of Shaanxi province (2017ZDCXL-GY-05-01).

References

1. Liu, L., Chen, C., Ren, Z., Shi, C.: A link transmission-quality based geographic routing in Urban VANETs. In: 2017 IEEE 28th Annual International Symposium on Personal, Indoor, and Mobile Radio Communications, pp. 1–6. IEEE (2018)
2. Eze, E.C., Zhang, S., Liu, E.: Vehicular ad hoc networks (VANETs): current state, challenges, potentials and way forward. In: 2014 20th International Conference on Automation and Computing, UK-CACS, pp. 176–181. IEEE (2014)
3. Hu, B., Gharavi, H.: DSR-based directional routing protocol for ad hoc networks. In: IEEE GLOBECOM 2007 - IEEE Global Telecommunications Conference, pp. 4936–4940. IEEE (2007)

4. Li, Y., Hu, W.: Optimization strategy for mobile ad hoc network based on AODV routing protocol. In: 2010 International Conference on Wireless Communications Networking and Mobile Computing, pp. 1–4. IEEE (2010)

5. Dua, A., Kumar, N., Bawa, S.: Elsevier Science Publishers B.V. (2014)

6. Vahdat, A., Becker, D.: Epidemic routing for partially-connected ad hoc networks, vol. 6, pp. 1571–5078. Research Gate (2000)

7. Karp, B., Kung, H.T.: GPSR: greedy perimeter stateless routing for wireless networks. In: 2000 International Conference on Mobile Computing and Networking, pp. 243–254. ACM (2000)

8. Qureshi, K.N., Bashir, F., Abdullah, A.H.: Real time traffic density aware road based forwarding method for vehicular ad hoc networks. In: 2017 10th IFIP Wireless and Mobile Networking Conference, pp. 2473–3644. IEEE (2017)

9. Zhang, J., Li, N., Liu, Z., Yang, Y.: Distributed toute recovery method in vehicle ad hoc networks. J. Electron. Meas. Instrum. (2014)

10. Lee, K.C., Le, M., Harri, J., Gerla, M.: LOUVRE: landmark overlays for urban vehicular routing environments. In: 2008 Vehicular Technology Conference, VTC, 2008-Fall, pp. 1–5. IEEE (2008)

11. Wang, H., Ni, D., Chen, Q., Li, J.: Stochastic modeling of the equilibrium speed–density relationship. J. Adv. Transp. **47**(1), 126–150 (2013)

12. Härri, J., Filali, F., Bonnet, C., Fiore, M.: VanetMobiSim: generating realistic mobility patterns for VANETs. In: 2006 International Workshop on Vehicular Ad Hoc Networks, pp. 96–97. ACM (2006)

13. Issariyakul, T., Ekram, H.: Introduction to Network Simulator NS2. Springer, Heidelberg (2011). https://doi.org/10.1007/978-1-4614-1406-3

The Knowledge Map Analysis of User Profile Research Based on CiteSpace

Danbei Pan, Hua Yin[✉], Yang Wang, Zhijian Wang,
and Zhensheng Hu

Information School, Guangdong University of Finance and Economics,
Guangzhou, China
yinhua@gdufe.edu.cn

Abstract. With the development of big data technology, user profile, as an effective method for delineating user characteristics, has attracted extensive attention from researchers and practitioners. Rich related literatures have been accumulated. How to find the key factors and the new direction from such a big library is a difficult problem for a new researcher entering the field. The knowledge map can be used to visualize the development trend, the frontier field and the overall knowledge structure from these researches. Therefore, we choose web of science database as the literature search engine and use CiteSpace to construct the user profile knowledge map. Through these maps, we analyze the important authors and countries, make the common word analysis and co-citation analysis, study the hot spots and important literatures. The time distribution shows that some foundational theories in user profile were produced at the second stage from 2004 to 2013. What's more, from the geographical distribution, we find that user profile, as an abstract concept, has no unified framework. Each country focuses on the different research points. From the knowledge map of keywords, we find that the top three algorithmic techniques used in constructing user profile are clustering, classification, and collaborative filtering. At the same time, user profile is also used in some specific applications, such as anomaly detection, behavior analysis, and information retrieval.

Keywords: User profile · CiteSpace · Knowledge map · Visualization
Big data

1 Introduction

In the era of big data, the amount of data has grown dramatically. Researchers in various fields have begun to realize the huge potential value behind these massive data, and gradually strengthen the application of big data analysis technology [1]. Particularly, for finding the potential users and supporting the user management, they urgently need to understand the characteristics, preferences and behavior of the users from the large amount of user-related data by accurate data analysis technologies.

User profile is an effective big data analysis method for delineating user characteristics and analyzing user needs, which aims to analyze and refine the users' demographic attributes, social interactions, behavioral preferences and other key

© Springer Nature Switzerland AG 2018
M. Qiu (Ed.): SmartCom 2018, LNCS 11344, pp. 311–320, 2018.
https://doi.org/10.1007/978-3-030-05755-8_31

information from the massive data [2]. At present, this technology is gradually being applied to many fields such as e-commerce, finance, insurance, and social media.

In the field of mobile communications, based on the user's log records, Zhu et al. analyze the scenarios and complete the construction of mobile user profile combined with the LDA topic model [3]. In the field of social networking, Marquardt et al. proposed a multi-label classification method based on Twitter tweets to improve the accuracy of user age recognition [4]. Mueller et al. constructed a variety of word structure features for Twitter username information, and relied on the support vector machine model to identify the gender of the user only from the user name [5].

Since user profile are used as basic technologies in various fields, there are various construction methods with different features. The knowledge map is an image that shows the relationship between the development process and structure of scientific knowledge in the knowledge domain. It can visually display the core structure, development history, frontier areas and overall knowledge structure [6].

Therefore, this paper hopes to use the visual map to find the construction rules and main methods of user profile to provide references for researchers. For this purpose, we use CiteSpace to analyze the time distribution and geographical distribution based on 1010 references in user profile. What's more, we find the most influential authors, identify hot topics and the most influential literature in this field.

2   Related Work

2.1   Research Methods

To get an overall overview from the research results, bibliometrics originated in the 1900s, which defined as the quantitative analysis of publications in the given field. It is a statistical analysis of article information regard to keywords, authors, references, journals, institutions, countries, and future directions and includes author co-citation analysis, document co-citation analysis, co-word analysis and other variations [7].

Nowadays, the development of technology has brought effective methods to support bibliometrics analysis. It is used to generate network images and provide visualized information rather than words. Knowledge map is a new visualization method of bibliometrics, which show many hidden complex relationships between knowledge domains such as network, interaction, intersection, evolution or derivative [6]. To create the knowledge maps and make visualization analysis, CiteSpace is one of the most popular software tools, which is developed by Chen [8]. It has been used for bibliometric studies in various areas such as informational sciences, regenerative medicine, electronic commerce, social commerce and so on [9].

Therefore, we use CiteSpace to draw the visual knowledge map for measuring and analyzing scientific literature, presenting a panoramic view of information, and identifying key literature, hot research and cutting-edge directions in the user profile.

2.2 Data Sources

The data used in this paper is from the Web of Science Core Collection recommended by CiteSpace, which contains more than 10,000 international, authoritative and academic journals.

We found that the articles may only contain "user" or "profile" if using "user profile" as a topic in the search engine. Thus, we set "user profile" or "user profiling" as title to obtain the target articles. And the time span is set from 1900 to 2018, including all available papers. What's more, we use the Science Citation Index Expanded and Social Sciences Citation Index as citation indexes. The search date is June 20, 2018, and the initial search result is 1502. Based on the classification function of Web of Science database, the results show that the selected records mainly come from 15 subject areas and have 14 research directions. The top three research directions, reaching 91.223% in total, are "Computer Science", "Engineering" and "Telecommunications", which separately accounted for 59.242%, 22.407%, and 9.574%. As we discuss user profile mainly from the technical perspective, we have chosen the top three research directions as research objects. In addition, "Book Review", "Conference Summary", and "Letter" as well as other "news reports" are excluded to make the samples more reliable. Finally, 1010 records were selected as the paper's data resources.

3 The Knowledge Map Analysis of User Profile Research

3.1 Time Distribution

The amount of publications over the years is an important indicator for evaluating the development of the discipline. Thus, we use the annual as horizontal axis and the number of publications per year as the vertical axis to draw a line graph shown in Fig. 1. Because the literature data in 2018 is still being entered, the graph shows the trend of user profile from 1994 to 2017. Through this line chart, the diachronic trend is obtained to reveal the current development of the field.

From the perspective of the number of publications over the years, the study of user profile began in 1994. And the numbers of articles grew slowly with no more than 20 articles in the following eight years. This shows that the field has not received enough attention in the first period of development. However, in this period, Pazzani made an innovative idea in the magazine published by Machine Learning in 1997. In the paper, "Learning and Revising User Profiles: The Identification of Interesting Web Sites", he has gotten the user's feedback on the interest of a set of web sites to learn a profile that would predict the interest of unseen sites [10].

Then there is a sudden increase in the publications in this field, from 17 articles in 2002 to 49 articles in 2004. But after that, the volume of publications has been fluctuating and maintained at around 50 per year until 2013. Although the number of articles has slowly increased in the second stage of development, the TOP 50 documents of high citations are almost in this period. This explains that many high-quality articles were produced at this stage and have important implications.

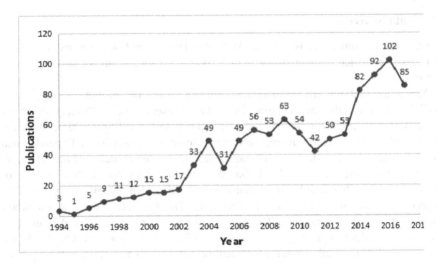

Fig. 1. Number of publications of user profile over years

Since 2013, with the continuous improvement of computer infrastructure and the increasing amount of data, the field has begun to receive widespread attention. The amount of publications increased significantly and peaked at 102 in 2016, followed by a slight decrease to approximately 85 in 2017. However, we predict that the publications may be maintained at more than 80 in the future with a small fluctuation as it has in the second period. What's more, we indirectly prove this point by drawing the amount of citations per year in Fig. 2. As shown in this figure, the amount of citations has been growing especially after 2013. It means that scholars have paid more and more attention to the study of user profile and the research has entered a stage of rapid development.

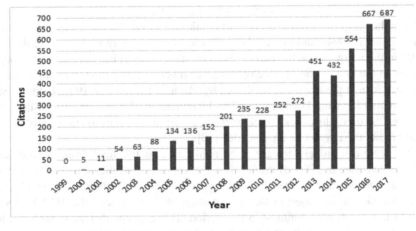

Fig. 2. Number of citations of user profile over years

3.2   Geographical Distribution

By drawing a visualization knowledge map of the countries, we get the spatial distribution of the user's profile literature, and understand the degree of attention and research status of each country.

According the statistical analysis of publications, it is concluded that about 25 countries have conducted research in this field. Among them, the top ten countries with large number of documents accounted for 67.556% of the total issued documents, which is listed in Table 1. There is no doubt that USA has the most articles.

Obviously, the country with the highest number of publications is the United States, since it has strong scientific research strength. But it is worth noting that the second place is China, which is closely related to China's vigorous development of big data technology in recent years. In addition, Italy, France, and India also have a high volume of publications showing the gap between countries is not large. In general, we can get that the user profile as an abstract idea has no mature technology, and each country attaches importance to come up with its own solution.

Table 1. The top 10 countries of user profile publications

Country	Total publication
USA	143
China	109
Italy	72
France	67
India	61
Korea	52
Germany	48
England	46
Spain	45
Japan	40

In addition, we analysis academic cooperation between countries by using CiteSpace software. After setting the node type as "country", the national partnership map is clearly display in Fig. 3. One node represents a country and the size of the node indicates how many publications the country has. With the collaborative links between the nodes, it shows the cooperation between the two countries. It is found that the academic exchanges and cooperation between these countries are very close and almost all countries have a cooperative relationship with the USA and China except Germany.

What's more, we combine national cooperation research with keyword research to find out the links between the country and keywords. It can help us to discover the main research points of each country. The similarities and differences between the main research keywords of countries are shown in the Table 2.

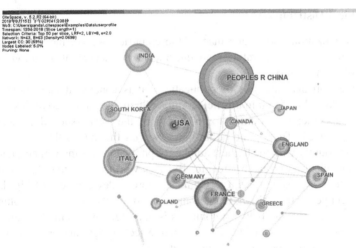

CiteSpace, v. 5.2.R2 (64-bit)
2018†9月15日 下午02时41分38秒
WoS: C:\Users\pands\.citespace\Examples\Data\userprofile
Timespan: 1994-2018 (Slice Length=1)
Selection Criteria: Top 50 per slice, LRF=2, LBY=8, e=2.0
Network: N=43, E=63 (Density=0.0698)
Largest CC: 30 (69%)
Nodes Labeled: 5.0%
Pruning: None

Fig. 3. Knowledge map of countries in user profile

Table 2. The main research keywords of top 5 countries

Country	Keyword
USA	Privacy, recommendation, information retrieval
China	Social network, big data, data mining
Italy	Ontology, collaborative filtering, privacy
France	Ontology, social network, bigdata, privacy
India	Ontology, data mining, personalization

3.3 Primary Author

The author's work citation indicates the impact of author. So, setting the node as "Author" can get the author cooperation network diagram as shown in Fig. 4.

It shows the influential scholars in this field are Marco Degemmis, Pasquale Lops and Giovanni Semeraro from the University of Bari. From the author's cooperation network map, these three scholars have close cooperation and have published large number of papers. In the paper with the most citations, they find that the traditional keyword-based method cannot capture the semantic information of user interest. Therefore, they propose a semantic user profile model that displays user preferences more effectively based on perceptual annotation. After that, a hybrid recommendation system based on content is proposed [11].

In addition, the other two influential authors, Mianowska and Nguyen from the Wroclaw University of Technology in Poland, have also published high-quality papers through close cooperation. One of the most cited papers proposes a method for constructing user profile by using hierarchical structure. At the same time, by clustering the user's basic statistical information, the user group which contains similar users can be analyzed. So the profile of new users can be constructed and the cold start problem can be solved [12].

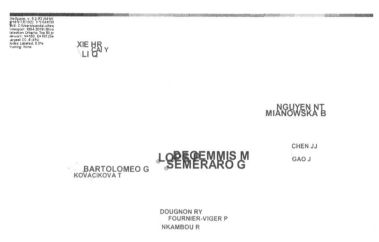

Fig. 4. Knowledge map of authors in user profile

3.4 Knowledge Map of Keywords

Word frequency refers to the number of occurrences of words in the document. In the scientific measurement research, the word frequency dictionary can be established according to the subject area to analyze the creative activities of the scientists. The word frequency analysis method is to extract the distribution of the keywords or the topic words, which expresses the core content of the literature in this field. The subject words are a high-level summary and refinement of the article's topic to study the development trends. The frequently-used keywords are regarded as a research hotspot in this field to a certain extent [13]. The keyword co-occurrence map drawn by setting the node as "keyword" in CiteSpace is shown in Fig. 5.

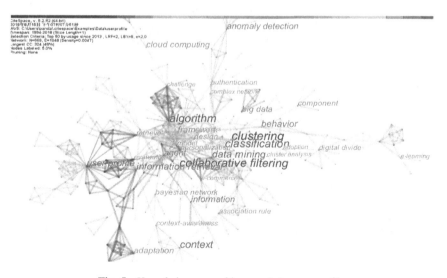

Fig. 5. Knowledge map of keywords in user profile

The main top ten keywords that appear in the research literature are: "clustering", "collaborative filtering", "algorithm", "classification", "context awareness", "Data mining", "information retrieval", "Behavior", " Anomaly detection", "Big data". The main hotspots of the researches include algorithmic techniques used to construct user profile such as clustering, classification, and collaborative filtering. They also include the application of user profile in major fields such as big data, data mining, anomaly detection, behavior analysis and information index.

3.5   Knowledge Mapping of Literature

To a certain extent, the cited quantity reflects the academic influence of the literature. And the co-citation analysis means that if two documents appear together in the reference list of the third literature, these two documents form a co-citation relationship. By analyzing the co-citation relationship of the literature data set, the literature information can be visualized and the information of literature influence and literature classification can be obtained [14]. Therefore, it is necessary to map the co-occurrence knowledge of the cited literature and analyze the highly cited literature. By setting the node as Cite references, we draw a knowledge map of the literature shown in Fig. 6.

The larger the node in the figure, the higher the amount of reference. It shows that the document with the highest citation is "Ontological user profiling in recommendation systems" written by Middleton in the journal ACM TRANSACTIONS ON INFORMATION SYSTEMS in 2004 [15]. This article mainly introduces a new ontology representation method for user analysis in the recommendation system to build an online academic paper recommendation system. Firstly, a basic document for researching user interest is constructed according to the user's web browsing history and related search results. And the topic representation is extracted according to ontology theory. Then, a set of topics and interest values are saved from these topics as user profile, which may adjust according to user feedback information. And the time decay function weights make the recently seen papers more important than the old ones to improve recommendation accuracy. Finally, the ontology relationships between the topics is used to infer topics that other users may be interested in. It is seen that based on ontology, it is possible to discover user interests that cannot be directly observed in user behavior.

At the same time, the node has a purple circle indicating that the research results are innovative. The most creative literature is Pazzani's "Learning and Revising User Profiles: The Identification of Interesting Web Sites" [10]. This article began to use the Bayesian classification algorithm to build user interest preferences by collecting user-interested web page tags to judge the user's interest. In addition, there is a document with high creativeness, Mislove's "You Are Who You Know: Inferring User Profiles in Online Social Networks" [16]. This article mainly combines the user's attribute set with the social network map to predict the attribute set of other users in the network. The author collects fine-grained data from two social networks and successfully infers the attributes of the remaining users with an accuracy rate of over 80% by only 20% of the users providing attributes.

In addition, using the CiteSpace software, we find a highly central article that reflects the importance of the article in the field. Among them, Xu's "Exploring Folksonomy for Personalized Search" published in 2008 reached a high centrality of 0.26 [17]. The article uses user-selected interests, web browser bookmarks, user personal document corpora, search engine click history, etc. to construct user profile. It describes user interests and improve search engine results. The ranking of the pages in the results depends not only on the terminology match between the query and the content of the page, but also on the topic matching between the user's interests and the page.

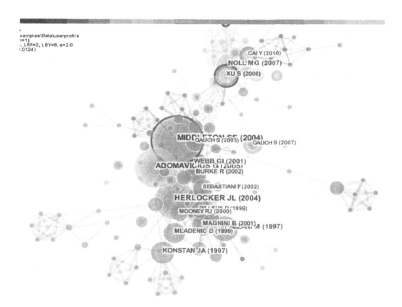

Fig. 6. Knowledge map of literature in user profile

4   Conclusions

User profile, as a hotspot problem, need comprehensive and visualized review for studying briefly and quickly. Thus, we take the literature related to user profile as the research object and uses CiteSpace to construct the knowledge maps by setting the nodes as Country, Author, Keyword and Cite references. However, it should be noted that this article selects the main research areas of user profile, such as Computer Science, Engineering and Telecommunications. Hence, the research results show that user profile is highly related to technologies in the computer science field. The emerging fields like big data and cloud computing, as well as the technical means such as collaborative filtering and text recognition, have an important impact on the user profile. We believe that with the new big data technologies such as deep learning, user profile can be further applied in the other areas. Therefore, in the future work, we should make further research on how to choose the appropriate technical methods to construct user images according to the application background.

Acknowledgments. This work was supported by Science and Technology Program of Guangzhou, China (No. 201707010495), Foundation for Distinguished Young Talents in Higher Education of Guangzhou, China (No. 2013LYM0032), Project supported by Guangdong Province Universities, China (No. 2015KTSCX046), and Foundation for Technology Innovation in Higher Education of Guangdong Province, China (No. 2013KJCX0085).

References

1. Chen, C.L.P., Zhang, C.Y.: Data-intensive applications, challenges, techniques and technologies: a survey on big data. Inf. Sci. **275**(11), 314–347 (2014)
2. Liu, W., Liu, J., Shi, C., et al.: User network profile of behavior. Publishing House of Electronics Industry, Beijing (2016)
3. Zhu, H., Chen, E., Xiong, H., et al.: Mining mobile user preferences for personalized context-aware recommendation. ACM Trans. Intell. Syst. Technol. **5**(4), 1–27 (2014)
4. Marquardt, J., Farnadi, G., Vasudevan, G., et al.: Age and gender identification in social media. In: Proceedings of CLEF 2014 Evaluation Labs, pp. 1129–1136 (2014)
5. Mueller, J., Stumme, G.: Gender inference using statistical name characteristics in Twitter. In: MISNC, SI, DS (2016)
6. Chen, Y., Chen, C.M., Liu, Z.Y., et al.: The methodology function of cite space mapping knowledge domains. Stud. Sci. Sci. **33**, 242–253 (2015)
7. Mayr, P., Scharnhorst, A.: Scientometrics and information retrieval: weak-links revitalized. Scientometrics **102**(3), 2193–2199 (2014)
8. Chen, C.: CiteSpace II: Detecting and Visualizing Emerging Trends and Transient Patterns in Scientific Literature. Wiley, Hoboken (2006)
9. Cui, Y., Mou, J., Liu, Y.: Knowledge mapping of social commerce research: a visual analysis using CiteSpace. Electron. Commer. Res. **18**, 837 (2018)
10. Pazzani, M., Billsus, D.: Learning and Revising User Profiles: The Identification of Interesting Web Sites. Kluwer Academic Publishers, Dordrecht (1997)
11. Degemmis, M., Lops, P., Semeraro, G.: A content-collaborative recommender that exploits WordNet-based user profiles for neighborhood formation. User Model. User-Adap. Inter. **17**(3), 217–255 (2007)
12. Maleszka, M., Mianowska, B., Nguyen, N.T.: A method for collaborative recommendation using knowledge integration tools and hierarchical structure of user profiles. Knowl.-Based Syst. **47**(3), 1–13 (2013)
13. Chen, Y., Chen, C., Hu, Z.: Principles and Applications of Analyzing a Citation Space. Science Press, Beijing (2014)
14. Hu, Z., Chen, C., Liu, Z.: The recurrence of citations within a scientific article. In: The International Society of Scientometrics and Informetrics Conference, 29 June–July 2015
15. Middleton, S.E., Shadbolt, N.R., Roure, D.C.D.: Ontological user profiling in recommender systems. ACM Trans. Inf. Syst. **22**(1), 54–88 (2004)
16. Mislove, A., Viswanath, B., Gummadi, K.P., et al.: You are who you know: inferring user profiles in online social networks. In: DBLP, pp. 251–260 (2010)
17. Xu, S., Bao, S., Fei, B., et al.: Exploring folksonomy for personalized search. In: Proceedings of the 31st Annual International ACM SIGIR Conference on Research and Development in Information Retrieval, SIGIR 2008, Singapore, 20–24 July 2008, pp. 155–162 (2008)

The Accuracy of Fuzzy C-Means in Lower-Dimensional Space for Topic Detection

Hendri Murfi$^{(\boxtimes)}$ [iD]

Department of Mathematics, Universitas Indonesia, Depok 16424, Indonesia
hendri@ui.ac.id

Abstract. Topic detection is an automatic method to discover topics in textual data. The standard methods of the topic detection are nonnegative matrix factorization (NMF) and latent Dirichlet allocation (LDA). Another alternative method is a clustering approach such as a k-means and fuzzy c-means (FCM). FCM extend the k-means method in the sense that the textual data may have more than one topic. However, FCM works well for low-dimensional textual data and fails for high-dimensional textual data. An approach to overcome the problem is transforming the textual data into lower dimensional space, i.e., Eigenspace, and called Eigenspace-based FCM (EFCM). Firstly, the textual data are transformed into an Eigenspace using truncated singular value decomposition. FCM is performed on the eigenspace data to identify the memberships of the textual data in clusters. Using these memberships, we generate topics from the high dimensional textual data in the original space. In this paper, we examine the accuracy of EFCM for topic detection. Our simulations show that EFCM results in the accuracies between the accuracies of LDA and NMF regarding both topic interpretation and topic recall.

Keywords: Topic detection · Clustering · Fuzzy c-means · Eigenspace
Accuracy

1 Introduction

Topic detection is automatic tools for discovering the thematic information from textual data called *topics* which are usually represented by a set of related words. This process is one important step to understanding the unstructured textual data. Moreover, with the discovered topics we can organize the textual data for many purposes, e.g., indexing, summarization, dimensionality reduction, trend analysis, etc. We can detect the topics manually by reading the contents of the textual data. However, the manual way is not feasible for big data collections or fast response time. From machine learning point of view, topic detection is unsupervised learning in the sense that it does not need labels of the textual data. In other words, the general problem of topic detection is to use the observed textual data to infer the set of related words implicitly representing the topics.

The standard methods for topic detection are *nonnegative matrix factorization* (NMF) [1–3] and *latent Dirichlet allocation* (LDA) [4–6]. NMF is a matrix factorization method of factoring matrix A into two matrices W and H, where all the elements are non-negative. If A is a word by data matrix, then W and H are interpreted as a word

© Springer Nature Switzerland AG 2018
M. Qiu (Ed.): SmartCom 2018, LNCS 11344, pp. 321–334, 2018.
https://doi.org/10.1007/978-3-030-05755-8_32

by the topic matrix and a topic by data matrix, respectively. In other words, the columns of W are sets of words interpreted as topics and columns of H are new representations of data with the topics as their features. It means that each textual data may contain multiple topics. LDA is a probabilistic model developed to fix some issues with a previously developed probabilistic model called *probabilistic latent semantic analysis* (pLSA) [7, 8]. LDA assumes that textual data typically represent multiple topics that are modeled as distributions over vocabulary. LDA is a generative probabilistic model where each word in the textual data is generated by randomly choosing a topic from a distribution over topics, and then randomly choosing a word from a distribution over the vocabulary.

Another method of topic detection is a *clustering* approach [9]. In this approach, the textual data are grouped in a way that members of the same cluster are more similar to each other than with members of other clusters. The centers of the clusters, called centroids, are means of their members. In a topic detection problem, the centroids are interpreted as topics of the textual data. *K-means* is a popular method for clustering in this scenario [10–12]. This method splits the textual data into k clusters in which each textual data belongs to the nearest cluster center. In other words, the k-means method assumes that each textual data contains only one topic. This assumption is rather weak and also different from the standard NMF and LDA method. Therefore, *fuzzy c-means* (FCM) is considered an alternative clustering based topic detection [13, 14]. In FCM, each textual data may belong to more than one cluster and hence may have more than one topics. The centroids are the weighted means of their members where some textual data contribute more than others. The weights are called the memberships which represent the inverse of the distance between data and centroids. Moreover, FCM contains a fuzzification constant to control the number of topics the textual data may have. We set the fuzzification constant approaches to one if the textual data may contain only one topic. For the textual data consisting more topics, we use a larger fuzzification constant.

In general, FCM only works well for low dimensional data and fails for high dimension data [15]. FCM generates only one centroid or one topic from high dimensional textual data for the topic detection problem. We can choose the smaller fuzzification constant to overcome the problem. However, this setting is only applicable to the textual data that contain a smaller number of topics. Another approach is transforming the textual data into lower dimensional space, i.e., Eigenspace, and called Eigenspace-based FCM (EFCM) [16]. Firstly, the textual data are transformed into an Eigenspace using truncated singular value decomposition. FCM is performed on the Eigenspace to identify the memberships. Using these memberships, we generate topics using the high dimensional textual data in the original space. In this paper, we evaluate the accuracy of EFCM and compare to the standard NMF and LDA. Our simulations show that EFCM results in the accuracies between the accuracies of LDA and NMF regarding both topic interpretation and topic recall.

The outline of this paper is as follows: In Sect. 2, we present the reviews of Eigenspace, FCM, and the EFCM. Section 3 describes the results of our simulations and discussions. Finally, a general conclusion about the results is presented in Sect. 4.

2 Methods

Let A be a word by document matrix and c be the number of topics. Given A and c, the topic detection problem is how to recover c topics from A. Clustering is one of the approaches to solving the topic detection problem. In this approach, the documents are grouped in a way that members of the same cluster are more similar to each other than with members of other clusters. The center of a cluster or a centroid equals to the mean of all of the documents assigned to the cluster. This centroid is interpreted as a topic for the topic detection problem. In this section, we describe our clustering based topic detection method called eigenspace-based fuzzy c-means. First, we review the concept of eigenspace and fuzzy c-means which are the main components of the method.

2.1 Eigenspace

Singular value decomposition (SVD) is one of the famous matrix factorizations that has many useful applications in data processing. Let A be any $d \times n$ matrix, then SVD of A is

$$A_{d \times n} = U_{d \times d} \Sigma_{d \times n} V_{n \times n}^{T} \tag{1}$$

where U is an $d \times d$ orthogonal matrix, Σ is an $d \times n$ pseudodiagonal matrix whose elements are nonnegative, and V is an $n \times n$ orthogonal matrix. The diagonal elements of the matrix Σ are called singular values of A and sorted from the largest to the smallest [17].

One important property of the SVD is that it allows us to get approximation matrices of A with the smaller size. The singular values on matrix Σ are sorted from the largest to the smallest, then the best p-rank approximation matrix to the matrix A can be formed by taking the first p singular values of matrix Σ where $p << min(d, n)$. Let A be an $d \times n$ matrix. The *truncated SVD* of A is

$$\tilde{A}_{d \times n} = \tilde{U}_{d \times p} \tilde{\Sigma}_{p \times p} \tilde{V}_{p \times n}^{T} \tag{2}$$

where $\tilde{U}, \Sigma, \tilde{V}$ are the first p columns of U, Σ, V, respectively, and $\left\| A - \tilde{A} \right\|$ equals to the $p + 1$-th singular value of Σ.

The SVD or truncated SVD use the principles of *spectral decomposition* to construct their factorization matrices. From Eq. (2), the SVD of A is $A = U\Sigma V^{T}$. AA^{T} is a symmetric matrix, that is, $AA^{T} = (U\Sigma V^{T})(U\Sigma V^{T})^{T} = U\Sigma V^{T} V\Sigma^{T} U^{T}$. Because V is an orthogonal matrix, then $V^{T} V = I$. Hence, $AA^{T} = U\Sigma^{T} \Sigma U^{T}$ where $\Sigma^{T} \Sigma$ is a diagonal matrix. According to the spectral decomposition, U is an orthogonal matrix whose i-th column is an eigenvector corresponding to the i-th eigenvalue of the diagonal matrix $\Sigma^{T} \Sigma$.

In data processing, truncated SVD is a method that commonly used for a dimension reduction. Because p is much smaller than d, $\tilde{\Sigma} \tilde{V}^{T}$ is lower dimensional representaions of A. The columns of $\tilde{U}$ are eigenvectors, so the columns of $\tilde{\Sigma} \tilde{V}^{T}$ are the coordinates of the columns of A relative to the subspace spanned by the eigenvectors. In other words, the columns of $\tilde{\Sigma} \tilde{V}^{T}$ are the coordinates of data in a lower dimensional *eigenspace*.

2.2   Fuzzy C-Means

In general, the problem of clustering is how to group data points into clusters such that the members of a cluster are more similar than the members of other clusters. An approach to solve the clustering problem is to partition the data points into some clusters which consist of data points whose inter-point distances are small compared with the distances to points outside of the clusters. Regarding the approach, the goal of fuzzy c-means (FCM) is to partition the data points into some clusters such that the sum of the squares of the distances of each data point to centers of clusters (centroids) is minimum. Different from k-means, FCM allows each data point is becoming members of multiple clusters. Therefore, a data point updates many centroids based on the membership of the data point in the clusters.

Given a dataset $A = [a_1 a_2 \ldots a_n]$ and the number of centroids c, the goal of FCM can be formulated as a following constrained optimization:

$$\min_{m_{ik}, q_i} J = \sum_{i=1}^{c} \sum_{k=1}^{n} m_{ik}^{w} \|\mathbf{a}_k - \mathbf{q}_i\|^2 \tag{3}$$

$$s.t. \quad \sum_{i=1}^{c} m_{ik} = 1, \forall k \tag{3a}$$

$$0 < \sum_{k=1}^{n} m_{ik} < n, \forall i \tag{3b}$$

$$m_{ik} \in [0, 1], \forall i, k \tag{3c}$$

where q_i is centroids, m_{ik} is the membership of data point a_k in cluster i, $w > 1$ is the fuzzification constant, and $\|.\|$ is any norm. The first constrains ensures that every data point has unit total membership in all clusters (Eq. 3a). Equation 3b constrains that all clusters are non empty [18].

The problem of the constrained optimization in Eq. 3 is to find m_{ik} and q_i so that to minimize J. The common approach to solve the constrained optimization is alternating optimization [19]. First, we choose some initial values for the q_i. Then we minimize J with respect to the m_{ik}, keeping the q_i fixed giving:

$$m_{ik} = \left[\sum_{j=1}^{c} \left(\frac{\|\mathbf{a}_k - \mathbf{q}_i\|}{\|\mathbf{a}_k - \mathbf{q}_j\|} \right)^{2/w - 1} \right]^{-1}, \forall i, k \tag{4}$$

Next, we minimize J on the q_i, keeping the m_{ik} fixed giving:

$$\mathbf{q}_i = \frac{\sum_{k=1}^{n} ((m_{ik})^w \mathbf{a}_k)}{\sum_{k=1}^{n} (m_{ik})^w}, \forall i \tag{5}$$

This two-step optimization are iterated until a stopping criterion is fulfilled, e.g., the maximum number of iteration, insignificant changes in the objective function J, the membership m_{ik}, or the centroids q_i. A FCM algorithm is decribed in more detail in Algorithm 1.

According to Eq. 4, the memberships m_{ik} are inversely related to the relative distance of a_k to the q_i. We can infer from Eq. 5 that a data point a_k can update many centroids q_i as long as its membership $m_{ik} > 0$. The memberships tends to 0 or 1 when the fuzzification constant w approaches 1. A larger fuzzification constant makes fuzzier membership. Therefore, not only the closest data that contributes to the centroids.

Algorithm 1. Fuzzy C-Means

Input   : A, c, w, max number of iterations (T), threshold (ε)

Output : m_{ik}, q_i

1.   set $t = 0$

2.   initialize q_i

3.   update $t = t + 1$

4.   calculate $m_{ik} = \left[\sum_{j=1}^{c} \left(\frac{\|a_k - q_i\|_2}{\|a_k - q_j\|_2} \right)^{2/w-1} \right]^{-1}, \forall i, k$

5.   calculate $q_i = \frac{\sum_{k=1}^{n}((m_{ik})^w a_k)}{\sum_{k=1}^{n}(m_{ik})^w}, \forall i$

6.   if a stopping, i.e., $t > T$ or $\|M^t - M^{t-1}\|_F < \varepsilon$, is fulfilled then stop, else go back to step 3

2.3 Eigenspace-Based Fuzzy C-Means

Given textual data, FCM may group the textual data into more than one cluster, and hence the textual data may have more than one topics. In this method, the centroids equal to the weighted mean of their members as described in Eq. 5. The weights are the memberships which are the inversed relative distance between documents and centroids. Moreover, FCM contains a fuzzification constant to control the number of topics the textual data may have as shown in Eq. 4. We set the fuzzification constant approaches to one if the textual data may contain only one topic. For the textual data consisting more topics, we use a larger fuzzification constant.

In general, FCM only works well for low dimensional data and fails for high dimension data. For the high dimensional data, FCM runs into the center of gravity of the entire data [15]. Therefore, FCM generates only one centroid or one topic from high dimensional textual data for the topic detection problem. We can choose the smaller fuzzification constant to overcome the problem. However, this setting is only applicable to the textual data that contain a smaller number of topics. Another approach is transforming the textual data into lower dimensional space, i.e., Eigenspace, using truncated SVD [16].

Truncated SVD decompose a matrix m x n A into $\tilde{U}\tilde{\Sigma}\tilde{V}^t$, where $\tilde{\Sigma}\tilde{V}^T$ is a p x n matrix with $p \ll min(m,n)$. If A is a feature by textual data matrix, then we interprete $\tilde{R} = \tilde{\Sigma}\tilde{V}^T$ as lower dimensional textual data of A in an eigenspace spanned by the eigenvectors of $\tilde{U}$. We denote this dimension reduction using the truncated SVD as follows

$$\tilde{R} = \text{TruncatedSVD}(A, p) \tag{6}$$

Next, we perform FCM in the eigenspace for the lower dimensional textual data $\tilde{R}$. In this step, we calculate the memberships m_{ik} for all textual data and all clusters. Using the memberships, we calculate the topics in the original space of A based on Eq. 5. We call this topic extraction method as *eigenspace based fuzzy c-means* (EFCM) described in Algorithm 2.

The weights of topic t_i indicate the degree of association of words on the topic. For the practical purpose, the topics are usually represented only by the top words, that is, the words with the highest weights, i.e., the top ten words.

Algorithm 2. Eigenspace-based Fuzzy C-Means

Input : A, c, w, max number of iterations (T), threshold (ε), p
Output: t_i
1. transform A : $\tilde{R} = \text{TruncatedSVD}(A, p)$
2. perform FCM : $m_{ik} = \text{FCM}(\tilde{R}, c, w, T, \varepsilon)$
3. calculate the topics : $t_i = \frac{\sum_{k=1}^{n}((m_{ik})^w a_k)}{\sum_{k=1}^{n}(m_{ik})^w}$

---

3   Results and Discussion

In this section, we examine the accuracy of the EFCM method. The accuracy is compared with the standard LDA and NMF method. For this purpose, we use two measurement units, i.e., *topic interpretability* and *topic recall*.

3.1   Topic Interpretability

The common quantitative method to measure the interpretability of a topic is to calculate the coherence scores of words constructing the topic. Pointwise mutual information (PMI) is one of the formulas to estimate the coherence scores [20]. Suppose a topic t consists of an n-word that is $\{w_1, w_2, \ldots, w_n\}$, the PMI of the topic t is

$$PMI(t) = \sum_{j=2}^{n} \sum_{i=1}^{j-1} \log\left(\frac{P(w_j, w_i)}{P(w_i)P(w_j)}\right) \tag{7}$$

where $P(w_j, w_i)$ is the probability of the word w_i appears together with the word w_j on the corpus, $P(w_i)$ is the probability of occurrence of word w_i in the corpus, and $P(w_j)$ is the probability of occurrence of word w_j in the corpus. The corpus is a database of textual documents that becomes a reference to calculate PMI. In this experiment, we use a corpus consisting of 3.2 million English Wikipedia documents.

For this simulation, we use the publicly available dataset for topic modeling in the UCI Machine Learning Repository [21]. The UCI datasets consist of NIPS, KOS, Enron, and NYTimes. NIPS is a dataset derived from various full papers, KOS is a dataset derived from various blog entries, Enron is a dataset derived from various emails, and NYTimes is a dataset derived from various news articles. All datasets have been preprocessed and provide the frequencies of words in documents. The NIPS dataset has 1500 documents and 12419 words, the KOS dataset consists of 3430 documents and 6906 words, the Enron dataset has 39861 documents and 28102 words, and the NYTimes dataset consists of 300000 documents and 102660 words. Figure 1 gives the statistics of the datasets.

The datasets have been in the form of a list of words and lists of occurrences of each word in each document. So, the process that needs to be done is only to form the word-document matrix A and do the weighting process. In this simulation, the weighting process is performed using the term frequency-inverse document frequency (TF-IDF) [22].

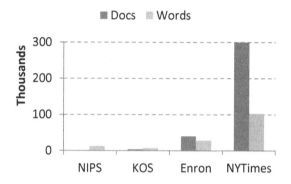

Fig. 1. The number of documents and words in the NIPS, KOS, Enron, and NYTimes datasets

In this simulations, we also examine two standard topic detection methods, i.e., LDA and NMF, in comparison with EFCM. The implementation uses a Python-based library called scikit-learn [23]. We use a batch variational implementation of LDA provided by the scikit-learn. This includes the default values for the Dirichlet parameters alpha and eta of $1/c$, where c is the number of topics. For NMF, the data vectors are normalized to unit length. The implementation of NMF uses a coordinate descent algorithm with default parameters provided by the scikit-learn. To reduce the instability of random initialization, the NNDSVD initialization is performed. For EFCM parameters, we set the fuzzification constant $w = 1.5$, the maximum number of iteration $T = 1000$, the threshold $\varepsilon = 0.005$ and the Eigenspace dimension $p = 5$.

The topic detection methods produce topics in the form of word vectors. For the evaluation of the methods, each extracted topic is represented only by the top 10 most probable words for LDA and the top 10 most frequent words for NMF and EFCM. These words are calculated by PMI in Eq. 7 to obtain the topic interpretability scores.

Figure 2 gives the comparison of the PMI scores in various numbers of topics for the datasets NIPS, KOS, Enron, and NYTimes, respectively. We select the optimal number of topics from a standard number set of {10, 20, ..., 100}. These procedures are known as the model selection in machine learning.

From Fig. 2(a), we see that the NMF and EFCM give a similar trend which tends to decrease with the increasing number of topics, while LDA shows a static trend. NMF achieves the maximum PMI score at the topic number of 20, while EFCM reaches the maximum PMI score at the topic number of 30. Figure 2(b) gives the PMI scores for the KOS dataset. Both EFCM and LDA decrease strictly for this dataset. It means that the maximum PMI scores for the methods are at the topic number of 10. NMF gives a fluctuating trend which decreases from 10 to 20 and increases from 20 to 30. After that, the trend tends to decrease strictly. From Fig. 2(c), we also see that both NMF and EFCM give the maximum PMI scores at the smallest topic number of 10. LDA needs more topics to reach the maximum PMI score for this Enron dataset. i.e., 20 topics. The last PMI scores of the NYTimes dataset are given in Fig. 2(d). For this dataset, the trends of all methods look different. The PMI scores of NMF grow fast from 10 to 20 and tend to stable after that. On the other hand, the PMI scores of EFCM shrink from 10 to 20 and increase after that. LDA gives more fluctuation trend and achieves the maximum score at the topic number of 30.

Table 1 gives a summary of the PMI scores for each method. For both NIPS and Enron datasets, EFCM archives the higher PMI score than LDA and the lower PMI score than NMF. EFCM can achieve the PMI score of 0.739 for the KOS dataset. This achievement is better than 11.80% of NMF and 114.83% of LDA. For the biggest NYTimes dataset, NMF results in the best PMI score of 0.561, while EFCM and LDA give comparable PMI scores, that is, 0.410 and 0.446, respectively.

3.2   Topic Recall

Twitter is one of the popular social media to spread information through the internet. In Twitter, users act not only as consumers of the information, but they can act as producer of the information also. This internet application facilitates users to send and read textual information known as *tweets*. Using the tweets, users may send information about real-world events almost in real-time. Therefore, Twitter may become *a real-time sensor* for real-world events [24]. Another similar use of Twitter is a real-time monitor in an urban area. The ability to monitor the situations may direct the local government to respond quickly or make public policy [25]. Determining which are the topics in tweets is the first step toward a human-understandable description of the tweets. However, finding topics in tweets is very difficult to do manually, because we must be observed a very large number of tweets. Therefore, we need automatic tools to such as topic detection. In general, the processes of sensing trending topics on Twitter as follows: firstly, users provide a set of words or location information to filter tweets containing at least one of them. Moreover, users determine a time slot for detecting trending topics, e.g., every 10 min. At the end of each time slot, the system gives topics in the time slot.

For this simulation, we use three datasets about a real-world event, i.e., FA Cup Final, Super Tuesday, and the US Elections [24]. FA Cup Final dataset consists of 13 one-minute slots, eight one-hour slots for Super Tuesday, and 26 ten-minute slots in US Election. There is an average of 1850 tweets in each time slot for FA Cup, an average of 30200 tweets in each time slot for US Election, and an average of 53500 tweets in each time slot for Super Tuesday. Statistics of the datasets is given in Fig. 3.

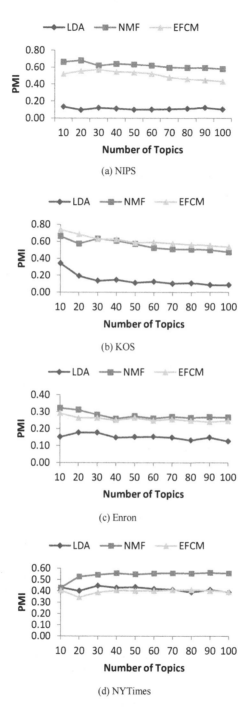

Fig. 2. The interpretability (PMI) scores for some numbers of topics, i.e., *[10, 20, ..., 90, 100]* for the NIPS, KOS, Enron, and NYTimes datasets.

Table 1. The comparison of the optimal topic interpretability (PMI) scores

	NIPS	KOS	Enron	NYTimes
LDA	0.121	0.344	0.177	0.446
NMF	0.681	0.661	0.322	0.561
EFCM	0.570	0.739	0.291	0.410

Each dataset has *ground truth* topics that are created manually by experts. Each slot of the datasets has at least one ground truth topic. In total, FA Cup comprises 13 ground truth topics, 64 ground truth topics in US Election, and 22 ground truth topics in Super Tuesday. Each method needs to produce topics for each slot of the datasets. Each extracted topic is represented only by the top 10 most probable words for LDA and the top 10 most frequent words for NMF and EFCM. These topics are compared to the ground truth topics of corresponding slots. We measure the accuracy of a method by using *topic recall*, that is, the percentage of ground truth topics successfully detected by the method. A ground truth topic is considered successfully detected in case the produced topics contain all mandatory words of the ground truth topic. To address the problem of word spelling variations, we use Levenshtein similarity, that is, a word in a detected topic matches a word in a ground truth topic when their Levenshtein similarity is greater than or equal to 0.8.

To convert tweets to vector representations, we do two main processes, i.e., pre-processing and word-based tokenization. The common pre-processing steps are used to three datasets. Firstly, we convert all words into lowercase, erase words containing domains such as www.* or https://*, and words containing @username, and erased # in #words. To standardize words with non-standard spelling, we replace two or more repeating letters with only two occurrences. Next, a lemmatizer is applied to remaining words. English stopwords and words that existed in lower than two tweets or more than 95% of tweets are filtered. Finally, we use the term frequency-inverse document frequency for weighting. Besides scikit-learn, we utilize the natural language toolkit [26] for these preprocessing and tokenizing steps.

Figure 4 shows the comparison of topic recall scores for the number of topic $c \in \{2, 3,..., 9, 10\}$. From Fig. 4(a), we see that the scores increase with the increasing number of topic. The NMF and EFCM methods approach the maximum topic recall scores for the FA Cup dataset. It means that the methods can extract almost all topics in the ground truth. However, each method extracts a different number of topics to reach the maximum topic recall scores. For this scores, NMF extracts only eight topics, while EFCM must extract more topic, that is, ten topics. LDA reach a slightly lower topic recall, i.e., 0.938.

Figure 4(b) gives the topic recall scores for the US Election dataset. The three methods present similar trends in the scores. With the increasing number of topics, the scores of the methods tend to increase. NMF increases strictly after the topic number of 3, while EFCM increases strictly after the topic number of 5. LDA also increases strictly. However, it grows slower than NMF and EFCM. Therefore, the LDA gives a lower topic recall than both NMF and EFCM.

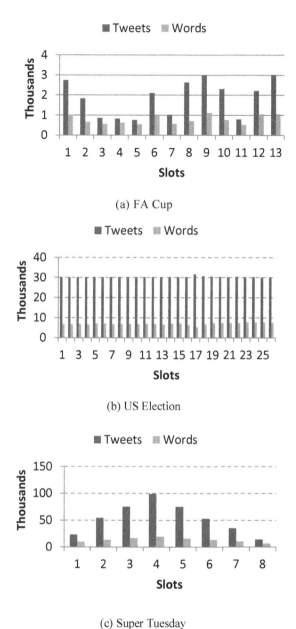

Fig. 3. The number of tweets and words in the FA Cup, US Election, and Super Tuesday datasets.

The last topic recall scores of the Super Tuesday dataset are given in Fig. 4(c). For this dataset, the trends of all methods look different. The scoring trend of NMF tends to fluctuate. The topic recall scores are decreasing from 4 to 6, and then they are

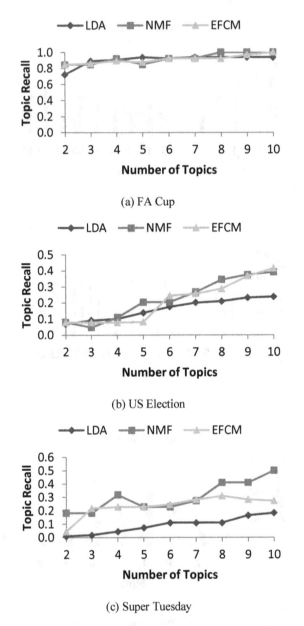

(a) FA Cup

(b) US Election

(c) Super Tuesday

Fig. 4. The topic recall scores for some numbers of topics, i.e., *{2, 3, ..., 9, 10}* for the FA Cup, US Election, and Super Tuesday datasets.

increasing again. The topic recall of EFCM grows fast from 2 to 3, and slower after that. Like the US Election dataset, LDA grows slower than both NMF and EFCM for this Super Tuesday dataset.

According to the results, we see that all methods need the maximum number of topics to achieve the maximum topic recall scores. It means that we still can increase the topic recall scores by increasing the number of topics. However, the numbers of available ground truth topics in each slot are limited. There are on average two ground truth topics in each slot with a minimum of one. Therefore, we limit the maximum number of topics to ten for these simulations.

Table 2 gives a summary of the topic recall scores for each method. From Table 2, we see that all methods work well and give comparable results for the small FA Cup dataset. NMF and EFCM can detect all ground truth topics in the dataset. For two other bigger datasets, EFCM can achieve the topic recall of 0.416 for the US Election dataset. This achievement is better than 6.39% of NMF and 74.79% of LDA. For the Super Tuesday dataset, the EFCM achievement is bigger than 69.78% of LDA, however, lower than 61.81% of NMF.

Table 2. The comparison of the optimal topic recall scores

	FA Cup	US Election	Super Tuesday
LDA	0.938	0.238	0.182
NMF	1.000	0.391	0.500
EFCM	1.000	0.416	0.309

4 Conclusions

In this paper, we consider the use of fuzzy c-means for topic detection. For high dimensional textual data, we examine the use of eigenspace-based fuzzy c-means method which performs the clustering process in the low dimensional eigenspace. Our simulations show that the eigenspace-based fuzzy c-means method achieves the accuracies between the accuracies of the standard methods, i.e., latent Dirichlet allocation and nonnegative matrix factorization, regarding both topic interpretation and topic recall.

Acknowledgment. This work was supported by Universitas Indonesia under PDUPT 2018 grant. Any opinions, findings, and conclusions or recommendations are the authors' and do not necessarily reflect those of the sponsor.

References

1. Lee, D.D., Seung, H.S.: Learning the parts of objects by nonnegative matrix factorization. Nature **401**, 788–791 (1999)
2. Cichocki, A., Phan, A.H.: Fast local algorithms for large scale nonnegative matrix and tensor factorizations. IEICE Trans. Fundam. Electron. Commun. Comput. Sci. **E92–A**, 708–721 (2009)
3. Févotte, C., Idier, J.: Algorithms for nonnegative matrix factorization with the β-divergence. Neural Comput. **23**, 2421–2456 (2011)
4. Blei, D.M., et al.: Latent Dirichlet allocation. J. Mach. Learn. Res. **3**, 993–1022 (2003)

5. Hoffman, M.D., Blei, D.M., Wang, C., Paisley, J.: Stochastic variational inference. J. Mach. Learn. Res. **14**, 1303–1347 (2013)
6. Hoffman, M.D., Blei, D.M., Bach, F.: Online learning for latent Dirichlet allocation. In: Proceedings of the 23rd International Conference on Neural Information Processing Systems, vol. 1, pp. 856–864. Curran Associates Inc., USA (2010)
7. Papadimitriou, C.H., Raghavan, P., Tamaki, H., Vempala, S.: Latent semantic indexing: a probabilistic analysis. In: Proceedings of the ACM Symposium on Principles of Database Systems, pp. 217–235 (1998)
8. Hofmann, T.: Probabilistic latent semantic analysis. In: Uncertainty in Artificial Intelligence, pp. 289–296 (1999)
9. Allan, J.: Topic Detection and Tracking: Event-Based Information Organization. Kluwer (2002)
10. Petkos, G., Papadopoulos, S., Kompatsiaris, Y.: Two-level message clustering for topic detection in Twitter. In: CEUR Workshop Proceedings, vol. 1150, pp. 49–56 (2014)
11. Nur'Aini, K., Najahaty, I., Hidayati, L., Murfi, H., Nurrohmah, S.: Combination of singular value decomposition and K-means clustering methods for topic detection on Twitter. In: 2015 International Conference on Advanced Computer Science and Information Systems, Proceedings, ICACSIS 2015 (2016)
12. Fitriyani, S.R., Murfi, H.: The K-means with mini batch algorithm for topics detection on online news. In: 2016 4th International Conference on Information and Communication Technology, ICoICT 2016 (2016)
13. Alatas, H., Murfi, H., Bustamam, A.: Topic detection using fuzzy c-means with nonnegative double singular value decomposition initialization. Int. J. Adv. Soft Comput. its Appl. **10**, 206–222 (2018)
14. Mursidah, I., Murfi, H.: Analysis of initialization method on fuzzy c-means algorithm based on singular value decomposition for topic detection. In: Proceedings of the 2017 1st International Conference on Informatics and Computational Sciences (ICICoS), pp. 213–218 (2017)
15. Winkler, R., Klawonn, F., Kruse, R.: Fuzzy c-means in high dimensional spaces. Int. J. Fuzzy Syst. Appl. **1**, 2–4 (2011)
16. Muliawati, T., Murfi, H.: Eigenspace-Based Fuzzy C-Means for Sensing Trending Topics in Twitter. In: AIP Conference Proceedings, vol. 1862, p. 030140 (2017)
17. Golub, G., Loan, C.V: Matrix Computation. The Johns Hopkins University Press (1996)
18. Bezdek, J.C.: Pattern Recognition with Fuzzy Objective Function Algorithms. Plenum, New York (1981)
19. Bezdek, J.C., Hathaway, R.J.: Convergence of alternating optimization. Neural Parallel Sci. Comput. **11**, 351–368 (2003)
20. Lau, J.H., Newman, D., Baldwin, T.: Machine reading tea leaves: automatically evaluating topic coherence and topic model quality. In: Proceedings of the 14th Conference of the European Chapter of the Association for Computational Linguistics, pp. 530–539 (2014)
21. Lichman, M.: UCI Machine Learning Repository (2013). http://archive.ics.uci.edu/ml
22. Manning, C.D., Schuetze, H., Raghavan, P.: Introduction to information retrieval. Cambridge University Press, Cambridge (2008)
23. Pedregosa, F., et al.: Scikit-learn: machine learning in Python. J. Mach. Learn. Res. **12**, 2825–2830 (2011)
24. Aiello, L.M., et al.: Sensing trending topics in Twitter. IEEE Trans. Multimed. **15**, 1268–1282 (2013)
25. Sitorus, A.P., Murfi, H., Nurrohmah, S., Akbar, A.: Sensing trending topics in Twitter for Greater Jakarta area. Int. J. Electr. Comput. Eng. **7**, 330–336 (2017)
26. Loper, E., Bird, S.: NLTK: the natural language toolkit. In: Proceedings of the COLING/ACL 2006 Interactive Presentation Sessions, pp. 69–72 (2006)

Information-Centric Fog Computing
for Disaster Relief

Jianwen Xu🆔, Kaoru Ota🆔, and Mianxiong Dong$^{(\boxtimes)}$🆔

Department of Information and Electronic Engineering,
Muroran Institute of Technology, Muroran 0508585, Japan
{17096011,ota,mxdong}@mmm.muroran-it.ac.jp

Abstract. Natural disasters like earthquakes and typhoons are bringing huge casualties and losses to modern society every year. As the main
foundation of the information age, host-centric network infrastructure is
easily disrupted during disasters. In this paper, we focus on combining
Information-Centric Networking (ICN) and fog computing in solving the
problem of emergency networking and fast communication. We come up
with the idea from six degrees of separation theory (SDST) in achieving Information-Centric Fog Computing (ICFC) for disaster relief. Our
target is to model the relationship of network nodes and design a novel
name-based routing strategy using SDST. In the simulation part, we
evaluate and compare our work with existing routing methods in ICN.
The results show that our strategy can help improve work efficiency in
name-based routing under the limitation of post-disaster scenario.

Keywords: Fog computing · Information-centric networking
Disaster management · Name-based routing · Six degrees of separation

1 Introduction

This year, a 6.6-magnitude earthquake occurred in Hokkaido, Japan [1]. As local
power system was seriously damaged, many areas have experienced network
connectivity interruption and communication service outage. Therefore, people
in affected areas are in urgent need of obtaining information about disaster relief
and getting in touch with the outside world.

First raised by *Cisco* [2] as an extension of cloud, fog computing focuses on the
computing resources near end users. Fog can provide a solution when we lose the
connection to central servers. As one of the future Internet models, Information-
Centric Networking (ICN) aims to build up a novel data-centric architecture
providing receiver-driven data retrieval services. ICN is not constrained by the
traditional network structures and can be used for fast networking [3]. As a
result, we believe that the Information-Centric Fog Computing (ICFC) fits the
requirements of emergency communication in disaster relief.

This paper is supported by JSPS KAKENHI Grant Number JP16K00117, and KDDI
Foundation.

© Springer Nature Switzerland AG 2018
M. Qiu (Ed.): SmartCom 2018, LNCS 11344, pp. 335–344, 2018.
https://doi.org/10.1007/978-3-030-05755-8_33

Name-based routing is one of the basic issues in ICN. Existing protocols including Named-data Link State Routing (NLSR) [4], Distance-based Content Routing (DCR) [5], and Diffusive Name-based Routing Protocol (DNRP) [6] rely on frequently message exchange between neighbor nodes to ensure the routing information is up-to-date. However, in consideration of the post-disaster scenario, available computing resources and bandwidths are limited. Under the constraints of power storage capacity, the nodes that making up the network may not be fixed, either. That is, name-based routing for disaster relief has to reduce the dependence of neighbor information and increase the scalability of network topology change.

Six degrees of separation refers to the theory that everyone and everything else in our world are in relation with each other by six steps away at most. In cyberspace, we are facing the situation similar to the real world. For example, if an ICN node receives the request and does have the waned file (or replica), it may choose to send it first to neighbor node most likely to save the file or most likely to know which one saves it. The basis for judgment used here is very easy to understand in the field of social networks. However, in ICFC for disaster relief, we need specific rules to model it with named data and realize efficient transmission under limited network resources.

To solve the problem of name-based communication for disaster relief, we believe that ICFC can achieve new breakthroughs with the help of SDST. The main contributions of our work are as follows.

- First, we design a 2-tier information-centric fog network model under the application scenario of disaster relief.
- Second, we model the relationships among ICN nodes based on delivered files, and propose a name-based routing to enable emergent communication. To the best of our knowledge, this is the first work to apply the idea from SDST in ICN and fog computing under the scenario of disaster management.
- Finally, we evaluate our work by carrying out simulations and comparing with DNRP under the same experimental settings. We choose number of forwarding hops and update messages in total as two metrics.

This paper is divided into six sections to cover all aspects of the research. Section 1 introduces the background and sorts out the whole work flow. Section 2 presents related work on ICN, fog computing, disaster management and six degrees of separation theory. Section 3 sets up the mathematical model and elaborates the details of raised problems. Section 4 proposes a name-based routing strategy using SDST for disaster relief. Section 5 gives the results of simulation and comparative analysis between our strategy and existing ones. Section 6 summarizes the previous work and draws conclusions.

2   Related Work

In this section, we present related work about ICN, fog computing, disaster management, and six degrees of separation theory.

As the current research hotspots, both fog computing and ICN are attracting extensive attention from academia and industry. Li *et al.* focus on the concept of edge-centric computing (ECC) to explore new possibilities in next generation wireless communication [7,8]. Wu *et al.* combine fog computing and ICN, and propose a security service architecture based on content-aware filtering [9]. Li *et al.* apply fog computing and deep learning in manufacture inspection to increase work efficiency [10]. Gai *et al.* present the framework of privacy-preserving communication in Internet of Things for system security improvement [11–13].

In the field of disaster management, there also have been many eye-catching research results with the emerging technologies. Erdelj *et al.* put forward a blueprint of unmanned aerial vehicles (UAV) assisted disaster management [14]. Han *et al.* pay attention to the localization in wireless sensor networks (WSNs) without geo-location information [15]. Li *et al.* focus on the distributed scene understanding by learning the depth images taken in disaster area [16]. Ernst *et al.* discuss the collaborative properties in crowdsourcing for emergency management [17]. Chung *et al.* put forward Peer-to-Peer cloud network services to provide disaster information from distributed IoT devices [18].

With this theory, we can expect to connect between any two people by a six-segmented (or less) path of "a friend of a friend". Besides the original application in social science, six degrees of separation theory (SDST) has already inspired many cross-disciplinary researches from mathematics to psychological analysis. Muldoon *et al.* discuss the small-world network properties for weighted brain networks [19]. Modern SNSs including Facebook and LinkedIn also apply SDST in designing some platform applications. In the field of computer networks, related work on efficient message delivery through user relationship networks has been around for a long time. Vespignani summarizes the development of network science in the past 20 years since Watts and Strogatz first proposed the small world model [20] in 1998 [21].

3   Problem Formulation

In this section, we design our ICFC network model and formulate the problem to solve. Symbols used in this paper are listed in Table 1.

A 2-tier information-centric fog network architecture is shown in Fig. 1. Fog Tier is made up of massive ICN nodes $F = \{f_1, f_2, ..., f_n\}$ providing limited services to users in User Tier ($U = \{u_1, u_2, ..., u_n\}$). Here we use the Watts-Strogatz model [20] from SDST to describe the properties of node distribution and relationship among them. In an undirected graph, a group n nodes first form a regular ring lattice one by one. Second, each node builds edges to its k (should be an even integer) neighbors, $k/2$ by left and right sides in a ring lattice. Third, each edge created by the current node can be rebuilt with a probability of β. As a result, for any two nodes n_i and n_j, there exists an edge if and only if

$$0 < |i - j| mod(n - \frac{k}{2} - 1) \leq \frac{k}{2} \tag{1}$$

Table 1. Notations in name-based routing using SDST for disaster relief.

Symbol	Meaning
F, f	Set of fog nodes in Fog Tier and one in it
U, u	Set of user nodes in User Tier and one in it
k	Number of edges built between neighbors in Watts-Strogatz model
β	Probability of edge rebuilt in Watts-Strogatz model
CL, cl	Content library and one file in it
n_u, n_f, n_{cl}	Number of users, fog nodes and files in CL
r	Popularity rank of cl in CL
s	An exponent to characterize the Zipf distribution
n_r^{hop}	Number of forwarding hops to get the rth file in CL

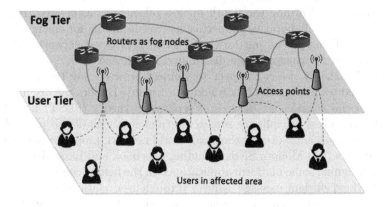

Fig. 1. A 2-tier information-centric fog network architecture.

A content library $CL = \{cl_1, cl_2, ..., cl_n\}$ includes all the files for requesting which are stored in Fog Tier. The popularity of files in CL obeys Zipf distribution.

$$f_{zipf}(r; s, n_{cl}) = \frac{1/r^s}{\sum_{i=1}^{n_{cl}}(1/i^s)} \tag{2}$$

Equation (2) shows the normalized frequency of cl_r in a CL with n_{cl} files in total. Here r stands for the popularity rank of cl_r in CL. s is the value of the exponent which characterizes the distribution. When any file is requested from User Tier for the first time, it has to be downloaded from the original node. After any file is being forwarded back, a replica can be left at any node it passes. Then from the second time, any ICN node has replicas also can answer the request.

As a result, our target is to design name-based routing strategy to answer the requests from users by finding out the suitable nodes having the wanted files or replicas with high work efficiency. The first metric we choose is the number of forwarding hops in total. That is, to cope with the same amount of user requests with as few forwarding hops as possible.

$$minimum \quad \sum_{r=1}^{n_{cl}} n_r^{hop} f_{zipf}(r; s, n_{cl})$$

$$= \sum_{r=1}^{n_{cl}} \frac{n_r^{hop}/r^s}{\sum_{i=1}^{n_{cl}}(1/i^s)} \qquad (3)$$

$$subject\ to \quad s \geq 0, r \in \{1, 2, ..., n_{cl}\}$$

Besides the efficiency on transmission, we also consider the number of update messages [22]. As discuss in the introduction section, existed routing protocols have to rely on frequent information exchange to ensure real-time mastery of network topology. Excessive messages for updating may not only occupy the limited network resources in disaster relief, but also bring the risk of losing effective information when encountering node changes. Thus, our second target is to integrate the inter-node relationships with SDST and reduce the number of update messages.

4   Name-Based Routing Using SDST for Disaster Relief

In this section, we design a routing strategy using SDST for providing information-centric fog services to users in affected area.

Algorithm 1. LRER: Limited Relationship Expansion Routing

$f\_next(f_i, cl_j) \leftarrow$ the name of next node to forward for f_i to find cl_j, $\emptyset$ means cl_i is
   already cached in CS of f_i
$n_{re}(cl_j) \leftarrow$ left number of replicas for each cl_j
$hop\_count \leftarrow$ record of forwarding hops in transmission
1: a user u_{this} send out a request to f_i ask for cl_j
2: $f_{this} \leftarrow f_i$, $hop\_count \leftarrow hop\_count + 2$
3: **while** $f\_next(f_{this}, cl_j) \neq \emptyset$ **do**
4:    **if** $find(f_{this}.CS = cl_j)$ **then**
5:       $hop\_count \leftarrow hop\_count + 2$
6:       **break**
7:    **else**
8:       $f_{this} \leftarrow f\_next(f_{this}, cl_j)$
9:    **end if**
10:   **if** $n_{re}(cl_j) > 0$ **then**
11:      **if** $!find(f_{this}.CS = cl_j)$ **then**
12:         push cl_j into $f_{this}.CS$
13:      **end if**
14:   **end if**
15: **end while**

Table 2. Experimental settings.

Parameter	Value
Number of files in CL	100
Number of users/fog nodes	200/50
β in Watts-Strogatz model	0.15/0.5
k in Watts-Strogatz model	2–20
s in Zipf distribution	1
Number of available replicas	0–4

As shown in Algorithm 1, to achieve name-based routing in ICFC for disaster relief, we minimize the conditions to be as close as possible to emergency communications in post-disaster environment. When traditional facilities such as cellular networks are no longer available, trapped users are in urgent need of getting in touch with the outside world, even if it is one-way communication. To cope with this situation, we first cover all areas where survivors may be present with multiple fog nodes. Instead of storing and managing a variety of information in FIB from neighbor reports, we only need the name of next node to search for file ($f\_next(f_i, cl_j)$).

As a result, the only thing a fog node needs to do when receiving request is to forward it to the next one. Update messages are being exchanged only when new node comes in. Even when any file is cached in the CS of passed node (line 12 in Algorithm 1), we do not need to update instantly. That is, we check the CS of each node if it has the wanted file (line 4) to reduce extra forwarding. Some periodic overall updates are also helpful in adapting to the topology changes of the network. When regarding the nodes as our own, to help deliver the request to its destination, in the case of limited knowledge of outside information, we always choose anyone most likely to be close to the target. Time complexity of Algorithm 1 is $O(n_f)$.

5   Performance Evaluation

In this section, we evaluate our proposed routing strategy for disaster relief through simulation experiments.

As shown in Table 2, in a open area after disaster, there are 200 users and 50 fog nodes. Users are sending requests for one of the 100 files in CL. All the files are originally saved in one of the fog nodes. When any file is delivered back to user, a replica can be left at the passed nodes. We limit the number of available replicas for each file within [0−4]. We repeat the process from requesting to getting satisfied 2000 times for each set with different β. We compare the metrics of forwarding hops and update messages with DNRP under the same experimental setups.

DNRP is proposed in 2018 [6] by the research team led by Garcia-Luna-Aceves. As one of the state-of-the-art name-based protocols, DNRP looks for current best path selection by recording and comparing the link cost at each step of forwarding. That is to say, neighbors know everything a node is doing under the premise of timely update. However, for emergency communication in post-disaster scenario, stable connections are often not guaranteed. As a result, how to make use of limited resources to complete minimal messaging is what LRER aims to do.

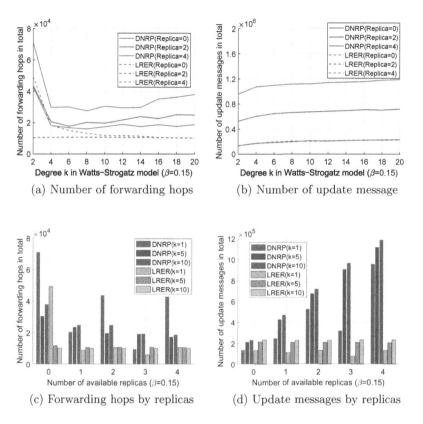

(a) Number of forwarding hops

(b) Number of update message

(c) Forwarding hops by replicas

(d) Update messages by replicas

Fig. 2. Results of name-based routing for disaster relief ($\beta = 0.15$). (Color figure online)

Figure 2 shows the results of name-based routing for disaster relief when β is 0.15. Here we use colors to indicate the number of different replicas allowed. Red is no replica, blue is 2 replicas and green is 4. When the rebuilt probability is low, fog nodes here own the similar degrees. Or we may look forward to a more regular network topology in which users are evenly distributed everywhere waiting for communication and rescue. First in Fig. 2a, we calculate the number of forwarding hops for answering requests from 200 users. In the case of the same number of replicas, LRER is always less frequently forwarded than DNRP. LRER with 2 or 4 replicas can even stay almost the same when k is changing. Second in Fig. 2b, LRER cuts most the overhead on update messages. DNRP with no replica nearly coincides with the results of LRER which can be explained that no frequent need to exchange information between neighbors. Figure 2c and d display the results by different numbers of available replicas. Compared with DNRP, nearly all results in LRER are lower in numerical values, which is consistent with the previous inferences.

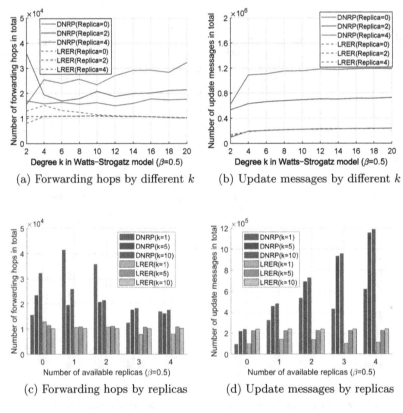

(a) Forwarding hops by different k (b) Update messages by different k

(c) Forwarding hops by replicas   (d) Update messages by replicas

Fig. 3. Results of name-based routing for disaster relief ($\beta = 0.5$).

In order to further simulate the adaptability of the proposed routing strategy in the Watts-Strogatz model, we add another set of results with $\beta = 0.5$. Compared with Fig. 2, Fig. 3 has higher randomness in network connectivity and may be closer to the disordered state in the scenario of disaster relief. The trend of the polylines also confirms this point. When each node only has a few connection options, not only will the nodes be differentiated from each other by degree, but they together may form some single long paths. Results of forwarding hops in Fig. 3a and c show more fluctuations. Especially when k is small, DNRP with no replica even has an increasing overall trend. LRER maintains high stability and does not receive too much influence from β. Finally in Fig. 3b and d, we do not observe any significant changes. Or we can say that under the current experimental settings, the randomness of network connections is not a major factor affecting the number of update messages in both strategies.

In summary, we compare the performance of our proposed LRER with the existing DNRP in numbers of forwarding hops and update messages through two sets of experiments. The results show that our strategy can achieve higher work efficiency and may be more suitable as a technology for network reconstruction in disaster relief.

6   Conclusion

In this paper, we focus on solving name-based routing for disaster relief by applying the idea from six degrees of separation theory. We first put forward a 2-tier information-centric fog network architecture under the scenario of post-disaster. Then we model the relationships among ICN nodes based on delivered files, and propose a name-based routing strategy to enable fast networking and emergency communication. We compare with DNRP under the same experimental settings and prove that our strategy can achieve higher work efficiency.

In the future, we are going to design real-world experiments to implement our work on information-centric fog computing for disaster relief. Our target is to consider more technical details in the process of system construction and evaluate the performance under different network sizes.

References

1. Wikipedia: 2018 hokkaido eastern iburi earthquake, September 2018. https://en.wikipedia.org/wiki/2018_Hokkaido_Eastern_Iburi_earthquake
2. Bonomi, F., Milito, R., Zhu, J., Addepalli, S.: Fog computing and its role in the internet of things. In: Proceedings of the First Edition of the MCC Workshop on Mobile Cloud Computing, MCC 2012, pp. 13–16. ACM, New York (2012). https://doi.org/10.1145/2342509.2342513
3. Xu, J., Ota, K., Dong, M.: Fast networking for disaster recovery. IEEE Trans. Emerg. Topics Comput. 1 (2018). https://doi.org/10.1109/TETC.2017.2775798
4. Hoque, A.K.M.M., Amin, S.O., Alyyan, A., Zhang, B., Zhang, L., Wang, L.: NLSR: named-data link state routing protocol. In: Proceedings of the 3rd ACM SIGCOMM Workshop on Information-Centric Networking, ICN 2013, pp. 15–20. ACM, New York (2013). https://doi.org/10.1145/2491224.2491231
5. Garcia-Luna-Aceves, J.: Name-based content routing in information centric networks using distance information. In: Proceedings of the 1st ACM Conference on Information-Centric Networking, ACM-ICN 2014, pp. 7–16. ACM, New York (2014). https://doi.org/10.1145/2660129.2660141
6. Hemmati, E., Garcia-Luna-Aceves, J.J.: Making name-based content routing more efficient than link-state routing. CoRR abs/1804.02752 (2018). http://arxiv.org/abs/1804.02752
7. Li, H., Ota, K., Dong, M.: ECCN: orchestration of edge-centric computing and content-centric networking in the 5G radio access network. IEEE Wirel. Commun. **25**(3), 88–93 (2018). https://doi.org/10.1109/MWC.2018.1700315

8. Li, H., Ota, K., Dong, M.: Learning IoT in edge: deep learning for the internet of things with edge computing. IEEE Netw. **32**(1), 96–101 (2018). https://doi.org/10.1109/MNET.2018.1700202

9. Wu, J., Dong, M., Ota, K., Li, J., Guan, Z.: FCSS: fog computing based content-aware filtering for security services in information centric social networks. IEEE Trans. Emerg. Topics Comput. 1. https://doi.org/10.1109/TETC.2017.2747158

10. Li, L., Ota, K., Dong, M.: Deep learning for smart industry: efficient manufacture inspection system with fog computing. IEEE Trans. Indus. Inform. 1 (2018). https://doi.org/10.1109/TII.2018.2842821

11. Gai, K., Choo, K.R., Qiu, M., Zhu, L.: Privacy-preserving content-oriented wireless communication in internet-of-things. IEEE Internet Things J. **5**(4), 3059–3067 (2018). https://doi.org/10.1109/JIOT.2018.2830340

12. Gai, K., Qiu, M.: Blend arithmetic operations on tensor-based fully homomorphic encryption over real numbers. IEEE Trans. Indus. Inform. **14**(8), 3590–3598 (2018). https://doi.org/10.1109/TII.2017.2780885

13. Gai, K., Qiu, M., Xiong, Z., Liu, M.: Privacy-preserving multi-channel communication in edge-of-things. Future Gen. Comput. Syst. **85**, 190–200 (2018). https://doi.org/10.1016/j.future.2018.03.043, http://www.sciencedirect.com/science/article/pii/S0167739X18300037

14. Erdelj, M., Natalizio, E., Chowdhury, K.R., Akyildiz, I.F.: Help from the sky: leveraging UAVs for disaster management. IEEE Perv. Comput. **16**(1), 24–32 (2017). https://doi.org/10.1109/MPRV.2017.11

15. Han, G., Yang, X., Liu, L., Guizani, M., Zhang, W.: A disaster management-oriented path planning for mobile anchor node-based localization in wireless sensor networks. IEEE Trans. Emerg. Topics Comput. 1 (2018). https://doi.org/10.1109/TETC.2017.2687319

16. Li, L., Ota, K., Dong, M., Borjigin, W.: Eyes in the dark: distributed scene understanding for disaster management. IEEE Trans. Parallel Distrib. Syst. **28**(12), 3458–3471 (2017). https://doi.org/10.1109/TPDS.2017.2740294

17. Ernst, C., Mladenow, A., Strauss, C.: Collaboration and crowdsourcing in emergency management. Int. J. Perv. Comput. Commun. **13**(2), 176–193 (2017)

18. Chung, K., Park, R.C.: P2P cloud network services for IoT based disaster situations information. Peer-to-Peer Netw. Appl. **9**(3), 566–577 (2016). https://doi.org/10.1007/s12083-015-0386-3

19. Muldoon, S.F., Bridgeford, E.W., Bassett, D.S.: Small-world propensity and weighted brain networks. Sci. Rep. **6**, 22057 (2016). https://doi.org/10.1038/srep22057

20. Watts, D.J., Strogatz, S.H.: Collective dynamics of "small-world" networks. Nature **393**, 440 (1998). https://doi.org/10.1038/30918

21. Vespignani, A.: Twenty years of network science. Nature **558**, 528–529 (2018). https://doi.org/10.1038/d41586-018-05444-y, https://www.nature.com/articles/d41586-018-05444-y

22. Hemmati, E., Garcia-Luna-Aceves, J.J.: A comparison of name-based content routing protocols. In: 2015 IEEE 12th International Conference on Mobile Ad Hoc and Sensor Systems, pp. 537–542, October 2015. https://doi.org/10.1109/MASS.2015.52

Smartly Deploying WeChat Mobile Application on Cloud Foundry PaaS

Zhihui Lu[1], Xiaoli Wan[2(✉)], Meikang Qiu[3], Lijun Zu[4],
Shih-Chia Huang[5], Jie Wu[6], and Meiqin Liu[7]

[1] School of Computer Science, Fudan University, Shanghai 200433, China
lzh@fudan.edu.cn
[2] Information Center, Zhejiang International Business Group Co., Ltd.,
Hangzhou, China
wanxl@zibchina.com
[3] Department of Electrical Engineering, Columbia University,
New York, NY 10027, USA
qiumeikang@yahoo.com
[4] Research Institute of Electronic Payment, China UnionPay, Shanghai, China
zulijun@unionpay.com
[5] Department of Electronic Engineering,
National Taipei University of Technology, Taipei, Taiwan
schuang@ntut.edu.tw
[6] Engineering Research Center of Cyber Security, Auditing and Monitoring,
Ministry of Education, Shanghai 200433, China
jwu@fudan.edu.cn
[7] College of Electrical Engineering, Zhejiang University,
Hangzhou 310027, China
liumeiqin@zju.edu.cn

Abstract. WeChat has become the mainstream social network mobile applications in China. Based on the WeChat API, there are many attached mobile applications. Cloud Foundry is a lightweight mainstream PaaS platform. In this paper, we studied how to develop and deploy WeChat applications on the Cloud Foundry platform to achieve lightweight development and deployment. The implementation of a product maintenance system proves the effectiveness of our deployment method with WeChat and Cloud Foundry.

Keywords: WeChat · Cloud Foundry · PaaS · Cloud computing
Smart computing

1 Introduction

According to the CNNIC survey report, the number of china mobile internet user reached at 0.62 billion at the end of 2015. The number has increased 8.4% compared with the data in 2014. And it has come to 0.788 billion in Q2 of 2018 [1]. The analysis says that the entire mobile internet business is still at the period of rapidly increasing.

Mobile application increases explosively, towards the direction of platformization and vertical. On one hand, internet magnate use their own super app to appeal to users,

M. Qiu (Ed.): SmartCom 2018, LNCS 11344, pp. 345–355, 2018.
https://doi.org/10.1007/978-3-030-05755-8_34

and build their own ecology circle based on it. The super app gradually become a platformization product. And it becomes the center of mobile internet application service by connecting different applications and scenery. For example, until the end of 2017, the monthly average active users of WeChat in the fields of mobile internet has covered about 93.9%, through WeChat, you can go shopping, play games, watching video, travel, music, and finance in this platform. On the other hand, as the development of industry internet, the fields is divided into more specific scenery. The mobile application WeChat is obviously one of the most popular mobile app nowadays. WeChat is a free instant messaging software launched by Tencent in 2011, and it becomes the most popular mobile application soon. Until the end of 2018 first quarter, the WeChat has covered 95% or more smart phones, so it has a big amount of users. WeChat is so popular because it can satisfy the social need of individuals, and obviously WeChat has become the biggest tool in mobile device users.

Based on WeChat, the Tencent Company offers many functions like public platform, moments, push notification and so on. Other company could develop their own services on the platform of WeChat. It is a win-win cooperation mode. For WeChat, it makes money by offering services. And through this way, they can attract more users to build their own ecosphere. For other developers, they can use this platform to develop their application. Users do not need to download another application and can easily access to services. The developers could take less effort to popularize the application. So this business mode will popularize in next several years. According to the prediction, WeChat will develop in these fields, as Fig. 1 shown. First, E-commerce. WeChat has launched the function named WeChat payment. And it also have its own e-commerce platform named Yixun. At the same time, sellers could open a WeChat store to sell their goods. Then, life service. You can pay your phone fee, call taxi, buy movie tickets, buy lottery and so on. With the help of WeChat, users could do these things without download other app. It is very convenient. And when users are accustomed to this mode, more services would be added to it. What is more, finance. Users could buy the financial products pushed by WeChat. They provide higher interest rate to appeal more users, and use these money to do other things. And there are many fields that are developing by WeChat, like games, O2O and so on. Upon on the huge amount users of WeChat, we could develop our own app on this platform, and it will be appeal to users easier than other ways.

Cloud Foundry is an open-source platform as a service (PaaS) that provides you with a choice of clouds, developer frameworks, and application services [2].

Cloud Foundry is licensed under Apache 2.0 and supports Java, Node.js, Go, PHP, Python and Ruby. The open source PaaS is highly customizable, allowing developers to code in multiple languages and frameworks [3]. This eliminates the potential for vendor lock-in, which is a common concern with PaaS. Developers choose Cloud Foundry for its free, open source nature and for the ability to use their own tools and code. Similar platforms and competitors to Cloud Foundry include OpenShift, Google App Engine and Heroku [3].

For infrastructure management, Cloud Foundry uses BOSH, an open source tool for deployment and lifecycle management.

In February 2014, Pivotal, EMC, IBM, Rackspace and VMware formed the Cloud Foundry Foundation, which currently has more than 50 members. The independent

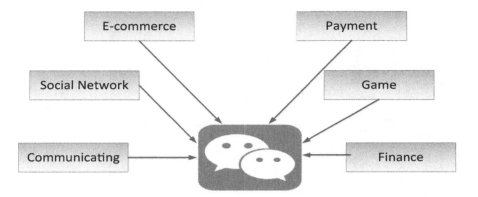

Fig. 1. WeChat application area

non-profit foundation has an open governance policy that allows any organization to contribute.

The Cloud Foundry Foundation's target is to utilize the efforts of the community to build a lightweight platform for cloud-native applications and software.

Cloud Foundry is a lightweight mainstream PaaS platform. In this paper, our contribution is that we develop and deploy WeChat applications on the Cloud Foundry platform to achieve smart and lightweight mobile application development and deployment.

The rest of the paper is organized as follows. We design Cloud Foundry architecture for WeChat application in Sect. 2. Section 3 gives detailed design of WeChat mobile application on Cloud Foundry PaaS. Section 4 describes module implementation and system demonstration. Section 5 concludes the paper and points out some future work.

2 Cloud Foundry Architecture Design for WeChat Application

The Fig. 2 shows our designed architecture of WeChat application combined with the Cloud Foundry PaaS and mBaas (mobile Backend-as-a-service).

2.1 mBaas-Loopback Module Design

LoopBack is a highly-extensible, open-source Node.js framework [4], and it can:

- Quickly create dynamic end-to-end REST APIs [4].
- Connect devices and browsers to data and services [4].
- Use Android, iOS, and AngularJS SDKs to easily create client apps [4].
- Add-on components for file management, 3rd-party login, and OAuth2 [4].
- Use StrongLoop Arc to visually edit, deploy, and monitor LoopBack apps.

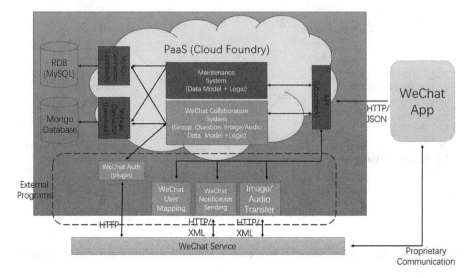

Fig. 2. The architecture of WeChat application combined with the Cloud Foundry PaaS and mBaas.

- StrongLoop API Gateway acts an intermediary between API consumers (clients) and API providers to externalize, secure, and manage APIs.
- Runs on-premises or in the cloud.

2.2   Work Flow Design

Our Platform as a Service is Cloud Foundry, and we execute a product maintenance system and a WeChat collaboration system on the Cloud Foundry.

While we open a WeChat App, we send message to the API which is made by the Loopback, and the Loopback communicate with the Maintenance System and WeChat Collaboration System on the PaaS layer. Whenever it need fetch some data, it will use the MySQL Connector or the Storage Connector created by the Loopback. And the Connect will to access to the database to get the data.

The Loopback API will also collaborate with the external program. When WeChat App need authentication, need to map the user or need to send information, it will connect to the WeChat Service with HTTP protocol which manage proprietary communication.

3   Detailed Design of WeChat Mobile Application on Cloud Foundry PaaS

3.1   Overall Architecture

The overall architecture is shown in Fig. 3, and the system consists of four parts. There are LoopBack server, WeChat client, WeChat public account server and WeChat server. The LoopBack server and WeChat public account server are both deployed on PaaS (Pivotal Cloud Foundry).

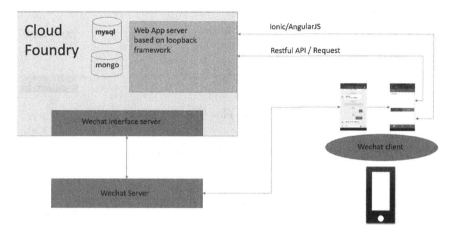

Fig. 3. Overall architecture of WeChat mobile application on Cloud Foundry PaaS

The responsibility of LoopBack server is to deliver the WeChat WebApp to the user and handle REST APIs calls. LoopBack is a Node.js API framework that quickly creates dynamic end-to-end REST APIs and connects devices and browsers to data and service. It eases the burden of the developers since it provides a way to link their applications to database.

WeChat client provides the interface of WeChat Official account service and the browser that the WeChat WebApp runs in. Users can do thing like sending texts, uploading pictures and receiving news feeds in the WeChat client. The user menu is where the users gain access to the WebApps and webpages. The WeChat public account server's job is to answer the request from the WeChat client and push messages to the user.

3.2   Dataflow Between Loopback and WeChat Browser

The following Figs. 4, 5, 6 and 7 illustrate the way that LoopBack and WeChat communicate with each other.

First the web browser requests the Webapp and LoopBack will return the HTML, Javascript, CSS files. After that, they mainly communicate with REST APIs.

For example, if a user wants to post a comment. After the user clicks the submit button, the Webapp will send a HTTP request through the POST method and data in JSON format in the HTTP body. The LoopBack server response with status code 200, which means the operation is successfully completed.

The REST APIs are automatically generated when models are created. However, users can define their own APIs if needed.

Fig. 4. First step

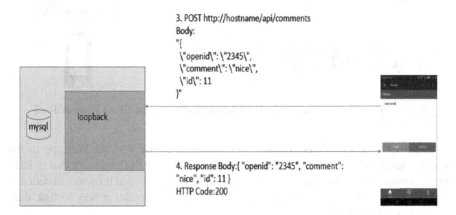

Fig. 5. Create a comment

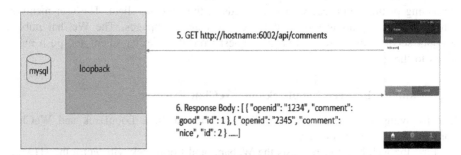

Fig. 6. Get all comments

3.3 Message Sending and Receiving Process

The following Fig. 8 illustrates the message sending and receiving process among WeChat client, WeChat server and public account server.

(1) The user sends a message to the public account. These message will be first transferred to the WeChat server via internet.

(2) After the WeChat server receives the message, it will transform it to xml format with a signature and forward to the public account server.

(3) First the public account server needs to authenticate the message. If it makes sure that the message does come from the WeChat server, the public account server parses the message and generates a response accordingly. It can choose to store the message.

(4) The WeChat server forwards that message to the client and the user can see the result.

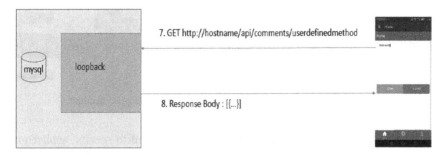

Fig. 7. User-defined-method

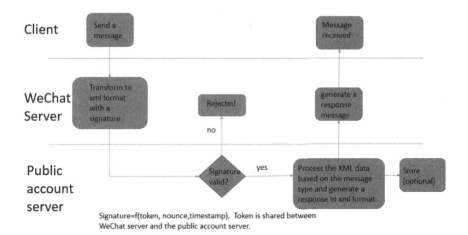

Fig. 8. Message sending and receiving process

4 Module Implementation and WeChat Maintenance System Implementation

4.1 Authentication Module

To achieve the authentication modules of mapping WeChat account and enterprise account, the modification of table structures in database and the specific logic processes of Web application are both necessary.

On the one hand, the attribute of WeChat account, name and etc. should be added to the table of customer information, or a new table of the map of WeChat account and enterprise account should be created.

On the other hand, the logic processes should be completed to achieve the map of the two accounts. Here are the data flows, as shown in Fig. 9.

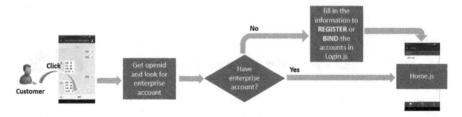

Fig. 9. Flows of mapping WeChat account and enterprise account

As the menu of WeChat public account has been bound to specific applications, when a follower click the button on the menu, the URL of application is called. Then the openid of WeChat user will be obtained by the interface provided by WeChat, and be sent with the URL as one of parameters to the application server.

In the application server, the openid will be used to search for enterprise account in the database. If the result is not null, the page is directed to the home page of the application, and customer can then use the application.

But if the result is null, it means that this follower is not one of customers of Hitachi, he or she doesn't have any enterprise account of Hitachi, or he or she hasn't bound this WeChat account to his or her enterprise account. Whichever situation is this follower in, the page is directed to the login page, where the follower can fill in some basic information to register or bind existed enterprise account to this WeChat account, and then redirected to the home page when succeed.

4.2   Image/Audio Uploading Module

The Fig. 10 shows how data flows in the image/audio transfer program. They are roughly divided into five flows, and then here are introductions.

(1) The user input some basic message, picture, and audio in the web. We can get the text and put it into database directly.
(2) In this step, we use the js-sdk which provided by WeChat. It can offer many interfaces, including uploading image, uploading audio and so on.
(3) Download the picture and audio from WeChat Server and save it to own database.
(4) Get data from database.
(5) Show data to web.

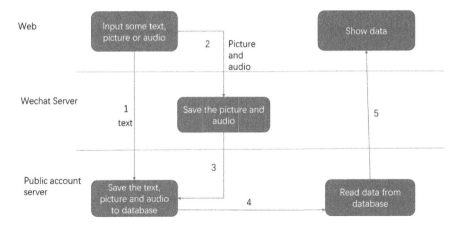

Fig. 10. Image/audio uploading module workflow

4.3 Underlying Technology of System Implementation

In order to implement the system introduced above, technologies listed below are required (Fig. 11).

	service	software	version	comment
1	mBaaS	Node.js	4.4.7	https://nodejs.org/en/
2		npm	3.10.6	npm -g install
3		LoopBack.io	6. 0. 1	Install using npm
4	Database	MySQL		provided by Cloud Foundry as a service
5	Develoment Machine	Node.js	4.4.7	https://nodejs.org/en/
		Android SDK		Android Studio with Android SDK
		Cordova SDK	6.3.1	Install using npm
		Ionic SDK	2.0.0	Install using npm
		AngularJS	1.3.2	

Fig. 11. Underlying technology of system implementation

4.4 Implementation of WeChat Maintenance System

Here are some GUI figures to show our implemented WeChat product maintenance system.

As Fig. 12 showing, when users want to maintain their products, they can click the button of maintenance application and fill in some information about the status of their products, including product number, reservation date, and submit it to apply for maintenance service. Then the request is sent to the manager to be handled offline. And

the maintenance processes will be monitored until the last step of certain-times satisfaction survey is completed to finish this task. And the user and manager can check
maintenance information of their products whenever they want, as Fig. 13 shown.

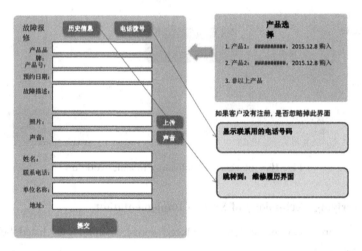

Fig. 12. Detailed maintenance operation menu-1

Fig. 13. Detailed maintenance operation menu-2

5   Conclusion and Future Work

In this paper, we focus on integrating mobile application with PaaS service, which will be better to have interaction with Chinese local popular services as well. Finally we decide to design WebApp of WeChat service with Cloud Foundry PaaS.

We have installed cloud foundry with OpenStack, then according to the requirements of the product maintenance system, we made basic designs for the WeChat maintenance system application over Cloud Foundry, including cloud foundry platform architecture design, WeChat application architecture design, work flows and GUIs design.

Next step, we will continue the developing work to realize all of the designed modules. And the bonus parts like customer satisfaction survey and customer forum would be considered carefully as well. As the final goal, when everyone access to WeChat through their own account, they can directly login and use our developed maintenance system service without other additional authentication.

Acknowledgments. This work is supported by the Fudan-Hitachi Innovative Software Technology Joint Laboratory. This work is also partially supported by National Natural Science Foundation of China under Grant No. 61572137-Multiple Clouds based CDN as a Service Key Technology Research, Grant No. 61728202-Research on Internet of Things Big Data Transmission and Processing Architecture based on Cloud-Fog Hybrid Computing Model, and Shanghai 2018 Innovation Action Plan project under Grant No. 18510760200- Research on smart city big data processing technology based on mixed mode. This work is also supported by the Ministry of Science and Technology, Taiwan under the Grant MOST 106-2221-E-027-126-MY2. This work also is partially supported by China NSFC 61728303 and the Open Research Project of the State Key Laboratory of Industrial Control Technology, Zhejiang University, China (ICT1800417).

References

1. CNNIC 42nd Report. https://tech.sina.com.cn/i/2018-08-20/doc-ihhvciiw6980104.shtml
2. https://docs.cloudfoundry.org/
3. https://searchcloudcomputing.techtarget.com/definition/Cloud-Foundry
4. https://loopback.io/
5. Bo, J.: Design and implementation of mobile library APP service system based on WeChat. J. Modern Inf. (2013)
6. Wu, L., Yang, X.: A research on the services of university mobile library based on the WeChat Public Platform. Res. Libr. Sci. (2013)
7. Che, H.L., Cao, Y.: Examining WeChat users' motivations, trust, attitudes, and positive word-of-mouth: evidence from China. Comput. Hum. Behav. **41**, 104–111 (2014)
8. Bernstein, D.: Cloud foundry aims to become the OpenStack of PaaS. IEEE Cloud Comput. **1**(2), 57–60 (2014)
9. Jiang, W., Ma, M., Li, X.: Design and implementation for building PaaS based on Cloud Foundry. Microcomput. Appl. (2014)
10. Introducing Cloud Foundry: Learn how to build and deploy cloud-native applications, This event took place live on July 14 2015, Presented by: Sujay Maheshwari, Sam Gazitt
11. Jiang, Y.L.: Design and implementation of bank data cloud platform based on WeChat Enterprise. Modern Comput. (2017)

Research on Arm Motion Capture of Virtual Reality Based on Kinematics

Shubin Cai[1], Dihui Deng[1], Jinchun Wen[1], Chaoqin Chen[1],
Zhong Ming[1(✉)], and Zhiguang Shan[2]

[1] College of Computer Science and Software Engineering, Shenzhen University,
Shenzhen, China
mingz@szu.edu.cn
[2] State Information Center of China, Beijing, China
shanzg@cei.gov.cn

Abstract. Virtual reality needs to simulate interaction scenes that are as consistent as possible with reality. Motion capture is the key to address this need. In this paper, a kinematic-based virtual reality arm motion capture scheme is designed on the HTC VIVE platform to achieve low-cost and high-precision motion capture. Based on the human skeleton model, an arm kinematic chain model suitable for VR environment is designed. The above human structure data is redirected to the VR arm to drive the VR arm movement in the virtual environment. Compared with existing motion capture solutions, the experimental results and user survey results show that the method proposed in this paper is able to restore the actual arm movements in virtual reality, showing higher accuracy, and the average satisfaction of the survey object reaches 85%.

Keywords: Virtual reality · Motion capture · Kinematics · Action recognition

1 Introduction

In order to promote the development of "Internet plus", Qiu et al. [1–3] have made many contributions in computing system and cloud system. At the same time, virtual reality is also driving the development of "Internet plus". Immersion is one of the important features of VR [4]. The use of motion capture to capture the movement of real people and then reconstruct the movement of characters in a virtual environment is one of the techniques to effectively solve the lack of immersion. Another important feature of VR is real-time interactivity [5]. In the virtual environment, intelligent human-computer interaction is performed by collecting human motion data, analyzing and identifying it, and then converting it into corresponding control behavior to operate the system. This interaction method based on human motion is more in line with human cognitive habits, and to some extent reduces the gap between human and equipment, which can improve user experience [6]. The premise of realizing intelligent human-computer interaction needs to obtain the user's motion information. Therefore, motion capture is important for the intelligent human-computer interaction in VR.

In this paper, a scheme based on kinematics for virtual arm motion capture is proposed. Based on this, the action recognition is studied. Aiming at the problem that

© Springer Nature Switzerland AG 2018
M. Qiu (Ed.): SmartCom 2018, LNCS 11344, pp. 356–365, 2018.
https://doi.org/10.1007/978-3-030-05755-8_35

there is no arm motion capture or arm motion capture is not good in the virtual reality application software, a method of mapping the data captured by the VR device to the real human body structure is proposed. The method specifically refers to initializing a predefined posture to obtain initial pose data when the human body wears the motion capture device. Then, the real-time posture data of the human body is captured, and the movement posture of the human arm is determined by the transformation matrix method of the arm linkage according to the real-time posture data and the initial posture data. Due to different coordinate axes of different 3D virtual images, this paper proposes a solution to redirect the above human structure data to VR arms. The joint data of the motion chain is converted to the joint coordinate system of the virtual character through redirection, which drives the character animation model and realizes the arm motion capture and tracking in the virtual environment. Design experiments, verification and analysis, the results show that the proposed method can effectively restore the actual arm movements in virtual reality and get a good user experience.

2   Arm Motion Capture Based on Kinematics

2.1   The Structure Model of VR Arm Motion Chain

For VR arm capture, in order to obtain the complete motion representation, it is not only necessary to capture the motion of the arm, but also the motion of the trunk. Therefore, the starting point of designing the movement chain of VR characters needs to start from the Root node, which is followed by Pelvis, Spine, Ribcage, and Clavicles. The movement chain of the left and right arms should be connected through the left and right Clavicles. As shown in Fig. 1, the arm skeleton chain designed in this paper consists of Shoulder Joint, Elbow Joint and Wrist Joint.

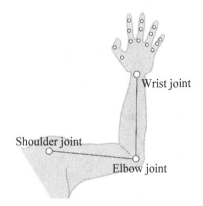

Fig. 1. Arm kinematic chain

Since different types of joints have different degrees of freedom, different joints are limited by their own structural characteristics, so the range of motion of each joint has a certain range of limits. According to Baerlocher [7] and other analysis of human joint anatomy, human joints can be divided into three types: rotary joints, hinge joints and ball joints. The arm joint angle is usually used to describe the important features of the specific posture of the arm. The relative angles of the sub-joints and the parent joints can be expressed by the Euler angles in the angular coordinate system [8].

2.2   Raw Capture Data

This program uses a standard VIVE product, including a head display, 2 handles, and then with 3 trackers, a total of 5 motion capture devices. During the motion capture process, both the head display and the handle are controlled in the normal way of wearing and holding. For the deployment of the tracker, one tracker is attached to the chest part of the body (above the waist), and the remaining two trackers are respectively bound to the left and right upper arm positions. The position of the tracker is not required to be accurate to a certain position, because the captured data is not absolute data, and the relative position of each joint needs to be calculated through the correlation between the device and joint space position information.

2.3   Predefined Posture

The predefined posture can be divided into two postures of "T" type and "I" type according to the angle of the arm and the trunk. Among them, the "T" posture is for the body to stand, and the two arms are stretched and extended; the "I" posture is for the body to stand and the two arms to sag naturally. In the "I" posture initialization, as shown in Fig. 2, the local coordinate system of the head, chest, shoulder and wrist can be determined. This coordinate information can be calculated by the quaternion method [9] using the information captured by the tracker.

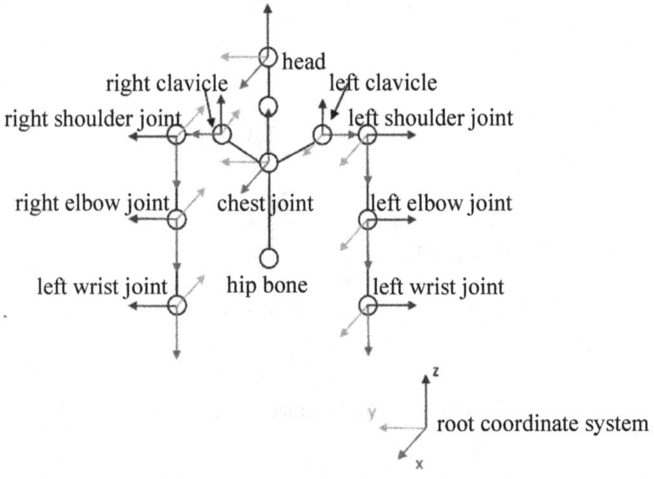

Fig. 2. Coordinate system of trunk and arm joints in "I" posture

2.4   Joint Pose Data Calculation

The posture of the head is directly obtained from the head, and the posture of the trunk is obtained by the following formula,

$$q_{Body} = q_{BTracker} \times \Delta q_{T2B} = q_{BTracker} \times \left(\left(q_{BTracker}^0 \right)^{-1} \times q_{Body}^0 \right) \tag{1}$$

Where $q_{BTracker}$ is the real-time pose of the trunk tracker, q_{Body} is the real-time pose of the trunk, q_{Body}^0 is the predefined pose and $q_{BTracker}^0$ is the initial tracker's pose. Similarly, the posture of the upper arm can be obtained by the following formula.

$$q_{Shoulder} = q_{STracker} \times \Delta q_{T2S} = q_{STracker} \times \left(\left(q_{STracker}^0 \right)^{-1} \times q_{Shoulder}^0 \right) \tag{2}$$

Where $q_{STracker}$ is the real-time pose of the upper arm tracker and $q_{Shoulder}$ is the real-time pose of the upper arm.

The formula for calculating the shoulder joint position $p_{shoulder}$ is as follows,

$$p_{shoulder} = p_{Ribcage} \pm {}_{Ribcage}^{world}T \times \frac{1}{2} L_{bodyWidth} \tag{3}$$

In the formula, $p_{Ribcage}$ is the center position of the chest. ${}_{Ribcage}^{world}T \times \frac{1}{2}L_{bodyWidth}$ is the offset of half the body width in the chest coordinate system.

Elbow position p_{elbow} is obtained by the following formula,

$$p_{elbow} = p_{shoulder} + {}_{shoulder}^{world}T \times L_{Upperarm} \tag{4}$$

Where p_{elbow} is the elbow joint position, $p_{shoulder}$ is the shoulder joint position, and ${}_{shoulder}^{world}T \times L_{Upperarm}$ is the upper arm length in the shoulder joint coordinate system.

It can be seen from Fig. 2 that the coordinate system of the elbow joint is the same as the coordinate system of the shoulder joint. In the arm model construction setting, the elbow joint is a swivel joint, and the degree of freedom of rotation is only one. Therefore, according to the shoulder joint position $p_{shoulder}$, the elbow joint position p_{elbow} and the handle position p_{hand},

$$\begin{aligned} V_{e2s} &= p_{shoulder} - p_{elbow} \\ V_{e2h} &= p_{hand} - p_{elbow} \end{aligned} \tag{5}$$

Where V_{e2s} represents the unit vector of the elbow joint pointing to the shoulder joint, and V_{e2h} represents the unit vector of the elbow joint pointing to the wrist joint. The angle α_{elbow} between V_{e2s} and V_{e2h} can be obtained by the cosine theorem,

$$\alpha_{elbow} = 180° - \arccos(V_{e2s}, V_{e2h}) \tag{6}$$

That is, the offset value α_{elbow} is added to the original elbow joint to generate a new elbow joint posture, realizing the forearm posture capture.

3   Human Model Movement Data Redirection

The animation system [10] is one of the essential subsystems of all current game graphics engines, used to create various character animations and other animation effects. Among them, skeletal animation [11] is the mainstream animation method used in animation systems. The description of the skeletal animation driver process can be explained by referring to the CMU defined ASF/AMC format file, in the present paper, the above ASF file corresponds to the skeleton model, and the AMC file corresponds to the capture data. For different bone models, the coordinate system that captures the data does not correspond to the bone model. Many researchers have done a lot of research on the matching problem between the joint points of different bones. Zhang et al. [12] proposed the automatic matching of bone joint points based on geometric feature points. Au et al. [13] proposed joint point matching for models with the same topology. In order to solve this problem, this paper adopts a capture data redirection algorithm.

3.1   Identifies the Coordinate System of the Joint Points in the Imported Skeleton Model

Because the bone model of different imported roles is not consistent with the coordinate system for capturing data, if the captured data is used directly in the skeleton model, the character animation will be confused. In order to solve the problem of the consistency between the bone model and the local coordinate system of the captured data, by constructing an intermediate built-in model that is independent of the local coordinate system of the imported model joint points, to identify the coordinate system of the imported model.

As shown in Fig. 3, pre-set the coordinate system of the joint points, and then use the coordinate system of the built-in model to identify the coordinate system of the bone joint points, to shield the difference of the local coordinate system in different bone models. The built-in model is represented by an orthogonal basis composed of the forward axis (XVector), the horizontal axis (YVector), and the vertical axis (ZVector).

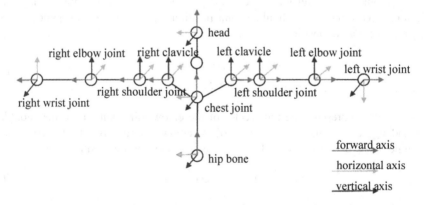

Fig. 3. Joint coordinate system convention for built-in models

3.2 Capture Data with Built-in Model Redirection

The joint coordinate system of the captured data model needs to be converted according to the joint coordinate system of the imported model, so that the axes of the captured data model are consistent with the axes of the imported model to correctly drive the imported model animation. The algorithm is as follows,

---

Algorithm 1 Capture Date Redirection Algorithm.

Input: The coordinate system $(x_d\ y_d\ z_d)$ of the captured data; The coordinate system $(x_n\ y_n\ z_n)$ of the build-in model; The coordinate system $(x_o\ y_o\ z_o)$ of the import model.

Output: The coordinate system $(x_{-d}\ y_{-d}\ z_{-d})$ of the captured data after redirection.

1: $(x_n\ y_n\ z_n)$ corresponds to $(x_d\ y_d\ z_d)$, determined by Fig.2 and Fig.3;

2: $(x_{-d}\ y_{-d}\ z_{-d}) \leftarrow$ Zero.Vector

3: if x_n is identified as x_d, $x_{-d} \leftarrow x_d$;

4:     else if x_n is identified as y_d, $x_{-d} \leftarrow y_d$;

5:     else if x_n is identified as z_d, $x_{-d} \leftarrow z_d$;

6: if y_n is identified as x_d, $y_{-d} \leftarrow x_d$;

7:     else if y_n is identified as y_d, $y_{-d} \leftarrow y_d$;

8:     else if y_n is identified as z_d, $y_{-d} \leftarrow z_d$;

9: if z_n is identified as x_d, $z_{-d} \leftarrow x_d$;

10:     else if z_n is identified as y_d, $z_{-d} \leftarrow y_d$;

11:     else if z_n is identified as z_d, $z_{-d} \leftarrow z_d$;

---

4 Experimental Analysis and Evaluation

4.1 VR Arm Motion Capture Experiment Verification

The technical research of this paper is realized through the development of UnrealEngine4 [14] platform. The hardware environment in which the system runs: Intel(R) Core (TM) i7-6700 K CPU, 32 GB RAM, NVIDIA GeForce GTX1080 graphics card and a set of HTC VIVE and 3 Tracker. Software environment: Windows 10 operating system, Microsoft Visual Studio 2017, UnrealEngine 4.18.

Action Picture Sequence Verification

The experiment selected four sets of simple movements of arm stretching, waving, elbow flexion and arm crossing as test actions [15]. In the course of the experiment, record the user's actual arm movements and VR arm movements simultaneously with a computer, and record the curve of the shoulder abduction angle $\alpha_{shoulder}$, the shoulder joint flexion angle $\beta_{shoulder}$, the shoulder joint internal rotation angle $\gamma_{shoulder}$ and the elbow joint flexion and extension angle α_{elbow} during exercise. The entire test process is as follows: After the tester wears the device, the left hand is taken as an example to collect the arm motion information. The real-time synchronously acquired video is intercepted as a sequence of synchronized action pictures, and time points are marked in the joint angle change curve for image comparison.

Through the comparison of the pictures of the four sets of action picture sequences t1 to t5 in Fig. 4, the virtual character arm movement is basically the same as the test character arm movement, and there is no misalignment of the joint position during the capture process, and the virtual character model basically tracks the real-time motion of the human body accurately.

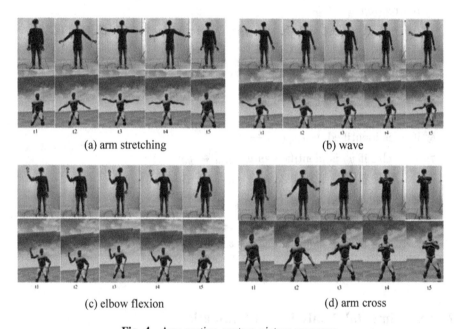

(a) arm stretching

(b) wave

(c) elbow flexion

(d) arm cross

Fig. 4. Arm motion capture picture sequence

In order to further analyze the changes in the angle of the arm joint during exercise, the curves in Fig. 5 are the time-dependent angular curves of the shoulder joint abduction angle $\alpha_{shoulder}$, the shoulder joint flexion angle $\beta_{shoulder}$, the shoulder joint internal rotation angle $\gamma_{shoulder}$, and the elbow joint flexion angle α_{elbow}, respectively. Each group of actions is periodically repeated three times, and one of the periods T (or half of the period of 0.5T) is selected for analysis, and a total of five time points from t1 to t5 are selected for analysis, corresponding to the sequence of motion pictures of Fig. 6. The experimental results show that the joint angle changes consistently with the motion, and the joint angle curve is smooth, indicating that the data is a smooth change.

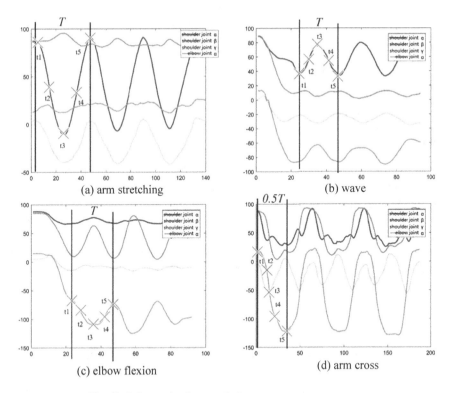

Fig. 5. Joint angle changes during arm movement capture

(a) bend the elbow horizontally   (b) bend the elbow vertically

Fig. 6. IK method (left hand) vs. this method (right hand) (Color figure online)

4.2   Compared with Existing Methods

Compared with IK Method

In order to facilitate the comparison, the tester's right hand adopts the IK method and the left hand adopts the scheme method.

It can be seen from the comparison of the left and right hands of the third figure in Fig. 6(a) that the real arm is in a flat state (shown by a red dotted line), and the right hand of the avatar's arm is tilted at a certain angle (yellow dotted line). The right-handed action using the IK method does not match the actual action. Similarly, as can be seen from the fourth image in Fig. 6(b), the real tester's arm is folded in a vertical state, and the right hand of the avatar's arm is tilted at a certain angle. The right-handed action using the IK method does not match the actual action.

Compared with Kinect-Based Motion Capture

The method using Kinect motion capture is compared with this method, and the results are shown in Fig. 7. It can be seen from the Fig. 7(a) the difference between virtual character movement and real character movement is obvious. At the same time, the palm position is slightly biased. But the virtual model in Fig. 7(b) is basically consistent with the action of real people. Figure 7(c) shows that the avatar's hand joints are misaligned, which is inconsistent with the actual; the two arms of the character model are inseparable, but the virtual model in Fig. 7(d) does not show a similar situation. Therefore, the data captured by Kinect does not reconstruct the joint coordinates of the avatar very well, and the capture effect is poor.

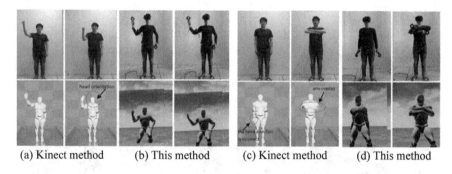

(a) Kinect method   (b) This method   (c) Kinect method   (d) This method

Fig. 7. Wave cross and arm cross motion capture effect

5   Conclusion

The kinematics-based virtual reality arm motion capture method proposed in this paper achieves low-cost and high-precision motion capture. Virtual characters can basically track the real-time movement of the human body and effectively restore the actual arm movements in virtual reality. Compared with the existing methods, it can make up for the shortcomings of the existing methods.

Acknowledgements. This work in this paper is supported by the National Natural Science Foundation of China (Nos. 61672358 and Nos. 61836005).

References

1. Li, Y., Gai, K., Ming, Z., Zhao, H., Qiu, M.: Intercrossed access controls for secure financial services on multimedia big data in cloud systems. ACM Trans. Multimedia Comput. Commun. Appl. **12(4)**, 10 (2016)
2. Li, Y., Dai, W., Ming, Z., Qiu, M.: Privacy protection for preventing data over-collection in smart city. IEEE Trans. Comput. **65**(5), 1339–1350 (2016)
3. Qiu, M., Ming, Z., Chen, Z., Qin, X.: Security-aware optimization for ubiquitous computing systems with SEAT graph approach. J. Comput. Syst. Sci. **79**(5), 518–529 (2013)
4. Biocca, F., Delaney, B.: Immersive virtual reality technology. In: Biocca, F., Levy, M.R. (eds.) Communication in the age of virtual reality, pp. 57–124. Lawrence Erlbaum Associates (1995)
5. Jiang, J., Li, Y.: Interactive model of virtual reality. Integr. Circ. Appl. **33**(12), 84–86 (2016)
6. Zhang, F., Dai, G., Peng, X.: Overview of virtual reality human interaction. Chin. Sci. Inf. Sci. (12), 1711–1736 (2016)
7. Baerlocher, P., Boulic, R.: Parametrization and range of motion of the ball-and-socket joint. In: Magnenat-Thalmann, N., et al. (eds.) Deformable Avatars, pp. 180–190. Springer (2001)
8. Craig, J.J.: Spatial descriptions and transformations. In: Introduction to Robotics: Mechanics and Control, 3rd edn. Pearson Education (1986)
9. Akenine-Möller, T., Haines, E., Hoffman, N.: Transforms. In: Real-Time Rendering, 3rd edn. A K Peter (2008)
10. Ye Jingfeng translation: Game Engine Architecture. Electronic Industry Press (2014)
11. Baran, I., Popovi, J.: Automatic rigging and animation of 3D characters. ACM Trans. Graph. **26**(3), 72 (2007)
12. Zhang, H., Sheffer, A., Cohen-Or, D., et al.: Deformation-driven shape correspondence. Comput. Graph. Forum **27**(5), 1431–1439 (2008)
13. Au, K.C., Tai, C.L., Cohen-Or, D., et al.: Electors voting for fast automatic shape correspondence. Comput. Graph. Forum **29**(2), 645–654 (2010)
14. Virtual engine animation system [EB/OL], 16 September 2017. https://www.unrealengine.com/
15. Zhang, D., Chen, X., Zhao, S., et al.: Posture recognition method based on Kinect Predefined bone. Comput. Appl. **34**(12), 3441–3445 (2014)

Financial News Quantization and Stock Market Forecast Research Based on CNN and LSTM

Shubin Cai[1], Xiaogang Feng[1], Ziwei Deng[1], Zhong Ming[1(✉)], and Zhiguang Shan[2]

[1] College of Computer Science and Software Engineering, Shenzhen University, Shenzhen, China
mingz@szu.edu.cn
[2] State Information Center of China, Beijing, China
shangzg@cei.gov.cn

Abstract. The changes of stock market and the predictions of the price have become hot topics. When machine learning emerged, it has been used in the stock market forecast research. In recent years, the vertical development of machine learning has led to the emergence of deep learning. Therefore, this paper proposes and realizes the CNN and LSTM forecasting model with financial news and historical data of stock market, which uses deep learning methods to quantify text and mine the laws of stock market changes and analyze whether they can predict changes. According to the results from this paper, this method has certain accuracy in predicting the future changes of the stock market, which provides help to study the inherent laws of stock market changes.

Keywords: Deep learning · Text quantification · CNN · LSTM
Stock market forecasting

1 Introduction

In domestic academic circle, as early as 2012, some people used machine learning to mine the content of news, which proved that news had a strong impact on the stock market [1].

Now deep learning has also been used in stock market investments. Deep learning neural network is a highly complex nonlinear artificial intelligence system. It is an artificial simulation of human brain abstraction and representativeness. It has the ability of self-organization and self-adjustment. It is suitable for dealing with complex nonlinear problems with multi-factors and random-like. At the same time, the content of financial news can be quantified into a word matrix by using neural network method. Thus, after quantifying the content of the news text, it can be added to the training in the deep learning neural network.

CNN and LSTM, as novel neural networks, each has their own characteristics. CNN can train the data set after the news text is converted into a numerical matrix. The LSTM has a timing concept, which can implement multiple inputs and outputs

© Springer Nature Switzerland AG 2018
M. Qiu (Ed.): SmartCom 2018, LNCS 11344, pp. 366–375, 2018.
https://doi.org/10.1007/978-3-030-05755-8_36

according to time series, train data with timing properties, and solve the vanishing gradient problem through the memory gate.

It was decided to use CNN and LSTM these two deep learning algorithms to study the forecast. The main problems solved in this paper include quantifying the title and content of financial news with machine learning, Baidu Index and tendency dictionary; combining the historical data of stock market into various training sets. This paper establishes two kinds of input data prediction models of CNN for text matrix and numerical value and LSTM for text quantization value: predicting the future ups and downs of individual stocks in the stock market, and setting trading strategies to calculate the rate of return.

By combining financial news with historical data of stock market, this paper applies deep learning to the analysis of stock market changes in order to predict the changes in the stock market. According to the forecasting results, we formulate trading strategies, calculate the return rate, and analyze the inherent law. And the deep learning method combined with financial news and stock market history applied to the forecast analysis of domestic stock market provides certain theoretical and practical value.

2 Related Work

2.1 Text Quantification Method

It is generally necessary to quantify text into numerical data for use in model input. From the article of Deep learning for stock market prediction from financial news articles [2], it is known that there are various methods for the quantitative processing of news texts, and get a variety of quantized data, such as: word embedding vector, sentence embedding vector, event embedding vector, word bag, and structured event tuple, etc.

In this paper, four text quantification methods are proposed, which refer to the common ways of many related literatures and the background of domestic stock market.

One is to quantify the news headline as a word vector. The second is to extract the keywords from each news by the TF-IDF method, and then quantize them into word vectors. The third is to extract the keywords from each news by the TF-IDF method, and then use the relevant weight calculation method to obtain a certain number of news set keywords to obtain the Baidu Index, that is, to quantify the news set into the Baidu Index. The last one is to use the relevant mathematical formula to deal with the word frequency of words in the news concentration, and quantify the value of the trend.

2.2 Deep Learning Model

CNN Model. Referring to the Internet short text classification method based on convolutional neural network [3], and based on text quantization and input data set structure, we constructed two kinds of CNN prediction models. The text type (word vector) data set (headline and keyword training set in news) and the numerical data set (Baidu Index, rise and fall tendency data set in news and historical stock market data set) are processed separately.

At the same time, it is tuned in terms of the number of convolution layers, the size of the convolution window, multiple convolutions, feature splicing, and the number of fully connected layers.

LSTM Model. LSTM mainly adds memory units to each unit. The entrance of these memory units is mainly controlled by three gates: input gate, forgetting gate and output gate. The operation functions include saving, writing and reading. These gates are logical units that use the error function of the selective memory feedback to correct the parameters as the gradient decreases, selectively forgetting and partially or fully accepting based on the weighted corrections of the feedback. In this way, each neuron will not be modified, so that the gradient will not disappear for many times, the weights of the previous layers can be modified accordingly, and the error function will descend faster with the gradient.

Adjusting the number of LSTM hidden layers and the probability of forgetting the memory unit gating can make the model get better results.

3   Text Quantification and Stock Market Prediction

3.1   Research Process

See the (Fig. 1).

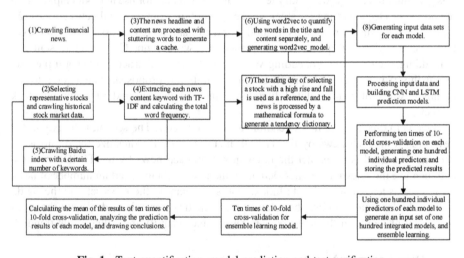

Fig. 1. Text quantification, model prediction and test verification

3.2   Financial News Quantification

The article Research on Web Text Mining Application of Machine Learning Algorithm [4], which has done research on information extraction, text classification, text clustering, has much reference value on the extraction and processing of financial news keywords based on machine learning.

It is important to note that this study not only calculates the prediction accuracy of the model, but also calculates the yield rate of the model. Therefore, based on the T + 1 trading system of the Chinese stock market, the data on the T day and the previous data will be used to predict the rise and fall of the T + 2 day compared to the T + 1 day. So the trading day is required to be a time series to build the corresponding training data set.

The financial news obtained by crawling is stored in a local database, quantified by various methods as follows, and then combined with stock market historical data to form input set data.

Headline Data Format in News. The headlines of all financial news of the day are concatenated with spaces as separators, and the word segmentation is used to perform word segmentation. The word2vec is used later to convert these words into a numerical matrix. It is used as a text quantification format for daily financial news.

Content Keyword Data Format in News. The main content of all financial news on the day is segmented using the TF-IDF method in the slogan segmentation method and the first 20 keywords are extracted for filtering as a key content of a news. Then link all the key words of the financial news content of the day, and then use word2vec to process, using it as a text quantification format for daily financial news.

Baidu Index Data Format in News. The main content of all financial news obtained by crawling is segmented by the TF-IDF method in the singular word segmentation and the first 20 keywords in each news are extracted. Then calculate the weights of the keywords in all the news, and select a certain number of important words to obtain the corresponding Baidu Index.

In this study, 50 words were selected, and after climbing the corresponding Baidu Index data, the rate of change of the corresponding index of all words per day was calculated.

Rise and Fall Tendency Data Format in News. Referring to *Stock Market Prediction Using Neural Network through News on Online Social Networks* [5], the mathematical method of converting daily news into stock market ups and downs, and quantifying financial news calculations into future stock market ups and downs, referring to its theory, make a slight adjustment to adapt to the training input, and the main mathematical formula is:

$$P(\mathrm{w}_i|\mathrm{c}) = \frac{1}{total_c} \sum\nolimits_{j=1}^{n_c} count(\mathrm{w}_i, \mathrm{m}_j) \tag{1}$$

First of all, because the performance of each stock in the market is not the same, it needs to be dealt with for individual stocks, and a special tendency reference dictionary is obtained.

All financial news is processed by word segmentation, then the weight of words in each category is calculated by (1), w_i represents a single word, m_j stands for single news, c is classification (rise or fall), and $total_c$ represents words in the classification.

The function of *count* counts the number of w_i in m_j, and thus $P(w_i|c)$ is the percentage of a word that appears in the c category.

$$P(m \in c) = P(c) \prod_{i=1}^{n_m} P(w_i|c) \tag{2}$$

(2) Calculate the tendency of a single financial news to rise and fall, where $P(w_i|c) = \frac{1}{total_c}$, and $P(c_1) = \frac{total_{c1}}{total_{c1} + total_{c2}}$.

$$v_{c_1} = p(m) = \frac{P(m \in c_1)}{P(m \in c_1) + P(m \in c_2)} \tag{3}$$

$$v_{c_2} = p(m) = \frac{-P(m \in c_2)}{P(m \in c_1) + P(m \in c_2)} \tag{4}$$

The two formulas here have changed compared with the original text, the (3) and (4) formulas can be used to calculate the tendency of each financial news to rise and fall.

$$V_{ci} = \frac{1}{n} \sum_{j=1}^{n_i} v_{cj} \tag{5}$$

Finally, the average value of (5) formula is used to get the tendency of daily financial news to rise or fall respectively.

Through the above series of calculations, the daily financial news can be converted into the trend of the future stock market ups and downs, which are two values: the rising tendency value and the falling tendency value. These two values are used as one of the textual quantization format on daily financial news.

3.3   Model Tuning

CNN Model Tuning

Textual Dataset Prediction Model. For the Chinese words in these two training sets, you need to use word2vec to convert them into numerical matrices before you can input them into the CNN model for training calculation.

CNN is mainly used to process and identify pictures in principle, so the input content is a matrix, and the number of rows and columns is certain. The number of columns is the number of words converted ito the value matrix by the word word2vec, and the number of lines is the number of words, which is the number of words in a piece of data (in a day's news). Because the number of news is different every day, it is necessary to cut off or supplement the number of words before word2vec processing to ensure that the number of training sets is certain.

The length and width of the convolution window in CNN are generally much smaller than the length and width of the input set. But in the text input here, one line represents a word, so the length of the convolution window should be consistent with the dimension of the word vector, only the width changes (i.e. the number of words included). The structure of the text data CNN prediction model is shown in Fig. 2.

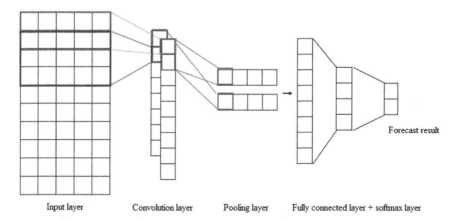

Input layer   Convolution layer   Pooling layer   Fully connected layer + softmax layer

Fig. 2. CNN text dataset prediction model structure

The predictive model is based on the CNN structure, mainly for parameter tuning. Based on the time of input data, the forecast is the closing price of the second trading day in the future. This is because the Chinese stock exchanges implement the T + 1 system, which means that after buying a stock, it takes a second trading day to trade, and the second trading day is expected to rise and fall in order to calculate the rate of return and conform to the actual situation.

It can be seen from the figure that the number of convolution kernels is consistent with the number of input matrix columns, and there are multiple convolution kernels (the number of rows is different), and then pooling to obtain various feature maps and spliced. Connecting a fully connected layer, mapping to a certain number of neurons, and then using the softmax layer to learn the classification result of the rise or fall.

The first step is to adjust the number of iterations of the training set, and then adjusting the size and number of convolution kernels and the number of single core feature maps. Replacing the activation function with the linear correction activation function ReLU to accelerate the training. Then using the pooled kernel with the size of 2 * 2 and the maximum value method for pooling, and then splicing the extracted feature matrix into the fully connected layer. Adjusting the number of neurons in the fully connected layer, and applying the abandonment technology to the whole connect layers to reduce overfitting. Adding L2 regularization at the softmax layer, and finally adjusting the model learning rate so that it can converge to better results.

Numerical Dataset Prediction Model. The input data in these two training sets are already numerical values, so no special processing is required. What needs to be done is to standardize the data. Different from the text word vector, the two training values are already the values obtained by the word conversion, so the length of the convolution window does not need to be fixed, and the length and width thereof are variable. The numerical data CNN prediction model structure is shown in Fig. 3.

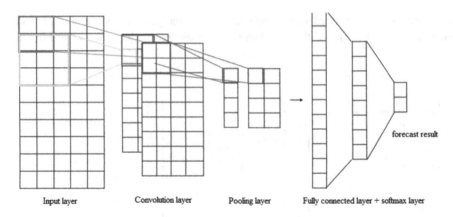

Input layer   Convolution layer   Pooling layer   Fully connected layer + softmax layer

Fig. 3. CNN numerical dataset prediction model structure

The structure of the numerical data set prediction model is similar to the text type, and the adjustment is basically the same. The main difference is that the number of columns of the convolution kernel is variable, so the convolution kernel with the same length and width is set. Because the number of rows and columns of the input matrix is small, multiple convolutions are not performed to reduce features, and feature splicing is also used to process the result of convolution pooling.

LSTM Model Tuning. The prediction model is based on the LSTM structure, which is mainly used for parameter tuning. Here, ten trading days are used to form a single time series, which predicts the closing price of the second trading day in the future.

The first is to adjust the number of iterations of the training set. As the training data is composed of time series data in days, and the data set is not large, so it only needs to iterate a certain number of times, but not too many times, otherwise it will be over-fitting. Then adjusting the number of hidden layer neurons, too little learning is insufficient, too much may ignore important data. Then the number of hidden layers is adjusted, which is the same as the number of neurons. Adjusting the bias of the input gate, output gate, and forgetting gate in the neuron, generally setting the offset of the forgetting gate and the proportion of the dropout output. Finally, adjusting the model learning rate so that it can converge to better results.

4   Experiments and Evaluation

The trading strategy adopts relatively simple and uniform rules. For example, in the CNN and LSTM models of this study, the output of model is a two-category result of whether the shock is rising or fall on the second trading day after holding the shock one day. If the predicted result is rising, then the rate of return is calculated in combination with the actual rate of change.

4.1   Prediction Model

TW-CNN: CNN architecture prediction model with the news title as input.
BW-CNN: CNN architecture prediction model based on the news keyword word vector.
BI-CNN:: CNN architecture prediction model based on Baidu Index with news content set as keyword.
BM&S-CNN: CNN architecture prediction model based on individual stock historical data and individual stock price change trend value calculated by the mathematical formula of news content.
S-LSTM: LSTM architecture prediction model based on individual stock historical data.
BI&S-LSTM: LSTM architecture prediction model based on Baidu Index and individual stock historical data.
BM&S-LSTM: LSTM architecture prediction model based on individual stock price change trend and historical data of individual stock.
EL-MODEL: The final model generated by ensemble learning.

4.2   Overall Analysis

In SAIC Motor and IFLYTEK, the prediction accuracy of the LSTM model is higher than that of the CNN model; while in PAIC, the prediction accuracy of the CNN model is higher than that of the LSTM model.

The difference is that the accuracy of the EL-MODEL is not the highest. Generally speaking, the effect of the model generated by ensemble learning is better than that of all individual models, but the result here is not the case. In fact, in all prediction models, only the S-LSTM model with stock market historical data has the best prediction effect.

The following shows some chart analysis of the forecast accuracy of each model, analysis of the unified trading day data, and the accuracy of each model in the forecast of each rise and fall (Figs. 4, 5 and 6).

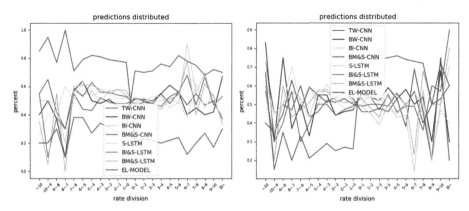

Fig. 4. Forecast accuracy of each model of SAIC Motor in each fluctuation range

Fig. 5. Forecast accuracy of each model of PAIC in each fluctuation range

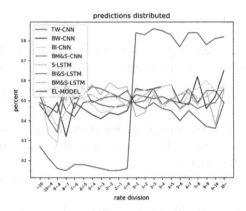

Fig. 6. Forecast accuracy of each model of IFLYTEK in each fluctuation range

As can be seen from the figure, except for the BM&S-CNN model and EL-MODEL, the curves of other models are similar, the accuracy of the high fall range is low, and the accuracy of the medium-low rise and fall is around 0.5, while the accuracy of the high gain range is slightly higher.

The BM&S-CNN model differs greatly from other models in SAIC Motor, with higher accuracy in the falling range and lower accuracy in the rising range. In PAIC and IFLYTEK, there are fewer differences from other model curves.

In the three stocks, EL-MODEL has a lower accuracy rate in the falling range and a higher accuracy rate in the rising range. Although the loss more because of the fall after buying, but also because there are more rises after buying, so that the yield is not low. In fact, the EL-MODEL performs well in the rising interval and has a higher accuracy. If it is possible to train in a targeted manner on the downside of trading day by EL-MODEL, it should be able to effectively improve the overall accuracy.

5   Conclusion

This paper implements a stock market prediction model based on CNN and LSTM neural network with multiple combinations of financial news and historical data of stock market.

We mainly developed four text quantification methods, which are quantification of news headline words, TF-IDF keyword quantification of news content, Baidu Index of news set keywords, and quantification of news content trend value.

The text quantitative prediction model and pure numerical prediction model are constructed for the two kinds of training sets of CNN. LSTM builds a prediction model, optimizes the parameters from various aspects, and finally generates seven prediction models. According to ensemble learning method, the seven models are constructed into an ensemble model to get a total model, and the accuracy and profitability of all models are tested by 10-fold cross-validation method ten times.

Unfortunately, all models have lower prediction accuracy. It is far lower than the accuracy of 66.7% obtained by scholars such as Meng [6] using KNN algorithm. Actually, from the research of scholars such as Vargas [7], CNN and LSTM models with financial news texts as input can have better prediction effects in US stocks and the predictive accuracy rate can reach 65.08%.

However, this study used 10-fold cross-validation method to evaluate the effect of the model better, rather than just selecting a more recent trading day as a test set in other literature studies. When dealing with text and generating tendency dictionary, we also consider the 10-fold situation, and generate different data sets, which makes the prediction more rigorous.

In fact, we should first apply the method of researching US stocks to the domestic stock market, analyze its effects and optimize it, and then add the characteristic factors which have great influence on the domestic stock market to study, so that we can get better results.

Acknowledgements. The research in this paper was supported by the National Natural Science Foundation of China (Nos. 61672358 and Nos. 61836005).

References

1. Zhao, L., Zhao, Q., Yang, J., Wang, T., Li, Q.: Quantitative analysis of the impact of financial news on Chinese stock market. J. Shandong Univ.: Sci. Ed. **47**(7), 70–75 (2012)
2. Chong, E., Han, C., Park, F.: Deep learning networks for stock market analysis and prediction. Expert Syst. Appl. **83**, 187–205 (2017)
3. Guo, D., Liu, X., Zheng, Q.: Internet short text classification method based on convolutional neural network. Comput. Modernization **4**, 78–81 (2017)
4. Chang, Q.: Research on application of web text mining based on machine learning algorithm. Master thesis, Tianjin University, Tianjin (2010)
5. Chen, W., Yan, Z., Chai, K., Lau, C.: Stock market prediction using neural network through news on online social networks. In: International Smart Cities Conference (2017)
6. Meng, X., Yang, Y., Zhao, X.: Financial news and stock market investment strategy research: text mining based on financial website. Invest. Res. **35**(8), 29–37 (2016)
7. Vargas, M., Lima, B., Evsukoff, A.: Deep learning for stock market prediction from financial news articles. In: IEEE International Conference on Computational Intelligence and Virtual Environments for Measurement Systems and Applications, pp. 60–65 (2017)
8. Li, Y., Gai, K., Ming, Z., Zhao, H., Qiu, M.: Intercrossed access controls for secure financial services on multimedia big data in cloud systems. ACM Trans. Multimed. Comput. Commun. Appl. **12**(4), 67:1–67:18 (2016)
9. Li, Y., Dai, W., Ming, Z., Qiu, M.: Privacy protection for preventing data over-collection in smart city. IEEE Trans. Comput. **65**(5), 1339–1350 (2016)
10. Qiu, M., Ming, Z., Chen, Z., Qin, X.: Security-aware optimization for ubiquitous computing systems with SEAT graph approach. J. Comput. Syst. Sci. **79**(5), 518–529 (2013)
11. Shun, R.: Research on price trend prediction model of US stock index based on LSTM neural network. Master thesis, Capital University of Economics and Business, Beijing (2016)

Correlation Coefficient Based Cluster Data Preprocessing and LSTM Prediction Model for Time Series Data in Large Aircraft Test Flights

Hanlin Zhu[1], Yongxin Zhu[1(✉)], Di Wu[1], Hui Wang[1(✉)], Li Tian[1],
Wei Mao[2], Can Feng[2], Xiaowen Zha[2], Guobao Deng[2], Jiayi Chen[2],
Tao Liu[2], Xinyu Niu[3], Kuen Hung Tsoi[3], and Wayne Luk[4]

[1] Shanghai Advanced Research Institute, Chinese Academy of Sciences,
Shanghai, China
{zhuyongxin, wanghui}@sari.ac.cn
[2] Commercial Aircraft Corporation of China Ltd., Shanghai, China
[3] Shenzhen Corerain Technologies Co. Ltd., Shenzhen, China
[4] Imperial College London, London, UK

Abstract. The Long Short-Term Memory (LSTM) model has been applied in recent years to handle time series data in multiple application domains, such as speech recognition and financial prediction. While the LSTM prediction model has shown promise in anomaly detection in previous research, uncorrelated features can lead to unsatisfactory analysis result and can complicate the prediction model due to the curse of dimensionality. This paper proposes a novel method of clustering and predicting multidimensional aircraft time series. The purpose is to detect anomalies in flight vibration in the form of high dimensional data series, which are collected by dozens of sensors during test flights of large aircraft. The new method is based on calculating the Spearman's rank correlation coefficient between two series, and on a hierarchical clustering method to cluster related time series. Monotonically similar series are gathered together and each cluster of series is trained to predict independently. Thus series which are uncorrelated or of low relevance do not influence each other in the LSTM prediction model. The experimental results on COMAC's (Commercial Aircraft Corporation of China Ltd) C919 flight test data show that our method of combining clustering and LSTM model significantly reduces the root mean square error of predicted results.

Keywords: Cluster · Time series · Correlation coefficient · LSTM

1 Introduction

As a recent development of Recurrent Neural Networks (RNNs), Long Short-Term Memory (LSTM) network has been applied to handle time series data in multiple domains such as speech recognition and financial prediction in recent years. LSTM often achieve high accuracy in many problems by containing a memory cell that can remember long term dependencies. A typical LSTM cell contains 4 gates, each with

© Springer Nature Switzerland AG 2018
M. Qiu (Ed.): SmartCom 2018, LNCS 11344, pp. 376–385, 2018.
https://doi.org/10.1007/978-3-030-05755-8_37

their own weights and biases, leading to a high computational cost during inference among time series data.

Real-time analysis of time series data is required in aircraft test flights as the safety and stability is of great concern in airplane. In anomaly detection for aircraft, acceleration data which are collected via dozens of sensors play an important role in real-time prediction and diagnosis. Each sensor can provide a high sampling frequency time sequence and we can get a high dimensional series through a large number of sensors. The purpose is to use past data to predict future data. If the gap between predicted data and measured data exceeds a threshold value, the position of sensor which records such data may trigger an anomaly at this time.

During the test flight of the COMAC (Commercial Aircraft Corporation of China, Limited) C919 airplane, terabytes of data are collected. The data have a character of high dimension and high frequency. In previous research, the long short term memory network has shown good performance in such kind of big data. However, the high dimensionality of the data complicates their architecture.

Moreover, uncorrelated features can lead to unsatisfactory analysis and complicated prediction models, due to the curse of dimensionality. Direct deployment of LSTM prediction model in previous research fails to ensure a satisfactory prediction performance.

To minimize the impact of uncorrelated features on time series data, we propose a novel method of clustering and predicting multidimensional aircraft time series to detect anomalies in flight vibration time series in this paper. Clustering is a branch of unsupervised machine learning. In clustering, different metric functions are used to measure the distance or similarity between data or clusters, so that close data or similar data can be gathered together.

In the area of time series analysis, traditional ARMA and GARCH model have limit in dealing with the high dimensional and complex problem. LSTM neural networks overcome the vanishing gradient problem through recurrent neural networks (RNNs) by employing multiplicative gates that enforce constant error flow through the internal states of special units called 'memory cells'. Because of the ability to learn long term correlations in a sequence, LSTM networks obviate the need for a pre-specified time window and are capable of accurately modeling complex multivariate sequences.

The contributions of this paper can be summarized as follows.

(1) A prediction model which combines clustering and LSTM together to minimize the impacts of uncorrelated features in time series data.
(2) Hierarchical clustering based on Spearman's rank correlation coefficient between two series to gather the monotonically similar series, and to remove the unrelated ones.
(3) Modification of the LSTM model for training and prediction in each cluster filtered in the clustering stage.
(4) Evaluation of our method with COMAC's C919 flight test.

The following outlines the rest of this paper. Section 2 introduces related work. Section 3 presents the basic algorithm and our combination model. Section 4 shows the experimental results and discussion. Section 5 draws a brief conclusion.

2   Related Work

There are many studies focusing on series tendency analysis, time series clustering and time series prediction.

Cao et al. [1] introduced a framework of real-time anomaly detection for flight testing. They used this method to solve other kinds of similar problems based on transfer learning. Their approach is to establish an anomaly detection model for dangerous actions of aircraft testing fights.

Hsu et al. [2] introduced a feature selection method through Pearson's correlation coefficient clustering. They used Pearson's correlation coefficient to measure the similarity between variables and clustered the features through hierarchical clustering. They used the UCI Arrhythmia dataset and SVM algorithm for experiment and analysis the validity of the method.

Gauthier [3] introduced a trends detection method through Spearman's rank correlation coefficient. He used the Spearman's rank correlation coefficient and Mann-Kendall test to analysis the similarity of MTBE data.

In the relevant area, cloudlet-based mobile cloud computing [8], reinforcement learning [12], K-means and PCA algorithm [6] are also used to analyze the data. In order to improve the efficiency of status detection, the FPGAs are used to accelerate Genetic programming [7], one-class SVM [9] and some other algorithms.

3   LSTM Joint Cluster Architecture

3.1   Spearman's Rank Correlation Coefficient

Spearman's rank correlation coefficient or Spearman's rho is similar to Pearson's correlation, which can be used to measure how well the relationship between two variables. It is a nonparametric measure of rank correlation. The difference between Spearman correlation and Pearson correlation is that the former can assess monotonic relationships (whether linear or not).

Suppose we have two series x_i and y_i, The Spearman's rank correlation coefficient can be calculated through the following equation:

$$r_s = 1 - \frac{6 \sum d_i^2}{n(n-1)} \tag{1}$$

where x_i is the difference between ranks for each x_i, y_i data pair and is the number of data pairs.

Spearman's coefficient can be applied to both continuous and discrete data. When there are no repeated data and each variables is a perfect monotone function of the other, a perfect Spearman correlation occurs. If data have a similar rank, Spearman correlation will get close to +1. On the contrary, if data have a dissimilar rank, it will decline to −1. Besides, if two series aren't related, it will close to 0.

3.2   Hierarchical Agglomerative Clustering

Hierarchical Agglomerative Clustering establishes a nested clustering tree according to the degree of similarity between data objects that do not belong to the same category [5]. Firstly, Hierarchical Agglomerative Clustering uses each raw data point as one class, and calculate the distance between different classes of data points. The smaller the distance, the higher the similarity. In our work, the closer the absolute value of correlation coefficient is to 1, the closer the two sequences are. This techniques involve aggregating the categories with the smallest distance and iterating through the process, until the number of categories reaches the expected value or other termination conditions are met.

There are three ways to calculate the distance between two categories of data: Single Linkage, Complete Linkage and Average Linkage. Single Linkage takes the distance between two data objects with the smallest distance among the data objects belonging to different categories as the distance between the data objects of the two categories. Complete Linkage just does the opposite, which takes the largest distance as the distance between different categories.

3.3   LSTM Prediction Model in Time Series

The Long Short-Term Memory (LSTM) architecture, which uses purpose-built memory cells to store information, is good at finding and exploiting long range dependencies in the data, which is very suitable for flight time series data [4]. Figure 1 illustrates a single LSTM memory cell.

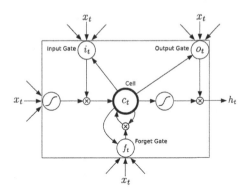

Fig. 1. Long Short Term Memory cell.

For the version of LSTM used in this paper, H is implemented by the following composite function:

$$
\begin{aligned}
i_t &= \sigma(W_{xi}x_t + W_{hi}h_{t-1} + W_{ci}c_{t-1} + b_i) \\
f_t &= \sigma(W_{xf}x_t + W_{hf}h_{t-1} + W_{cf}c_{t-1} + b_f) \\
c_t &= f_t c_{t-1} + i_t tanh(W_{xc}x_t + W_{hc}h_{t-1} + b_c) \\
o_t &= \sigma(W_{xo}x_t + W_{ho}h_{t-1} + W_{co}c_t + b_o) \\
h_t &= o_t tanh(c_t)
\end{aligned}
\tag{2}
$$

where σ is the logistic sigmoid function, and i, f, o and c are respectively the input gate, forget gate, output gate, cell and cell input activation vectors, all of which are the same size as the hidden vector h. W_{hi} is the hidden-input gate matrix, W_{xo} is the input-output gate matrix etc. The weight matrices from the cell to gate vectors (f.g. W_{ci}) are diagonal. So element m in each gate vector only receives input from element m of the cell vector. The bias terms (which are added to i, f, c and o) have been omitted for clarity [10].

The original LSTM algorithm adopts a custom designed approximate gradient calculation that allows the weights to be updated after each time step. However, the full gradient can instead be calculated with back propagation through time.

3.4   Combination of Cluster and LSTM Analysis Model

After data preprocessing, we calculate the Spearman's rank correlation coefficient between each two series and get the correlation coefficient matrix. The heat map of this matrix is shown in Fig. 2:

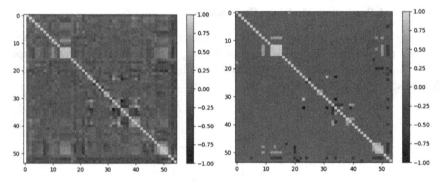

Fig. 2. The left figure is Spearman's rank correlation coefficient matrix heat map. The right figure is the Spearman's rank correlation coefficient matrix heat map which set the correlation coefficient that the absolute of it less than 0.5 be 0.

As is shown in Fig. 2, the brighter or darker point means that two series linked to this point is correlated. The brighter one shows the similar tendency of two series, while the darker ones shows the opposite but related tendency. In the process of clustering the series, our aim is gathering the series whose Spearman's rank correlation coefficient between them is closed to +1 or −1. Similar to the hierarchical group method in [11], this process is described in Table 1.

In the clustering process, we gather the high related series together. At the same time, we abandon the series which are not related to any other series.

After the preprocessing, we build an LSTM prediction model to analyse the data. Our LSTM model includes LSTM layers and full connected layers. We use 128 LSTM layers to get the information from input data and 19 dense layers to export the predicted output. The loss function as MAE (Mean Absolute Error) and the optimizer is Adam. The whole framework is shown in Fig. 3.

Table 1. Pseudo-code of clustering based on the Spearman's rho

---

Input Parameters: series set=$\{x_1, x_2, \ldots, x_m,\}$;
Similarity function: Correlation_Coefficient (a_i, a_j);
Threshold value:λ;
Aim number of cluster:k

---

for i $= 1,2,\ldots,$ m do
  $C_i = \{x_i\}$
  for j $= 1,2,\ldots,$ m do
    $r_{i,j} = $ Correlation_Coefficient (x_i, x_j);
  end for
end for
for i $= 1,2,\ldots,$ m do
  for j $= 1,2,\ldots,$ m **do**
    $M(i,j) = r_{i,j}$;
    $M(j,i) = M(i,j)$
  end for
end for
set original cluster number: q $= $ m
while q $>$ k do
  find two cluster C_{i^*} and C_{j^*} whose absolute value of Spearman's rho is biggest
    if Abs(M(i^*, j^*)) $< \lambda$ do
      break whole process
    /* When all the distance between two clusters are
    less than the threshold, the similarity between the two
    clusters are small. */
    else do
      merge C_{i^*} and C_{j^*} : $C_{i^*} = C_{i^*} \cup C_{j^*}$
      for j $= j^* + 1, j^* + 1, \ldots, q$ do
        renumber the C_j to C_{j-1}
      end for
      delete the j^{*th} row and j^{*th} column
      for j $= 1,2,\ldots,q-1$ do
        for i in C_{i^*} do
          $r_{i,j} = $ Correlation_Coefficient (x_i, x_j)
        end for
        M(i^*, j)=max(r_{*j})
      end for
    q $= $ q $- 1$
end while

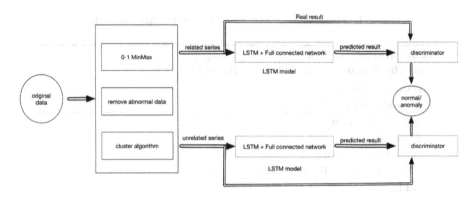

Fig. 3. Correlation coefficient based cluster and LSTM prediction model.

4   Experimental Results and Analysis

We set up our experiments to evaluate the effectiveness of our method for anomaly detection of time series. The settings are as follows.

The operating system we use is Ubuntu16.04. Our server has "Intel(R) Xron(R) CPU E5−2680 v4 2.40 GHz" CPU and "NVIDIA Tesla K80" GPU. The language we choose is python3.5 and the main toolkit we use is Keras, Tensorflow, matplotlib, numpy and pandas.

We use the real data of the COMAC C919 aircraft during a test flight. The data contain the time series of 56 sensors at a 6K sampling frequency. We deal with the data using the MinMaxScaler method. During the process, we find certain sample values to be constant. These abnormal data are eliminated in the preprocess. We extract the preprocessed data from 54 sensors at 10,000 sample points for further processing.

After calculating the correlation coefficient and the clustering algorithm is in operation, we get the required classes. Figure 4 shows two clusters with strong correlations obtained by clustering. For comparison, we also draw a sequence group with weak correlation (Fig. 5).

In the comparison of the two figures, it can be found that clustering results in a highly correlated sequence, which also has a visually related growth trend. Among them, the orange line in the second cluster (Fig. 4 bottom) means that the line has an opposite but very relevant trend with other sequences.

Before training, we change the format of data. We use the data of previous 10 sampling points to predict the data of later sampling point. Since each sampling point has 19 dimensions of data, our input is a 10×19 matrix and output is a 1×19 matrix.

In the next experiment, we design the LSTM model for training and predictive analysis. We put the closely related sequences and the sequences which are used in [1] into our LSTM model. After several rounds of training, we get the maps of MAE and training rounds, as shown in Fig. 6.

After error calculation, we get the following RMSE (Root Mean Square Error) in Table 2.

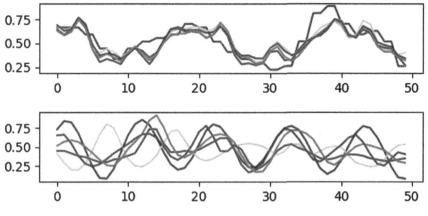

Fig. 4. Two clusters of related series.

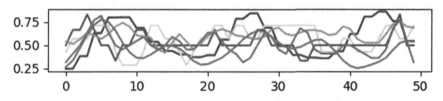

Fig. 5. Example of unrelated series.

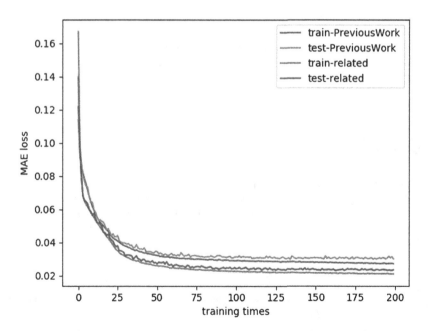

Fig. 6. MAE loss of related series and previous used series during the LSTM training.

Table 2. RMSE of the previous model and our model

	Training dataset	Test dataset
Series in reference [1]	0.002232	0.002378
Series selected via our clustering method	0.001731	0.001790

Through comparative experiments, we find that the more relevant data sets have faster convergence rate and less loss of convergence results than the randomly selected series used in previous work. Models based on clustering and LSTM have better performance in high latitude time series analysis.

5   Conclusion

We propose a novel method of clustering and predicting multidimensional aircraft time series whose analyses are challenging in data science. Given COMAC's C919 flight test data, we observe that uncorrelated information and data redundancy in high latitude sequences can interfere with the analytical capabilities of the LSTM based prediction model for the time series of flight test data. With these observations, our method integrates clustering with an LSTM model to select time series with high correlation from high latitude sequences, which improves the accuracy of the LSTM prediction model compared with recent work. Our research can be further extended to other scenarios of time series data analyses.

Acknowledgment. This work is partially supported by National Key Research & Development Program of China (2017YFA0206104), Shanghai Municipal Science and Technology Commission and Commercial Aircraft Corporation of China, Ltd. (COMAC) (175111105000), Shanghai Municipal Science and Technology Commission (18511111302, 18511103502), Key Foreign Cooperation Projects of Bureau of International Co-operation Chinese Academy of Sciences (184131KYSB20160018) and UK EPSRC (EP/L016796/1, EP/N031768/1 and EP/P010040/1).

References

1. Cao, Z., Zhu, Y., et al.: Improving prediction accuracy in LSTM network model for aircraft testing flight data. In: IEEE International Conference on Smart Cloud (2018)
2. Hsu, H., Hsieh, C.: Feature selection via correlation coefficient clustering. J. Softw. 5(12), 1371–1377 (2010)
3. Gauthier, T.: Detecting trends using spearman's rank correlation coefficient. Environ. Forensics 2, 359–362 (2001)
4. Nanduri, A., Sherry, L.: Anomaly detection in aircraft data using recurrent neural networks. In: Integrated Communications Navigation and Surveillance (ICNS) Conference (2016)
5. Grabusts, P., Borisov, A.: Clustering methodology for time series mining. Sci. J. Riga Tech. Univ. 40(1), 81–86 (2009)
6. Singhal, A., Seborg, D.: Clustering multivariate time-series data. J. Chemom. 19, 427–438 (2005)

7. Funie, A.-I., Grigoras, P., Burovskiy, P., Luk, W., Salmon, M.: Run-time reconfigurable acceleration for genetic programming fitness evaluation in trading strategies. J. Signal Process. Sys. **90**(1), 39–52 (2018)
8. Gai, K., Qiu, M., Zhao, H., et al.: Dynamic energy-aware cloudlet-based mobile cloud computing model for green computing. J. Netw. Comput. Appl. **59**, 46–54 (2016)
9. Bara, A., Niu, X., Luk, W.: A dataflow system for anomaly detection analysis. In: International Conference on Field Programmable Technology (2014)
10. Graves, A.: Generating sequences with recurrent neural networks. https://arxiv.org/abs/1308.0850
11. Cui, L., Luo, Y., Li, G., Lu, N.: Artificial bee colony algorithm with hierarchical groups for global numerical optimization. In: Qiu, M. (ed.) SmartCom 2016. LNCS, vol. 10135, pp. 72–85. Springer, Cham (2017). https://doi.org/10.1007/978-3-319-52015-5_8
12. Gai, K., Qiu, M., Liu, M., Zhao, H.: Smart resource allocation using reinforcement learning in content-centric cyber-physical systems. In: Qiu, M. (ed.) SmartCom 2017. LNCS, vol. 10699, pp. 39–52. Springer, Cham (2018). https://doi.org/10.1007/978-3-319-73830-7_5

PSPChord - A Novel Fault Tolerance Approach for P2P Overlay Network

Dan Nguyen[1], Nhat Hoang[1], Binh Minh Nguyen[1(✉)], and Viet Tran[2]

[1] School of Information and Communication Technology,
Hanoi University of Science and Technology, Hanoi, Vietnam
`dannguyen2511@gmail.com`, `nhat.hqh@gmail.com`, `minhnb@soict.hust.edu.vn`
[2] Institute of Informatics, Slovak Academy of Sciences, Bratislava, Slovakia
`viet.tran@savba.sk`

Abstract. In this paper, we propose a novel approach called PSPChord to provide efficient fault tolerance solution for Chord-based P2P overlay networks. In our proposal, the successor list is removed, instead, we design the partition-based data replication and modify finger tables. While the partition strategy is used to distribute data replicas evenly on Chord ring to reduce and balance the cost of lookup request, the finger table is added links to successor and predecessor of neighboring nodes to pass over faulty nodes. By simulating, our experiments already showed the performance of PSPChord as compared with original Chord in resolving fault tolerance problem on P2P overlay network.

Keywords: Chord · Peer-to-peer · Overlay network · Fault tolerance
Data replication · Lookup · Partition

1 Introduction

In recent years, the explosion of digital data as well as the increasing demand of data accessibility brings a requirement of large-scale systems which allow either storing a massive amount of data or serving a huge number of users. Peer-to-peer (P2P) overlay networks have emerged as viable solutions for this demand. P2P networks provide scalability due to the feature that all nodes in P2P networks play an equal role of accessing as well as sharing their resource with others. When a user requests to obtain a data at any node, P2P routing algorithm would help to find the desired data stored on other nodes and return it to the user. As a result, in principle, this allows the system to be extended limitlessly in horizontal by increasing the number of nodes instead of being dependent on the vertical limits of computation and storage capacities of a central point. In this study, we focus on fault tolerance of Chord [9].

Chord is a popular structured P2P network that was applied in many problems in different fields such as distributed and high performance systems [7], file sharing [4], key-value storage scheme [6], IoT resource discovery [8], and so on. Chord uses a distributed hash table (DHT) in form of finger table to provide a

© Springer Nature Switzerland AG 2018
M. Qiu (Ed.): SmartCom 2018, LNCS 11344, pp. 386–396, 2018.
https://doi.org/10.1007/978-3-030-05755-8_38

simple and efficient resource lookup service that require a path length $O(logN)$ for an N-node network, and also uses a successor list including a set of consecutive nodes immediate following each node for its fault tolerance. Dealing with the problem (1), data is replicated on the successor list and would be retrieve when the node storing the data gets faulty. And for the problem (2), Chord takes advantages of both the successor list and the finger table to pass over the faulty node during lookup process. Both of those approach work quite well but we argue two main shortcomings of them. Firstly, replicas are only used when the primary node storing the data gets faulty, causing the node may get overloaded while leading a waste of memory resources for the successor list. Secondly, when existing many faulty nodes, the finger table becomes inefficient to route over faulty nodes.

Therefore, with the aim of enhance Chord's fault tolerance, we propose a novel approach namely PSPChord including two contributions. Firstly, we design a partition strategy to distribute replicas of data evenly on Chord ring instead of centralize them on the successor list to reduce and balance the cost of lookup request. Secondly, we add into the finger table 2 fields pointing to successor and predecessor of each entry to provide more overlay links associated to a node, improving cost-efficient of lookup request.

2   Related Work

There are many existed works to enhance the Chord protocol. According to their approaches, we classify roughly these works into several groups as follows.

Data Replication. Data replication is a widely used strategy to avoid data loss. In [5], the authors proposed a duplication scheme to replicate the state of service components around the Chord ring. Each state of service component associated with a key k is replicated on $r-1$ nodes being responsible for keys $k + nKS/r$, where n ranges from 1 to $r-1$ and KS is the key space size (i.e. 2^m). This paper demonstrates how stateful-Byzantine-Fault-Tolerance services may be hosted on Chord ring. For each $get()$ or $put()$ operation, the node sends requests to all replica nodes. It then waits for replies from the replica nodes. Until an appropriate number of consistent replies are received, the operation is considered to be complete.

Fault Handling. Most of the proposed studies referred mechanisms of passing over a faulty node directly by finding another node to forward the request, for example [1,2], and [10]. However, those studies still worked based on finger table and successor list. Otherwise, detecting nodes at risk of fault was another approach. In [11], MR-Chord was designed with the aim of keeping the finger table fresh. The authors proposed a modified finger table by adding three new fields: the *Succ* field, the Fail field and the WeakNode field. If a lookup process through a finger entry i^{th} was successful, the *Succ* field of the entry would increase by 1. Otherwise, the fail field would increase by 1. A finger node would be considered as weak or not, depending on $Fail[i] - Succ[i] > Threshold$ is

True or False, where $Threshold$ was a predefined value. If True, the finger node i would be set to be a weak node, i.e. $WeakNode = True$, otherwise $WeakNode = False$. As a result, lookup process could avoid those weak nodes. This proposal improved lookup success rate and lookup delay time comparing the original Chord. However, in fact the $Succ$ and Fail values of an entry in finger table did not reflect the current state of that finger node (i.e. finger node is weak or not) and threshold value influences the P2P network performance.

Chord Optimization. In [1], authors proposed a scheme called NN-Chord (Neighbor's Neighbor Chord) to shorten the routing path length. Their research focused on enhancing the number of overlay links among nodes in ring by adding a routing table namely learn table. Because each node has an addition learn table, so the node holding the desired data would be reached more quickly. Beside, a variant of NN-Chord is described in [2]. The authors proposed a routing algorithm called Bidirectional Neighbor's Neighbor Chord based on NN-Chord to improve the lookup efficiently. In their scheme, each node has additionally a W_finger table and a W_learn table (like finger table and learn table but in anticlockwise). Moreover, the redundant overlay links in those tables are pruned to simplify them. The lookup process is performed in both clockwise and anticlockwise at the same time to obtain a better lookup direction. Similar to the above approaches, [10] also used two finger table for each node in two opposite directions to shorten the routing path length. Furthermore, Z-Chord system structure proposed in [3] divide Chord ring into many partitions. Each partition is managed by a super node. There are two types of routing tables, namely foreign-super-nodes-routing-table and local-area-routing-table, in this study. The foreign-super-nodes-routing-table helps to point out all super nodes on ring, while local-area-routing-table determine all nodes on a partition. Due to those routing tables, it only requires maximum 3 hops to find out the desire data. However, some drawbacks of this proposal are those: high cost for updating and difficulty for extending.

In this our study, we propose an approach namely PSPChord, that consists of two main contributions: firstly, the data replication mechanism using partition strategy, that not only solves the unbalance problem of original Chord's mechanism, but also enhances the lookup efficiency. Secondly, the modification of the finger table in order to deal with the problem of passing over faulty nodes on Chord ring.

3   Partition-Based Data Replication Mechanism on Chord Ring

As mentioned, instead of replicating data on a set of consecutive nodes like the successor list of the original Chord, we replicate data on multiple nodes which are successors of evenly distributed replica keys. Each data item now is represented by a set of $\mathcal{P}$ of $p + 1$ keys consisting of 1 identifier key and p replica keys. In order to evenly distribute these keys, the distance between two adjacent keys is a *partition* $= \frac{2^m}{p+1}$, in which 2^m is the key space size. As such, if a data item is identified by a key k, its set of representative keys is $\mathcal{P} = \{k, k + partition, k + 2 * partition, ..., k + p * partition\}$. Algorithm 1 describes the procedure of inserting a data item as follows.

- **Step 1:** Assigning identifier key k for the data.
- **Step 2:** Generating set $\mathcal{P} = \{k, k + partition, k + 2 * partition, ..., k + p * partition\}$ of representative keys for the data (see Algorithm 2).
- **Step 3:** For each key in $\mathcal{P}$, find the corresponding successor to insert data.

Algorithm 1. Key Insert

1: **function** N.INSERT(data, p)
2:    $k \leftarrow hash(data)$;
3:    $\mathcal{P} \leftarrow generateKeys(k, p)$;
4:    **for** each $key \in \mathcal{P}$ **do**
5:        $succ \leftarrow n.find\_successor(key)$;
6:        $succ.insert(k, data)$;
7:    **end for**
8: **end function**

In this direction, when looking up a data item with a given key k, the query node only needs to lookup the closest replica key of the data in the set $\mathcal{P}$ instead of looking up the key k. This reduces the maximum possible distance (in key space) between the query node and the node holding data from $2^m - 1$ down to no more than $\frac{2^m - 1}{|\mathcal{P}|}$ - the size of a partition between by two adjacent replicas. As a result, the path length of lookup process is also decrease significantly. Theoretically, the average path length of lookup process can be reduced from $\frac{1}{2}logN$ to about $\frac{1}{2}log\frac{N}{|\mathcal{P}|}$ and we would verify this by experimenting.

Algorithm 2. Replica Keys Generation

1: **function** N.GENERATEKEYS(k, p)
2:    $\mathcal{P} \leftarrow \{\}$;
3:    $\mathcal{P}.append(k)$;
4:    **for** each i from 1 to p **do**
5:        $replicaKey \leftarrow (k + i * \frac{2^m}{p+1}) mod 2^m$;
6:        $\mathcal{P}.append(replicaKey)$;
7:    **end for**
8:    **return** $\mathcal{P}$
9: **end function**

In addition, the evenly distributed replicas of data enable load balancing for lookup requests. While the destination of a same data lookup processes from any nodes in Chord always is the successor of key k, the partition-based mechanism helps to balance this burden with multiple other nodes which are the successor of the replica keys. Algorithm 4 describes the procedure of data lookup, shorten in 3 steps as follow.

– **Step 1:** Generate set $\mathcal{P}$ corresponding the key k and rearrange $\mathcal{P}$ in the closest order to the query node in clockwise.
– **Step 2:** Find the successor of the closest key in $\mathcal{P}$. If the successor is faulty, perform the finding successor for the next closest key.
– **Step 3:** Return the data received from the first found alive successor.

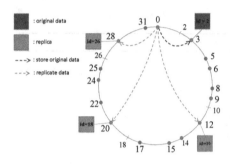

Fig. 1. Partition-based data replication

In order to provide a clear explanation, Fig. 1 illustrates an example about replication of a data item identified by key $k = 2$ on a 2^5-key-space-size ring maintained by 16 nodes. It is configured that each data is replicated to $p = 3$ replicas, thus the size of a $partition = \frac{2^5}{3+1} = 8$. Suppose that node 0 receives the request for the data insertion. According to the algorithm presented above, the set $\mathcal{P}$ of the data is 2, 10, 18, 26. As such, node 3, 12, 20 and 28 are responsible for storing the data, in which node 3 is the primary node corresponding to the identifier key $k = 2$ and the remaining nodes are replica nodes corresponding to the replica keys. If node 15 receives a key $k = 2$ lookup request, it routes to the closest replica node 20 first instead the primary node 3 whose distance (in key space) is nearly four times greater.

4   Successor-Predecessor Modification of Finger Table

With the purpose of broadening overlay links among nodes to enhance cost efficiency and fault tolerance for key lookup on Chord ring, we add two new

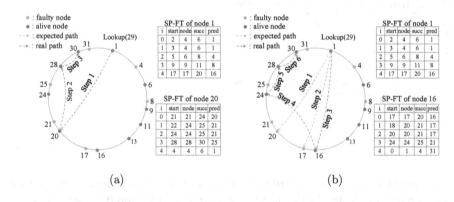

Fig. 2. SP Chord lookup process examples

fields into each entry of the finger table, one points to successor and one points to predecessor of the finger node. We call these new fields as *succ* node and *pred* node (to distinguish with finger node) and name this modified finger table as SP finger table. Due to this change, each node in the ring now associates to maximum $3 * m$ nodes, influencing effectively to the closest preceding node finding procedure during lookup process. On the one hand, SP finger table helps to shorten the lookup path length. In considering which is the closest preceding node to the key in SP finger table, the *succ* node obviously tends to be the better candidate than the finger node. Especially, when the density of nodes on ring is sparse or the gap between the finger node and the *succ* node is large, choosing the *succ* node can narrow significantly the distance to the key. On the other hand, when encounter a faulty node during lookup process, SP finger table provides more options to pass over the faulty node by considering the *succ* node or the pred node as an alternative route. SP finger table even gives a beneficial step of overcoming the failure by getting closer to the key in some cases. Algorithm 3 describes the pseudocode of the closest preceding node finding procedure when applying SP finger table.

Algorithm 3. Finding The Closest Preceding Node

 1: **function** N.CLOSEST_PRECEDING_NODE(k)
 2:     **for** $i \leftarrow m - 1$ down to 0 **do**
 3:         **if** $finger[i].succ \in (n, k)$ **and** $finger[i].succ.status == alive$ **then**
 4:             **return** $finger[i].succ$;
 5:         **end if**
 6:         **if** $finger[i].node \in (n, k)$ **and** $finger[i].node.status == alive$ **then**
 7:             **return** $finger[i].node$;
 8:         **end if**
 9:         **if** $finger[i].pred \in (n, k)$ **and** $finger[i].pred.status == alive$ **then**
10:             **return** $finger[i].pred$;
11:         **end if**
12:     **end for**
13:     **return** n;
14: **end function**

In order to explain clearly the usage of SP finger table, Fig. 2a illustrates a typical example which SP finger table expresses better efficiency than the cooperation of finger table and successor list in the original Chord. In the example, node 1 performs the lookup for key 29. Firstly, it checks its SP finger table and sees at 4th entry the *succ* node 20 is closest to the key. Because node 20 is alive, node 1 sends the request to node 20. Then, node 20 searches in its finger table and realizes node 28 at 3th entry is the closest node to key 29. Similarly, the rest of this lookup process goes through node 28 and ends at node 30 where the desired data is stored. The route of this lookup is briefed in the order: node 1 $\rightarrow$ node 20 $\rightarrow$ node 28 $\rightarrow$ node 30. There are only 3 hops in this lookup process, while the original Chord requires 5.

Given a more challenging circumstance in this example by assuming that node 20 is also faulty. In this case, node 1 would ignores both node 20 and node 17, because they are faulty, and selects the pred node 16 at its 4th entry of SP finger table. In the same way, the lookup process is completed after totally 4 hops in the order: node 1 → node 16 → node 24 → node 28 → node 30, as shown in Fig. 2b. Even if node 16 also gets faulty, the path length of lookup process is still 3 hops by going though the *succ* node 11 at 3th entry in SP finger table of node 1, the finger node 28 at 4th entry in SP finger table of node 11, and ending at node 30.

Dealing with fault tolerance on Chord, both partition-based data replication mechanism and SP finger table show its efficiency in their own ways. Therefore, we combine these two solutions into PSPChord model as a novel approach to provide fault tolerance for Chord-based overlay network, as well as to overcome the existing shortcomings of Chord using successor-list. We spend the remainder of this paper presenting the experiments to test and evaluate the efficiency of PSPChord.

Algorithm 4. Key Lookup

1: **function** N.LOOKUP(k, p)
2:     $\mathcal{P} \leftarrow generateKeys(k, p)$;
3:     $\mathcal{P} \leftarrow reorderKeys(n, \mathcal{P})$;
4:     **for each** $key \in \mathcal{P}$ **do**
5:         $succ \leftarrow n.find\_successor(key)$;
6:         **if** $succ.status == alive$ **then**
7:             **return** $succ.retrieveData(k)$;
8:         **end if**
9:     **end for**
10: **end function**

---

5   Experiments

5.1   Experimental Setup

Due to the difficulties to have a real testbed for a huge number of nodes (up to more than 4000 nodes), we build a simulation tool, where ring, node, key are considered as programming objects. In this approach, a strong configuration and control interface was developed using Python language for all our tests as well as evaluations. In each test, we use a same dataset, which describes how nodes and keys are distributed on the rings, for every different mechanisms and configurations to ensure the obtained results as fair as possible. Otherwise, although in a real P2P system, the time-based cost plays the important role in performance assessment for entire system, but with the goal of experimenting PSPChord in theoretical, in this work, we focus on measuring the proposal effects by using the path length as the main metrics. We also calculate the success rate of lookup request to evaluate and prove the efficiency of PSPChord.

5.2   Key Lookup Test on PSPChord with Various Ring Sizes in Case of Existing of Faulty Nodes

We carry out the key lookup test on PSPChord with the replica set $\mathcal{P}$ sized of 12 replicas and various ring sizes N (512, 1024, 2048, 4096), however, there are faulty nodes located among alive nodes on ring. For each turn of lookup test on a specific sized ring, we also vary the percentage of faulty nodes from 0% to 90% then measure both the path length of each successful lookup and the number of partitions the process passed to obtain the desired data. The means path length of a lookup process for each size of ring are shown in Fig. 3a. Likewise, the means number of partitions are shown in Fig. 3b. Concretely, the mean theoretical path length is calculated as formula: $mTheoPL = mP * mPL$, where mP is the mean number of partitions calculated for each size of ring in this experiment and mPL is the quantile path length of a lookup process. The mean theoretical path lengths are also illustrated in Fig. 3a by the dashed line along with the mean practical path lengths.

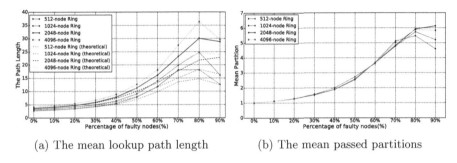

(a) The mean lookup path length   (b) The mean passed partitions

Fig. 3. The lookup on PSPChord with various ring sizes with the percentage of faulty nodes from 0% to 90%

There are some comments gained from the results of the experiment. Firstly, Fig. 3a shows that the mean path length increases when the ring size is greater. This is reasonable because when the number of nodes increases, the lookup process would have to hop through more intermediate nodes. Secondly, at low percentage of faulty nodes from 0% to 40%, the mean path lengths for all ring sizes are quite low (under 10 hops) and very close to the theoretical values. This increase in the mean path lengths are due to the fact that the closest replica node is probably faulty, leading the lookup process to query the second closest replica at high probability, and even the third or fourth closest replicas at low rate, as seen in Fig. 3b. However, the partitions for all ring sizes rise rapidly as the faulty nodes appear more densely and reach the peaks nearly 6 partitions in average. This caused a significant increase in the mean path lengths, which are predictable according to our theoretical formula. The practical values of the mean path lengths are almost higher than the theoretical ones because we estimate the values in the best case which ignores the encounters to faulty nodes, in fact, the lookup process requires some more hops to pass over faulty nodes. Finally, at 90% of faulty nodes on ring, both the mean path lengths and the mean partitions for all ring sizes tend to decrease because only very few lookup requests success in this case and they also require low costs of path length.

5.3   Key Lookup Test on PSPChord with Various Sizes of Replica Set in Case of Existing Faulty Nodes

This test is carried out to evaluate the performance of PSPChord. We configure the ring size as 1024 nodes and increase the percentage of faulty nodes from 0% to 90%. There are 5 sizes of replica set $|\mathcal{P}|$ (5, 8, 10, 12, 15) chosen in this test to analyze the impacts of replica sizes on the efficiency of PSPChord. We also try the dataset on the original Chord in both version of using successor list and non-using successor list to compare with our proposal in terms of the path length and the success rate. The achieved results are illustrated in the Fig. 4.

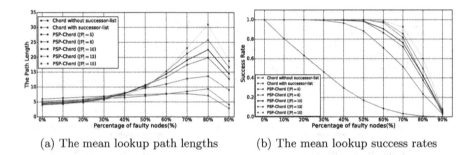

(a) The mean lookup path lengths   (b) The mean lookup success rates

Fig. 4. The lookup on PSPChord with various number of replicas with the percentage of faulty nodes from 0% to 90%

From the Fig. 4a, it can be observed that PSPChord with various partitions requires the lower path lengths compared to Chord at low rate of faulty nodes. However, when the number of faulty nodes increase, the cost of PSPChord tend to rise significantly compare with Chords. The cause of this raise is explained according to results of experiment in Sect. 5.2. Beside, while the path lengths of higher replica size is lower at low percentage of faulty nodes, they gradually become higher at high faulty rate. Nonetheless, the Fig. 4b demonstrates that larger number of replicas leading higher rate of success. PSPChord with $|\mathcal{P}| = $ (15) still reaches more than 90% of success at 70% of faulty nodes. In contrast, PSPChord with $|\mathcal{P}| = $ (5) has success rate decreasing quickly after 50% of faulty rate. In conclusion, our PSPChord approach shows a good performance at low and medium rate of failure. But at high percentage of faulty nodes, the assurance of success also entails costly lookup path length.

6   Conclusion and Future Work

The works presented in this document concentrate on proposing a novel approach to resolve fault tolerance on Chord-based P2P overlay network. This approach deepens the fault tolerance problems of Chord in two directions: data replication mechanism enhancement and lookup efficiency optimization. In our proposal, the successor list of the original Chord is removed due to its shortcoming of unbalanced data replication, instead, we design a balanced data replication mechanism by distributing replicas evenly on the ring based on partition strategy. In addition, we conduct a finger table modification by adding two fields pointing to the successor and predecessor of the finger node on each entry. In this way, each node on the ring is provided more options to pass over faulty nodes during the lookup process. With the goal of providing efficient fault tolerance solution for Chord ring, we make a combination of these two approaches and perform many experiments with various parameters. The achieved results prove the operability, feasibility of our proposal as well as the efficiency it brings. In the future, this work can be continued to improve the resilience to failures, namely failure detection and failure recovery.

Acknowledgments. This research is supported by projects: the Vietnamese MOET's "Research and development of software framework to integrate IoT gateways for fog computing deployed on multi-cloud environment", the Slovak VEGA 2/0167/16 "Methods and algorithms for the semantic processing of Big Data in distributed computing environment" and the Slovak APVV-17-0619 U-COMP "Urgent Computing for Exascale Data".

References

1. Bin, D., Furong, W., Ma, J., Jian, L.: Enhanced chord-based routing protocol using neighbors' neighbors links. In: 2008 22nd International Conference on Advanced Information Networking and Applications-Workshops. AINAW 2008, pp. 463–466. IEEE (2008)
2. Chao, F., Zhang, H., Du, X., Zhang, C.: Improvement of structured P2P routing algorithm based on NN-CHORD. In: 2011 7th International Conference on Wireless Communications, Networking and Mobile Computing (WiCOM), pp. 1–5. IEEE (2011)
3. Chen, Y., Sun, L.Z., Liu, H.L., Xiao, W.Z.: The improvement of chord protocol about structured P2P system. TELKOMNIKA (Telecommun. Comput. Electron. Control) 11(2), 393–398 (2013)
4. Dabek, F., et al.: Building peer-to-peer systems with Chord, a distributed lookup service. In: Proceedings Eighth Workshop on Hot Topics in Operating Systems, pp. 81–86, May 2001. https://doi.org/10.1109/HOTOS.2001.990065
5. Dearle, A., Kirby, G., Norcross, S.: Hosting byzantine fault tolerant services on a Chord ring. arXiv preprint arXiv:1006.3465 (2010)
6. DeCandia, G., et al.: Dynamo: amazon's highly available key-value store. In: ACM SIGOPS Operating Systems Review, vol. 41, pp. 205–220. ACM (2007)

7. Hluchy, L., Nguyen, G., Astalos, J., Tran, V., Sipkova, V., Nguyen, B.M.: Effective computation resilience in high performance and distributed environments. Comput. Inform. **35**(6), 1386–1415 (2017)
8. Nguyen, B.M., Hoang, H.N.Q., Hluchy, L., Vu, T.T., Le, H.: Multiple peer Chord rings approach for device discovery in iot environment. Procedia Comput. Sci. **110**, 125–134 (2017)
9. Stoica, I., et al.: Chord: a scalable peer-to-peer lookup protocol for internet applications. IEEE/ACM Trans. Netw. (TON) **11**(1), 17–32 (2003)
10. Wang, J., Yang, S., Guo, L.: A bidirectional query Chord system based on latency-sensitivity. In: null, pp. 164–167. IEEE (2006)
11. Woungang, I., Tseng, F.H., Lin, Y.H., Chou, L.D., Chao, H.C., Obaidat, M.S.: Mr-Chord: improved chord lookup performance in structured mobile P2P networks. IEEE Syst. J. **9**(3), 743–751 (2015)

Studying Weariness Prediction Using SMOTE and Random Forests

Yu Weng[1,2], Fengming Deng[1,2(✉)], Guosheng Yang[1,2],
Liandong Chen[3], Jie Yuan[1,2], Xinkai Gui[1,2], and Jue Wang[4]

[1] School of Information Engineering, Minzu University of China,
Beijing 100081, China
Fengmingdeng_bj@163.com
[2] National & Local Joint Engineering Lab for Big Data Analysis and Computing
Technology, Beijing 100190, China
[3] State Grid Hebei Electric Power Company, Shijiazhuang 050022, Hebei, China
[4] Computer Network Information Center, Chinese Academy of Sciences,
Beijing 100190, China

Abstract. This article is aimed at the low accuracy of student weariness prediction in education and the poor prediction effect of traditional prediction
models. It was established the SMOTE (Synthetic Minority Oversampling
Technique) algorithm and random forest prediction models. This study puts
forward to useing the SMOTE oversampling method to balance the data set and
then use the random forest algorithm to train the classifier. By comparing the
common single classifier with the ensemble learning classifier, it was found that
the SMOTE and Random forest method performed more prominently, and the
reasons for the increase in the AUC value after using the SMOTE method were
analyzed. Using Massive Open Online Course (Mooc) synthesis student's
datasets, which mainly include the length of class, whether the mouse has
moved, whether there is a job submitted, whether there is participating in discussions and completing the accuracy of the assignments. It is proved that this
method can significantly improve the classification effect of classifiers, so
teachers can choose appropriate teaching and teaching interventions to improve
student's learning outcomes.

Keywords: Education · SMOTE · Random forest

1 Introduction

The education community needs to have an approximate pre-admission knowledge to
predict their academic performance in the future. It helps them to identify prospective
students and provides them with an opportunity to focus on and improve those students
that may have lower scores. Education is one of the most promising responsibilities for
any nation to its fellow citizens. Quality education does not mean a high level of
knowledge. However, it means that education is effectively provided for students so
that they can learn without any problems. For this reason, quality education includes
teaching methods, continuous assessment, similarities in student classification and
other characteristics, so that students have similar goals, educational background, etc.

© Springer Nature Switzerland AG 2018
M. Qiu (Ed.): SmartCom 2018, LNCS 11344, pp. 397–406, 2018.
https://doi.org/10.1007/978-3-030-05755-8_39

In this context, the current main goal is to provide students with high quality education and improve the quality of management decisions. This study analyzes the main attributes that affects student's performance which helps academic planners provide constructive suggestions to enhance their decision on making process, to improve student's academic performance and trim down failure rate, to better understand student's behavior, to assist instructors, to advance teaching and many other benefits.

The study found that in this era of big data, a large number of structured and unstructured student data are generated daily. Most of the data is difficult to handle. This model proposes applying data mining techniques to predict student dropouts and failures. In many practical applications, the object of classification processing is mostly unbalanced data sets, that is some types of samples have more samples than other types of samples. Among them, a small number of classes are often referred to as a minority class; a large number of classes are referred to as a majority class. Traditional classifiers tend to prefer the most classes when categorizing decisions, while ignoring a small number of classes, leading to overall performance degradation of the classifier. Therefore, how to effectively improve the classification accuracy of the minority classes and the overall performance of the classifier has become a hot spot on the field of data mining.

At present, the research on the classification of unbalanced data sets mainly focuses on the algorithm layer and the data layer [1–3]. The algorithm layer processing method is mainly to modify the bias of the algorithm on the data set, so that the decision plane is biased towards a few classes, and the identification rate of a few classes is improved, such as an integrated learning method, a feature selection method. The core idea of the data layer approach is to resample data, including undersampling technique and oversampling technique. The basic idea of the undersampling technique is to delete some of the majority of the samples, which will result in the loss of classification information. The oversampling technique is mainly to add a few samples, and the original classification information can be better preserved. Therefore, oversampling technology is usually selected in some areas where the classification accuracy of various types of samples requires high accuracy.

This study uses the SMOTE oversampling method and the random forest algorithm to solve the unbalanced classification problem of student data sets. By comparing the experimental results of several representative single classifiers and integrated classifiers, it is found that the classification results using the integrated classifier are generally better than the single classifiers, and that the SMOTE combined with the random forest method performs best. According to the experimental results, the important parameters in the method are optimized, and the main reasons for the SMOTE method to improve the classification effect of student data sets are analyzed.

The outline of the paper is as follows: Sect. 2 literature review on SMOTE and Random forest methods applied to distance education; Sect. 3 includes the proposed SMOTE oversampling Method and Random Forest Algorithm; Sect. 4 shows the experimental set and result analysis, and finally Sect. 5 presents the discussion and conclusion with a future work.

2 Related Works

As the learning environment is widely available on the Internet, students can learn their lessons anywhere and indulge in learning activities, such as the recent flipping of classes largely dependent on the Internet's online activities. Students create a large amount of data onto learning management system activities that can be used to develop a learning environment that helps students learn and improve the overall learning experience. In addition to the data obtained from student activities, educational institutions also use applications to manage courses and students. The amount of data provided with the above cases is very large and conventional processing techniques cannot be used to process them. Due to the limitations of traditional data processing applications, educational institutions have begun to explore "big data" technologies to process educational data.

One way for the education system to achieve the highest level of quality is by studying knowledge from this education data to study the main attributes that may affect student performance. Angie Parke [4] said that the college offers courses for both traditional and distance students. In the semester, the drop-out rate of traditional classes was less than 3%, and the dropout rate of remote classes exceeded 17%. The authors propose a control scale to determine the combination of variables that can be considered as predictors of dropouts in the distance education. Finally, the variables are retained in the discriminant analysis and the results are re-examined.

In recent years, it is undeniable that there are a large number of unbalanced data in the distance education. These unbalanced learning problems have attracted academics, industry, and government-funded institutions [5]. The literature [6] did a good theoretical analysis of the learning of unbalanced data and promoted the development of unbalanced data set learning. Domestic literature also analyzes unbalanced data. At present, the relevant methods of classifying imbalanced data are mainly studied from the following aspects: algorithm layer, data layer and judgment criteria.

The data level research method is a key research method of classifying unbalanced data. There are mainly two methods: oversampling and undersampling. The theoretical point of sampling technology is to add and subtract data and balance the distribution of unbalanced data sets by adding or deleting data, such as adding a small number of class samples. The SMOTE algorithm [7] proposed by Chaw La et al. is an unbalanced data processing algorithm proposed to this basis. The algorithm solves the classification problem of unbalanced data well.

Random Forest is a classification and prediction algorithm proposed by Breiman [8] in 2001. The algorithm is a set of multiple unpruned decision trees, The training set of each decision tree originates from the Bagging method and is sampled from the original training set. During the construction of each tree, each node selects the best splitting feature based on the information gain. The difference is that this paper proposes an integrated classification model that integrates multiple random forests and uses a threshold majority voting method to determine the final prediction results.

3 Design Algorithm

3.1 SMOTE Oversampling Method

There is a large amount of umbalancing in distance education data. For these unbalanced datasets, it refers to the data onto a large number of sample points in the dataset. The use of traditional data mining algorithms to deal with unbalanced data sets has the problem of low accuracy and poor classification. There are two main ideas of solving the classification problem of unbalanced data sets. One is to balance the data set, the other is to improve the learning algorithm. SMOTE is one of the representative methods of balancing data sets. The SMOTE method is an intelligent oversampling technique proposed by Nitesh V Chawla et al. for unbalanced data sets [7]. It has significantly improved classification overfitting caused by traditional oversampling methods, therefore that are widely used in unbalanced applications which the data set is classified [9–12]. The main idea of SMOTE are to insert "man-made" samples of rarer samples that are closer together, thereby increase the number of rare samples and improving the imbalance of the data set.

SMOTE detailed algorithms and assessments can be seen in [13], we only describe the subject here part of the SMOTE algorithm.

```
Algorithm 1: SMOTE (T, N, K)
Inputs: Number of minority class samples T; Amount of SMOTE N%;
Number of nearest neighbors k
Output: (N/100) * T synthetic minority class samples
Step 1: Begin
Step 2:    for i ← 1 to T
                Populate (N, i, nnarray)
Step 3:    Populate (N, i, nnarray)
Step 4:    While N!= 0
                for attr ← 1 to numattrs
                Compute: dif=Sample[nnarray][nn][attr] - Sample[i][attr]
                Compute: gap=random number between 0 and 1
                Synthetic[newindex][attr] = Sample[i][attr] + gap * dif
Step 5:    newindex++
Step 6:    N = N -1
Step 7:    return SMOTE
Step 8: End
```

The main steps of the SMOTE method are as follows:

1. First find K nearest neighbors for each rare sample based on the oversampling ratio N, and randomly select N sample among them.
2. Each rare class example and its selected N examples generate N new rare class examples according to formula (1).

3. Add new samples to the original training data set to form a new training data set.

$$x_{new} = x + rand * (y[i] - x) \tag{1}$$

Where $i = 1, 2,..., N$, rand represents a random number between 0 and 1; x_{new} represents a new sample of addition; x represents a rare sample; y[i] represents the i-th neighboring sample of x.

3.2   Random Forest Algorithm

After balancing a large number of umbalanced datasets in the distance education through the SMOTE algorithm, the data needs to be classified. In the article, random forests (RFs) [14] was used for classification. RF is an integrated classifier composed by multiple decision tree classifiers proposed by LeoBreiman in 2001. It has the advantages of high classification accuracy, high learning speed, and strong adaptability to data imbalance, which has been widely used in information retrieval, bioinformatics and other fields [15, 16]. It uses CART as a meta-learning algorithm, and generates a number of different sub-training data sets through the Bagging method, which is used to train individual classifiers, and finally adopts a voting method to determine the final classification result from a simple majority. The complete definition of the random forest is as follows: The random forest is a set of decision tree classifiers $\{h(X, \theta_k), k = 1...\}$ and the meta classifier $h(X, \theta_k)$ is constructed without clipping using the CART algorithm. Categorical Regression Trees: X is the input vector, and the independent and identically distributed random vector θ_k determines the growth process of a single tree; the final output of the random forest are obtained by the simple majority vote method. In order to construct k decision trees, k random vectors must be generated at first. These random vectors $\theta_1, \theta_2,..., \theta_k$ are independent and identically distributed. The random vector constructs the decision classification tree $\{h(X, \theta_i)\}$, which is abbreviated as $h_i(X)$. give k classifiers $h_1(X), h_2(X),..., h_k(X)$ and a random vector X, Y denotes class labels, defining edge functions

$$mg(X,Y) = av_k I(h_k(X) = Y) - max_{j \neq Y} av_k I(h_k(X) = j) \tag{2}$$

In the formula (2), $I(\cdot)$ is an indicative function, and $av_k(\cdot)$ represents a mean function. The edge function specifies the degree to which the vector X is correctly classified as the Y-average number of votes over any other type of average votes. The greater the value of the function, the higher the confidence in the classification. The classifier's generalization error is defined as

$$PE^* = P_{X,Y}(mg(X, Y) < 0) \tag{3}$$

The above results are generalized to random forests. If the number of decision trees in a forest is large enough, the following theorems can be obtained using the laws of large numbers and the structure of decision trees. Theorem 1 As the number of decision trees increases, for all random vectors θ_i, PE* tends to

$$P_{x,y}(P_\theta(h(X,\theta) = Y) - \max_{j \neq y} P_\theta(h(X,\theta) = j) < 0) \qquad (4)$$

Theorem 1 has been shown in [15], which shows that random forests do not overfit. This is an important feature of random forests, and as the tree increases, the generalization error PE* will tend to be an upper bound, indicating that random forests have a good extension of unknown instances.

RF detailed algorithms and assessments can be seen in [15], we only describe parts of the RF algorithm here.

Algorithm 2: RandomForests (node, V)

```
Input: node from the decision tree, if node.attribute = j then the split
       is done on the j'th attribute and V a vector of M columns where
       Vj = the value of the j'th attribute.
Output: label of V
Step 1: Begin
Step 2:   If node is a Leaf then
              Return the value predicted by node
Step 3:   Else
              Let j = node.attribute
              If j is categorical then
RandomForests (childv,V)
              Else j is real-valued
                  If Vj < t then
                        Return RandomForests (childLO,V)
                  Else
                        Return RandomForests (childHI,V)
Step 4:End
```

The algorithm process is divided into two parts. First, when the leaves in the divided forest are null, Then select the class where the majority tuple is located as the node. Otherwise, all the data onto the sample does not belong to the same category. It is necessary to select the class where the majority tuple is located as the node, and divide the attribute with the greatest information gain.

3.3   Combine SMOTE with Random Forest Algorithm

The main idea of this study are to first use the SMOTE method to oversample the data set to balance the proportion of rare and large data onto the data set, then use the random forest algorithm to train the new balanced training data set, and finally generate the classifier. Specific steps are as follows:

1. Sampling the original student training data set S, first find K nearest neighbors for each student sample based on the oversampling ratio N, and select N sample among them randomly.

2. Each student sample and N examples selected by it generate N new student examples according to formula (1).
3. Addingnew examples to the original training data set to form a new training data set S'.
4. Using the Bagging method, N_{all} samples of the new training set S' are randomly selected from the N_{all} samples as the training set for decision tree growth.
5. Assuming that the attribute features has M dimensions, the mtry dimension features are randomly selected from the M-dimensional features as candidate features, and the best splitting method on the mtry features is used to split the nodes. The value of mtry remains unchanged during the growth of random forests.
6. To maximize the growth of each decision tree without pruning.

4 Experiment Settings and Result Analysis

4.1 Datasets and Evaluation Criteria

A good model must stand the test, so when it comes to building a model, we must choose a better data set. Since this paper studies an improved unbalanced data over-sampling algorithm, the data set should not only reflect the real state of the system, but also have an imbalance. In order to meet the two requirements in the previous paragraphs, Mooc synthesis student's datasets are used in this paper. At the same time, the attribute features provided for the student dataset are content-based features, which mainly include the length of class, whether the mouse has moved, whether there is a job submitted, whether there is Participate in discussions and complete the accuracy of the assignments. The specific conditions after the completion of statistical analysis are shown in Table 1.

Table 1. Experimental data set in this table

	Number of students	Study hard	Do not study hard
Training data set	3849	208	3641
Test data set	1948	113	1835
Total	5797	321	5476

From Table 1, it can be seen that there is a serious imbalance in the number of data sets. The proportion of the number of samples in training data set, the serious study in the test data set and the non-conscientious learning is approximately 18:1. Such a serious imbalance leads to training results tending to divide all data into a large number of categories, resulting in degraded classifier performance. Therefore, solving the serious imbalance of Mooc synthesis student dataset is one of the key issues to improve the classifier classification effect. Specific evaluation criteria include precision (pre), recall (recall), F1 measure (F1), and AUC (area under roccurve) values. Compare with other evaluation criteria, AUC values can treat rare and large classes more fairly, so they are very suitable as a classification evaluation indexes for Mooc synthesis student data sets.

4.2   Experiment Settings and Result Evaluation

The experiments in this study were conducted at Weka, a data mining and machine learning platform developed by the University of Waikato, New Zealand.

Comprehensive comparison of single classifiers and integrated classifiers In order to make a comprehensive comparison of the performance of single classifiers and integrated classifiers on experimental data sets, this study selected two typical single classifiers and two integrated classifications. The classifiers are the C4.5 decision tree classifier and the c-svm classifier in Libsvm, while the integrated classifiers are the Bagging classifier and Adaboost classifier, respectively. The experimental comparison values are the averages obtained by weighted average of student classification results.

Table 2. The experimental results are shown in this table

Classifier	Pre	Rec	AUC
C4. 5	0.914	0.923	0.533
c-svm	0.887	0.942	0.500
Bagging	0.937	0.948	0.788
Adaboost	0.936	0.948	0.751

As shown in Table 2, the overall performance of the two integrated classifiers is better than that of the two single classifiers, and all the indicators have been improved. The average values of TP and TN for the two single classifiers were 0.9005 and 0.9325. The average values of TP and TN for the two integrated classifiers were 0.9365 and 0.9480, which showed a significant increase, indicating that the ensemble learning method has a strong classification ability for student data sets. After using the Bagging and Adaboost integration methods, the AUC values of the C4.5 single classifiers were increased by 47.8% and 40.9% respectively, indicating that the effect of the classifier was significantly improved after the integration method was used. For the two ensemble classifiers, the highest AUC value is Bag-ging (0.788), but Bagging performs best on TPR, TNP, and AUC values, indicating that its AUC value (0.788) is obviously affected. Imbalanced dataset effects, so later experiments attempted to use the SMOTE method to balance the dataset. In order to verify the effectiveness of the SMOTE method of different algorithms, this study compared the above four algorithms with the SMOTE method respectively. The experimental results are shown in Table 3.

Table 3. The experimental results are shown in this table

Classifier	Pre	Rec	AUC
SMOTE + C4. 5	0.925	0.919	0.679
SMOTE + c-svm	0.887	0.940	0.449
SMOTE + Bagging	0.932	0.941	0.782
SMOTE + Adaboost	0.928	0.931	0.773

From Table 3, it is found that the overall classification effect of each classifier is improved after it is combined with the SMOTE method. The average AUC value of the four classifiers increased by 3.6%, but the performance was not the same. The increase was more pronounced in C4.5 and Adaboost, and the AUC values were increased by 27.3% and 2.9%, respectively. However, classifiers have also shown a significant decline, and the results of other algorithms have not changed significantly.

5 Conclusions and Future Work

Based on the combination of the SMOTE oversampling method and the random forest classification algorithm under the big data platform, this study put forward an integrated classification method for unbalanced data sets. The purpose is to analyze the factors that affect academic performance and help predict students' academic performance. This is useful for identifying vulnerable students who may not perform well in learning. An educational institution needs to have an approximate pre-admission knowledge to predict their academic performance in the future. Various data mining techniques [17] can be effectively implemented on educational data. From the above results, it is clear that the research method has greatly improved the classification effect compared with other single classifiers and integrated classifiers. Even if compared with the random forest algorithm after the optimization parameters, the AUC value of the main classification index has also been improved. It can be applied to predict student outcomes and improve their performance. The system has high classification accuracy and performance. This experiment shows that the proposed system is more efficient than the existing system. However, there is blindness in the SMOTE algorithm. The inability to finely control the number of synthesized samples, changing the distribution of the raw data of a few class samples and blurring the positive and negative class boundaries is also a deficiency of the algorithm.

Without perfection, algorithms often fail to achieve desirable results when classifying unbalanced data sets. At the same time, in the face of massive data on distance education, the traditional random forest algorithm will inevitably face enormous challenges. How to improve the efficiency of forest algorithms in colleges and universities has become an imperative.

Finally, The next step in our research is to experiment with more data and improved algorithms to test whether different classification methods are used to achieve better performance results.

As future work, we can mention the following points:

First: Assume student failure as quickly as possible. The sooner the better, so that students at risk can be found in time.

Second: The SMOTE and Random Forest algorithms were improved to satisfy the massive data and improve the classification efficiency.

Third: Propose actions to help identify students in risk groups. Then, in order to check the ratio of time, previously detected students can be prevented from failing or being out of school.

Acknowledgments. This work was partly supported by the National Key R&D Program of China (No. 2017YFB0203102), the State Key Program of National Natural Science Foundation of China (No. 91530324).

References

1. Japkowicz, N., Stephen, S.: The class imbalance problem: a systematic study. Intell. Data Anal. J. **6**(5), 429–450 (2012)
2. Batista, G.E.A.P.A., Prati, P.C., Monard, M.C.: A study of the behavior ofseveral methods for balancing machine learning training data. SIGKDD Explor. **6**(1), 20–29 (2014)
3. He, H., Garcia, E.A.: Learning from imbalanced data. IEEE Trans. Knowl. Data Eng. **21**(9), 1263–1284 (2010)
4. Parker, A.: A study of variables that predict dropoutfrom distance education. Int. J. Educ. Technol. **1**(2), 1–11 (1999)
5. He, H., Garcia, E.A.: Learning from imbalanced data. IEEE Trans. Knowl. Data Eng. **21**(9), 1263–1284 (2015)
6. Japkowicz, N.: Learning from imbalanced data sets: a comparison of various strategies. In: AAAI Workshop on Learning from Imbalanced Data Sets, vol. 68, pp. 10–15 (2010)
7. Chawla, N.V., Bowyer, K.W., Hall, L.O., et al.: SMOTE:synthetic minority over-sampling technique. J. Artif. Intell. Res. **16**(1), 321–357 (2002)
8. Loughlin, W.A., Tyndall, J.D., Glenn, M.P., et al.: Update 1 of: beta-strand mimetics. Chem. Rev. **110**(6), 2017
9. Luengo, J., Fernndez, A., Garcia, S., et al.: Addressing data complexity for imbalanced data sets: analysis of SMOTE-based oversampling and evolutionary undersampling. Soft. Comput. **15**(10), 1909–1936 (2011)
10. Bunkhumpornpat, C., Sinapiromsaran, K., Lursinsap, C.: Safe-level-SMOTE: safe-level-synthetic minority over-sampling technique for handling the class imbalanced problem. In: Theeramunkong, T., Kijsirikul, B., Cercone, N., Ho, T.-B. (eds.) PAKDD 2009. LNCS (LNAI), vol. 5476, pp. 475–482. Springer, Heidelberg (2009). https://doi.org/10.1007/978-3-642-01307-2_43
11. Ramentol, E., Caballero, Y., Bello, R., et al.: SMOTE-RSB*: a hybrid preprocessing approach based on oversampling and undersampling for high imbalanced data-sets using SMOTE and rough sets theory. Knowl. Inf. Syst. **33** (2), 245–265 (2012)
12. Cutler, A., Cutler, D.R., Stevens, J.R.: Random forests. Mach. Learn. **45**(1), 157–176 (2004)
13. Kandaswamy, K.K., Chou, K.C., Martinetz, T., et al.: AFP-Pred: a random forest approach for predicting antifreeze proteins from sequence-derived properties. J. Theoret. Biol. **271**(1), 56–62 (2011)
14. Chuanke, X., Chen, Y., Zhao, Y.: Prediction of protein-protein interaction based on improved pseudo amino acid composition. J. Shandong Univ.: Nat. Sci. **44**(9), 17–21 (2016)
15. Kotsiantis, S.: Educational data mining: a case studyfor predicting dropout-prone students. Int. J. Knowl. Eng. Soft Data Parad. **1**(2), 101–111 (2009)
16. Heinz, S., Zobel, J., Williams, H.E.: BurstTries: a fast, efficient data structure for string keys. ACM Trans. Inf. Syst. **20**(2), 192–223 (2012)
17. Groot, S., Kitsuregawa, M.: Jumbo: Beyond MapReduce for workload balancing. In: 36th International Conference on Very Large Data Bases (2010)

Design of Heterogeneous Evaluation Method for Redundant Circuits

Huicong Wu[1(✉)], Jie Yu[1], Yangang Wang[2], and Xiaoguang Wang[2]

[1] College of Information Science and Engineering,
Hebei University of Science and Technology, Shijiazhuang, Hebei, China
whc@hebust.edu.cn
[2] Computer Network Information Center, Chinese Academy of Sciences,
Beijing 100190, China

Abstract. Fault-tolerant mechanisms have been an essential part of the electronic equipment in extreme environments such as high voltage, extreme temperature and strong electromagnetic environment etc. Accordingly, how to improve the robustness and disturbance rejection performance of the circuit has become the primary problem in recent years. In this paper, a heterogeneous evaluation method based on relational analysis is proposed. It uses genetic algorithm and evolutionary hardware to get the required sub-circuit structures and uses relational strategy to evaluate heterogeneous degree of redundant circuit system. Finally, the sub-structures with large heterogeneous degree are selected to build redundant circuit system. In the experiments, we designed short-circuit fault and parameter drift fault to validate the heterogeneous evaluation method. The experimental results show this method can not only enhance the heterogeneous degree, but also maintain high robustness. Compared with random heterogeneous redundant system and homogeneous redundant system, the Average Fault-free Probability of redundant fault-tolerant circuit system based on relational method is 8.9% and 21.7% higher respectively in short-circuit fault experiments, and it is 9.1% and 23.9% higher respectively in parameter drift fault experiments.

Keywords: Fault-tolerance · Redundancy · Algorithm
Heterogeneous evaluation method · Relational strategy

1 Introduction

With the increasing demand for electronic technology and performance, some problems such as tedious design, poor performance and low versatility have gradually produced. System reliability and circuit stability become new challenges in circuit system design. Once the system fails, the function of local control will be lost, even the operation of the entire electronic equipment will be endangered. In some special areas, such as spacecraft and underwater vehicle, due to the uncertainty of its work and the harshness of the environment, the system is required to have better adaptive ability. Therefore, it is necessary to improve the self-repairing and self-adapting ability of electronic system to improve reliability and enhance versatility. In this paper, a heterogeneous circuit evaluation method based on relational analysis is proposed, and a redundant system

© Springer Nature Switzerland AG 2018
M. Qiu (Ed.): SmartCom 2018, LNCS 11344, pp. 407–416, 2018.
https://doi.org/10.1007/978-3-030-05755-8_40

with stronger fault tolerance and disturbance rejection ability is constructed by using substructures with higher heterogeneous degree. The stability of the system under random, short-circuit and open-circuit faults is simulated to verify the feasibility and effectiveness of the system.

Relational analysis is mainly a systematic analysis method for a variety of influencing factors. By analyzing the data of each influencing condition, relationship between these factors and the results in changing trend, speed, etc. will be found [1, 2], thus relevance and tightness can be judged. Many scholars have explored the structure and properties of the grey relational analysis model, furthermore, have achieved periodic results. Chen et al. [3] proposed to improve grey correlation by spline, which was equivalent to using cubic spline difference method to obtain curves with behavior characteristics, at last, calculating correlation degree by integral. Jiang et al. [4] proposed an area correlation method to construct the correlation degree, which used the area between the selected scheme and the ideal scheme to construct a block of small area, and "turning the whole into zero" to verify the rationality of the model and the effectiveness of the algorithm.

Fault tolerance means that when one or more controls of the device fail, it can continue to work at the expense of other aspects [5–8]. Redundant circuit system is designed to ensure the normal operation of the circuit under the condition of introducing fault, so that the circuit has certain self-repairing ability and immunity [9–12]. Liu et al. [13] proposed an ENCF model, and the experiments showed that the proposed method can automatically evolve negative correlation analog circuits under uncertain fault conditions, and the circuit is robust. And Liu et al. [14] also proposed a feature mapping and heterogeneous evaluation scheme to design redundant fault-tolerant circuits, and it was proved by experiments that heterogeneous redundancy has better fault-tolerance and robustness. Zhang et al. [15] analyzed the relationship between angle and fault tolerance from the direction of vector, and the experimental results showed that the larger the angle, the stronger the fault tolerance of the circuit.

Research on fault-tolerant circuit design method is an important work, therefore, for heterogeneous circuit design, this paper proposes a new heterogeneous evaluation method by using the relational selection strategy. In addition, we define four factors that affect heterogeneous degree, and then these factors are applied to set weights by correlation method to improve the evaluation of heterogeneous degree. At last the validity and feasibility of this method are verified by the simulation experiments of injection fault. The rest of this paper is organized as fellows. Section 2 shows the evaluation criteria of influencing factors and heterogeneous evaluation schemes. Section 3 presents the experimental results and analysis. Section 4 concludes the whole paper.

2   Design of Heterogeneous Circuit Evaluation Scheme

2.1   Analysis of Influencing Factors

With circuit evolution, multiple groups of individual circuits can be generated. Through the analysis of these circuits with different topological structures, it is found that there are many factors that lead to circuit failure, such as the life cycle of device, the combination method of the circuit, the influence of the harsh environment and so on. The influence factors of the circuit heterogeneous evaluation, such as the number of components and the distance between input and output, are studied.

Euclidean Distance. If the input and output modes of the circuit are set as vectors, and the input mode of the k circuit is x_k and the output mode is y_k, the distance between the circuits is:

$$d_k = \sqrt{(x_k - y_k)^2} \tag{1}$$

With the decrease of d_k, the circuit structure is simpler. On the contrary, The larger the d_k, the more complex the system structure.

Statistics of Components. Calculate the number of logical function units. In the process of circuit function design, if two sub-circuits meet the design requirements through evolution, and they use n logic gates and m logic gates respectively. In this case, it is considered as two different circuit systems. If the first group is n logic gates and m logic gates, the second group is n logic gates and k logic gates. If m < k, the second group has higher heterogeneous degree than the first group.

Exclusive OR Method. The circuit structure is expressed in the form of tree, and then the heterogeneous degree is calculated through XOR. The root node of the tree acts as the logic function of the gate circuit. The left and right sub-nodes represent the input of the gate structure. The left child is set as the small value of the setting result, the right child is the large value, and the node without branch is set as −1. If the nodes of the two circuit structures are the same, the nodes in the tree structure are defined as 0, otherwise this result is 1. The sum of all nodes in a tree structure is the heterogeneous degree of the circuit.

Reliability Calculation. Reliability means the probability that the logic device in the circuit system can the correct execution of the system under certain time and conditions. If there are n components in the circuit system 1 and m components in the circuit system 2, and each component may have an error of p. And then if $n > m$, the probability of failure in the circuit system 1 is greater than that in the circuit system 2, and the reliability of circuit 1 is lower than circuit 2. The calculation methods of circuit reliability are as follows:

$$R = \prod_{i=1}^{n} r_i \tag{2}$$

In Formula (2), R means the reliability of the circuit system, r_i represents the reliability of the i component. The system reliability evaluation is to integrate the reliability of each component, in other words, to calculate the product reliability of each component. As the increase of the reliability of the circuit, the probability of circuit failure decreases and the system becomes more stable. Conversely, the possibility of circuit failure increases in the system.

2.2 Design of Relational Method

For the relational analysis of data, it is necessary to pre-process the statistical data to eliminate the impact caused by different units.

$$x_i'(k) = \frac{x_i(k)}{\frac{1}{n}\sum_{k=1}^{n} x_i(k)} \tag{3}$$

In Formula (3), $x_i(k)$ denotes the k-th parameter value of the i-th influence factor. $x_i'(k)$ represents the k-th value of the i-th influence factor after averaging. The processed data can reduce the impact of different data levels, and do not cause loss to the original data information. It successfully retains the characteristics of the original information.

The influence factors and the experimental results are compared and analyzed. If the change trend between the correct value of the experimental results and the influence factor is consistent, the factor has important effect on the system output results. On the contrary, the difference of the two is the greater, the influence of this factor become the weaker on the system output results. The calculation of correlation coefficient γ is as follows:

$$\gamma_i(j) = \frac{\Delta\min + \rho\Delta\max}{\Delta(j) + \rho\Delta\max} \tag{4}$$

In formula (4), ρ is a coefficient of resolution with a range of 0, 1. $\gamma_i(j)$ represents the correlation coefficient between the experimental results and the i-th factors in the j-th experiment. The greater the γ_i, the closer the correlation between the probability of failure and the influence factor. The influence of this influence factor on the stability of the circuit system is greater. On the contrary, it on the robustness of the circuit system is smaller. The correlation between the failure probability and the influencing factors increases with the increase of γ_i value, which has a greater impact on the stability of the circuit system.

$$\Delta(j) = |x_0' - x_i'| \tag{5}$$

$$\Delta\max = \max_m \max_n |x_0' - x_i'| \tag{6}$$

$$\Delta\min = \min_m \min_n |x_0' - x_i'| \tag{7}$$

$$\Gamma_i = \frac{1}{n}\sum_{j=1}^{n} \gamma_i(j) \tag{8}$$

In formulas (5–7), x_i' is the initialized value of the group i influence factor. x_0' is the initialized value of the test result. Δmax represents the maximum difference between the experimental result and the influence factor. Δmin represents the minimum difference between the experimental result and the influence factor.

Formula (8) is the calculation method of the correlation degree Γ_i. Γ_i represents the average correlation coefficient of n experiments, that is, the correlation degree between the experimental result and the influence factor. The correlation between the experimental result and the influence factor is stronger as the increase of Γ_i.

2.3   Design of Heterogeneous Selection Method

The performance of the circuit is expressed in terms of weights, such as formula (9). The complexity of the circuit structure increases with the increase of ψ value.

$$\psi = \sum_{i=1}^{n} (\Gamma_i \bullet x_i')$$

(9)

If there are n sub-circuit structures that meet the design requirements and m of them are selected for redundant combination, then there are C_n^m kinds of combinations. The three sub-circuits are considered as a group, and the ψ-value are presented as space distances in the form of vectors in the three-dimensional space coordinate system. The area of the sub-circuits is taken as heterogeneous degree of the logic circuits (see Fig. 1).

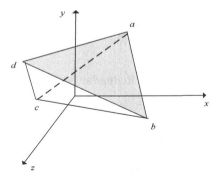

Fig. 1. Heterogeneous evaluation method

The largest set of heterogeneous degree is constructed as the three sub-structures of the triple modular redundancy system. The area represents the heterogenous degree of logic circuit and it changes with the change of ψ value. Following the increasement of the area, the Heterogenous Degree between sub-circuits increases. In Fig. 1, there are four heterogeneous combinations. The area of the shaded portion Δabd is the largest, that is, it has the largest heterogeneous degree, so the redundant fault-tolerant system is constructed with three sub-circuits a, b and d.

3   Experimental Results and Analysis

In the experimental section, we take the binary comparator as an example, heterogeneous degree is evaluated. The experimental parameters are shown in Tables 1 and 2. Heterogeneous degree increases with the increase of the numbers of the logic units needed in the evolution circuit. But heterogeneous degree reaches saturation when the numbers of the logic units increases to a certain extent. Figure 2 gives the evaluation result of heterogeneous degree of the logic units in the circuit structure when the number of logic units reaches 15.

Table 1. The setting of the evolutionary parameters

Category	Value
Population size	10
Cross probability	0.6
Mutation probability	0.3
Maximum evolution times	1000

Table 2. The output of the binary comparator

Compare (A_1A_0 and B_1B_0)	Value ($C_2C_1C_0$)
$A_1A_0 > B_1B_0$	100
$A_1A_0 < B_1B_0$	010
$A_1A_0 = B_1B_0$	001

3.1   The Heterogeneous Degree of Redundancy Circuit System

Three sub-circuits with the same function but different structures are combined into a heterogeneous circuit system. A redundant system is constructed by finding out the largest heterogeneous sub-circuit structure among circuit individuals. We construct 6 heterogeneous redundant systems, and each has 3 circuit modules. Heterogeneous circuit systems are evaluated by heterogeneous degree of active nodes, topology, and relational selection strategy, respectively. In Fig. 2, the X coordinate represents 10 different combinations and Y coordinate represents heterogeneous degree between substructures.

Figure 2 shows that heterogeneous degree obtained by different heterogeneous evaluation methods is different in the same combination. Compared with the method of the active node and topology heterogeneous evaluation, the correlation selection strategy method has higher heterogeneous degree. The evaluation scheme of relational strategy integrates various factors with different judgment structures to increase the difference between circuits. Therefore, it is easier for the relational method to find out the larger heterogeneous circuit structure and build redundant system.

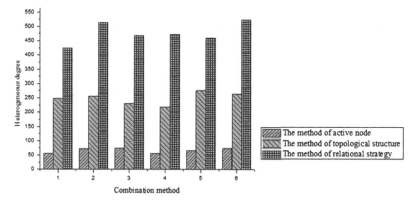

Fig. 2. Comparison experiment of heterogeneous degree

3.2   The Experiment of Fault Simulation

Considering the type of fault and the probability of occurrence are uncertain, the fault is simulated by random injection. Firstly, the SA fault is injected randomly in this experiment. The results of each successful evolution are recorded as the number of injected failures is changed. Then, we observe the effect of the number of faults on the minimum population fitness and evolution algebra, as shown in Fig. 3.

Figure 3 shows that as the increasing number of fault injection, the evolving algebraic curve presents a trapezoidal upward trend. The main reason is that for the same search space, with the increasing number of faults, the maximum evolution algebra and the minimum evolution algebra gradually increase, the probability of circuit device errors increases, and the influence of faults on the evolution algebra increases. With the increase of the number of fault injection, the fitness value decreases and the accuracy of the circuit declines. In fact, the robustness of the circuit is reduced. The number of evolutionary algebras is not only related to the design of evolutionary algorithms, but also closely related to the number of introduced faults.

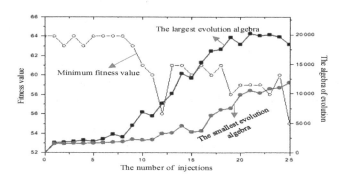

Fig. 3. The experimental curve of SA fault

The components of the circuit are injected into random short-circuit fault and parameter drift fault, and the actual output is recorded. Then compared with the expected output information in the truth table, the fault-free probability is calculated. That is, the fault-tolerance of the circuit is validated. After repeating the experiment 20 times, the average failure-free probability is calculated. In Figs. 4 and 5, the X coordinates represent the number of experiments, and the Y coordinates represent the fault-free probability values corresponding to the system.

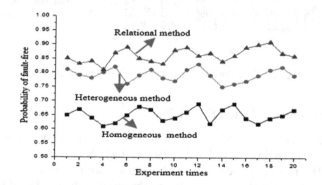

Fig. 4. The short-circuit fault simulation experiment

Figure 4 shows that the fault-free probability of redundant circuits constructed by relational method is higher than that of heterogeneous redundant circuits and homogeneous redundant circuits when the short-circuit fault is introduced. It shows that this method has better fault-tolerant performance. In 20 times short-circuit fault experiments, the average failure-free probability of heterogeneous systems with relational strategy is 86.2%, that of randomly combined heterogeneous systems is 79.2%, and that of homogeneous redundant circuits is 65%. Compared with random heterogeneous redundant system and homogeneous redundant system, the fault-free probability of redundant fault-tolerant circuit system based on relational method is 8.9% and 21.7% higher, respectively. Redundant fault-tolerant circuit system based on relational method has better anti-disturbance ability in the face of the short-circuit fault, which is helpful to improve the fault-tolerant ability and stability of circuit system.

In parameter drift fault experiments, the average failure-free probability of systems is shown in Fig. 5. Compared with random heterogeneous redundant system and homogeneous redundant system, the fault-free probability of redundant fault-tolerant circuit system based on relational method is 9.1% and 23.9% higher, respectively. Redundant fault-tolerant circuit system based on relational method has better anti-disturbance ability in the face of the parameter drift fault, which is helpful to improve the fault-tolerant ability and stability of circuit system.

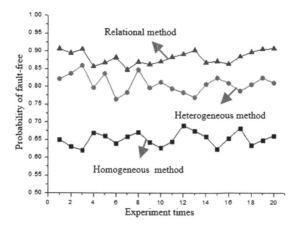

Fig. 5. The parameter drift fault simulation experiment

4   Conclusion

This paper aims at improving the fault tolerance of the system from the point of improving heterogeneous degree between sub-circuits. In this paper, the factors affecting the variation of heterogeneous is analyzed during evolutionary design. Secondly, the weight of each factor is obtained according to the relational analysis method. Finally, heterogeneous degree of sub-circuits is evaluated. In the experiment, the heterogenous degree of redundant circuits are obtained by different evaluation methods with the same combination. Sub-circuits with large heterogeneous is chosen to construct the redundant system, and then the random short circuit fault and parameter drift fault are applied to verify the feasibility and effectiveness of the method. Experimental results show that the heterogenous degree of the relational strategy method is better than that of the active node and topology structure whereas the fault-free probability of redundant system constructed by relational strategy is higher than fault-free probability of the random heterogeneous redundant system and the homogeneous redundant system. That is, the circuit has high accuracy and robustness. The relational heterogeneous redundancy circuit system played its function more stably in the complex environment. There are, however, some issues that need resolving. For example, how to improve the fault-tolerant ability of the system in uncertain faults and quickly get the required circuit system and so forth.

Acknowledgments. This work was partly supported by the National Key R&D Program of China (No. 2017YFB0202202), the State Key Program of National Natural Science Foundation of China (No. 91530324).

References

1. Liu, S.F., Cai, H., Yang, Y.J.: Advance in grey incidence analysis modelling. Syst. Eng. Theory Pract. **33**(8), 2041–2046 (2013)
2. Liu, Z., Dang, Y.G., Zhou, W.J.: New grey nearness incidence model and its extension. Control. Decis. **29**(6), 1071–1075 (2014)

3. Chen, Y.M., Zhang, M.: Cubic spline based grey absolute relational grade model. Syst. Eng. Theory Pract. **35**(5), 1304–1310 (2015)
4. Jiang, S.Q., Liu, S.F., Liu, Z.X.: Grey incidence decision making model based on area. Control Decis. **30**(4), 685–690 (2015)
5. Zhang, M., He, J.: Vector analysis on the fault-tolerant abilities of combined analog circuit systems. In: proceeding of International Congress on Image and Signal Processing, Biomedical Engineering and Informatics, pp. 2020–2025 (2017)
6. Chang, H., He, J.: A novel fault-tolerance design model for automatic synthesis of circuit robust to unknown fault. In: Proceeding of Conference Anthology, pp. 1–6. IEEE (2014)
7. Chang, H., He, J.: Swarm intelligence: making differences in analogue circuits structure for fault-tolerance. Int. J. Comput. Appl. Technol. **46**(3), 210–219 (2013)
8. Zheng, Y., He, J.: Learning the distance between circuit structures for fault tolerance of redundant system. In: proceeding of Seventh International Symposium on Computational Intelligence and Design, pp. 207–211 (2015)
9. Chen, Z., Ni, M.: Reliability and security analysis of triple-module redundancy system. Comput. Eng. **38**(14), 239–241 (2012)
10. Gao, G.J., Wang, Y.R., Yao, R.: Research on redundancy and tolerance of system with different structures. Transducer Microsyst. Technol. **26**(10), 25–28 (2007)
11. Shi, W., Yuan, L., Xie, S.J.: Research on selective redundancy of evolved circuits using negative correlation. Microelectron Comput. **30**(6), 71–74 (2013)
12. Wu, H.C., Wang, J.Z., Liu, C.C.: Research of circuit evolution design based on adaptive HereBoy algorithm. J. Hebei Univ. Sci. Technol. **36**(3), 293–299 (2015)
13. Liu, M., He, J.: An evolutionary negative-correlation framework for robust analog-circuit design under uncertain faults. IEEE Trans. Evol. Comput. **17**(5), 640–665 (2013)
14. Wu, H.C., Wang, J.Z., Zhou, W.Z.: Redundancy fault-tolerant circuit design based on feature map clustering and heterogeneous selection strategy. High Volt. Eng. **43**(4), 1362–1369 (2017)
15. Zhang, J.B., Cai, J.Y., Meng, Y.F.: A design technology of fault tolerance circuit systems facing complex electromagnetic environments. J. Xi'an Jiaotong Univ. **51**(2), 53–59 (2017)

Senior2Local: A Machine Learning Based Intrusion Detection Method for VANETs

Yi Zeng[1], Meikang Qiu[2(✉)], Zhong Ming[2], and Meiqin Liu[3]

[1] College of Electronic and Information Engineering, Xidian University,
Xi'an, Shaanxi, China
zengyi_xidian@163.com
[2] College of Computer Science, Shenzhen University, Shenzhen, Guangdong, China
{mqiu,mingz}@szu.edu.cn, qiumeikang@yahoo.com
[3] College of Electrical Engineering, Zhejiang University, Hangzhou, China
liumeiqin@zju.edu.cn

Abstract. Vehicular Ad-hoc Network (VANET) is a heterogeneous network of resource-constrained nodes such as smart vehicles and Road Side Units (RSUs) communicating in a high mobility environment. Concerning the potentially malicious misbehaves in VANETs, real-time and robust intrusion detection methods are required. In this paper, we present a novel Machine Learning (ML) based intrusion detection methods to automatically detect intruders globally and locally in VANETs. Compared to previous Intrusion Detection methods, our method is more robust to the environmental changes that are typical in VANETs, especially when intruders overtake senior units like RSUs and Cluster Heads (CHs). The experimental results show that our approach can outperform previous work significantly when vulnerable RSUs exist.

Keywords: ML · Intrusion detection · VANETs · RSUs
Game theory

1 Introduction

The Vehicular Ad-hoc Network (VANET) is an emerging type of Mobile Ad-hoc Networks (MANETs) with excellent applications in the intelligent traffic system. Despite the promising future of VANETs, they are known to be sensitive to various misbehaves, ranging from malicious attacks to random failures [15]. Considering the safety of vehicles is directly related to human lives, security is one of the main challenges in VANETs. Various detection methods have been proposed in the past decade to detect and mitigate Intrusions in VANETs. Most of these presented methods overlook the security of senior units or just simply rely on a set of predefined and fixed threshold(s) to secure the senior units.

However, senior units, Road Side Units (RSUs) and Cluster Heads (CHs) (see Sect. 2.1), are not guaranteed to be safe in a VANET. Although RSUs are built to be robust, yet intruders can still impair the system through physical

© Springer Nature Switzerland AG 2018
M. Qiu (Ed.): SmartCom 2018, LNCS 11344, pp. 417–426, 2018.
https://doi.org/10.1007/978-3-030-05755-8_41

attacking RSUs or impersonating as an RSU [8]. Not to mention that CHs are easier than RSUs to be impersonated or overtook [10]. The overlook of those senior units' security can lead to serious consequences [10]. Furthermore, considering the highly dynamic nature of VANETs, it is not achievable to find a set of fixed thresholds to detect malicious nodes. In contrast, our online Machine Learning based (ML-based) intrusion detection method can automatically determine whether a node is malicious or not considering all available data from the VANET.

In addition, we argue that RSUs cannot be marked simply as either malicious or cooperative, taken that cooperative RSUs might behave abnormally due to the nature of VANETs. One example is illustrated in Fig. 1. We find that RSU 2 drops packets from all CHs that connected to because different reasons, which will make it be detected as an intruder without further investigation. However, it is actually a cooperative RSU which dops packages out of malicious intent. Meanwhile, RSU 1 pretends to be a normal RSU and answers requests from CH 4 and CH 2, which will be classified as a cooperative RSU by most of the methods presented, yet it is an intruder who might spoof other units in the VANET [3]. Both misclassifications will lead to extra costs and dangerous outcomes. Hence, we clearly see from this example that a trust system, where RSUs are motivated to provide trustworthy information, is required in order to mitigate the influence of vulnerable nodes and fake RSUs.

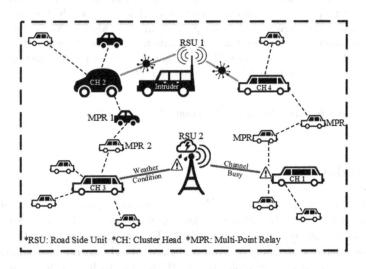

Fig. 1. Trust system is required for RSUs

In this paper, we proposed an Intrusion Detection method based on Machine Learning (ML) and game theory for VANETs. Our method securing the VANET ranging from senior units (RSUs and CHs) to local vehicles level to level. A trust system is built to credit RSUs. Then, Artificial Neural Network (ANN) is presented in RSUs to detect malicious CHs. Finally, in local scale, online Support Vector Machine (SVM) is trained and implemented to detect malicious vehicles inside clusters.

This paper's contribution can be summarized as follows: **(1)** We apply game theory to secure senior units which proved to be more reliable than presented works under the dramatically changing environment in VANETs. **(2)** ANN is implemented in our methods in RSUs, which is known to be more precise than most presented classification methods in VANETs. **(3)** We apply simplified SVM in vehicles, which is a light-weight detection method that suits the resource-constrained nature of vehicles. **(4)** To our best knowledge, this is the first through intrusion detection method that concerning each level of nodes in detail. This presented method is proved to outperform presented methods dramatically when senior level nodes are damaged.

The rest of this article is divided into five sections. Section 2 presented background information and problem statements. The Senior2Local detection method is elaborated in Sect. 3. The experimental result is shown in Sect. 4. Finally, Sect. 5 gives the concluding remark of this paper.

2   Problem Statement

2.1   Backgrounds of VANETs

A VANET as a whole consists of RSUs, CHs, Multi-Point Relays (MPRs), and normal vehicles. Each vehicle, including CH and MPR, is equipped with technologies that allow communications between each point possible.

Globally, RSUs are capable of communicating with other RSUs via physical networks, e.g., data center network [6]. This character also empowers RSUs to use cloud computing and regardless of the resource constraint. An RSU can connect to every vehicle in the area that covered by its wireless network directly. All those RSU-based connections together build up the global view of a VANET.

From the local perspective, this connection between RSU and its correlative cars usually including several vehicular clusters. These clusters follow Vehicular Ad-Hoc Network Quality of Service Optimized Link State Routing (VANET QoS-OLSR) [13], which is a clustering protocol that considers a trade-off between the QoS requirements and the high mobility metrics in VANET. For every cluster concerned, a CH is selected to facilitate the management of each cluster. Then, these heads are responsible for selecting a set of specific vehicles charged of transmitting the network topology information through messages called Topology Control (TC) and forwarding the packets. Such nodes are called MPRs.

Problems can arise no matter globally or locally to impair the VANET due to the vulnerability of RSUs and vehicles.

2.2   Problems and Challenges in VANET

Globally, RSUs can be physically damaged by malicious actions or accidents [8]. In this scenario, the accuracy of analyzing CHs can be dampened. If there is a specific RSU which is physically vulnerable, then, there are chances that the data transmitted through this RSU is not trust-worthy. Another issue is the impersonation [8]. Intruders can impersonate as RSUs, spoofing service advertisements or safety messages. Those two major issues with RSUs are illustrated in Fig. 2.

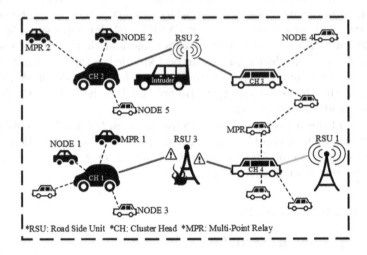

Fig. 2. Global intrusion examples in VANETs

In Fig. 1, only RSU 1 is working properly. RSU 1 can exchange data with CH 4 and oversees the related cars in the cluster continuously. Hence security actions can take place as expected, a high security of this area can be ensured.

RSU 2 is actually a vehicular intruder impersonating as a normal RSU. Firstly, this leads CH 3 and other cooperative cars in the area covered by RSU 2, e.g., NODE 4 and NODE 5, try to exchange important data with this intruder, hence important information of cars can be leaked, and extra transporting consumption is required. Secondly, this intruder can take cover for CH 2, which is a malicious CH performing malicious actions. This directly leads MPR 2 and NODE 2, which all are malicious vehicles, take malicious actions barbarically, which might even cost massive death.

RSU 3 is an RSU which is physically damaged which cannot receive packages from CH 1 or CH 4. Despite the driving experience in the related area is dampened, the malicious CH 1 will remain undetected. This failure of detecting CH 1 leads NODE 1 and MPR 1 continuously perform malicious actions barbarically, which surely will damage the whole VANET.

Locally, if intruders remain undetected, especially when intruders play a roll in the cluster, serious consequences can happen [9]. One dangerous scenario is when the head of the cluster is malicious. As a CH, it can perform malicious actions without being detected by other vehicles. Malicious CHs can send fake data or spam to other members in the cluster. More dangerously, a malicious CH can take cover for other malicious nodes in the cluster. It can choose a malicious node as an MPR, which can perform Denial of Service (DoS) or inject fake data to other clusters. If the CH is not malicious, however, malicious nodes in the cluster can be isolated and a trust-worthy node can be chosen as MPR. Hence, the guarantee of CH is trust-worthy is important for the whole cluster.

As RSUs are not guaranteed to be cooperative constantly, we assume RSUs can be intruders or real RSUs which have chances to perform packages drop, like examples mentioned in [8]. As for CHs, different from other presented methods which regard them as trust-worthy all the time, we treat them same as other normal vehicles, which can be overtaken by intruders.

3 The Senior2Local Intrusion Detection Method

In this section, we will illustrate the details of our proposed ML-based intrusion detection method for VANETs. Senior2Local Intrusion Detection method is divided into two functional modules: *Global Intrusion Detection and Propagation, Local Intrusion Detection and Propagation.*

3.1 Global Intrusion Detection and Propagation

In this process, our presented model will firstly analyze all the CHs in the cluster based on pre-trained ANN that is implemented in RSUs. Although ANNs can detect intruders effectively, they normally require a high computational resource to train and implement. In a VANET, only RSUs are concerned as unlimited in the resource, which is suitable to use ANN to detect malicious CHs. The ANN in our proposed method is firstly trained and tested on a fuzzification dataset which was collected from a trace file that was generated utilizing GloMoSim 2.03 [14] to model the VANET and its environment. This fuzzification ANN-based detector is inspired by the work [1], yet we will only use this ANN in RSUs to detect malicious CHs. Furthermore, we trained our ANN to output a real number ranging from -1 to 1, which denotes the belief of the CH being cooperative or malicious. If the number is positive, then the CH is marked as cooperative, otherwise, it is marked as malicious. The absolute value of the number $BasBili$, denotes the basic belief of CH being that way. The total accuracy of the training process is 99.97%. The true positive rate on testing data is 99.91%, and the true negative rate on testing data is 99.84%.

After we implement this well-trained ANN, RSUs are able to detect malicious CHs that connected directly to themselves individually. Then, a trust system is built up to evaluate each RSU's credit. Trust is constructed by exchanging detection belief about CHs based on their previous interactions. Practically, fake RSUs may be tempted to collusion with each other to provide fake detection results over CHs, which may lead to misleading results. To overcome scenarios that most multiple RSUs are imprisoned by intruders, we adopt the credibility update function and a belief function transplanted from [11] with the aim of encouraging RSUs, even fake ones, to participate in the trust establishment process and provide truthful analyze results over CHs.

The proposed trust system for RSUs works as follow. The belief function represents the total analyze belief results globally considering all RSUs. We let RSU_x be the xth RSU of the VANET, $Clus^i$ be the Custer i, and CH^i be the CH of $Clus^i$. For example, $Beli^i_x(H)$ is a belief function, whihc will indicate the belief from RSU_x over a hypothesis, e.g., CH^i is H (H is a hypothesis, cooperative, malicious, or uncertain). This belief is a real number ranging from 0 to 1. Let $LRes^i_x = \{Co, Ma, Un\}$ denote the local analyze results over CH^i by RSU_x. Co denotes the possibility of CH^i being cooperative; Ma is the possibility of CH^i being malicious, and Un is an expression of uncertainty. Primarily, $LRes^i_x$ is acquired from the out put of aforementioned ANN. For instance, the ANN output a negative number 0.78, then we set $BasBili$ as 0.78, Co as 0, Ma as 0.78, and Un is equal to $1 - BasBeli$, which is 0.22. The belief function of RSU_x in CH^i will be updated according to the belief updat function presented in [11] after consulting two other RSUs, RSU_1 and RSU_2.

Thus, the problem of establishing the common belief over CHs in the VANET can be achieved after computing, consulting, and combining all the believes. This purposed technique is proved in [11] that it can overcome the problem where malicious RSUs are the majority.

Primarily, we set the credits of each RSU to 1. and now, we can reset the credits of each RSU_x after judging CH^i in favor of RSU_s based on the credibility update function from [11]. After conducting this iteration globally with all the RSUs in the VANET, a reward for consistency and a punishment for inconsistency can be achieved.

The last step is the global propagation process. And more details of this function model as a whole is explained in Algorithm 1. After conducting this model, senior units, e.g., RSUs and CHs, are motivated to perform cooperatively. This can facilitate future local detection since detected malicious CHs are no longer participate in the VANET.

3.2   Local Intrusion Detection and Propagation

Taken that vehicles are resource constrained [4], an intelligent trigger for vehicles to detect the intruder in the local cluster is required. In our presented model, the trigger would go off when package dropping is detected in the cluster. In this trigger detecting process, each vehicle in the cluster would be designed as watchdogs [7] to constantly monitoring and analyzing the behavior of MPRs that within their transmission range. Hence, we are capable to monitor the number of packages that an MPR to send and the number of packages that an MPR actually sent. When a mismatch of those two number happens, we will mark such a MPR as malicious primarily. After every vehicle has its own observation about MPRs in its vicinity, we will let each vehicle in the cluster to exchange and integrate those observations to generate a dataset to train our light-weight SVM in the following process. After this process, a basic perspective over malicious nodes in the cluster is acquired.

Algorithm 1. Global Intrusion Detection and Propagation

Input:

Pre-trained ANN classifier.

Extracted features' data of every CH.

Output:

A updated trust system of RSUs.

A secured set of CHs where acknowledged malicious CHs are banned.

Procedure:

1: **for** each RSU_j in the VANET **do**
2:   **for** each CH^i that directly connects to RSU_j **do**
3:     Transmit Behavioral Data to RSU_j
4:     Transmit Contextual Data to RSU_j
5:     Apply pre-trained ANN classifier to analyze CH^i
6:     Save analyze result to $LRes_x$
7:   **end for**
8: **end for**
9: Computing, consulting, and comparing classification believes of CH^i globally according to the belief updat function from [11]
10: **for** each RSU_j in the VANET **do**
11:   Reward or Punish the RSU according to the credibility update function from [11]
12: **end for**
13: Broadcast the trust credit of each RSU globally
14: based on common belief, mark every acknowledged malicious CH
15: **for** every acknowledged malicious CH^m **do**
16:   Ban node CH^m from the network
17:   Select a new CH^m from $Clus^m$ randomly
18: **end for**

After a trigger, a dropping of packages is detected in the previous process, the *Local Intrusion Detection and Propagation* process will initiate. In this part, similar to [12], we integrate the support vectors from the previous training process and the observation from other vehicles in the cluster except the vehicle that running this detection as training data, and the observation of this vehicle is set as the testing dataset. Notice that Gaussian Radial Basis Function kernel is selected in our model, taken that it was experimental proved to be best fitting scenarios in VANETs [12]. In order to conduct a high accuracy in detection, our model will work in an online fashion, which means it will be trained incrementally. Considering the resource constraint in vehicles, the online training process will only keep the support vectors from the previous iteration. Each testing process works as a detection from an individual vehicle, and the final results from all the nodes in the cluster will be integrated after all the detection is done. This integrated list of vehicles can be divided into two parts, the *MaliSet*, which is a list of malicious nodes, and the *CoopSet*, which is a list of cooperative nodes. Those two sets will be stored in the CH of the cluster. In order to reach a regional security, those two sets will be exchanged and integrated between CHs only when two CHs contacts. This exchange of the *MaliSet* and the *CoopSet* can prevent malicious vehicles run away from a cluster to a new cluster without being noticed. After the detection and propagation, further monitoring will only concern those cooperative nodes, and malicious nodes will be banned from cluster to cluster for security reasons.

4   Experimental Results and Analysis

In this section, we evaluate the performance of the Senior2Local intrusion detection method using network simulation and the performance is compared with two novel ML-based intrusion detection methods. The first baseline mechanism is the SVM-based Context-Aware Security Framework (SVM-CASE) that proposed in [5], which is a well-known ML-based method for intrusion detection in VANET. The other based line is CEAP (Collection, Exchange, Analysis, and Propagation) that proposed in [12], which is another ML-based detection method for VANETs.

4.1   Simulation Setup

The experimental platform we use is GloMoSim 2.03 [14]. We set the simulation area as $600\,m \times 600\,m$. The total number of nodes we used is 50, 100, 150, and 200 for each iteration. The total number of RSUs in our simulation is 6. For each iteration, we set 10%, 20%, 30%, and 40% nodes as intruders. The transmission range we used is $120\,m$. The moving speed is set from $5\,m/s$ to $30\,m/s$ randomly for each vehicle. The total simulation time was set to $900\,s$.

The parameters used to evaluate the performance of the different methods are the accuracy rate and attack detection rate. Accuracy Rate is the number that results when the number of correctly detected malicious nodes is divided by the total number of detected malicious nodes. The attack detection rate is the number results when the total number of correctly detected malicious nodes is divided by the total number of malicious nodes.

$$\text{Accuracy Rate} = 100\% \times \frac{\text{Number of Correctly Detected Malicious Nodes}}{\text{Total Number of Detected Malicious Nodes}} \tag{1}$$

$$\text{Attack Detection Rate} = 100\% \times \frac{\text{Total Number of Correctly Detected Malicious Nodes}}{\text{Total Number of Malicious Nodes}} \tag{2}$$

We compare different parameters under one possible scenario in the VANET. In this case, half of the RSUs are fake RSUs collude together to provide fake data in order to interfere with the detection process [2]. Futhermore, one of the RSU is physically broken (denying all the detection requests), which is a possible scenario chould happened in VANETs [8]. In our simulation, one of the RSU from the six RSUs is selected randomly and start to denying all the detection requests as a simulation of the physically broken scenario. Then, we selected 3 RSUs randomly from the other 5 RSUs and let them transmit some similar fake data with others. The fake data is actually generated from the real detection results, yet we let those fake RSUs report malicious when they detect cooperative nodes, and vice versa.

4.2   Experimental Results

Firstly, we can learn from Fig. 3 that the Senior2Local method can outperform the SVM-CASE method and CEAP method dramatically when RSUs are not trustworthy. We can see a dramatic decline in the accuracy performance of SVM-CASE [5] and CEAP [12] in our experimental scenario comparing to their original experimental result, which was at least 98.7% and 98.9% respectively. Yet, the Senior2Local's accuracy is more robust, the average accuracy is 98.37% even when most of the functional RSUs are fake. From Fig. 4, we can observe a higher ability to detect attacks of the Senior2Local method. This ability is much higher than SVM-CASE and CEAP in the same environment. The average attack detection rate of the Senior2Local method is 98.25%, which means even most of the RSUs cannot provide trustworthy detection data, Senior2Local still can secure the VANET. Those two results can reflect the ability of Senior2Local to overcome impersonation and physical vulnerability, which can be a more suitable detection method to implement in the VANET.

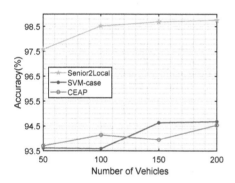

Fig. 3. Accuracy rate comparison

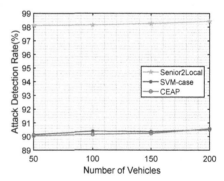

Fig. 4. Attack detection rate comparison

5   Conclusion

In this paper, we presented Senior2Local, a novel ML-based intrusion detection method for VANETs. We used game theory to build a trust system for RSUs. ANN is implemented in our model based on trust-worthy RSUs to securing CHs. After removing malicious CHs, a light-weight SVM is used to detect malicious MPRs cluster to cluster locally. The experimental result shows that Senior2Local is more robust and trust-worthy comparing to presented ML-based detection methods.

Acknowledgement. This work is supported by China NSFC 61836005 and 61672358; China NSFC 61728303 and the Open Research Project of the State Key Laboratory of Industrial Control Technology, Zhejiang University, China (ICT1800417).

References

1. Alheeti, K.M.A., Gruebler, A., McDonald-Maier, K.D.: An intrusion detection system against black hole attacks on the communication network of self-driving cars. In: 2015 Sixth International Conference on Emerging Security Technologies (EST), pp. 86–91. IEEE (2015)
2. Chim, T.W., Yiu, S., Hui, L.C., Li, V.O.: Security and privacy issues for inter-vehicle communications in vanets. In: 6th Annual IEEE Communications Society Conference on Sensor, Mesh and Ad Hoc Communications and Networks Workshops, 2009, SECON Workshops 2009, pp. 1–3. IEEE (2009)
3. Gai, K., Qiu, M., Ming, Z., Zhao, H., Qiu, L.: Spoofing-jamming attack strategy using optimal power distributions in wireless smart grid networks. IEEE Trans. Smart Grid **8**(5), 2431–2439 (2017)
4. Kumar, N., Chilamkurti, N.: Collaborative trust aware intelligent intrusion detection in vanets. Comput. Electr. Eng. **40**(6), 1981–1996 (2014)
5. Li, W., Joshi, A., Finin, T.: SVM-case: an SVM-based context aware security framework for vehicular ad-hoc networks. In: 2015 IEEE 82nd Vehicular Technology Conference (VTC Fall), pp. 1–5. IEEE (2015)
6. Liu, J., Wan, J., Zeng, B., Wang, Q., Song, H., Qiu, M.: A scalable and quick-response software defined vehicular network assisted by mobile edge computing. IEEE Commun. Mag. **55**(7), 94–100 (2017)
7. Marti, S., Giuli, T.J., Lai, K., Baker, M.: Mitigating routing misbehavior in mobile adhoc networks. In: Proceedings of the 6th Annual International Conference on Mobilecomputing and Networking, pp. 255–265. ACM (2000)
8. Qian, Y., Moayeri, N.: Design of secure and application-oriented VANETs. In: 2008 IEEE Vehicular Technology Conference, VTC Spring 2008, pp. 2794–2799. IEEE (2008)
9. Qiu, M., Gai, K., Thuraisingham, B., Tao, L., Zhao, H.: Proactive user-centric secure data scheme using attribute-based semantic access controls for mobile clouds in financial industry. Futur. Gener. Comput. Syst. **80**, 421–429 (2018)
10. Sharma, S., Kaul, A.: A survey on intrusion detection systems and honeypot based proactive security mechanisms in VANETs and VANET cloud. Vehic. Commun. (2018)
11. Wahab, O.A., Bentahar, J., Otrok, H., Mourad, A.: Towards trustworthy multi-cloud services communities: a trust-based hedonic coalitional game. IEEE Trans. Serv. Comput. **11**(1), 184–201 (2018)
12. Wahab, O.A., Mourad, A., Otrok, H., Bentahar, J.: CEAP: SVM-based intelligent detection model for clustered vehicular ad hoc networks. Expert. Syst. Appl. **50**, 40–54 (2016)
13. Wahab, O.A., Otrok, H., Mourad, A.: Vanet QoS-OLSR: QoS-based clustering protocol for vehicular ad hoc networks. Comput. Commun. **36**(13), 1422–1435 (2013)
14. Zeng, X., Bagrodia, R., Gerla, M.: GloMoSim: a library for parallel simulation of large-scale wireless networks. In: ACM SIGSIM Simulation Digest, vol. 28, pp. 154–161. IEEE Computer Society (1998)
15. Zhu, M., et al.: Public vehicles for future urban transportation. IEEE Trans. Intell. Transp. Syst. **17**(12), 3344–3353 (2016)

Depth Prediction from Monocular Images with CGAN

Wei Zhang$^{(\boxtimes)}$, Guoying Zhang, and Qiran Zou

Department of Electrical and Information Engineering,
China University of Mining and Technology (Beijing), Beijing 100089, China
Zhangwei_1@126.com, Zhangguoying1101@163.com,
zouqiran@student.cumtb.edu.cn

Abstract. Depth prediction from monocular images is an important task in many computer vision fields as monocular cameras are currently the majorities of the image acquisition equipment, which is used in many fields such as stereo scenes understanding and Simultaneous Location and Mapping (SLAM). In this paper, we regard depth prediction as an image generation task and propose a new method for monocular depth prediction using Conditional Generative Adversarial Nets (CGAN). We transform the corresponding depth images of RGB images as the Relative depth images by dividing the maximum value, then we use an encoder-decoder as the generator of CGAN, which is used to generate depth images corresponding to input RGB images, the discriminator is constituted by an encoder, which is used to discriminate whether the input images are true or fake by evaluating the difference between input images. By learning the potential correspondence between pixels of RGB images and depth image, we could finally obtain the corresponding depth images of test RGB images with our CGAN model. We test our model with different objective functions in TUM RGB-D dataset and NYU V2 dataset, and the result shows excellent performance.

Keywords: Depth prediction · CGAN · Image generation
Relative depth images · Encoder-Decoder

1 Introduction

Depth prediction is one of the fundamental tasks in computer vision, which could be widely used in many fields such as SLAM, autonomous driving, augmented reality (AR) and stereo scenes understanding. Also, many other computer vision tasks such as object detection, semantic segmentation can benefit from depth prediction. Depth prediction is mainly used for monocular or stereo images which depth can't be obtained directly. At present, depth sensors such LiDARs, Kinect and stereo cameras are the main image depth acquisition equipment, however, these depth sensors have limitations in application such as cost-prohibitive, sparse measurement, sunlight-sensitive and power-consuming. Meanwhile, monocular cameras are still the majorities of the image acquisition equipment and are widely used in our lives. Thus, monocular depth prediction now becomes an important task to be solved.

© Springer Nature Switzerland AG 2018
M. Qiu (Ed.): SmartCom 2018, LNCS 11344, pp. 427–436, 2018.
https://doi.org/10.1007/978-3-030-05755-8_42

Traditional depth prediction methods are mostly based on mathematical or physical theories, such as Triangulation, that is, for two or more monocular images, through the feature matching between adjacent images, we could obtain the real distances according to the corresponding feature points by Trangulation. Methods based on physical theories, such as Structure-from-Motion (SFM) [1], Shape-from-Shading (SFS) [2], are mostly relied on the Lambertian Surface reflection Model. These methods discard most information of images, which lead to the lack of effective constraints and large errors.

There is another kind of methods of depth prediction, the probabilistic graphical models. In [3], images are divided into sub-pixel blocks of the same category, and the depth information between sub-pixel blocks of the image is inferred by global MRF, which could finally estimate the 3D structure of objects in images. Saxena et al. [4] obtains the depth map of the image using MRF and Laplacian Model.

Recent years, some excellent depth prediction methods based on deep convolutional neural network (deep CNN) have been proposed. Eigen et al. [5] uses two deep network stacks: Global Coarse-Scale Network and Local Fine-Scale Network to predict the predicts the depth of the scene at a global level and local level respectively. Laina et al. [6] uses the fully convolutional residual network to obtain the depth images by its up-sampling blocks.

In this paper, we propose a depth prediction method based on CGAN [7]. Compared with other methods based on deep convolutional neural network, we regard depth prediction as an image generation task, by calculating the relative depth of image pixels and forming then into the target images, the constraint from the discriminator is added into the depth prediction process, which will increase the accuracy of the prediction. At the training step, we train CGANs with different objective functions to evaluate the performance of our models. We test our model on TUM RGBD dataset [8] and NYU V2 dataset [9]. We introduce the related work about our research in Sect. 2 and the architecture of our method will be described in Sect. 3.

2   Related Work

Before Traditional depth prediction from monocular images mostly relied on the motion of cameras or objects, such as Structure-from-Motion (SFM) [1], Shape-from-Shading (SFS) [2] or Shape-from-Defocus (SFD) [10]. These traditional methods are based on the ideal physical model, i.e., Lambertian Surface reflection Model, by making ideal assumptions about imaging conditions and optical features, we could obtain the 3D information by converse-solving the reflection equation based on Lambertian Surface reflection Model. These methods are convenient and fast, however, they require high quality light and other constraints, these weaknesses result in the inability to reconstruct curved objects which have concave or convex surfaces.

There are other depth prediction methods which are mainly relied on hand-crafted features and probabilistic graphical models. For instance, Saxena et al. [4], uses a linear regression and MRF to infer depth from local and global features extracted from images, [11] proposes a non-parametric method, that is, given an input image, a candidate similar to it is found in the candidate database, the depth of the input image is estimated using the existing depth information of the candidate based on a kNN transfer mechanism, [12] trains a factored autoencoder which is based on learning about the interrelations between images from multiple cameras on image patches to predict depth from stereo sequences, [13] uses supervised learning to train the MRF in order to model the depth information of the image and the relationships between different parts of the image, [14] formulates the depth prediction as a discrete-continuous optimization problem with CRF models. [15] trains a Markov random field (MRF) as a separate depth estimator for semantic classes labeled by semantic segmentation. These probabilistic graphical models are based on the premise that similarities between regions in the RGB images imply also similar depth cues, which normally need to compare the similarity between image patches with unknown depth information and the patches whose depth values are known.

Recent years, some excellent methods of depth prediction based on deep convolutional neural networks are proposed. [5] directly regress on the depth using a neural network which is constituted by two CNN stacks: the Global Coarse-Scale Network predicts the overall depth map structure in a global view, while the fine-scale network receives the coarse prediction and align with local details such as object and wall edges. [16] uses a cascaded network which is constructed with a sequence of three scales to generate features and refine depth predictions. [17] combines CNN and CRF and proposed a deep convolutional neural field model for depth prediction, which could learn the unary and pairwise potentials of continuous CRF in a unified deep network. [18, 19] formulates depth estimation in a two-layer hierarchical CRF to refine their patch-wise CNN predictions from superpixel levels down to pixel levels. [20] proposes a neural regression forest (NRF) model, combines random forests and CNNs and predicts depth values in the continuous domain via regression. [6] trains a convolutional residual network and replaces the fully-connected layer with up-sampling blocks, which could generate the corresponding depth images of input images directly. [21] predicts depth values with the semantic information of pixels by training a semantic depth classifier.

3 Model Architecture

In this paper, we use CGAN [7] as the producer of depth images which is proposed in 2014 by Mirza and Osindero. Original GAN [22] doesn't need a hypothetical data distribution when generate images, this method is too simple, which leads to the uncontrollable of generating process. In the contrary, CGAN is an improvement of turning unsupervised GAN into a supervised model. CGAN adds the tag information in the process of image generation, which adds the constraints and pertinence in generating process. In this section, we will introduce our model based on CGAN. The pipeline of our method is shown as Fig. 1.

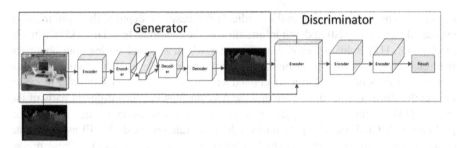

Fig. 1. The pipeline of our method.

3.1 Principle of CGAN

A CGAN is the abbreviation of conditional Generative Adversarial Nets, which is a variant of GAN. The objective function of CGAN is written as follow:

$$\min_{G} \max_{D} V(D, G) = E_{x \sim p_{data}(x)} [\log D(x|y)] + E_{z \sim p_z(z)} [\log(1 - D(G(z|y)))] \quad (1)$$

where $p_{data}(x)$ means the distribution of input images, $p_z(z)$ means the distribution of generated images.

We define our model architecture similar as used in [23], which is described in the following sections.

3.2 Architecture of Generator

In this paper, we use the U-net as the generator of our CGAN model. The U-net can be regarded as an encoder-decoder model which concatenates corresponding feature maps in different layers together between encoder and decoder. The architecture of generator is shown as Fig. 2.

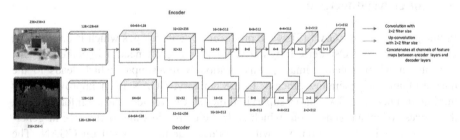

Fig. 2. The architecture of generator.

3.3   Architecture of Discriminator

The discriminator is constituted as a encoder, which learns to classify between real and fake images pairs. The discriminator will supervise the generation of depth images. When training the discriminator, real depth images and fake images are sent into the network and the differences between real and fake images will be learnt by minimize the objective function. The prediction will be obtained by a sigmoid function at last. The architecture of discriminator is shown as Fig. 3.

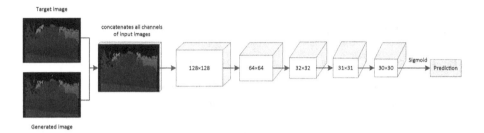

Fig. 3. The architecture of discriminator.

3.4   Loss Function

The common objective function of a CGAN is expressed as formula (1) shows. For the training of the generator, the purpose is to minimize the value of the objective function, which means the prediction of generated data by the discriminator approaches to 1. On the contrary, the purpose of discriminator training is to maximize the value of the objective function, which means the prediction of generated data approaches to 0.

In reality, the objective function of discriminator is usually remains in its original form as formula (1), however, the objective function of generator is expressed as:

$$V_G = \max_G \left(E_{z \sim p_z(z)}[\log(D(G(z)))] \right) + \lambda F_{y \sim p_{data}(y)}(y, G(z)) \qquad (2)$$
$$z \sim p_z(z)$$

where function F means a kind of traditional loss, such as $L1$ or $L2$ distance of input data y and generated data $G(z)$, λ is the weight of F.

In this paper, we choose the reverse Huber (BerHu) function as F, which is written as:

$$BerHu(x) = \begin{cases} |x| & |x| \leq c, \\ \frac{x^2 + c^2}{2c} & |x| > c, \end{cases} \qquad (3)$$

c means the threshold value, which is defined as:

$$c = 0.2 \times \max_i |\tilde{d}_i - d_i| \qquad (4)$$

where i means all pixels of images in every training batch, $\tilde{d}_i$ means the depth prediction value of one pixel, d_i means the real depth value of this pixel.

Thus, the final objective function of generator is written as:

$$V_G = \min_G \left(-E_{z \sim p_z(z)}[\log(D(G(z)))] + \lambda BerHu(y - z) \right) \tag{5}$$

λ means the weight of BerHu function.

When training our model, we test several different objective functions, such as the BerHu function and L1, Huber function.

4   Data Augmentation

4.1   Foreground Clipping for Image Pre-processing

As described in [6], the depth values of image follow heavy-tailed distribution, that is, in the whole depth range of an image, most depth values are in a few depth ranges, while the other depth ranges contains only a small part of the total depth values, which means that the regularities of image depth distribution are mostly included in these areas. Thus, we clip the foreground images and train our model firstly, then the model is trained with the original images. The results of foreground clipping are shown in Fig. 4.

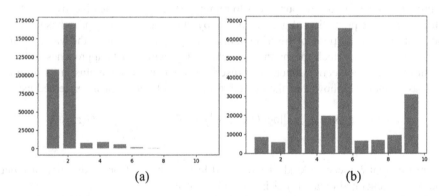

Fig. 4. The distribution of depth values in different dataset. (a) means the distribution in TUM RGBD dataset; (b) means the distribution in NYU V2 dataset.

Based on this phenomenon, in this paper, we propose the method of foreground clipping to increase the amount of images. Specifically, we count all depth values of pixels in images and divide the whole depth range into ten subranges, compute the foreground of images in which the depth values of pixels is responsible for 85% of all pixels. The results of foreground area cut are shown in Fig. 5.

Fig. 5. The results of foreground cut tested on TUN RGBD dataset. Images on the lefts side are the original images in dataset, images on the right side are the result images.

4.2   Training Data Augmentation

Before training our model, we downscale the input RGB images to 286×286, and clip patches of 256×256 randomly as inputs of the generator, we also set a 50% chance to flip the clipping images left and right to augment the input images.

During training process, we first train the model in foreground images for 200 epochs, then we apply the checkpoint on raw dataset for further training.

5   Experiments

We estimate our method on two datasets, the TUM-RGBD dataset and the NYU indoor dataset. In our experiments, we evaluate the performance of three functions: L1, Huber and the reverse Huber (BerHu), prior works [5, 6, 14, 18, 19, 24] are also compared with our experimental results.

When comparing with other works, we choose several measures commonly used in works such as [6, 16, 20], which is shown as:

root mean squared error (rms): $\sqrt{\frac{1}{T}\sum_{i \in T} \left\| \tilde{d}_i - d_i \right\|^2}$

average relative error (rel): $\frac{1}{T}\sum_{i \in T} \left| d_i - \tilde{d}_i \right| / d_i$

average log 10 error (log10): $\frac{1}{T}\sum_{i \in T} \left| \log_{10} d_i - \log_{10} \tilde{d}_i \right|$

root mean squared log error (rmslog): $\sqrt{\frac{1}{T}\sum_{i \in T} \left\| \log \tilde{d}_i - \log d_i \right\|^2}$

accuracy with threshold *thr*: (%) of $\tilde{d}_i$ s.t.max$\left(\frac{d_i}{\tilde{d}_i}, \frac{\tilde{d}_i}{d_i} \right) = \delta < thr$

5.1   TUM-RGBD Dataset

The TUM RGBD dataset contains a series of continuous RGB image and depth images, the ground truth file are given to associate the RGB images and their corresponding depth images.

We test our models with different objective functions, and the results are shown as Table 1 and Fig. 6.

In Table 1, we test our model with 3 different objective functions of the generator in CGAN, and the results shows that, the BerHu function works best in the depth prediction task. The result images of different objective functions are shown in Fig. 6.

Table 1. The results of our model with different objective functions on TUM-RGBD dataset.

Loss function	rms	rel	Log10	rms(log)	δ_1	δ_2	δ_3
L1	0.986	0.247	0.098	0.286	0.845	0.868	0.881
Huber	0.822	0.281	0.075	0.259	0.879	0.889	0.929
BerHu	**0.525**	**0.188**	**0.064**	**0.235**	**0.917**	**0.936**	**0.952**

Fig. 6. The results with different object functions tested on TUM RGBD dataset.

5.2 NYU V2 Dataset

We train our model in NYU V2 dataset, and test our model in test image set compared with other works and the results are shown in Table 2 and Fig. 7.

We compare our model with other depth prediction works, and the results of these measures are shown in Table 2. The results show that the performance of our model are better than other works. And the generating images of our method with different objective functions of generator are shown in Fig. 7.

Table 2. The results of our model with different objective functions on NYU V2 dataset.

	rms	rel	Log10	Rms(log)	δ_1	δ_2	δ_3
Liu et al.[14]	1.06	0.335	0.127	–	–	–	–
Liu et al.[24]	0.824	0.230	0.095	–	0.614	0.883	0.971
Liu et al.[18]	0.821	0.232	0.094	–	0.621	0.886	0.968
Laina et al.[6]	0.573	0.127	0.055	0.195	0.811	0.953	0.988
Wang et al. [19]	0.745	0.220	0.094	0.262	0.605	0.890	0.970
Eigen et al. [5]	0.907	0.215	–	0.285	0.611	0.887	0.971
Ours(L1)	0.474	0.080	0.126	0.445	0.680	0.741	0.844
Ours(Huber)	0.373	0.133	0.053	0.253	0.814	0.912	0.934
Ours(BerHu)	**0.192**	**0.066**	**0.028**	**0.126**	**0.921**	**0.975**	**0.992**

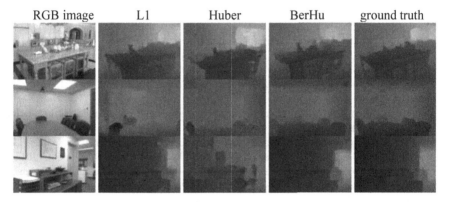

RGB image   L1   Huber   BerHu   ground truth

Fig. 7. Test results on NYU V2 dataset with different objective functions.

6 Conclusion

In this paper, we propose a new method of depth prediction based on CGAN. We regard depth prediction as an image generation task and use an encoder-decoder as the generator of CGAN, which is used to generate depth images corresponding to input RGB images. The discriminator supervises the generation of depth images in training steps. We train our model on TUM RGBD dataset and NYU V2 dataset with the image argumentation such as foreground clipping. Finally, we test our model compared with other works. The results of experiments show the excellent performance of our method.

References

1. Szeliski, R.: Structure from motion. In: Computer Vision, Texts in Computer Science, pp. 303–334. Springer, London (2011). https://doi.org/10.1007/978-1-84882-935-0_7
2. Zhang, R., Tsai, P.S., Cryer, J.E., Shah, M.: Shape-from-shading: a survey. IEEE Trans. Pattern Anal. Mach. Intell. **21**(8), 690–706 (1999)

3. Saxena, A., Sun, M., Ng, A.Y.: Make3D: learning 3D scene structure from a single still image. IEEE Trans. Pattern Anal. Mach. Intell. (PAMI) **12**(5), 824–840 (2009)
4. Saxena, A., Chung, S.H., Ng, A.Y.: Learning depth from single monocular images. In: NIPS (2005)
5. Eigen, D., Puhrsch, C., Fergus, R.: Depth map prediction from a single image using a multi-scale deep network. In: Proceedings of Advances in Neural Information Processing systems (2014)
6. Laina, I., Rupprecht, C., Belagiannis, V., Tombari, F., Navab, N.: Deeper depth prediction with fully convolutional residual networks. In: 3DV (2016)
7. Mirza, M., Osindero, S.: Conditional generative adversarial nets. arXiv preprint arXiv:1411. 1784 (2014)
8. TUM RGB-D dataset. http://vision.in.tum.de/data/datasets/rgbd-dataset
9. Silberman, N., Hoiem, D., Kohli, P., Fergus, R.: Indoor segmentation and support inference from RGBD images. In: Fitzgibbon, A., Lazebnik, S., Perona, P., Sato, Y., Schmid, C. (eds.) ECCV 2012. LNCS, vol. 7576, pp. 746–760. Springer, Heidelberg (2012). https://doi.org/ 10.1007/978-3-642-33715-4_54
10. Suwajanakorn, S., Hernandez, C.: Depth from focus with your mobile phone. In: Proceedings of the IEEE Conference on Computer Vision and Pattern Recognition (2015)
11. Karsch, K., Liu, C., Kang, S.B.: Depthtransfer: depth extraction from video using non-parametric sampling. IEEE Trans. Pattern Anal. Mach. Intell. **36**, 2144–2158 (2014)
12. Konda, K., Memisevic, R.: Unsupervised learning of depth and motion. arXiv:1312.3429v2 (2013)
13. Saxena, A., Chung, S.H., Ng, A.Y.: 3-D depth reconstruction from a single still image. Int. J. Comp. Vis. **76**, 53–69 (2007)
14. Liu, M., Salzmann, M., He, X.: Discrete-continuous depth estimation from a single image. In: Proceedings of the IEEE Conference on Computer Vision and Pattern Recognition (2014)
15. Liu, B., Gould, S., Koller, D.: Single image depth estimation from predicted semantic labels. In: 2010 IEEE Conference on Computer Vision and Pattern Recognition (CVPR), pp. 1253–1260. IEEE (2010)
16. Eigen, D., Fergus, R.: Predicting depth, surface normals and semantic labels with a common multi-scale convolutional architecture. In: Proceedings of the IEEE International Conference on Computer Vision (2015)
17. Liu, F., Shen, C., Lin, G., Reid, I.D.: Learning depth from single monocular images using deep convolutional neural fields. IEEE Trans. Pattern Anal. Mach. Intell. **38**, 2024–2039 (2016)
18. Li, B., Shen, C., Dai, Y., van den Hengel, A., He, M.: Depth and surface normal estimation from monocular images using regression on deep features and hierarchical CRFs. In: Proceedings of the IEEE Conference on Computer Vision and Pattern Recognition (2015)
19. Wang, P., Shen, X., Lin, Z., Cohen, S., Price, B., Yuille, A.L.: Towards unified depth and semantic prediction from a single image. In: Proceedings of the IEEE Conference on Computer Vision and Pattern Recognition, June 2015
20. Roy, A., Todorovic, S.: Monocular depth estimation using neural regression forest. In: Proceedings of the IEEE Conference on Computer Vision and Pattern Recognition (2016)
21. Ladicky, L., Shi, J., Pollefeys, M.: Pulling things out of perspective. In: CVPR (2014)
22. Goodfellow, I., et al.: Generative adversarial nets. In: NIPS (2014)
23. Isola, P., Zhu, J.Y., Zhou, T., Efros, A.A.: Image-to-image translation with conditional adversarial networks. In: CVPR (2017)
24. Liu, F., Shen, C., Lin, G.: Deep convolutional neural fields for depth estimation from a single image. In: Proceedings of the IEEE Conference on Computer Vision and Pattern Recognition, pp. 5162–5170 (2015)

Anomaly Detection for Power Grid Based on Network Flow

Lizong Zhang[1], Xiang Shen[1], Fengming Zhang[1], Minghui Ren[1],
and Bo Li[2(✉)]

[1] State Grid Shaoxing Power Supply Company, Zhejiang, China
zlz951@163.com, shx8022@163.com, zhangfm712@163.com,
17226656@163.com
[2] School of Computer Science and Engineering, Beihang University,
Beijing, China
libo@act.buaa.edu.cn

Abstract. As an important part of the national infrastructure, the power grid is facing more and more network security threats in the process of turning from traditional relative closure to informationization and networking. Therefore, it is necessary to develop effective anomaly detection methods to resist various threats. However, the current methods mostly use each packet in the network as the detection object, ignore the overall timing pattern of the network, cannot detect some advanced behavior attacks. In this paper, we introduce the concept of network flow, which consists of the same end-to-end network packets, besides the network flow fragmentation divides the network flow into pieces at regular intervals. We also propose a network flow anomaly detection method based on density clustering, which uses bidirectional flow statistics as features. The experimental result demonstrate that the methodology has excellent detection effect on large-scale malicious traffic and injection attacks.

Keywords: Power grid · Anomaly detection · Network flow · Density cluster

1 Introduction

Over the past few decades, the emergence and development of the next generation smart grid has enabled the grid to improve in all aspects of power generation, transmission, distribution and consumption. It improves the energy efficiency, maximizes the utility, reduces the cost and controls the emission [1]. However, the smart grid breaks the previous physically isolated power network, causing the adversary has more possible access points and intrude the entire network. Recently, cyber-attacks against the power grid are gradually increasing, among which the Ukrainian grid event is the most concerned. On December 23, 2015, the Ukrainian Kyivoblenergo's seven 110 kV and 23 35 kV substations were disconnected for three hours. After investigation, this event was considered to be due to a foreign attacker remotely controlled the SCADA distribution management system [2]. The incident exposed the Ukrainian grid with many security vulnerabilities, for example, VPNs into the ICS from the business network lacks the two-factor authentication, and there is no abnormal detection or

© Springer Nature Switzerland AG 2018
M. Qiu (Ed.): SmartCom 2018, LNCS 11344, pp. 437–445, 2018.
https://doi.org/10.1007/978-3-030-05755-8_43

active defense devices. This reflects the necessity of anomaly detection and defense in the smart power grid.

As an important industrial control system, the power grid is a key national infrastructure. In the development process from traditional closed architecture to informationization and networking open architecture, numerous vulnerabilities are gradually exposed. To protect national security, many countries are investing in industrial security (including power system security) and make certain progress [3]. Existed research work includes behavior-based, rule-based detection methods such as [4, 5], which is mainly based on the deep analysis of the industrial control protocol, extracts the key field information(combined of expert experience partially), and detects through the access control list such as whitelist and blacklist. In addition, the model-based anomaly behavior detection uses the system model parameters and features to establish mathematical models to detect intrusion anomaly, such as AAKR, CUSUM, ARIMA [6–8], besides the formal models can be constructed for anomaly detection by extracting programmable logical controller code logic [9, 10]. Lastly, the machine learning methods are also studied widely in industrial control anomaly detection, mainly divided into supervised learning, unsupervised learning and semi-supervised learning, including K-means, fuzzy C-means, support vector machine, intelligent Markov Chains, etc. [11–13].

The above methods have made progress in the detection, but the data elements are in units of packets, lacking the correlation feature of time dimension. The state machine model only pays attenuation to the order of the packets, but ignores the time limit. In this paper, we consider the same end-to-end network packet collection as a network flow, divide the network flow to form fragments at regular intervals, and extract time-related statistical features from the fragment. We use unsupervised density clustering as a machine learning method. In the training phase, we use the normal samples as input, the normal network flow segmentation will be clustered into non-quantitative clusters according to the distance between features. The boundary of each cluster constitutes the anomaly detection model. In the detection phase, when the network flow feature is too far away from any clusters, it is considered abnormal.

In summary, the contributions of this paper as follows:

(1) We introduce the concept of network flow and fragmentation, which allows us to extract and exploit time dimension features.
(2) We propose a network flow anomaly detection method based on density clustering, which is intuitively effective to differentiate between network flows and construct the model of network flows.

The rest of the paper is organized as follows: Sect. 2 provides the background on network flow and density clustering. Section 3 presents the algorithm's framework and its entire training phase and execution phase. Section 4 presents experimental results in terms of model's construction and detection performance. Finally, in Sect. 5 we present our conclusion.

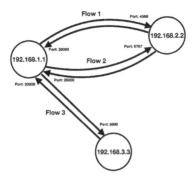

Fig. 1. Network flow diagram

2 Background

2.1 Network Flow and Fragment

A network flow is a collection of end-to-end bidirectional packets in the network. In the most common TCP/IP architecture, the collection of packets in each TCP session constitutes a network flow. However, it should be noticed that different connections between two nodes are not the same network flow (different ports in TCP), because the tasks they perform are not same necessarily, the communication mode may be different. Besides, during extracting the network flow features, since the two-way communication mode is not same necessarily, each direction packets will be feature-extracted separately to avoid mixing. Finally, it should be noted that the TCP session ends after the four-way handshake, or after the timeout expires, the flows ends, regardless of subsequent network flows. Network flow diagram shown in Fig. 1.

However, it is unacceptable to perform statistical feature extraction until the end of each network session to, especially the network session in the industrial control system (including the power grid) will last for a long time. In order to enable feature extraction and detection, we introduce the concept of network flow fragmentation, which divide the network flow at regular intervals, the packets in every interval.

2.2 Density Clustering

Density clustering can cluster irregular shapes without requiring to predetermine the number of clusters, and discrete point noise data can be processed better. Density clustering assumes that the clustering structure can be determined by the tightness of the sample distribution. In general, density clustering determines the connectivity between samples by their density, and the clusters are expanded continuously by connectable samples to obtain the final clustering results.

DBSCAN is a representative algorithm of density clustering, which use (ε, MinPts), two neighborhood parameters to describe the degree of distribution between cluster samples, the following will define several basic concepts by the data set $S = \{x_1, x_2, ..., x_n\}$:

ε Neighborhood. For each $x_i \in S$, its neighborhood ε represents a set of samples in which distance from x_i is no greater than ε, denoted as $N_\varepsilon(x_i) = \{x_j \in S | dist(x_i, x_j) \leq \varepsilon\}$;

Core Object. If the ε neighborhood of x_i contains at least MinPts samples, i.e. $|N_\varepsilon(x_i)| \geq$ MinPts, then x_i can be called the core object;

Density Directly Reachable: If x_i is a core object, and x_j is in the ε neighborhood of x_i, then x_j can be density reached directly by x_i;

Density Reachable: If there is a sample sequence $\theta_1, \theta_2, \ldots, \theta_n, \theta_1 = x_i, \theta_n = x_j$, and any θ_{k+1} in the sequence can be density reached directly by θ_k, the x_j is determined by x_i density reachable;

Density Connection: If x_k for x_i, x_j, such that x_i, x_j, are all density reachable by x_k, then x_i is connected to x_j density [14].

Through the above definitions, a cluster can be described as a sample set consisting of a density-reachable, maximum density connected. In DBSCAN clustering algorithm, it is necessary to determine all the core objects in a given data set by neighborhood parameters (ε, MinPts), find out the objects whose density is reachable for each core object, and form cluster clusters. If an object is reachable by more than one core object simultaneously, these core objects and their clusters are merged into the same cluster. When all core objects are traversed and expanded, the density clustering result is obtained, besides the objects which do not belong to any cluster are considered noise.

3   Anomaly Detection Model

3.1   Overview

The industrial control system network mainly performs timing data acquisition and scheduling control, which has high periodicity and certainty. During normal operation of the system, the statistical information of each network flow should be in a stable interval, and the characteristic values of each network flow should be gathered in a tight cluster, it is natural to build a model using density clustering to detect abnormal.

3.2   Feature Extraction and Preprocessing

The network flow we propose is bidirectional, and the nodes at both ends are divided into a server and a client according to whether or not the service is provided. Therefore, the network flow has two directions: toClient and toServer. In addition, the two-way network flow has different communication modes, so it is necessary to distinguish and extract features separately.

In the two directions of network flow, we extract the number of bytes of each packet and the interval time of the packets, and calculate the mean and variance respectively to better fit the distribution. In addition, we also extract the information entropy of the byte, which indicates the distribution of ASCII code per byte in each packet, which is the implicit mode of network transmission. In Table 1, the specific characteristics are shown.

Table 1. Network flow features

	Feature	Quantity	Meaning
Statistical features (toServer and toClient)	Bytes.avg	2	Mean of packet bytes
	Bytes.std	2	Standard deviation of packet bytes
	Intervals.avg	2	Mean of packet intervals
	Intervals.std	2	Standard deviation of packet intervals
	Be	2	Byte information entropy

In this paper, the characteristics of network stream extraction are all numeric types, which are comparable float numbers. However, the difference of the original data magnitude of each feature is large, so that the weights of the features of the final clustering result are different, so it is necessary to normalize the features. In this paper, the Sigmoid curve is selected as the function of the normalization operation, the mean and standard deviation parameters are introduced in the basis of the original formula, so that the normalized feature data is concentrated near 0.5 and has certain linearity.

$$\sqrt{y = \frac{1}{1 + e^{-\frac{x - avg}{std}}}}$$

3.3 Training Phase

The process of constructing the cluster anomaly detection model is roughly as follows:

Step 1: Data acquisition, obtaining sample data for constructing the model through the network flow engine (samples composed of 11 statistical class features);

Step 2: Data preprocessing, calculating the mean avg of each feature, the standard deviation std, and normalizing each feature of each sample using a Sigmoid function;

Step 3: Density clustering, given empirical neighborhood parameters (ε, MinPts), performing density clustering on the normalized sample data to obtain cluster clusters to which each sample belongs;

Step 4: According to the clustering result, the range value is obtained by calculating the maximum value of each feature in each cluster. As the cluster boundary of the normal model, the network flow anomaly detection model of the normal mode is constructed.

3.4 Detection Phase

After the cluster anomaly detection model is constructed, it will consist of the following steps in the model detection phase:

Step 1: Data acquisition, through the network flow engine, whenever the network flow reaches the fragmentation time, obtain the statistical sample data;

Step 2: Data preprocessing, the obtained sample data, the mean value avg calculated by the model construction step, and the standard deviation std parameter are normalized by the Sigmoid function;

Step 3: Anomaly detection, comparing the normalized sample data with the cluster boundary one by one, and obtaining the degree of abnormality of the sample from each cluster feature boundary (Euclidean distance, if a certain feature of the sample is at Within the cluster boundary, the feature and its boundary distance are recorded as 0). If there is a cluster such that the sample abnormality is less than the abnormal threshold, the detection result is normal; if the abnormality of all cluster samples is greater than the abnormal threshold, the detection result is abnormal.

4   Experiment

4.1   Experiment Procedure

This experiment is completed on the laboratory industrial control system simulation platform, which mainly includes the following steps:

(1) Start the HMI and PLC to enter the normal communication mode, and observe the data of the HMI interface is in a normal state;

(2) Perform network stream data buffering, calculate the mean value and variance of each feature after the buffer amount is satisfied, to perform data normalization;

(3) Training the pre-processed samples to construct a network flow clustering model;

(4) The simulated HMI suffers from DDos attack (distributed denial of service attack, through a large number of legitimate requests, preempting network resources, causing the server network to smash), a large number of network flows should occur in a short time, but the network flow characteristics and industrial control under normal mode. There is a huge difference in network traffic, and it is observed whether the network flow clustering model can detect anomalies;

(5) Simulate a large number of malicious injection attacks on PLC. A large number of injection attacks will bring about changes in network flow statistics, observe whether the network flow clustering model can detect abnormalities.

4.2   Experiment Results

The experimental results and analysis are as follows:

(1) In a highly periodic industrial control network, network flow features are densely distributed at multiple points, so the clustering target is to gather multiple small clusters to precisely represent the feature range. In the algorithm implementation, the parameters in the density cluster are set to $\varepsilon = 0.05$ and MinPts = 10, respectively. Moreover, the algorithm will normalize the 12 features of the selected network flows, represent the clustering results in the form of maximum and minimum values of each cluster, as shown in Fig. 2. Analysis of network flow data in normal mode, including a total of 1 Modbus connection, 3 S7 connections, so the clustering of 4 clusters is a

reasonable result. Figure 3 shows the results of network flow clustering mapping each cluster's features to the radar graph.

```
● ● ●                          Network flow cluster — -bash — 99×24
ABB-iMac:Network flow cluster apple$ python dbscan.py flow_5_5 ddos

cluster result(4 clusters):
max: [0.414, 0.692, 0.696, 0.439, 0.437, 0.39, 0.621, 0.659, 0.451, 0.439]
min: [0.411, 0.689, 0.695, 0.438, 0.437, 0.388, 0.57, 0.618, 0.448, 0.438]
avg: [0.412, 0.69, 0.696, 0.439, 0.437, 0.389, 0.595, 0.639, 0.45, 0.439]

max: [0.56, 0.485, 0.481, 0.425, 0.425, 0.604, 0.591, 0.549, 0.419, 0.424]
min: [0.553, 0.484, 0.48, 0.425, 0.425, 0.597, 0.589, 0.548, 0.419, 0.424]
avg: [0.556, 0.484, 0.48, 0.425, 0.425, 0.601, 0.59, 0.548, 0.419, 0.424]

max: [0.679, 0.45, 0.431, 0.423, 0.423, 0.65, 0.48, 0.439, 0.419, 0.423]
min: [0.665, 0.446, 0.429, 0.423, 0.423, 0.639, 0.474, 0.438, 0.419, 0.423]
avg: [0.672, 0.448, 0.43, 0.423, 0.423, 0.645, 0.477, 0.439, 0.419, 0.423]

max: [0.362, 0.366, 0.383, 0.811, 0.719, 0.37, 0.336, 0.363, 0.811, 0.719]
min: [0.36, 0.366, 0.383, 0.702, 0.704, 0.369, 0.334, 0.363, 0.701, 0.704]
avg: [0.361, 0.366, 0.383, 0.756, 0.712, 0.369, 0.335, 0.363, 0.756, 0.712]
```

Fig. 2. Cluster result

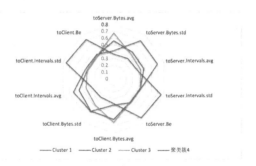

Fig. 3. Cluster result radar graph

(2) The simulated HMI is subjected to a DDoS attack, and a large number of spurious S7 request packets with a destination port of 102 are sent, so that a large number of network flows occur in a short period of time, each network flow contains only a small number of packets. There is a notable difference between the industrial control network flow and the normal mode. Figure 4 shows the abnormal results detected by the network flow clustering model, its feature deviation exceeds the threshold.

```
● ● ●                          Network flow cluster — -bash — 99×24
detection failed(deviation: 0.46198878296 ):
original features: [0.033, 16.0, 16.0, 0.001, 0.0, 0.017, 0.0, 0.0, 0.0, 0.0]
normalized features: [0.316, 0.871, 0.511, 0.383, 0.419, 0.422, 0.368, 0.326, 0.358, 0.416]

detection failed(deviation: 0.461987813927 ):
original features: [0.033, 16.0, 16.0, 0.002, 0.0, 0.017, 0.0, 0.0, 0.0, 0.0]
normalized features: [0.316, 0.871, 0.511, 0.383, 0.419, 0.422, 0.368, 0.326, 0.358, 0.416]
```

Fig. 4. Detection result

(3) The simulated PLC suffers from a large number of malicious injection attacks, which will generate statistical changes to the network flow. Figure 5 shows the detection result of the network flow clustering model for the injected attack network flow.

```
detection failed(deviation: 0.280568849205 ):
original features: [6.733, 9.238, 5.052, 0.122, 0.073, 8.817, 9.023, 8.023, 0.093, 0.112]
normalized features: [0.678, 0.702, 0.41, 0.384, 0.421, 0.605, 0.6, 0.46, 0.359, 0.419]

detection failed(deviation: 0.357851693023 ):
original features: [1.3, 34.09, 34.133, 0.626, 0.681, 0.717, 15.558, 26.723, 1.143, 0.79]
normalized features: [0.381, 0.991, 0.673, 0.389, 0.439, 0.436, 0.748, 0.761, 0.369, 0.439]
```

Fig. 5. Detection result

5 Conclusion

This paper proposed a novel approach to detect abnormality in the industrial control system network. Based on the density clustering method of network flow statistical information, the number of clusters is determined autonomously according to the distribution density of sample points, the cluster results are tight, and abnormal noise can be found in the training process. The experiments shown that the model has excellent detection effect on large-scale traffic attacks and injection attacks, also can perform well when the system faces unknown proprietary protocols.

References

1. Fang, X., Misra, S., Xue, G., et al.: Smart grid — the new and improved power grid: a survey. IEEE Commun. Surv. Tutorials **14**(4), 944–980 (2012)
2. E-ISAC, SANS ICS: Analysis of the Cyber Attack on the Ukrainian Power Grid, p4, 18 March 2016. http://www.nerc.com/pa/CI/ESISAC/Documents/E-ISAC_SANS_Ukraine_DUC_18Mar2016.pdf
3. Shang, W., An, P., Wan, M., et al.: Summary of research and development of industrial control system intrusion detection technology. Appl. Res. Comput. **34**(2), 328–333 (2017)
4. Khalili, A., Sami, A.: SysDetect: a systematic approach to critical state determination for Industrial intrusion detection systems using Apriori algorithm. J. Process Control **32**(11), 154–160 (2015)
5. Choi, S., Chang, Y., Yun, J.H., et al.: Traffic-Locality-Based Creation of Flow Whitelists for SCADA Networks (2015)
6. Yang, D., Usynin, A., Hines, J.W.: Anomaly-based intrusion detection for SCADA systems (2005)
7. Mo, Y., Chabukswar, R., Sinopoli, B.: Detecting integrity attacks on SCADA systems. IEEE Trans. Control Syst. Technol. **44**(1), 11239–11244 (2011)
8. Zhang, Y., Tong, W., Zhao, Y.: Improvement of CUSUM anomaly detection algorithm and application in industrial control intrusion detection system. Metallurgical Industry Automation (2014)
9. Guo, S., Wu, M., Wang, C.: Symbolic execution of programmable logic controller code. In: ACM SIGSOFT Symposium on the Foundations of Software Engineering. ACM (2017)

10. Stephen, M., et al.: A trusted safety verifier for process controller code. In: NDSS Symposium 2014, pp. 1–3, February 2014
11. Zhou, C., Huang, S., Xiong, N., et al.: Design and analysis of multimodel-based anomaly intrusion detection systems in industrial process automation. IEEE Trans. Syst. Man Cybernet. Syst. **45**(10), 1345–1360 (2017)
12. Ponomarev, S., Atkison, T.: Industrial control system network intrusion detection by telemetry analysis. IEEE Trans. Dependable Secure Comput. **13**(2), 252–260 (2016)
13. Macdermott, A., Shi, Q., Merabti, M., et al.: Intrusion detection for critical infrastructure protection. In: The 13th Post Graduate Symposium on the Convergence of Telecommunications, Networking and Broadcasting (PGNet 2012) (2012)
14. Zhou, Z.: Machine Learning. Tsinghua University Press, Beijing (2016)

A K-Anonymous Full Domain Generalization Algorithm Based on Heap Sort

Xuyang Zhou[1](✉) and Meikang Qiu[2]

[1] International Department, Beijing National Day School, Beijing 100039, China
2191168228@qq.com
[2] Department of Computer and Information Science,
Harrisburg University of Science and Technology, Harrisburg, PA 17101, USA
qiumeikang@yahoo.com

Abstract. K-Anonymity algorithms are used as essential methods to protect end users' data privacy. However, state-of-art K-Anonymity algorithms have shortcomings such as lacking generalization and suppression value priority standard. Moreover, the complexity of these algorithms are usually high. Thus, a more robust and efficient K-Anonymity algorithm is needed for practical usage. In this paper, a novel K-Anonymous full domain generalization algorithm based on heap sort is presented. We first establish the k-anonymous generalization priority standard of information. Then our simulation results show the user's data privacy can be effectively protected while generalization efficiency is also improved.

Keywords: K-anonymity · Privacy · Generalization · Protection
Quasi-identifier · Generalization priority

1 Introduction

With the rapid development of cloud computing and big data technology, data mining and data publishing are widely used. Thus, data collected by the individuals, the companies, and the governments are increasing as people's daily life has been digitized [6]. This data mining analysis, on the one hand, provides support for government and enterprise decision-making, and provides better service for the public. On the other hand, how to protect private data, especially prevent the leak of student information has become a topic of increasing concern.

In a telephone survey conducted in the United States, 87% of the people said the law should prohibit organizations from providing medical data without the permission of the patients [9]. Today, health data disclosure is strictly regulated in many countries, and institutions are legally required to enhance the privacy of health data before it is disclosed to researchers. For example, the U.S. Health Insurance Portability and Accountability Act (HIPAA) [1] and Canada's Personal Health Information Protection Act (PHIPA) [2] are recognized privacy

© Springer Nature Switzerland AG 2018
M. Qiu (Ed.): SmartCom 2018, LNCS 11344, pp. 446–459, 2018.
https://doi.org/10.1007/978-3-030-05755-8_44

laws that protecting the confidentiality of electronic medical data. This algorithm can help relevant institutions and platforms to strengthen the protection of sensitive data, avoid information leakage in use.

The k-anonymous algorithm is commonly used to protect the sensitive information of customers. The k-anonymity means that at least k records in a customer information data table have the same quasi-identifier value, and each record in the customer data table should be at least similar to $(k-1)$ records to ensure personal privacy. Generally, k-anonymity is achieved by generalization and suppression of the quasi-identifiers.

There are several commonly used k-anonymous algorithms. Sweeney's [10] algorithm is a greedy algorithm based on local region search, but it is not necessarily the most advantageous for full domain searching. Samarati's [8] algorithm is a full domain generalization algorithm, it uses the Binary Search method to search the nodes. Kodam's [7] algorithm is a parallel Samarati's algorithm. Since Kodam's algorithm is an improvement on Sweeney and Samarrati's algorithm, this paper focuses on the analysis of examples of Kodam's three quasi-identifier models.

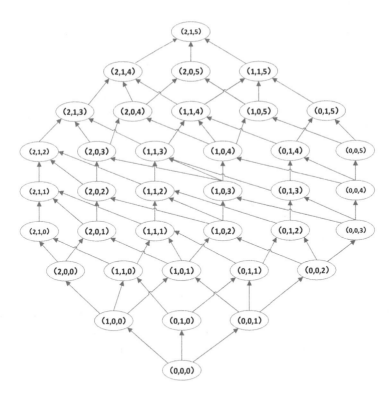

Fig. 1. Generalization relation model of 3 quasi-identifiers for Kodam

As seen in Fig. 1, when generalizing the three quasi-identifiers (2, 1, 5) of age, sex and zip code, this algorithm started a binary search from the middle layer with the greedy algorithm to find the most appropriate nodes. The algorithm constructed a 3D model map when generalizing the data table of three quasi-identifiers. For instance, there are five incoming and outgoing connections on the nodes (1, 0, 3), (1, 0, 4), (1, 1, 2), and (1, 1, 3). But the algorithm did not give the criteria for finding the most suitable nodes and the shortest generalization path [5].

If more than three quasi-identifiers are generalized, for example, ten quasi-identifiers are generalized, we will need a ten-dimensional model. The data model structure will be very complicated at this time. The nodes will be crisscrossed, and the nodes connections will be difficult to determine [3]. It will be difficult to draw the data model and flow chart. It also will be difficult to program and verify the correctness of the program. In fact, Kodam did not draw more than three-dimensional general algorithm models.

In Sweeney's, Sameriti's and Kodam's algorithms, the minimum inhibition values were used to determine the search results. However, how to define minimum inhibition variables, they did not give specific solutions. This paper will build the k-anonymous priority table and the generalization rule table below.

This paper's contribution can be summarized as follows: (1) We proposed a novel K-Anonymous Full Domain Generalization Algorithm Based on Heap Sort which can outperform related state-of-art algorithms. (2) One possible real life problem is solved and demonstrated in this paper to elaborated the effectiveness.

The rest of this article is divided into four sections. The novel K-Anonymous Full Domain Generalization Algorithm Based on Heap Sort is elaborated in Sect. 2. The experimental set up and the result is shown in Sect. 3. Finally, Sect. 4 gives the concluding remark of this paper.

2   A K-Anonymous Full Domain Generalization Algorithm Based on Heap Sort

2.1   Basic Definitions

$$ILoss = \frac{\|Vg\| - 1}{\|Da\|} \tag{1}$$

The $\|Vg\|$ is the number of generalization nodes, and the Da are the number of quasi-identifiers. If $ILoss = 0$, it means that the data table has not started generalization yet. For example, there are 3 quasi-identifiers, age is generalized to two digits.

$$ILoss = \frac{(2-1)}{2} = \frac{1}{2} \tag{2}$$

After generalization, any recorded ILoss can be calculated. Obviously, information loss is directly proportional to the value of ILoss.

Table 1. Definition

Notions	Description
Quasi-identifier	The combination of a set of attributes of the client privacy information table, which can be used to identify different records in the privacy table
Generalization	Generalization modifies the initial values of the quasi-identifiers into the values of the specific description. The full domain generalization generalize all the records and the quasi-identifiers in the data tables. The local generalization generalize part of the records and quasi-identifiers in the data tables
Inhibitory and inhibitory values	A part of the attribute values of the quasi-identifier are covered up, which be called inhibition. There are two levels of inhibition, Value and Unit inhibition
Value level inhibition	Suppress all records of a specific value in the table
Unit level inhibition	The records of the given value in the table are inhibited
Information loss (ILoss)	When information is generalized, the loss needs to be assessed. This can be measured by ILoss [4]

2.2   Algorithm Design

For a basic information data table with n quasi-identifiers, a quasi-identifier set A is set up, where $A = a, b, \ldots, n$, $a, b, \ldots, n$ are the character attribute of the quasi-identifiers. Set the length of the quasi-identifier characters in set A to A', where $A' = a', b', \ldots, n'$, a' is the character length of character a, b' is the character length of character b, and n' is the character length of character n. Let $S = (a'+1)*(b'+1)*\ldots*(n'+1)$. Let the arrangement of elements in A' has the meaning of increasing order from right to left, that is, a's position bigger than b's position and bigger than every following positions. When a generalization is done, it is always generalized from right to left, that is, from small to large.

At the same time, we divided the nodes according to the number of the generalization, zeroth layers are not generalized any bits, and the first level generalizes one bit, and so on, the S level generalizes the S bits. Set $S' = a' + b' + \ldots + n' + 1$. We can divide S generalization into S' layer. So, I have set up the following heap sort k-anonymous generalization model for this purpose.

In Table 2, the column numbers represent the generalized permutation position of the quasi-identifier, and the row numbers represent the generalized digits of the quasi-identifiers in each layer. For example, the zeroth level $(0, 0, \ldots, 0n)$ has only one node, which indicates that the number of generalization is 0. The first level represents the generalization of 1 bit, and I level indicates the generalization of I bits. For any node, generalize from the rightmost node of the row

Table 2. The k-anonymous full domain generalization algorithm based on heap sort model diagram

	Node 1	...	Node j	...		Node n
Layer s'			$(a',b',\ldots,n')$			
...						
...						
Layer I	$(a'_i,\ldots,n'_{(n-i)})$	...	$(0,\ldots,j'_i,\ldots,n'_{(n-i)})$	...		$(0,0,\ldots,n')$
...						
Layer 1	$(1,0,0,\ldots,0)$	...		...	$(0,0,\ldots,1,0)$	$(0,0,\ldots,1)$
Layer 0			$(0,0,\ldots,0_n)$			

to the left in turn, and the sum of the digits generalized by each node is the number of rows. The top S' layer has only one node, which means that the node values are all generalized, that is, the maximum generalization.

Therefore, in the algorithm model of Table 2, considering the possibility of generalization operation for each bit of quasi-identifier, there is a total generalization of $(a'+1)*(b'+1)*\ldots*(n'+1)$. From the 0 level to the S' level, the data values are arranged in ascending order, and the data values of each layer from right to left nodes are arranged in ascending order. So, Table 2 is an ordered 2-D table, which have $S'+1$ rows and $a'+b'+\ldots+(n-1)'+1'$ columns.

For example, in Table 2, the value of the nodes in layer $0(0,0,\ldots,0n)$ is smaller than that of the nodes in layer $S'(a',b',\ldots,n')$, and the value of the nodes in layer $1(0,0,\ldots,n')$. The value of 1 is smaller than that of $(1,0,\ldots,0)$. For all nodes in the S' layer, the values in the lower layer are smaller than those in the upper layer, and the values on the right side of the same layer are smaller than those on the left.

Because the values of each node are different, and there are size and order. Thus, Table 2 can be transformed into one dimensional ordered array. We can construct a complete two binary tree in the S generalization mode according to the order of arrangement values. The root node of this tree is the maximum value in the set S, and each leaf node is a permutation value in the set S. Sort the whole two binary tree, that is a heap sort. For example, there is a student information table with two quasi-identifier fields: the age and the zip code.

Table 3. Student information table with age and zip code quasi-identifier.

Age	Zip code
18	271500
18	271501
16	271510
10	274200
7	274201

Table 4. The nodes table of two quasi-identifiers.

	Column 1	Column 2	Column 3
Layer 8		(2, 6)	
Layer 7	(2, 5)		(1, 6)
Layer 6	(2, 4)	(1, 5)	(0, 6)
Layer 5	(2, 3)	(1, 4)	(0, 5)
Layer 4	(2, 2)	(1, 3)	(0, 4)
Layer 3	(2, 1)	(1, 2)	(0, 3)
Layer 2	(2, 0)	(1, 1)	(0, 2)
Layer 1	(1, 0)		(0, 1)
Layer 0		(1, 0)	

We set up a quasi-identifier set $A = (age, zipcode)$. The set of character lengths in set A is set to $A' = (2, 6)$. Where '2' is equal to the character length of the age, meanwhile, '6' is equal to the length of the Chinese Zip Code. We can compute that $S = (2 + 1) * (6 + 1) = 21$ and $S' = 2 + 6 + 1 = 9$. We can tell that the number of columns L is 3. We have generalized these 21 generalizing ways to generate data tables of 9 rows and 3 columns as shown in Table 4.

Then we counted the nodes, and built an ordered array with 21 nodes is arranged from large to small.

$$\{(2,6), (2,5), (1,6), (2,4), (1,5), (0,6), (2,2), (1,3), (0,4),$$
$$(2,1), (1,2), (0,3), (2,0), (1,1), (0,2), (1,0), (0,1), (0,0)\}$$

This is an array that is arranged from large to small, and the smallest distance is between array elements. We can build a complete two binary tree and then search for the minimum inhibitory node by using heap traversing.

2.3 The Priority Rule Base of the Heap Sort K-Anonymous Full Domain Generalization

(1) **The weight principle of the student classification:** The generalization of student information quasi-identifier is divided into 5 levels of weights, corresponding to different priority weights respectively. (a) Kindergarten students 5 > primary school students 4 > junior high school student 3 > high school student 2; (b) In the same school age, younger students have higher generalization priority; (c) In the same school age, younger students have higher generalization priority. The detail of this principle is shown in Table 5.

(2) **The weight principle of the k value priority:** The k value priority > suppression value priority. Firstly, we selected the k value, if the k values are same, then we selected the generalization inhibition value. The priority weight of the level was the k value. The default k value was 3.

Table 5. The table of weight principle of the student classification.

Age	Degree	Priority (PRI)
0–6	Kindergarten	5
6–13	Primary school	4
13–16	Middle school	3
16–18	High school	2

(3) **The threshold weighting principle for student data size:** We set some thresholds for the size of the data, which is divided into seven thresholds from bigger to smaller: classes, grades, schools, districts, cities, provinces (municipalities directly under the Central Government). More detail of this principle is elaborated in Table 6.

Table 6. The table of the threshold weighting principle.

Size of data	Threshold
Class	2
Grade	3
School	4
District	5
City	6
Province	7

(4) **The weight principle of the concise generalization:** When we dealt with a small amount of the student information, the priority of the attribute with smaller suppression value is higher. In order to improve the computer system processing efficiency, under the premise of satisfying the anonymity effect, fewer generalization nodes and smaller generalization values are better than more generalization for more nodes. More details are shown in Table 7.

Table 7. The table of weight principle of the concise generalization.

Size of data	Weight of concise generalization	Generalization values	Generalization nodes
Smaller than 30 people	2	Smaller	Smaller

(5) **The weight principle of the field type precedence:** Binary data type 7 > Digital data type 6 > Monetary data type 5 > Character data type 4 > Unicode data type 3 > Date and time data type 2 > Special data type 1.

(6) **The weighted principle of the generalized equilibrium distribution on the same level:** When dealing with data larger than class size, nodes in the same layer suppress more quasi-identifier field attributes > nodes with less quasi-identifier field attributes. For example, (1, 1, 1) is superior to (0, 0, 3) priority is the number of layers. The default value is 3.

(7) **The weight principle of the quasi-identifier attribute priority:** Generalize a quasi-identifier for a record, age 5 > sex 4 > zip code 3 > mobile phone number 2 > other quasi-identifiers 1.

(8) **The principle of regional classification weight:** Class A area > B class > C area. Priority is higher in developed and central cities with large population density. (a) The A area includes Beijing and 11 provinces and municipalities. (b) The B area includes 10 provinces and cities such as Chongqing. (c) The C area includes 10 provinces such as Inner Mongolia. More details are shown in Table 8.

Table 8. The table of regional classification weight.

Area class	Classification weight
A	5
B	3
C	1

(9) **The weight principle of heavy disease:** The priority of students suffering from major infectious diseases is higher than that of students suffering from common infectious diseases, and the priority of sick students is higher than that of healthy students. This principle is further elaborated in Table 9.

Table 9. The table of weight principle of heavy disease.

Physical testing data	Weight
Serious and dangerous infectious diseases	5
Serious infectious diseases	4
General infectious disease	3
Healthy	0

(10) **The other priority weights for the students:** This case can further prioritize student's basic information, such as the basic information of the family members, the physical examination report information of the students and the family members. If we prioritize customers other than students, we can also prioritize them in terms of their occupation, income, ethnicity, urban and rural areas, social connections, risk assessment, interests, and hobbies. This priority is elaborated in Table 10.

Table 10. The table of other priority weights for the students.

Data	Scope of weight	Describe	Manual adjustment and confirmation
Name			
Number			
Sex			
Birthday			
Mobile number			
Degree			
Zip code			
Family member			
Family income			
Student's physical testing data			
Family's physical testing data			
Nation			
Risk assessment factor			
Social contact information			

Hence, we can come up with the numbered table of the priority weight which is shown in Table 11. The average weight P is computed follow:

$$P = \frac{(p1 + p2 + p3 + p4 + p5 + p6 + p7 + p8 + p9 + p10)}{10}$$

For the model, the maximum value is 4, the minimum value is 1.2. According to the principle of rounding, there are 4 levels.

If we add tenth considerations, and the K value is greater than 7. The priority weights greater than 4 are placed at level fifth. So, the PRI is divided into 5 priorities. When generalizing multiple nodes in the same layer, it is necessary to note the corresponding rule node parameters, which records in the data table are generalized, and what is the original value before generalization, so as to restore the data table parameters. This is elaborated in Table 12.

Table 11. The numbered table of the priority weight.

Priority (PRI)	PRI weight type	PRI weight
1	Student classification	
2	K value	
3	K threshold	
4	Concise	
5	Field type precedence	
6	Generalized equilibrium distribution on the same level	
7	Quasi-identifier property	
8	Three types of regional classification	
9	Priority of disease priority	
10	Other priority of students	

Table 12. The weight operation table.

Priority (PRI)	Operation	Manual adjustment and confirmation
5	If K $\geqslant$ 5 and generalization $\geqslant$ 5, generalizing all nodes oil the same level	
4	K $\leqslant$ 4, generalization $\geqslant$ 4, generalizing all nodes on the same level	
3	K $\leqslant$ 3, generalization $\geqslant$ 3, generalize $\leqslant$ 3 nodes on the same level	
2	K $\leqslant$ 3, generalization $\geqslant$ 2, generalize $\leqslant$ 2 nodes on the same level	
1	K $\leqslant$ 2, generalization $\geqslant$ 1, generalize $\leqslant$ 1 node on the same level	

2.4 Establishing Generalization Rule Table C

For the student information table with n quasi-identifiers, a generalization rule table C is established. Where $C = (a_g, b_g, \ldots, n_g)$, where $a_g, b_g, \ldots, n_g$ are the generalization rule of the quasi-identifiers.

This generalization rule is formulated in accordance with the definition explained in Table 1. There are the generalization rules: 1. Partial inhibition 2. All inhibition 3. Set inhibition range

So far, depending on the different requirements for using k-anonymity, we have established a generalized priority table rule base containing and corresponding to each node, and given the node attribute with the highest priority value. At the same time, a generalization rule table C is established.

When each time we do heap sort lookup, we compare the priority values in the priority table to find a node that satisfies the k-anonymous minimum suppression condition. If we find a priority node that meets the set requirements,

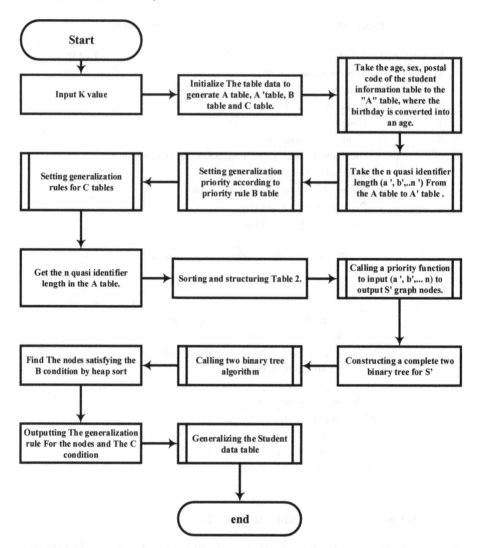

Fig. 2. A flowchart of generalization program for student vaccination information.

we will output the priority of this node and the parameters of the generalized rule table C. This is the best anonymous generalization node we want to find. The system will generalize the corresponding quasi-identifiers in accordance with pre-set rules. More details are elaborated in Algorithm 1 and Fig. 2.

2.5   Comparison Between Related Algorithms

In summary, there are 10 differences between our presented algorithm and those related algorithms shown in Table 13. Reference Table 13: The table directly

Algorithm 1. *Heap Sorting K-anonymous Full Domain Generalization Algorithm*

Procedure:

1: **Initialization:** Ordered set $A=a, b, \ldots, n$ has n quasi-identifiers. The set of character lengths in A is A'. $A'=a', b', \ldots, n'$. a' is length a, b' is length b, $\ldots, n'$ is the length n
2: Establishing a complete two fork tree according to the rules of section 2.2.
3: Optimal node parameters are calculated based on a K-anonymous generalization priority algorithm.
4: Searching for optimal nodes by heap sort.
5: Finding and outputting priority node parameters and generalization rules to meet generalization requirements.
6: Generalizing the data tables according to rule table C.

---

refers to the basic definitions of the time complexity and space complexity of the computer data structure principle, and no longer proves the definitions.

Table 13. Algorithm analysis and comparison table.

	Lookup method	Generalization principle	Generalizatio n range	Generalizati on standard	Time complexity	Space complexity	Model complexity	Model visualizatio n	Model maintainabilit y	Generalizatio n value extensibility
Sweeney	Binary search	Local greedy algorithm	Local generalization	No	O (log n)	O(n)	Complex	Difficult	General	Difficult
Samarati	Binary search	Greedy algorithm	Full domain generalization	No	O (log n)	O(n)	Complex	Difficult	General	General
Kodam	Parallel binary search	Greedy algorithm	Full domain generalization	No	O (log n)	O(n)	Very complex	Difficult	Difficult	Very difficult
This algorithm	Heap sorting	Priority algorithm	Full domain generalization	Yes	O (log n)	O (1)	Simple	Easy	Good	Easy

(1) Comparing with the basic algorithm, the heap sort algorithm in this paper is better than the binary search algorithm.
(2) Comparing with the generalization principle, the priority algorithm is superior to the greedy algorithm without priority.
(3) Comparing with generalization range, full domain generalization is better than local generalization.
(4) Comparing with the generalization standard, the algorithm in this paper establishes the generalization standard, and other algorithms have no executable standard.
(5) Comparing with the average time complexity, the heap sort algorithm is the same with other algorithms.
(6) Comparing with the space complexity, the heap sort algorithm is better than other algorithms.

(7) Comparing with the model complexity, the heap sort algorithm is simple and clear, and other algorithms are too complicated.

(8) Comparing with the visualization, this algorithm transforms the complex graph theory model into a simple one-dimensional array, which is easy to be vitalized and revised by human being. Other algorithms are formidable to be visualized when multiple quasi-identifiers are used.

(9) Comparing with the model maintenance, this algorithm supports arbitrary setting of K value, and the generalized priority standard can be maintained manually. The suppression method is not constrained by asterisks and can be defined in the rule base. There are no standard libraries and rule libraries available for the other algorithms.

(10) Comparing with the scalability of quasi-identifiers, the heap sort algorithm can support all the multi-character standard and can support big data and all the multi-quasi-identifier extension. Other algorithms tend to crash when quasi-identifiers increase to a certain number, such as 100 quasi-identifiers.

Hence, we can have the following conclusion, compared with the integrated application effects, the k - anonymous full domain generalization algorithm based on heap sort is better than the other algorithms.

3   Demonstration

In this section we will demonstrate how to solve the Generalization Problem of Student Immunization Data by the Heap Sort K-anonymous Full Domain Generalization Algorithm. We also presented the conclusion of simulation process.

The operating system is above windows7, Intel corei7-3520M CPU, memory RAM 8 GB. Programming language Python3.6.5. We have set up 100 basic data samples for students, ranging in age from 1 to 18 years. Input k value from any number between 1–100, take priority weight value 1–10 between any number, take generalization Rule 1–3. The output results fully meet the requirements of the heap sort k-anonymous full domain generalization algorithm.

We have made inferences in Table 13 that other algorithms do not have priority weights and generalization rules, which made it difficult to model multidimensional models. Therefore, there is no direct comparability of running speed.

4   Conclusion and Future Work

In summary, we have studied a new model to implement a k-anonymous generalization algorithm and proposed a K-anonymous full domain generalization algorithm based on heap sort. Comparing with other basic k-anonymity algorithms in ten aspects, and through practical programming experience and verification, this algorithm has more integrated application advantages in many aspects.

At the same time, referring to the principle of CRM and further put forward ten priority weights, five-level standardized operation standards is made up for the lack of common k-anonymity basic algorithm generalization standards. For quasi-identifiers containing sensitive student information, this algorithm can find out the optimal generalization solutions of different k-anonymity. After we generalize the student vaccination information table, this algorithm can produce the desired results. For the future work, we will continue working on improving the heap sort based K-anonymous full domain generalization algorithm by deploying machine learning algorithms.

References

1. Adusumalli, S.K., Kumari, V.V.: Attribute based anonymity for preserving privacy. In: Abraham, A., Mauri, J.L., Buford, J.F., Suzuki, J., Thampi, S.M. (eds.) ACC 2011. CCIS, vol. 193, pp. 572–579. Springer, Heidelberg (2011). https://doi.org/10.1007/978-3-642-22726-4_59
2. Berčič, B., George, C.: Identifying personal data using relational database design principles. Int. J. Law Inf. Technol. **17**(3), 233–251 (2008)
3. Gai, K., Qiu, M.: Blend arithmetic operations on tensor-based fully homomorphic encryption over real numbers. IEEE Trans. Ind. Inform. **14**(8), 3590–3598 (2018)
4. Gionis, A., Tassa, T.: k-anonymization with minimal loss of information. IEEE Trans. Knowl. Data Eng. **21**(2), 206–219 (2009)
5. Li, Y., Dai, W., Ming, Z., Qiu, M.: Privacy protection for preventing data over-collection in smart city. IEEE Trans. Comput. **65**(5), 1339–1350 (2016)
6. Qiu, M., Gai, K., Thuraisingham, B., Tao, L., Zhao, H.: Proactive user-centric secure data scheme using attribute-based semantic access controls for mobile clouds in financial industry. Futur. Gener. Comput. Syst. **80**, 421–429 (2018)
7. Sai Kumar, K.: Achieving k-anonymity using parallelism in full domain generalization. Ph.D. thesis (2015)
8. Samarati, P., Sweeney, L.: Protecting privacy when disclosing information: k-anonymity and its enforcement through generalization and suppression. Technical report, SRI International (1998)
9. Shi, P., Xiong, L., Fung, B.: Anonymizing data with quasi-sensitive attribute values. In: Proceedings of the 19th ACM International Conference on Information and Knowledge Management, pp. 1389–1392. ACM (2010)
10. Sweeney, L.: Achieving k-anonymity privacy protection using generalization and suppression. Int. J. Uncertain. Fuzziness Knowl.-Based Syst. **10**(05), 571–588 (2002)

Author Index

Printed in the United States
By Bookmasters